Effective Literacy Instruction K–8

Implementing Best Practice

FIFTH EDITION

Donald J. Leu, Jr.
University of Connecticut

Charles K. Kinzer
Vanderbilt University

Upper Saddle River, New Jersey
Columbus, Ohio

Library of Congress Cataloging-in-Publication Data

Leu, Donald, J.
    Effective literacy instruction, K–8/Donald J. Leu, Jr., Charles K. Kinzer.—5th ed.
      p. cm.
    Includes bibliographical references and index.
    ISBN 0-13-099541-X
      1. Reading (Elementary)—United States. I. Kinzer, Charles K. II. Title.

    LB1573 .L445 2003
    372.4—dc21   2002016676

Vice President and Publisher: Jeffery W. Johnston
Editor: Linda Ashe Montgomery
Editorial Assistant: Evelyn Olson
Development Editor: Hope Madden
Production Editor: Linda Hillis Bayma
Text Design and Production Coordination: Amy Gehl, Carlisle Publishers Services
Design Coordinator: Diane C. Lorenzo
Cover Designer: Brenda Grannan
Cover Image: Corbis Stock Market
Production Manager: Pamela D. Bennett
Director of Marketing: Ann Castel Davis
Marketing Manager: Krista Groshong
Marketing Assistant: Tyra Cooper

This book was set in Palatino by Carlisle Communications, Inc. It was printed and bound by Courier Kendallville, Inc. The cover was printed by Phoenix Color Corp.

Photo Credits: Tom Watson, pp. 3, 135, 477; P. G. Schrader, pp. 6, 36, 239, 321, 352, 378; Charles Kinzer, pp. 14, 20, 31, 47, 68, 76, 86, 100, 112, 120, 139, 148, 158, 169, 192, 200, 211, 218, 231, 241, 252, 274, 280, 287, 310, 328, 335, 366, 394, 414, 429, 445, 448, 457, 467, 480, 487, 493, 512, 519, 533; Judy Dill, pp. 9, 127 (bottom), 171 (center), 255, 359, 463, 486; KS Studios/Merrill, p. 25; Hope Madden/Merrill, pp. 41, 81, 127 (top), 171 (left, right), 325; Anne Vega/Merrill, p. 61; Scott Cunningham/Merrill, pp. 95, 236, 265, 345; Anthony Magnacca/Merrill, pp. 183, 299, 389; Nikki Robinson, pp. 205, 283, 413, 525; Frank Siteman/PhotoEdit, p. 441; Frank Johnston/Getty Images, Inc./PhotoDisc, Inc., p. 509.

Pearson Education Ltd.
Pearson Education Australia Pty. Limited
Pearson Education Singapore Pte. Ltd.
Pearson Education North Asia Ltd.
Pearson Education Canada, Ltd.
Pearson Educatión de Mexico
Pearson Education—Japan
Pearson Education Malaysia Pte. Ltd.
Pearson Education, *Upper Saddle River, New Jersey*

Copyright © 2003, 1999, 1995, 1991, 1987 by Pearson Education, Inc., Upper Saddle River, New Jersey 07458. All rights reserved. Printed in the United States of America. This publication is protected by Copyright and permission should be obtained from the publisher prior to any prohibited reproduction, storage in a retrieval system, or transmission in any form or by any means, electronic, mechanical, photocopying, recording, or likewise. For information regarding permission(s), write to: Rights and Permissions Department.

10 9 8 7 6 5 4 3 2 1
ISBN: 0-13-099541-X

To Alexandra, Debbie, and Rita—
We thank you, once again, for your support and understanding as we developed these ideas during many late nights, early mornings, and weekends on the computer.

To Our Readers—
Each of you is part of a very long and important chain that began with your parents and teachers, includes your current professors, and will continue as you serve in the noblest of professions—teaching.

To Our Undergraduate and Graduate Students—
We greatly appreciate the opportunity to participate in your development and the ideas you shared, that contributed to our own development.

To Teachers Around the World—
Our heartfelt thanks for allowing us to enter the special worlds you create for children. Your insights have been especially helpful as we seek to support the development of literacy educators.

Donald J. Leu, Jr. is the John and Maria Neag Endowed Chair in Literacy and Technology in the Neag School of Education at the University of Connecticut. He served in the Peace Corps, teaching English in the Marshall Islands of Micronesia. He also was an elementary classroom teacher and a reading specialist in California. He received an Ed.M. degree in reading and human development at Harvard and a Ph.D. in language and literacy at the University of California, Berkeley. He edits a column on literacy on the Internet for *The Reading Teacher*, teaches graduate courses in literacy education, and is currently studying the integration of Internet technologies within school classrooms. Professor Leu has published articles on literacy in a variety of journals, including *Reading Research Quarterly, The Reading Teacher, The Journal of Reading Behavior*, and *The Journal of Educational Psychology*. He co-edited *The National Reading Conference Yearbook* for six years and co-authored the recent book, *Teaching with the Internet: Lessons from the Classroom*. He currently serves on the editorial review boards for *Reading Research Quarterly, The Reading Teacher*, and *Reading Online*. He enjoys dressage, fly fishing, and spending time with his family.

Charles K. Kinzer is associate professor in the department of teaching and learning and a research scientist at the learning and technology center at Peabody College of Vanderbilt University. He teaches graduate and undergraduate courses in literacy education and works extensively with technology as it relates to literacy instruction. He has taught reading and remedial reading in middle and junior high schools. He received his M.A. in education from the University of British Columbia, Canada, and his Ph.D. in language and literacy at the University of California, Berkeley. Professor Kinzer's research includes reading comprehension, vocabulary acquisition, teacher cognition, and the application of technology in education. He has published articles about reading education, technology, and expert systems development in journals such as *The Journal of Reading Behavior, The Journal of Reading, Reading Research and Instruction*, and *Applied Cognitive Psychology*. He co-edited *The National Reading Conference Yearbook* for six years and the *Electronic Classroom* (for *Reading Online*) for three years. He serves on numerous editorial boards, including *The Reading Teacher, The Journal of Literacy Research, The Journal of Special Education Technology*, the *NRC Yearbook* and *Reading Online*, and he has directed several nationally funded projects. He enjoys photography, traveling, and spending time at the beach with his wife and daughter.

Preface

Our Approach

We write this book for students in a reading/literacy methods course. The central idea of this book is a simple proposition: *We believe children learn best when they have an insightful teacher capable of making professional judgments about what each child requires.*

We seek to develop insightful teachers, empowered to make thoughtful decisions about children and literacy instruction. We believe the insights teachers possess about literacy, children, and best practice instruction largely determine their effectiveness as literacy educators. We show readers how to develop these insights by *understanding central principles of best practice instruction derived from research and related to state standards.*

Therefore, this book seeks to move away from prescriptive literacy programs. Instead, we support teachers who recognize that knowing "why" is just as important as knowing "what" and "how." Children and literacy are too complex to provide a simple, "one-size-fits-all" instructional solution. Instead, children require the very best insights teachers possess. Our approach seeks to accomplish this.

We have organized this edition around the principles of best practice instruction derived from research and commonly found in state standards for reading/literacy education. Each chapter begins with a central principle of best practice instruction based on the research literature and commonly reflected in state standards. It then explores a wide variety of instructional practices that support this principle.

Goals in This Revision

We have several goals for this revision.

First, we want teachers to understand the research bases for best practice instruction. Each chapter is organized around an important, research-based, best practice principle common to all state standards for reading/language arts. It explains how this principle is implemented in effective classrooms around the country through powerful classroom examples and extensive instructional practices. Links on our website (www.prenhall.com/leukinzer) take you to the standards for your state, so you can see how this principle gets enacted in your state standards.

Second, we want to help teachers develop the insights about literacy and literacy instruction that permit them to meet their individual needs. We show you how to develop a personal "literacy framework," a set of beliefs and insights to inform the decisions each teacher must make in the classroom. This literacy framework is a powerful tool. It helps you develop the insights critical to successful literacy instruction. We believe an insightful teacher, making thoughtful decisions, is far more important than any instructional approach, any set of materials, or any mandated prescription for instruction.

Third, we seek to help teachers integrate Internet technologies into classroom lessons to prepare children for the literacy futures they deserve. The International Reading Association recently approved a position statement explaining the important need to prepare our students for the new literacies emerging from the Internet and other technologies (available at http://www.reading.org/pdf/technology_pos.pdf). Drawing on extensive research in this area, we have created the *first* textbook that shows how to systematically integrate traditional aspects of literacy instruction with new technologies such as the Internet. We have been careful not to include technology for technology's sake, focusing instead on simple and practical strategies to incorporate technology into widely recognized practices for literacy instruction. Additionally, we have been sensitive to the needs of teachers without access to technology or teachers in a single-computer classroom. We present the use of technology as one of many different options for constructing a literacy program.

Finally, we want to show teachers how to use literacy to celebrate the diversity that increasingly defines our world. We demonstrate how to teach literacy in the context of our increasingly global and multicultural society by using a variety of resources: new works of children's literature that share important cultural perspectives; new teaching strategies that help children understand and value diversity; and the Internet, which enables students to communicate with others around the world and helps them discover alternative perspectives.

New to This Edition

Here are just a few of the many changes we have made in this edition to meet the rapidly changing nature of literacy and the new expectations parents and children have for every teacher:

▶ Each chapter now focuses on a research-based, best practice principle common to nearly all state standards.
▶ Videos of effective classroom practice are now available for students to view over the Internet, showing them how to implement best practice instruction in their classroom. Visit www.prenhall.com/leukinzer
▶ Chapters contain new instructional models showing how a central research principle is implemented in different classrooms.
▶ Throughout the text we have revised the instructional models used to integrate Internet technologies into the reading program. These include Internet Workshop, Internet Project, WebQuests, and Internet Inquiry.
▶ We have expanded our comprehensive coverage on how best to develop the foundations of early literacy, including the development of phonemic awareness, phonics, and fluency.
▶ We have updated our comprehensive coverage of how best to integrate children's literature and writing into a balanced reading program.
▶ We provide a new listserv only for students and professors who are using this text, providing a common forum for conversations with the authors who wrote the book and for discussions among students at different institutions who explore the challenges, joys, and anxieties of becoming a teacher of reading. For information about this resource, visit www.prenhall.com/leukinzer

Special Features

Becoming an insightful and effective literacy educator is not easy. Our greatest concern in this edition was to craft the revision in a manner considerate of your needs. We include a number of special features to support this important work.

Useful Teaching Ideas

▶ Online videos of best practice instruction may be viewed over the Internet.
▶ We describe more than 300 teaching ideas in the **Practical Teaching Strategies** feature boxes.
▶ In a continuing feature, **E-mail from the Classroom,** literacy educators share stories and teaching ideas that really work.
▶ A special feature, **Celebrating Diversity,** describes powerful strategies to use diversity to promote literacy and learning.

▶ We show how to integrate the Internet in your classroom around **Internet Workshop, Internet Project, WebQuests,** and **Internet Inquiry.**

▶ Samples of **thematic units** integrating children's literature, multicultural perspectives, and literature discussion groups are provided.

▶ In each **Comments from the Classroom** feature, experienced teachers share stories of classroom teaching and learning.

Developing Literacy Insights

▶ **Belief inventories** in chapter 3 help readers identify their beliefs about literacy and learning.

▶ We show **how beliefs inform teaching decisions** about what to teach and how to teach. Tables and discussion at the end of each chapter show these relationships for the topic of that chapter.

▶ **Model lessons demonstrate how teachers adapt instructional practices** to meet individual needs in their classrooms. Alternative ways to teach the same lesson are also described.

▶ A section in each chapter, **Making Instructional Decisions,** invites readers to apply their understanding of each chapter's contents.

Supporting the Learning Process

▶ Each chapter begins with a list of **key concepts** and **chapter goals** that help students organize concepts before reading.

▶ **Key terms are highlighted** in the text and **definitions appear in the margins** to assist in the initial comprehension and later review.

▶ **Internet locations are highlighted** to make it easier to locate important resources and explore the potential of this new literacy resource.

Ancillary Resources

▶ An **instructor's guide** includes **summaries of each chapter; additional activities** to complete individually or within cooperative groups; **blackline masters** for use with an overhead projector to facilitate class discussion; and an **extensive set of examination questions and quizzes.**

▶ To enhance discussion and understanding, a **videotape** showing classroom examples of best practice instruction is also available. Segments from these videos are also available online.

▶ To prepare readers for their electronic futures we have developed a **Companion Website** available at www.prenhall.com/leukinzer, as well as a special **listserv.** Directions for subscribing to this listserv are available on pages 89 and 90.

Acknowledgments

As in any major project, the quality of the finished product results from the effort, encouragement, and sacrifices of many individuals. We greatly appreciate everyone who has supported this work and beg the indulgence of any we may inadvertently fail to acknowledge.

This revision has benefited from an extensive review by many talented colleagues who were gracious enough to share their many useful insights. We wish to recognize the important work contributed by these distinguished reviewers: Steve Arndt, Warner Pacific College; Betty Goerss, Indiana University East; Steve Hansell, Wright State University; and Tim Shanahan, University of Illinois at Chicago.

Finally, we wish to thank our editors at Merrill/Prentice Hall and Carlisle Communications for all their support and excellent assistance. Authors could not ask for more capable editors.

To everyone, our deepest thanks!

A Final Note

Finally, we wish to share a personal note. Working together on this project has been an especially important experience for each of us. Neither the previous editions, nor this fifth edition, would have its depth of coverage without the combined knowledge of each author. This book is a joint effort in the fullest sense of a partnership—a co-authored volume with both authors participating equally throughout the project. Author order was determined randomly.

Donald J. Leu, Jr.
University of Connecticut

Charles K. Kinzer
Vanderbilt University

Discover the Companion Website Accompanying This Book

Effective Literacy Instruction Companion Website: A Virtual Learning Environment

In building on our goal to help teachers integrate Internet technologies into classroom lessons to prepare children for the literacy futures they deserve, we have developed an online learning environment for students and professors alike—a Companion Website and listserv—to support *Effective Literacy Instruction K–8: Implementing Best Practice.* These tools provide professors with effective technologies for supplementing classes, provide an environment for teachers to become familiar with all the Internet has to offer them and their literacy classrooms, and help users grow comfortable with technology while they ground their learning.

In creating this virtual environment, our goal is to build on and enhance what our textbook already offers. For this reason, the content for this user-friendly website is organized by chapter and provides the professor and student with a variety of meaningful resources.

For the Professor—

The Companion Website integrates **Syllabus Manager**™, an online syllabus creation and management utility.

- **Syllabus Manager**™ provides you, the instructor, with an easy, step-by-step process to create and revise syllabi, with direct links into the Companion Website and other online content without having to learn HTML.
- Students may logon to your syllabus during any study session. All they need to know is the web address for the Companion Website and the password you've assigned to your syllabus.
- After you have created a syllabus using **Syllabus Manager**™, students may enter the syllabus for their course section from any point in the Companion Website.
- Clicking on a date, the student is shown the list of activities for the assignment. The activities for each assignment are linked directly to actual content, saving time for students.
- Adding assignments consists of clicking on the desired due date, then filling in the details of the assignment—name of the assignment, instructions, and whether it is a one-time or repeating assignment.
- In addition, links to other activities can be created easily. If the activity is online, a URL can be entered in the space provided, and it will be linked automatically in the final syllabus.
- Your completed syllabus is hosted on our servers, allowing convenient updates from any computer on the Internet. Changes you make to your syllabus are immediately available to your students at their next logon.

For the Student—

▶ **Key Concepts**—outline key concepts from the text
▶ **Interactive Self-quizzes**—complete with hints and automatic grading that provide immediate feedback for students

After students submit their answers for the interactive self-quizzes, the Companion Website **Results Reporter** computes a percentage grade, provides a graphic representation of how many questions were answered correctly and incorrectly, and gives a question-by-question analysis of the quiz. Students are given the option to send their quiz to up to four e-mail addresses (professor, teaching assistant, study partner, etc.).

▶ **Video Footage**—clips of classroom instruction, accompanied by essay questions, familiarize students with the implementation of best practice
▶ **Web Destinations**—links to all Internet sites discussed in the text
▶ **Chat**—real-time chat with anyone who is using the text anywhere in the country— ideal for discussion and study groups, class projects, etc.
▶ **Listserv**—dedicated to users of this text alone and maintained by the text's authors, this listserv provides a common forum for conversations among students at different institutions who explore the challenges, joys, and anxieties of becoming a teacher of reading.

The Companion Website is developed and maintained by Prentice Hall and includes a privacy policy statement for that location.

To take advantage of the many available resources, please visit the *Effective Literacy Instruction K–8: Implementing Best Practice,* 5th Edition, Companion Website at

www.prenhall.com/leukinzer

Brief Contents

Contents

PART 2   Developing a Knowledge Base   93

CHAPTER 12   Including All Children in Your Literacy Classroom   440

Disclaimer: We have devoted great time and energy to providing accurate and current information in this book. Nevertheless, in an environment as constantly changing as the Internet, it is inevitable that some of the information provided here will also change, and we cannot be responsible for these changes. Information provided at one Internet location may move to another, sometimes without any indication it has moved. If you notice changes to the Internet locations described in this book, please keep us informed so that we may update the links on the accompanying home page to this text (http://www.prenhall.com/leukinzer).

Also, the authors and the publisher do not assume responsibility for errors or omissions with regard to the Internet resources identified in this book, nor do they assume liability for any damages resulting from the use of any information identified in this book or from links listed at sites that are described. As we state in this book, the best way to protect children from viewing inappropriate sites or receiving inappropriate messages is to implement a sound, acceptable use policy and to carefully monitor student use of the Internet in your classroom, at school, and at home.

Finally, the Internet and non-electronic citations in this book are used as examples only. We do not endorse specific sites or products, whether commercial or not-for-profit.

Entering the World of Literacy Learning

CHAPTER 1

The Challenge and the Rewards

✉ **E-mail from the Classroom**

Subject: Becoming a Great Teacher!
From: Merritt Johnson, mj137@aol.com

I've always wanted to be a reading teacher, probably because I love reading so much myself and want to help open up this wonderful world for others. Everybody knows that helping children learn to read and write is about the most important things teachers do. I, personally, don't remember how I learned to read, but I do remember the teachers who helped me love books! Ms. Jackoby in first grade had all these books in her room and let me choose the ones I wanted to read and talk about. She had some neat-looking worksheets that I loved filling out and then she'd post them around the room. And then there was Mr. Williams in third grade, who kept using storybooks together with our textbooks in social studies. Oh yes! I remember how we used to play games with reading and writing in kindergarten with Ms. Franklin, even though I know now that these games were really good teaching. It seems like they all did slightly different things, but everything they did helped me learn to read and developed my love of reading.

What I want to know now is what will make me the best teacher that I can be! I want to be a great teacher, one children will remember. I want to learn about all the things that will make me successful. I'm excited about my methods course and about learning to teach reading well—it's a responsibility that I'm looking forward to. I KNOW I'm going to love watching the children in my class become joyful readers and writers! I'm excited about finding out how to become the great teacher that I want to be!

—Merritt

After reading this chapter, you should be able to:

1. Discuss effective instructional principles for teaching reading.
2. Describe how your personal definition of reading will influence literacy instruction in your classroom.
3. Explain why different teachers reach different decisions about how to teach reading.
4. Evaluate different definitions of reading and how these affect instruction.
5. Discuss instructional frameworks and how these inform instructional decisions about literacy education.

⌨ Becoming an Outstanding Teacher of Reading: Principles of Effective Literacy Instruction

In her chapter-opening e-mail, Merritt Johnson shares her excitement about opening up the world of literacy to her students. Her excitement may be similar to your own. You may also feel that teaching is a challenging and rewarding profession, that teachers have a significant influence on their students' lives, and that literacy educators can have an especially lasting impact. The importance of reading and writing is seen in every subject area and in nearly every aspect of life. The decisions you make in these areas are critical to your students' future success. We are sure you share Merritt's goal of being a great teacher and perhaps also wonder, as she does, about how to teach reading most effectively to a range of children.

This book, and your coursework, will provide you with the basis to be a great teacher of reading. In order to provide you with this foundation, we have organized this book around a core set of research-based instructional principles. These principles are an essential part of effective reading instruction; knowing how to structure your teaching so that these principles of effective instruction are incorporated into your teaching will help make you the effective teacher you want to be.

While no two teachers teach in exactly the same way, the following instructional principles have been found to be instrumental in effective teaching:

1. **Teachers' insights are central to effective instruction.** Effective literacy educators use their insights about literacy to meet individual needs (Anders, Hoffman, & Duffy, 2000; Duffy & Hoffman, 1999; Snow, Burns, & Griffin, 1998). This is perhaps the most important and least understood principle of effective literacy instruction, and is elaborated in chapters 2 and 3. Insightful teachers are critical to children's success in reading—it is knowledgeable and insightful teachers who implement effective instructional principles, and who use materials, methods, and management strategies to ensure the literacy futures of children. Teachers make a difference. Chapters 1 through 3 explore this principle.

2. **Teach decoding skills.** Beginning reading instruction should integrate a systematic program in decoding knowledge that includes, when appropriate for individuals, the development of phonological awareness, phonemic awareness, phonic knowledge, sight word knowledge, context use strategies, and fluency. (Adams, 1990; Anderson, Hiebert, Scott, & Wilkinson, 1985; National Reading Panel, 2000; Snow, Burns, & Griffin, 1998). Systematic instruction in decoding knowledge is related to reading success. Instructional procedures that focus on various aspects of decoding knowledge, and when these should occur in the early grades, are highlighted in chapter 4.

3. **Early literacy and home experiences are important.** Early experiences with literacy in a variety of situations and contexts are important to later reading achievement; building on students' sociocultural and linguistic backgrounds is related to reading achievement and positive reading attitudes in all students (Gee, 2000; National Reading Panel, 2000; Snow, Burns, & Griffin, 1998; Yaden, Rowe, & MacGillivray, 2000). Early experiences with literacy—being read to as a young child, having chances to explore print and print materials, and being a part of a discussion about picture and print books—are related to later reading acquisition. Chapter 5 discusses the importance of early literacy experiences, the importance of acknowledging children's literacy backgrounds, and the implications of these aspects for teachers of reading.

4. **Use exceptional works of literature and other text types.** Exceptional children's literature, including a variety of text types, is essential to include in an effective literacy program (Anderson, Hiebert, Scott, & Wilkinson, 1985; Galda, Ash, & Cullinan, 2000; Snow, Burns, & Griffin, 1998). Stories are essential to passing down knowledge across generations, to providing common links across human experiences, and to literacy learning. Stories are motivational, and so are well-written texts of different

types—narrative, expository, and literature across genres. Exposure to texts of many types allows children to discover the structure of stories and of informational texts, and provide an important vehicle to embedding the concepts important to learning how to read and write. Chapter 6 explores the essentials of children's literature in effective literacy instruction.

5. **Integrate reading and writing.** It is important to integrate writing with reading experiences to support children's literacy development (Calkins, 2000; Gavelek, Raphael, Biondo, & Wang, 2000; Yaden, Rowe, & MacGillivray, 2000). Reading and writing are related language processes, and children are motivated to communicate their ideas through writing and reading. As you will see in chapter 7, there are at least four reasons why integrating reading and writing can enhance reading instruction.

6. **Vocabulary knowledge helps comprehension.** Vocabulary knowledge is closely related to reading comprehension, and vocabulary instruction can help build background knowledge and word attack strategies that lead to increased reading achievement (Anderson & Freebody, 1981; Nagy, 1988; Nagy & Scott, 2000; Smith, 1997). Fluent reading of words and understanding the concepts they represent result from effective instruction and concept development linked to word recognition. Chapter 8 explores effective techniques you will be able to use in your classroom to help your students learn the meanings for unfamiliar words and to recognize these words fluently.

7. **Teach reading comprehension.** An effective literacy program should integrate systematic instruction in reading comprehension (Anderson, Hiebert, Scott, & Wilkinson, 1985; National Reading Panel, 2000; Snow, Burns, & Griffin, 1998). Readers' comprehension can be enhanced through the instruction of strategies targeted at understanding the structure of text, the accessing of a reader's background knowledge, and fluent reading of text. Chapter 9 explores instructional strategies that result in effective reading comprehension.

8. **Teach reading using different kinds of texts.** Different strategies are required for reading different kinds of texts; teaching strategies that are most appropriate for texts in the various content areas will result in more effective comprehension of materials that rely less on narrative text patterns (Bean, 2000). Stories and other materials that are typically read in language arts have a different text structure than expository materials, word problems in mathematics, maps, charts and graphs, and other materials that are encountered in various subject areas. The most appropriate strategies for different content-area texts are presented in chapter 10.

9. **Good assessment strategies help teachers teach.** Monitoring children's success in reading enhances the probability of providing appropriate, individualized instruction for all readers (Pellegrino, Chudowsky, & Glaser, 2001; P.L.107-110 (H.R.I), 2002). Chapter 11 presents a range of assessment strategies, from informal techniques to standardized measures, that will be useful to you as you decide on appropriate instructional strategies for the children in your class.

10. **Meet individual needs, including children with special needs.** An effective literacy program should seek to meet as wide a range of individual needs as possible within the classroom, including the needs of those who are formally designated as children with special needs (Allington, 1991; Allington & Johnston, 1989; Au, 2000). Chapter 12 provides a discussion of individual needs and includes strategies for teaching reading to address special populations.

11. **Organize your classroom to maximize learning.** A teacher's ability to orchestrate instruction to meet the varying needs of individuals and groups is critical to success in the literacy classroom (Anderson, Heibert, Scott, & Wilkinson, 1985; Snow, Burns, & Griffin, 1998). Effective classroom organization and management allows more time to be spent on instruction and is related to children's learning. Various classroom organization patterns and the integrations of literacy instruction within these patterns are presented in chapter 13.

12. **Teach for children's literacy futures.** Integrating computer and Internet technologies in literacy instruction allows children to use their emerging literacy abilities in

Incorporating technology into literacy instruction is becoming increasingly important at all grade levels.

Check your ongoing understanding of chapter concepts by using the guided review for this chapter on http://www. prenhall.com/leukinzer

the most current literacies that are valued in society and can enhance children's learning of both conventional and emerging literacies (Labbo & Reinking, 2000; Leu & Kinzer, 2000; Reinking, 1998). Teaching in ways that prepare children for emerging communication and literacy demands is important. This principle is a part of each chapter in this book and is emphasized in chapter 14.

Each chapter in this book highlights one or more of the previous principles and explains its importance to effective instruction. Each chapter also describes effective instructional procedures that will allow you to incorporate each principle into your literacy instruction. In this way, we will answer Merritt's question about how to teach reading effectively.

Teaching Reading Effectively: Preparing Children for Their Literacy Futures

We live in a world where the technologies of literacy are rapidly changing and where new technologies of literacy regularly appear (Kinzer & Leu, 1997; Leu & Kinzer, 2000). Thus, you need to keep in mind an important point: Effective literacy educators must prepare children for their literacy futures. Throughout this book, we will help you accomplish this important challenge. We include traditional elements of literacy education such as children's literature, decoding and fluency practices, reading and writing workshop, language experience approaches, and big book activities. We integrate these with important new elements of literacy education made possible through the new technologies of literacy: Internet Workshop, Internet Projects, Internet Inquiry, keypals, and talking storybook activities.

However, helping children acquire literacy is not just a matter of becoming familiar with children's literature, new technologies, or even outstanding instructional practices. Instead, we believe *the most important element of effective literacy instruction will be the decisions you make in the classroom as you work with children to support their individual needs.* In a complex classroom community, you will need to insightfully orchestrate effective literacy learning opportunities for each child in your classroom. As an insightful teacher, *you* will be the most important component of your reading and writing program.

TABLE 1-1

World Wide Web sites available to teachers and their students to support literacy learning

> **The Children's Literature Web Guide** (http://www.ucalgary.ca/~dkbrown/) is a wonderful resource for children's literature on the Internet. It includes discussions about books, pages where authors discuss their books, and links to many related sites. Stop by for a visit!
>
> **Keypals** (http://www.keypals.com/) contains a master list of mailing lists (listservs) from different organizations. The mailing lists link teachers to teachers, students to students, and classes to classes. You may subscribe to these lists directly from the Keypals site.
>
> **Literacy** (http://www.oswego.org/staff/cchamber/literacy/index.cfm) is a nicely organized resource with links to exceptional resources for teaching reading and writing.
>
> **Yahooligans** (http://www.yahooligans.com/) contains an extensive collection of resources for young children. It screens sites for appropriateness and child safety issues.
>
> **Reading Online** (http://readingonline.org/) is an electronic journal of the International Reading Association. It presents articles, critical issues, developments in literacy, and other aspects that will support your teaching and professional knowledge. It also has a section that provides discussion areas for readers to post responses and talk with authors.

To help you make the decisions essential to effective literacy instruction, we will focus more on reading than writing in these early chapters. After we explore reading instruction in the first six chapters, we will integrate the other central aspect of literacy—writing. We take this approach for several reasons. First, the important debates taking place within the literacy community focus on the nature of early reading. By understanding these debates, you will better understand your own beliefs about both reading and writing. Second, reading is central to all literacy acts; even when we write, we must read. Third, it is easiest to develop literacy insights by first exploring your beliefs about reading. Understanding these beliefs will help you to see why different instructional practices are effective for both reading and writing. Finally, we believe successful early reading experiences are the greatest gift you can give to children. Learning to read prepares children for their literacy futures, enabling them to succeed on life's journey.

As a teacher, you will sense the importance of reading as parents ask about their children's progress; as administrators provide in-service workshops on reading; as you see your school's test scores reported in the local newspaper; and especially as you look at the faces of your students, who want very much to learn to read. Reading is a critical part of the elementary school curriculum, and many people will be watching closely as you work to support your children in this area.

Fundamental changes are taking place in the nature of literacy learning within school classrooms. Most classrooms have at least one computer connected to the Internet, opening up a world of opportunities to your students. These opportunities include exchanging messages with keypals (electronic penpals) around the world, communicating with authors about their books, discussing an experiment with a scientist, communicating with astronauts, and many other exciting experiences. In addition, World Wide Web (WWW) locations provide you and your students with many new information resources. Throughout this book we will show you WWW locations where you can discover lesson plans for upcoming units and where your students can publish their writing, read wonderful works by other students, explore biographies of prominent children's authors, and engage in important multicultural experiences. It is hard not to get excited about these new opportunities available to children in your classroom, which can be explored by visiting the sites shown in Table 1-1. Upcoming chapters will show you how to use these locations, and many more, to support literacy learning. Internet resources will increase, not decrease, the central role you will play in orchestrating literacy experiences for your students.

reading process Active
and internal operations
involved in reading.

As we focus on reading instruction at the beginning of this journey, we will guide you to develop your beliefs about reading and reading instruction. The relationship between your beliefs about the **reading process** and the instructional decisions you make is one we will revisit often.

Understanding this relationship is important to developing the insights that are so crucial to effective literacy instruction. As you read this text, you will explore questions such as these:

▶ How do readers construct meaning as they read stories, articles, and books?
▶ How can technology, including the Internet, be helpful in supporting literacy learning in my classroom?
▶ What materials should I use to help children learn about literacy?
▶ How can I best organize my classroom to provide for the individual differences in my classroom?
▶ How can I use assessment tools to teach more effectively?
▶ What are the characteristics of effective teachers?
▶ What must I do to become an effective literacy educator?

As you develop your own beliefs about reading, you will more clearly articulate answers to these and other important questions. One way to explore these issues, and to provide additional support as you move toward becoming an effective literacy educator, is to join the electronic mailing list available to users of this book. This mailing list, LITERACY, provides an opportunity to discuss thoughts and experiences related to your development as a literacy educator and to explore issues raised in this book with peers from around the country. Instructions for joining this mailing list appear on page 88. Please join us.

One issue you may want to address on the mailing list is the diversity of the children that teachers encounter in every classroom. Some children will be far beyond their classroom peers in reading ability; others will be somewhat below the class average. All will have individual needs. Some will have difficulty in recognizing words, others will need help understanding word meanings, and other students will require assistance in interpreting or evaluating what is read. This diversity of needs and abilities makes teaching in general—and the teaching of reading in particular—both challenging and exciting.

The final challenge for you as a teacher will be to make appropriate instructional decisions while attending to the many events that take place during the course of a lesson. Learning to manage classroom activities and provide the best possible learning environment is an important part of becoming a teacher. Can you remember how you felt when you were learning to drive a car? You were confronted with important decisions that had to be made while you attended to many other things—the cars in front of and behind you, the actions of your passengers, the condition of the road, and so on. You probably drive skillfully now, and any uneasiness you felt has likely disappeared. With a solid knowledge base and concentrated practice, you will also master both the decision-making process and the management functions that will make your classroom a haven for learning.

As a literacy educator, you face several challenges. To be successful, you need a clear understanding of this complex subject, the ability to make informed decisions, and the management skill to accomplish your instructional goals in a busy classroom environment. Across the nation teachers are meeting these and other challenges, giving us one of the highest literacy rates in the world. When we compare the percentage of people who can read now to the percentage from 50 years ago, it is clear that others have learned to teach reading effectively, just as you will. With the help of this text and your own work and practice, you can develop into a successful teacher who will be repeatedly rewarded as your students become eager readers.

How does a teacher make appropriate decisions in the classroom? The answer lies partly in a teacher's beliefs about the reading process. In the next section we discuss definitions of the reading process and how respective definitions influence the choices and decisions that teachers make. We then introduce literacy frameworks and explain how they will help you to make instructional decisions in your classroom.

JUDY'S

COMMENTS FROM THE CLASSROOM

Because I have been teaching many years, I am often asked to explain how children learn to read. I try my best to explain that there is no one, prescribed way. Learning to read is a multifaceted process and, as each child is different with different abilities and learning styles, teachers must figure out what strategies work best with individual children.

One thing I have learned is that the most challenging part of teaching reading is to develop a love of reading. Children will not undertake the struggle to learn to read if they do not have a strong desire to do so.

A big key in getting children to learn to love reading is to tap into their interests. Obvious? Not always. It is easy to choose books you like, but that might not match a child's interests. As an example, this year my first-grade class had a tremendous interest in dinosaurs. A science buff I am not, but I accessed **Curse of the T-Rex** (one of Nova's locations at http://www.pbs.org/wgbh/nova/trex/) and found out a lot about dinosaurs and the time in which they lived. Along with this resource, we read books and poems and wrote songs about dinosaurs. Several children brought in models of dinosaurs and compared them to artwork, models, and fossils that had been posted on the Internet. We also found a site where artwork and other items about dinosaurs are featured (http://www.sofweb.vic.edu.au/STUDENTS/KIDS/vclass/dino.htm). The children then wrote and published their

own stories and we all learned how fascinating these creatures are. Therefore I was able to introduce some wonderful, enriching vocabulary words, including carnivore, herbivore, and paleontologist. My first graders loved learning these big words.

My advice to beginning teachers who want to open the world of reading for children is to find where each child is developmentally. Then, match books and reading-related activities to *their* interests—not yours. Be prepared to find that children's development and their interests will be as varied as flowers in a garden. The role of a teacher is to know what nourishment will allow each child to grow and flourish and how to nurture children so they blossom into good readers.

Source: When Judy Dill made these comments, she was a teacher at Strong Elementary School in a consolidated school district in rural Maine. She served as director of a preschool for several years before moving on to teach kindergarten.

Featured Teacher

Jack Fontanella

One of the teachers you may meet on the Internet is Jack Fontanella, a kindergarten teacher in Juneau, Alaska. As is quickly seen at his website (http://www.jsd.k12.ak.us/hbv/classrooms/Fontanella/fontanejhbvHome.html), he has a commitment to teaching children the literacies that have traditionally been associated with paper, as well as the new literacies that are increasingly encountered in our technological society. Jack Fontanella realizes that integrating technology into his students' learning has motivational as well as practical benefits. His students really enjoy making suggestions about the class website, and seeing their work appear there. In addition, Mr. Fontanella uses his website as a communications tool for parents and as an outreach center to others beyond his classroom. We encourage you to take a look at his website, where you will find samples of kindergartners' work, newsletters to parents, a summary of class projects, and useful links to other websites.

Go to:
Welcome to Kindergarten:
Everything You Need to Know
Our Photo Album
Our On-line Alphabet Book
Some of Our Work
Some of Our Block Projects
Our Seasons Project
Our Parent's Page
Class Newsletters
Links to Kindergarten Classes
Mr. F's Bookmarks
Our Teacher
Our Principal
Our School's Home Page
Our School District

A KINDERGARTEN CLASS—
MR. FONTANELLA'S
WELCOME!!!

Hi! We are a class of five and six year old girls and boys. We live in Alaska's Capital City, Juneau, Alaska. We go to school from 9:00 in the morning to 2:00 in the afternoon. We all like to have fun and play at school, but we are also learning how to read and write.

Click on a link below to learn more about us.

The Importance of Establishing a Perspective

Your view of reading—the factors involved, their relative importance, and the way the process takes place and develops—will have a direct and significant impact on your decision making. This, in turn, will affect how you teach reading. In fact, the relationship between a personal view of reading and teaching practices has been discussed for some time. About 40 years ago, Strang, McCullough, and Traxler (1961) stated:

> If we think of reading primarily as a visual task, we will be concerned with the correction of visual defects and the provision of legible reading material. If we think of reading as word recognition, we will drill on the basic sight vocabulary and word recognition skills. If we think of reading as merely reproducing what the author says, we will direct the student's attention to the literal meaning of the passage and check his comprehension of it. If we think of reading as a thinking process, we shall be concerned with the reader's skill in making interpretations and generalizations, in drawing inferences and conclu-

sions. If we think of reading as contributing to personal development and effecting desirable personality changes, we will provide our students with reading materials that meet their needs and have some application to their lives. (pp. 1–2)

Teachers are often left to discover their view of the reading process on their own; they are not advised how various viewpoints will affect their instructional decisions. This text provides guidance in establishing and making explicit your view of reading. It also helps you incorporate your view into a framework that will guide your instructional decisions. This will allow you to later modify your beliefs and your classroom instruction as appropriate for your students' learning. First, however, let us look at how others have defined reading and how reading is defined in this text.

Some Definitions of Reading

As knowledge about the reading process has evolved, definitions of reading have become more complex. Although "getting the author's message" is one way to define reading, such simplified definitions do not adequately describe the richness of this process. Look at the following definitions. As you consider them, think about the kinds of instructional choices each might imply. How might the classrooms of teachers with the following definitions of reading look different from one another?

Most current definitions of reading acknowledge the social, communicative nature of reading and writing and the fusion of the reading and writing process. Such viewpoints assume that learning takes place as children see the importance of communication and are based on beliefs that teaching should maximize communicative intent. Harste (1990), for example, notes that "language is a social event" (p. 317), and Shanahan (1990) stresses its communicative purpose:

> We read an author's words and are affected by the author's intentions. We write with the idea of influencing or informing others. . . . The fusion of reading and writing in the classroom offers children the possibility of participating in both sides of the communication process and, consequently, provides them with a more elaborate grasp of the true meaning of literacy. (p. 4)

The relationship between reading and writing and between readers and writers has been called interactive by some, transactional by others. For example, Rosenblatt (1985, 1988) has described this relationship as a transaction between the text and the reader, during which both are changed and become more than the sum of their parts. Rosenblatt's (1994) transactional view has had a major impact on reader-response theory; that is, thoughts about how readers react to a text—socially, psychologically, and morally:

> For the individual, then, language is that part, or set of features, of the public system that has been internalized through that person's experiences with words in life situations. . . . The residue of the individual's past transactions in particular natural and social contexts constitutes what can be termed a linguistic-experiential reservoir . . . this inner capital is all that each of us has to draw on in speaking, listening, writing, or reading. We "make sense" of a new situation . . . by applying, reorganizing, revising, or extending public and private elements selected from our personal linguistic-experiential reservoirs. (pp. 1060, 1061)

Other, generally older definitions equated reading with mechanics and pronunciation. Definitions such as the one shown below de-emphasized personal aspects such as motivation and background knowledge:

> Learning to read is like learning to drive a car. . . . The child learns the mechanics of reading, and when he's through, he can read. (Flesch, 1981, p. 3)
>
> [We should teach the child phonics] letter-by-letter and sound-by-sound until he knows it—and when he knows it he knows how to read. (Flesch, 1955, p. 121)

Is a knowledge of letters and sounds all there is to reading? In the case of a blind law student, the job of a paid reader is to read assigned class material to the student. Who would you say is reading—the sighted person who is pronouncing the material or the blind student who is comprehending it? Most people would agree that reading includes, but goes beyond, decoding symbols:

> Reading cannot occur unless the pupil can identify and recognize the printed symbol, and generally the pupil must also give the visual configuration a name. Even so, it is only one aspect of the reading process. Meaning, too, is an absolute prerequisite in reading. Perhaps too much emphasis in reading instruction has been placed on word identification and not enough on comprehension. (Dechant, 1982, p. 166)

If we assume that reading goes beyond pronunciation and involves understanding, we can see that the process of reading is more than a mechanical skill; it is active and internal. In fact, teaching reading may be thought of as teaching thinking because readers must organize information, recognize cause and effect, assess the importance of what is being read, and fit the material into their own beliefs and knowledge base. Consider, for example, these definitions:

psycholinguistic
Referring to the psychological and linguistic processes involved in language.

syntactic   Referring to the ordering of words that makes meaningful phrases and sentences.

semantic   Referring to the meanings of words.

pragmatic   Referring to the social appropriateness of speech acts in certain contexts.

> Reading is a **psycholinguistic** guessing game. It involves an interaction between thought and language.
>   Efficient reading does not result from precise perception and identification of all elements, but from skill in selecting the fewest, most productive cues necessary to produce guesses [about meaning] which are right the first time. (Goodman, 1976, p. 498)

> Reading is the process of understanding written language. It begins with a flutter of patterns on the retina and ends (when successful) with a definite idea about the author's intended message . . . a skilled reader must be able to make use of sensory, **syntactic, semantic,** and **pragmatic** information to accomplish his task. These various sources of information interact in many complex ways during the process of reading. (Rumelhart, 1994, p. 864)

As you have seen, the definitions presented in this section view reading differently. The definitions range from a mechanical sounding-out process to an interaction between what is read and what is already known to a social and emotional experience. Different instructional decisions result in part from varied definitions of reading. For example, a teacher who defines reading as strictly sounding out letters usually spends more time at the early grade levels teaching letter-sound relationships and less time reading to students.

All definitions of reading are personal, based on an individual's view of the reading process and the way in which reading ability develops. In order for you to understand the assumptions we make about reading throughout this book, it is important to share our definition of reading with you:

> Reading is a social, developmental, and interactive process that involves learning. It is a process incorporating a person's linguistic knowledge and can be powerfully influenced by an insightful teacher as well as other nonlinguistic internal and external conditions. It can be developed by self-directed learning experiences as well as by direct instruction and is increasingly important in the information age in which we live.

Several principles follow from this definition and inform succeeding chapters in this book.

1. *Reading and learning to read are fundamentally social actions.* Reading is a communicative and social act that occurs between individuals or groups. Moreover, a reader's social context helps to define the way in which reading is viewed and the function it serves. In addition, children learn much about reading from one another, from you, and from other significant adults in social contexts. We need to recognize the social nature of reading as we consider how best to support children on the road to literacy.

2. *Reading is a meaning construction process.* Readers construct meaning as they read, using both the meaning in a text and the meaning they bring to a text in an interactive process. Both decoding knowledge and prior knowledge are essential to effective reading. Because individual knowledge and expectations are not identical, different readers may interpret an identical text in varying ways.

Celebrating Diversity

Using Internet Resources

The diversity of students in your classroom will provide opportunities for meeting individual needs, as well as opportunities to learn from each other. You will have many opportunities to celebrate diversity as you encounter children with different dialects, backgrounds, abilities, concerns, motivations, interests, and reading levels. One way to celebrate this diversity is by using resources available on the Internet. These include:

Around the World
(http://www.yahooligans.com/Around the World/)

Cultures of the World
(http://www.ala.org/parentspage/greatsites/people.html#b)

K-5 CyberTrail: Multicultural Curriculum Resources
(http://www.wmht.org/trail/explor02.htm)

KidLink
(http://www.kidlink.org/english/general/intro.html)

Multicultural Pavilion
(http://curry.edschool.virginia.edu/go/multicultural/)

Wonderful Tales
(http://www.angelfire.com/ma3/mythology/introduction.html)

3. *Reading and writing are closely related and develop together.* Children learn much about reading through their writing. Conversely, they also learn much about writing through their reading. Since both reading and writing are linguistic processes, classroom learning should seek, wherever possible, to integrate reading and writing experiences.

4. *Children learn best when teachers take an approach that uses a range of strategies to teach reading.* Classroom literacy learning should recognize that children often travel different paths to reach the same destination. Children sometimes appear to do best by directing their own learning about reading. At other times, children appear to do best when you direct their learning about reading.

5. *The more children read, the better they read.* As children read interesting and authentic texts, they become actively engaged and seek out additional reading experiences. And, as children read, they learn many important things about reading. Every classroom reading program needs to include opportunities for independent reading of self-selected materials, ensuring that children read, read, and then read some more.

6. *We need to prepare children for the new information and communication technologies of their futures.* The nature of reading and writing is changing in an information age with many new technologies. We need to ensure our children's success in these new worlds by engaging them in successful experiences with the Internet as well as other information and communication technologies. As important new technologies appear, we need to prepare ourselves for using these in the classroom as well.

7. *Classrooms rich in literacy materials and literacy experiences are central to effective learning.* By creating a classroom rich in literature and informational resources, you do much to communicate the importance of reading and writing. By modeling effective use of these materials you provide important learning experiences for children.

8. *The most important element in any literacy program is an insightful teacher.* Insightful teachers understand the literacy needs of their children. They know what and how to teach. Most importantly, they know *why* they do what they do during literacy lessons.

Children love being read to, and their expressions as they listen to stories and learn to read them on their own are among the many rewards for teachers of literacy.

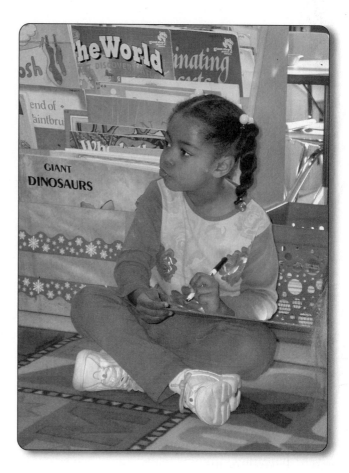

Specifying a definition and personal framework to develop and improve instructional strategies is an important part of being a literacy educator and will help you meet the challenges outlined here. Guiding you in this task is one of our major goals. As you read through the following chapters, look back periodically at our definition of reading. Add to it or delete from it as your knowledge changes and as you continue to clarify your own definition of reading and the reading process. Throughout this text we will remind you that your view of reading will determine how you teach.

Literacy Frameworks and Instructional Decisions

Teachers provide effective reading instruction in busy classroom environments by relying on different types of literacy frameworks. Frameworks help teachers decide what and how to teach. Such frameworks consist of the materials, methods, and beliefs about reading that teachers use to make their instructional decisions. Literacy frameworks provide structure and reduce the number of conscious decisions that teachers must make during interactions with students.

Literacy frameworks guide teachers in planning and teaching their reading lessons in much the same way that road maps guide drivers in their travels, or grocery lists guide shoppers at the supermarket. Consider how a road map provides a general sense of direction and goals as well as specific instructions along the way and how this sense of direction and goals helps a driver who encounters an unexpected detour. A literacy framework can provide you with a reference point from which instructional decisions can be quickly made when unexpected things are encountered in a reading lesson—perhaps a student who is not reaching certain expectations or materials that might be inappropriate for one or more students. Literacy frameworks promote individual decisions that are consistent with your overall instructional goals.

FIGURE 1-1

A procedural outline for a directed reading–thinking activity

1. _Predicting._ During this first step, ask students what they expect to find when they read. At the beginning ask questions like, "What might a story with this title be about? Why?" Later in the story ask questions like, "What do you think will happen next? Why?" Each student should form a prediction and be able to support it.
2. _Reading._ During this second step, ask students to read up to a specified point in the story and check their predictions. They may read either orally or silently.
3. _Proving._ During this third step, ask students to evaluate their predictions within the context of a discussion. Ask questions like, "Was your prediction correct? Why or why not?" At the end of the discussion, begin the procedural cycle again, and have students predict what will take place in the next portion of the story. Continue in a similar fashion until students finish reading the story.

Three Types of Frameworks

Teachers use three types of frameworks to meet the instructional and organizational challenges of reading instruction:

▶ Frameworks based on a set of instructional materials, called _material frameworks._
▶ Frameworks based on instructional methods, called _method frameworks._
▶ Frameworks based on your beliefs about what to teach and how to teach, called _literacy frameworks._

Our experiences suggest these frameworks are often developmental. That is, some new teachers often rely on material frameworks early in their careers. Later, these teachers come to rely less on lesson-planning information in these materials as they develop their own method frameworks to guide instructional activities. Later still, many teachers come to understand more fully why they do what they do during literacy lessons. These teachers have developed literacy frameworks to inform their instructional decision making.

A **material framework** is based on the materials and lesson-planning information available in the teacher's guide to a published set of instructional tools, which may include a kit of graded activity cards, computer software, or a complete reading program. Because the lesson-planning information in the teacher's guide has a sequence of procedures and plans to follow, many decisions are already made or suggested. A material framework, based on a detailed description of how to teach reading (provided as part of the instructional materials), reduces the number of instructional decisions that a teacher must make.

> **material framework**
> A framework used to teach reading, based on a published set of materials and lesson-planning information.

Adopting a material framework typically means becoming familiar with the teacher's manual for a particular reading program and following its directions quite closely. Many new teachers begin with a material framework because they have little time to develop or modify their own plans for instruction.

Other teachers primarily make instructional decisions from a **method framework.** These teachers follow certain methods for teaching reading, and they implement these methods as needed to meet instructional goals. Each instructional method includes procedural steps as well as options that may be selected at each step. Thus, instructional decision making revolves around the procedural steps specified by a particular method. Figure 1-1 presents an example of one type of method framework, a **directed reading–thinking activity (DRTA).**

> **method framework** A framework used to teach reading, based on procedural steps for teaching and options for completing each step.

> **directed reading–thinking activity (DRTA)** A method framework used to assist students in predicting outcomes and drawing conclusions, which involves predicting, reading, and proving.

A method framework provides a general description of the steps to follow during instruction and a general indication of the activities that might be used at each step. Nevertheless, it is not usually tied to a specific set of materials. Instead, a method framework may be used with almost any set of materials, from selections found in published reading programs, to ways to incorporate technology and the Internet, to selections written by teachers or provided by students. If the teaching procedures suggested by particular materials differ from a teacher's preferred method, then the teacher following a method framework would substitute the preferred method to replace the suggestion.

Often teachers employ several different method frameworks, using each for different instructional purposes. For example, a particular method might be chosen for enjoying a work of children's literature, while another might be chosen to teach decoding skills, and yet another might be chosen to teach study skills. Some of the more frequently used method frameworks include directed reading activities, language experience activities, and activities associated with deductive and inductive instruction. These and other common method frameworks are presented in chapter 3.

literacy framework   A framework used to teach reading, based on beliefs about what to teach and how to teach.

A **literacy framework** is the most powerful and flexible of the three frameworks discussed here. It provides wonderful insights about your teaching and about individual children in your classroom, allowing you to thoughtfully individualize instruction.

A literacy framework is what most effective teachers strive toward and is where we will guide you in the following chapters. It is more abstract than either a material framework, where teachers follow the suggestions and decisions as found in a teacher's manual, or a method framework, where teachers follow the procedures and options specified as part of a particular teaching method. A literacy framework, based on an understanding of reading comprehension and response, organizes your beliefs about literacy around two issues: (1) What should I teach? and (2) How should I teach? To teach from a literacy framework you will need to become knowledgeable about a wide range of materials and methods and articulate your beliefs around these two issues.

Literacy frameworks are used in two major ways: (1) to select appropriate materials and methods and (2) to inform your decisions about what to teach and how to teach. Thus, a literacy framework will help you to adapt lesson plans and activities in a set of materials and to select several different methods to teach a reading lesson. Each choice or decision would be deliberate, reasoned, and consistent with your beliefs.

Given the complexity of developing a literacy framework, why should it be preferred to a material or a method framework? Teaching from a literacy framework is preferable for at least six important reasons:

1. A literacy framework will inform your decisions as you choose materials and methods appropriate for individual children in your class. With a literacy framework, you will not rely only on one predominant approach for each student. Most importantly, you will know why you are individualizing instruction.
2. A literacy framework provides a clear sense of direction, especially as you decide how and when to modify instructional resources. All teachers adapt and supplement available instructional materials, and a literacy framework guides the necessary decision making.
3. A literacy framework provides more strategies for meeting individual needs and for working with diverse and challenged learners. Within material or method frameworks, individual needs are met by altering the pace of instruction and/or the amount of practice. Within a literacy framework individual needs can also be met by altering instructional materials, methods, and even what is taught.
4. A literacy framework helps explain why certain decisions are made during reading instruction, whereas frameworks based on materials or methods simply tell teachers what to do. Knowing why something is being done will allow you to more effectively alter instruction for particular students and more accurately evaluate the success of an instructional activity.
5. Literacy frameworks can be used in many more situations than frameworks based on materials or instructional methods. For example, specific material and method frameworks often are helpful only if a teacher's preferred methods or materials are those favored by the school district in which they are to be used. A literacy framework can be used in any instructional situation.
6. Literacy frameworks offer more flexibility in instructional decision making than either material or method frameworks. The illustration in Figure 1-2 indicates that teachers making decisions based on literacy frameworks choose from the full range

FIGURE 1-2

An illustration showing the inclusiveness of a literacy framework

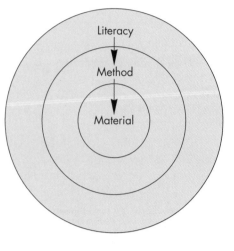

FIGURE 1-3

An illustration of the framework modification cycle

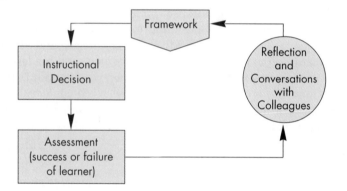

of methods and materials. Teachers using method frameworks are somewhat less flexible but may choose any materials appropriate to their chosen method(s). However, teachers with material frameworks are completely constrained by their chosen instructional materials.

Developing a literacy framework is more difficult than developing a material or method framework, partly because of the broad knowledge base required. Nevertheless, such wide-ranging knowledge certainly results in a more effective teacher, and knowing in advance that your goal is to develop a literacy framework will facilitate that development. Knowing where you are going always makes the journey shorter and easier. Thus, learning about reading instruction from the perspective of a literacy framework should make your learning process more effective and efficient.

Decision Making and the Modification of Literacy Frameworks

Literacy frameworks are not static devices; they are modified as knowledge about materials, methods, and the reading process develops and changes. You will continually modify your literacy framework as you reflect on what does and does not help children learn to read. This process, combining experiences of teaching literacy with reflection, is shown in Figure 1-3.

As you progress, it is important to remember that your framework will also be influenced by professional conversations you will have with colleagues in your school and

FIGURE 1-4

The Doucette Index (http://www.educ.ucalgary.ca/litindex/), an Internet resource page to help teachers and children find resources for children's literature

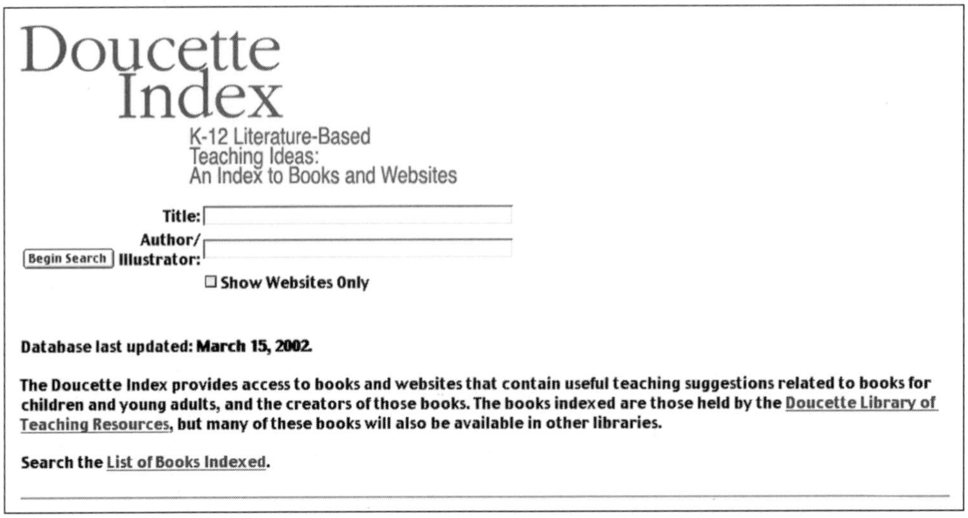

Doucette Index

K-12 Literature-Based
Teaching Ideas:
An Index to Books and Websites

Title: [   ]
Author/
Illustrator: [   ]
[Begin Search]

☐ **Show Websites Only**

Database last updated: March 15, 2002.

The Doucette Index provides access to books and websites that contain useful teaching suggestions related to books for children and young adults, and the creators of those books. The books indexed are those held by the Doucette Library of Teaching Resources, but many of these books will also be available in other libraries.

Search the List of Books Indexed.

Note: Courtesy of University of Calgary, Doucette Library.

over the Internet. You will find support and ideas from across the nation as you join mailing lists where teachers discuss issues important in their work as they help children learn to read. Many teachers will share ideas as you influence each other's literacy framework. There are also many resources available, including resources on the Internet, that will enable you to implement your literacy framework. For example, the Doucette Index, shown in Figure 1-4, allows you to search the Internet for instructional resources for many works of children's literature, and the resources available through SCORE: Cyberguides (http://www.sdcoe.k12.ca.us/score/cyberguide.html) provide guidance for web-delivered units of instruction centered on core works of literature that are keyed to California State Standards.

Frameworks are central to the decisions you will make as a teacher of reading. They reduce complexity, allow you to make decisions quickly, and most important, help you meet the challenges encountered in reading instruction. As you learn about ways to teach reading effectively, you will define and clarify your own framework, which will guide your teaching decisions.

⌨ What Are the Rewards?

Classroom teaching—particularly the teaching of reading—is not only challenging, but is also immensely rewarding. Good readers often forget how difficult it may have been to learn to read. Reading affects our everyday lives; we take for granted the many times we use this ability during the day. Look around you right now. How many things need to be read? At home there may be a newspaper, a guide of television listings, a cereal box, or mail. At school there may be a bulletin board, posters, books, or class notes. Think of all the things you have already read so far today. If you view reading in the broadest terms, perhaps as making meaning from abstract symbols, then you may have read your watch, the morning paper, road signs, a map or some other set of directions, or the numbers and letters on a dollar bill. Reading touches all aspects of life.

It is also rewarding to know that reading ability positively influences our lifestyles. For example, teaching children to read well will be a key factor in determining their later employment opportunities. Moreover, reading can positively impact depression and boredom as well as provide role models and inspiration. It can answer our questions, give us directions, teach and transform, provide pleasure, and stimulate original thought. As a literacy educator you will have a lasting impact on your students' personal and professional lives.

E-mail from the Classroom

Subject: Advice
From: Paul and Therese Forster, paulyj@whidbey.net

Hi! Welcome to the real world of teaching. I've been teaching now for 13 years, but I still remember my first year of teaching reading, and it was an eye-opener! I believe it will take a few years in the classroom (at least it did for me) for you to really know what your own personal beliefs are about how kids learn, and especially how they learn to read. It also will take a few years for you to gather, collect, and glean the supplemental materials that you will want to use to supplement or support whatever the adopted curriculum is in your school/district.

That said, my best advice to you is to hook up with an experienced teacher at your grade level. Sad to say, not all teachers will want to share their things, but there are plenty of us that are more than willing. Find one who is willing to share and use anything or everything that that person will share with you. They have probably already developed some units, word lists, art projects, multicultural ideas, grouping ideas, teaching strategies, and so on. You don't have to copy everything they do or say (especially if it really goes against your philosophy), but it certainly gives you a place to start and you don't end up reinventing the wheel. That way you free up at least some of your time to develop your own ideas and ways of doing things. During your second year, you will really feel much more comfortable doing things because every little thing won't be new. Additionally, by then, you'll have the advantage of knowing what didn't work the year before and what needs to be changed.

Good luck. Remember, we all had to start somewhere!

Therese Forster

In school, reading cuts across every subject area. The ability to read a textbook, do research in the library or on the Internet, or read a teacher's notes on the chalkboard directly affects the quality of a child's learning. It is not surprising, then, that teachers, parents, and children are greatly concerned that reading be effectively taught—and that teachers feel an immense sense of satisfaction as they see their students' growth in reading.

You will play a central role in helping children gain access to the pleasure and power of reading. What you do in the classroom will profoundly shape your students' lives. Helping your students acquire needed skills and knowledge to develop into self-confident adults provides a feeling of reward and accomplishment rare in other professions. Perhaps it can best be described by Darren Johnson, a parent whose former teacher made several instructional decisions that helped him enter the world of readers.

Darren Johnson's Reflections on Learning to Read

"You know the stories about parents who used to go through snowdrifts and walk 10 miles to school? Well, I feel something like that! I used to have to get up early and ride the bus for what seemed like hours. And I know that lots of what we called 'white kids' were doing the same. So my first grade wasn't anywhere close to my hood. And though I could (and still do) talk up a storm, I really wasn't much for reading. It's different now, but it wasn't important to me then. I remember Momma telling me that my report cards and notes from the teacher always said I needed to pay more attention.

"I also remember that I got more interested about halfway through the year. For one thing, Momma told me she had a long conference with my teacher. But what I remember most was a book that my teacher started reading to us—*Charlotte's Web*. It was about a farm and pigs and spiders and animals. I was a city kid, but the friendships in that story made me cry. There were a lot of people moving in and out of where we lived then,

Current definitions of literacy must take into account affective factors as well as decoding and comprehension of text.

and my best friend had just moved away. That book really tore at me. I guess my teacher let Momma have it [the book], because she would read a bit to me, and we would talk about it every night.

"My teacher would also find things for me to do that made more sense to me and that helped me read. Like I said, I talked a lot, and I also loved to draw. So I started drawing pictures and then writing down what they were about. And I got to talk more to my teacher, who would write down what I said and let me draw on those pages. My teacher put them in a notebook that I would take home and read to my Momma.

"Looking back, I think that's what turned things around. The interest my teacher showed in me by letting me do things that meant something to me and taking the time to learn how I felt about things.

"Now I see my own son doing amazing things in school because of the teacher he has. They have three computers in their class connected to the Internet. Above the computers is a map of the world with string marking all of the places they have received e-mail from. Amazing! And last night at Back to School Night, his teacher was showing us their reading project about space. They follow the shuttle missions, send messages to the astronauts, and monitor the science experiments they are conducting in space at the **NASA Shuttle web site** (http://spaceflight.nasa.gov). They also take **The Nine Planets Tour,** traveling to each of the planets, and they are reading to see what it is like there (http://seds.lpl.arizona.edu/billa/tnp/).

"But, you know, it isn't just this fancy technology they have in class that is helping my son. It's his teacher who knows what to do with it to get him excited about learning and about reading. Teachers really do make the difference."

Use the self-test questions on http://www.prenhall.com/leukinzer to review the material presented in this chapter.

Major Points

- Literacy is important. It is a key factor in job opportunities and quality of life for each one of us.
- The teacher is a continual decision maker in the classroom, using observational skills to gather information with which to guide instruction.

- Reading is a social, linguistic, developmental, and interactive process that involves learning.
- A teacher's beliefs about what and how to teach informs central decisions about reading instruction.
- Keeping up with changing literacy demands is an important part of becoming a teacher of reading.
- Teaching reading to children in the elementary grades is one of the most rewarding tasks anyone can perform. Teachers of reading have the potential to help young children achieve one of their most important and exciting accomplishments.

Making Instructional Decisions

1. Different teachers, using the same information about their students, often make different instructional decisions. How would you explain such differences?

2. Look at **The Children's Literature Web Guide** (http://www.acs.ucalgary.ca/~dkbrown/index.html). Using the information found there (including links to other sites), put together a set of children's books that are thematically linked—perhaps books about common folktales, dinosaurs, or another topic you think might be of interest to primary-grade students. How do you think the Internet might be useful to you as you develop lessons for your future students?

3. Interview at least two teachers and two parents. Ask them: (a) what they think reading is and (b) how important they think reading is now and will be in the future. Ask the teachers how their beliefs about reading and its importance influence their instructional decisions. Ask the parents what they would emphasize if they were teaching reading. What implications do any similarities or differences have for students and for teachers?

4. During the past several years a tremendous change has taken place in education, partly because of the rapid spread of technology in our society (in general) and in our schools (in particular). This ever-increasing emphasis on technology has raised speculation that reading and writing will become obsolete as we know them because sophisticated and easy-to-use technology will read for us and type words as we speak into our computers. Others (Bruce, 1997; Reinking, 1998) have argued that reading will be even more important in the years ahead. In an information age, they argue that the race will be won by those who can acquire information in a faster manner and use it in effective ways. According to this view, we need to show children how to effectively integrate and adapt traditional reading abilities to the increasingly rich resources available in digital contexts such as the Internet. Do you feel that reading and writing will be more important or less important in the years ahead? Why?

5. What are literacy frameworks and how are they modified? Which is the most powerful and flexible framework? Why?

Further Reading

Baumann, J., & Duffy, A. M. (2001). Teacher-researcher methodology: Themes, variations, and possibilities. *The Reading Teacher, 54*(6), 608–615.

Through a readable analysis of teacher research studies, this brief paper shows the scope of choice that teachers can make in their efforts to examine questions in their classrooms, and provides a list of possibilities for teachers to use as guidelines for their classroom inquiries.

Iannone, P. V. (1998). Just beyond the horizon: Writing-centered literacy activities for traditional and electronic contexts. *The Reading Teacher, 52*(5), 420–427.

Explores writing opportunities for students and teachers on the Internet. This article includes a number of locations to help your students with their writing, including many locations to publish student work.

Kinzer, C. K., & Leu, D. J. (1997). The challenge of change: Exploring literacy and learning in electronic environments. *Language Arts, 74*(2), 126–136.

Explores the challenges we all face as digital technologies open up new opportunities for literacy and learning in the classroom.

Spielman, J. (2001). The family photography project: "We will just read what the pictures tell us." *The Reading Teacher, 54*(8), 762–770.

Describes a project to collect evidence about learning in the "life school" of families, specifically a session where people shared artifacts representing learning in their homes. Shows how families and teachers became more aware of the importance of home experiences in literacy education.

Taylor, D. (1993). How do you spell dream? You learn—with the help of a teacher. *The Reading Teacher, 47,* 8–16.

Presents an autobiographical account of school experiences and highlights the importance of teachers in children's lives

Worthy, J. (2001). A life of learning and enjoyment from literacy. *The Reading Teacher, 54*(7), 690–691.

Discusses the different kinds of texts people read and write, and relates these texts to a wide variety of personal and societal literacy goals. Argues that different kinds of texts should be available for students in classrooms, and provides a list of such materials.

References

Adams, M. J. (1990). *Beginning to read: Thinking and learning about print.* Urbana-Champaign, IL: Center for the Study of Reading.

Allington, R. L. (1991). Children who find learning to read difficult: School responses to diversity. In E. H. Hiebert (Ed.), *Literacy for a diverse society: Perspectives, practices, and policies* (pp. 237–252). New York: Teachers College Press.

Allington, R. L., & Johnston, P. (1989). Coordination, collaboration, and consistency: The redesign of compensatory and special education interventions. In R. Slavin, N. Karweit, & N. Madden (Eds.), *Effective programs for students at risk* (pp. 320–354). Boston: Allyn & Bacon.

Anders, P. L., Hoffman, J. V., & Duffy, G. G. (2000). *Teaching teachers to teach reading: Paradigm shifts, persistent problems and challenges.* In M. L. Kamil, P. Mosenthal, P. D. Pearson, & R. Barr (Eds.), *Handbook of reading research, Volume III* (pp. 719–742). Mahwah, NJ: Lawrence Erlbaum Associates.

Anderson, R. C., & Freebody, P. (1981). Vocabulary knowledge. In J. T. Guthrie (Ed.), *Comprehension and teaching: Research reviews* (pp. 77–117). Newark, DE: International Reading Association.

Anderson, R. C., Hiebert, E. H., Scott, J. A., & Wilkinson, I. A. G. (1985). *Becoming a nation of readers: The report of the commission on reading.* Washington, DC: National Academy of Education.

Au, K. H. (2000). A multicultural perspective on policies for improving literacy achievement: Equity and excellence. In M. L. Kamil, P. Mosenthal, P. D. Pearson, & R. Barr (Eds.) *Handbook of reading research, Volume III* (pp. 835–851). Mahwah, NJ: Erlbaum.

Bean, T. W. (2000). Reading in the content areas: Social constructivism dimensions. In M. L. Kamil, P. Mosenthal, P. D. Pearson, & R. Barr (Eds.), *Handbook of reading research, Volume III* (pp. 629–644). Mahwah, NJ: Erlbaum.

Bruce, B. C. (1997). Current issues and future directions. In J. Flood, S. B. Heath, & D. Lapp (Eds.), *Handbook of research on teaching literacy through the communicative and visual arts* (pp. 875–884). New York: Macmillan.

Calkins, L. M. (2000). *The art of teaching reading.* NY: Longman.

Dechant, E. (1982). *Improving the teaching of reading* (3rd ed.). Englewood Cliffs, NJ: Prentice Hall.

Duffy, G., & Hoffman, J. (1999). In pursuit of an illusion: The flawed search for a perfect method. *The Reading Teacher, 53.*

Fingeret, A. (1983). A new perspective on independence and illiterate adults. *Adult Education Quarterly, 33,* 133–146.

Flesch, R. (1955). *Why Johnny can't read.* New York: Harper & Brothers.

Flesch, R. (1981). *Why Johnny still can't read.* New York: Harper & Row.

Galda, L. Ash, G. E., & Cullinan, B. E. Children's literature. (2000). In M. L. Kamil, P. Mosenthal, P. D. Pearson, & R. Barr (Eds.), *Handbook of reading research, Volume III* (pp. 361–380). Mahwah, NJ: Erlbaum.

Gavelek, J. R., Raphael, T. E., Biondo, S. M., & Wang, D. (2000). Integrated literacy instruction. In M. L. Kamil, P. Mosenthal, P. D. Pearson, & R. Barr (Eds.), *Handbook of reading research, Volume III* (pp. 361–380). Mahwah, NJ: Erlbaum.

Gee, J. P. (2000). Discourse and sociocultural studies in reading. In M. L. Kamil, P. Mosenthal, P. D. Pearson, & R. Barr (Eds.), *Handbook of reading research, Volume III* (pp. 195–208). Mahwah, NJ: Erlbaum.

Goodman, K. S. (1976). Reading: A psycholinguistic guessing game. In H. Singer & R. Ruddell (Eds.), *Theoretical models and processes of reading* (2nd ed., pp. 497–508). Newark, DE: International Reading Association.

Harste, J. C. (1990). Jerry Harste speaks on reading and writing. *The Reading Teacher, 43,* 316–318.

Heath, S. B. (1980). The functions and uses of literacy. *Journal of Communication, 30,* 123–133.

Kinzer, C. K., & Leu, D. J. (1997). The challenge of change: Exploring literacy and learning in electronic environments. *Language Arts, 74*(2), 126–136.

Labbo, L. D., & Reinking, D. (2000). Once upon an electronic story time. *New Advocate, 13,* 25–32.

Leu, D. J., Jr. (2000). Continuously changing technologies and envisionments for literacy: Deictic consequences for literacy education in an information age. In M. L. Kamil, P. Mosenthal, P. D. Pearson, & R. Barr (Eds.), *Handbook of reading research, Volume III.* Mahwah, NJ: Erlbaum.

Leu, D. J., & Kinzer, C. K. (2000). The convergence of literacy instruction with networked technologies for information, communication, and education. *Reading Research Quarterly, 35*(1), 108–127.

Miller, P. (1982). Reading demands in a high-technology industry. *Journal of Reading, 26,* 109–115.

Nagy, W. E. (1988). *Teaching vocabulary to improve reading comprehension.* Newark, DE: International Reading Association.

Nagy, W. E., & Scott, J. A. (2000). Vocabulary processes. In M. L. Kamil, P. Mosenthal, P. D. Pearson, & R. Barr (Eds.) *Handbook of reading research, Volume III* (pp. 269–284). Mahwah, NJ: Erlbaum.

National Reading Panel. (2000). *Teaching children to read: An evidence-based assessment of the scientific research literature on reading and its implications for reading instruction.* Available: http://www.nichd.nih.gov/publications/nrp/smallbook.htm.

P. L. 107-110 (H.R.1). (2002). *No Child Left Behind: Reauthorization of the Elementary and Secondary Education Act.* Available Online [http://thomas.loc.gov/cgi-bin/query/z?c107:h.r.l.enr:]. Accessed 01/29/02.

Pellegrino, J. W., Chudowsky, N., & Glaser, R. (Eds.). (2001). *Knowing what students know: The science and design of educational assessment.* Washington, DC: National Academy Press.

Reinking, D. (1998). Synthesizing technological transformations of literacy in a post-typographic world. In D. Reinking, M. McKenna, L. D. Labbo, & R. Kieffer (Eds.), *Handbook of literacy and technology: Transformations in a post-typographic world.* Mahwah, NJ: Lawrence Erlbaum Associates.

Rosenblatt, L. M. (1985). The literary transaction: Evocation and response. *Theory into Practice, 21,* 268–277.

Rosenblatt, L. M. (1988). *Writing and reading: The transactional theory* (Tech. Rep. No. 416). Urbana, IL: Center for the Study of Reading.

Rosenblatt, L. M. (1994). The transactional theory of reading and writing. In R. B. Ruddell, M. R. Ruddell, & H. Singer (Eds.), *Theoretical models and processes of reading* (4th ed., pp. 1057–1092). Newark, DE: International Reading Association.

Rumelhart, D. (1994). Toward an interactive model of reading. In H. Singer & R. Ruddell (Eds.), *Theoretical models and processes of reading* (4th ed., pp. 864–894). Newark, DE: International Reading Association.

Samuels, S. J., & Kamil, M. L. (1984). Models of the reading process. In P. D. Pearson (Ed.), *Handbook of reading research* (pp. 185–224). White Plains, NY: Longman Publishing Group.

Shanahan, T. (1990). Reading and writing together: What does it really mean? In T. Shanahan (Ed.), *Reading and writing together: New perspectives for the classroom* (pp. 1–18). Norwood, MA: Christopher-Gordon.

Smith, C. B. (1997). Vocabulary and reading comprehension. *ERIC Clearinghouse on Reading, English, and Communication Digest* #126. Available Online [http://www.indiana.edu/~eric_rec/ieo/digests/d126.html]. Accessed 12/29/01.

Snow, C. E., Burns, M., & Griffin, P. (Eds.). (1998). *Preventing reading difficulties in young children.* Washington, DC: National Academy Press.

Stanovich, K. E. (1980). Toward an interactive compensatory model of individual differences in the development of reading fluency. *Reading Research Quarterly, 16,*(1) 32–71.

Stanovich, K. E. (1986). Matthew effects in reading: Some consequences of individual differences in the acquisition of literacy. *Reading Research Quarterly, 21*(4) 360–407.

Strang, R., McCullough, C., & Traxler, A. (1961). *The improvement of reading* (3rd ed.). New York: McGraw-Hill.

Yaden, D. B., Rowe, D. W., & MacGillivray, L. (2000). Emergent literacy: A matter of polyphony. In M. L. Kamil, P. Mosenthal, P. D. Pearson, & R. Barr (Eds.), *Handbook of reading research, Volume III* (pp. 425–454). Mahwah, NJ: Erlbaum.

2

Developing Insights: Using Material and Method Frameworks for Literacy Instruction

✉ E-mail from the Classroom

Subject: Thoughts on Using a Published School Reading Program (A Basal Reading Series)
From: Jessica Juda, jjuda@hotmail.com

Hi!

We use a published school reading program (basal reading series) in grades K-6. The program includes many things I learned in my college classes like guided reading, leveled reading selections, Internet activities, phonics instruction, children's literature, and running records. We can supplement our program with other works of literature or even choose not to use this reading program if we wish. Everyone, however, must have students complete the periodic unit tests that come with this program. These are aligned with our state reading assessment. I used our reading series more when I was a new teacher. It saved me lesson-planning time when I was beginning my career. I also learned new teaching ideas from the TM (teacher's manual). Now, however, I am confident that I know my students' needs better than the person who wrote the lesson plans in our basal series. I also know how to meet their unique needs in a variety of ways. As a result, I use our reading series but I also integrate additional works of children's literature and different method frameworks to teach my second-grade students. My students get really excited about reading when they choose their own books to read from the library. I make certain to include this time for independent reading in my class. My insights about individual students and how best to meet their needs make me an effective reading/literacy educator, not the materials or the methods I use.

Jessica

After reading this chapter, you should be able to:

1. Revise the lesson plans in a published school reading program to meet the individual needs of your students.

2. Explain why method frameworks often are more useful than published school reading programs for literacy learning.

3. Teach with a variety of method frameworks, including:

- reading workshop
- guided reading
- read-aloud response journals
- cooperative learning groups
- deductive instruction
- Internet Workshop
- Internet Project
- Internet Inquiry

Meeting Individual Needs: A Principle of Effective Literacy Instruction

You will recall from chapter 1 that one of the most important, but often overlooked, principles of effective literacy instruction is this:

1. **Teachers' insights are central to effective instruction (Anders, Hoffman, & Duffy, 2000; Duffy & Hoffman, 1999; Snow, Burns, & Griffin, 1998).**

Many teachers believe that there is one set of materials or one instructional practice that is "best" when teaching reading or writing. Becoming an effective literacy teacher would be easy if this were true. Unfortunately, there is no single set of instructional materials that is best for teaching every child to read and write. Similarly, there is no single method of instruction that is best at teaching every child to read and write. In reading, one size does not fit all. It is not the materials or the methods that make the difference in teaching every child to read and to write; it is you, the teacher. And what is it that makes you an effective teacher in the literacy classroom? Effective teachers make insightful instructional decisions that meet the individual needs of each of their students.

In order to develop these insights and meet each child's individual needs, effective literacy educators develop core knowledge in at least three areas:

1. material frameworks
2. method frameworks
3. literacy frameworks

These three elements provide the foundation for effective literacy instruction. They permit you to insightfully orchestrate instruction in your classroom to meet the individual needs of your students. We will help you to develop this foundation for effective literacy instruction in this chapter and chapter 3.

This chapter will develop your understanding of one type of material framework: published school reading programs, one of the most common types of instructional materials used in school classrooms today. We will also show you how to modify these programs to meet your individual needs. In addition, this chapter will develop your understanding of the major method frameworks used to teach reading. Thoroughly understanding these material and method frameworks will provide important core knowledge as you seek to become an effective literacy educator, meeting the needs of each student in your classroom.

The next chapter will provide you with a third type of core knowledge important for your development as an effective literacy educator. It will help you to develop a literacy framework, an organized system of insights into how children read and how children learn to read.

Check your ongoing understanding of chapter concepts by using the guided review for this chapter on http://www.prenhall.com/leukinzer

Material Frameworks

Teaching will require you to make many decisions as you work with children. Elementary classrooms are busy and complex places. As Jessica Juda points out, many teachers, especially new teachers, rely on lesson planning information in **published school reading programs.** A published school reading program is a comprehensive, graded set of published materials used to teach reading in kindergarten through grades 6 or 8. They often are called basal reading programs, basal readers, or simply basals. The information in these teacher's manuals reduces the complexity of classroom decision making for you.

A published school reading program is the most common example of a **material framework.** A material framework consists of a published set of instructional materials with lesson planning information found in a teacher's manual. New teachers sometimes find material frameworks useful because they provide simple "recipes for teaching." The lesson plans in the teacher's manual of a published school reading program will tell you exactly which materials you need and how to use them. You, too, may find this attractive. As Jessica indicates, however, following the same directions for all children does not al-

published school reading program A published school reading program is a comprehensive, graded set of published materials used to teach reading in kindergarten through grades 6 to 8.

material framework An instructional framework used to teach reading; includes a published set of materials and lesson planning information.

FIGURE 2-1

A lesson from the first-grade level of McGuffey's readers

LESSON XXVI.

fạll	īçe	skātes	erȳ
wĭth	hăd	stōne	dĭd

ạ   ç   sk

The boys are on the ice with their skates.

There is a stone on the ice. One boy did not see it, and has had a fall.

But he is a brave boy, and will not cry.

Source: From *McGuffey's Eclectic Primer, Revised Edition* (New York: American Book Company, 1909, p. 31).

ways meet their individual needs. Increasingly, teachers like Jessica are replacing these material frameworks with method frameworks as they bring their own insights to instructional decisions and make learning to read more meaningful to youngsters.

Published school reading programs have been used to teach reading since 1836, when McGuffey's readers first appeared in the United States. An example of a lesson from that early program can be seen in Figure 2-1.

The use of material frameworks and published school reading programs is decreasing as many teachers turn toward more "authentic" types of reading experiences such as original works of children's literature. Still, well over half of all elementary school classrooms have a published school reading program available.

Today, reading programs are developed by several large publishers such as Scott Foresman, Houghton Mifflin, Open Court, and others. Developing a published school reading program is a major undertaking, with the initial cost estimated between $50–$100 million. A major revision in each program usually occurs every 5 to 6 years, coinciding with state adoptions in Texas and California, the two largest states that regularly review published school reading programs for their schools.

Published school reading programs reduce the complexity of classroom decisions in at least three ways. First, they contain a wide variety of instructional materials used to teach reading. This reduces the time teachers require to select materials for reading instruction. Second, they systematically organize reading materials around well-defined grade levels, skill sequences, and thematic units. This reduces the time a teacher needs to develop integrated sequences of instruction. Finally, published school reading programs contain a teacher's manual with step-by-step directions for teaching reading, which reduces planning time. We will describe each of these aspects of published school reading programs: the instructional materials, organization, and teacher's manuals.

Instructional Materials

Teachers often believe a published school reading program, or basal series, contains all of the materials necessary to teach reading in the elementary grades. While this is never the case, we should not be surprised at this perception. A published school reading program contains many materials for teachers and students: teacher's manuals, student books, student workbooks, an assessment package, duplicating masters, and even multimedia software.

During the 1990s, several important changes were made to the nature of materials included in published school reading programs (McCarthey & Hoffman, 1995). First, these programs now contain more original works of children's literature. Publishers are paying attention to evidence that children's literature selections are central to supporting reading development (Tunnell & Jacobs, 1989). While many of these selections are excerpts from a longer work and many of them have been reillustrated, published school reading programs now contain relatively few changes to the language of the original work (Leu & Ayre, 1992)—changes that were common during the 1980s.

In addition, published school reading programs now include interactive multimedia selections, Internet experiences, and other electronic learning resources as a part of their series. These support traditional reading skills as they develop the new forms of literacy students require for reading and writing within newly emerging information and communication technologies (Leu & Kinzer, 2000).

Some teachers are attracted to published school reading programs because they contain a variety of instructional materials. Having all of these materials at your fingertips clearly saves time and reduces the complexity of making decisions about what and how to teach.

Organization

A second way in which published school reading programs reduce decision making is by systematically organizing materials. Published school reading programs are designed around three organizational structures: thematic units, grade levels, and skills. Systematically organizing materials around these three structures can save teachers time as they plan integrated reading experiences in busy classrooms.

thematic units
Instructional units organized around a single issue or theme that usually contain children's literature as well as integrated experiences in reading, writing, speaking, and listening.

Thematic Units.   Published school reading programs are almost always organized by **thematic units** that integrate reading, writing, and discussion experiences around a single topic or author such as "Making Friends," "Celebrating Differences," "Fantastic Tales," or "Laura Ingalls Wilder." Organizing instruction around thematic topics permits teachers and children to engage in purposeful experiences as they find connections between reading selections, post-reading conversations, and writing experiences (Strickland & Morrow, 1990). Some programs have been criticized, though, for paying only minimal attention to substantive issues when defining their thematic structure. These programs organize instruction around thematic titles such as "Teddy Bears, Teddy Bears," "Wishes," or other thematic topics that fail to provide opportunities for reading, writing, and thinking about substantive issues.

Organizing a thematic unit on your own requires considerable time (Staab, 1991). When thematic units are designed appropriately in published school reading programs, they reduce the amount of time teachers must spend to develop these units.

Grade Levels. Ever since the McGuffey readers, published school reading programs have been organized according to levels of difficulty, traditionally designated by grade levels. In kindergarten most children receive early literacy materials with many listening and discussion experiences. First-grade children typically receive five different levels of materials: three preprimers (PP1, PP2, and PP3); a primer (P); and a first reader. In second and third grades most children receive a first-semester reader and a second-semester reader, identified by a numbering system such as 2.1 or 3-1, and so on. Finally, children in fourth through eighth grades generally read from a single book. You usually can locate a table that defines the grade-level-to-book-title correspondence at the beginning of most teacher's manuals. Organizing materials for reading instruction by difficulty level reduces the amount of time teachers need to spend gathering appropriately challenging materials.

Skills. Published school reading programs are also organized around a set of reading skills developed in a particular sequence. The range of skills taught in any one program is referred to as the program's *scope;* the order in which skills are introduced is referred to as its *sequence.* Each published reading series will provide you with a scope and sequence table showing when each skill is introduced and reviewed. This allows teachers to see which skills receive emphasis during each unit of instruction. It also makes it easier to plan instructional activities designed to support particular needs.

Teacher's Manuals

A third way in which published school reading programs reduce the complexity of classroom instruction is by providing teachers with detailed lesson plans. Each teacher's manual contains elaborate lesson planning information, which can save time while planning instructional lessons.

If you compare lessons from several series, they will look very different; each will use different labels for the sections of the lesson plan. If you look closely, though, all series tend to follow an identical, underlying structure in lesson planning. You will notice that teaching plans in published school reading programs are usually organized something like this:

I. Preview information for the teacher
   A. Summary of the selection
   B. New vocabulary for students
   C. Instructional objectives
   D. Instructional materials
II. Preparation activities for the students
   A. Developing vocabulary
   B. Developing reading skills
   C. Defining a purpose for reading
III. Reading and discussing the selection
   A. Reading the selection silently and then sometimes orally
   B. Discussing the selection
IV. Skill development and practice activities
V. Extension activities

The first portion of most teaching plans contains **preview information.** This section includes a story summary, new vocabulary words in the story, instructional objectives, and necessary instructional materials. Preview information allows you to understand the instructional purposes of a particular lesson and to decide whether, and how, a lesson should be taught. It also permits you to collect and prepare the necessary materials for each lesson.

The second portion of most teaching plans is a **preparation section.** The preparation section of a lesson describes useful activities that prepare children to read the selection. New vocabulary words are listed, along with suggestions for how the new

preview information
The first section of most teaching plans in a published school reading program; explains the purpose of the lesson and provides an overview.

preparation section
The second section of most teaching plans in a published school reading program; provides activities that prepare students to read the selection.

words should be taught. Specific reading skills are often developed during the preparation section. Skills such as developing useful reading strategies, monitoring comprehension, or recognizing common sight words in context may be taught because they are important in reading and discussing the story selection. Finally, the preparation section defines a purpose for reading. You may be directed to have children read and think about connections with a previous selection, to read and see what they would have done in a situation related to the story, or to read and enjoy the way an author uses a stylistic feature such as humor.

The third section of most teaching plans suggests how to conduct a reading and discussion of the passage. These reading experiences usually take place in one of two ways. Children often read an entire selection silently, after which you initiate a discussion that may include an oral reading of portions of the story. In an alternative strategy, children read the story silently, a page or two at a time. After each portion is read, you initiate a discussion that, again, may include an oral reading. In both cases children have an opportunity to read stories silently before they are asked to read them aloud (Harris & Sipay, 1990).

skill development and practice   The fourth section of most teaching plans in a published school reading program; provides directions for specific skill instruction.

After the guided reading section, many teaching plans provide suggestions for **skill development and practice.** These sections often consist of a response journal or practice activities for children to complete at their desks. For example, in a lesson where meanings of new vocabulary words are developed, children might be asked to work together in small groups to complete a crossword puzzle containing these words.

extension activities The fifth section of most teaching plans in a published school reading program; contains enrichment activities.

Extension activities are often included in the lesson plans of a published school reading program. Extension activities include functional and enjoyable activities related to content or skills associated with a selection. These may contain a variety of additional reading and writing experiences related to the literature selection that was just read. For example, after reading a selection from *The Voyage of the Dawn Treader* by C. S. Lewis, children in your class might be asked to work in small groups to draw a map of a fantasy kingdom. Or, after reading an excerpt from *Charlotte's Web,* children might be asked to create a spider's web on a piece of construction paper with cotton fiber and glue, weaving one word into the web that best describes their classroom. Afterward you might display these in a prominent place in the room. Other similar experiences will be found at the end of each lesson.

Material Frameworks: The Controversy

If published school reading programs reduce the complexity of instructional decisions and make reading instruction easy, why does a controversy surround their use? Shouldn't we all seek to make our work less complex? Unfortunately, reducing the complexity of classroom life by relying solely on a published school reading program appears to be a double-edged sword. Although a published school reading program reduces the complexity of classroom decisions, it also forces you to rely on judgments made by others, rather than seeking to cultivate your own professional insights about individual students (Shannon, 1986). Most decisions about which stories to use and how to use them have been made for you. Thus, some believe that published school reading programs make so many decisions that teachers will be discouraged from thinking about important instructional issues. Blindly following the directions in a teacher's manual may lead you to abdicate your developing ability as an insightful and skilled educator who responds to individual needs. One problem with published school reading programs, then, is they disempower teachers, resulting in teachers who don't always trust their special insights about children—insights crucial to effective instruction.

A second criticism of published school reading programs is associated with teachers' different beliefs about how children learn to read. Teachers who object to using published school reading programs believe that children learn best by reading authentic works to accomplish personal, purposeful, and practical tasks. They believe published school reading programs teach too many skills, provide too many drills, and isolate the teaching of reading from other subject areas. According to these teachers, published

Published reading programs are often modified by teachers to more closely match their literacy framework.

school reading programs provide students too few opportunities to make personal and authentic reading choices. They prefer that children select their own works of children's literature from a school or classroom library as teachers use a variety of method frameworks to develop reading proficiency.

Some teachers, though, value the use of published school reading programs. These teachers believe in the importance of direct instruction in teaching reading strategies and argue that published school reading programs provide important support and direction for new teachers; such programs save new teachers from having to assemble all their own reading materials and activities. Also, these teachers note that published school reading programs have recently changed and now include literature selections. They point out that several programs are actually anthologies of children's literature and include classroom libraries of children's books. Finally, they argue that published school reading programs have decreased instruction in isolated skills and increased the integration of reading with subject areas by organizing individual lessons within thematic units.

As you can see, the decision whether to use a published school reading program is closely associated with your beliefs about reading. Teachers who believe that children learn best by reading authentic materials to accomplish significant and functional tasks do not value published school reading programs; those who believe that children learn to read best through more direct instruction value published school reading programs. Teachers who believe that children learn best through a combination of these approaches value a published school reading program used in conjunction with additional, self-selected reading and writing experiences.

Who decides whether to use a published school reading program? In many situations, that decision is made by the local school district or the building principal. Increasingly, however, teachers are actively seeking a voice in the decision-making process. This trend is as true today as when it was initiated by the recommendations made in the *Report Card on Basal Readers*, written by the Commission on Reading of the National Council of Teachers of English. These recommendations are listed in Figure 2-2. As a result, decisions about the use of published school reading programs are more frequently made by building-level or district-level teams of teachers, parents, and administrators.

FIGURE 2-2

Recommendations from the National Council of Teachers of English

1. Teachers should develop, individually or with others, a clear position of their own on how reading is best taught.
   ▶ They should continually examine this position as they work with children.
   ▶ They should examine policies and instructional materials from this professional perspective.
   ▶ They should keep themselves well-informed about developments in research and practice.
   ▶ They should communicate to administrators their own professional views.
2. Teachers individually and collectively need to take back the authority and responsibility to their classrooms for making basic decisions.
   ▶ They need to make their own decisions about how to use materials, including, or not including, basals to meet the needs of their pupils.
   ▶ They need to be willing to take risks while asserting their professional judgments.
3. Teachers, through their professional organizations, should reject the use of materials, including basals, which make them less-than-responsible professionals.
4. Teachers should communicate their professional judgments about what they need in the way of resources to administrators, publishers, and others.
   ▶ They should make clear to publishers the strengths and weaknesses of programs as they work with them.
   ▶ They should plan material purchases with administrators.
   ▶ They should demand a voice in text adoption decisions and policies.

Source: From K. S. Goodman, Y. Freeman, S. Murphy, and P. Shannon, *Report Card on Basal Readers* (Evanston, IL: National Council of Teachers of English, 1988). Reprinted by permission of Richard C. Owen Publishers, Inc.

Whatever your beliefs about reading instruction, it is likely that published school reading programs will continue to be available in many schools. It may be useful, then, to consider both their advantages and disadvantages carefully as you determine their role in your classroom. Some of the major conclusions about published school reading programs that have appeared in professional literature are presented in Table 2-1.

TABLE 2-1

Advantages and disadvantages associated with the use of published school reading programs

Advantages	Disadvantages
Published school reading programs save time. Having a complete set of stories, instructional activities, assessment instruments, and answer keys means that teachers do not have to spend large amounts of time developing or acquiring each of these components (McCallum, 1988).	Selections in published school reading programs often lack educational content. Stories and articles often are selected to teach a particular skill rather than to provide children with substantive knowledge about their environment (Schmidt, Caul, Byers, & Buchmann, 1984).
Published school reading programs include a comprehensive set of reading skills (Osborn, 1984).	Selections in published school reading programs often are uninteresting. They tend not to interest young readers to the same extent as unabridged children's literature (Goodman, Freeman, Murphy, & Shannon, 1988).
Published school reading programs provide for regular and systematic review of skill development (Harris & Sipay, 1990).	Published school reading programs direct teachers to assess children's performance more frequently than they teach children how to read (Durkin, 1981).
Published school reading programs provide support for new teachers. They are thought by some to be more important than university courses in educating new teachers in reading instruction (McCallum, 1988).	Published school reading programs are associated with an abdication of responsibility for classroom decisions. Teachers often believe that these materials must be correct because professionals prepared them (Shannon, 1986).

Modifying Material Frameworks to Meet Individual Needs

If you use a published school reading program, it is essential to remember that *teachers should always modify published school reading programs in order to best meet the unique needs of their students.* Lesson plans in teacher's manuals are intended to provide a range of suggestions and instructional ideas. They should never be followed completely from beginning to end; if you do, you will quickly discover there is insufficient time to complete any lesson.

In addition to modifying the lessons in a published school reading program to meet your students' unique needs, some other reasons to change these lessons include: (a) to be more consistent with your beliefs about reading, (b) to increase children's interest in reading, (c) to integrate reading instruction with other subject areas, and (d) to include instructional activities known to be successful. How should you do this? The following Practical Teaching Strategies feature summarizes a number of strategies teachers have used to modify published school reading programs.

PRACTICAL TEACHING STRATEGIES

Modifying Teaching Plans in Published School Reading Programs

It is essential to modify the lesson plans in every published school reading program (basal series) to meet the many individual needs in your classroom. As Jessica Juda pointed out in her e-mail message at the beginning of this chapter, you will know the children in your class better than the person who wrote these lesson plans. Here are several suggestions to get you started:

- Replace story selections in your published school reading program with individual choices from children's literature. Visit your school library and assist your students in making these choices.

- Reorganize the reading selections in your published school reading program to create new combinations of thematic units related to your science and/or social studies programs. Integrate your reading experiences with these other content areas.

- Check to be certain that the skills taught in each lesson actually are useful for reading and understanding that selection. If not, skip them or look for other instructional experiences that *are* useful for reading the story. Teach these instead.

- Instead of having students complete skill experiences individually, have them work together in small groups to accomplish these tasks and learn from each other.

- Skip or replace lessons when students are proficient at the skills in those lessons. Use the reading selection for another reading, writing, listening, or speaking activity.

- Replace the preparation activity at the beginning of a lesson with an activity from the extension section at the end of a lesson. Preparation activities tend to emphasize a specific skill taught directly by the teacher. Extension activities often can be used to develop important prior knowledge about a story in a more engaging fashion (Reutzel, 1991).

- Divide students into several heterogeneous groups. Have each group read one story from a thematic unit and then plan a method for presenting it to the other groups. This might involve a dramatic reading of the story, a rewritten version of the story to be read by others, a dramatic pantomime of the story as one person reads it aloud, or a choral reading of the story. After the presentations, have each group discuss the common relationships between each of the selections. Share the results of these discussions in a large group and then engage students in a common experience requiring them to read each of the selections and then write something in response to their reading.

- Have students ask discussion questions of the teacher after reading the story. Explain your reasoning processes for each answer. Show students how you figured out each answer.

- Skip preparation activities that teach a specific reading strategy. Instead, have students read the passage and then describe in their journals the parts that were hard to understand. Share this information. Use it to begin a discussion on which strategies to use when a story doesn't make sense.

Making More Substantial Changes to Published School Reading Programs

Modifying published school reading programs based on your developing insights about reading can be useful for both you and your students. Thoughtful changes will allow you to adjust the program to more closely meet your needs and those of individual students. Still, you may wish to make more substantial changes than those described in the Practical Teaching Strategies feature on page 33. If you wish to make more substantial changes, at least two options are available.

One strategy uses the reading selections in your program but reorganizes them around instructional units in at least one other content area such as social studies or science. For example, a Native American folktale by Paul Goble, *The Girl Who Loved Horses,* might appear in the thematic unit "Folktales" in a published school reading program. Instead of using it here, though, you may wish to use it during a social studies unit on Native Americans. Similarly, a selection about a woman who decides to plant lupine flowers wherever she goes, *Miss Rumphius* by Barbara Cooney, might appear in the published school reading program during a thematic unit on "Bringing Beauty to the World." It could also be used just as easily in a science unit on ecology. With this approach, you may follow some of the instructional suggestions for each story or create your own. Tightly linking reading and language arts experiences with content area study is thought to be especially useful to growth in both areas (Herber & Herber, 1993).

Another strategy is to use the reading selections in your published school reading program as a resource anthology. Some teachers, for instance, do not use the lesson planning information from a published school reading program. Instead, they rely on children's self-selected literature experiences from a school or classroom library. Sometimes, though, these teachers use a few of the selections from the published school reading program to supplement ongoing reading and writing activities. A story in a published school reading program, for example, might be used as a read-aloud experience. The teacher might read the selection aloud to initiate a discussion on a topic or to illustrate an author's writing style. Before a short lesson on the use of dialogue, for example, you may wish to read an excerpt aloud from *James and the Giant Peach* by Roald Dahl to show students how this master of dialogue handles his craft. At another time, you might have everyone read an excerpt to begin a discussion of an author. For example, to introduce author Jean Craighead George, you may have your students read the excerpt in your published school reading program from her book, *My Side of the Mountain.* Many other uses for the selections in a published school reading program can be developed if you approach the stories as a resource anthology. The advantage of this technique is that it permits each of your students to have a copy of the same selection—something that is at times hard to do when children are reading individual choices from the school library.

You may choose not to use a published school reading program. You may feel that it is more important for students to read literature selections of their own choice. Some authors have pointed out that it may be less expensive to purchase children's literature for a classroom library than it is to purchase a published school reading program (Jachym, Allington, & Broikou, 1989). If you decide not to use a published school reading program, you should pay particular attention to the method frameworks presented in the next section and in each of the subsequent chapters. These will help you organize your instructional reading program.

⬛ Method Frameworks: Procedural Guides

method frameworks
Instructional frameworks used to teach reading; contains procedural steps for teaching and options for completing each step.

While a material framework reduces the complexity of instructional decisions by telling you exactly what to do throughout a lesson, this often is achieved at the expense of your insights about individual children. It also can become repetitive and boring.

A more engaging way to structure reading experiences is through another type of instructional framework, **method frameworks.** Method frameworks contain: (a) procedural steps for completing a learning activity and (b) options for completing each of the procedural steps.

Teachers employ many different method frameworks to guide instructional decisions. Listen to several teachers talking about the method frameworks they use in their classrooms, and see if you can determine the steps in each one:

> "I used guided reading in my class. I find that work in reading groups, organized around students' levels, helps me to meet individual needs best. First we read and discuss a familiar selection from the day before, then I introduce the new selection, then we read this selection on our own, and then I teach a mini-lesson." (A master teacher explaining to a student teacher how she uses guided reading.)

> "I really like to do read-aloud response journals each day as we work in thematic units. I begin by reading a book or a chapter aloud to the whole class. It is always a book related in one way or another to the thematic topic. Then I give students a writing task to complete and we take about 10 minutes to make an entry in our read-aloud response journal. Afterward, we share some of our entries. Later on, we will use some of these entries and work them up into larger pieces of writing." (A seventh-grade teacher talking to parents at "Back to School Night.")

> "We're doing a language experience story today. We do one almost every day. It's easy. First we do a fun activity. Then we talk about it. As they tell me about it, I write their words down on the chalkboard. Then I use their words to teach them something about reading. Watch me." (A first-grade teacher preparing her student teacher for the first day of class.)

> "We do the writing process in our class. First we prewrite. Then we write a draft. Next we revise. Then we proofread. And last we publish. The writing process helps the reading process because students are reading their own and each other's writing so much. I use it as often as possible." (A fourth-grade teacher overheard at a state reading conference.)

Why are method frameworks so common in literacy instruction? They are popular because they help to reduce the complexity of instructional decisions while still permitting teachers to take advantage of their special insight about children. Method frameworks consist of clearly defined procedures that are easily learned; as a result, they reduce the complexity of instructional decisions. Knowing automatically what the next instructional step will be permits you to pay closer attention to your students' needs—one child's inability to understand a particular word, another child's failure to make an inference, or a third child's limited range of reading interests. Method frameworks free teachers to make appropriate instructional decisions for individual children in busy classrooms.

Method frameworks empower teachers. With method frameworks, you decide when each will be used and which options you will select for any lesson. This allows you the opportunity to redefine method frameworks around the unique needs of your students. As a result, you can exploit the special insights you develop about children to assist them in their journey.

Common Method Frameworks

This section presents 10 common method frameworks used to help youngsters develop into avid and proficient readers and writers. In addition, it provides model lessons to demonstrate how these method frameworks are used in classrooms. Many other method frameworks are presented throughout the rest of this book. Becoming familiar with each method framework is important. Each reduces the complexity of your instructional decisions, yet allows you to use insights about children to meet their individual needs.

Reading Workshop

Reading workshop is a method framework often used in place of a published school reading program by teachers who wish to provide students with greater choice in reading selections and response opportunities. There are probably as many different definitions of reading workshop as there are teachers who use this method. Generally, reading

reading workshop A method framework often used in place of a published school reading program. Contains these steps: sharing responses, providing a mini-lesson, reviewing reading progress, self-selected reading and response, and sharing reading experiences.

Many method frameworks provide opportunities for individual or group work.

PRACTICAL TEACHING STRATEGIES

Responding to Literature during Reading Workshop

Responding to works of children's literature is an important part of reading workshop. There are probably as many different ways to respond to a work as you and the children in your class have creative ideas. As you progress through the year, post a chart with a list of possibilities you and your class discover. It might include some of these ideas we have observed in classrooms around the country:

▶ Read aloud to the class an exciting episode from your selection. Do not tell the other students what the ending is, but do encourage them to check the book out and read it for themselves.

▶ Make an advertisement for your book that tries to sell others on reading it. Put your ad up with others on a bulletin board labeled "Great Buys on Great Books."

 ▶ Make a crossword puzzle using vocabulary words found in your reading selection. You may wish to use a computer program to help you. Have the next person reading the book attempt to complete the puzzle—with your help, if possible.

▶ Come to school dressed as one of the major characters in your book. When people ask you about your character, be certain to describe what the person did and how he or she acted.

▶ Write a different ending to your reading selection. Make it the final chapter. Post it on the bulletin board.

▶ Create a shoebox diorama illustrating one of the scenes from your reading selection. Attach a page to it listing the author, title, and illustrator of the book as well as a description of the scene you have created.

▶ Write a letter to the author of your reading selection; send it to the author in care of the publisher.

▶ Write a letter to one of the characters in your reading selection. Put this with letters from other children on a bulletin board labeled "Letters to Characters in Books We Have Read."

▶ Read several books on the same theme written by different authors. Then write one review, comparing all of the books. Post your review on a bulletin board labeled "Critics' Corner."

workshop consists of a substantial block of time each day where self-selected literature is read, enjoyed, and used as a vehicle for learning (Atwell, 1998). Reading workshop is described in a variety of ways but often includes the following steps:

1. Share reading responses.
2. Provide a reading strategy mini-lesson.
3. Review reading progress.
4. Engage in self-selected reading and response.
5. Share reading experiences.

The first step is to provide a few minutes each day for children (and you) to share responses to what you are reading. This can be accomplished in a variety of ways. Sometimes children may share a project related to the book they have just read, hold up a good book they are reading and provide a brief overview of the plot, or read an especially evocative or exciting passage aloud to classmates. Sharing reading experiences like this often serves to interest children in reading additional works of literature.

The second step in reading workshop is to orchestrate a short mini-lesson on an important reading strategy. This can be done with the entire class if you think everyone could benefit from the strategy session. Some teachers prefer to conduct this mini-lesson in small groups with children they believe will especially benefit from a particular strategy. Others will conduct several mini-lessons with different groups of children during reading workshop. In either case, strategy lessons will focus on items your students need assistance with. These might include lessons on reading strategies such as:

▶ Skimming to find specific information in a lengthy book or article.
▶ What I should do when I can't recognize a word.
▶ Reading between the lines and making inferences.
▶ How to choose a book that is not too hard, not too easy, but just right.
▶ Understanding cause-and-effect relationships.
▶ Drawing conclusions.
▶ Predicting outcomes.

The third step in reading workshop is to review the reading progress of your students. You can often accomplish this in short, individual conferences with children, during which you have several goals: monitor the progress a child is making in self-selected reading, briefly evaluate the child's ability to use effective reading strategies, and discuss ideas for sharing the book when the child completes it. You will usually conduct 3 to 5 individual conferences during each reading workshop session. This allows you to meet with each child at least once or twice each week. A form like that in Figure 2-3 is typically used during these conferences. This allows you to record information you discover about a child's progress, the use of effective reading strategies, and plans for sharing a work of literature.

While you are meeting with children in individual conferences, other children are completing the fourth step in reading workshop—engaging in self-selected reading and response. Here children choose the works of literature they wish to read, read them, and then prepare a response to the work. In reading workshop, children determine what they will read based on their own interests and achievement levels. Teachers, however, help children identify interest areas and put them in touch with a range of books in each area. You should have a classroom library that contains four to five books for each child to effectively initiate a reading program such as this (Harris & Sipay, 1990). This is often achieved by taking advantage of the resources at your school or local library.

After reading a work of literature, children engage in a short response activity. The nature of these response activities usually is discussed with you during the conference session. The response might be something as simple as keeping a response journal, reading the book aloud to a class at a lower grade level, illustrating a central scene, or sharing an evocative passage aloud with the class. Suggestions for many different types of

FIGURE 2-3

A sample conference record to be completed during reading workshop

Name: _____   Date: _____

Title: _____   Author: _____

Response evaluation: _____

_____

_____

_____

Decoding evaluation: _____

_____

_____

_____

Comprehension evaluation: _____

_____

_____

_____

Other observations: _____

_____

_____

_____

Will the book be shared? How? _____

_____

_____

_____

Ideas for additional support: _____

_____

_____

_____

responses are listed in the Practical Teaching Strategies feature on page 36. Literature response activities for several specific books can be found in Table 2-2.

The fifth and final step in reading workshop is to share additional reading responses. Providing children with a second, short period to share their reading experiences is a nice way to begin and end reading workshop. The model lesson on page 40 describes how reading workshop is used in one classroom.

Guided Reading

guided reading A method framework used to teach reading to students in small groups.

Guided reading is used in many different ways, depending upon the teacher. Essentially, though, it is a method framework used to scaffold the development of

TABLE 2-2

Responses that might be used with a specific book during reading workshop

Literature Selection	Activity
Where the Wild Things Are by Maurice Sendak	Make a map describing the route Max took to get to the place of the "wild things."
Alexander and the Terrible, Horrible, No Good, Very Bad Day by Judith Viorst	Write a book about yourself that follows the predictable pattern in this story, entitled *(Your Name) and the Terrible, Horrible, No Good, Very Bad Day.*
James and the Giant Peach by Roald Dahl	Make a paper-mâché model of the peach in which James flew away with all of his insect friends. Use a balloon to mold the basic shape. Then cut out an opening and show James and his friends the inside of their home.
The Very Hungry Caterpillar by Eric Carle	Make a "book caterpillar" around the walls of your classroom. Make a head for your caterpillar and post it on the wall. Then cut out a pattern for a segment of the caterpillar's body. Have students write the title and author of each book they read on one of these segments and post them on the wall in sequence behind the head. Your caterpillar can even go out into the hallway, announcing your reading to the rest of the school.
Frog and Toad Are Friends by Arnold Lobel	Draw a picture of your favorite story in this book and write a sentence underneath the picture describing what happened. Post this and other illustrations on a bulletin board entitled "Friendship."
Little House in the Big Woods by Laura Ingalls Wilder	Write a book of pioneer recipes using the descriptions found in this book. Possible entries might include: head cheese, smoked ham, and sugar snow.
The Little Prince by Antoine de Saint-Exupery	Make a paper-mâché model of the asteroid where the Little Prince lived. Use a balloon to mold the basic shape.

reading ability in small groups of students who are reading at approximately the same level. Teachers will often have three-to-six guided reading groups. They will choose guided reading selections at the level of the average student in each group. Guided reading lessons for groups and individuals, when necessary, are often organized around these steps:

1. Reread a familiar text to practice developing skills.
2. Introduce the new reading selection.
3. Read the new selection with support, when necessary.
4. Conduct a mini-lesson to teach a new strategy or review a previous strategy.

At the beginning of a guided reading lesson, teachers often have students reread a familiar passage, often the passage from the previous guided reading lesson. By rereading a familiar passage, you scaffold the new skills students are acquiring as they practice these skills within a familiar passage. This helps students extend newly emerging skills and pay closer attention to the plot, words, sentences, major ideas, language structure, writing style, and other elements of a passage.

The second step in a guided reading selection is to introduce the new reading selection. Often you will have students do a quick "book walk," skimming through the story quickly to see what it is about. Then you will engage your students in a discussion about what they think will happen in the selection. You might also have them try to locate

MODEL LESSON

Reading Workshop in Joan Simonetta's Class

Sharing Reading Responses. Joan Simonetta likes to begin each day's reading workshop session with what she calls "formal responses." These are more formal presentations of responses students have prepared after reading a selection. Today one student has come dressed as Dee Willis in *Hold Fast to Dreams*. She presents herself and then invites the rest of the class to interview her with questions like: "What's your name?" "Where do you live?" "What problems do you experience in the story?" "Did you try to 'act white'?" The questions lead to a wonderful discussion about the book as well as issues of racism. Several other students also share their responses. One has developed a bulletin board display, another has created a diorama, and another shares a letter she received from an author.

Providing a Reading Strategy Mini-Lesson. Today Joan teaches two brief mini-lessons on reading strategies as other students read their literature selections or work on their response projects. She shows one group how to recognize words by their surrounding context. These children have difficulty with recognizing words, attending solely to grapho-phonic (letter-sound) relationships. She wants these children to think more about the meaning of what they are reading so they can sometimes predict upcoming words accurately. A second group receives a short mini-lesson on "reading between the lines" to see how meaning is not always stated in the text. She uses several short paragraphs and asks children what they know that isn't stated in the words themselves. As each child finds meaning that must be inferred from the paragraph, she asks that child to explain the "clues" that helped him or her to "read between the lines." Each lesson lasts about 5 minutes. Afterward, she begins meeting with other individuals to review their reading progress.

Reviewing Reading Progress. Joan tries to hold individual conferences with at least five children each day. This allows her to meet once a week with each child in her class. In each session, she asks children to share a favorite portion of the story. She uses this time to evaluate comprehension and response strategies. She often will show children a useful reading strategy when she believes this would help their reading. She keeps track of this information on the form in Figure 2-3. Finally, she considers responses to the work that children are reading. Students in Ms. Simonetta's class share a formal response for every two or three books they have read. The nature of this response project is decided jointly by Joan and the child, in keeping with each child's interests and needs. Around the room are several recent response projects: a poster advertising the book *I Was a Second Grade Werewolf* by Daniel Pinkwater, a diorama of a scene from *Mufaro's Beautiful Daughters* by John Steptoe, and a crossword puzzle made by one child and completed by another after each had read *Number the Stars* by Lois Lowry.

Engaging in Self-Selected Reading and Response. As Joan conducts mini-lessons and conferences, other children read the books they have selected and work on their response projects. In her classroom, children usually read at their desks or in one of the beanbag chairs in the reading corner. They choose their books from Ms. Simonetta's classroom library (collected over the years) or from the school library.

Sharing Reading Experiences. The final 5 minutes of reading workshop are spent with sharing what Joan calls "informal responses." During this time several students spontaneously share brief responses about what they have read that day. This provides other children with ideas for books and authors to read in the future.

several of the more challenging words in the story to see if they can pronounce them and determine each word's meaning.

The third step is to have students read the new selection on their own. During this time, students read to themselves and work their way through the selection. When they experience difficulty with a word or with comprehension, they should ask for your support. That way, you can provide individual attention to students when they need it. After reading the story, engage your students in a short discussion about what they have read. This helps to check comprehension.

The final step is to conduct a mini-lesson on a reading skill or strategy that students in your group need. This might help them to recognize a new word beginning with a particular letter pattern (*th, wh, ph*) or it might help students with a comprehension strategy ("Stories always have a problem. What do you think was the problem in this story?").

One way in which guided reading seeks to meet individual needs is to ensure that each group reads selections that are at their level of difficulty. Teachers use **leveled**

leveled books Books that have been evaluated for their approximate reading level.

SUSAN'S

COMMENTS FROM THE CLASSROOM

9:00 A.M.

Centers begin. For the next 2 hours (with a 20-minute break for snack and recess) the children rotate in groups of four-to-six through four 25-minute centers designed to enhance literacy learning.

Our school has chosen a published school reading program that is literature-based. We have multiple copies of books available, leveled from prereading through fluent reading stages. A test individually administered at the beginning of the year identifies each child's reading level. I use the test results to form reading groups. I also use the results both to choose the books we will be reading in groups and to help children identify the books they may read during independent reading time. For example, suppose a child has performed at a level L on the assessment. That child will be reading books in group that are at an L or M level and may choose books for independent reading that are at a J, K, or L level. As the children progress through the year and their reading improves, their book levels in group and independent reading change accordingly. Student groupings are also fluid. As for the centers themselves, we have four: reading group, writing, independent reading, and Internet Workshop.

11:00 A.M.

Centers are completed. We gather in the back of the room to share our writing. On some days the children sit in the "author's chair" to entertain and enlighten us with thoughts they've put to paper. Other days I commandeer the chair and lead interactive writing. During this time we

all "share the pen" to compose a story. (Our class hamster has successfully starred in many adventures.) This time has led to many productive discussions on "how" to write, with topics ranging from the basic mechanics of writing and editing to the use of vivid imagery. On Friday, we always use this time to conduct our workshop session for Internet Workshop. We share and compare the information each of us has gathered. We also share new strategies each of us discovered for using the Internet. These new literacies are important to me.

11:20 A.M.

Lunch! If my hair is disheveled and my clothes askew, it's been a good morning. Lunch bell marks the time to take a break and regroup for the afternoon.

Source: Susan Weber has been teaching for many years in a variety of grade levels. She currently teaches second grade in a K–4 school in Grandview Heights, Ohio. She believes that a combination of gaining experience and continuing her own education has helped her to grow as a teacher.

books, books that have been evaluated for their approximate reading level, and then match these books with the ability of their guided reading groups. As a general rule, students in any group should be able to read 90 percent of the words in their selections with accuracy. To assist teachers in these decisions, many schools have leveled the books that they use for reading instruction, using one of several systems for leveling books. The guided reading system uses an alphabetic system (levels A–Z), the Reading Recovery system uses a numerical system (levels 1–50), while Accelerated Reader also uses a numerical system (1.0–10.0). On the Internet, you may discover a number of databases that contain the levels for most of the books you will use in your classroom by searching for "leveled books." Examples include a searchable database developed by the Beaverton, Oregon School District (http://registration.beavton.k12.or.us/lbdb/default.htm) or the one located at http://www.leveledbooks.com/booksearch.html. These will tell you the level of most books you may use in your classroom.

Read-Aloud Response Journal

read-aloud response journal activity   A method framework containing five steps: read a selection aloud, engage students in a writing task, have students write, share the responses, and, at a later point, use some of the entries to develop larger writing projects.

Many believe you should read quality literature aloud to children each day they are at school (Trelease, 2001). Often, you will want to combine these read-aloud experiences with journal writing opportunities. This is what a **read-aloud response journal activity** accomplishes. Exploring responses to works of children's literature through journal writing is thought to provide important support for literacy learners (Barrentine, 1996; Hancock, 1993).

A read-aloud response journal activity includes the following steps:

1. Read a quality work of children's literature aloud.
2. Share a writing task related to the reading selection.

TABLE 2-3

Examples of children's literature and writing prompts for read-aloud response journal activities in several different thematic units

Thematic Unit	Title	Author	Writing Prompt
Courageous Acts	*John Henry*	Ezra Jack Keats	In this story, John Henry's courage was tested and he paid with his life. Can you think of a challenge that you would be willing to take on even if it cost you your life? Describe this challenge and describe why you believe it to be so important.
	Number the Stars	Lois Lowry	Define the meaning of the term "courage." Apply this definition to one of the many acts of courage you found in this story and explain why it was a courageous act. Or, describe an act in which you were courageous.
	Dear Mr. Henshaw	Beverly Cleary	Did Leigh Botts lead a courageous life? Did his mother? Did his father? Choose one of the main characters and explain your conclusion.
The Nature of Friendship	*The Cat in the Hat*	Dr. Seuss	Compare *The Cat in the Hat* and a friend. What makes them the same? What makes them different?
	The Giving Tree	Shel Silverstein	Can you think of anyone who is a friend to you the way the apple tree was a friend to the boy? Describe this person.
	Frog and Toad Are Friends	Arnold Lobel	Whom do you think was the better friend, Frog or Toad? Why?

3. Have children write responses in their journals.
4. Share the responses.
5. Later encourage children to go back to some of their earlier entries and expand these into larger writing projects.

The initial step in a read-aloud response journal activity is to read a selection aloud to the children in your class. This usually is a work of children's literature, either a short picture book or a chapter from a longer work. In either case, the selection is often thematically related to work you are doing in your classroom.

The second step is to share a writing task related to the reading selection. Plan a short writing activity that allows children to think about the reading selection and write a short response. These writing activities allow children to connect their own thoughts or previous experiences with something that took place in the read-aloud passage. Teachers often will develop several activities and encourage students to select the one they wish to use in their responses. Table 2-3 shows examples of writing activities for several literature selections.

In the third step, children make an entry in their read-aloud response journal, a spiral notebook for recording responses to literature selections. Sometimes teachers will encourage students to make their entries in a common format. An example of a response journal entry is shown in Figure 2-4.

FIGURE 2-4

An example of a response journal entry by a fifth-grade student

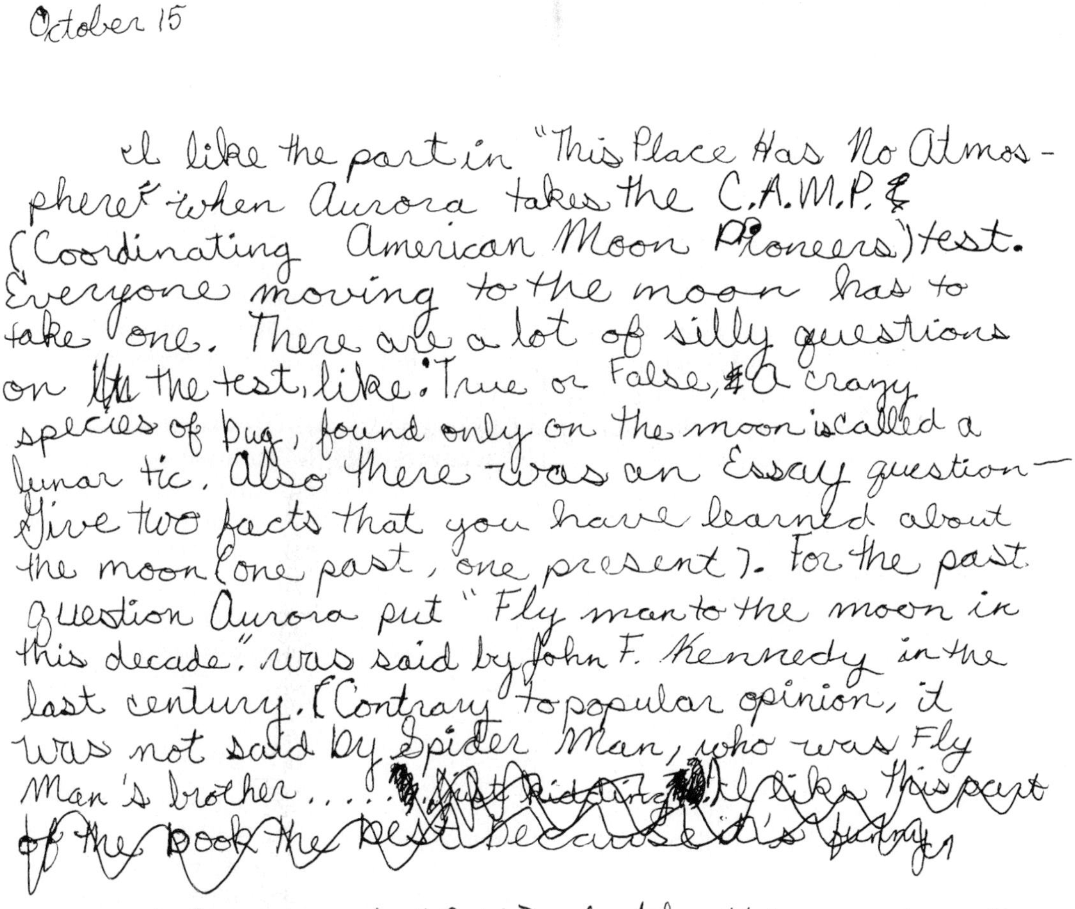

October 15

I like the part in "This Place Has No Atmosphere" when Aurora takes the C.A.M.P. (Coordinating American Moon Pioneers) test. Everyone moving to the moon has to take one. There are a lot of silly questions on the test, like: True or False, A crazy species of bug, found only on the moon is called a lunar tic. Also there was an Essay question—Give two facts that you have learned about the moon (one past, one present). For the past question Aurora put "Fly man to the moon in this decade." was said by John F. Kennedy in the last century. (Contrary to popular opinion, it was not said by Spider Man, who was Fly Man's brother... ~~Just kidding I like this part of the book the best because it's funny~~

...just kidding! A.B.W.) I like this part of the book the best because it's funny.

MODEL LESSON

A Read-Aloud Response Journal Activity in Juanita Esquevarra's Class

Read a Selection Aloud. Juanita's sixth-grade class is exploring a thematic unit called "The Nature of Courage." She begins each day's experiences with a read-aloud response journal activity. Today she is reading a chapter from the book *Hatchet* by Gary Paulson, a story of wilderness survival. The chapter describes how the main character, Brian, is afraid of running into a bear in a raspberry patch.

Engage Students in a Related Writing Task. After reading this chapter, Juanita encourages children to brainstorm several possible writing tasks about fear and courage. She writes these on the chalkboard: (a) Describe a time when you were afraid. (b) Write a definition of courage using examples to explain your definition. (c) How would you have handled being afraid in this situation? (d) Does being courageous also mean that you are afraid? Explain how this applies or does not apply to this chapter. Then, she encourages children to write an entry in their journal about one of these ideas.

Children Write in Their Journals. Students are given about 10 minutes to write responses. Toward the end, Juanita reminds them that writing time is drawing to a close and that they have 2 to 3 minutes remaining. This reminds students to wrap up their entries.

Share the Responses. Juanita has children form groups with members who have written on different topics. She does this to allow each child the opportunity to hear ideas that were generated on each topic. As children read their entries, she circles the classroom, reminding them to provide a positive comment to each child who reads an entry. When this first sharing session is completed, she has children form groups with members who have written on the same topic. Again, children read their entries, providing each other with positive comments.

Encourage Students to Expand Their Entries. A week before the unit ends, Juanita shows children how to select one of their entries to revise and expand into a larger writing project. She supports them as they develop an initial draft of the expanded work, as they revise this draft, as they edit the final draft, and as they share their "magnum opus" with the entire class.

The fourth step is to encourage children to share their responses with others by reading them aloud. This may take place in pairs, in small groups, or with the entire class as students read their entries to others. After individuals share their work, you may wish to encourage listeners to make several positive comments about each entry. This helps children feel more comfortable about sharing their writing and usually results in children wanting to write even better the next time.

Finally, after children in your class have completed a number of journal entries, encourage them to review some of their earlier entries and expand these into larger writing projects. The short entries in read-aloud response journals can be seen as an artist's "sketchbook" where the images of thoughts, feelings, and ideas are quickly jotted down. After children make several short entries, you might show them how to reread their entries, looking for writing ideas that can be elaborated on and more thoroughly developed. Children in your class can work these up into larger units of writing and share them with everyone. The model lesson illustrates how Juanita Esquevarra used a read-aloud response journal activity in her classroom.

Cooperative Learning Groups

Cooperative learning groups is another method framework that supports children during literacy lessons, often through discussions of literature selections. Group discussion about children's literature and other texts has been shown to have a powerful effect on learning (Leal, 1993).

You may have heard people use other terms for this method framework: cooperative learning, collaborative learning, cooperative learning strategies, cooperative inte-

cooperative learning groups A method framework containing these four steps: define a learning task, assign students to groups, have students complete the learning task in their groups, and have students share their results with other groups.

PRACTICAL TEACHING STRATEGIES

Using Cooperative Learning Groups

Nearly every aspect of your classroom curriculum may be enhanced through the use of cooperative learning groups. Cooperative learning groups prepare children for their futures in an increasingly diverse society where we will all have to learn from one another. Here are just a few ways in which cooperative learning groups might be integrated into your classroom to support children during literacy learning:

▶ Before children in your class read a story or an article, have small groups list everything they already know about the topic. Then get together as a whole class and compare notes.

▶ After children read the story, have them work in their groups to develop a short script from one portion of the selection. Let them practice reading this script several times before reading it to the class.

▶ Before they read an unfamiliar passage, give children a list of words from the story that may be unfamiliar. Have each group try to define the words and generate one sentence that uses each word correctly. Then get together as a class to compare definitions and sample sentences.

▶ After children read a chapter in a content area text, give them a list of statements about the topic. Have each group determine whether each statement is supported by the information in the chapter. Have them record evidence from the chapter that supports their decisions.

▶ After children read a chapter in a content area text, give them a list of statements about the topic. Have each group determine whether each statement is explicitly supported by the information in the text or whether they must "read between the lines" to infer the statement.

grated reading and composition, cooperative reading teams, or collaborative learning groups. Depending on the definition, cooperative learning may also have many different sets of procedural steps. We use the term cooperative learning groups to refer to a method framework with these procedural steps:

1. Define a learning task.
2. Assign children to groups.
3. Children complete the learning task together through cooperative group activity.
4. The results of the learning task are shared with other groups.

The first step is to define a learning task. You could, for example, ask your children to compare the main character in one story with a character in another story they have just read. Or, they could discuss a critical episode in a story and explore ways they might handle the situation differently. The Practical Teaching Strategies feature on page 45 provides more examples of tasks that might be used within cooperative learning groups.

With the second procedural step, you assign children to groups. Cooperative learning groups may consist of any reasonable number of children but they almost always include a range of reading abilities. Heterogeneous grouping allows children to benefit from the unique insights of each group member. It also avoids the motivational problems that result when lower-achieving children are placed in a single group. Cooperative learning groups often change their composition with every task.

During the third step, you direct children to complete the learning task together in their groups. Each group usually designates one person to serve as a recorder/reporter who keeps a written account of the group's decisions. Recording this information is important because the results of the group's work often are shared in a brief oral report to the rest of the class.

The fourth step, sharing the results of the learning task with the entire class, allows children to compare their thinking with the thinking that took place in other groups. During this step, you will often summarize each group's report on the chalkboard.

MODEL LESSON

Using Cooperative Learning Groups in Ellen Gallagher's Class

Ellen Gallagher likes to use cooperative learning groups in her sixth-grade class to organize the reading of children's literature. These groups are sometimes referred to as literature discussion groups or literature study groups (Keegan & Shrake, 1991).

Define a Learning Task. During the next 4 weeks, Ellen's class works in four different groups, each organized around popular reading interests: mysteries, biographies, and books by Virginia Hamilton and Lois Lowry.

The Virginia Hamilton group reads and discusses books by this important author, getting together every fourth day to share what they have read with others. Ellen has gathered a number of outstanding books from the school library, including *Virginia, The House of Dies Drear, Cousins, M.C. Higgins the Great,* and many others. During the final week, this group prepares a presentation for the class based on their readings. Using information from the Internet and the school library, the presentation includes summaries of each book and a report on the life of Virginia Hamilton.

Children in the mysteries group read and discuss mysteries from another collection Ellen has brought to class. They also meet every fourth day to share what they have read with others. During the final week, members of this group select an exciting episode from one of the mysteries, write a script for the episode, practice reading their parts, and then perform it for the entire class.

The Lois Lowry group reads from a collection of books by this important author, getting together every few days to share the books they are reading. Ellen has gathered a number of books, including *Number the Stars, The Giver, Anastasia Krupnik, Anastasia Absolutely, Attaboy, Sam, Rabble Starkey,* and others. During the final week, they develop a bulletin board display about this author and give an oral presentation to the class.

The biographies group reads books from a set collected by Ellen, including *Eleanor Roosevelt: A Life of Discovery, Franklin Delano Roosevelt, Lincoln: A Photobiography,* and others. Children in this group get together regularly to share their reading experiences. During the final week, they develop and present another bulletin board display.

Assign Children to Groups. Two days before the groups are assigned, Ellen explains the group projects and distributes sign-up sheets to everyone. Children get to select the group in which they wish to work. Ellen limits each group to seven members.

Children Complete the Learning Task Together. During the 4 weeks, Ellen circulates through the classroom during reading time, assisting students with their particular needs. She does a short lesson for some children on the use of the library's card catalog. She helps others select an interesting mystery. Ellen remains available to help as children near the completion of their group's project.

The Results of the Learning Task Are Shared with the Entire Class. At the end of the 4-week period, time is set aside for each group to display the results of its work. The other sixth-grade class in the school is also invited to this session.

Deductive Instruction

deductive instruction
A method framework containing these four steps: state the skill or rule, provide examples of the skill or rule, provide guided practice, and provide independent practice.

Deductive instruction is a method framework commonly used to directly teach a specific reading skill to students. Deductive instruction contains four procedural steps:

1. State the skill.
2. Provide examples of the skill or rule.
3. Provide guided practice.
4. Provide independent practice.

The first step is to state the skill that students will learn. For instance, you may wish to teach strategies for using an index at the end of an informational book. In this case, you might begin the lesson by having students open to the index in their social studies textbook and explain how an index is used.

The second step is to provide examples of the skill you are teaching. If you were teaching children how to use the index to find information in a textbook, you might

Cooperative learning groups are sometimes used during the guided or independent practice phases of deductive instruction. This provides support for students as they practice important literacy strategies.

MODEL LESSON

Using a Deductive Method Framework in Jeff Gordon's Class

Jeff Gordon wants the children in his class to understand how newspaper articles are organized. He is starting a unit where students will be asked to write articles for a class newspaper and he wants his students to understand the characteristics of this form.

State the Skill. Jeff explains that most newspaper articles are written to inform readers about important current events. He explains that this form of writing is usually organized around these questions: Who? What? When? Where? and Why? He tells them they will learn how to write this type of article.

Provide Examples. Jeff has his class read two short newspaper articles. He helps children to identify each of these elements (Who? What? When? Where? and Why?) by underlining and labeling them on the articles.

Provide Guided Practice. Jeff provides his students with another short article and asks them to find and underline information about who, what, when, where, and why. He writes these categories on the chalkboard and the class then discusses their selections. Jeff writes each bit of information on the chalkboard next to the appropriate category. He has children check their work as he does this.

Provide Independent Practice. Jeff divides the class into cooperative learning groups and gives each group a different article. Then he has the groups identify each type of information in the article. Afterward, one person from each group shares his or her article and his or her decisions with another group.

write several topics and their associated page numbers on the chalkboard. Then you might show them how to use this information to look up items in their textbook.

The third step is to provide guided practice in using the skill. Here you allow children the opportunity to practice what you have taught them so you can assist them if they need help. In our previous example, you might have children turn to the index in

E-mail from the Classroom

Subject: A Method Framework for Kindergartners
From: Lauren Mellone, lmellone@FM.CNYRIC.ORG

Hi!

I teach kindergarten. In terms of phonics instruction, I work with the names of the children in my class a lot. Every day we pull a child's name from an envelope one letter at a time. As each letter appears, the children guess whose name it is. We predict what letter might be next while we are pulling it out. We call it the Mystery Name and it is one of the kids' favorite morning activities. The children are already starting to recognize each other's names! Last year the children knew each other's names and would be able to spot them anywhere in the room. Also, they would often make connections to children's names in our class while writing. For example, Marla said, "Cookie starts with a *c* like Connor." It is very helpful! You can also introduce vowels using names! It makes it so meaningful for the kids and they start using last names also!

Lauren

their social studies book and ask them to find the page where information about Frederick Douglass might be found. Once they have located this information, you might have them turn to that page to find out why he was a famous American. After several practice opportunities like this, you can make it a bit more challenging by asking children to locate the answers to several questions with the help of their index. The questions might include items like: When did Hawaii become a state? Who was Thurgood Marshall? Whose rights did Cesar Chavez demonstrate for? If children have trouble, you would provide the assistance necessary for them to develop the skill.

The final step in a deductive method framework is to provide independent practice opportunities. After you are certain children know how to use the skill, ask them to practice it without your support. Continuing with our example of the index, you might provide your students with a page containing questions such as those previously listed and ask them to locate the information by using the index. Note that this step could be done by individuals working alone or by using a cooperative learning group method framework as described earlier.

Literacy on the Internet: Method Frameworks

The Internet is redefining what it means to be literate (International Reading Association, 2002; Leu, 2000; Leu & Kinzer, 2000b). If we are to prepare children for their tomorrows, we need to embrace the opportunities the Internet provides for new forms of literacy. School districts are quickly recognizing the importance of these new forms of literacy by investing in the technology required for Internet connections and by expecting their teachers to develop expertise in the new literacies of the Internet.

A fundamental issue related to Internet use is how to best integrate the Internet into classroom instruction to support literacy and learning. Three important method frameworks will assist you in these efforts: Internet Workshop, Internet Projects, and Internet Inquiry.

Internet Workshop

Internet Workshop
A method framework containing these steps: locate a site with content related to instruction, develop an activity requiring the use of this site, assign the activity, and have students share their work.

Your class has just received several Internet connections along with several new computers. How do you begin to integrate the Internet into your classroom? Many teachers start by using **Internet Workshop** (Leu, 2002; Leu & Leu, 2000). This is an easy way to

MODEL LESSON

Using Internet Workshop in Rebecca Field's Class

Rebecca Field obtained two new computers with Internet connections in her fifth-grade classroom at the beginning of the year. Since this was the first year she used the Internet in her classroom, she was moving forward gradually, using Internet Workshop. Each Friday, the class met together in Internet Workshop to share the results of their Internet work, to raise questions that arose during the week, and to gather the advice of colleagues.

As she explored this method framework, she discovered new ideas about its use. One powerful insight came during the spring, while the class was enjoying a book on the *Titanic* disaster. Rebecca decided to try a simulation approach with Internet Workshop. She planned a simulation of the Senate hearings on the *Titanic* disaster. Four students would be U.S. senators. These students would hear testimony from other students who would play the part of *Titanic* survivors or newspaper reporters. The survivors would have to select a survivor, do research on the Internet to discover that survivor's story, and then come to the hearings prepared to tell the story of their survival and answer any questions the senators might have. The newspaper reporters would have to report on their experiences interviewing the survivors.

Rebecca enlisted the help of the schools' technology specialist. The specialist created a web page for this Internet Workshop (http://www.sp.uconn.edu/~djleu/titanic.html), with links to many useful resources including the **Encyclopedia Titanica** (http://www.encyclopedia-titanica.org/index.shtml).

The research for the simulation took several weeks to complete. Each week they held a workshop session on Friday. This provided opportunities for students to share their discoveries about the *Titanic* and to exchange new reading and writing skills they were developing with Internet technologies. Some of these questions initiated useful discussions about navigation strategies on the Internet. Others provided opportunities for other students to share the new information they were learning about the disaster. Internet Workshop quickly became a favorite time at the end of the week, and Rebecca started to see students prepare themselves for this time, underlining new information they had recorded in their journals they thought no one else knew and writing down questions about things with which they needed help.

Finally, the day of the simulation arrived. Rebecca invited another class to join as spectators in the gallery. It was a huge success as students dressed up for their parts and told their stories about survival in the cold North Atlantic.

---

begin using the Internet for instruction. Internet Workshop is especially useful to introduce children to sites that will be used in your class for an upcoming unit.

Internet Workshop has many variations. Generally, though, it contains these steps:

1. Locate a site, or several sites, on the Internet with content related to a classroom unit of instruction and set a bookmark for the location(s).
2. Develop an activity related to the learning goals of your unit(s).
3. Assign this activity to be completed during the week.
4. Have children share their work, questions, and new insights at the end of the week during a workshop session.

The first step is to locate a site on the Internet with content related to your instructional unit. How do you do this quickly? One strategy is to simply use a search engine or a directory organized for teachers and children, one that also screens out inappropriate sites for children. You might begin with one of these locations:

- **Yahooligans** (http://www.yahooligans.com/)—This is a directory and a web guide designed for children. Appropriate sites are selected for children ages 7–12.
- **Ask Jeeves for Kids** (http://www.ajkids.com/)—This is a directory and a search engine based on natural language. This means you simply type in a question and it finds the best site with the answer. It contains sites selected for appropriate use by children.

▶ **Searchopolis** (http://www.searchopolis.com/)—Searchopolis is a directory and a search engine organized for students in the elementary grades, middle grades, and high school.

▶ **KidsClick!** (http://sunsite.berkeley.edu/KidsClick!/)—KidsClick is a directory and search engine for kids, developed by the Ramapo Catskill Library System.

central Internet site
A location on the Internet with extensive and well-organized links about a specific topic.

A second strategy is to begin your search at a **central Internet site,** a location on the Internet with extensive and well-organized links about a specific topic. Visiting a central Internet site often will give you many useful resources for your instructional unit, some of which may be used for Internet activities. Most are located at stable sites that will not quickly change. As you explore the Internet, you will discover these well-organized treasure troves of information. They will become homes to which you will often return. Here are some of the better central sites within content areas common to schools:

• Reading	The Literacy Web	http://www.literacy.uconn.edu
	Children's Literature Web Guide	http://www.ucalgary.ca/~dkbrown/index.html
	Cyberguides	http://www.sdcoe.k12.ca.us/score/cyberguide.html
• General	Blue Web'n	http://www.kn.pacbell.com/wired/bluewebn/
• Science	Eisenhower National Clearinghouse	http://www.enc.org:80/
	Science Learning Network	http://www.sln.org/index.html
• Math	Eisenhower National Clearinghouse	http://www.enc.org:80/
	The Math Forum	http:www.mathforum.org
• Social Studies	History/Social Studies Website for K–12 Teachers	http://www.exepc.com/~dboals/boals.html

After you locate an Internet site with information related to your instructional unit, set a bookmark for this site so you and your students may find it easily.

The second step is to develop an activity related to the learning goals of your lessons and the Internet resource you have identified. Sometimes this will be used to introduce children to a site you will use in your instructional unit; other times this will be used to develop central content in your unit. And, sometimes, this will be used to develop navigation strategies for Internet use. Teachers often will prepare an activity page for children to complete and bring to Internet Workshop. Figure 2-5 shows an example of an activity page created by Mary Osborne, a second-grade teacher, to culminate a short unit on poetry and to support recent experiences with long vowel sounds. It uses **Poem Pack** (http://www.bbc.co.uk/education/wordsandpictures/longvow/poems/fpoem.shtml), an exceptional resource developed by the BBC in the United Kingdom and one of many resources located at **Long Vowel Sounds** (http://www.bbc.co.uk/education/wordsandpictures/longvow/). Poem Pack contains a number of humorous poems, each of which contains many key words with long vowel patterns. Each poem is read aloud for children and provides them with many exciting activities. Mary set a bookmark to this site on her classroom computers.

Notice how the tasks on the activity page are open-ended, inviting students to select their own poem at this location and bring this to Internet Workshop to share at the beginning of the unit. This is an essential aspect of any assignment prepared for Internet Workshop. Open-ended activities invite students to bring many different types of experiences and information to Internet Workshop for discussion. Little discussion will take place if you have all students read the same poem or only search for literal-level facts such as "How high is Mt. Fuji?" Discussion is at the heart of Internet Workshop.

FIGURE 2-5

An activity page developed for Internet Workshop to review long vowel patterns and extend responses to poetry

POETRY FROM ENGLAND

Internet Researcher: _____   Date: _____

Objectives

This Internet Workshop will share some funny poems from England and review the use of long vowel patterns. You should use the bookmark I have set to **Poem Pack** (http:www.bbc.co.uk/education/wordsandpictures/longvow/poems/fpoem.shtml).

Choose One Poem and Complete These Activities

• Go to the bookmark I have set for **Poem Pack**
  (http:www.bbc.co.uk/education/wordsandpictures/longvow/poems/fpoem.shtml). Then, for each poem, do these activities by clicking on the button at the bottom of the screen.
• 1. **Hear It.** Listen to the poem being read aloud for you.
  2. **Read It.** Read the poem to yourself or with a partner.
  3. **Sound Search.** Did you find all the sounds?
  4. **Find the Word.** How many words did you find in your poems?
  5. **Print It.** Print out your poem. Practice reading it. We will ask you to read your poem during Internet Workshop on Friday.

Your Choice

Visit at least one of the many other locations at Poem Pack. You decide where to go! Write down notes of what you discovered and share your special discoveries with all of us during Internet Workshop.

_____
_____
_____
_____
_____
_____

Evaluation Rubric

8 points—You completed all of your activities for your poem and you read it in class to your group.

2 points—You shared new information that you discovered at Poem Pack with our class or in your group.

10 points—Total

The third step is to complete the research activity during the week. If you have access to a computer lab at your school you may wish to schedule a period to complete the activity in that facility. This will be essential if you have a departmentalized program in the upper grades and you only see your students for one or two periods each day.

In self-contained classrooms with one or two Internet computers, you may wish to assign students to a schedule such as the one in Figure 2-6. This provides each student with one hour of access on the Internet each week, 30 minutes alone and 30 minutes with a partner. This is usually sufficient time to complete the research activity for Internet Workshop.

The concluding experience each week is a short workshop session where students get to share and compare the information they discovered, discuss newly developing skills, and raise new questions or new activities to be explored in the upcoming weeks.

FIGURE 2-6

A weekly computer schedule posted for Internet Workshop

	Monday	Tuesday	Wednesday	Thursday	Friday
8:30–9:00	Michelle	Michelle/Becky	Chris/Emily	Shannon/Cara	Cynthia/Alana
9:00–9:30	Chris	Julio/Miguel	Jeremy/Tyna	Kati	Patti
9:30–10:00	**Internet Workshop**	Ben	Aaron	Lisa	Julia
10:00–10:30	Shannon	**PE**	Paul	**PE**	Andy
10:30–11:00	**Library**	Mike	Scott	Faith	Melissa
11:00–11:30	Cynthia	Eric	James	Linda	Sara
11:30–12:30	**Lunch**	**Lunch**	**Lunch**	**Lunch**	**Lunch**
12:30–1:00	Alana	Tyna	Miguel	Cara	Emily
1:00–1:30	Becky	Jeremy	Ben/Sara	Mike/Linda	Julio
1:30–2:00	Eric/James	Aaron/Melissa	**Music**	Paul/Scott	**Class Meeting**
2:00–2:30	Kati/Lisa		Faith/Andy	Patti/Julia	

In the example using Poem Pack, students brought their copy of the poem they had enjoyed and shared it in small groups by reading it aloud. They also shared the many new resources they discovered at this location.

Often, Internet Workshop will conclude with ideas to explore in the next experience or research activity and the Internet Workshop cycle continues. Over time, as students become familiar with the purpose and practices of Internet Workshop, they may begin inquiry projects as groups or individuals and bring the information they discover back to the next workshop session.

Internet Project

Internet Project A method framework with these steps: develop a collaborative project, post a description on the Internet, arrange collaboration details with participating teachers, and complete the project.

Internet Project (Leu, 2001; Leu & Leu, 2000) is a collaborative learning experience between two or more classrooms that takes place over the Internet. Internet Project is especially useful for several reasons. It provides opportunities for students to work together—a skill increasingly important in an interdependent world. It also provides special opportunities to integrate language arts with other subject areas such as science, math, and social studies; communicating via Internet technologies is often a central part of any Internet Project. Finally, Internet Project often provides unique opportunities to learn about different cultural contexts; sharing a learning experience with students in other parts of the world leads to important insights about cultural differences.

There are many definitions of Internet Project. Each, however, engages students in classrooms at different locations in collaborative work to solve a common problem or explore a common topic. As a result, Internet Project helps children acquire skills in the collaborative problem solving, information use, and communication activities they will use when they enter the world of work. At least two different types of Internet Project exist: more permanent website projects and temporary projects.

Website projects are more permanent projects, coordinated by an individual or group at a website. They are a wonderful starting point for teachers just beginning their Internet journey since they are precisely defined with clear directions for participation and a complete set of instructional resources. One example of a website project for the youngest literacy learners is the **Flat Stanley Project** (http://flatstanley.enoreo.on.ca/), developed and maintained by Dale Hubert, a third-grade teacher in London, Ontario.

The Flat Stanley project is based on the book, *Flat Stanley*, by Jeff Brown. In this delightful story, a young boy, Stanley Lambchop, is flattened by a falling bulletin board. He quickly discovers a special advantage of being flat, however, when his parents mail him to California in an envelope. This leads to all kinds of wonderful adventures.

In most Flat Stanley projects, small groups make a Flat Stanley on paper and contribute several entries in a journal about his experiences. Then they arrange with a collaborating class to receive their Flat Stanley by mail. The recipient class adds several journal entries describing Stanley's experiences with them and return Flat Stanley and the journal back to the sender. Sometimes, a class will plan a route for Flat Stanley, with several classes in a chain hosting Flat Stanley, reading the previous entries, and creating their own journal entries before sending Flat Stanley on his way. After visiting a host of locations, Flat Stanley returns home.

Many classrooms send Flat Stanley journal entries by e-mail to all classrooms participating in the project. Thus, a new journal entry arrives each morning via e-mail describing the adventures Stanley had the previous day.

This project may be conducted in the youngest grade levels, with journal entries composed together by the class in a language experience activity. Journal entries that arrive from a participating classroom may be shared within the context of a morning message or a message-of-the-day activity.

At older grade levels, students may work in groups, sending and receiving Flat Stanley journal entries on a regular basis and sharing the results with the class. Often, classrooms will put up bulletin boards containing maps and messages they have received on their various Flat Stanley projects.

If you are interested in reading about the experiences of teachers who have conducted a Flat Stanley project in their classroom, be certain to visit **Success Stories** at http://flatstanley.enoreo.on.ca/success_stories.html. You will get many great ideas for your classroom. More complete directions are available at **How Does it Work?** at http://flatstanley.enoreo.on.ca/how.html. If you are looking for classrooms that might be interested in receiving a Flat Stanley, visit **Participants** at http://flatstanley.enoreo.on.ca/list_map.htm.

Website Internet projects are coordinated by an individual at a website. They are a good starting point for teachers new to the Internet because they are often precisely defined with clear directions for participation. Table 2-4 lists examples of website Internet projects. To participate, simply visit the site and follow the directions.

TABLE 2-4

Examples of website Internet Projects and their locations

Title and Location	Description
Book Raps (http://reite.ed.qut.edu.au/oz-teachernet/projects/book-rap/index.html)	Here you can visit the schedule of upcoming books that will be discussed via e-mail (http://www.pa.ash.org.au/rite/projects/book-rap/form1/displayrec2.asp) or you may sign up to coordinate an e-mail discussion of a book your class will read. It's the perfect way to broaden the conversations of books you and your class are reading throughout the year.
Mind's Eye Monster Project (http://www.monsterexchange.com)	Useful for primary grade classrooms. Classrooms and students are matched. Then one student draws a monster and writes a detailed description. The description is sent to the student's partner who must draw the monster from the description. Then, both pictures are posted in the monster gallery. Both reading and writing skills are supported.
Monarch Watch (http://www.MonarchWatch.org/)	Raise monarch butterflies, tag them, release them, record observations about monarchs in your area, and then watch as your data and those compiled by others are used to track the annual migration of this wonderful creature!
Earth Day Groceries (http://www.earthdaybags.org/arborhts/earthday.html)	Students decorate grocery bags with environmentally friendly messages and distribute them at local grocery stores just before Earth Day. Classrooms report on their experiences.
Journey North (http://www.learner.org/jnorth/)	Journey North is a resource for the study of seasonal change. Recently, more than 250,000 students from all 50 states and seven Canadian provinces participated. Students track the arrival of the first robin, red-winged blackbird, hawks, eagles, or other migratory species and then contribute this information to a common database. The database at Journey North displays the information on migrations for everyone to use.
My Hero Project (http://myhero.com/home.asp)	This site celebrates our many heroes and heroines in this world. Your students can read about the many heroes and heroines nominated by others around the world as they come to understand what it means to make a difference in this world. Then, your students can write about their own hero or heroine and post their description at this site.

Temporary Internet projects developed by teachers are currently more common than website Internet projects. Temporary projects are created by teachers who then advertise for collaborating classrooms at one of several locations. After one or several teachers communicate their interest via e-mail, children in each classroom complete the project together and then share their work. These projects often lead to further collaboration between classrooms on other projects.

Temporary Internet projects have many variations. Generally, they follow these procedures:

1. Develop a clear description of your project.
2. Post the project description and timeline.
3. Arrange collaboration details with teachers in other classrooms who agree to participate.
4. Complete the project, exchanging information with your collaborating classrooms.

The first step requires you to do some advance planning, at least several months before you begin the project. Recent projects on the Internet include the following:

▶ *Teddy Bear Travels the World.* Each participating class will host the teddy bear sent out by the initiating classroom for 1 week. While the bear is with a classroom, children will write a description of its adventures in their classroom and send these out each day via e-mail to all participating classrooms. Individual students in other classrooms may write e-mail letters to Teddy about its adventures. These will be answered by students in the host classroom.

▶ *The Eric Carle/Katherine Patterson/Lois Lowry/etc. Book Club.* Participating classes will read books by the book club author. Students in each class will share their responses to the books via e-mail with participating classes. Students reading the same book at the same time will have opportunities to e-mail their responses to their reading partners. Classes will be polled about their favorite books by this author and the results will be shared and graphed.

▶ *Passage to Hiroshima.* A teacher in Nagoya, Japan proposed this project and sought collaborating classrooms interested in studying about the importance of peace and international cooperation. This class proposed to exchange useful sites on the Internet related to world peace and solicited interview and research questions to be used during their trip to Hiroshima. They volunteered to interview citizens of Hiroshima and then share the results, including photos, on their return.

The second step is to post the project description and timeline at one of several locations of the Internet where teachers advertise their projects, seeking collaborating classrooms. This should be done several months in advance so that other teachers have time to find your project. Project descriptions may be posted at several locations, including:

▶ **Global SchoolNet's Internet Project Registry** (http://www.gsn.org/pr/index.cfm)
▶ **SchoolNet's Grassroots Project Gallery** (http://www.schoolnet.ca/grassroots/e/project.centre/search-projects.html)
▶ **Australian Curriculum Projects Registry** (http://rite.ed.qut.edu.au/oz-teachernet/registry/index.html)

If you are new to Internet Project, you may wish to review the project descriptions at these locations and participate in one or two as a collaborating classroom before developing your own project.

The third step in Internet Project is to arrange collaboration details with teachers in other classrooms who agree to participate in the project. Internet Project requires close coordination; it is important to confirm procedures and timelines with everyone involved.

Finally, you complete the activities in the project, exchanging information with all of the collaborating classrooms. This step provides you and your students with opportunities to read, write, and critically evaluate information related to the project. It often leads to longer-term relationships with your classroom partners and with new insights about different cultural contexts, especially if you are fortunate enough to collaborate with classrooms abroad.

Internet Inquiry

For students and classrooms with some experience using the Internet, **Internet Inquiry** is a useful method framework (Leu & Leu, 2000). During Internet Inquiry, individuals or groups identify an important question and gather information as they seek answers to their question. It turns over much of the responsibility for learning to children who pursue answers to questions that are important to them. Internet Inquiry often supplements part of traditional content area instruction.

Internet Inquiry A method framework with these phases: question, search, analyze, compose, and share.

Internet Inquiry consists of five phases:

1. Question
2. Search
3. Analyze
4. Compose
5. Share

During the question phase, children identify an important question they wish to explore. You can support this phase by engaging in group or individual brainstorming

Featured Teacher

Mary Kreul

Another of the talented literacy educators you may find on the Internet is Mary Kreul, a second-grade teacher at Richards Elementary School in Whitefish Bay, Wisconsin. Exploring her classroom home page (http://www.wfbschools.com/RICHARDS/richardsindex.html see Figure 2-7) will reveal many lessons about becoming an effective literacy educator. You will discover the many Internet Projects she uses to develop reading and writing skills as she connects her students to the world around them. You will also discover the many other ways in which she connects literacy and technology. Recently, these included having students make and print their own personalized stationery; having a team of students write and edit their weekly classroom newsletter; publishing student writing on the classroom web page; and much more. Take a few minutes to explore this site. You will discover many new methods and materials to use in your classroom. Teachers like Mary Kreul are preparing their students for the new literacies that will be an important part of their future.

FIGURE 2-7

The home page for Mary Kreul's second-grade classroom in Whitefish Bay, Wisconsin

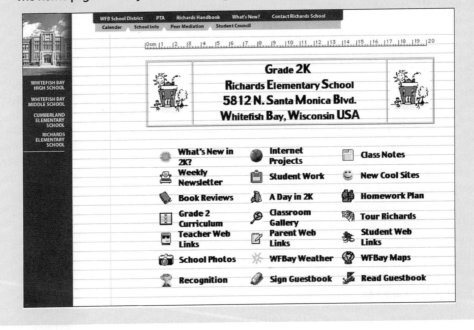

sessions or by setting a bookmark to a central Internet site for the general topic area and allowing students to explore the area, looking for an issue.

Once children have decided on a question they wish to explore, the search phase begins. Students may search on the Internet for useful information related to their question and should be reminded to use more traditional resources found in their classroom or school library during their search.

During the third phase, children should analyze all of the information they have located and respond to the question they initially posed. Sometimes this will lead students to address another question they discover to be more important than their initial question. When this happens, they should be encouraged to repeat the search and analyze phases.

The fourth phase of Internet Inquiry requires students to compose a presentation of their work. There are many ways to do this: a traditional written report, a poster session, a multimedia presentation, or an oral report.

During the final phase, children have an opportunity to share their work with others and respond to questions about their work. Some teachers set aside a regular time each week for sharing inquiry projects as they are completed. Sometimes this takes place during Internet Workshop or during a special science or social studies fair where students have an opportunity to share their work with other classes at school.

Internet Inquiry can be an exciting part of your curriculum because it offers students important opportunities to read, analyze, and write within content areas such as math, science, and social studies. It allows you to integrate traditional subject areas with language arts in powerful ways.

Material and Method Frameworks: A Final Word

This chapter provides you with initial frameworks for conducting reading instruction in your classroom. Material and method frameworks are commonly used by teachers as they seek to prepare their students for future literacy demands. These are useful starting points as you consider literacy instruction in your classroom. Additional method frameworks will be explored in upcoming chapters, providing you with an extensive set of instructional tools. However, by themselves, material and method frameworks only get you started on the road to effective literacy instruction. To develop the insights so critical to success, you need to begin developing a literacy framework, the subject of the next chapter.

Use the self-test questions on http://www.prenhall.com/leukinzer to review the material presented in this chapter.

Major Points

▶ Teachers employ a material framework when they follow lessons in the teacher's manual of a published school reading program. This reduces the complexity of decision making but may sometimes result in teachers abdicating their responsibility as insightful, reflective professionals. There are several ways in which insightful teachers modify the nature of these lessons to more effectively meet the needs of individual students.

▶ Method frameworks consist of two common elements: procedural steps for completing an activity and options for completing each one of the procedural steps. Like material frameworks, method frameworks reduce the complexity of classroom decisions but provide teachers with more of an opportunity to use their special insight about students.

▶ Each of the following method frameworks is commonly used to teach reading: reading workshop, guided reading, read-aloud response journal activities, cooperative learning groups, and deductive instruction. You should be familiar with the procedural steps for each method framework and some of the options that are possible for each step.

▶ Several method frameworks are useful for integrating the Internet into your literacy classroom: Internet Workshop, Internet Project, and Internet Inquiry. Each can be used to help children develop the literacies of their futures.

Making Instructional Decisions

1. It is your first year of teaching. Your principal has required all teachers to use the Scott Foresman reading program. You are allowed to replace, refine, supplement, or even skip lessons in the teacher's manual, but student growth will be regularly measured and monitored by the skills tests that accompany this program. Your evaluation is also related to your students' performance on these tests. You believe, however, that basals teach too many skills and you feel uncomfortable with the decision

that has been made about their use. This is a common situation for teachers who find that decisions about instructional materials contradict their own beliefs. Mosenthal (1989) describes it as putting teachers between a rock and a hard place. How do you think teachers should handle this situation? Would you closely follow lesson plans in the program to be certain your students pass the tests? Would you adapt the lessons? If so, how would you do this? Would you replace basal lessons with method frameworks? What would these be? How would you explain these changes to your principal?

2. Which of the method frameworks used for traditional reading experiences do you think will be most useful to you? Why?

3. Develop an Internet Workshop. Use one of the central Internet sites listed in this chapter to find an appropriate location for this activity.

4. Specify a grade level. Develop an Internet Project that would be especially useful for integrating the Internet into your reading and language arts program.

Further Reading

Au, K. H. (1997). *Literacy instruction in multicultural settings.* Belmont, CA: Wadsworth.

Describes ways to make changes to typical instruction to meet the needs of students with diverse backgrounds. Topics covered include the nature of literacy, cultural and linguistic variation, multiethnic literature, and writing experiences in multicultural classrooms.

Hancock, M. R. (1993). Exploring and extending personal response through literature journals. *The Reading Teacher, 46,* 466–475.

Describes the importance of response opportunities for readers transacting with literature and discusses a wide variety of prompts that may be used to support students' responses to works of literature. These may also be used to structure read-aloud response journal experiences.

Leu, D. J., Jr. (2000). Our children's future: Changing the focus of literacy and literacy instruction. *The Reading Teacher, 53,* 424–431.

Explains how and why the nature of reading and writing are changing as the Internet generates new literacies, which are important for our students to acquire.

Leu, D. J., Jr., & Leu, D. D. (2000). *Teaching with the Internet: Lessons from the classroom, K-12* (3rd ed.). Norwood, MA: Christopher-Gordon Publishers, Inc.

Shows how the Internet is used in classrooms around the world to support literacy and learning. It features instructional models including: Internet Workshop, Internet Project, and Internet Inquiry.

References

Anders, P. L., Hoffman, J. V., & Duffy, G. G. (2000). Teaching teachers to teach reading: Paradigm shifts, persistent problems, and challenges. In M. L. Kamil, P. Mosenthal, P. D. Pearson, & R. Barr (Eds.), *Handbook of reading research, Volume III* (pp. 719–742). Mahwah, NJ: Lawrence Erlbaum Associates.

Atwell, N. (1998). *In the middle: New understandings about writing, reading, and learning with adolescents* (2nd ed.). Portsmouth, NH: Boyton/Cook.

Barrentine, S. J. (1996). Engaging with reading through interactive read-alouds. *The Reading Teacher, 50,* 36–43.

Duffy, G. G., & Hoffman, J. V. (1999). In pursuit of an illusion: The flawed search for a perfect method. *The Reading Teacher, 53,* 10–34.

Durkin, D. (1981). Reading comprehension instruction in five basal reader series. *Reading Research Quarterly, 16,* 515–519.

Goodman, K. S., Freeman, Y., Murphy, S., & Shannon, P. (1988). *Report card on basal readers.* Evanston, IL: National Council of Teachers of English.

Hancock, M. R. (1993). Exploring and extending personal response through literature journals. *The Reading Teacher, 46,* 466–475.

Harris, A. J., & Sipay, E. R. (1990). *How to increase reading ability* (9th ed.). New York: Longman Publishing Group.

Herber, H. L., & Herber, J. N. (1993). *Teaching in content areas.* Boston, MA: Allyn & Bacon.

International Reading Association. (2002). *Preparing students for their literacy future: A position statement on literacy and technology.* Newark, DE: IRA.

Jachym, N. K., Allington, R. L., & Broikou, K. A. (1989). Estimating the cost of seatwork. *The Reading Teacher, 43,* 30–35.

Keegan, S., & Shrake, K. (1991). Literature study groups: An alternative to ability grouping. *The Reading Teacher, 44,* 542–547.

Leal, D. J. (1993). The power of literary peer-group discussions: How children collaboratively negotiate meaning. *The Reading Teacher, 47,* 114–121.

Leu, D. J., Jr. (2000). Our children's future: Changing the focus of literacy and literacy instruction. *The Reading Teacher, 53,* 424–431.

Leu, D. J., Jr. (2001). Internet Project: Preparing students for new literacies in a global village. *The Reading Teacher, 54,* 568–585.

Leu, D. J., Jr. (2002). Internet Workshop: Making time for literacy. *The Reading Teacher, 55,* 466–472.

Leu, D. J., & Ayre, L. (1992). *Changes to children's literature in the basals of the 1980's and the 1990's.* Paper presented at the 42nd annual meeting of the National Reading Conference, San Antonio, Texas.

Leu, D. J., Jr., & Kinzer, C. K. (2000b). The convergence of literacy instruction and networked technologies for information and communication. *Reading Research Quarterly, 35,* 108–127.

Leu, D. J., Jr., & Leu, D. D. (2000). *Teaching with the Internet: Lessons from the classroom, K–12* (3rd ed.). Norwood, MA: Christopher-Gordon Publishers, Inc.

McCallum, R. D. (1988). Don't throw out the basal with the bathwater. *The Reading Teacher, 42,* 204–209.

McCarthey, S. J., & Hoffman, J. V. (1995). The new basals: How are they different? *The Reading Teacher, 49,* 72–75.

Mosenthal, P. B. (1989). The whole language approach: Teachers between a rock and a hard place. *The Reading Teacher, 42,* 628–629.

Osborn, J. (1984). Workbooks that accompany basal reading programs. In G. G. Duffy, L. R. Roehler, & J. Mason (Eds.), *Comprehension instruction: Perspectives and suggestions.* New York: Longman Publishing Group.

Reutzel, D. R. (1991). Understanding and using basal readers effectively. In B. L. Hayes (Ed.), *Effective strategies for teaching reading* (pp. 254–280). New York: Allyn & Bacon.

Schmidt, W. H., Caul, J., Byers, J. L., & Buchmann, M. (1984). Content of basal text selections: Implications for comprehension instruction. In G. G. Duffy, L. R. Roehler, & J. Mason (Eds.), *Comprehension instruction: Perspectives and suggestions.* New York: Longman Publishing Group.

Shannon, P. (1986). The use of commercial reading materials in American elementary schools. *Reading Research Quarterly, 19,* 68–85.

Snow, C. E., Burns, S., & Griffin, P. (1998). *Preventing reading difficulties in young children.* Washington, DC: National Academy Press.

Staab, C. (1991). Classroom organization: Thematic centers revisited. *Language Arts, 68,* 108–113.

Strickland, D. S., & Morrow, L. M. (1990). Integrating the emergent literacy curriculum with themes. *The Reading Teacher, 44,* 604–605.

Trelease, J. (2001). *The Read Aloud Handbook* (5th ed.). New York: Penguin.

Tunnell, M. O., & Jacobs, J. S. (1989). Using "real" books: Research findings on literature based reading instruction. *The Reading Teacher, 42*(7), 470–477.

CHAPTER 3

Developing Insights: Defining Your Literacy Framework

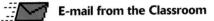 **E-mail from the Classroom**

Subject: Literacy Insights
From: Tamika Jones, tjones54@hotmail.com

I think I'm beginning to understand what it means to have insights about literacy. I had been using a deductive method in one group to teach how stories contain problems that get resolved.

Everyone got this idea except for Julian. He just wasn't interested. It showed in his reading comprehension and in the stories he wrote, none of which had a problem or a resolution. I changed to a more inductive approach with Julian for a few days. We read a few short stories together and we took turns guessing what the problem would be. When we guessed the problem, we tried to guess the solution. He got it right away. His comprehension has increased, and his written stories are now nicely structured, containing problems and resolutions. Developing insights, like the ones I used with Julian, are the most important part of my preparation. They help me to know how to change instruction to fit what a student needs.

I have been following the e-mail messages on the RTEACHER listserv (http://www.reading. org/publications/rt/rt_listserv.html). I really like what one teacher recently wrote, "I teach children, not reading programs. I focus on the outcome, not the materials."

Good luck everyone! Make a difference in the lives of children!

Tamika

Key Concepts

affective aspects

automaticity

balanced literacy framework

decoding knowledge

discourse knowledge

emergent literacy

holistic language learning explanations

integrated explanations

interactive explanations

literacy framework

metacognitive knowledge

phonics instruction

reader-based explanations

social aspects

specific skills explanations

syntactic knowledge

text-based explanations

vocabulary knowledge

After reading this chapter, you should be able to:

1. Use your literacy framework to develop insights about reading and help you meet the individual needs of students in your classroom.
2. Understand how each component of the reading process contributes to successful reading.
3. Develop your beliefs about how children read and use this to inform decisions about *what* to teach.
4. Develop your beliefs about how children learn to read and use this to inform decisions about *how* to teach.
5. Show how a balanced perspective supports diverse student needs.

Developing Insights: A Principle of Effective Literacy Instruction

This chapter completes our introduction to the first, and most important, principle of effective literacy instruction:

1. **Teachers' insights are central to effective instruction (Anders, Hoffman, & Duffy, 2000; Duffy & Hoffman, 1999; Snow, Burns, & Griffin, 1998).**

You will recall from previous chapters that research demonstrates that effective literacy educators use their insights about literacy to meet individuals needs.

In chapter 2, we indicated that effective literacy educators develop three important types of frameworks:

1. Material frameworks
2. Method frameworks
3. Literacy frameworks

You have now developed important beginning understandings about material and method frameworks, a journey that will continue throughout this book. In this chapter, you will develop your insights about how children read and how children learn to read.

You will develop these insights by identifying your initial literacy framework. A literacy framework consists of your beliefs about how children read and how children learn to read. Your beliefs about these two important issues will inform your insights and your instructional decisions. Your beliefs are also critical to understanding students' individual needs and to developing strategies to meet them. As you observe the effects of your instructional decisions, you will regularly modify your beliefs based on what succeeds with your students. This is what effective literacy instruction is all about. The very best literacy educators are always testing their beliefs about effective instruction in the classroom, developing new insights that permit them to become even more effective teachers.

This chapter will help you to develop your literacy framework and the insights necessary to become an effective literacy educator. Because a literacy framework provides you with powerful insights about your students and their instructional needs, it is one of the most important tools you can develop. Thus, the information in this chapter is critical to your developing ability as a literacy educator.

Check your ongoing understanding of chapter concepts by using the guided review for this chapter on http://www.prenhall.com/leukinzer

What Are My Current Beliefs about Reading Comprehension and Response?

As Tamika Jones indicates in her e-mail message, some teachers hold strong views about the best way to teach reading. Debates about reading instruction take place every day on the Internet. Educators tend to be very polarized in their views about reading. Some argue for approaches that use more **phonics instruction.** Others argue for approaches consistent with a **more holistic** perspective. Later, we will show you why we believe this is a false dichotomy. Nevertheless, many in the field of reading take one side or the other in this fierce debate.

Let us be very clear about our position: There is no single best method for teaching reading. *What appears to help children most is an insightful teacher—not a particular instructional practice nor a particular set of instructional materials. Reading and children are both too complex for a single instructional practice or a single set of materials to meet every child's needs.* Insightful teachers help children learn to read, even if it means abandoning a favorite approach when it is not working. Insightful teachers are not limited to one approach or another.

But what is an insightful teacher? An insightful teacher understands how children read and uses this information to make informed decisions about *what to teach.* An insightful teacher also understands how children learn to read and uses this information to make informed decisions about *how to teach.* Developing insights about these two is-

phonics instruction Teaching practices designed to help students acquire knowledge of the relationships between letters and sounds and the ability to blend combinations of letter-sounds.

FIGURE 3-1

Beliefs about how children read

1. When children cannot recognize a word during reading, a useful strategy is to help them sound it out.
2. Children's knowledge about the world is more important to reading comprehension and response than their ability to correctly sound out words.
3. To understand what they read, it is important that children be able to read most words correctly.
4. Computers are most useful because they help students discover more about the world around them.
5. When we ask children a question about a story they have read, there usually is one answer that is better than others.
6. When children cannot recognize a word during reading, a useful strategy for them is to read the sentence again, look at the first letter of the difficult word, and make a guess about what it might be.
7. In the early grades, teachers should spend roughly equal amounts of time teaching children how to sound out unfamiliar words and how to make reasonable guesses about words they cannot recognize.
8. Reading is really the interaction between what an author intended to mean and the meaning a reader brings to that text.
9. Teachers should encourage each child to have a different interpretation and response to a story.
10. When we think about comprehension, it is important to keep in mind that the meaning an author intended usually is what we should encourage children to take away from their reading experience.
11. Teachers should always find out what children know about the topic of a story before asking them to begin reading.
12. Talking storybook software is useful for younger children because it will pronounce unfamiliar words during reading experiences on CD-ROMs.
13. During the reading process, guesses often are as important as accurate word recognition.
14. Authors and readers understand a story in their own ways.
15. When children cannot recognize a word, a useful strategy for them is to read the sentence again and make a guess.

sues helps you understand why you should use different instructional strategies for different children in different situations.

What should I teach children about reading? How should I teach it? As a classroom teacher, you will face these two issues as well as many other important decisions. Each will be fundamentally influenced by your beliefs (Richardson, Anders, Tidwell, & Lloyd, 1991). These beliefs can be a powerful tool for developing insights about your students and your teaching (Goodman, 1986, 1992; Spiegel, 1992). It is important to become aware of your beliefs about reading and to think about how they will affect your instruction and your students.

What are your beliefs about these two important issues: how children read and how children learn to read? Here is a brief activity designed to identify your current beliefs. First, read the 15 statements in Figure 3-1. Mark the five statements in the figure that best represent your current ideas about how children read. Next, identify your beliefs about how children learn to read by looking at the 15 statements in Figure 3-2. Mark the five statements in this figure that best represent your current ideas about this second issue. Do this now before you read any further. Think about your choices as you read the remainder of this chapter. At the end of this chapter, you will be asked to come back and determine how the choices you made here can help inform the important decisions you must make during literacy instruction: What should I teach? and How should I teach?

FIGURE 3-2

Beliefs about how children learn to read

1. It is important for teachers to provide clear explanations about many aspects of reading.
2. Students should receive many opportunities to select and read materials unrelated to school learning.
3. Reading instruction should include both teacher-directed and student-directed learning opportunities.
4. Students learn the most about reading when they engage in reading experiences that are personally meaningful, accomplish an important function, and are self-directed.
5. An effective reading program is one where both teachers and students have a clear understanding of essential reading skills.
6. Assessment is essential to a literacy program. This assessment should closely match the skills that have been developed in class.
7. Some children seem to learn about reading best when they determine their own literacy experiences; others seem to learn best through more structured experiences designed by a teacher.
8. Computers are most useful when they are used for communication.
9. To provide children with a reason to read and write, teachers need to create personally meaningful literacy experiences for them.
10. Teachers need to regularly determine which children will benefit from teacher-directed instruction and which children will benefit from self-directed learning experiences.
11. Teachers should have a minimal list of literacy learning goals for students in their classrooms.
12. Computers are most useful when many practice activities are used at the appropriate level for each child.
13. Both students and teachers should define appropriate classroom literacy experiences.
14. Children learn much about literacy by watching their parents at home.
15. No single approach to literacy learning will fit each child perfectly. Teachers need to modify their programs to meet each child's unique needs.

Understanding the Components of Reading

Before we go any further, let's take a look at the components of the reading process. Understanding these components is a good place to begin thinking about how children read.

Most agree the nine components illustrated in Figure 3-3 contribute in a major way to reading comprehension and response (Anderson, Hiebert, Scott, & Wilkinson, 1985; Snow, Burns, & Griffin, 1998). Although people may disagree about which components are most important, most would agree these components define much of the reading process.

Reading instruction consists of activities designed to help children acquire the components in Figure 3-3. For example, teachers try to establish a social context for reading in their classrooms that communicates the joys, knowledge, and excitement that comes from reading. These teachers are supporting social aspects of reading—an important component of the reading process. In addition, teachers often discuss the meanings of unfamiliar words before asking children to read a selection. These teachers are teaching vocabulary knowledge, another component of the reading process, in order to help children understand the upcoming story or article. Similar instructional activities are used to develop each of the other components. Understanding each of these components will give you many insights about what to teach.

social aspects Readers comprehend and respond to a passage depending on a number of social aspects, including the social context you establish for reading in your classroom, the social context parents establish for reading at home, the larger social context of how reading is used in a society, and the social significance of a particular story.

Social Aspects

There are many **social aspects** to literacy (Dyson, 1993; Vygotsky, 1978). These include the social context you establish for reading in your classroom, the social context parents

FIGURE 3-3

FIGURE 3-3

Major components of reading comprehension and response

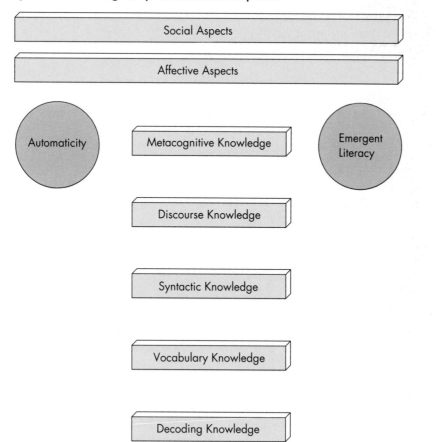

establish for reading at home, the larger social context of how reading is used in a society, and the social significance of a particular story. Readers comprehend and respond to a story depending on each of these social aspects.

For example, you may enjoy reading stories like *The Giving Tree* by Shel Silverstein because you fondly recall the social context of read-aloud time during your own elementary school years. You may also appreciate the social significance of this story since you see it as a story about friendship: an apple tree continues to give of herself to the boy who becomes a man until, at last, the apple tree is only a stump.

However, your memories of the social context of reading may not be happy ones. You may recall reading stories like *The Giving Tree* as unpleasant times, when you had to read stories aloud in front of your friends and reveal your reading weaknesses in public. Moreover, you may have a negative view about the social meaning that some feel is presented by this story: a story about men always taking from—never giving to—women.

In addition, the social context for reading at home may have been a positive one, with everyone reading in the afternoon and evening, often discussing what they had read. Alternatively, the social context for reading at home may have not been so positive, with little reading and much television viewing.

There is also the larger social context of how reading is used in a society. You may believe that reading is a liberating experience, enabling all people to learn and accomplish anything they wish. Or, you may view reading as an experience that enforces prevailing social classes, being widely available to those in positions of power and less available to those who are not privileged. Yes, reading and response may contain all of these important social aspects.

PRACTICAL TEACHING STRATEGIES

Developing Social Aspects of Reading

Helping Your Child Learn to Read (http://www.ed.gov/pubs/parents/Reading/index.html). This wonderful resource on the Internet is an online book for parents written by nationally recognized experts in reading instruction for the U.S. Department of Education. It is written in an easy to understand style, containing information for parents about how they may help their children to read at home. Print out copies of several chapters and distribute these at "Back to School Night." Invite parents to support your classroom reading program with the social context they establish for reading at home.

Read-Alouds. Spend 15 minutes each day reading aloud an exciting work of children's literature. Establish a warm and pleasant context for reading by inviting younger students to gather around you on a rug in a special corner of the room. To draw your students into the story, invite them to share their responses as the story unfolds.

Affective Aspects

affective aspects
Children get excited about reading when affective aspects such as interest and attitude increase motivation and facilitate comprehension and response.

We all read better when we have a positive attitude toward reading and when we are interested in reading a particular story. We refer to these elements as **affective aspects.** Students' attitudes and interests about reading play an important role in the way they approach reading experiences and how they respond to them (Holdaway, 1979; Madden, 1988; Oldfather, 1993). Affective aspects often are established by the social context you establish for reading.

All readers comprehend and respond better when they are interested in reading; the difference is especially noticeable among less-proficient readers. As teachers, we need to make certain we make reading an exciting experience for everyone. Often this is done by sharing your own enthusiasm for reading and by providing students with opportunities to select their own reading experiences. By encouraging students to choose selections that are personally interesting, teachers seek to increase their students' attitudes and interests about reading.

Metacognitive Knowledge

We use many different strategies as we read. For example, you may have decided to start reading this chapter by reading the summary at the end to get a sense of its content. Or perhaps you leafed through the pages, looking at the sequence of section headings. You may even have decided to read this page again if you got to the end of it and did not understand parts of what you had read. All these strategies are used by good readers.

metacognitive knowledge   The knowledge readers have about the strategies used during reading.

Metacognitive knowledge is strategic knowledge (Baker & Brown, 1984; Palincsar & Ransom, 1988). This is a third component we use during reading. Metacognitive knowledge consists of all the strategies you use to actively construct the meaning of a passage while you are reading. It is very useful for comprehension; good readers stop to look at a figure, sound out an unfamiliar word, reread a troublesome sentence, think about what they have read, underline important information, and read chapter summaries first. Metacognitive knowledge is important in all aspects of reading, including reading on the Internet since your students must learn strategies to efficiently find useful locations on the Internet.

Discourse Knowledge

There is a special magic in the four words, "Once upon a time . . . ." What happens when you read the first four words of a book that begins this way? It is likely you expect to find many things. You know, for example, that this is probably a fairy tale, not a chapter in a social studies book. You also expect the location of this story to be a kingdom "long ago and far away." In addition, you probably expect to find a prince and princess as central charac-

PRACTICAL TEACHING STRATEGIES

Developing Affective Aspects

Storybook Character Days. Designate a day as "Storybook Character Day." Encourage students to come dressed as their favorite character in a book they have recently read and keep a box of clothing and hats for those who may not have extra clothing at home. Come dressed as a character yourself. Have a contest to see who can identify the greatest number of characters. Encourage children to talk about their chosen characters and the books from which their characters come. Such an activity will increase interest in reading and will lead students to books they might not have considered reading before.

Book Talks. At the beginning of every week, introduce several new books to your students. You may wish to bring these from your own library, your local library, or your school's library. As you introduce each book, talk about it as if you were trying to "sell" it to your students. Tell them the title, author, general plot of the story, and something special about the book or author that will interest your students in reading the book (e.g., "If you are really interested in books about outdoor adventures, this is the book for you!"). After you have introduced all of the books, set them in a visible location in your room for students to explore.

PRACTICAL TEACHING STRATEGIES

Developing Metacognitive Knowledge

Internet Workshop. As you engage children in reading experiences on the Internet, periodically conduct Internet Workshop. Invite children to bring the new strategies they have learned and the things that cause problems to the workshop session. Gather students weekly for a short session where they share their new strategies and seek advice about how to do things on the Internet. Sharing Internet strategies in this manner can be very effective in helping your children use this resource effectively (Leu & Leu, 2000).

Think-Alouds. Periodically model your own reading strategies in a think-aloud. To conduct a think-aloud, begin reading a passage and then share aloud each of your thoughts as you are reading. These might be questions you have about what is going to happen next, surprise at something happening in the story, or strategies you use to monitor your understanding. Think-alouds help your students to see what is happening inside your head as you read. Encourage students to conduct a think-aloud as well.

ters as well as a king and queen. Finally, you may expect the hero or heroine to resolve some problem in the story, which will conclude with a happy ending. Why do you have these expectations from just four words? All of these expectations are generated because your **discourse knowledge** includes an understanding of how fairy tales are organized.

Discourse knowledge is knowledge about how different language forms are structured. Each language form has its own internal structure: a fairy tale, a business letter, a memo, a newspaper article, a story, and even an Internet browser. Discourse knowledge tells you what to expect while you are reading a familiar form. Knowing the discourse structure tells you many things about what you are likely to find in that text.

discourse knowledge
The knowledge readers have about how different language forms are structured.

Syntactic Knowledge

How do you know these two sentences, with the same words, contain different meanings?

"The dog bit the man."

"The man bit the dog."

You know that in each sentence a different agent is acting on a different object. This is an example of **syntactic knowledge** at work during reading. Syntactic knowledge

syntactic knowledge
The knowledge readers have of word order rules that determine meaning in sentences.

Discourse knowledge is developed as children experience the structure inherent in the books they read.

refers to your knowledge of rules that determine meaning within individual sentences. Knowledge of sentence syntax is crucial to the comprehension process (Irwin, 1986).

You can see the importance of syntactic knowledge for comprehension by doing an experiment with children at different age levels. Write the following sentence on the chalkboard:

> David, John's father, went outside.

Then read this sentence to children who are about 5 years old and ask them how many people went outside. Most 5-year-olds will tell you that three people went outside: David, John, and father. Now do the same thing with 10-year-olds. Most 10-year-olds, because they are familiar with this type of sentence structure, will tell you that only one person went outside. Most 10-year-olds possess the syntactic knowledge to comprehend this sentence correctly; most 5-year-olds do not.

Children's oral language ability is fairly well developed when they come to school at 5 or 6 years of age. Nevertheless, many complex sentence patterns, like the one in the previous experiment, are unfamiliar to most children when they begin school. Young children need to develop familiarity with many new elements of sentence syntax when they come to school. Understanding more complex syntactic patterns becomes especially important as readers mature and their reading selections contain more complicated types of sentence structures.

Vocabulary Knowledge

vocabulary knowledge
The knowledge readers use to determine word meanings, including the ability to use context to determine word meanings.

Of course, understanding the meanings of words you read is also very important. We refer to this as **vocabulary knowledge.** Vocabulary knowledge includes two elements: (1) the knowledge readers have of word meanings and (2) the knowledge readers use to determine the meanings of unfamiliar words from the surrounding context. Both elements are essential to the reading process. Consider this sentence in a brief passage:

> Joan's problem is with her ethmoid.

PRACTICAL TEACHING STRATEGIES

Developing Discourse Knowledge and Syntactic Knowledge

Developing Discourse Knowledge

Teaching Fable Characteristics. Read a different fable aloud each day for several consecutive days. Discuss each one. After students have listened to a number of fables, ask them to help you list the characteristics that are common to all. Write these observations on the board. They may respond, for example, with the following observations: animals are the main characters, the animals talk and act like people, there usually is a lesson (moral) at the end of each story, or the fables did not really happen. Read (or have students read) another fable to see whether the same structural elements also appear. Discuss the ones they noticed. Finally, have students write or dictate a fable themselves, being sure to incorporate the structural elements of this type of writing.

Developing Syntactic Knowledge

Conducting a Style Study. Help your students become familiar with the writing style of an outstanding author. Read a book together by this author and look for the syntactic characteristics of the author's style. The author may often use a sequence of descriptive adjectives or participial phrases to evoke more complete images in the mind of the reader. The author may use the word "and" frequently during conversations to make these seem more natural and consistent with the way people speak. Perhaps the author uses very short and compact sentences to paint a precise picture of what took place. The author may also frequently use a semicolon. Find one common syntactic characteristic and have students discuss why they think the author used this feature. Then have them respond to a short writing task that allows them to try using this same feature in their own writing. Afterward, have students share their work in small groups. After each student shares a piece of writing, encourage students to make at least one positive comment about the writing that was shared.

Unless you know the meaning of the final word in this sentence, you cannot understand the sentence. This is the first element of vocabulary knowledge—knowing word meanings.

However, you may not know the meaning of a word but are able to determine its meaning from the surrounding information, or context. The context of the second sentence in this brief passage can help you determine the meaning of *ethmoid*:

> Joan's problem is with her ethmoid. She broke this bone at the point where the nose joins the skull.

The meaning of the second sentence, not your knowledge of the word *ethmoid*, helped you discover that ethmoid refers to a bone connecting the nose and the skull. Knowing how to use context is a second element of vocabulary knowledge.

Helping students develop vocabulary knowledge is important at all grade levels (Harris & Sipay, 1990; Johnson & Pearson, 1984). It is particularly important as children explore less-familiar subject areas that use specialized vocabularies.

Decoding Knowledge

Decoding knowledge is the knowledge readers use to determine the oral equivalent of a written word; that is, sound it out. Knowing how to sound out, or decode, a written word often enables a beginning reader to determine its meaning. Phonic knowledge is one element of decoding knowledge, but not the only one, as we will see in chapter 4.

Sometimes decoding knowledge is important for comprehension and response; at other times, it is not. Decoding knowledge is important when recognizing the sound of a word can help a reader determine its meaning. Decoding knowledge is not important when a word's sound does not help a reader identify the word's meaning. For example, just knowing how to decode an unfamiliar word like *taligrade* usually is not helpful to understanding its meaning.

decoding knowledge
The knowledge readers use to determine the oral equivalent of a word.

PRACTICAL TEACHING STRATEGIES

Developing Vocabulary Knowledge

Internet Vocabulary Workshop. Each week, select a list of 10 vocabulary words that will be important in up-coming units of instruction. Post these next to a classroom computer connected to the Internet if you have one. As students have a few moments, have them use a search engine to locate the top two or three sites containing each word. Provide each student with a journal to record the meaning for each word he or she uncovers, and have the students organize these into weekly lists. Bring journals and share discoveries during Internet Workshop once a week. This activity is especially useful to introduce content related to upcoming units. For child safety concerns, you may wish to limit searches to resources available with the search engine at **Yahooligans!** (http://www.yahooligans.com/). Yahooligans! screens sites for child safety and appropriateness (see Figure 3-4).

A Synonym Tree. If you do not have access to the Internet, make a synonym tree in your classroom and have students look for words similar in meaning to the words on your tree. On a bulletin board, put up the outline of a large tree made from construction paper. Cut out blank word cards in the shape of a leaf. Write challenging words on the word cards (one per card), then pin each card on the tree. As students discover synonyms in their reading, have them write them on blank word cards and pin them to the original words on the tree so they can see the appropriate synonym pairs.

FIGURE 3-4

Yahooligans! is a useful resource on the Internet because it screens locations for child safety and appropriateness (http://www.yahooligans.com)

Note: Courtesy of Yahooligans!.

PRACTICAL TEACHING STRATEGIES

Developing Decoding Knowledge

Using an Inductive Method Framework. Use an inductive method framework to teach students that *-ake* usually represents the sound /ache/. Inductive instruction allows students to induce a rule or principle from a set of data and then provides them with practice opportunities.

1. *Provide examples of the rule.* Present riddles in which the answers rhyme with *make* and end in *-ake*. For example, "I'm thinking of a word that rhymes with *make* and is something you eat at a party." (cake) "I'm thinking of a word that rhymes with *make* and is something that crawls in the grass." (snake) As students guess each riddle, write the answers on the board until you have four or five words that end in *-ake: cake, snake, rake, lake, bake.*

2. *Help students discover the rule.* Help students see that all of the words on the board end in *-ake* and sound like /ache/. Use the words on the board to help students induce the decoding generalization: the letters *-ake* usually represent the sound /ache/.

3. *Provide guided practice.* Help students apply this generalization to read other, similarly spelled words such as *take, fake,* or *wake.*

4. *Provide independent practice.* Provide independent practice that allows students to practice this generalization. This activity may include the reading of a short literary selection containing the *-ake* pattern or a writing experience where this pattern is likely to appear.

Developing decoding knowledge is almost always included in instructional programs. It is an important part of beginning reading instruction (Adams, 1990; Anderson, Hiebert, Scott & Wilkinson, 1985; Chall, 1983; Cunningham, Hall, & Defee, 1991).

Automaticity

You often read without being aware of what you do while you read. At times it seems that meaning almost magically pops into your head as you move through a story. This is an example of **automaticity** at work. Automaticity describes situations where we perform a complex activity without paying attention to any of the components of that activity. Consider, for example, the physical movements of a concert pianist during a performance. Playing a piece of music requires many complex sequences of movement. Proficient pianists have learned how to perform these movements automatically without attending to any of the components such as finger movement. Similar explanations may be given to other complicated activities such as solving a long division problem, throwing a football, hitting a golf ball, or driving a car. In each, you perform a complex task without attending to the components of that task.

automaticity The ability to perform a complex task like reading without attending to any of the components of that task. Fluent reading is a result of automaticity.

Learning each of these complex tasks, though, requires conscious awareness of each of the component parts at the beginning. You initially think about your grip on a football, keeping your left arm straight in a golf swing, or which direction you move the turn signal for a right-hand turn. Gradually, though, you learn to perform each action without attending to each of the components. That is, you develop automaticity with respect to each of the component parts.

Reading is also a complicated process like playing a piano or driving a car. As such, it requires attention to the many components of the process when first learning how to read. As one practices the many aspects of this process, these components become increasingly automatic (Samuels & Eisenberg, 1981; Stanovich, 1980). This explains why good readers can read without thinking about what they are doing.

Understanding reading as the development of automaticity provides insights about many things in your classroom. You understand why students forget to correctly spell an easy word when they are writing quickly, trying to capture the essence of a thought before they forget it. The children's attention is devoted to the content of the writing—not the

PRACTICAL TEACHING STRATEGIES

Developing Emergent Literacy with Texts that Scaffold Early Reading Experiences

Reading Predictable Texts. Read predictable texts aloud to your young students. Predictable texts are storybooks that contain a repeated element—a sentence pattern, a rhyming pattern, or some other pattern—that makes the language highly predictable. Examples include *Brown Bear, Brown Bear; The Cat in the Hat; The Little Red Hen; Henny Penny; The House that Jack Built;* and *The Gingerbread Boy.* When you read predictable texts aloud to your students, they will quickly notice the repeated pattern. As they do, occasionally leave out the repeated pattern, and have students complete it for you. Afterward, place that book out on a table for your students to enjoy. Even your weakest readers will be able to read many such books on their own as soon as they discover the predictable and repeated patterns.

Reading Wordless Picture Books. Enjoy wordless picture books with very young readers in kindergarten and first grade. Then, invite individuals to "read" these books to a partner. Use books such as *Shopping Trip* by Helen Oxenburg and *Up a Tree* by Ed Young. You may locate others in this genre by checking with your school librarian.

form. Knowing about automaticity will permit you to encourage a child to go back later and attend to the spelling and punctuation when he or she revises the piece. You also understand why some beginning readers attempt to recognize the oral equivalent of a written word by sounding out individual letters. These readers do not yet have automatic decoding skills; therefore, you seek ways to assist them. Finally you understand why some students know how to use an encyclopedia or navigate efficiently on the Internet: These students are automatic with navigation strategies for these contexts. Understanding reading as an automatic process generates many insights about your students.

Emergent Literacy

emergent literacy   A view of literacy as a continuously emerging and evolving ability that results from one's experiences and experiments with language in literacy contexts.

Does anyone ever complete the "learning to read" process? This is the question posed by an emergent literacy perspective. **Emergent literacy** refers to a belief that literacy is a continuously emerging and evolving ability (Teale & Sulzby, 1986, 1989). According to an emergent literacy view, each of us—from preschool to adulthood—continues to emerge in our ability as a reader. Each of us is constantly learning something new about the reading process. For example, you continue to develop electronic literacy skills on the Internet as you discover how different search engines work. A preschooler who is read to at home each night may be discovering some of the more rudimentary aspects of reading such as how to hold a book, the names of several letters, or the left-to-right sequence in our writing system. Each of us, however, is always growing as a reader.

Understanding reading as emergent literacy also provides insights about many things you see in your classroom. One important insight is that every child can benefit from reading experiences no matter how inexperienced they are. All youngsters, for example, are ready to engage in reading experiences such as read-alouds, regardless of whether they are ready for more demanding types of reading experiences. As teachers, an emergent literacy view suggests the need to engage each student in appropriate types of reading experiences so that each may grow and develop as a reader. We should not exclude any child from reading experiences.

scaffolding   Temporary support provided to students that enables them to perform a task they might not normally be able to do on their own.

zone of proximal development   Learning that can be accomplished with the support of another individual such as an adult or more knowledgeable child. A term developed by Vygotsky (1978).

As you consider how to create developmentally appropriate types of reading experiences for students, it is also important to understand the notion of **scaffolding,** or scaffolded instruction. Scaffolding refers to intentional support provided to children as we engage them in literacy tasks they might not be able to accomplish on their own (Meyer, 1993). For example, you might point to the initial letter in a word to assist a child with reading it aloud. Likewise, parents might read a story aloud at bedtime to provide their very young child with a sense of what books and reading are all about. Scaffolded learning is especially powerful when children are acquiring literacy strategies within their **zone of proximal development,** a term used by Vygotsky (1978) to describe learning that can be accomplished with the support of another individual, such as an adult or more knowledgeable child. This temporary support is very important in assisting literacy learners as they accomplish more challenging tasks for the first time. Scaffolding strategies are important to understand as you seek to support all literacy learners who are emerging in their development. Activities with books containing a repeated sentence pattern provide important support in emergent literacy among very young readers.

Literacy Frameworks

Now that you understand the components of reading comprehension and response, let's begin to look at literacy frameworks. A **literacy framework** organizes your beliefs around two central issues in reading instruction: (1) What should I teach? and (2) How should I teach? It also generates important insights as you help your students become more enthusiastic and proficient readers. As you plan experiences for your students, you will continually make decisions about these two issues—they are central to your reading program.

> **literacy framework** A means to organize your beliefs about two central issues in reading instruction: What should I teach? and How should I teach? This helps develop insights and informs instructional decisions about reading.

By developing a literacy framework, you are in a powerful position to assist children. You understand exactly how to help each child in your classroom become a better reader. Let's look at the two central issues in reading instruction and see how your beliefs may be used to inform instructional decisions.

What Should I Teach? Which Components Are Most Important?

Because of extensive work conducted by researchers since the late 1800s, most people today agree that social aspects, affective aspects, metacognitive knowledge, discourse knowledge, syntactic knowledge, vocabulary knowledge, decoding knowledge, automaticity, and emergent literacy are all parts of the reading process. Nevertheless, disagreement exists over which components are most important to reading comprehension and response. These views have been articulated into several theories about how one reads.

These theoretical explanations and their association with the various components of the reading process can be seen on the continuum in Figure 3-5. We present beliefs in this manner because a wide variety of beliefs exist at various points along a continuum. Where your beliefs fall on this continuum depends on the emphasis you assign to the components of background knowledge or to decoding knowledge.

As you read more about each theoretical explanation, remember the five statements you selected at the beginning of this chapter in Figure 3-1 and try to determine your own beliefs about how a child reads and which components are most important to teach. Your beliefs will inform your decisions about *what* to teach students about reading.

FIGURE 3-5

Explanations of how a child reads and which components are most important

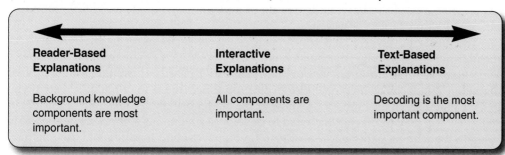

Reader-Based Explanations	Interactive Explanations	Text-Based Explanations
Background knowledge components are most important.	All components are important.	Decoding is the most important component.

Reader-Based Explanations: Teaching Background Knowledge

Goodman (1992, 1993) and Smith (1988) believe the components of background knowledge are most important during reading: metacognitive knowledge, discourse knowledge, syntactic knowledge, and vocabulary knowledge. Adopting a reader-based explanation of how a person reads, they believe meaning has more to do with what readers bring to a text rather than the text itself. According to this view, readers do not sound out every word they see; instead, readers use background knowledge and the evolving meaning of a text to make predictions about upcoming words and construct meaning. In addition, readers first make a prediction about the meaning of a word and only then perceive the word's letters. According to **reader-based explanations,** readers continuously predict upcoming words and, when necessary, look at the letters in those words to see whether their predictions were correct.

One way to understand this explanation is to consider how we might read a popular novel. Before reading, we probably have clear expectations about the story structure. Our expectations of the plot are strong and most of the words are familiar. We do not even notice the words at the end of some sentences (e.g., "Courtney gracefully dove into the swimming _____"). We fly through the story, skimming the incidental portions to get to the more interesting sections. Indeed, we may finish the book in a single night.

Another way to understand this theory is to look at a process model, describing what takes place in the mind of a reader. A reader-based explanation for how children read is illustrated in Figure 3-6, which shows how a child might read the beginning of a fairy tale. In this example, the child has started to read—"Once upon a time, a princess kissed a . . ."—and is now ready to read the word "frog."

In this case, social aspects initially establish the context in which the story is read. The story was chosen by the child during reading workshop, known as a pleasurable time for reading. This social context influences the affective aspects of the reading experience, causing the child to be very interested in reading the story to see what happens.

While reading the opening sentence, the child's strategic knowledge causes him or her to think about how this sentence might end and what the final word might be. Several expectations are then generated from discourse knowledge: First, this story is probably a fairy tale. Moreover, the beginnings of most fairy tales contain information about the main characters. And, because a princess is about to kiss someone (or something, in this case), the child expects the second character to be mentioned next.

Expectations from discourse knowledge limit the child's expectations from syntactic knowledge: The child expects a noun, the recipient of a kiss. These, in turn, limit expectations from vocabulary knowledge. The word must be a person who is a potential main character in a fairy tale and is likely to be kissed by princesses. This includes kings, queens, and princes. It also includes frogs, if the child is familiar with the princess-kisses-a-frog-and-finds-a-prince pattern of some fairy tales.

Finally, vocabulary knowledge limits the child's expectations from decoding knowledge. The child analyzes the text for the graphic representation of one of the expected nouns, finds the initial "f" in frog, and concludes that *frog* is the final word, perhaps without even analyzing the other letters. Sometimes readers have such strong expectations they do not even look at any letters in a word. Instead, they continue reading until some evidence in the story indicates their prediction was wrong. In any event, this child continues to read by using background knowledge and the evolving meaning of the text to make additional predictions about upcoming words. There is little sounding out of individual words or letters.

Teachers who believe that components such as social aspects, affective aspects, metacognitive knowledge, discourse knowledge, syntactic knowledge, and vocabulary knowledge are most important adopt more of a reader-based explanation for the process of reading and focus on helping children develop expectations for what they read. If you believe that meaning is based more in what the reader brings to a text than in the text itself, then you may think children need to develop useful sources of prior knowledge to bring to the reading experience. As a result, you may spend instructional time helping

reader-based explanation The belief that people read by using background knowledge to predict upcoming words and construct meaning.

FIGURE 3-6

A reader-based model of comprehension and response

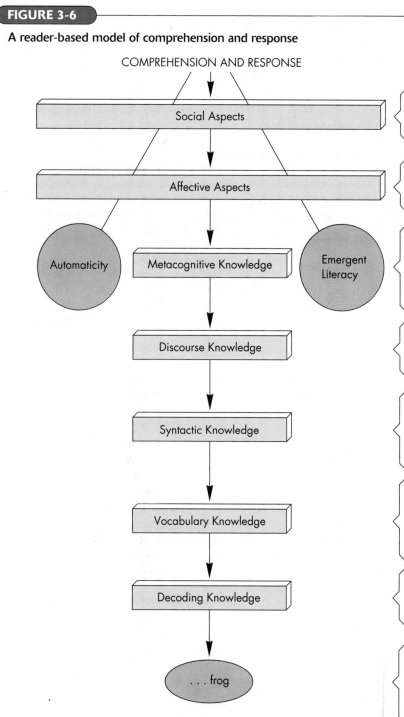

Step 1: Social aspects establish the context in which this story is being read and influence affective aspects.

Step 2: Affective aspects influence a child's initial response and interest in reading this passage.

Step 3: While reading the first sentence, strategic knowledge directs the child to think about how this sentence might end and what the final word might be.

Step 4: After reading the beginning of this sentence, discourse knowledge leads to the expectation that this is a fairy tale.

Step 5: Given the syntactic structure of this sentence and the expectation that this is a fairy tale, the child expects to find a noun and a recipient of a kiss, who will be a main character.

Step 6: Only a limited set of meanings fit previous discourse and syntactic constraints: king, queen, prince, frog. The child expects to find "frog" since (s)he knows another version of this fairy tale.

Step 7: Since the meaning is likely to be "frog," decoding knowledge tells the child to expect the sequence of letters: f r o g.

Step 8: The child analyzes the text and finds the letters f r o g. The child concludes that the meaning of the first sentence is, "Once upon a time, a princess kissed a frog."

students develop these components of prior knowledge and spend relatively little time teaching decoding knowledge.

Text-Based Explanations: Teaching Decoding Knowledge

Another theory is that decoding knowledge is more important than any other component. These theorists adopt a **text-based explanation** of how children read (Gough, 1993). They suggest that meaning is more *in* the text than in what a reader *brings* to the

text-based explanation
The belief that people read by translating print into sounds as they construct the meaning in a text.

Classrooms are organized to facilitate instruction consistent with a teacher's literacy framework.

text. As a result, a person reads by decoding, or sounding out, words on a page. According to a text-based explanation, readers translate print into sounds to uncover the meaning that exists in a text.

One way to understand this theory is to think about how we might read unfamiliar words in a Russian novel like *Roskolnikov, Ekaterinburg,* or *Fedorachovna.* Many of us would find ourselves attempting to sound out these difficult Russian names, hoping that hearing them would help us to remember them. Such an approach (translating the print into sounds) supports a text-based explanation.

Another way to understand a text-based explanation is to return to our earlier example of the fairy tale and look at Figure 3-7, which shows a process model describing how a young child might read this story according to a text-based explanation. Again, the child has started to read—"Once upon a time, a princess kissed a . . ."—and is now ready to read the word "frog."

According to a text-based explanation, a child first uses decoding knowledge to determine the oral equivalent of this word. Once the sound /frog/ has been constructed, the child uses that sound to search vocabulary knowledge. In vocabulary knowledge, the child is familiar with two meanings: (1) "a small green amphibian" and (2) "frog like" (e.g., frog legs). Both meanings are passed on to syntactic knowledge, where the child decides the word *frog* is being used as a noun, not an adjective. Consequently, the first meaning for the word is chosen (e.g., "a small green amphibian").

At this point, discourse knowledge concludes the selection is a fairy tale because the beginning is consistent with that story type. Metacognitive knowledge is then activated; strategic knowledge directs the child's attention to the first word of the next sentence to see what will happen next.

While this is happening, affective aspects influence the initial response the child has to this story. If the child enjoys fairy tales and frogs, he or she will probably become more engaged in the story to see how it ends. If the child thinks that fairy tales are uninteresting or is already familiar with the story, he or she may become less engaged.

Ultimately, social aspects influence the meaning the child draws from the story. Perhaps the social context suggests a traditional interpretation: the princess kisses a frog and finds happiness. However, older children might be aware of social contexts that suggest a feminist interpretation for this tale, finding little value in this solution to happi-

FIGURE 3-7

A text-based model of comprehension and response

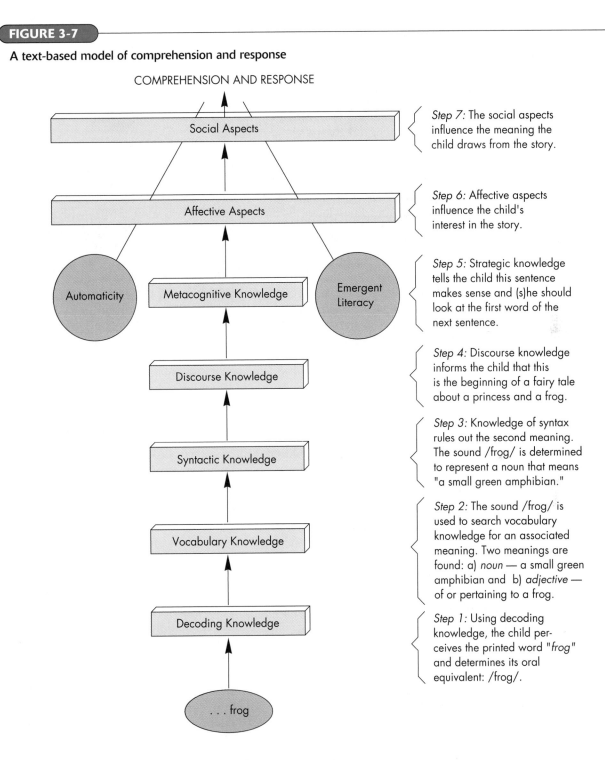

COMPREHENSION AND RESPONSE

Social Aspects

Step 7: The social aspects influence the meaning the child draws from the story.

Affective Aspects

Step 6: Affective aspects influence the child's interest in the story.

Automaticity

Metacognitive Knowledge

Emergent Literacy

Step 5: Strategic knowledge tells the child this sentence makes sense and (s)he should look at the first word of the next sentence.

Discourse Knowledge

Step 4: Discourse knowledge informs the child that this is the beginning of a fairy tale about a princess and a frog.

Syntactic Knowledge

Step 3: Knowledge of syntax rules out the second meaning. The sound /frog/ is determined to represent a noun that means "a small green amphibian."

Vocabulary Knowledge

Step 2: The sound /frog/ is used to search vocabulary knowledge for an associated meaning. Two meanings are found: a) *noun* — a small green amphibian and b) *adjective* — of or pertaining to a frog.

Decoding Knowledge

Step 1: Using decoding knowledge, the child perceives the printed word *"frog"* and determines its oral equivalent: /frog/.

. . . frog

ness. The reading process would continue in this manner, moving always from the lowest to highest component of the reading process.

Those who believe decoding knowledge is the most important component of the reading process adopt a text-based explanation for how children read. If you think that children must become proficient in sounding out written words, you may also think that meaning is more in the text than in the prior knowledge that readers bring to a text. As a result, you may spend much instructional time helping children develop fluency in their reading by developing decoding knowledge.

Interactive Explanations: Teaching All Components

interactive explanation
The belief that we read by
simultaneously translating
print into sounds and
using background
knowledge to predict
upcoming words; a
combination of reader-
based and text-based
explanations.

Some individuals believe all components are important to reading and have an **interactive explanation** for how a person reads (Anderson, Hiebert, Scott, & Wilkinson, 1985; Rumelhart, 1976; Stanovich, 1980). They believe we read by simultaneously sounding out words while at the same time developing expectations for words from vocabulary, syntactic, discourse, and metacognitive knowledge. Thus, reading comprehension is a product of the interaction between text and reader.

One method of understanding an interactive explanation is to consider your own reading behavior. When your background knowledge is extensive about a topic, reading is easy and you are able to anticipate the words that come next. In this case, the meaning you bring to the page closely matches the meaning that exists on the page. However, when your background knowledge is limited, reading is somewhat difficult and you may attempt to sound out an unfamiliar word to see if its oral equivalent helps you recall its meaning. Readers who shift quickly back and forth between predicting words and decoding them are reading in an interactive fashion.

Consider once again, this time from an interactive perspective, how a young reader is apt to read the final word in the sentence, "Once upon a time, a princess kissed a . . . ." Children who are unfamiliar with fairy tales and who have never heard the princess-kisses-a-frog-and-finds-a-prince pattern must depend on decoding knowledge to recognize this word. They will read the word *frog* in a text-based fashion, as depicted in Figure 3-7. However, children familiar with fairy tales and with the princess-kisses-a-frog-and-finds-a-prince pattern can generate accurate predictions. Consequently, they will depend on metacognitive, discourse, syntactic, and vocabulary knowledge and will use decoding knowledge only to check predictions. They will read the word *frog* in a reader-based fashion, as shown in Figure 3-6.

Teachers who believe all components of reading are equally important tend to adopt an interactive explanation for how children read. The major task of a reader, according to these teachers, is to develop knowledge in a broad range of components that can assist the reading process. As a result, these teachers spend instructional time helping students develop each of the components of the reading process, depending on their individual needs.

A Historical Perspective

The issue of how a child reads was very controversial during the 1970s. The three theories we've discussed in this chapter were developed to explain how people read and to explain which components were most important to teach. At the beginning of this period, people's beliefs tended to fall at either end of the continuum in Figure 3-5. Most had either strong text-based or strong reader-based explanations for the reading process. Over time the issue has become less divisive. Many people have concluded that neither a text-based nor a reader-based explanation is sufficient to explain how children read. At times, especially with unfamiliar or difficult texts, the evidence suggests that children read more by sounding out words; at other times, especially with familiar or easy texts, children read more by making predictions about upcoming words. Only an interactive explanation seems to account for both types of evidence. As a result, many people today believe it is important to help students develop all components of reading. Some children, though, need greater assistance in some areas than in others. This is why insightful teachers are so important to reading success. Balance doesn't mean equal. It means meeting individual needs as appropriate for each child.

How Should I Teach? How Do Children Learn to Read?

The second part of a literacy framework consists of your beliefs about how children learn to read. Such beliefs will determine how you will teach reading and which method frameworks you will use. Of the different explanations that exist concerning how children learn to read, the three most common are shown on the continuum in Figure 3-8.

FIGURE 3-8

Explanations of how children learn to read

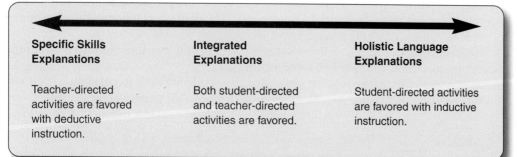

Specific Skills Explanations	Integrated Explanations	Holistic Language Explanations
Teacher-directed activities are favored with deductive instruction.	Both student-directed and teacher-directed activities are favored.	Student-directed activities are favored with inductive instruction.

At one end of this continuum are explanations based on the idea that children best learn to read when they direct their own reading experiences, engaging in functional and holistic reading tasks within authentic contexts. At the other end are explanations based on the idea that children best learn to read when specific reading skills are taught. Somewhere in the middle are explanations based on the idea that children best learn to read through an appropriate combination of self-directed, holistic reading experiences in authentic contexts and teacher-directed instruction in specific reading skills.

It is clear that a wide variety of beliefs exist at various points along this continuum. As you read about each theoretical explanation, remember the five statements you selected at the beginning of this chapter in Figure 3-2 and try to determine your own beliefs about how children learn to read.

Holistic Language Learning Explanations

One theory about how students learn to read is a **holistic language learning explanation.** A holistic language learning explanation is based on two assumptions: (1) students learn best as they direct their own holistic literacy experiences in authentic contexts and (2) students learn best inductively. Reading comprehension and response are perceived as holistic entities that are difficult to break down into a fixed set of separate skills (Clay, 1980; Goodman, 1993; Holdaway, 1979). Comprehension and response are viewed as holistic processes; separating them into isolated skills is thought to give young children the wrong idea about reading. Moreover, students are believed to induce most of the components required for reading during their self-directed learning experiences with print and their observations of others interacting with print in authentic reading contexts. Inductive teaching and learning is favored.

According to this explanation, children should be supported in directing authentic reading experiences and provided with a social context in which others are also engaged in literacy tasks. If these conditions exist, children will induce all the necessary generalizations they need to become proficient readers; therefore, reading should develop in a natural manner.

How would you teach if you believed in a holistic language learning explanation for how children learn to read? You would seek out those method frameworks that allow students to: (1) direct their own holistic literacy experiences in authentic contexts and (2) provide inductive learning experiences. You would probably find these method frameworks to be especially useful: reader's workshop, read-aloud response journal activities, inductive instruction, and Internet Inquiry. Each allows students to direct many of their own literacy experiences in authentic contexts and provides opportunities for inductive learning.

holistic language learning explanation The belief that students learn best as they: (1) direct their own holistic literacy experiences in authentic contexts and (2) learn inductively about important literacy principles.

Specific Skills Explanation

specific skills explanation   The belief that students learn best: (1) as teachers provide instruction in specific skills and (2) as they learn deductively about important literacy principles.

A **specific skills explanation** of how students learn to read is based on two assumptions: (1) students learn best as teachers provide instruction in specific skills and (2) students learn best deductively. Thus, students are assumed to learn best when the development of reading skills is carefully directed by the classroom teacher.

Teachers with a specific skills explanation of how children learn to read often organize instruction around an explicit set of reading skills, sometimes sequenced according to the level of difficulty. Easier reading skills usually are taught first; harder reading skills are taught last. A teacher with a specific skills explanation might target skills such as:

1. Students will develop familiarity with different forms of narratives such as fables, fairy tales, science fiction, contemporary realistic fiction, and fantasy.
2. Students will develop a wide range of response patterns in relation to both narrative and informational prose.
3. Students will develop effective strategies for learning the content of informational articles.

Such skills are often taught separately from the reading of stories and articles. Reading experiences are viewed either as opportunities to practice the specific skills that have been taught or as opportunities to develop greater interest in reading.

How would you teach if you believed in a specific skills explanation for how children learn to read? You would seek out those method frameworks that: (1) have teachers provide instruction in specific skills and (2) provide deductive learning experiences. You would find deductive instruction especially useful as a method framework since it teaches skills directly. If you use the Internet in your classroom, you would have children complete Internet assignments, check their work to see that they have mastered the learning activity you targeted for instruction, and then proceed to the next lesson.

Integrated Explanations

integrated explanation   The belief that students learn best: (1) as they direct their own experiences in authentic contexts and as teachers provide instruction in specific skills and (2) as they receive both deductive and inductive learning experiences.

Teachers who develop an **integrated explanation** believe that both holistic language learning and specific skills explanations are, alone, too limited to explain the complex nature of reading development among diverse students. These teachers believe that a specific skills explanation confines students too narrowly to the mastery of isolated reading skills, often in reading contexts that are not authentic. Although some students benefit from this structure, others become bored and lose interest in reading. However, a holistic language learning explanation places too much responsibility on students for their own development. Although some students benefit from this freedom, others get lost in opportunities for self-development.

An integrated explanation combines aspects of both of the previous explanations. It makes these assumptions: (1) students learn best as they direct their own experiences in authentic contexts and as teachers provide instruction in specific skills when it is necessary, and (2) students learn best in a program where both deductive and inductive learning experiences are provided.

Teachers following an integrated explanation of reading development include elements from both holistic language learning and specific skills perspectives. They provide students a rich written-language environment and examples of others engaged in authentic literacy tasks in rich social contexts. Moreover, they provide direct instruction in reading skills as these appear necessary to support children's development.

How would you teach if you believed in an integrated explanation for how children learn to read? You would individualize instruction as much as possible. You would seek to provide students who learn best in self-directed contexts with opportunities common to method frameworks like readers' workshops, read-aloud response journal activities, inductive instruction, and Internet Inquiry. You would seek to provide students who learn best in specific skill contexts with method frameworks like deductive instruction. You would also use Internet Workshop and Internet Project,

SUSAN'S

COMMENTS FROM THE CLASSROOM

Every decision I make in terms of what to present in reading group, how to respond to a child's reading, and what a child needs to become an avid reader is based on my literacy framework.

The process varies widely from grade level to grade level and child to child. I first observe and analyze what each child is doing in his or her attempts to read. I use a running record to reveal which cues the child attends to during reading. Some children rely heavily on phonetic cues to "sound out" the words on the page. Some discard phonetic cues altogether and just "make up" the words they think should appear on the page. Ideally, a child will use phonetic, contextual, and syntactic cues to determine the author's message. This is the work of the first-grade teacher—to facilitate the child's integration of all cueing systems so that the message is accurately and fluently read. And hard work it is.

At second grade, children enter the classroom with a wide range of reading abilities. Some still need the instructional focus on the mechanics of reading. Others are ready for more in-depth comprehension work. Still others are able to read and comprehend far above grade level. The task becomes one of meeting each child as close to his or her level as possible. It also becomes one of facilitating joy in reading.

For group reading, I like to have the children sit at a reading (semi-circle shaped) table. I've found their attention to the work we are doing that much more focused when they are at the table. For independent reading, however, I have pillows scattered throughout the room. When children are in the independent reading center they may grab a pillow, find a comfortable spot, and immerse themselves in their books. I've found a reading program's success is validly measured by the collective groan that occurs when it's time to put the books away.

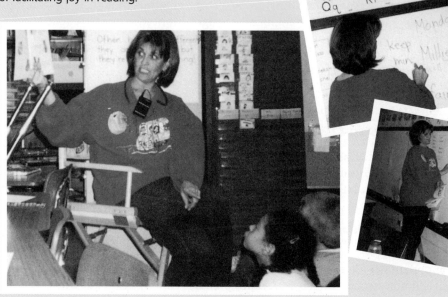

providing opportunities for children to direct their own learning during the discussion that takes place. At the same time, you would provide more direct instructional experiences when these appeared necessary.

A Historical Perspective

Far less agreement exists about how children learn to read than there is about which components of reading are most important to teach. In fact, the question of how children learn to read continues to be one of the most controversial issues in the field of reading instruction. Individual explanations can be found at nearly every point on the continuum. A specific skills perspective had a strong influence on the field of reading; traditionally, students were thought to learn best when presented with a skills-based curriculum taught directly by a teacher. The composition of many published reading programs tends to reflect the assumptions of this perspective. It is also found in instructional recommendations that emphasize direct teaching in specific skill areas (Bauman & Schmitt, 1986).

During the recent past, however, evidence has demonstrated that children acquire literacy skills inductively through holistic, purposeful, and functional reading tasks in authentic contexts (Goodman, 1992; Harste, Woodward, & Burke, 1984). As a result, many teachers have associated themselves with what has come to be known as a whole language point of view—a movement that has powerfully influenced the development of new instructional materials and methods.

The term *whole language* is, however, quickly coming to represent many things to many people (McKenna, Robinson, & Miller, 1993). For some, it represents an extreme position on the continuum (illustrated in Figure 3-8) as holistic language learning, characterized by classrooms rich in literacy experiences where students direct their own learning and induce from these self-directed experiences the generalizations necessary to learn to read. For others, the term *whole language* represents the middle of the continuum and is characterized by classrooms that combine students' self-directed learning experiences with direct instructional experiences whenever students experience difficulty in a particular aspect of reading. In each representation, though, is the assumption that students will acquire important literacy insights from self-directed experiences with authentic reading and writing experiences that take place in rich social contexts. In some cases this will also include some teacher-directed learning experiences around specific skills or strategies. In others, it will not.

Using a Literacy Framework to Inform Instructional Decisions

Developing a literacy framework is not easy; reading comprehension and response are abstract and complex concepts. Nevertheless, a literacy framework is a practical tool that can provide assistance with the instructional choices you need to make as a teacher of reading. As such, it is central to your ability to integrate our first principle into your classroom:

1. **Teachers' insights are central to effective instruction (Anders, Hoffman, & Duffy, 2000; Duffy & Hoffman, 1999; Snow, Burns, & Griffin, 1998).**

Most importantly, a literacy framework provides you with important insights about what to teach and how to teach as you seek to meet the individual needs in your classroom.

Developing Insights about What to Teach

The first portion of your literacy framework concerns insights that are useful as you consider the "what" of reading instruction: What should you teach about reading to assist your students? Your beliefs about the most important components of the reading process will inform your decisions about what to teach and emphasize during reading instruction. Text-based, reader-based, and interactive beliefs lead to different conclusions about what to teach during reading.

Teachers with a text-based explanation stress the acquisition of decoding knowledge more than any other type of knowledge, believing that strong decoding skills lead to a successful translation of text meaning. Instruction, especially for younger readers, emphasizes activities that help students to sound out individual words.

Teachers with a reader-based explanation of how a child reads stress the acquisition of metacognitive, discourse, syntactic, and vocabulary knowledge, believing that adequate background knowledge leads to accurate explanations of upcoming meaning and richer response patterns. As a result, instruction emphasizes activities like those described earlier under metacognitive knowledge, discourse knowledge, syntactic knowledge, and vocabulary knowledge. Any activity designed to help students generate expectations, such as the reading of predictable texts, is especially valued.

Teachers with an interactive explanation of how a person reads devote relatively equal attention to the acquisition of metacognitive, discourse, syntactic, vocabulary, and decoding knowledge during instruction. These teachers believe that readers need to develop accurate expectations of upcoming meaning, richer response patterns, and automaticity with decoding processes. All activities described earlier in this chapter might be used by these teachers, depending on their individual needs.

Developing Insights about How to Teach

The second portion of a literacy framework concerns insights that are useful as you consider the "how" of reading instruction. How should you teach reading to assist your students? Your beliefs about how children learn to read best will inform your classroom decisions about how to teach reading. Holistic language learning, specific skills, and integrated explanations lead to quite different conclusions about how best to support students' development as literacy learners.

Teachers with holistic language learning beliefs about how children learn to read allow students to direct their own reading experiences, always in the context of authentic social contexts and always with authentic reading materials. These would include literature selections students might choose from the school or classroom libraries. Reading skills are not frequently taught in a direct fashion. Instead, teachers develop classroom experiences where self-directed, inductive learning is emphasized—children learn to read by reading. Popular method frameworks include those that allow for much student direction during learning experiences: reader's workshop, read-aloud response journal activities, inductive instruction, and Internet Inquiry.

Teachers with specific skills beliefs about how children learn to read provide students with direct instruction on progressively more difficult reading skills. These teachers often use published reading series that provide for skill instruction. These teachers also organize their classroom reading program around a set of reading skills that need to be mastered during the year. The most popular method framework is deductive instruction since this provides direct instructional experiences. Other method frameworks are modified to include more direct instruction in these learning experiences.

Teachers with integrated beliefs about how children learn to read provide opportunities for students to direct their own reading and writing experiences. In addition, these teachers give direct instruction on specific skills as students require such support. These often take place in mini-lessons with individuals or small groups around a particular skill or strategy. These teachers tend to shift between teacher-directed and student-directed learning experiences as appropriate to meet particular student needs. All method frameworks are used, depending on individual need.

What Is My Literacy Framework?

You can see that a literacy framework is extremely helpful as you make instructional decisions. However, it is often difficult to understand that a literacy framework combines beliefs about two different issues and that these beliefs inform two different instructional issues. Figure 3-9 shows how beliefs about *what* to teach interact with beliefs about *how*

FIGURE 3-9

A matrix illustrating the range of different types of literacy frameworks possible in response to two major issues: What should I teach? and How should I teach?

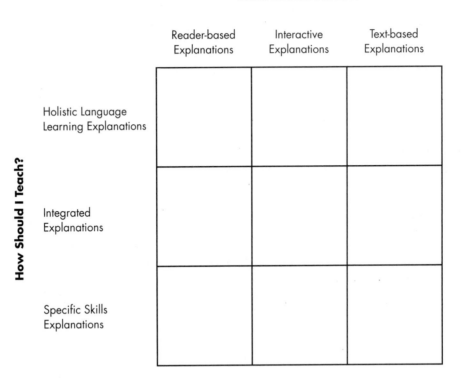

to teach. Because both issues are represented by a continuum, innumerable combinations are possible.

Let us now determine what your literacy framework looks like at this point in your development. Look back at the statements you marked in Figure 3-1, which contains statements reflecting different beliefs about which components of reading are most important. Your beliefs about this issue will inform your decisions about *what* to teach. Some statements assume that prior knowledge components are most important. These are statements 2, 4, 9, 11, and 15. If the majority of your statements came from this category, your beliefs are most consistent with a reader-based explanation, and you will probably be most interested in helping students develop the ability to bring prior knowledge to a passage and use this to comprehend and respond during reading.

Other statements assume that decoding knowledge is most important during reading. These are statements 1, 3, 5, 10, and 12. If the majority of your statements came from this category, your beliefs are most consistent with a text-based explanation; you will probably be most interested in helping students develop the ability to accurately decode words and use this to comprehend and respond during reading.

A third set of statements assumes that both prior knowledge and decoding components are important during reading. These are statements 6, 7, 8, 13, and 14. If the majority of your statements came from this category or if you have a diverse set of statements, your beliefs are most consistent with an interactive explanation; you will probably be most interested in helping students develop proficiency with all components of reading, depending on their individual needs. Your responses to Figure 3-1 should help you develop beginning insights about what you think is most important to teach about reading.

Now look at your responses to the statements in Figure 3-2, which contains statements reflecting different beliefs about how best to teach reading. Some statements assume that children learn best when they direct their own learning in authentic reading contexts. These are statements 2, 4, 8, 9, and 14. If the majority of your statements came from this category, your beliefs are most consistent with a holistic language learning theory of how one learns to read. You probably believe that students learn best when they are engaged in meaningful and self-directed literacy experiences and you will be most interested in creating purposeful and functional opportunities for students to read. You will probably find method frameworks most useful if they support students in directing their own literacy experiences in rich social contexts and with authentic reading experiences.

Other statements assume that children learn best when taught specific skills in a direct fashion. These are statements 1, 5, 6, 11, and 12. If the majority of your statements came from this category, your beliefs are most consistent with a specific skills theory of how one learns to read. You will probably be most interested in directing students' literacy experiences and teaching specific skills. You will find method frameworks most useful if they provide these types of teaching opportunities.

Some statements assume that children learn best when they are engaged in self-directed reading experiences and when they are taught specific skills at appropriate moments. These are statements 3, 7, 10, 13, and 15. If the majority of your statements came from this category or if you have a very diverse set of statements, your beliefs are most consistent with an integrated theory of how one learns to read. You will probably be most interested in helping students to direct their own literacy experiences in rich social contexts, using authentic reading experiences. You will also be interested in directly teaching some components of literacy when the need arises. You will find method frameworks most useful if they provide both types of opportunities.

Why We Believe a Balanced Perspective Helps More Children

Recently the debate about the best approach for teaching children to read has become polarized. Some argue that approaches consistent with a whole language perspective are best. Others argue for approaches that use more phonics instruction. We believe this is a false dichotomy.

There is nothing logically incompatible with using phonics instruction within a whole language approach. Advocating for phonics instruction is advocating about *what* to teach; you believe decoding knowledge is the most important component to teach beginning readers. Advocating for whole language is advocating for *how* to teach; you believe that student-directed learning experiences in print-rich environments are best. There is nothing incompatible with including both within the same classroom; each addresses a different issue about learning to read.

We believe the intense arguments about these views miss an essential point: No single approach will meet all children's needs. Reading and children are both so incredibly diverse that no single solution will ever meet each individual child's needs in your classroom. Instead of a single approach to reading instruction, we believe children learn best when they have an insightful teacher with a literacy framework to make professional judgments about what each child requires to achieve the benefits literacy bestows. We believe that insightful teachers—not politicians—should make these decisions in the classroom.

Because we believe that children have very diverse learning needs, we believe in a balanced literacy framework. A **balanced literacy framework** includes an interactive explanation for which reading components are most important. As you consider *what* to teach, you believe that both prior knowledge and decoding components are important for children to acquire but that each child is likely to have slightly different needs in these areas. You will find some children do best when they receive instruction in decoding knowledge (including phonics) and others do best when they receive instruction in prior knowledge components.

A balanced literacy framework also includes an integrated explanation for how children learn to read best. As you consider *how* to teach, you believe that both student-directed learning in print-rich classrooms and teacher-directed learning of specific skills

balanced literacy framework A combination of interactive and integrated beliefs. You believe that both prior knowledge and decoding components are important but that each child is likely to have slightly different needs in these areas. You also believe in both student-directed, inductive learning in authentic contexts and teacher-directed, deductive learning in specific skills, depending on individual needs.

A perspective that provides many, varied opportunities to read and write allows teachers to address all aspects of the reading process.

are important, but that each child has slightly different needs. At times, you want students to engage in self-directed reading experiences. At other times, you will call a small group of students together to teach them directly a specific skill they appear to need.

The advantage of a balanced literacy framework is that you can focus on successful learning outcomes and avoid a fixed ideological stance about reading instruction, neglecting students' needs at the expense of ideological purity. A balanced literacy framework allows you to provide decoding (including phonics) instruction to children who require it. It also allows you to encourage children to make predictions about upcoming words based on prior knowledge. A balanced literacy framework allows you to provide student-directed literacy experiences as students discover many important lessons about literacy on their own. At the same time, though, it allows you to step in and provide direct skill instruction when you see that children will gain from lessons in specific skills. With a balanced literacy framework, you do what is necessary to ensure your students' success, such as observing your students and using your insights about literacy to guide you.

We believe, like Michael Bradley and his colleagues in Quebec, that we need to keep our eyes focused clearly on helping each of our students achieve the rewards of literacy. His posting to the RTEACHER mailing list (*http://www.reading.org/publications/ rt/rt_listserv.html*) provides compelling evidence for a balanced approach.

The Internet as a Professional Resource: Continuing to Develop Your Literacy Framework

As you grow professionally, you will find your literacy framework continuing to develop, providing you with many new insights about children and learning to read. Your students will teach you many important lessons if you watch closely. You will also acquire new insights from conversations with colleagues, attending conferences, and read-

E-mail from the Classroom

E-mail from the Classroom

Subject: The Phonics vs. Whole Language Debate
From: Michael Bradley, kobra@netrover.com
To: RTEACHER@BOOKMARK.READING.ORG

For the past 3 years the first-grade teachers at my school have made a conscious decision that no student would slip through our classrooms unable to read at level (meaning somewhere in a normally acceptable range of reading ability for the end of grade 1). Once the decision was made, it meant careful, regular monitoring of children using Clay's Observation Survey initially and then doing weekly Running Records of each child in each class for the balance of the year.

The lower third of each class was immediately placed in small groups (of 5 students) in October and given direct instruction. These children left these groups as soon as they caught up with their peers. This tended to be in January or so. They were replaced by any students who seemed to be slipping based on their Running Record scores. This year, one class canceled these small groups as everyone is at or above level . . .

We avoided the "Phonics vs. Whole Language" debate entirely by deciding to use whatever method seemed to work, either by itself or in combination. We also swallowed our pride and quickly abandoned any method which wasn't producing results within a couple of weeks. We also switched children from one group and one teacher to another if that seemed to work.

The key for us was not to give up on any child, and to monitor constantly for both signs of weakness, which we used to modify our teaching, and signs of success, which we celebrated with the child and class. The results have been gratifying. Five years ago, up to a third of the first-grade students did not meet the minimum requirements in reading. Many of these either repeated their year or entered second grade in a remedial class. Today, the only children falling outside the minimum requirements have a good, solid, medically, psychologically, or neurologically substantiated reason for their inability to read. Out of 60 children, this has meant 1 or 2 children per year, and they can read, but not at level requirements.

Interestingly enough, we did not need to purchase exotic materials or develop new methods or go back to 'basics,' but instead relied on known teaching methods, the research findings of Marie Clay and others like her, and high quality children's literature. That some people choose to still argue that one method or book is better than another is sad. Their time could be better spent. . . .

Michael Bradley

Lennoxville, Quebec, Canada

ing professional materials. In addition, you should also become familiar with the use of professional mailing lists (listservs) to continue to develop the critical insights so important to effective literacy instruction.

Mailing Lists

A **mailing list** is an e-mail discussion group you may join if you have an e-mail account. Mailing lists are sometimes referred to as listservs or discussion lists. A message sent to the posting address for a mailing list is distributed to all members who have subscribed to that list. This enables you to participate in conversations about areas that interest you among a wide circle of colleagues. The message from Michael Bradley appeared on the RTEACHER mailing list. There are thousands of other mailing lists, each organized around a different interest area.

mailing list An e-mail discussion group you may join if you have an e-mail account; sometimes referred to as listservs or discussion lists.

Featured Teacher

🍎 *Marci McGowan*

Marci McGowan, a first-grade teacher at Mountz Elementary School in New Jersey, is an excellent example of a teacher who has developed many important insights about literacy and young children during her career. She has also developed many insights about how to use Internet technologies to prepare her students for the new forms of reading and writing appearing on the Internet. Her classroom web page in Figure 3-10 (http://myschoolonline.com/site/0,1876,34898-119831-38-21589,00.html) appears at one of several sites hosting classroom web pages for teachers when their districts do not yet have the technology resources to do so.

Exploring Marci's classroom page will teach you much about early reading instruction. She has many valuable links to important reading resources. In addition, Marci has developed a number of Internet Projects that she posts at her site. Explore these wonderful instructional models and discover the exceptional curriculum projects that teachers like Marci are creating.

Marci is a member of the RTEACHER listserv and shares her insights on that list. In addition, she has links to a number of classroom web rings. These are classroom web pages that agree to be linked to one another. You may circle around these web rings to discover even more classroom websites that will give you even more great ideas to use in your classroom.

FIGURE 3-10

The home page for Marci McGowan's first-grade classroom in Spring Lake, New Jersey (http://myschoolonline.com/site/0,1876,34898-119831-38-21589,00.html)

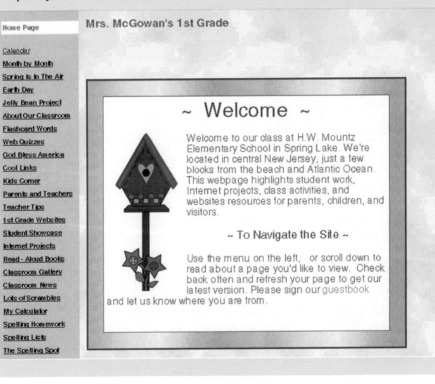

As a teacher, mailing lists are very useful. They allow you to ask questions about instructional practices, locate teachers interested in collaborative projects between classrooms, and much more. Mailing lists are especially useful as you seek to develop your beliefs about the two central issues in reading. Reading and participating in discussions on a mailing list will help to inform your own beliefs about reading. We invite you to join us on LEUKINZER, the mailing list we developed for readers of this book. The directions for joining appear below.

Mailing lists have two addresses: the administrative address and the posting address. To subscribe to a list, you need only to send a subscription message to the administrative address of the computer that manages the list. Type the administrative address in the "To:" box of your e-mail window. To subscribe to the LEUKINZER list, for example, you would address your message to: listserv@pearsoned.com Leave the "Subject" box blank. Then, type a subscription message in the first line of the "Message" box. Your message should contain the following information:

To join the LEUKINZER listserv, simply visit our Companion Website at www.prenhall.com/leukinzer and click on the home page's listserv link.

> subscribe [listname] [your first name] [your last name]

For example, Don Leu would subscribe to the LEUKINZER mailing list by sending the following message to listserv@pearsoned.com:

> subscribe LEUKINZER Don Leu

Do not include any other information in this message. If you have an automatic signature, you should disable or delete this. Sometimes a mailing list will have a different procedure; this is usually indicated on the list's web page. Shortly, you will receive a welcome message. Save this message! It usually explains procedures for posting messages and directions for getting off a list.

Most lists follow similar procedures to "unsubscribe" or to leave a list. You should address the message to the administrative address and then send the message:

> unsubscribe [listname]

The posting address is the address you use to post a message and have it distributed to everyone on a list. You may only use a posting address after you have subscribed to a mailing list. The posting address usually begins with the title of the mailing list. You will receive the posting address in the "Welcome" message after you subscribe to a list.

It is usually best to "listen" a bit on a mailing list before you post a message. Each list will have its own social context; it is often helpful to understand who is on the list, which issues are being discussed, and how members on the list respond to one another.

If you are interested in continuing to think about your beliefs and your literacy framework, some of the most useful mailing lists include the ones in Table 3-1. You may also wish to visit one of the following Internet sites that contain master lists of mailing lists and then conduct a search for a list that meets your specific needs:

Liszt Select (http://www.liszt.com)—This is probably the most comprehensive WWW site for mailing lists, containing over 50,000 lists as well as a search engine for the extensive database.

EdWeb E-mail Discussion Lists and Electronic Journals
(http://www.edwebproject.org/lists.html)—This is a great set of mailing lists that focus solely on education. It also contains background information about mailing lists and an example for subscribing.

Use the self-test questions on http://www.prenhall.com/leukinzer to review the material presented in this chapter.

TileNet (http://tile.net/lists/)—This is another extensive set of mailing lists. It also contains an excellent search engine.

TABLE 3-1

Mailing lists to support your professional development

Mailing List	Administrative Address	Description
LEUKINZER	listserv@pearsoned.com (if problems, send a message to djleu@uconn.edu)	A discussion group for readers of this textbook and the authors. It extends your reading to explore issues related to literacy learning and instruction.
RTEACHER	rteacher@bookmark.reading.org Directions are located at: http://www.reading.org/publications/rt/rt_listserv.html Archives are located at: http://www.reading.org/archives/rteacher.html	A discussion group of teachers, publishers, professors, and others who explore topics related to literacy learning in traditional and electronic contexts. A very supportive group. Sponsored by the International Reading Association.
TAWL	listserv@listserv.arizona.edu Archives are located at: http://listserv.arizona.edu/archives/tawl.html	A discussion group on teaching from a whole language perspective.
READPRO	readpro-subscribe@topica.com Visit the ReadPro web page for directions on subscribing to this list at: http://www.indiana.edu/~eric_rec/gninf/readpro.html	A discussion forum devoted to the analysis of issues facing reading professionals of all types, whether they are reading specialists, elementary or secondary classroom teachers, college professors, librarians, or researchers.
ECENET-L	listserv@listserv.uiuc.edu Visit the ECENET-L web page for directions on subscribing to this list: http://ericps.ed.uiuc.edu/eece/listserv/ecenet-l.html	A discussion group on early childhood education.
KIDSPHERE	kidsphere-request@vms.cis.pitt.edu Visit the KIDSPHERE web page for directions on subscribing to this list: http://www.hale.ssd.k12.wa.us/friends/kidsphere.html	A discussion group for a wide range of people interested in education: kids, parents, teachers, and administrators.
MIDDLE-L	listserv@listserv.uiuc.edu Visit the MIDDLE-L web page for directions on subscribing to this list: http://ericps.ed.uiuc.edu/eece/listserv/middle-l.html	A discussion group for anyone interested in middle schools and middle school students.

Major Points

▸ There is no single best method for teaching reading. What appears to help students most is an insightful teacher, not a particular instructional practice. Reading and children are both too complex for a single instructional practice to meet every student's needs. An insightful teacher understands the nature of the reading process and uses this information to make informed decisions about *what to teach*. An insightful teacher also understands how reading ability develops and uses this information to make informed decisions about *how to teach*.

▸ The reading process involves a number of important components: social aspects, affective aspects, metacognitive knowledge, discourse knowledge, syntactic knowledge, vocabulary knowledge, decoding knowledge, automaticity, and emergent literacy. Reading instruction promotes the development of these components through carefully designed learning activities.

▸ A literacy framework organizes your beliefs around two central issues in reading instruction: What should I teach? and How should I teach?

▶ Your beliefs about the most important components of reading inform decisions about *what* to teach. Beliefs exist along a continuum ranging from reader-based beliefs about how a child reads to text-based explanations, with interactive explanations somewhere near the middle.

▶ Your beliefs about how children learn to read inform decisions about *how* to teach. These beliefs exist along a continuum ranging from holistic language learning beliefs about how children learn to read best to specific skills beliefs, with integrated explanations somewhere near the middle.

▶ The debate about the best approach for teaching children to read has recently become very polarized. Some argue that approaches consistent with a whole language perspective are best. Others argue for approaches that use more phonics instruction. We believe this is a false dichotomy.

▶ A balanced literacy framework consists of integrated beliefs about the components of reading and integrated beliefs about how children best learn to read. The advantage of a balanced literacy framework is that you can focus on successful learning outcomes and avoid a fixed ideological stance about reading instruction, neglecting students' needs at the expense of ideological purity. With a balanced literacy framework, you do what is necessary to ensure your students' success by observing your students and using your insights about literacy to guide instruction.

▶ In addition to classroom observation, reading, and talking with colleagues at your school, mailing lists (listservs or discussion lists) are useful for developing the insights so important to effective literacy instruction.

Making Instructional Decisions

1. Identify your beliefs about how children read on the continuum in Figure 3-5. Use the statements you selected in Figure 3-1 to help identify your beliefs. Describe the consequences of your beliefs for decisions about what you will teach during literacy lessons. Which components of the reading process will you be most concerned about? Why?

2. Identify your beliefs about how children learn to read on the continuum in Figure 3-8. Use the statements you selected in Figure 3-2 to help identify your beliefs. Given your beliefs about how reading ability develops, how will you teach reading? Which method frameworks will you most likely use? What will characterize the nature of the classroom reading experiences you develop?

3. If you believe that children have different reading needs and that it is important to individualize the nature of reading instruction, what will your literacy framework be like? Why?

4. Visit the RTEACHER archives (http://www.reading.org/archives/rteacher.html) and print out several postings about instruction with which you agree and several with which you do not agree. What do your selections indicate about your developing literacy framework?

Further Reading

Duffy, G., & Hoffman, J. (1999). In pursuit of an illusion: The flawed search for a perfect method. *The Reading Teacher, 53,* 10–34.

Explains how research demonstrates that the classroom teacher, not any specific instructional method, makes the difference in whether or not children learn to read.

Goodman, K. (1992). I didn't found whole language. *The Reading Teacher, 46* (3), 188–199.

A pioneer of whole language describes the theoretical, historical, and social context of his beliefs.

Schirmer, B. R., Casbon, J. C., & Twiss, L. L. (1997). Teacher beliefs about learning: What happens when the child doesn't fit the schema? *The Reading Teacher, 50* (8), 690–692.

This article discusses how teachers' beliefs need to consider individual students' needs first. It is a wonderful story of how a teacher needed to accommodate her beliefs about whole language to the instructional needs of a student who learned best through more direct instructional experiences.

Spiegel, D. L. (1992). Blending whole language and systematic direct instruction. *The Reading Teacher, 46* (1), 38–47.

Describes ways to combine both holistic language learning approaches and specific skill approaches in an integrated classroom reading program. The article shows how this more integrated approach leads to gains in both students' and teachers' learning.

Wharton-McDonald, R., Pressley, M., Rankin, J., Mistretta, J., Yokoi, L., & Ettenberger, S. (1997). Effective primary-grades literacy instruction: Balanced literacy instruction. *The Reading Teacher, 50* (6), 518–521.

This article reviews research of highly effective literacy teachers in the primary grades. It concludes that the best teachers include instructional methods from a wide range of perspectives, taking a balanced perspective.

References

Adams, M. J. (1990). *Beginning to read: Thinking and learning about print.* Urbana-Champaign, IL: Center for the Study of Reading.

Anders, P. L., Hoffman, J. V., & Duffy, G. G. (2000). Teaching teachers to teach reading: Paradigm shifts, persistent problems, and challenges. In M. L. Kamil, P. Mosenthal, P. D. Pearson, & R. Barr (Eds.), *Handbook of reading research, Volume III* (pp. 719–742). Mahwah, NJ: Lawrence Erlbaum Associates.

Anderson, R. C., Hiebert, E. H., Scott, J. A., & Wilkinson, I. A. G. (1985). *Becoming a nation of readers: The report of the commission on reading.* Washington, DC: National Institute of Education.

Baker, L., & Brown, A. (1984). Metacognitive skills and reading. In P. D. Pearson (Ed.), *The handbook of reading research.* New York: Longman Publishing Group.

Bauman, J. F., & Schmitt, M. C. (1986). The what, why, how, and when of comprehension instruction. *The Reading Teacher, 39,* 640–645.

Chall, J. S. (1983). *Stages of reading development.* New York: McGraw-Hill.

Clay, M. M. (1980). *Reading: The patterning of complex behavior* (2nd ed.). London: Heinemann.

Cunningham, P. M., Hall, D. P., & Defee, M. (1991). Non-ability grouped multilevel instruction: A year in a first-grade classroom. *The Reading Teacher, 42,* 194–199.

Duffy, G., & Hoffman, J. (1999). In pursuit of an illusion: The flawed search for a perfect method. *The Reading Teacher, 53,* 10–34.

Dyson, A. H. (1993). *Social worlds of children learning to write in an urban primary school.* New York: Teachers College Press.

Goodman, K. (1986). *What's whole in whole language?* Portsmouth, NH: Heinemann.

Goodman, K. (1992). I didn't found whole language. *The Reading Teacher, 46,* 188–199.

Goodman, K. S. (1993). Reading: A psycholinguistic guessing game. In H. Singer & R. Ruddell (Eds.), *Theoretical models and processes of reading* (4th ed.). Newark, DE: International Reading Association.

Gough, P. B. (1993). One second of reading. In H. Singer & R. Ruddell (Eds.), *Theoretical models and processes of reading* (4th ed.). Newark, DE: International Reading Association.

Harris, A. J., & Sipay, E. R. (1990). *How to increase reading ability* (9th ed.). New York: Longman Publishing Group.

Harste, J., Woodward, V., & Burke, C. (1984). *Language stories and literacy lessons.* Portsmouth, NH: Heinemann.

Holdaway, D. (1979). *The foundations of literacy.* Exeter, NH: Heinemann.

Irwin, J. W. (1986). *Teaching reading comprehension processes.* Englewood Cliffs, NJ: Prentice Hall.

Johnson, D. D., & Pearson, P. D. (1984). *Teaching reading vocabulary* (2nd ed.). New York: Holt, Rinehart & Winston.

Leu, D. J., Jr., & Leu, D. D. (2000). *Teaching with the Internet: Lessons from the classroom* (2nd ed.). Norwood, MA: Christopher-Gordon Publishers, Inc.

Madden, L. (1988). Improve reading attitudes of poor readers through cooperative reading teams. *The Reading Teacher, 42,* 194–199.

McKenna, M. C., Robinson, R. D., & Miller, J. S. (1993). Whole language and research: The case for caution. In D. J. Leu & C. K. Kinzer (Eds.), *Examining central issues in literacy research, theory, and practice: Forty-second yearbook of the National Reading Conference* (pp. 141–152). Chicago, IL: National Reading Conference.

Meyer, D. K. (1993). What is scaffolded instruction? Definitions, distinguishing features, and misnomers. In D. J. Leu & C. K. Kinzer (Eds.), *Examining central issues in literacy research, theory, and practice: Forty-second yearbook of the National Reading Conference* (pp. 41–54). Chicago, IL: National Reading Conference.

Oldfather, P. (1993). What students say about motivating experiences in a whole language classroom. *The Reading Teacher, 46,* 672–681.

Palincsar, A. S., & Ransom, K. (1988). From the mystery spot to the thoughtful spot: The instruction of metacognitive strategies. *The Reading Teacher, 41,* 784–789.

Richardson, V., Anders, P., Tidwell, D., & Lloyd, C. (1991). The relationship between teachers' beliefs and practices in reading comprehension instruction. *American Educational Research Journal, 28* (3), 559–586.

Rumelhart, D. (1976). *Toward an interactive model of reading (Report No. 56).* La Jolla, CA: University of California, San Diego, Center for Human Information Processing.

Samuels, S. J., & Eisenberg, P. (1981). A framework for understanding the reading process. In F. J. Pirozzolo & M. C. Wittrock (Eds.), *Neuropsychological and cognitive processes in reading.* New York: Academic Press.

Smith, F. (1988). *Understanding reading: A psycholinguistic analysis of reading and learning to read* (4th ed.). Hillsdale, NJ: Lawrence Erlbaum Associates.

Snow, C. E., Burns, S., & Griffin, P. (1998). *Preventing reading difficulties in young children.* Washington, DC: National Academy Press.

Spiegel, D. L. (1992). Blending whole language and systematic direct instruction. *The Reading Teacher, 46* (1), 38–47.

Stanovich, K. E. (1980). Toward an interactive-compensatory model of individual differences in the development of reading fluency. *Reading Research Quarterly, 16,* 32–71.

Teale, W. H., & Sulzby, E. (Eds.). (1986). *Emergent literacy: Writing and reading.* Norwood, NJ: Ablex.

Teale, W. H., & Sulzby, E. (1989). Emergent literacy: New perspectives. In D. S. Strickland & L. M. Morrow (Eds.), *Emerging literacy: Young children learn to read and write.* Newark, DE: International Reading Association.

Vygotsky, L. S. (1978). *Mind in society.* Cambridge, MA: Harvard University Press.

PART 2

Developing a Knowledge Base

Decoding Knowledge: Phonological Awareness, Phonemic Awareness, Phonics, Sight Words, Context Use, and Fluency

✉ E-mail from the Classroom

Subject: The Role of Decoding Knowledge
From: Christina Gracey, cgracey@hotmail.com

I teach first grade and, for me, decoding knowledge is an important aspect of my reading program. However, since I take a balanced point of view, decoding knowledge is not the only part. I integrate all elements of the reading process into the curriculum. Nevertheless, acquiring the ability to accurately and fluently decode print is a major developmental hurdle for first graders, so this becomes more important in my class than if I were teaching sixth grade. In sixth grade, there may be only a few students who have not acquired adequate decoding knowledge and fluency. In first grade, most students are beginning to develop these skills. Some are still developing the precursor skills of phonological awareness and phonemic awareness; some are developing phonic knowledge, sight word knowledge, context use strategies, and fluency. To me, a sound program in developing decoding knowledge is just as important as using the finest works of children's literature, connecting reading and writing, developing comprehension skills, and instilling the joy of reading in each and every child in my classroom.

I often hear that principals put their best teachers at the first-grade level. I don't know if I fit this category, but I do everything I can to get my first graders off to a successful start in reading. Part of this challenge is to ensure that everyone develops solid decoding skills including phonological awareness, phonemic awareness, phonics, sight word knowledge, context use, and fluency.

Key Concepts

context knowledge

decoding knowledge

deductive instruction

developmental spelling phases

fluency

inductive instruction

making words

onset

phonic knowledge

rime

sight word knowledge

talking storybook software

After reading this chapter, you should be able to:

1. Describe the nature of decoding knowledge and explain how it contributes to literacy.

2. Implement strategies for developing phonological awareness.

3. Implement strategies for developing phonemic awareness.

4. Implement strategies for developing phonic knowledge.

5. Implement strategies for developing sight word knowledge.

6. Teach children strategies for using context knowledge.

7. Implement strategies for developing fluency.

8. Use your literacy framework to inform instructional decisions about decoding instruction.

Teach Decoding Skills: A Principle of Effective Literacy Instruction

It is a rainy day and you are reading a wonderful book, thinking only about what is taking place in the story. Suddenly you come across the word *indefatigable* and your mind shifts from what is taking place in the story to sounding out this word. You quickly, almost effortlessly, break the word into its constituent sound elements (in-deh-fuh-teeg-ah-bul) and then put these sounds together to determine its pronunciation. Whenever you focus your attention on determining the pronunciation of an unfamiliar word like this, you are using **decoding knowledge,** the knowledge we use to determine the pronunciation of a written word. We use decoding knowledge when we encounter an unfamiliar word and attempt to determine its pronunciation. We also use it when we read aloud.

As a mature reader, you seldom are aware of using decoding knowledge until you encounter unfamiliar words like *indefatigable;* you recognize most words automatically and fluently because they are familiar. Younger readers, for whom many printed words are unfamiliar, consciously rely on decoding knowledge much more often to construct the meaning of texts they read. Often, hearing the pronunciation helps them to understand its meaning since so many words they read are familiar when they can hear them.

As Christina Gracey notes in her e-mail message, developing decoding knowledge is an essential component of beginning reading instruction. Her observation reflects the second principle of effective literacy instruction:

> 2. **Teach decoding skills.** Beginning reading instruction should integrate a systematic program in decoding knowledge that includes, when appropriate for individuals, the development of phonological awareness, phonemic awareness, phonic knowledge, sight word knowledge, context use strategies, and fluency (Adams, 1990; Anderson, Hiebert, Scott, & Wilkinson, 1985; National Reading Panel, 2000; Snow, Burns, & Griffin, 1998). As a teacher of reading, you should carefully consider the nature of your decoding instruction.

The nature of decoding instruction has historically been one of the most controversial topics in reading. Many states have mandated instruction in specific elements of decoding knowledge, especially phonics instruction. Others believe these decisions should be left in the hands of educators, not politicians. Regardless of the intensity of this debate, it is important to keep in mind that the development of decoding knowledge is not an end in itself. Instead, we develop decoding skills so that students are able to construct the meaning of the texts they read.

Decoding knowledge contributes to reading comprehension when a printed word is within the listening vocabulary of the reader. Decoding knowledge does not contribute to reading comprehension when the meaning of a word is unfamiliar to the reader. How, for example, would decoding knowledge help you to comprehend a word like *indefatigable* if you didn't already know its meaning?

All reading approaches for young children develop decoding knowledge, including holistic approaches, though each goes about it in a different fashion (Stahl, 1992). Consider, for example, what to teach—some emphasize phonic strategies, and some emphasize context use strategies, and some emphasize sight word strategies. Consider also how to teach—some emphasize student discovery of decoding principles and some emphasize direct instruction of these principles by the teacher. Both what, and how, to teach decoding knowledge are highly dependent on your literacy framework.

Decoding knowledge is especially important to beginning readers (Adams, 1990; Snow, Burns, & Griffin, 1998). Since beginning readers know the meanings of many words they encounter in print, determining the oral equivalent of a printed word gives them a reasonable opportunity to determine its meaning. Consequently, instruction in decoding knowledge receives the greatest attention in the primary grades (kindergarten through third grade). Helping young readers develop decoding knowledge will enable them to meet with early success as they begin their journey to literacy (Strickland, 1998).

decoding knowledge
The knowledge a reader uses to determine the oral equivalent of a word; includes phonological awareness, phonemic awareness, phonic knowledge, sight word knowledge, context use, and fluency.

Check your ongoing understanding of chapter concepts by using the guided review for this chapter on http://www. prenhall.com/leukinzer

FIGURE 4-1

The developmental nature of several important elements of phonological awareness

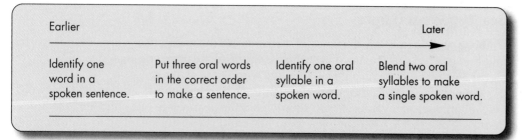

Earlier   Later

| Identify one word in a spoken sentence. | Put three oral words in the correct order to make a sentence. | Identify one oral syllable in a spoken word. | Blend two oral syllables to make a single spoken word. |

The development of decoding knowledge begins as young children develop **phonological awareness** and then **phonemic awareness.** These important early achievements in oral language enable students to become proficient at mapping sounds to letters and letters to sounds in written language as young children begin to read.

Phonological Awareness

What does it mean to possess phonological awareness? When young children first develop oral language, they use speech to communicate and accomplish many goals that are important to them ("Eat now, daddy"). Usually, however, they are not consciously aware of language as an abstract object that can be manipulated, taken apart, and reconstituted in different ways and held up for analysis. Being able to identify one word in a sentence as a separate word would be one example of being aware of language as an object. Initially, this might happen when very young children play the "I wanna game" with an adult. An adult initiates this word game by saying, "I wanna *book,*" thereby attempting to get the child to imitate him or her while substituting a different noun at the end ("I wanna *peanut/Snuffleuppagus/*" and so on) as each tries to use a sillier and sillier word at the end until they both end up laughing.

Being able to manipulate language like this, substituting a number of different words in the same slot without any intent other than to play with language, is an example of phonological awareness. Another example of phonological awareness takes place when children can clap or tap each word in a sentence as they say it, indicating their awareness of individual words that actually appear in oral language as a continuous stream of sound. Phonological awareness also exists when a child can clap or tap each syllable in a sentence or word ("I want a ba-na-na"). When children achieve phonological awareness, they are aware of language as an object, something that can be analyzed and manipulated. This is an important first step in their journey to develop word analysis skills and reading ability.

Many children, but not all, come to school with at least the initial stage of phonological awareness. They may, for example, be able to identify one word in a sentence but they may not be able to identify one syllable in a word, which is a more challenging task. Figure 4-1 shows the developmental sequence of these, and several other, elements of phonological awareness. Usually phonological awareness of words as separate objects precedes phonological awareness of syllables as separate objects.

Teaching Phonological Awareness

If you have children in a kindergarten or first-grade class who have yet to develop phonological awareness, there are many games and activities that may be used to develop this important area. You might also wish to visit these resources on the Internet for additional instructional ideas and activities:

▶ **The Literacy Web** (http://www.literacy.uconn.edu)
▶ **PALS Activities** (http://curry.edschool.virginia.edu/curry/centers/pals/pals-activities.html)

phonological awareness When children achieve phonological awareness, they are aware of language as an object that can be analyzed and manipulated, especially at the word and syllable level.

phonemic awareness Phonemic awareness is being aware of the smallest units of speech sound (phonemes) as objects that can be analyzed and manipulated.

▶ **Phonological Awareness: Instructional and Assessment Guidelines** (http://ldonline.com/ld_indepth/reading/chard_phono_awareness.html)

Beanbag Word Games

Beanbag word games are very useful, considering the energetic nature of kindergarten and first-grade children. As you gently toss the beanbag from one person to another, you signal the child whose turn it is to play the word games you chose.

One simple way to introduce the nature of beanbag games and to develop word-level phonological awareness is to simply pass the beanbag to one child and ask him or her to say one word. After saying a word, the child passes the beanbag to another child, who must do the same. To make the game a bit more challenging, you may wish to limit word choices to words related to a topic or theme (e.g., food items such as apple, orange, chocolate, and carrots or games such as basketball, baseball, and soccer). Be certain choices only contain a single word, not, for example, words like hamburgers and fries, apple pie, or macaroni and cheese.

After children are successful at saying one word, you can then say a short sentence for students ("I like to play"), gently toss the beanbag to a student, and ask that student to identify a single word ("soccer"). Then, ask the child with the beanbag to say a new sentence and toss the beanbag to another child who must say one word from the new sentence. Continue the game in a similar manner, practicing the ability to identify a single word in a sentence.

You can also play the beanbag game to develop phonological awareness of syllables. Simply say a word with two syllables ("ta-ble"), gently toss the beanbag to a child, and ask that child to say one of the syllables. That child then says a word with two syllables, tosses the beanbag, and asks the next child to identify one of the syllables. To help the students think of two-syllable words, you may wish to set up objects or pictures of 5 to 10 two-syllable words.

Finally, you may play the beanbag game with the most challenging task in phonological awareness, having students blend several syllables together to make a word. Gently toss the beanbag to a student, saying two syllables that compose one word ("ap-ple"). Ask that child to say the word from the two portions. That child then repeats the task with a new child. Again, the game is made easier when you set up objects or pictures of 5 to 10 two-syllable words. This syllable game can be made even more challenging by moving to three-syllable words.

Counter Games

You may also develop phonological awareness of words and syllables by playing counter games. With counter games, you provide an individual child or a group of children with counter tokens. These might be Unifix cubes from your math program, pennies, small wooden blocks, paper clips, or other small objects. Show the children how we can line up one counter, from left to right, for each word in a sentence. A sentence such as "I like singing" would have three counters. After they have lined up the counters, have children then touch each one, saying the word it represents, as they say the complete sentence. Start with two- or three-word sentences and then work up to longer, and harder, sentences.

Counter games may also be used to develop the phonological awareness of syllables. Begin with two-syllable words and have children line up one counter for each syllable. Advance to three-syllable words, and perhaps even longer words to help students hear the segmented speech sounds that comprise syllables in our language.

Word and Syllable-Strip Games

Use a sentence strip to write a short sentence (I like reading). Then, cut the sentence up into individual words. (You may write these separate words on note cards if you do not have sentence-strip materials.) Give one word to each child, saying "Nora, you have the word *I*," and so on, having them then stand up in a line to form the sentence, with each child holding a word. Have each child say his or her word and then have the other children, who are sitting down, read the individual words as you point to them.

Phonemic Awareness

Phonemic awareness is being aware of the smallest units of speech sound, known as phonemes. You can, for example, identify the three separate phonemes in the word *can* (/k/, /a/, and /n/). Put somewhat simply, when you possess phonological awareness, you are aware of individual words and syllables as objects that can be analyzed and manipulated. When you possess phonemic awareness, you are aware of individual sounds or phonemes as objects that can be analyzed and manipulated. With phonological awareness, you can identify the two syllables in the spoken word *today*. With phonemic awareness, you can hear these two syllables and you can also identify the two separate phonemes in the syllable *to*, as well as the two phonemes in *day*. Having phonemic awareness allows you to succeed in developing phonic knowledge because you can identify the individual sounds in syllables and words. This helps you to map individual sounds to a letter or letters, and then map a letter or letters to individual sounds. If you can't hear the individual sounds, or phonemes, phonics will provide little help.

Teaching Phonemic Awareness

It is likely that you will have children in your kindergarten or first-grade class who have yet to develop phonemic awareness. There are a number of games and activities that may be used to develop phonemic awareness. You might also wish to visit these resources on the Internet for additional instructional ideas and activities:

▶ **The Literacy Web** (http://www.literacy.uconn.edu)
▶ **PALS Activities** (http://curry.edschool.virginia.edu/curry/centers/pals/pals-activities.html)
▶ **Phonemic Awareness Activities for Collaborative Classrooms** (http://ldonline.com/ld_indepth/teaching_techniques/cld_hownow.html)

Beanbag Rhyme Games

You may use beanbag games to develop phonological awareness, but you may also use them to develop phonemic awareness with rhyming games. When children can rhyme one word with another (e.g., "bat" and "hat"), they have developed phonemic awareness since they are changing the beginning sound of one word to create another word. That is why rhyming games are often an excellent way to develop phonemic awareness. In a beanbag game, simply toss the beanbag to one child as you say a single syllable word, such as "top." The child who receives the beanbag must then say a word that rhymes, such as "hop." The child with the beanbag then repeats the task, saying a single-syllable word and tossing the beanbag to a new child, who must then say a rhyming word.

Beanbag rhyming games can be made a bit more challenging by saying first the initial sound in a single-syllable word and then the ending sound (e.g., "b" and "at") before gently tossing the beanbag to a child. That child then has to blend the initial phoneme and the ending sound together to form the word (e.g., "bat").

Odd One Out

Have children cut out pictures of three objects that rhyme (e.g., "bone," "cone," and "phone"). Then, paste or laminate these pictures on card stock and add in one picture of an object that does not rhyme with each set. Now show a set of the four cards, three that rhyme and one that doesn't, to a student, asking him or her to say each word and find the one word that does not rhyme.

Many activities can help provide practice in matching sounds to letters and words.

Going on a Rhyme Hunt

Gather a small group of children and take them on a rhyme hunt. Tell them one word (e.g., "hook") and then have them look all around the room for any objects that rhyme with the word you said (e.g., "book"). Then have one of the children say another word for everyone to find a rhyming object from somewhere in the classroom.

Phonic Knowledge

Phonological and phonemic awareness contribute in important ways to children discovering an insight critical to successful reading and writing performance: Written language in English is somewhat predictable and rule governed. The fact that many letters in English map quite consistently onto sounds is referred to as the alphabetic principle. The alphabetic principle is important for readers to recognize. While not all letters map perfectly to sounds the way they might in other languages (such as Spanish, for example), the patterns that do exist in English provide important information for children when they encounter an unfamiliar word.

Understanding the patterns that relate letters to sounds in English is often referred to as phonics or **phonic knowledge.** As children come to analyze letter–sound relationships and uncover the patterns that exist, they also come to more fully develop initial phonological and phonemic awareness. Thus, phonological and phonemic awareness support the development of phonic knowledge, and phonic knowledge supports the development of phonological and phonemic knowledge. Phonic knowledge consists of two elements: (1) knowledge of the relationship between letters and sounds and (2) the ability to put together, or blend, the sounds represented by letters. English letters do not always represent a single sound; nevertheless, knowledge of the more regular letter–sound relationships helps us to recognize many of the words we encounter. Under-

phonic knowledge
Knowledge of letter–sound relationships and the ability to blend the sounds represented by letters.

FIGURE 4-2

A graphic representation of the categories of phonic elements

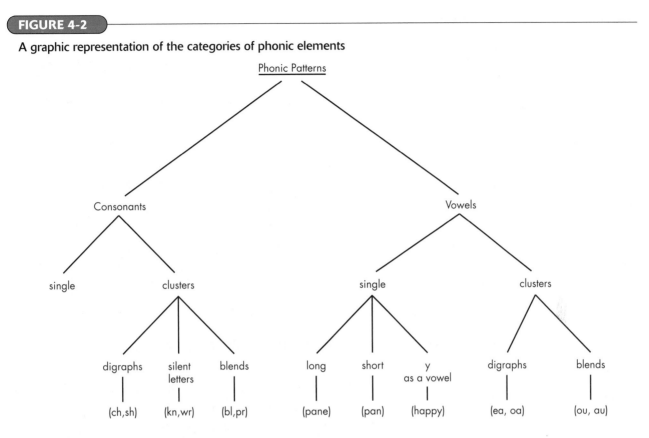

standing the basic elements of phonic knowledge is especially important for teachers of beginning readers (Lapp & Flood, 1997; Morrow & Tracey, 1997; Stahl, 1992).

No other topic in reading inspires more controversy and less agreement than that of phonics instruction (Adams, 1990; Chall, 1983). Some have argued against the utility of extensive phonics instruction because the English language does not contain a perfect one-to-one relationship between letters and sounds (Hittleman, 1988; Smith, 1988). These individuals tend to have reader-based beliefs about how we read; they feel prior knowledge elements are more important to support than phonic knowledge. However, enough regularity exists in the relationship between English letters and sounds that other individuals support instruction in phonic knowledge (Adams, 1990; Harris & Sipay, 1990; Snow, Burns, & Griffin, 1998). These individuals tend to have text-based or interactive beliefs about how we read; they feel phonic knowledge is essential for beginning readers to develop.

Even the experts who advocate phonics instruction, however, have different ideas about which letter–sound relationships need to be taught. We will describe those letter–sound relationships most consistently included in instructional programs. Consonant generalizations are presented first, followed by vowel generalizations. A diagram of the categories of phonic patterns is presented in Figure 4-2.

Consonants

Linguistically, **consonants** are sounds produced by a restriction in the airstream. In English, single consonants contain the most consistent relationship between letters and sounds. As a result, those relationships usually are taught to beginning readers. Even teachers who teach few phonic generalizations will help their students develop an understanding of phonic relationships for single consonants.

It is hard for young children to sound out long strings of letters; it is easier for them to begin using what are called onset and rime patterns. Initial consonant letters and

consonants Sounds produced by a restriction in the air stream.

FIGURE 4-3

Letter–sound relationships for single consonants included in most instructional programs

b as in *boy*	*c* as in *cent, cat*	*d* as in *did*
f as in *feet*	*g* as in *gem, go*	*h* as in *home*
j as in *job*	*k* as in *king*	*l* as in *like*
m as in *make*	*n* as in *no*	*p* as in *pan*
q as in *queen*	*r* as in *rat*	*s* as in *sat, has*
t as in *time*	*v* as in *very*	*w* as in *we*
x as in *six*	*y* as in *yes*	*z* as in *zoo*

onset patterns Initial consonant letters and consonant combinations.

rime patterns The most common endings to syllables and words (e.g., -ake, -ack, -ail, -ame, and so on).

consonant combinations are usually referred to as **onset patterns** (e.g., b, c, d, f, g, sn, st, str, and so on). These are found at the beginning of syllables and words. **Rime patterns** usually include a limited set of the most common endings to syllables and words (e.g., -ake, -ack, -ail, -ame, and so on). By combining onset and rime patterns, children can quickly begin to apply the alphabetic principle to unlock the sounds of many written words (e.g., bake, cake, fake, snake, stake, back, snack, stack, and so on). Onset and rime patterns are often an early component of phonics instruction.

Figure 4-3 presents the single consonant relationships included in most instructional programs. The letters *c* and *g* are unique single consonants; the sound for each is dependent on the vowel that follows. When *c* is followed by *e*, *i*, or *y*, it usually represents the *soft c* sound, /s/, as in *cent, city*, or *cymbal*. When *c* is followed by *a*, *o*, or *u*, it usually represents the *hard c* sound, /k/, as in *cat, coat*, or *cut*.

The same pattern follows for the letter *g*. When *g* is followed by *e*, *i*, or *y*, it usually represents the *soft g* sound, /j/, as in *gem, ginger*, or *gym*. When *g* is followed by *a*, *o*, or *u*, it usually represents the *hard g* sound, /g/, as in *game, go*, or *gun*. The patterns of *g*, however, have a number of exceptions, such as *finger, get, forget, give, forgive*, and *girl*.

consonant clusters Two or three consonant letters that often appear together.

In addition to single consonants, there are also **consonant clusters,** which consist of two or three consonant letters that often appear together. The different types of consonant clusters include consonant digraphs, silent letter combinations, and consonant blends. **Consonant digraphs** are two different consonant letters that together represent a single sound not usually associated with either letter—for example, *ch* (*child*), *ng* (*sing*), *ph* (*phone*), *sh* (*fish*), and *th* (*thin*). **Silent letter combinations** contain two different consonant letters that represent the sound of only one of the letters—for example, *kn* (*knit*), *wr* (*write*), *ck* (*check*), *gn* (*sign*), *mb* (*comb*), or *gh* (*ghost*).

consonant digraphs A type of consonant cluster in which two different consonants together represent a single sound not represented by either letter alone.

silent letter combinations A type of consonant cluster in which two consonants express the sound of only one of the letters.

consonant blend A type of consonant cluster in which two or more consonants blend together their separate sounds.

A third type of consonant cluster is called a **consonant blend.** It contains two or more consonant letters, each with a separate sound blended together. Consonant blends include combinations such as the following: *bl* (*blue*), *br* (*brick*), *sc* (*scare*), *scr* (*scream*), *sk* (*skip*), *sm* (*smile*), *str* (*street*), and *thr* (*three*).

Vowels

vowels Sounds produced without a restriction in the airstream.

Vowels are sounds produced without a restriction in the airstream. Vowel letters include *a, e, i, o, u,* and sometimes *y*. Like consonants, vowels are divided into single vowels and vowel clusters. Single vowels include long vowels, short vowels, and *y* (when it functions as a vowel). A **long vowel sound** is identical to the vowel names of the five traditional vowel letters—*a, e, i, o,* and *u*. Long vowel sounds occur most frequently in two positions: (1) when a vowel occurs at the end of a syllable—*me, no, pa*-per, *ce*-dar, or *ci*-der; and (2) when a vowel is followed by a consonant and the letter *e*—*mane, theme, time, rope,* or *cute*. The final *e* in this pattern is usually silent.

long vowel sound A sound identical to the name of each of the five traditional vowels: *a, e, i, o,* and *u*.

short vowel sound One of the five vowel sounds found at the beginning of each of these words: *apple, egg, ink, octopus,* and *umbrella*.

Each of the five traditional vowel letters also has a **short vowel sound.** These sounds are usually learned with a set of key words, each with a short vowel sound at the beginning:

E-mail from the Classroom

Subject: Phonics: How It Is Taught
From: Alan Frager, frageram@muohio.edu

Phonics is useful in decoding new words—anyone who has taught reading knows there is an important place for phonics. To me, the main issue is how phonics is taught.

I believe it is important to assess who needs phonics instruction and who doesn't. Many children teach themselves to read: These children don't need the same type of phonics instruction as those who barely read a few words. The beginning readers who read many words are often attuned to word patterns and need confirmation and extension of their knowledge from phonics instruction. This entails much different instruction from the lock-step phonics approach, which starts at beginning consonants and ends three years later with syllabication. However, children who can't or haven't yet taken the path of recognizing patterns in words might benefit greatly from a systematic program of phonics instruction, at least until they become independent at recognizing patterns and can then learn phonics in an accelerated way.

Al Frager

> *a* as in *apple*
>
> *e* as in *elephant*
>
> *i* as in *ink*
>
> *o* as in *octopus*
>
> *u* as in *umbrella*

Short vowel sounds occur most frequently in syllables that end in a consonant or consonant cluster, such as *let, win, ot*-ter, or *fun.*

Functioning as both a consonant and a vowel, the letter *y* works like a consonant in words such as *yes, yellow,* and *yet.* There are two positions, however, when *y* functions as a vowel: (1) when it appears at the end of a word with more than one syllable, *y* usually represents a long *e* sound, as in *sandy, baby,* or *sixty*; and (2) when it appears at the end of a word with only one syllable, *y* usually represents the long *i* sound, as in *try, my,* or *cry.*

Like consonants, vowels also appear in clusters. **Vowel clusters** consist of two or three vowel letters that often appear together, such as *ou, ee, ai,* and *oy.* **Vowel digraphs** are two different vowel letters that together represent a single sound—for example, *oo* (*boot*), *au* (*caught*), *ea* (*each*), and *oa* (*boat*). Some vowel digraphs represent sounds not usually associated with either vowel letter: *oo* (*shoot*) or *au* (*auto*). Other vowel digraphs represent sounds usually associated with one of the letters: *ay* (*say*), *ea* (*beach*), *ee* (*see*), *oa* (*coat*), *ai* (*bait*), or *ei* (*sleigh*). Vowel blends, or **diphthongs,** are two vowel letters that represent a blending of the sounds often associated with each letter: *oi* (*soil*), *oy* (*toy*), or *ou* (*mouse*).

vowel clusters Two or three vowels that often appear together.

vowel digraphs A type of vowel cluster in which two different vowels together represent a single sound.

diphthongs A type of vowel cluster in which two or more vowels blend together their separate sounds.

Phonics Instruction

In his posting at a *Reading Online* discussion forum, Alan Frager reminds us of an important insight related to phonics instruction: Only teach phonic relationships to those who require it.

Several additional insights also apply. These include the following:

▶ *Provide many opportunities for students to apply phonic generalizations in meaningful reading experiences.* Make sure students have opportunities to read widely and often outside regular instructional materials.

▶ *Be consistent.* Students benefit from consistency in the labels used in your phonics program and in the way in which you state phonic generalizations.

▶ *Encourage students to be flexible in their application of phonic strategies.* Students need to know that exceptions exist to every rule. They should also try alternative letter–sound relationships when the application of one generalization fails to yield a familiar word.

▶ *Spend more time on consonants than on vowels.* Consonants have more consistent letter–sound relationships than vowels. Consonants also carry more information about words, as can be seen in the examples that follow. The same sentence is shown first with only its vowels and then with only its consonants. Notice which one is easier to decode.

_ _e_ _ _ o _ e _ i _ e o_ _o _ _ o _a _ _ _ !

Sp_nd m_r_ t_m_ _n c_ns_n_nts!

▶ *Be sure students actually can use a phonic generalization.* Do not assume students can use a generalization when they are able to verbalize it. The point of learning any phonic generalization is not to parrot back a verbal rule, but to have a strategy for determining the pronunciation of a difficult word.

Several instructional practices often are used to develop phonic knowledge: making words, writing experiences, deductive instruction, and inductive instruction.

Making Words

making words A method framework for developing decoding knowledge; provides students with a limited number of letters and then guides their manipulation of these letters to make words.

Making words is a wonderful method framework, developed by Cunningham and her colleagues (Cunningham, 1995; Cunningham, Hall, & Defee, 1991) to teach children awareness of phonemes, phonic knowledge, and spelling patterns. This method (see Model Lesson on page 105) provides students with a limited number of letters and then guides their manipulation of these letters to make words of increasing length. The active manipulation of letters and sounds appears to be helpful for many young children and for older students experiencing difficulty with decoding. Making words contains several procedural steps.

During the first step, identify a word that is central to a previous or future reading experience for students. This word should have five or six letters so that many words can be created from combinations of the individual letters. For example, if students will soon read *Anansi the Spider* by Gerald McDermott, you might select a word like *spider*.

Next, create letter sets for each student and one for yourself. These letter sets consist of letters in the target word printed on stiff paper such as oak tag. You can quickly make a master with each of the letters in the word and duplicate sufficient copies for your students. In the previous example, this would include the letters *s, p, i, d, e,* and *r*. You or the students can then cut out the individual letters to make one set for each student. The teacher's letter set should consist of larger letters on individual index cards so that all students can see the words you form with your letter set.

Third, call out a two-letter word that can be created from the letter set and use it in a sentence. In the previous example, this might be the word *is*, and you might say the sentence, "The car *is* red."

Next, have each student try to create this word from his or her letter set. As each student does so, ask one student to come to the front and make the word using your letter set so that everyone can see it. After the student has made the correct word at the front, encourage your students to check their own work and correct any mistakes.

Continue with three-, four-, five-, and six-letter words that are possible using this letter set. Three-letter words might include the words *red, rid, dip,* and *sip*. Four-letter words might include *ride, side, rise,* and *drip*. Five-letter words might include *drips* and *pride*. And finally, the six-letter word would include, of course, *spider*.

After all of the words have been created and checked, you can provide students with meaning clues or sound pattern clues to see if they can create the appropriate word as you review the words they have already made. For example, "Make the word that tells us the color of Benito's shirt" (red), or "Make a word that has the silent *e* at the end" (ride, side, or rise), or "Make the word that tells us what you do when you drink a hot cup of cocoa" (sip).

MODEL LESSON

Using the Making Words Approach to Teach Phonic Knowledge in Arpina McIntosh's Classroom

Arpina McIntosh was looking for new ideas for teaching phonic knowledge to students in her second-grade class. Several were experiencing difficulty recognizing unfamiliar words. They had not yet become fluent in oral reading. They often labored over words that others could quickly recognize. Arpina had a balanced literacy framework with interactive beliefs about what to teach and integrated beliefs about how to teach. She was seeking ways to help these students acquire phonic knowledge. Arpina posted a message on the RTEACHER mailing list (http://www.reading.org/publications/rt/rt_listserv.html), a mailing list she had subscribed to last year. Colleagues in Vancouver, Wyoming, and Delaware suggested she try the making words approach and provided her with references in several journals and books. They also posted the address for several on-line bookstores where she could order these books (http://www.amazon.com and http://www.bn.com). After reading about this approach, Arpina decided to use it during mini-lesson time in reading workshop with those students who needed it.

Identify an Important Word from a Recent or Future Reading Experience with Literature. Tomorrow, Arpina was planning on conducting a read-aloud of *Miss Rumphius* by Barbara Cooney, a story about a woman who made the world beautiful by planting lupines, a type of flower. She decided to use the word *flowers* as the base word for her making words activity, relating it to the story. From the letters in this word, she developed the following word sets:

Two letters: *so, we, of, or*

Three letters: *few, low, row, for, owe*

Four letters: *flow, sore, rose, lose, slow*

Five letters: *lower, rower, loser*

Six letters: *flower, slower, lowers*

Seven letters: *flowers*

Create Letter Sets for Students and Yourself. First, Arpina wrote this list on a single index card to guide her during the lesson. Then she made the letter sets for children, duplicating 10 sets of the letters in *flowers* on oak tag and cutting each letter into a single square. She also made a separate set for herself with larger letters on index cards. She put all of these materials into a single envelope, labeling the envelope with the base word: *flowers.* She decided to use envelopes like this to organize her sets for each word.

Call Out a Two-Letter Word from the Letter Set. The next day, she invited six children to get together with her during reading workshop time for a 10-minute mini-lesson. She passed out letter sets to the children and explained the activity. Then she started by calling out the two-letter words: *so, we, of,* and *or.*

Have Each Student Attempt to Make that Word with the Letter Set. As each word was called, students attempted to make it with the letters in their letter set. This first stage was relatively easy for her students and gave them confidence.

Have One Student Make the Word with the Teacher's Letter Set. Every time a word was called, Arpina asked one student to come up and make the word with her larger letter cards on the railing below the chalkboard. This allowed her students to check their work and correct any mistakes.

Repeat for All Two-, Three-, Four-, Five-, and Six-Letter Words in the Letter Set. Arpina repeated this for each of the letter groupings.

Help Students Make Words According to Meaning and Sound Patterns. At the end, Arpina gave meaning or phonic cues and asked students to make the words they had made earlier: "Make the word that is the name of a red flower." (*rose*) "Make a word that has a silent *e* at the end." (*sore, rose, lose, owe*) "Make the word that means the opposite of fast." (*slow*) "Make the word that means the opposite of many." (*few*)

Making words is a great way to help beginning readers become familiar with the relationships between letters and sounds. It fits especially well with reading workshop, where you conduct these experiences during mini-lesson sessions. There are several ways to make this procedure more student-directed and consistent with holistic language beliefs about how to teach. To start, you can encourage individual students to provide the meaning or sound pattern clues during the final step of the activity, or ask students to select the base word for you and help you develop the two-letter, three-letter, four-letter, and so on word sets the day before you complete the activity. Finally, give the list of words to a student and have him or her take the role of the teacher during the activity. Each day, you could rotate this responsibility.

Making words is a useful way to get all students involved in thinking about individual letters and their function in representing sounds in our language. It often is used in groups containing students with a range of abilities so that more-proficient students can help the less-proficient ones. It is also a wonderful way to integrate decoding instruction with the use of children's literature if you choose words from the literature selections used in your classroom.

Writing Experiences

Writing experiences provide important opportunities to help children develop knowledge of letter–sound relationships. They should not be overlooked as a strategy to develop phonic knowledge. As children consider the spelling of words, they must consider the relationships between letters and sounds. Writing invites many reflective moments to analyze these relationships, consolidate previous learning about phonic knowledge, and develop new insights about letters and sounds. There is something very special about writing that engages students in this important thinking.

In addition to the general benefits provided by regular writing experiences, two specific methods can be used to develop knowledge about letter-sound relationships through writing: (1) editing conferences and (2) language experience writing activities. Both are consistent with more holistic language learning explanations of how children learn to read and write since each invites students to direct more of their own learning about phonic knowledge.

Editing conferences are an important aspect of the writing program you develop for your classroom (See chapter 7). Peer editing conferences allow both author and editor to talk about important letter–sound relationships and to correct spelling in a work before it is published. With younger children, it is important to model these conferences carefully so that all understand how an editor looks for spelling corrections and other details that need to be corrected. Some teachers will ask students to complete at least two editing conferences before beginning their final draft of an important work. Asking editors to initial the draft in the upper right-hand corner helps you keep track of each editor's work and to ensure that all students engage in editing conferences.

language experience writing activities   A method framework used to develop decoding knowledge through writing; students draw, write, and share.

Language experience writing activities are a less-formal, but equally important, opportunity to have students reflect on letter–sound relationships in their writing. This method framework is especially useful for beginning writers and readers. As a method framework, language experience writing activities usually contain three procedural steps:

1. Encourage students to draw a picture.
2. Have students write something about their picture.
3. Have students share their work.

During the first step, children are encouraged to draw a picture about something they have recently experienced. Sometimes teachers will use this activity as a follow-up activity to a shared reading experience with a big book. In this case, students might be encouraged to draw a picture about something that happened in the story. At other times, students may be encouraged to draw a picture about a classroom visitor, an experience at home, or an activity completed in class.

Next, students are encouraged to write something about their picture. Here, the important point is not to worry about correct spelling but, rather, to support children as they attempt to create a written representation of their ideas. As students attempt to spell unfamiliar words, they naturally consider relationships between letters and sounds. This is why language experience writing activities are so useful for developing phonic knowledge in a natural way.

Finally, encourage children to share their work by asking them to read their writing to you, a friend, a small group, or the entire class. Figure 4-4 shows one example of how a kindergartner completed a language experience writing activity after one year of completing this activity on a daily basis.

FIGURE 4-4

FIGURE 4-4

The writing of a kindergarten student completed during a language experience writing activity. He read this work as "I love Dad and Mom and my Taurus, that was a car, and me and Mom and Dad watch TV."

Deductive Instruction

We encountered the method framework known as **deductive instruction** in chapter 2. This approach is a useful way to directly teach insights about literacy and is consistent with the specific skills belief about how children learn to read and write. It is often used to teach phonic generalizations. The model lesson on page 108 describes how Bob Burns used deductive instruction in his second-grade classroom to teach phonic knowledge.

deductive instruction
A method framework containing these four steps: state the skill or rule, provide examples of the skill or rule, provide guided practice, and provide independent practice.

Inductive Instruction

Instead of teaching a skill directly to students as with deductive instruction, **inductive instruction** presents examples and supports students as they determine the pattern that applies to these examples. Inductive instruction often is used by teachers who want to teach a skill or strategy but wish to provide students with more control of their learning than is available with deductive instruction. Teachers who use inductive instruction have more integrated or holistic language learning beliefs about how children learn to read and write. Inductive instruction contains four procedural steps:

inductive instruction
A method framework containing these four steps: provide examples, help students discover the insight, provide guided practice, and provide independent practice.

1. Provide examples.
2. Help students discover the pattern, the rule, or the principle that applies.
3. Provide guided practice.
4. Provide independent practice.

You will notice the procedural steps in inductive instruction are identical to those in deductive instruction with one exception: The order of the first two steps is reversed.

MODEL LESSON

Deductive Instruction to Teach the Vowel Sounds of Y

Bob Burns has interactive beliefs about what to teach. He has integrated beliefs about how to teach. With his balanced perspective, he also tried to meet individual needs. However, Bob had several second-grade students who were confused about the two sounds of *y* at the ends of words. He decided to bring them together for a mini-lesson during reading workshop to help them learn about these letter–sound relationships. Because he had seen these children do well when presented with direct instruction on a specific skill, he decided to employ deductive instruction.

State the Skill or Rule. Bob began by stating the phonic generalization: "Sometimes you will find words ending with the letter *y*. *Y* has the /i/ sound at the end of a one-syllable word. *Y* has the /e/ sound at the end of a word with more than one syllable. Look at these examples."

Provide Examples of the Skill or Rule. Bob wrote the following words on the board:

try	baby
my	quickly
cry	sticky
sky	pretty

He read some of the words aloud and helped children to read others. As they read the words, Bob pointed out that one-syllable words ending in *y* had the /i/ sound, whereas the words with more than one syllable had the /e/ sound.

Provide Guided Practice. Bob then presented a new set of words to his students: *pry, why, fry, silly, rainy,* and *sunny.* He wanted to be sure that his students had acquired the rule and he wanted to show them how the rule applied to other words. He asked individual children to read each new word aloud, tell the group which column it should go in, and explain why. Bob helped when someone had difficulty.

Provide Independent Practice. Bob then provided his students with a short cooperative learning group task, using a worksheet he had made and duplicated. He gave each child a copy of the page but explained that it should be completed by the group. He appointed one child to serve as the leader of the discussion and asked that they let him know when they were finished so they could go over the page together. The page looked like this:

Directions: Put each of the following words in the correct column according to the sound of *y* at the end of each word.

happily	cry	dry	runny	shy
Christy	silly	sly	spy	windy

Words like MY   **Words like BABY**

How would you turn this method framework into one that was more student directed and consistent with more holistic language learning beliefs?

Inductive instruction begins with examples and then uses those examples to help students discover the rule or principle for themselves.

Thus, the first step in inductive instruction is to provide students examples of the rule they are about to discover. Consider, for example, a situation where you wish students to learn that the letter *c* usually represents the "hard sound" of *c* (as in *cat*) when it is followed by *a, o,* or *u.* Here, you would provide examples of words where this pattern applies and read each one. You might even group the words:

cat	cot	cut
can	corn	cup
cap	come	cub

The second step in an inductive framework is to use these examples to help students discover—or induce—the insight you want them to acquire. Continuing with our illustration, you might engage students in a discussion focusing on the phonic principle somewhat similar to this: "What is the same in all of these words? Yes, they all begin with the letter *c.* Is the sound for *c* the same in all these words? Do you notice anything else about these words? Which letters follow the letter *c?* That's right, the letters *a, o,* or *u.* Let's see if *c* always makes this sound when it is followed by *a, o,* or *u.* Here are some more words." Working in this way, you would help students to discover the pattern, state it in a rule, and then write it on the chalkboard.

The third procedural step is the same as deductive instruction: to provide guided practice with the insight students have just discovered. In our previous example, you might list additional words that followed this pattern and have students use their new principle to decode them:

cab	cold	curl
car	cod	cure
camp	coal	curb

The fourth procedural step is to provide independent practice and is identical to that of deductive instruction. In our example, you might have students independently read a story where this pattern appeared frequently, asking them to keep track of any words they find following this pattern. These words might be shared when you get together after everyone has read the story. See the Model Lesson on page 110.

Developing Sight Word Knowledge

Sight word knowledge refers to the ability to recognize the pronunciation of words automatically, without conscious application of other decoding strategies. It is another element of decoding knowledge.

Mature readers recognize most words by relying on their extensive sight word knowledge. Beginning readers have far less sight word knowledge and, in some cases, have none at all. If beginning readers knew they had to recognize so many different words by sight, they might give up. Memorizing the pronunciation of thousands of separate items would be a tremendous challenge.

Fortunately, however, two considerations reduce the difficulty of developing extensive sight word knowledge. First, a small set of words appears frequently in writing. By knowing how to recognize these 200 to 400 words by sight, readers can immediately recognize 50 to 65 percent of the words in nearly any reading selection (Harris & Sipay, 1990). Second, most of the other words that become part of sight word knowledge are acquired experientially over an extensive period of time. Initially, readers attempt to recognize each new word by using either a context or phonic strategy. However, after a number of such experiences with a particular word, a reader becomes able to recognize it automatically—without using a conscious strategy to determine its pronunciation (Stahl, 1992). Many more sight words are acquired from reading experience and use than from deliberate instruction. With beginning readers, then, it is not our goal to teach automatic recognition of all of the words in our language. Instead, we want to provide many opportunities for our students to acquire sight word knowledge independently, teach a limited set of sight words that appear with high frequency, and monitor each child's development of sight word knowledge. The sight word knowledge necessary for beginning readers consists of a limited set of words that share several characteristics.

sight word knowledge
One aspect of decoding knowledge; the ability to automatically recognize the pronunciation of words without conscious use of other decoding strategies.
Sight word knowledge continues to develop through our reading experiences, as we continue to interact with print.

MODEL LESSON

Inductive Instruction to Teach the Vowel Sounds of Y

Bob Burns had several other second-grade students who were confused about the two sounds of *y* at the ends of words. These students, he had discovered, seemed to do better at literacy tasks when they had greater opportunities to direct their own learning. He decided to bring them together for a mini-lesson during reading workshop to help them learn about the sounds of *y*, only he decided to use an inductive approach.

Provide Examples of the Skill or Rule. Bob began by writing the following words on the chalkboard for his students to analyze. He read each word aloud as he wrote it, emphasizing the multiple syllables in the second column.

try	quickly
cry	baby
my	sticky

Help Students Discover the Skill or Rule. Bob asked questions to help his students notice the two sounds of *y* at the ends of words: "Which letter is at the end of all these words? That's right! *Y* is at the end, isn't it? Now, which sounds do you hear at the ends of these words? Yes, we hear the sound /i/ at the end of the words like *try* and the sound /e/ at the end of the words like *baby*. Can anyone state a rule that would apply to these words?" Bob helped the children state the rule and then wrote it on the board: "When *y* is at the end of a word, it can have two sounds: /i/ as in *try* or /e/ as in *baby*." Then he asked questions to help the children notice where each of those sounds occurred. "What is the same about all these words in the first column, where *y* has the long *i* sound? That's right! They are all short words, aren't they? How many syllables does each word have? Right, only one syllable. Now look at the second column, where *y* has the long *e* sound. What is the same about all of these words? That's right! They all have more than one syllable. Can anyone help us change our rule to include this new information?" Bob helped the children state the new rule and then wrote it on the board: "*Y* has the /i/ sound at the end of a word with one syllable. *Y* has the /e/ sound at the end of a word with more than one syllable."

Provide Guided Practice. Bob then presented a new set of words to see whether children had acquired the rule and to show them how the rule applied to other words: *pry, why, fry, slowly, rainy,* and *sunny*. He asked individuals to read each new word aloud, tell the group which column it should go in, and explain why. Bob helped the students when they had difficulty.

Provide Independent Practice. Bob then provided the children with a short cooperative learning group task, using the same worksheet he made for the other group.

Directions: Put each of the following words into the correct column according to the sound of *y* at the end of each word.

happily	cry	dry	runny	shy
Christy	silly	sly	spy	windy

Words like MY	**Words like BABY**
_____	_____
_____	_____
_____	_____
_____	_____
_____	

With a balanced literacy framework, Bob Burns provided some students with deductive instruction, and others with inductive instruction, and was able to focus on how each of his students learned best.

FIGURE 4-5

Sight words that should be familiar to first graders by the end of the school year

a	day	had	let	off	table	want
above	days	hand	like	old	than	wanted
across	did	hard	little	one	that	was
after	didn't	has	look	open	the	way
again	do	have	love	or	then	we
air	don't	he		out	there	well
all	door	help	make	over	these	went
am	down	her	making		they	what
American		here	man	past	think	when
and	end	high	may	play	this	where
are		him	me	point	those	which
art	feet	home	men	put	three	who
as	find	house	miss		time	why
ask	first	how	money	really	to	will
at	five		more	red	today	with
	for		most	right	too	work
back	four	if	mother	room	took	
be		I'm	Mr.	run	top	year
before	gave	in	Ms.		two	years
behind	get	into	must			
big	girl	is	my	said		yet
black	give	it		saw	under	you
book	go	its	name	school	up	your
boy	God	it's	never	see		
but	going		new	seen	very	
	gone	just	night	she		
came	good		no	short		
can	got	keep	not	six		
car		kind	now	so		
children				some		
come				something		
could				soon		
				still		

Source: From *Teaching Reading Vocabulary*, second edition by Dale D. Johnson and P. David Pearson. Copyright 1984 by CBS College Publishing. Reprinted by permission of Thomson Learning.

▶ *High frequency.* Words taught as initial sight words should appear frequently in print. Thus, words like *is, a, the, to,* and *she* should be taught, but not words like *excavation.*

▶ *Familiar meanings.* The meanings of initial sight words should be familiar to beginning readers; that is, they should know the words from their oral language. Thus, words like *car, come, good,* and *school* are better candidates than words like *turbine* or *nucleus.*

▶ *Phonic irregularity.* Words taught as initial sight words often cannot be recognized by applying phonic generalizations. Words like *one, said, where,* and *some* are thus more appropriate for early instruction than words that can be identified by applying common phonic generalizations.

Which specific words, then, should be familiar to beginning readers? Published reading programs usually have their own list of words that students are expected to know as sight words. In addition, several different lists of sight words are based on a wider range of reading material. The list in Figure 4-5 above includes words that appear frequently in the oral language of kindergarten and first-grade students, as well as a variety of published materials.

Sight word knowledge continues to develop through our reading experiences, as we continue to interact with print.

Instruction

Many teachers will tell you, "The best way to learn to read is to read." This advice is sound because the more opportunities children have to read, the more they will encounter high-frequency words in our language. It is important, therefore, for them to have many opportunities to read during daily classroom activities. Reading promotes the development of sight word knowledge; in turn, sight word knowledge promotes the development of reading.

Creating a literacy environment in the classroom can do much to develop sight word knowledge. Labeling objects, pictures of objects, and artwork provides excellent exposure to the sight words students should know. Teachers might also consider prominently displaying weather charts, calendars, and job charts. The teaching strategies previously listed offer further suggestions.

In addition to extensive reading opportunities, sight word knowledge may be developed through a number of more formal instructional practices, always occurring within meaningful contexts. Children are more certain about a word's meaning when it appears in a sentence or phrase. Confusion about meaning can be great among words that look or sound alike, and it is important to establish the habit of using context to identify words. These examples illustrate the potential for confusion.

> The book was *red*. The book was *read*.

> That play was *close*. That play will not *close*.

A second reason for teaching sight words in context is to more closely approximate the reading experience. Presenting words in isolation sometimes leads children to think that reading is simply a process of recognizing the pronunciations of separate words. Slow, inefficient, word-by-word reading without attention to meaning often is the result.

A useful way for younger readers to develop sight word knowledge in context is to follow a **sight word learning routine** developed by Johnson and Louis (1987). This method framework contains seven procedural steps:

sight word learning routine A method framework for developing sight words by using familiar stories, poems, songs, or chants.

1. Help students learn an engaging story, poem, song, or chant.
2. Help students prepare a chart or book version.

3. Help students recognize familiar lines of text.
4. Help students recognize familiar words.
5. Help students identify familiar lines of text.
6. Help students identify words.
7. Encourage individuals to read portions of the text by themselves.

The first step is to help your students learn an engaging story, poem, song, or chant. Often this step is completed by reading a predictable text together that has been published in a big book. The predictability of repeated sentence patterns makes learning the story easier for younger children.

If students did not use a big book, you will next want to make a chart or big book version of the text. This can be as simple as writing the text on a large sheet of chart paper. It could also be as elaborate as helping your class to make its own big book from the story. Here, you will need to write the text on large sheets of construction paper and encourage groups of children to illustrate each page. Use yarn or metal rings to bind the big book together and display it in a prominent place.

Next, assist students in recognizing familiar lines of text. As you read the text together, point to the words. As you encounter familiar or repeated lines, help your students recognize them by pointing them out or providing verbal clues. As you have repeated reading experiences with this text over several days, continue to point to familiar lines and encourage children to identify them.

After several lines are familiar to students, frame one of the words in the line with your hands and help students read it. Their familiarity with the line will help them to quickly spot the individual words within that line. Continue with other words in that line and then move on to other familiar lines.

As students engage in rereading experiences, help them identify some of the familiar lines by asking questions such as, "Now where does it say, 'Yellow duck, yellow duck, what do you see?'" Encourage individuals to locate the lines of text you call out.

After each line is located, ask students to identify individual words within that line. Let all of the children have an opportunity to do this, saving the last word in a line for the student who is weakest at recognizing words. This is usually the easiest to recognize.

Finally, encourage individuals to read the words in entire lines by themselves. By rereading the students' favorite stories, this will become a popular activity, one for which you will have many volunteers. Sight word knowledge can also be developed by using **individualized word banks.** Such banks consist of index card boxes (shoeboxes make an inexpensive substitute) with cards inside. Words that children have not completely learned are written on those cards; on one side, the words may be written in isolation, and on the other side, in a sentence context. The words can be practiced individually or with a partner. In addition, cooperative learning group activities can be designed using these boxes. When a sufficient number of words are accumulated, the cards can be organized alphabetically to develop familiarity with alphabetical order. Figure 4-6 shows an example of a word bank.

individualized word banks One means of developing sight word knowledge; uses words written on index cards and filed in index card boxes.

FIGURE 4-6

A word bank for sight words

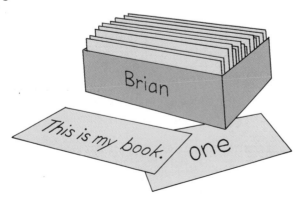

PRACTICAL TEACHING STRATEGIES

Integrating Sight Word Development within Primary Grade Classrooms

Talking Storybooks. An increasing number of talking storybook products are appearing on CD-ROM, including *Living Books,* a product containing a number of well-known works of children's literature. These provide children with opportunities to hear unfamiliar words pronounced for them as they read. Preliminary evidence suggests these are helpful in supporting decoding knowledge, though highly interactive illustrations sometimes distract students from the storyline.

A Word Wall. Set aside a wall or bulletin board at the beginning of the year for posting new sight words. Each day, put up three new sight words at this location using small index cards before your students arrive. At the end of each day, see whether anyone has found and can read all three new words. At the beginning of the year, this will be easy. However, as words begin to cover the wall or bulletin board with time, it will be difficult to find the three new words. The real benefit of this activity is that students will be reading all the words on your wall as they search for the three new words each day. One variation on this activity is to assign a different student each week to select the three new words and post them for others to find. Try to use words that students often ask to be spelled. Then, encourage them to check the word wall each time they ask for the spelling of these words.

Individualized word banks often are used in student-centered programs in which students decide which words they need to practice and learn (Ashton-Warner, 1963). In conjunction with writing activities, a teacher might write a new word on a card whenever a student asks for its spelling. That word card could then go into that student's word bank after it was used in the writing activity.

Context Knowledge

context knowledge
One element of decoding knowledge; the reader's ability to use information in the text, along with background knowledge, to predict upcoming words.

Context knowledge refers to a reader's ability to use information from the text in conjunction with background knowledge to predict upcoming words. Readers often use context knowledge to determine the oral equivalent and meaning of a word. For example, notice how you decode the italicized words in the following sentence:

Alexandra will *read* the book after you have *read* it.

Even though this word is spelled the same each time it appears, you decoded it differently at the two locations. You decoded the first instance as /reed/ and the second instance as /red/. In each case, you relied on the surrounding context to determine the appropriate pronunciation. In other words, you used context knowledge. Readers frequently use context knowledge like this to determine the oral equivalent as well as the meaning of words.

Sometimes readers use context knowledge so proficiently that they do not even perceive certain words as they read. Consider this sentence with a missing word:

Sarah, an only child, had always wanted a younger brother or _____.

In this example, you again rely on the surrounding context to determine that the missing word is probably *sister.* The text indicates the word is something that an only child wants. It is also a noun and must be an alternative to *brother.* Your background knowledge tells you the word *sister* fits all these conditions and is therefore a likely candidate. Thus, readers are frequently able to use context knowledge to predict upcoming words.

Teaching Context Strategies

Working with students on context strategies helps them to form expectations for upcoming words. An activity with context use is often an enjoyable activity because it is very much like a game: predicting a missing word and then explaining the reasoning be-

Celebrating Diversity

Using Predictable Texts to Provide Everyone with a Successful Reading Experience

Some students in a first- or second-grade class will be able to recognize many words. They have extensive decoding knowledge. Other students will have limited decoding knowledge, and be unable to recognize many words. In this situation, the use of predictable texts with repeated sentence patterns can be very useful to provide everyone with a successful reading experience. Leu, DeGroff, & Simons (1986) found that low-achieving readers read predictable texts as quickly and as accurately as high-achieving readers. They also comprehended stories at the same high level. Low-achieving readers used context strategies while high-achieving readers were able to accurately recognize words with a minimum use of context. Thus, predictable texts allow each child to meet with success even though they might use different decoding strategies. Consider using some of these predictable literature selections in your beginning reading program:

Polar Bear, Polar Bear, What Do You Hear? by Bill Martin, Jr.

The Very Hungry Caterpillar by Eric Carle

Brown Bear, Brown Bear, What Do You See by Bill Martin, Jr.

Is Your Mama a Llama? by Deborah Guarino

Goodnight Moon by Margaret Wise Brown

The House that Jack Built by Janet Stephens

Today Is Monday by Eric Carle

Chicken Soup with Rice by Maurice Sendak

The Little Old Lady Who Was Not Afraid of Anything by Linda Williams

Go Tell Aunt Rhody by Aliki

hind the prediction. Several instructional practices can help students develop better context use strategies while reading: written cloze activities, oral cloze activities, and integrating cloze activities into ongoing reading instruction.

Written Cloze Activities

Written cloze activities present a reader with writing that contains at least one missing word, as in this example:

> The team left the field excited because they had _____ the game.

The reader's task is to use the information in the text, along with background knowledge, to determine the missing word—or to provide closure to the sentence. Cloze activities provide children with situations they might experience when they cannot recognize a word during reading. It helps them practice using the surrounding context to figure out what this word might be.

The use of written cloze activities probably is the most common technique used to develop context knowledge. If you use this approach, be certain to provide opportunities for discussing the strategy and clues used to make the prediction; simply completing cloze exercises does little to develop this ability.

Teachers can select commercial materials or make their own materials to develop written cloze activities. Simply find or create materials where words are periodically replaced by blank lines. Then ask children to complete the blank spaces with words they think make sense at that location and discuss their choices.

Longer selections may be used to provide instruction in using multiple cues to predict what an unfamiliar word might be and are easier to complete than single sentences

written cloze activities
Used to develop context knowledge; the reader is asked to determine, in writing, a missing word by using text information and background knowledge.

because more information is provided in the text. This can be seen in the following two examples:

1. The _____ didn't stick around to see which nasty spell the witch had in mind.

2. "I'm the Frog Prince."
"That's funny. You don't look like a frog. Well, no matter. If you're a prince, you're a prince. And I'll have to cast a nasty spell on you. I can't have any princes waking up Sleeping Beauty before the hundred years are up."
    The _____ didn't stick around to see which nasty spell the witch had in mind. (*The Frog Prince* by J. Scieszka, 1991, p. 11)

A second element to vary is the target word location. Putting the target word at the end provides practice in using preceding context to recognize a word; putting it near the beginning helps teach students to read past an unknown word and to use the contextual information that appears after it. Notice the different reading strategies required in these two examples:

A _____ is a person who flies an airplane.

A person who flies an airplane is a _____.

A third element to vary is the information available at target word locations. Traditionally, only a blank space is provided; however, the task can be made easier by providing the first letter or two of the target word. It can be made easier still by placing two or more words underneath the blank and having students choose the correct word. Notice the task becomes progressively easier in each of the following examples:

We went to the   _____.

We went to the   st_____.

We went to the   _____.
                    (run, store)

Oral Cloze Activities

oral cloze activities
Cloze activities used to develop context knowledge but completed orally, often while the teacher reads a storybook aloud.

Cloze activities usually take place in written contexts, but they may also be completed in oral contexts. Many teachers use **oral cloze activities** as they read a story aloud to young children, stopping just before a highly predictable word and then cueing children to make a guess as to what it might be. Oral cloze activities engage children in the story and give them greater confidence in their own reading ability. Consider, for example, how students might be invited to predict the final word on this page from *The Very Busy Spider* by Eric Carle:

"Oink, Oink!" grunted the pig. "Want to roll in the mud?"

The spider didn't answer. She was busy spinning her _____.

Integrating Cloze Activities into Ongoing Reading Instruction

Often the best way to provide instruction on context use is to incorporate this aspect of decoding knowledge into ongoing reading experiences, thus encouraging students to make a habit of context use. This approach is useful as you engage students in a "Message of the Day" activity, a language experience story, or a big book activity. Consider, for example, how you might read and point to the words in this language experience story, dictated by your class, leaving the final word in each sentence for children to read aloud as you point to it:

Our Trip to the Farmer's Market

We went on the bus.

We went to the farmer's market.

We saw all the fruits and vegetables.

We got to eat a big red apple.

Katrina found a flower and it had a caterpillar.

PRACTICAL TEACHING STRATEGIES

Integrating Context Use into Classroom Instruction

Oral Cloze Activities with Predictable Texts. Use oral cloze activities as you read texts with repeated sentence patterns, which make them highly predictable. Periodically omit the final word in a sentence or the repeated phrase, and then ask students to complete the sentence for you. This experience is especially enjoyable with younger readers. Try using these selections with first-grade students:

Suddenly! by Colin McNaughton

Two Bad Ants by Chris Van Allsburg

The Piggy in a Puddle by Charlotte Pomerantz

Cookie's Week by Cindy Ward

The Napping House by Don Woods and Audrey Woods

Mary Wore Her Red Dress by Merle Peek

Small Green Snake by Libba Moore

The Cake that Mack Ate by Rose Robart

The Cat on the Mat by Brian Wildsmith

Introducing New Vocabulary Words with Cloze Activities. If you are introducing new words to children, present each word in a cloze sentence. See if children can guess its meaning from the surrounding context. Then write the word for students and see if they can pronounce it.

Pirates often carry a long, sharp _____.

The pirates had to pull up the _____ before the ship could leave.

Keeping Track of Successful Context Use Strategies. Encourage students to share their successful strategies for context use. As they share a strategy, write it on chart paper with the title "Context Use Strategies." Keep this posted in a prominent location in the room.

We bought a big orange pumpkin for our class.

We ate our lunch in the park.

If you left out the final word in each sentence, students would likely predict it accurately; students would be sufficiently familiar with the experiences from the field trip to fill in the final word for you.

Other teachers will prepare a mini-lesson for reading workshop using literature selections or other written materials. With literature selections, simply invite students to read different portions of a story aloud. As they experience difficulty reading a word aloud, invite readers to reread the sentence from the beginning and then guess what the troublesome word might be, making certain it makes sense in the sentence. Wrap up this short activity by reminding children of one strategy to use while they are reading: Reread the sentence and use the meaning to help make a prediction about an unrecognized word.

Additional examples of integrating context use instruction into classroom reading experiences are described above.

Fluency

A major goal of decoding instruction, from the early beginnings with phonological and phonemic awareness to the later stages of phonic knowledge, sight word knowledge, and context use strategies, is to enable students to read text fluently. **Fluency,** or the ability to read aloud grade-appropriate text accurately and rapidly, is a necessary, but not sufficient, condition for comprehension.

fluency The ability to read aloud grade-appropriate text accurately and rapidly.

Listen to several beginning readers read a passage aloud. You will find that some read each word haltingly, slowly, and with many errors. You may wonder how they can recall the meaning at the beginning of the sentence by the time they come to the end of the sentence. In fact, this lack of fluency does impede the construction of comprehension. Other students read the passage smoothly, quickly, and with few errors. These students have achieved fluency, since they automatically recognize each word and can devote their thought to the meaning of the passage, not to deciding what sound is represented by the letter at the beginning of a word or how to blend several letter–sound combinations.

Students who have not yet achieved fluency in their reading of grade-appropriate passages will usually also struggle with the comprehension of the passage. That is why fluency is so important. Students are less able to focus their attention on the meaning of the passage since they must spend so much time consciously thinking about how to de-code individual words.

Fluency is not something that can be taught directly, except as you support the de-velopment of the foundational skills of decoding knowledge, phonological awareness and phonemic awareness, and as you teach the components of decoding: phonic knowl-edge, sight word knowledge, and context use strategies. Fluency is achieved as more and more individual words become a part of a student's sight word vocabulary and as students are able to quickly orchestrate the effective use of phonic knowledge and con-text use strategies when they are unable to recognize a word by sight. This is achieved through good instruction of the basic components and by making certain that students have many opportunities to read, perhaps by using method frameworks in chapter 6 such as Drop Everything And Read (DEAR), readers theater, and independent reading opportunities within a guided reading framework.

Supporting the Decoding Needs of Linguistically Diverse Children

It is likely you will have the opportunity to work in a classroom where several different dialects of English are spoken. To support the decoding needs of children from diverse linguistic backgrounds, it is important to understand several important principles of language variation.

dialect   An alternative language form used by a regional, social, or cultural group and understood by speakers of the same major language.

What is a **dialect?** Dialects are alternative language forms commonly used by regional, social, or cultural groups. Dialects can be understood by speakers of the same language group, but they feature important differences in sounds (for example, *this* or *dis*), vocabu-lary (for example, *soda* or *pop*), and syntax (for example, "He is tired" or "He tired"). Nearly every major language incorporates a number of different dialects. All are equally logical, precise, and rule-governed; no dialect is inherently superior to another. However, one di-alect usually becomes the standard language form in a society because it is used by the so-cially, economically, and politically advantaged members of that society.

In the United States the standard language form has sometimes been called Stan-dard American English (SAE). Although it is difficult to define precisely, Standard American English is commonly identified as the form of English spoken by newscasters in most parts of the United States. It is thought to be most similar to the main dialect found in the midwestern states.

Many nonstandard dialects are spoken in the United States. One is common to the southern United States. Another is common to the Appalachian region. And one is com-monly found in New England. Speakers of these dialects share certain language con-ventions, but some degree of variation remains within each dialect.

One of the more popular dialect variations recently has been referred to as Ebonics. As with other dialects, much variability exists in this dialect. Ebonics is considered in the following discussion, but everything said about it also applies to other dialects.

Decoding Instruction and Dialect Differences

When students who speak a dialect read aloud, they often alter the sounds, words, and syntax of the writing to be consistent with their own dialect. A speaker of Ebonics, for

TABLE 4-1

A partial summary of common differences between Standard American English and Ebonics

Language Trait	Standard American English	Ebonics
	Phonological Differences	
Initial		
th (becomes d)	this	dis
th (becomes t)	thin	tin
str (becomes skr)	stream	scream
thr (becomes tr)	three	tree
Final		
sks (becomes ses)	tasks	tasses
sk (becomes ks)	ask	aks
th (becomes f)	teeth	teef
l (has no sound)	tool	too
r (has no sound)	four	foe
General		
Final consonant	best	bess
clusters simplified	walked	walk
	books	book
	talks	talk
i (becomes e before nasals)	pin	pen

example, might read the sentence "He is playing" as "He playing." Although it may appear that the child has not decoded the sentence correctly, there is no evidence that this behavior interferes with comprehension. Indeed, it reflects an attempt to understand the text in the dialect of the reader and should not be discouraged. To do so would force the student to attend to the surface conventions of writing at the expense of comprehension.

At the same time, it is important to encourage students to self-correct any decoding mistakes that interfere with comprehension and are unrelated to a dialect (for example, "He painting" instead of "He is playing"). Thus, teachers need to be aware of the dialects of their students and distinguish between oral reading patterns reflecting dialect differences and oral reading patterns reflecting comprehension difficulties.

To become familiar with some of the more common dialect differences between Standard American English and Ebonics, study Table 4-1. Every dialect contains differences that are regular and predictable. By listening to your students speak, you should be able to discover those regularities and then let your knowledge of dialect differences guide your decisions during oral reading and decoding instruction.

Instruction

Some assume that nonstandard dialects interfere with reading comprehension. That assumption, which was common before 1970, is referred to as a **deficit explanation.** According to a deficit explanation, nonstandard dialects are not only different from the standard dialect, but are also illogical, imprecise, and unsystematic. In an attempt to overcome the perceived deficit that nonstandard speakers faced in their use of dialect, several instructional practices were recommended:

deficit explanation A view of nonstandard dialects as less logical, less precise, and less rule-governed when compared to standard dialects.

- Teach children with reading materials that match their dialect.
- Use dialect-neutral stories and reading materials that do not conflict with the nonstandard dialect.
- Teach children to speak Standard American English before teaching them to read.

Many young children learn to read and write more than one language.

None of these approaches was particularly effective in increasing students' reading ability (Simons, 1979). In addition, because each proposal assumed that the children had deficits, they were implicitly being told that their language was inferior. The result was a negative impact on self-image and motivation.

difference explanation
A view of nonstandard dialects as being different from the standard dialect but equally logical, precise, and rule-governed.

Research during the 1970s led most educators to accept a **difference explanation** of dialect differences. In other words, nonstandard dialects are now recognized as different but equally logical, precise, and rule-governed. Dialect differences—by themselves—are not the cause of reading failure.

Today, five instructional practices usually are encouraged in classrooms with nonstandard dialect speakers.

1. Language experience approaches are used in the beginning stages of reading to help children see the close connection between their language and printed words.
2. Culturally relevant materials are used to provide a supportive environment for reading and to increase interest and motivation. Such materials also ensure that students' background knowledge is consistent with the background knowledge required to comprehend a text. Most importantly, they provide multicultural reading experiences for all of the students in a class. Literature selections portraying different cultural and ethnic groups are described in chapter 6.
3. Children's background knowledge is carefully considered in relation to the texts they read (Maria, 1989). During vocabulary instruction, children's understanding of key concepts is probed to determine what they need to know about key terms. Instruction then helps children understand word meanings with which they are unfamiliar (appropriate techniques are described in chapter 8). Semantic mapping activities are especially useful.
4. Cooperative learning group activities are frequently used, again to provide a supportive environment in which children can accomplish tasks they might be unable to complete alone (these techniques are described in chapter 3). Discussion and debate often serve to clarify understanding.

miscue   A difference between what a reader reads aloud and the expected word on the page.

5. During oral reading, teachers ignore a reading **miscue** when it does not alter the underlying meaning of a text but merely reflects a child's dialect.

This last point is an especially important one when it comes to oral reading experiences with children who speak a variety of Ebonics. Teachers often will attempt to correct

---

PRACTICAL TEACHING STRATEGIES

Developing Familiarity with Different Dialects

Writing Conferences. Use writing conferences to direct students' attention to the conventions of the standard dialect. Because writing makes language permanent and concrete, it is easier to discuss differences between standard and nonstandard dialects during writing experiences.

Read-Aloud Sessions. Incorporate culturally appropriate materials into read-aloud sessions. Use these to generate discussions of dialect differences. You might want to write down examples of how each dialect communicates the same message.

Two-Sided Stories. Have students write stories in dialect, putting a few sentences and an illustration on one side of each page. Then help them rewrite the story in standard dialect on the reverse side of each page. This activity could also be carried out as a language experience story, with you writing the sentences as the students dictate them.

---

the oral reading of past tense verbs where two consonant sounds appear at the end of the word, such as *skipped, picked, hopped,* or *turned.* A very common rule within Ebonics is referred to as "consonant simplification." The rule requires speakers of this dialect to simplify multiple consonant sounds at the ends of words to a single consonant sound. Thus, words like *skipped* are pronounced as *skip* /SKIP/. Similarly, *picked* becomes *pick, hopped* becomes *hop,* and *turned* becomes *turn.* Children who pronounce words like this during oral reading understand the correct tense of the word and the correct meaning of the sentence; they are simply following the phonological rules of their dialect. These oral reading behaviors should not be corrected. To correct them during oral reading interferes with the comprehension process. In addition, if you do try to correct them, children will follow the logical rules of their dialect and begin pronouncing words like *skipped* as *skip-ed* /SKIP-ED/. This will happen because their dialect simply does not permit two consonant sounds to appear at the end of a word without putting a vowel sound between them.

Does all of this mean that teachers should never try to develop oral competency in the standard dialect? On the contrary, teachers should provide learning experiences that promote such competency because the standard dialect provides access to power and influence in any society. However, the appropriate time for such efforts is not when children are demonstrating competence in decoding and comprehension during oral reading. Since dialect variation in writing is concrete, many teachers will work on students' dialect differences through writing activities. This allows you and your children to talk about differences more precisely. Often teachers will correct dialect variation during many writing activities and not during reading. Activities such as those previously described may be used to direct children's attention to the conventions of the standard dialect.

Developing Decoding Knowledge with Computer and Internet Resources

Computer resources may be used to support the development of decoding knowledge in important ways (Labbo, 1996; Miller, Blackstock, & Miller, 1994). Increasingly, new electronic resources can assist you and your students in this area.

For the youngest literacy learners, symbol-making software such as Kid Pix Deluxe may be used to support early insights into letters and sounds (Labbo, 1996). Providing young children with software that supports initial attempts at making meaning through drawing and writing appears to be especially powerful. Context knowledge, phonic knowledge, and sight word knowledge all may be developed and refined as children create their own meanings on the computer and then share these messages with others. Typing one's own name or the name of a friend, labeling objects, and writing messages

---

MODEL LESSON

Responding to Dialect Errors during Oral Reading in Peter Stanton's Class

Peter Stanton is reading and discussing a story with a small group of his sixth-grade students. Darleen, who speaks a variation of Ebonics, reads the following sentences:

Text: They won't ask for the two books. They are afraid.

Darleen: Dey woan aks for duh two book. Dey [pause] after?

As Darleen reads, Peter must quickly decide how to respond. He does not want to correct a word that simply reflects a pattern in Darleen's dialect and does not interfere with comprehension. However, if a word changes the meaning of the story, Peter needs to point that out to her.

Peter ignores miscues each time she reads *they* as *dey.* Darleen's dialect uses /d/ to represent the /th/ sound in Standard American English. He also ignores Darleen's reading of *the* as *duh* and *ask* as *aks.* None of these deviations interfere with comprehension and each reflects the pronunciation patterns of Darleen's dialect.

Peter also ignores the reading of *won't* as *woan* because Darleen's dialect simplifies final consonant clusters such as /nt/. The same basic principle applies to her reading of *books* as *book;* the final consonant cluster /ks/ was simplified to /k/. Peter is confident this change did not alter Darleen's comprehension because she correctly read the word *two* just before she read *book.* Peter also ignores Darleen's omission of the word *are* since *to be* verbs are sometimes dropped in her dialect.

However, Peter is concerned about the last word. Darleen reads *afraid* as *after,* and the question intonation gives Peter a clue that Darleen is uncertain of that word. He also notices this miscue is not based on a pronunciation rule in her dialect. And, most importantly, this miscue changes the meaning of the sentence. Consequently, he asks Darleen to look at the ending sound of the word, especially the last four letters. When she notices the word *raid,* he asks her to read the sentence again. Darleen reads the final sentence correctly in her dialect: "Dey afraid."

---

require children to think about principles associated with decoding knowledge. A child in the Labbo study (1996) puts it best: "You gotta spell it like grown-ups if someone's really gotta read it" (p. 378).

Programs like Kid Pix are very useful in the early primary grades. Often teachers will set up a computer with a program like this as a literacy center activity. At their assigned time, individuals, pairs, or groups visit the center and use the software for writing and drawing. Teachers with a specific skills explanation for how children learn to read and write will assign a specific writing project to be completed during this time. Teachers with a holistic language learning explanation for how children learn to read will simply invite children to create their own meanings and messages with the software.

Often software used in the early grades will include the ability to read back to students the writing they create. This includes the software product, Kidspriration, which allows students to develop concept maps, character maps, and story maps. As they construct their maps, the program can be set up to read their work back to them.

A product sometimes used to provide the extensive, independent reading experiences necessary for the development of fluency is Accelerated Reader. This software has students take a short comprehension test after reading a book on the list of books listed in the program. The program is intended to provide motivation for students to read many books independently, thus developing greater fluency. You will discover varied evaluations of this product from teachers. Some like the management system it contains to track and record books that students have read. Some will question the relatively simple assessments of comprehension and point out that authentic response experiences are seldom accomplished with this program.

Another important resource used in the primary grades to support decoding knowledge is **talking storybook software.** This is sometimes found as a component of an integrated learning system such as the ones found in products of the Classroom Computer Corporation. They are also found on separate CD-ROMs. Examples of the latter include

talking storybook software Software products containing works of literature, interactive animations, and the ability to pronounce any word a child wishes to hear, often in several languages.

FIGURE 4-7

Some talking storybook software is beginning to integrate writing and letter–sound activities as you can see in this beginning screen from Wiggleworks. These experiences develop decoding knowledge

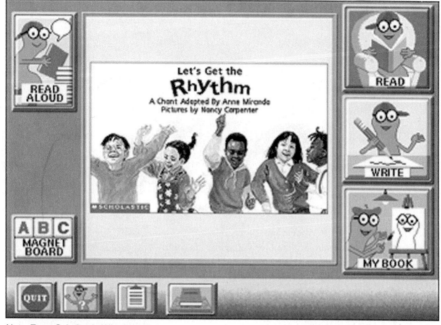

Note: From Scholastic Wiggleworks.

software such as *Multimedia Literature, Magic Tales, Living Books,* and *Wiggleworks.* Talking storybook software contains works of literature, interactive animations, and the ability to pronounce any word a child wishes to hear, often in several languages. This software will also "read" the entire story, a page, or a single sentence should your student select one of these options. Experiences like these, especially clicking on an unfamiliar word to hear its pronunciation, appear to increase children's ability to independently decode words (Miller, Blackstock, & Miller, 1994). Programs combining literature experiences, a writing component, and spelling or phonemic awareness activities such as *Wiggleworks* (Figure 4-7) may be especially useful.

Developmental Spelling: Insights into Your Students' Decoding Knowledge

Children's nonstandard spelling progresses through a series of phases until more standard forms appear. If you understand the developmental progression of these spelling phases, you will develop insights into children's decoding knowledge. Children's writing tells you what they know and what they have yet to learn about letter–sound relationships and sight words.

Consider the developmental spelling checklist shown in Figure 4-8. By checking the school quarter when you find evidence of each element, you will be able to track the growth of phonic knowledge and sight word knowledge among your students.

Children usually begin writing in a **precommunicative phase.** Writing during this phase usually is characterized by not having a consistent, communicative intent. If you ask children to tell you about their work, they usually will not give you the same interpretation. Initially, children engage in squiggle writing and then you will begin to see some left-to-right order in organized lines. Also at this time, lines representing the components of letters begin to appear (circles, straight lines, slant lines). This is followed by actual letters, though these often are randomly distributed over a page. At

precommunicative phase The first phase in developmental spelling where writing usually does not express a communicative intent.

FIGURE 4-8

A developmental spelling checklist used to gain insight into decoding development

Developmental Spelling Checklist

Student _____

School Year _____

A. Precommunicative Phase

Pattern

1. Random drawing
2. Organized lines

3. Letter components
4. Random letters

What the child knows

Tool knowledge
Left to right/There is a system here, but what are the rules?
Letters are central elements
Letter formation

School Quarter

I	II	III	IV

B. Semi-Phonetic Phase

Pattern

1. Some systematic meaning

2. Sounds of letters are names of letters
3. Consonants and long vowels, few short vowels
4. Spaces between words

What the child knows

Writing is for communication. Letters represent sounds/sounds represent meaning
Letter names are letter sounds

Consonants carry most information

What a written word is

School Quarter

I	II	III	IV

C. Phonetic Phase

Pattern

1. Most sounds are represented in writing
2. Phonic strategies are used

What the child knows

Recognizes most phonological segments

English is phonetic

School Quarter

I	II	III	IV

D. Transitional Phase

Pattern

1. Some irregular, high-frequency sight words spelled correctly

What the child knows

English is not phonetic

School Quarter

I	II	III	IV

E. Standard Phase

Pattern

1. Most words spelled correctly
2. Misspellings follow these patterns:

_____
_____
_____
_____

What the child knows

English is (and is not) phonetic

School Quarter

I	II	III	IV

this phase, it is clear that children have not yet acquired an understanding of letter–sound relationships.

Next, children usually enter a **semi-phonetic phase.** At this time, children discover that writing has a communication intent and that letters represent sounds, which in turn represent meaning. This is an important milestone. During this phase, students often believe that the names of letters are the sounds they represent. Thus, writing like "IM5" (I am five) is common. Consonants and long vowels are more common than short vowels; vowels in the middle of words usually are omitted.

If you see writing that looks like the child is sounding out every word, it is likely that they are in a **phonetic phase** of developmental spelling. Here, writing like "I LUV MI KAT" is common. Notice how more vowels now begin to appear, indicating that children have developed an understanding of these letter–sound relationships. The difficulty in this phase, however, is that children often believe that English is completely phonetic. They will soon learn this is not always true.

In the **transitional phase,** you will begin to see some irregular, high-frequency sight words spelled correctly. This is an important milestone since it indicates the child is discovering that English is not completely phonetic. Writing often looks like this, combining phonetic strategies and sight word knowledge: "ME AND MY FRNDZ LIK TO PLA." Often the sight words that first appear are either very common words (*and, I, me*) or words that are very important to the individual child (their name, the name of their friend, Mom, Dad, the name of a pet).

During the **standard phase** of developmental spelling, students are able to effectively combine phonetic strategies and sight word strategies. For most of us, though, there will still be some words spelled incorrectly. These often follow a particular pattern such as misspellings of double consonant words (*commitment, curriculum*) or certain short vowel sounds.

See if you can use the developmental spelling checklist to develop insights from the writing of kindergarten and first-grade students in Figure 4-9. What do these students know about phonic knowledge and sight word knowledge? What have they yet to learn? In general, which phase best characterizes each writing selection? As you consider these issues, note how common words or important personal words often appear very early.

Using a Literacy Framework to Inform Instructional Decisions about Decoding

As with other areas, you will face two basic decisions as you consider decoding instruction. First, you will need to decide *what* to teach about decoding knowledge. Second, you will need to decide *how* to teach decoding knowledge. Your literacy framework will inform both of these decisions.

What Should I Teach?

To guide decisions regarding what to teach about decoding, consider your beliefs about how one reads. Table 4-2 summarizes how these beliefs can be used to guide instructional decisions.

If you have reader-based beliefs about how a person reads, you believe that reading consists largely of expectations for upcoming words. Thus, you believe that extensive prior knowledge leads to successful reading because readers are able to accurately predict upcoming words. As a result, you will probably spend little time on the development of decoding knowledge. The limited time that you do spend will be devoted to developing context knowledge, and you will encourage children to use contextual analysis strategies to decode words. Context knowledge, of course, helps students use their prior knowledge to develop more accurate expectations for upcoming words.

semi-phonetic phase
The second phase in developmental spelling where students often believe that the names of letters are the sounds they represent.

phonetic phase   The third phase in developmental spelling where children believe that English is completely phonetic.

transitional phase   The fourth phase in developmental spelling where children discover that English is not completely phonetic; some high-frequency sight words are spelled correctly.

standard phase   The final phase in developmental spelling where students are able to effectively combine phonetic strategies and sight word strategies.

FIGURE 4-9

Examples of developmental spelling from children in kindergarten and the beginning of first grade and how each child reads his or her writing

(a) "I love my Kitty." Precommunicative Phase.

(b) "The cat and the person." Semi-Phonetic Phase.

(c) "Me and Jeffrey Beard are friends." Phonetic Phase.

(d) "I love my cousins." Transitional Phase.

SUSAN'S
COMMENTS FROM THE CLASSROOM

"A-a apple; B-b balloon; C-c cat. . . ." Children in first-grade classrooms all over the country often read the alphabet chart. Why? Letter knowledge is crucial to reading. Sound–symbol association is one of the keys to unlocking the code of print. Decoding instruction is an important element of reading instruction. While I agree with these tenets, I believe I must link decoding instruction to a contextual setting whenever possible. Here is what happened one day in my classroom, for example:

Susan: Let's say you're reading along in this book (I hold up a book) and you come to a word you don't know that begins with this letter. (I point to a *T.*) What's the first sound you'd make to read that word?

Class: t-t-t-t-t-t-t-t-t-t (producing the letter-sound as well as copious amounts of saliva).

Susan: (Brightly) Right! Suppose that word you don't know starts with this letter? (I point to *h.*) What sound would start the word?

Class: h-h-h-h-h-h-h-h.

Susan: Excellent. Now I've got a tricky one for you. (Of course!) What if the word begins with the *th* chunk? How do you get your mouth ready then?

Class: th-th-th-th-th-th-th (those tongues are dancing now).

Susan: Right again! Let's try something else. I'll read a sentence and stop right before I've read the last word. Then I'll say the first sound in the missing word and you tell me what that word might be. Let's try one together so you can understand what we're doing. What if I were to read the sentence, "Please come *h* . . ." (I end the sentence with the sound of *h*). What might the last word be? "Please come *h* . . ." (again, the *h* sound ends the sentence).

Class: Here! Home! To school!

Susan: Good guesses! Let's try one of those guesses—*here.* Does it make sense to say, "Please come here?" Sure it does! Now let me write the word that came at the end of the sentence. (I write *home* on the board.) Do the letters in this word match the ones you'd find in *here?* No (with great disappointment), that won't work because there's an *r* in *here* and there's no *r* in this word (I point to the mystery word on the board). Great guess, but it won't work. Someone said home. Let's try home. Does it make sense to say "Please come home?" OK, look at the word on the board again. Does this word look like it could be *home?* We know it starts with an *h*, there's an *o* for the o sound in home, and there's the *m.* This must be home! Please come home! (Cheers all around.)

By taking the knowledge fostered by the learning of initial consonant patterns and demonstrating how that knowledge is used in a book context, I help the children link phonics to actual reading experiences.

TABLE 4-2

A summary of how a literacy framework can be used to inform decisions about what to teach in decoding

Beliefs about How One Reads	Related Assumptions	Probable Time Spent on Decoding Instruction	What Is Taught?
Reader-based	Meaning exists more in what the reader brings to the text.	Little	Context knowledge
	Reading is a result of expectations.		
	Reading begins with elements of prior knowledge.		
Text-based	Meaning exists more in the text.	Much	Phonemic awareness
			Phonological awareness
	Reading is translation.		Phonic knowledge
	Reading begins with decoding.		Sight word knowledge
			Fluency
Interactive	Meaning exists in both the text and the reader.	Average	Phonemic awareness
			Phonological awareness
	Reading is both translation and expectation.		Context knowledge
			Sight word knowledge
	Reading uses each knowledge source simultaneously.		Phonic knowledge
			Fluency

If you have text-based beliefs about how a person reads, you believe that reading consists largely of translating words into sounds. You believe that readers use decoding knowledge before any other knowledge sources. As a result, you will probably decide to spend much more time on the development of decoding knowledge, especially with beginning readers. And you will probably emphasize phonological awareness, phonemic awareness phonics, sight word instruction, and fluency rather than the development of context knowledge. Instruction in these areas facilitates the translation of printed words into sounds.

If you have interactive beliefs about how a person reads, you believe that readers do both; they bring their own meaning to a passage through expectations and they uncover meaning in a passage by sounding out words. As a result, you will probably spend an average amount of time on decoding instruction, about as much as you will spend developing the other knowledge sources associated with comprehension and response: vocabulary, syntactic, discourse, and metacognitive knowledge. In addition, you will probably teach all aspects of decoding knowledge: phonological awareness, phonemic awareness, context, phonics, sight words, and fluency. You do not, however, provide everyone with the same type of decoding instruction. Your insights allow you to see what individual children require in this area, and then you seek to provide it in your classroom.

TABLE 4-3

A summary of how a literacy framework can be used to inform decisions about how to teach decoding knowledge

Beliefs about How Children Learn to Read	Related Assumptions	Favored Method Frameworks and Instructional Activities
Holistic language learning	Students learn best in an inductive fashion as they direct their own learning and reading experiences. Students learn best during holistic, meaningful, and functional experiences with authentic writing and literature.	Inductive instruction Integrated sight word development into daily literacy activities. Writing used to develop phonic knowledge.
Specific skills	Students learn best when they are taught directly by the teacher in a deductive fashion. Students learn best when they master specific reading skills.	Deductive instruction A sight word learning routine to teach sight word knowledge.
Integrated	Students learn best as a result of both student-directed, inductive experiences and teacher-directed, deductive experiences. Students learn best when they engage in meaningful, functional, and holistic experiences with authentic texts and when they acquire specific reading skills.	Both inductive and deductive instruction are used. Writing experiences to develop phonic knowledge. Making words, sight word learning routine, individualized word banks, all used to develop sight word knowledge.

How Should I Teach?

To guide decisions about how to teach decoding knowledge, consider your beliefs about how children learn to read. Table 4-3 summarizes how these beliefs can be used to inform instructional decisions about which method frameworks to use.

If you have holistic language learning beliefs, you believe children learn best by directing their own reading experiences. As a result, you use inductive methods to teach phonological awareness, phonemic awareness, context knowledge, or phonic knowledge. In addition you integrate sight word development into daily classroom activities, perhaps by using individualized word banks and letting your students determine the words to enter into the banks. You also favor the use of writing experiences to develop phonic knowledge since this also allows children to direct their own learning of decoding principles.

If you have specific skills beliefs, you favor learning experiences that are deductive in nature and focus on specific skills. As a result, you use deductive methods. In general, you organize instruction around a set of specific decoding skills, which you teach directly to children.

If you have integrated beliefs, you use both deductive and inductive methods to develop decoding knowledge. You also find writing experiences and making words useful to develop phonic knowledge. To develop sight word knowledge, you use some combination of individualized word banks, making words, and a sight word learning routine. Importantly, however, you will seek to provide more teacher-directed or student-directed learning experiences as benefits individual children in your class.

Use the self-test questions on http://www.prenhall.com/leukinzer to review the material presented in this chapter.

Featured Teacher

🍎 *Mrs. Dunkerley*

To develop an understanding of how important decoding knowledge is to the first-grade curriculum, pay a visit to Mrs. Dunkerley's classroom web page (http://www.teachingfirst.net/). This classroom website from La Hambra, California, contains many examples of how decoding instruction can be accomplished in a meaningful fashion using both Internet and traditional classroom resources. If you visit the link to "Word Wall Activities" you will find an extensive list of instructional ideas that may be used with word walls for developing sight word knowledge. You should also explore the link to "Fun Learning Sites for Kids" where you will discover an exceptional collection of links to reading resources on the Internet, including many links to support your decoding program. In addition, be certain to visit the links to many other exceptional classroom websites that Mrs. Dunkerley has placed on her website. You will discover many other exceptional teachers who integrate the Internet into their first-grade classrooms. Mrs. Dunkerley's classroom page can teach each of us important lessons about effective literacy instruction.

Major Points

▶ Decoding is the process readers use to determine the oral equivalent of written words. Decoding knowledge includes phonological awareness, phonemic awareness, phonics knowledge, context knowledge, sight word knowledge, and fluency. Decoding contributes to the reading process when a word's pronunciation helps a reader determine its meaning. Decoding knowledge is especially important for beginning readers.

▶ Several instructional practices can be used to develop context knowledge: written cloze activities, oral cloze activities, and integrating cloze activities into ongoing reading instruction.

▶ Several instructional approaches are used to develop phonic knowledge: making words, writing experiences, inductive instruction, and deductive instruction.

▶ Sight word knowledge can be developed by providing extensive reading experiences, using a sight word learning routine, and using individualized word banks.

▶ It is important to consider issues of language diversity as you plan decoding instruction.

▶ Computer and Internet resources may be used to support the development of decoding knowledge.

▶ An analysis of children's developmental spellings can provide insight into the development of their decoding knowledge.

▶ A literacy framework can be used to guide decisions about the content and manner of decoding instruction. Your beliefs about how one reads can inform decisions about *what* to teach. Your beliefs about how children learn to read can inform decisions about *how* to teach.

Making Instructional Decisions

1. Consider the following list of decoding skills taught in one particular reading program. Identify the type of decoding knowledge represented by each listed skill: context knowledge, phonic knowledge, or sight word knowledge:
   a. Recognizes mastery words in isolation and in context.
   b. Decodes the appropriate sound for *f*.
   c. Uses picture context.
   d. Uses meaning and syntax to recognize words.
   e. Knows that one sound is represented by different letters.
   f. Recognizes these common words: *the, a, one, he, she, here, we, run,* and *goes*.

2. Develop a lesson to teach some aspect of context use, such as reading past a troublesome word. Use an inductive method framework, and then develop another lesson using a deductive method framework to teach that same aspect. When would you use each?

3. How important is phonics to your instructional program? What should be taught? How should it be taught? Why? As you think about these issues, consider the nature of your literacy framework, especially your beliefs about which components are most important and how you believe children learn to read.

4. Specify how you will develop sight word knowledge in your instructional program. Which methods and activities will you use? Explain how your literacy framework has informed your decisions.

5. Which miscues will you ask children to correct during oral reading: miscues that don't change the meaning or ones that do change the meaning? Why? Which decoding strategy(ies) will you support: sounding out strategies, context use strategies, or both? Why? As you think about these issues, consider the nature of your literacy framework, especially your beliefs about whether meaning is more in the text or in what students bring to the text. Can you see how your beliefs might inform these decisions?

6. Describe the literacy framework of a second-grade teacher who makes these decisions about decoding instruction:
   a. Decoding will receive far less attention than the development of vocabulary, syntactic, discourse, or metacognitive knowledge.
   b. Context knowledge will receive greater emphasis than the development of phonic or sight word knowledge.
   c. Inductive methods will be used to develop context knowledge.
   d. Sight word knowledge will be developed through writing experiences and the use of individualized word banks.

   Explain how this teacher's literacy framework has guided these instructional decisions.

Further Reading

International Reading Association (1997). The role of phonics in reading instruction: A position statement of the International Reading Association. *Reading Online* (http://www.readingonline.org/critical/phonics/full.html).

> *This statement defines the balanced stance taken by the largest organization devoted to reading instruction. A great discussion forum accompanies the statement where professionals contribute their responses to this statement.*

Lapp, D., & Flood, J. (1997). Where's the phonics? Making the case (again) for integrated code instruction. *The Reading Teacher, 50,* 696–700.

> *Describes a teacher using a balanced approach to phonics instruction in a first-grade classroom.*

Lehman, N. (November 1997). The reading wars. *The Atlantic Monthly.* (http://www.theatlantic.com/atlantic/issues/97nov/read.htm).

> *Describes the history and politics of the whole language–phonics debate in California.*

Wilson, R. M., Hall, M., Leu, D. J., Jr., & Kinzer, C. K. (2001). *Phonics, phonemic awareness, and world analysis for teachers.* Upper Saddle River, NJ: Prentice Hall.

> *An interactive tutorial for teachers.*

Stahl, S. A. (1992). Saying the "p" word: Nine guidelines for exemplary phonics instruction. *The Reading Teacher, 45,* 618–625.

> *Discusses the principles that should guide phonics instruction in the primary grades. Illustrates each principle with an episode from classroom practice.*

References

Adams, M. J. (1990). *Beginning to read: Thinking and learning about print.* Champaign, IL: Center for the Study of Reading.

Anderson, R. C., Hiebert, E. H., Scott, J. A., & Wilkinson, I. A. G. (1985). *Becoming a nation of readers: The report of the commission on reading.* Washington, DC: National Institute of Education.

Ashton-Warner, S. (1963). *Teacher.* New York: Simon & Schuster.

Burmeister, L. E. (1983). *Foundations and strategies for teaching children to read.* Reading, MA: Addison-Wesley.

Chall, J. S. (1983). *Stages of reading development.* New York: McGraw-Hill.

Cleary, B. (1968). *Ramona the pest.* New York: Scholastic Book Services.

Clymer, T. (1963). The utility of phonic generalizations in the primary grades. *The Reading Teacher, 16,* 252–258.

Cunningham, P. M. (1995). *Phonics they use: Words for reading and writing.* New York: HarperCollins.

Cunningham, P. M., Hall, D. P., & Defee, M. (1991). Nonability grouped, multilevel instruction: A year in a first-grade classroom. *The Reading Teacher, 44,* 566–571.

Dolch, E. W. (1960). *Teaching primary grade reading.* Champaign, IL: Garrard Press.

Durkin, D. (1983). *Teaching them to read* (4th ed.). Boston, MA: Allyn & Bacon.

Fry, E. (1980). The new instant word list. *The Reading Teacher, 34,* 284–289.

Harris, A. J., & Sipay, E. R. (1990). *How to increase reading ability* (9th ed.). New York: Longman Publishing Group.

Hittleman, D. R. (1988). *Developmental reading* (3rd ed.). Columbus, OH: Merrill.

Johnson, T., & Louis, D. (1987). *Literacy through literature.* Portsmouth, NH: Heinemann.

Labbo, L. D. (1996). A semiotic analysis of young children's symbol making in a classroom computer center. *Reading Research Quarterly, 31* (4), 356–387.

Lapp, D., & Flood, J. (1997). Where's the phonics? Making the case (again) for integrated code instruction. *The Reading Teacher, 50,* 696–700.

Lesiak, J. (1984). There is a need for word attack generalizations. In A. J. Harris & E. R. Sipay (Eds.), *Readings on reading instruction* (3rd ed.). New York: Longman Publishing Group.

Leu, D. J., Jr., DeGroff, L. J. C., & Simons, H. D. (1986). Predictable texts and interactive compensatory hypotheses: Evaluating differences in reading ability, context use, and comprehension. *Journal of Educational Psychology, 78,* 347–352.

Miller, L., Blackstock, J., & Miller, R. (1994). An exploratory study into the use of CD-ROM storybooks. *Computers and Education, 22,* 187–204.

Morrow, L. M., & Tracey, D. H. (1997). Strategies used for phonics instruction in early childhood classrooms. *The Reading Teacher, 50,* 644–651.

National Reading Panel (2000). *Teaching children to read.* Washington, D.C.: National Institute of Health.

Resnick, L. B., & Beck, I. L. (1984). Designing instruction in reading: Initial reading. In A. J. Harris & E. R. Sipay (Eds.), *Readings on reading instruction* (3rd ed.). New York: Longman Publishing Group.

Rey, H. A. (1952). *Curious George rides a bike.* Boston, MA: Houghton Mifflin.

Samuels, S. J., & Eisenberg, P. (1981). A framework for understanding the reading process. In F. J. Pirozzolo & M. C. Wittrock (Eds.), *Neuropsychological and cognitive processes in reading.* New York: Academic Press.

Scieszka, J. (1991). *The Frog Prince—continued.* New York: Viking.

Smith, F. (1988). *Understanding reading* (4th ed.). Hillsdale, NJ: Lawrence Erlbaum Associates.

Snow, C., Burns, M., & Griffin, P. (Eds.) (1998). *Preventing reading difficulties in young children.* Washington, DC: National Academy Press.

Stahl, S. A. (1992). Saying the "p" word: Nine guidelines for exemplary phonics instruction. *The Reading Teacher, 45,* 618–625.

Strickland, D. (1998). *Teaching phonics today.* Newark, DE: International Reading Association.

CHAPTER 5

Emergent Literacy

E-mail from the Classroom

Subject: Student Teaching: First Week Reflections
From: Jenny Chiang, jechiang@MAILBOX.SYR.EDU

The very thought of empowering one to read, write, speak, and listen is beyond incredible. My student-teaching encounter with the 5- and 6-year-olds this week was an eye-opening experience as well as a time to really reflect upon the idea of what literacy is.

The excitement of seeing the very first child in my classroom was thrilling. My duty was to make sure all of the kids had a name tag. How easy is that, right? At least, you would think so.

The first child approached with a gleaming smile, a smile that stretched beyond mountains. I greeted her with a smile I haven't felt in years and introduced myself as Ms. Chiang. Then I proceeded with the question of, "What is your name?" She responded in a shy but proud manner: "Jessica."

We walked over to the table of name tags and I asked her to find her name. After watching her for a minute or two and hearing several random guesses, I realized that she didn't know her alphabet or how to read. I soon learned that most of the children were in the same shoes as Jessica. At that very moment, I felt deeper about teaching, its importance, and my value to these children than ever before.

Jenny Chiang

After reading this chapter, you should be able to:

1. Capitalize on the literacy abilities children have when they enter school within your instructional program.
2. Use appropriate method frameworks to teach literacy to young children.
3. Use the Internet in appropriate ways to enhance your literacy instruction for young children.
4. Explain how emergent literacy perspectives differ from traditional views of reading readiness.
5. Use evaluation procedures appropriate for beginning readers.

⌨ Early Literacy and Home Experiences Are Important: A Principle of Effective Reading Instruction

One of the basic principles of effective instruction, shown in chapter 1, is reprinted below:

3. **Early literacy and home experiences are important.** Early experiences with literacy in a variety of situations and contexts are important to later reading achievement; building on students' sociocultural and linguistic backgrounds is related to reading achievement and positive reading attitudes in all students.

This principle highlights the importance of teachers being knowledgeable about the processes of literacy development, and the factors that affect literacy development—both in and out of school environments. Critical to teachers' understanding of literacy development, and thus to understanding one's literacy framework, is how to develop children's literacy in ways that are based on their strengths. In all situations, but especially in the early grades, instruction must take into account what children know and bring to the kindergarten and first-grade classroom. The strengths children bring to the classroom have been developed outside school situations, in social and linguistic environments that influence literacy development and that will affect your teaching. The strengths that children bring with them range across many areas, and appear throughout the children that you will find in your classroom. Children will have different capabilities in areas from letter name knowledge, phonemic awareness, and concepts about print, to social aspects of learning. All of these will affect your teaching and your students' learning.

Building on Children's Strengths: What Beginning Readers Already Know

Although children learn a great deal about reading and writing in school, much has already been learned before they enter kindergarten or first grade. Before formal schooling begins, children have the perceptual abilities to discriminate among different letters, words, and sounds. They are already good users of their native language and are able to understand almost all basic types of sentences, including questions, statements, and exclamations. In addition, children in the early elementary grades have highly developed speaking vocabularies. Early studies indicated that a first grader's vocabulary averaged about 2,500 words; other studies have put that estimate as high as 8,000 words (Anderson & Freebody, 1985; Dale, 1965). Teachers use all of these language-related abilities to advance their students' reading development.

However, mature readers do many things automatically that beginning readers must still discover. For example, beginning readers are developing **phonemic awareness,** including an awareness that speech is made up of separate sounds

phonemic awareness
An awareness that speech is comprised of separate sound elements and the ability to segment speech into constituent parts.

Examples of this awareness can be seen as young children repeat and make up rhyming words, as they notice and comment on the sounds or patterns of words, and as they play games that involve clapping as they say words or syllables. Beginning readers also must develop the convention that English text is read from left to right and top to bottom on a page, must be able to understand the relationships of punctuation to meaning, and are learning the concepts of "word" and "sentence." All of these are incorporated in the following general behavioral goals often targeted by reading programs for beginning readers (Durkin, 1987):

▶ To acquire an understanding of what reading and learning to read are all about.
▶ To learn to want to be a reader.
▶ To learn what is meant by "word."
▶ To understand the function of empty space in establishing word boundaries.
▶ To learn about the left-to-right, top-to-bottom orientation of written English. (pp. 110–111)

More recently, Teale and Yokota (2000, p. 7) have identified seven points that they feel should be present in effective early literacy programs:

1. An emergent literacy approach provides the foundation.
2. Comprehension instruction is a core feature.
3. A multifaceted word study program [including decoding] is essential.
4. Writing—integrated and separated—is central.
5. Reading fluency must be developed.
6. Children need to practice by reading connected text.
7. The early reading program is conceptualized as developmental.

As both lists imply, literacy programs for beginning readers do not wait for readiness to occur spontaneously in young children. Years ago, however—beginning in the early 1920s and continuing for 15 to 20 years—readiness was defined by mental age, largely because of the work of Morphett and Washburn (1931). It was thought that a child without a mental age of 6.0 to 6.5 was not ready to read and instruction would be wasted. Mental age was determined by this formula:

$$\text{Mental age} = \text{intelligence quotient (IQ)} \times \text{chronological age (CA)}/100$$

Readiness for reading gradually was viewed as something that could be developed rather than awaited; measures of mental age stopped being used as a criterion for entry into kindergarten. Today there is increasing emphasis on the idea that literacy develops continually and emerges from a child's ongoing exploration of the environment and of print—a concept known as **emergent literacy.** There is also an understanding that systematic instruction in decoding and comprehension, in meaningful contexts, is a necessary part of effective early literacy instruction. (Decoding aspects are discussed in detail in chapter 4.)

Check your ongoing understanding of chapter concepts by using the guided review for this chapter on http://www.prenhall.com/leukinzer

emergent literacy   A view that literacy develops continually through children's interaction and exploration of writing and reading.

A Brief Look at "Whole Language" Issues

"Whole language" instruction has been debated throughout the 1990s. As a teacher, you will continue to encounter discussion and questions about the impact of whole language on literacy education, and will continue to hear questions about the whole language approach. For example, some say there may be little difference between what are called whole language programs and what have been known as good teaching practices for the past two decades. Good teachers usually have incorporated writing with reading activities in meaningful contexts, often at the suggestion of basal reader programs, which McCallum (1988) cautions may be discarded prematurely. Others argue there is little difference between whole language programs and language experience approaches (LEA) if the LEA lesson is expanded to encompass more of the instructional program. Stahl and Miller (1989) are among those who have, at least to some extent, equated language experience and whole language. In addition, an increasing number of theorists believe that terminology such as emergent literacy and whole language is problematic since, in fact, all approaches hold that literacy acquisition is developmental or emergent (Bransford, 1988; Rowe, 1989; Rowe & Harste, 1990). An associated concern is the lack of consistent, comparative evidence regarding the value of whole language as opposed to that of other approaches. According to Catterson's (1989), Stahl and Miller's (1989), McKenna, Stahl, and Reinking's (1994), and McKenna, Robinson, and Miller's (1993) views of research evidence, whole language programs appear no more effective than traditional programs. Counterarguments appear in Smith (1994).

Another related area of discussion focuses on whether reading and writing should be equally stressed in kindergarten programs or whether writing should receive greater emphasis. Durkin, for example, finds "particularly troublesome the assumption that all children should do a lot of writing right away . . . what one child finds easy and meaningful and is successful with is not going to be the same for another child. . . . I think we're a little lopsided now about the way we look at some things. I think we need to be vigilant about unverified assumptions about reading and writing and the reading and writing connections" (Aaron, Chall, Durkin, Goodman, & Strickland, 1990). Strickland responded to Durkin's comments by affirming the close relationship between reading and writing but agreed that to "place undue emphasis on one or the other is probably misplaced . . . offering opportunities for both reading and writing is very different from pressuring or requiring that children engage in writing early on" (Aaron et al., 1990).

However, research and descriptions of children learning to read and write in child centered settings, both at home and in preschool and first-grade programs, support holistic and language-based, integrated approaches (for example, see DeFord, 1986; Harste, Woodward, & Burke, 1984; Holdaway, 1979; Mason, 1989; Rowe, 1994, 1998; Wells, 1986). Furthermore, these and other researchers have linked integrated language and child centered approaches to theories of learning, classroom management, and functional, communicative uses of literacy. For this reason, the literacy curriculum takes into account the close relationship between reading and writing, the importance of contextualizing learning, and the beneficial effects of social aspects of learning, while not ignoring the more skills-based and systematic components of decoding and comprehension instruction.

Understanding Emergent Literacy and the Shift from "Readiness" Perspectives

Traditional views often present reading readiness as a stage children pass through before they become readers. In effect, proponents of this view look at nonreaders as not having the required skills or abilities necessary for reading to occur. Consequently, traditional readiness programs attempt to provide activities aimed at developing those prereading skills, and often do so with deductive methods.

reading readiness Traditionally, the time when a beginning reader acquires the skills and knowledge needed for reading instruction.

Reading readiness identifies that period of time in which students acquire the specific skills and abilities that allow reading to take place. *A Dictionary of Reading and Related Terms* (Harris & Hodges, 1981) defines readiness as "preparedness to cope with a learning task" and states that readiness for learning of any type at any level is determined by a complex pattern of intellectual, motivational, maturational, and experiential factors in each individual, which may vary from time to time and from situation to situation (p. 263)—a definition consistent with *The Literacy Dictionary* (Harris & Hodges, 1995). In the past, kindergarten reading programs focused on developing readiness for reading through prereading activities, activities designed to result in later, fluent reading.

In contrast, proponents of emergent literacy believe all literacy-related activity is part of the reading and writing process. For example, scribbling is viewed as writing, especially if the child thinks it is. Children's scribbles and descriptions of pictures in a book are seen as part of an evolution toward mature reading and are not separated from "real" literacy activities. Instruction from an emergent literacy perspective usually occurs in functional situations (without segmenting or isolating skills) and is usually based on inductive strategies and **functional literacy experiences.**

functional literacy experiences Literacy tasks and activities that are meaningful, not artificial.

Some have argued that little theoretical difference exists between traditional and emergent literacy philosophies because both view children's literacy as moving from less mature to more mature forms of reading and writing (Harris & Sipay, 1990). Others disagree, citing the theoretical base of emergent literacy, which stresses the social nature of literacy acquisition (Luria, 1976; Vygotsky, 1978, 1986) and the emotional and psychological responses, included in reader-response theory, that are a part of reading and writing (Galda, 1988; Rosenblatt, 1988; Willinsky, 1988; see also Robeck & Wallace's 1990 presentation of the similarities and differences between Piaget's and Vygotsky's views). Indeed, emergent literacy views of reading development have brought into sharp focus the social, communicative nature of literacy (Rowe, 1989, 1994, 1998) and have made teachers of literacy look at the continuum of literacy activities, especially writing activities, as being meaningful and continually evolving. Nonetheless, a major difference between traditional views of reading readiness and emergent literacy perspectives is in the method frameworks (deductive versus inductive, respectively) that influence reading instruction.

Oral language evolves in clear stages, from babbling to mature speech; this has been accepted by language and educational theorists for some time. Teachers and parents

Providing opportunities to interact with print through literacy-related activities is an important part of reading development.

generally accept toddlers' halting verbalizations as attempts at communication and refer to these attempts as talking. Until recently, however, there was little formal recognition that reading and writing might also proceed through stages. Teachers and parents often were unwilling to refer to young children's scribbles as writing. Few teachers were ready to acknowledge work such as that pictured in Figures 5-1 and 5-2 (on pages 140–141) as meaningful attempts at writing.

More recently, there has been increasing evidence that even very young children participate in and initiate literacy-related play in an environment that includes adults who model, answer questions, and encourage children's curiosity about reading and writing (J. Goodman, 1990; Harste, Woodward, & Burke, 1984; Rowe, 1998; Teale & Sulzby, 1986, 1989). Such play can include writing activities that appear quite distant from what adults perceive as "real" writing, yet are part of the experimentation and growth common to all learning.

Trial and error during literacy learning are especially visible in writing, which has many subcomponents. For example, mature writing is thought to consist of legible penmanship and attention to correct grammar and spelling, straight lines of text, consistent margins and indentation of paragraphs, punctuation, and capitalization. As children experiment with writing, many or all of these items may be missing or incomplete, yet one essential component is present—the products have meaning and are intentionally created as a form of expression and literary activity (Rowe, 1994; Teale & Sulzby, 1986). In other words, even young children are not randomly scribbling; they are intentionally writing products that have clear meaning to them.

Thus, an emergent literacy perspective implies that children's experiments with language are evolving communicative acts. Figure 5-1(a) shows a letter that Lauren (age 3 years, 2 months) wrote to her grandmother. Lauren had just spent time watching her parents write a series of letters and Christmas cards. She took an envelope and

FIGURE 5-1

Sample of preschool writing products

(a)

(b)   (c)   (d)

went to her room. When she returned, she gave her parents her letter and addressed envelope, read her letter to them, and asked that it be mailed along with those her parents were writing. When asked to reread her letter about 30 minutes later, she did not deviate substantially from her earlier reading. Thus, even though adults would not be able to read Lauren's letter or addressed envelope, for her they were meaningful and had a purpose.

In the samples shown in Figure 5-1(b) and 5-1(c), Alexandra (age 2 years, 8 months) has drawn an apple tree and signed her name. The drawing in 5-1(b) preceded the finished product in 5-1(c), and when questioned, Alexandra explained she had rejected the "practice" tree in 5-1(b) for several reasons; when finally satisfied, she signed her name. The sample in Figure 5-1(d) also shows **intentionality.**

intentionality The purposefulness of an activity, in contrast to random behavior or accidentally occurring responses that might be appropriate.

Alexandra had stated that she was going to practice making a list using As, Os, and Ps; although the letters are by no means perfectly formed, it is easy to see that she is practicing these letters and that her completed list fulfills her goal.

Figure 5-2 shows other examples of children's written work. The sample in Figure 5-2(a) shows a shopping list (student age 2 years, 6 months), whereas 5-2(b) and 5-2(c) show two kindergartners' correspondence with each other. Even though they could not read their friend's note, they read their own notes to each other and happily kept their friend's note. All these examples demonstrate that children express meaning in their written work, regardless of how unpolished it might seem to an adult. Clearly, these children have conceptualized and used certain literacy **conventions:** Lauren's letter and en-

convention A common way language is used by a particular group of people.

FIGURE 5-2

Samples of emergent writing and invented spelling: (a) a preschooler's shopping list, (b) a kindergartner's note to a classmate ("I got a haircut"), and (c) the classmate's response ("I hope you had a good time—I hope I can come") [in response to an earlier question about a sleep-over.]

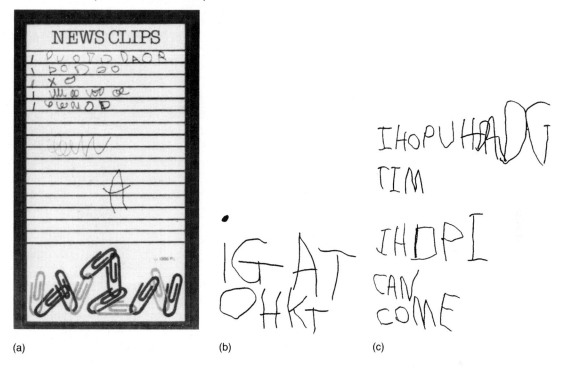

(a)   (b)   (c)

velope in Figure 5-1(a) are in correct form (the envelope even has a stamp on it), the signature with the apple tree is in a suitable location, the shopping list is in list form, and so on. Such conventions will be refined through further practice.

Instructional Implications

The concept of emergent literacy has resulted in an instructional approach often called language-based, child centered, holistic, or **whole language.** In general, these terms encompass is a view that instruction is based on all aspects of language (speaking, listening, reading, and writing) and imply that literacy instruction is integrated across language processes—that instruction does not break language learning into isolated skill components. Instead, learning occurs in the context of meaningful literacy activities. For example, reading and writing skills often are taught within the context of complete stories. Thus, children's literature plays a large part in reading instruction in language-based settings; traditional published reading programs, which are viewed as fragmenting skills, are de-emphasized. However, as discussed in chapter 2, the recent emphasis on child centered instruction has resulted in published reading programs that incorporate children's literature, involve fewer worksheets and less teaching of isolated skills, incorporate children's oral language abilities, and emphasize the shared reading model (Hoffman et al., 1994).

> **whole language** The philosophy that all literacy and language processes interact and thus can be used to reinforce each other.

The following list encompasses aspects of programs supportive of children's developing literacy:

1. Children should be allowed to control the focus and sequence of their literacy learning. This ensures that they are participating in activities they see as linked to their existing concepts about literacy.
2. Activities should be open-ended. Variation in learning outcomes should be expected.

Celebrating Diversity

Enhancing Literacy Activities through Children's Diverse Backgrounds

Consider how children's diverse backgrounds, abilities, interests, and cultures can enhance meaningful literacy activities. For example, if your class is creating books or big books, encourage children from diverse backgrounds to make books that will let others learn about their language, backgrounds, and interests. (Internet sites such as **How a Book Is Made** at http://www.harperchildrens.com/index.htm provide helpful information that can enhance children's interest in bookmaking and writing activities; see Figure 5-3.)

Consider also that "meaningful" literacy activities may differ for students, depending on their interests and on the value their particular cultural group places on specific activities. Also, children whose literacy abilities are less developed may view some activities as less meaningful or important than readers with more highly developed literacy abilities. That is, sending a letter to a children's literature author might be meaningful and motivating to some children, but sending a reminder note to a family member might be more relevant to many other readers or writers.

3. Children should be encouraged to form and test their own hypotheses about literacy, rather than to master performed generalizations presented by the teacher.
4. Children should have opportunities to explore their hypotheses in many different types of literacy events over a long period of time.
5. Children should be encouraged to present their newest ideas and to push beyond what they currently know to explore new ways of using literacy.
6. Rough draft thinking and communication should be valued.
7. Teachers should be familiar with children's current interests and hypotheses so they can present invitations and demonstrations related to that learning. (Rowe, 1994, p. 203)

All of the literacy-related activities in student-centered classrooms are intended to be relevant and meaning-based. Such activities need not always be shared, however. For example, a child might want to write a very private fantasy story that would not be shared even with friends or parents. The writing activity for this child would be meaningful and motivational even without sharing. However, literacy activities certainly can be shared—in general, children want to do so. Writing activities especially might lead to student conferences in which student writers share their "work in progress" with other children, eliciting comments, reactions, and suggestions from friendly but knowledgeable readers (Calkins, 1983; Graves, 1983). The resulting dialogue between writers and readers can lead to significant insights for each about both reading and writing. Meaningful activities can also be teacher-assigned tasks that are purposeful rather than purely artificial. For instance, if students are dictating a letter the teacher transcribes, the letter should be delivered or mailed to a real person and the response shared and posted. In this way, children learn that writing is purposeful, and the motivation for both writing and reading remains high.

The concept of emergent literacy also implies that children's written products are communicative acts in a state of evolution. Thus, children's written work should be considered meaningful and should be encouraged, shared, and highlighted. Teachers in student-centered classrooms encourage children to ask questions as they work and to elaborate orally on what they are attempting to convey through their writing. According to an emergent literacy view, teachers should be tolerant of variations in form as children write and read their work. Nonstandard handwriting, spacing, margins, letter formation, and spelling are considered parts of the developmental process. Through teacher model-

FIGURE 5-3

A sample page from HarperCollins' site, **How a Book Is Made** (http://www.harperchildrens. com/hch/picture/features/aliki/howabook/book1.asp)

Note: Reprinted by permission of HarperCollins.

ing, instruction, and ongoing attempts by the child, such variations will continue to more closely approximate traditional forms until the correct form appears. In short, variations in form are treated as normal stages of learning; and as in all learning, mistakes are made along the way toward expertise. Figure 5-4 shows some of the **invented spellings** children use as their writing evolves.

Many of the method frameworks implied by an emergent literacy perspective are immediately apparent in a child-centered environment. Classroom walls are often covered with children's writing and illustrations, and children in a class often have their own bulletin board. Children are busy with literacy-related play and reading/writing activities, including the revision of previous work. In addition, the classroom probably has many things conducive to reading and writing in plain view and in use by the children: mobiles, reading corners, writing corners, and, in particular, much print everywhere—on the walls, in books on bookshelves, in magazines on tables, and in the artwork area. Drawings that have been posted on Internet sites such as **Kids' Corner** (http://kids.ot.com/; see Figure 5-5) should also be posted in the classroom.

invented spellings
Children's spellings that are meaningful to them but are inconsistent with the spellings accepted as correct by mature readers and writers.

FIGURE 5-4

Sample of two first-graders' writing products. These pieces of writing demonstrate the invented spellings present in many beginning readers' and writers' products.

(a) Little Kitten, by Alexa. She was a tabby gray and her name was Shea, and she slept by the fire. And my name is Alexa. My kitten is not full grown and I love my kitten and I got her for my birthday. My and she is fluffy and I do not have to share [her] with my family, and my kitten has white spots.

(b) I had great fun roller skating because it was my party. We had pizza for lunch and then we had cake and then we opened up the presents.

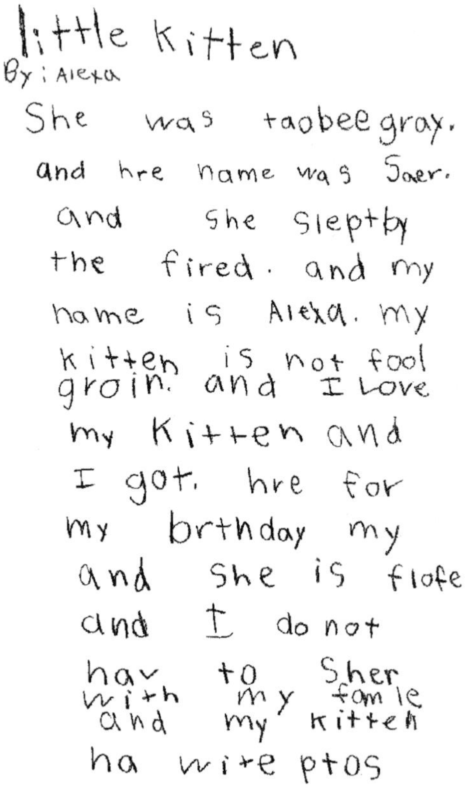

little Kitten
By: Alexa
She   was   taobee gray.
and   hre   name was Saer.
and   She Sleptby
the   fired. and my
name is Alexa. my
kitten is not fool
groin. and I Love
my Kitten and
I got. hre for
my   brthday my
and   She is flofe
and   I do not
hav   to   Sher
with   my   famle
and   my   kitten
ha wire ptos

(a)

I had   gaet fun   rooler skating
bekus   It was   my paerty
we   had pizza for luche
and   then we had cake and
then   we open up the presen.

(b)

Method Frameworks for Use with Beginning Readers and Writers

Although the activities throughout this book can be modified for use with beginning readers and writers, the activities in this section are especially appropriate for kindergarten classrooms that focus on meaningful literacy activities.

The Language Experience Approach.   Many individuals have demonstrated the power of oral language and personal experiences in helping children learn to read (for example, Allen & Allen, 1976; Ashton-Warner, 1963, 1972; Nessel & Jones, 1981; Stauffer, 1980). The generic term **language experience approach (LEA)** represents those efforts to teach reading that use children's language and experiences as a base.

language experience approach (LEA)   A method framework for teaching reading based on children's language and experiences.

At beginning levels the language experience approach uses transcriptions of children's oral language to help them learn about reading. The most common language experience activity at this level is an experience story, as detailed in chapter 3. A language experience story begins with a memorable experience that you would elicit a description of, or story about, from the experience of the children. You then transcribe each child's contribution on paper, a chalkboard, or a computer. When the story is completed, it may be used to teach a variety of reading-related concepts.

With beginning readers, you might simply read back the language experience story, moving a hand under each word as it is read. You might also comment about frequently

FIGURE 5-5

The home page for **Kids' Corner** (http://kids.ot.com:80/)

Note: Courtesy of Oasis Telecommunications.

occurring words or point out the left-to-right progression of the words. Another approach is to read a portion of the story and then stop before a predictable word and ask a child to read the word. Later on, a letter-sound pattern might be pointed out. Saving language experience stories over a period of time will allow you and your students to revisit, reread, and possibly extend these enjoyable accounts of memorable experiences. An experience story is not the only language experience activity that can be used at beginning levels. Other examples are listed on the following page.

The Morning Message.   A favorite technique that uses literacy in a meaningful way is the morning message (for example, see Kawakami-Arakaki, Oshiro, & Farran, 1989). This is typically the first instructional activity of the school day and comes right after attendance is taken. In this activity, the children watch as you write the date and several short messages or announcements pertaining to the day's activities on the chalkboard or on chart paper. At the beginning of the school year, the messages are relatively short, increasing in length as the year goes on.

The morning message on page 147 is often part of a daily **community meeting,** where the entire class comes together, usually in the morning. Announcements are

community meeting
A gathering of all participants in a class (teachers, students, aides, parents, and others) to discuss upcoming events or to share general thoughts and information.

MODEL LESSON

A Language Experience Story in Margie Platt's Class

Margie has reader-based beliefs that influence her decisions about *what* to teach. Because reader-based beliefs imply that meaning is greatly influenced by what readers bring to a text, Margie often uses a language experience approach (LEA) in her kindergarten classroom. This allows her children to use their own knowledge and experiences as a basis for a story. Margie also has integrated beliefs about *how* to teach. Thus, she uses student-directed and teacher-directed experiences and inductive and deductive method frameworks. The LEA allows her to encourage her children to present their ideas, which she then uses as a basis for instruction. Here is an example of an LEA in Margie's classroom:

Margie: Boys and girls, let's write a story about our field trip today. We can use it to practice our reading, and then we can put it in the hall to tell the rest of the school where we went and what we did. What do you think we should call our story? What about a title?

Jaime: I know. Let's call it "Apples, Apples, Everywhere!"

Margie: [Writing.] Good, Jaime. I like that. Look at these capital letters. Titles always have capitals at the beginning of each word. Now, how shall we start our story?

Maggie: I want to start: We had a special day. We had an apple day.

Margie: [Writing.] Good. Now what shall we say?

Tom: We went to Beak and Skiff Apple Farm. [Margie writes.]

Pam: And we got to ride on the tractor. [Margie writes.]

Katie: We got to pick apples. [Margie writes.]

Jason: And we got to eat apples. [Margie writes.]

Sarah: And Tom got his shoes wet. [Margie writes.]

Kerrie: We saw bees. [Margie writes.]

Del: When we got back, we were tired, and we got ready to go home. [Margie writes.]

Margie explains to the students that they can sometimes use other words to help them read. She reads the first two sentences, stopping at the last word.

We had a special day. We had an apple _____.

Margie lets the students read the last word together. Then she gives them a chance to practice using context as she reads each sentence and lets the students supply the last word. Sometimes the children say an entire sentence along with her or "read" a sentence on their own, especially if it is the sentence that they contributed to the story. At the end Margie restates the generalization about context use.

Margie then has each student draw a picture of the trip. As she walks around the room, she helps some students copy words or a short sentence from the experience story to serve as a caption for their picture. With other students Margie transcribes their dictated sentences or words on the bottom of their pictures. Finally, she places the experience story on the bulletin board in the hall and surrounds it with the students' pictures.

made by both the teacher and the children, show-and-tell activities take place, a new book in the classroom library might be discussed, decisions are made about ordering more paper or other materials for the writing center, and so on. The community meeting is a time when students can share and help make decisions and when you can focus on the significant, everyday literacy activities required to keep the classroom organized.

The Shared Book Experience.   The shared book experience (Holdaway, 1979; Slaughter, 1993) has its roots in the bedtime story, where parents and children share a literacy activity in a supportive, secure, and pleasant way. In schools, the book used by individual

---

MODEL LESSON

The Morning Message in Warren Titus's Class

Warren Titus has text-based beliefs about *what* to teach and holistic language learning beliefs about *how* to teach. His text-based beliefs (which imply that meaning resides in a text) lead him to use this morning message activity to develop punctuation and capitalization knowledge. His holistic beliefs (which emphasize inductive learning and student-directed activities) lead him to encourage children to notice what *they* want to discuss in the message and to use learner-directed activities based on the morning discussion. Here is a summary of one morning message activity in Warren's classroom.

Write a Message to the Class. After taking attendance, Warren writes the following message on chart paper, reading each word as he writes it:

November 4

Today is Thursday. Mr. Paolo will be here at storytime. He will tell us a story about Brazil.

You can take your art projects home today!

Read the Message to the Class. After the message is complete, Warren reads it to the class. The children are encouraged to read along if they are able. Warren runs his hand under the words as he reads them. Then the whole message is read in chorus. He notices that most of the children are able to repeat it from memory at this point.

Discuss the Form and Content of the Message. Warren asks whether the children notice anything interesting about the written message itself. Tom says that the first letter is the same as the first letter of his name. Janie notices the exclamation mark and says that the message doesn't end "in a dot." Warren uses this input to draw the parallel between Tom, Today, and Thursday. He explains that these words begin with capital Ts and points out the lowercase Ts in *storytime*. Then he explains why he used an exclamation mark instead of a period (the artwork is so good that he's excited about letting them take it home). Finally, the message itself is discussed. Mr. Paolo heard some interesting folktales while he was in Brazil recently and he is coming to share those stories with the class. Warren tells the children they will be able to choose activities that will allow them to listen to other folktales, or to tell their own, after Mr. Paolo's visit.

---

parents with their children is usually replaced with a big book, discussed below, but the shared book experience still provides a model of reading and includes discussion in a nonthreatening and supportive way.

In kindergarten classrooms, many reading activities center around big books, which usually reproduce in large format (sometimes as large as chart paper pads) children's literature selections. Big books are colorful, motivational, and are found in traditional readiness programs as well. Even though big books are complete stories and are longer than language experience stories, you read them to your students in much the same way you read language experience stories—running your hand under the print as you read, commenting on a particular word, or asking children to read a word or phrase. Big books are available from most educational publishers but can also be created by a teacher and students. To create a big book, write down on chart paper what children dictate (perhaps suggesting story lines the children can refine). Then have the children draw illustrations that can be inserted into the book, create a cover and copyright page, and use a hole punch and twine to bind all the pages together.

In the shared book experience, children are encouraged to read along and to predict words or events as the story is read (this works especially well with repetitive texts). The model lesson on page 150 provides an example of a shared book experience with a **big book.**

big books Children's literature selections reproduced in large format.

Journal and Process Writing. As noted earlier and throughout this text, there is a close relationship between reading and writing; beginning readers must be provided opportunities to do both. Partly for this reason, the physical classroom environment noted in

PRACTICAL TEACHING STRATEGIES

Developing Print-Vocabulary through Language Experiences

Student Name Cards. Make name labels for all the children in your class. Allow them to place the labels on their desks on the first day of school.

Labeling. Have children give the names of important items in the classroom and watch you as you make labels for those objects. A similar activity is having children suggest labels for magazine pictures. Have them watch as you make the labels. Post the pictures and labels around the classroom or on a bulletin board.

Word Walk. Take the children on a walk around the playground or around the block. Talk about what is around them. Later, make up word cards about some of the things they saw. Use the word cards as triggers for oral language. Let children randomly pick a card, think of the walk, and talk about the specific word on the card. Be ready to read the card for some children.

Internet Experience. Let children explore sites such as **Kids Zone** from the National Wildlife Federation (http://www.nwf.org/kids/; see Figure 5-6). There they will find games, puzzles, *Ranger Rick* samples, and pictures and descriptions of animals. If they take the tour, or even if they only do one of the activities, they will encounter words and pictures and can later use their experiences in an LEA activity, dictating to you their activities and feelings. As is true for several sites, an option for using a Spanish language version is available.

Art-Based Stories. When children come to school in the fall (or after winter vacation), have them draw a picture of an exciting summer (or winter) experience. Circulate and ask children to dictate a sentence or two about their pictures. Write their sentences on their pictures, ask them to read their sentences, and then bind the art stories into a book for the reading center.

Class Diary. Keep a regular class diary, making entries each day. Include photos of class activities wherever you can. Keep the diary in the reading center for children to read and remember class events. A class diary can also be compiled and updated using a computer and word processing software and can be reprinted on a regular basis.

Helper Chart. Construct helper charts with movable name tags. Rotate the names regularly.

Dictated Letter Writing. Write class-dictated letters to authors of books you have read to your children.

Shared experiences are often the basis for a later, language experience story.

FIGURE 5-6

A sample page from *Ranger Rick's* **Kids Zone,** a website from the National Wildlife Federation (http://www.nwf.org/kids/)

Note: Courtesy of National Wildlife Federation.

Figure 5-7 on page 151 includes space for a designated writing center. Each day, students should be given many opportunities to write new material and to extend what they have previously written.

Writing on a daily basis is often accomplished through journal writing. The journals should be kept in a designated area where children can have access to them at any time. Creating covers for journals is a motivational activity that personalizes and provides a sense of ownership. Usually, 5 to 15 minutes each morning (often after the community meeting or morning message) are set aside for journaling. During this time, children can write on a topic of their own choosing or respond to a topic suggested by the teacher. They might write to extend something from the previous day's journal page or move to a new subject. In any case, this time should be used for writing by all participants in the class, including the teacher and any visitors.

MODEL LESSON

A Shared Book Experience (Using a Big Book) in Nanci Clark's Classroom

Nanci Clark has reader-based beliefs about *what* to teach and holistic language learning beliefs about *how* to teach. Her reader-based beliefs guide her to activities that allow children to predict, set expectations, and link what is read to children's prior knowledge. Her holistic language learning beliefs lead her to find opportunities for students to direct their learning—in the following case, by choosing the book to be read.

Choose a Big Book. Nanci usually allows the children to choose the book from those available in her classroom. This might be a book that has been read before and that the children have enjoyed but have not tired of, a new book that relates to a theme of interest to the class, or a book on display in her classroom that has captured the attention of one or more children.

Introduce the Story. Nanci often discusses the theme of the book by allowing students to predict what might be in the story after she reads the title or as part of a discussion about the cover illustration. If the book has been read previously, she asks a few questions that allow the children to remind each other about what the book is about or has several children tell which episode in the story is their favorite. During this discussion, Nanci talks about and writes down on chart paper specific words that will (or might) be found in the story as it is read. During the discussion, she always makes sure to credit the author and illustrator of the big book.

Read the Book. With the children sitting comfortably around her, Nanci holds the big book (or places it on a stand) so that the children can easily see the words and illustrations. She runs her hand under the words and phrases as they are being read, stopping occasionally to state what she is thinking as she reads or to comment on particular aspects of the story. Nanci asks several children to predict upcoming story episodes and to read along at appropriate points of the story. She tries hard to ensure that the reading experience is enjoyable, that the story remains meaningful, and that it is not too broken up with tangential discussions.

Discuss the Story. After reading, Nanci and the children talk about the story. First, Nanci models her approach to thinking about what was read, providing appropriate reasons for her opinions. Then she asks the children what they thought about the story and branches out into how they felt about the characters and their actions. Nanci ties in the children's backgrounds by asking if they have experienced things similar to what went on in the story. As appropriate, she goes back to certain words to point out interesting vocabulary and how certain words have similar spelling patterns. Nanci usually ends by asking if the story reminds the children of any other book that they have read before and whether they would like to read the book again.

Initially, the children's writing will consist of drawings and/or a few letters. Later, the writing will include more letters, eventually clustered together in groups. Still later, more recognizable words with invented spellings will appear. All of these forms are meaningful and should be supported, as should copying, if children wish to do so. Often, especially for beginning readers and writers, illustrations predominate in their journals. The illustrations can serve as wonderful discussion starters during sharing times throughout the day, but children should have the option to keep their journals private if they wish to do so.

Journal writing and free writing of all types are especially common in programs with emergent literacy perspectives. However, many teachers also use what has been called **process writing,** which includes prewriting, drafting, revising, editing, and sharing. These stages are applicable both to writers in kindergarten and to more mature writers. The products look different, but the process for kindergartners as well as adult writers moves through the steps noted above. In particular, you will have to be especially supportive during the drafting, revising, and editing stages. Young writers should know they can revisit earlier work—a piece of writing is never truly "finished."

Writing should begin when children first arrive in the kindergarten classroom and should be modeled early and often. Modeling can include how a topic is chosen and can precede each of the steps in the writing process. Choose one of the steps (perhaps

process writing When focusing on writing, teaching that addresses stages of prewriting, drafting, revising, editing, and sharing as part of the writing episode.

FIGURE 5-7

Drawing of a typical kindergarten classroom

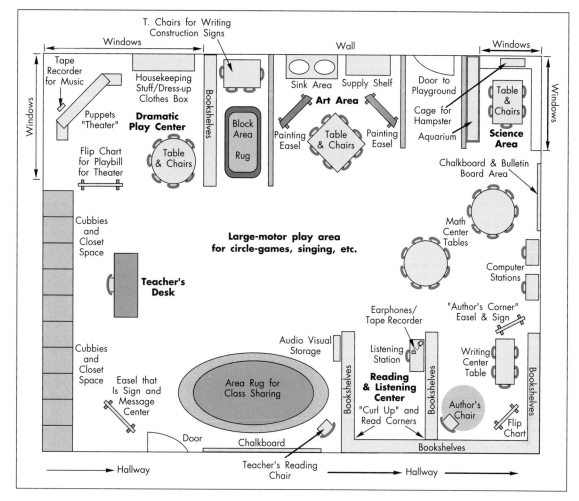

drafting or editing) and show how you work through this step. Model the process on chart paper, talking through your thoughts as you write. Show the children that writing is valuable to an author, even if others cannot read everything on the page. That is, writing is still writing, even if the children can't read it! But do encourage each author, especially during sharing time, to share and read what was written to the rest of the group or to the whole class. Then allow time for constructive discussion about the writing, as well as time for authors to edit their work. Many different writing activities can be used to create excitement in the kindergarten classroom. Several of these are listed in Table 5-1.

Broader Applications. Even though emergent literacy/readiness concepts are most often applied to beginning readers, they can also relate to proficient readers. For example, even mature readers are apt to have difficulty understanding the following passage:

> Comprehensive allocation is more consistent with the accounting for liabilities than roll over, such as accounts payable. New accounts payable continually replace accounts being paid, much the same as originating timing differences replace timing differences that reverse. Each creditor's account is accounted for separately, even though aggregate accounts payable continue to roll over. Consistency requires that timing differences related to a particular asset or liability likewise be accounted for separately. (Davidson, Stickney, & Weil, 1980, pp. 20–26)

TABLE 5-1

Examples of types and categories of writing

advertisements	labels
agendas	letters
announcements	lists
banners	maps
books	menus
bumper stickers	messages
captions	notes
cards	poems
cartoons	postcards
CD covers/song titles	posters
certificates	questions
coupons	reminders
descriptions	requests
diaries	riddles
directions	rules
envelopes	signs
fact sheets	stories
fortune cookie inserts	telegrams
invitations	tickets
jokes	websites

How well did you comprehend the concepts in the above passage? Try to answer the following questions:

1. Why is comprehensive allocation more consistent with liabilities than roll over?
2. What is the concept of timing differences and what is their importance to accounts payable?
3. What is the paragraph about? Explain it in your own words.

You are a fluent reader, yet you may not be "ready" to read such a passage from an accounting text (an accountant would have had no difficulty with it). You could probably have used some prereading activities—perhaps targeting background knowledge, definitions of new vocabulary, and maybe discussion of overall meaning. The point is that emergent literacy/readiness does not stop with the acquisition of decoding knowledge. A broader view acknowledges that we all may encounter text we are unprepared to read, given our current level of knowledge.

Internet Method Frameworks.   We often hear comments implying that computers and the Internet are most appropriate for children above third grade. This is a misconception, however, because all of the method frameworks discussed in chapter 2 (Internet Workshop, Internet Inquiry, and Internet Project) can be used in kindergarten classrooms. Some researchers (e.g., *Education Week on the Web*, 1997) advocate exposing children as young as age 3 to computers, using much the same reasoning used by those who support emergent literacy perspectives. All of the aspects that support children's developing literacy, as shown on pages 141 and 142, can be applied to uses of the Internet. Table 5-2 presents that list again, with comments showing how the Internet can facilitate each aspect.

In the rest of this section, we provide some specific Internet sites and suggestions for using them with young children. The sites we list represent what is available—they are not intended to be comprehensive lists. Publications such as Leu & Leu (2000) contain many sites appropriate for elementary-age and kindergarten children. We recommend you consult such resources as you integrate technology and the Internet into your literacy instruction. Also, software packages such as *Storybook Weaver* and *Kidpix* are moti-

TABLE 5-2

Internet features that support children's developing literacy

Aspects of Programs Supportive of Children's Developing Literacy (Rowe, 1994)	Internet Applications
1. Children should be allowed to control the focus and sequence of their literacy learning. This ensures they are participating in activities they see as linked to their existing concepts about literacy.	The Internet allows young children to explore a range of activities, from coloring to sequencing to learning the alphabet to acquiring background knowledge.
2. Activities should be open-ended. Variation in learning outcomes should be expected.	The Internet is an open-ended resource where each child can move in different paths and directions. Variation is the norm as Internet users rarely take identical paths during a session—even if they begin at the same site.
3. Children should be encouraged to form and test their own hypotheses about literacy rather than to master performed generalizations presented by the teacher.	As young children move to different Internet sites and explore different resources and activities related to literacy, they can test hypotheses and, in interactive sites, see the outcomes of their hypotheses.
4. Children should have opportunities to explore their hypotheses in many different types of literacy events over a long period of time.	The Internet provides multiple sites and multiple resources within a given topic area. Children are not limited to one way of playing alphabet games or playing games to learn animal names. The rich variety of activities within and across topics allows hypothetically unlimited time periods to be spent in given domains.
5. Children should be encouraged to present their newest ideas and to push beyond what they currently know to explore new ways of using literacy.	The Internet allows children to post their ideas in writing, through artwork, or through audio clips and to receive feedback on those ideas. Using multimedia capabilities, literacy is being redefined in new ways.
6. Rough draft thinking and communication should be valued.	The Internet is a wonderful way to post formative thoughts and ideas for feedback. Communication through listservs, bulletin boards, and e-mail is available to users of all ages.
7. Teachers should be familiar with children's current interests and hypotheses so they can present invitations and demonstrations related to that learning.	The Internet provides many resources specifically for teachers. It is easy to find Internet sites related to children's interests.

vating, easy to use, and appropriate for use by young readers to create and publish stories and artwork. Software and CD-ROM books are discussed in chapter 14.

Internet Workshop assignments for young children can be based around the following representative sites:

Carlos' Coloring Book (http://www.coloring.com/pictures/choose.cdc) and **TV Ontario Coloring Book** (http://www.tvo.org/cb_eng/). Coloring books are often used in kindergarten classrooms because they are motivational and allow children to work with books. Often coloring books are used as story starters and to stimulate discussion around the pictures. Internet sites such as these provide both interactive, on-line pictures to color as well as pictures that can be printed and colored later. Pictures change regularly and such sites provide a cost-effective way to find pictures and to introduce young children to the Internet in a meaningful way (see Figure 5-8).

FIGURE 5-8

Sample screen from **Carlos' Coloring Book** (http://www.coloring.com/pictures/choose.cdc)

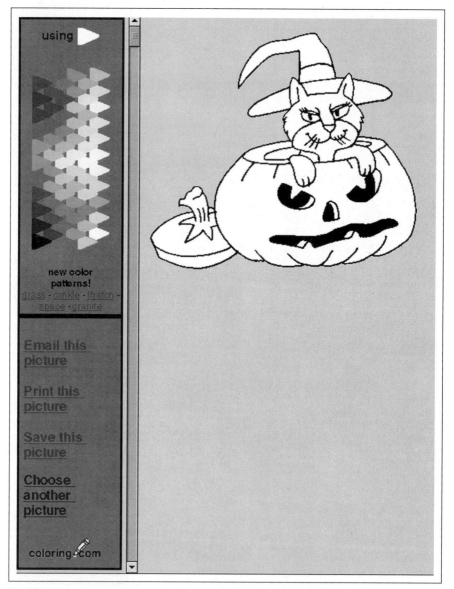

Note: Courtesy of Ravenna Communications Corporation.

Alex's Scribbles—Koala Trouble (http://www.scribbles.com.au/). This site contains a collection of illustrated stories about a koala bear, written by Alex Balsom (at age 5) and his dad. The stories include hyperlinks within the illustrations. This is a wonderful way to introduce stories from a peer, to discuss Australia and koala bears, and to provide a springboard for your students to write their own stories about animals.

Hangman at Kids Corner (http://kids.ot.com/hangman). This site provides practice with words and decoding through an on-line "hangman" game. The size of the letters and the words to solve are appropriate and motivating for young children (see Figure 5-9).

Internet Project activities are available to you and your students through sites such as The **Mind's Eye Monster Exchange Project** (http://www.monsterexchange.org/, see also http://www.csnet.net/mindseye/mindseye.htm). Children draw pictures of mon-

FIGURE 5-9

Sample screen from **Hangman at Kids Corner** (http://kids.ot.com:80/cgi/kids/hangman?)

Note: Courtesy of Oasis Telecommunications.

sters and write descriptions to go with their drawings. Paired classes of students trade descriptions and then try to draw pictures, based on the descriptions, of what the other class's monsters look like. When completed, all images of the monsters are posted to the Monster Exchange site so that children can see the original drawings, the descriptions, and their own drawings based on the descriptions. Lesson plans and resources for teachers are also listed there. Other sites where you may locate Internet Projects include **The Global Schoolhouse's Internet Projects Registry** (http://www.gsn.org/pr/) and **KIDPROJ** (http://www.kidlink.org/KIDPROJ/).

Internet Inquiry projects, as discussed in chapter 2, involve independent exploration of the Internet. This might be less desirable, due to child safety and logistical issues, for children in kindergarten classes. However, Internet Inquiry projects can certainly be done with the help of a parent aide or with small groups of children with a teacher. Using search engines such as **Yahooligans** or going through sites such as **Berits Best Sites for Children** (http://www.cochran.com/theosite/Ksites.html), where sites are prescreened, offers one way to conduct a modified Internet Inquiry. Internet Workshop, where children share their experiences and search strategies, can occur around the Internet Workshop, Internet Project, and Internet Inquiry activities described above.

FIGURE 5-10

The home page for Earlychildhood.com (http://www.earlychildhood.com/)

Note: Courtesy of Earlychildhood.com.

You should also know that numerous professional resources are available that can help you to teach young children. A quick search using the key words "early childhood education" returns an extensive list of sites: those operated by the federal government, special interest groups, and publishers of children's books. One useful resource site is **Earlychildhood.com** (http://www.earlychildhood.com/), which provides useful links, resources, and articles on a wide variety of topics intended for educators as well as parents (see Figure 5-10).

Creating Supportive Literacy Environments

Teachers begin to make instructional decisions well before their students arrive at school. One of the first decisions you will have to make is how to set up your classroom so that literacy learning will occur in supportive, meaningful environments. Creating a learning environment that will facilitate your students' emerging literacy processes has to do with organizing materials and physical room layout to support the desired activities and instruction. The room arrangement is important because it can facilitate or de-emphasize social interaction and exploration of literacy by children.

A Typical Kindergarten Classroom

Although teachers are always constrained by the physical space provided to them, there are some common features of kindergarten classrooms that facilitate literacy learning. For example, it seems intuitive that young children need room to move, explore, and

E-mail from the Classroom

 Subject: Computer Lab Activities for My Young Children
From: Lauren Mellone, Lauren.Mellone @FM.CNYRIC.ORG

Hello everyone!

I took an in-service this week on creating templates for instruction. The in-service was called Tool Software. It was wonderful, and I left with many ideas for how to use it with my kindergarten children.

I have a half day program, and I am often frustrated with trying to fit everything in. We have computers on Fridays and, most of the time, there isn't any software that correlates with my weekly theme. Now that I have taken the in-service, I am able to create templates that will teach computer skills and also continue my theme into the computer lab.

For example, this week my class is studying Native Americans. We have been learning the Native American symbols and writing messages to each other. They love it! For computers this week, I created a template that will allow them to click on Native American symbols and drag them to the bottom of the screen to create messages! I drew the pictures in the painting and then pasted them on the drawing program in Clarisworks. The computer teacher put a copy of it on each child's shared folder so they will each be able to do the activity! This was so beneficial to me because my kindergarten program is based on a theme, even in the computer lab, and I feel like it helps put my computer time to better use.

Lauren

play; desks that are fixed in rows would be inappropriate. Also, the kindergarten curriculum includes art, music, and other aspects that can be incorporated into literacy development, assuming that the room is structured in a way that allows this to occur.

Figure 5-7 on page 151 shows a room layout fairly typical of a kindergarten classroom. As you see, the room is divided into areas that serve as a holding space for materials needed for specific activities. The art area is where art supplies are kept and where tables and work areas allow children to explore and be messy while painting, working with clay, making collages, using glue, and so on. Similarly, the room has centers for science and mathematics, where materials and work space are allocated to facilitate these activities. In addition, there are areas where the whole class can come together, where the teacher can read to the class, and where show-and-tell and other sharing activities can easily occur. The dramatic play area includes space for dress-up clothes and props. The reading and listening center has been placed next to the author's corner. These areas include tape recorders and tapes to be used for listening activities with headphones; chart paper on a stand; lots of writing materials (paper, pencils, markers, crayons); and many, many books. Books and other reading materials might include wordless picture books, caption books, big books, minibooks, predictable-text books, magazines, brochures, reference books, tactile books, pocket-chart stories, flannel boards, and so on. Computer stations are close to the author's corner so that software to illustrate stories and simple word-processing programs can be used by students if they wish.

Missing from the drawing in Figure 5-7 are the touches that make the room feel cozy and inviting. For example, most kindergarten rooms have a rug, overstuffed pillows, and an armchair where students can read. A rocking chair is often seen in kindergarten classrooms—one large enough for you to sit with a child and read together. Stuffed animals, donated by parents or older students, often provide a warm feeling, as do appropriate bulletin boards, good use of color, and personalizing touches such as photographs of each student (and perhaps pictures of their pets) in the class. Of course, a major part of the kindergarten room will include books and reading material of all types. Keep in mind that the room is there for the children—they should feel that it is their room. The

Rugs, author's chairs, and other cozy touches help to make children feel special and at home in a kindergarten literacy environment.

TABLE 5-3

Sample daily time plan

8:00	Morning sign-in (perhaps a snack, if needed)
8:15	Circle/community meeting time (whole group activities, sharing, daily calendar, morning message)
8:35	"Center" time (art area, computer area, dramatic/creative play area, science area, math area, writing/author's area, reading/listening area)
10:45	Music/singing/story time (large group)
11:15	Lunch
11:45	Outdoor/indoor active play
12:15	Journal writing/silent reading time
12:45	Nap/rest time
1:00	"Center" time (as above, but includes time for sharing/reporting to others or to the whole group, as needed)
2:30 or 3:00	Home

environment should not make them feel like visitors. Also keep in mind that young children will not be able to see things on walls if items are too high. Post important things close to children's eye level. When setting up your room, look for items that will impart a cozy, supportive feeling.

Also important, of course, is the general organization of the day (a typical daily structure for a kindergarten room is shown in Table 5-3). However, many school districts provide instruction on a "half day" basis; others require teachers to provide more time for rest periods. The decision about specific time allotments will depend, in some sense, on your particular school district and the needs of your students. Although the activities and time breakdown in the table are consistent with many programs, you may want to vary the order of the items. For example, journal writing might occur in the morning rather than after lunch.

▣ Factors Affecting Emergent Literacy/Reading Readiness

A number of factors interact to affect literacy development. Some, such as cognitive factors, are thought of as *internal* to the reader; others, such as home environment, are thought of as *external* factors. All, however, influence prereaders and continue to influence their reading throughout life. These interacting factors are presented separately here for ease of discussion.

Cognitive Factors

Psychologists Jean Piaget and Lev Vygotsky have been instrumental in shaping educators' views about the relationship between thought and language. While Vygotsky has enjoyed a greater influence more recently, Piaget's work indicated that all human beings have the capability of progressing through four levels of **cognition,** often defined as thought processes: sensorimotor, preoperational, concrete operational, and formal operational (Inhelder & Piaget, 1964; Piaget, 1963). Among the cognitive operations related to reading are: **seriation,** ordering, **temporal relations, conservation,** one-to-one correspondence, spatial relations, classification, and number relations (Almy, Chittenden, & Miller, 1966; Bybee & Sund, 1982; Waller, 1977).

> **cognition** Knowing; thought processes.

> **seriation** The ability to logically order a set of objects.

Seriation and ordering, for example, play a part in learning left-to-right progression and in realizing that letters and words go together in sequence. To understand the importance of these cognitive operations, first consider the following sentences:

> The boy was hungry. He stole some food. When the lady came in, he hid under a table that had a large pot of flowers on it.

> **temporal relations** A relationship based on either the passage of time or a particular interval of time.

Now, answer these related questions, for which Bybee and Sund (1982) have identified the required cognitive operations:

> What happened first—the boy being hungry or his stealing the food? (seriation, ordering, and temporal relations)
>
> What do you think the boy will do next? (ordering)
>
> Where was the boy at the end of the story? (spatial relations)

> **conservation** The ability to keep an unchanging property of something in mind when perceptual conditions are changed.

Questions like these are often asked without adequate attention given to the cognitive demands involved. Although questions that extend and appropriately challenge children are necessary for learning, questions that are too difficult can frustrate and prompt them to give up prematurely. Thus, teachers must be careful not to use concepts beyond the level of beginning readers. Many kindergarten programs, especially more traditional ones, try to provide activities to build many of the concepts adults take for granted—concepts designated by terms such as *before, in front of,* or *under.* You can demonstrate such concepts in everyday teaching routines. For example, there are ample opportunities for students to stand *beside* one student and *in front of* another. Children can also be asked to manipulate objects: placing them on, under, and around other objects. They might also perform a sequence of activities, allowing other children to describe the order of events. These activities often occur normally in the classroom; simply drawing children's attention to this terminology during such activities provides a basis for learning in context. Teachers have found activities such as those listed on page 160 to help students learn sequencing and direction following.

Following directions is another potentially difficult cognitive task. Forgetting that some young children may have difficulty grasping multiple directions, children are often asked to do several things at once—for example, "Put your pencils down, close your books, and pass your journals forward before you line up for recess." Again, many kindergarten programs provide specific activities targeting listening skills and following directions. Simple games such as "Simon Says" or a classroom treasure hunt that requires students to follow instructions can help students to sequence and follow directions. Keep in mind, however, that activities tied to literacy are most valuable.

PRACTICAL TEACHING STRATEGIES

Helping Children with Sequencing and Following Directions

Left-to-Right Sequencing

Observing Writing. Ask children to point to the places on the chart paper where you start and stop writing. Then ask them to watch as you write—perhaps transcribing a simple story or sentence they dictate to you. Draw their conscious attention to where you start and stop each line.

Picture-Story Sequencing. Cut simple cartoon strips into individual frames, then have the children arrange the frames from left to right so the story is told. After the frames are arranged, have children tell the story in their own words, frame by frame, pointing to each frame as appropriate.

Meaning Match. Have the children draw lines from left to right between two pictures that, when joined, make sense. For example, pictures on the left might show a squirrel, a car, and a boat; pictures on the right might show a nut, a garage, and a lakeshore. Say to the children, "Help the squirrel [car, boat] get to the nut [garage, water] by drawing a line from left to right between the two."

Sequencing and Following Directions Games

- Supply children with labeled pictures and ask them to follow specific, sequential instructions (for example, "Put an X below the house and then circle the dog"). Then help the children label their pictures.

- Have children give directions to you or another student to perform a simple task.

- Present a simple board game and explain the directions. Have children repeat the directions to check for understanding. After they have played the game, change the directions and discuss the effect on the game. Write down the directions and post them for future use.

- Bring a simple recipe to class (for example, popcorn or Jell-O). Make the item by reading and following the directions step by step. Discuss how important the directions were.

---

cognitive development
Growth in mental abilities and thought processes.

Although Piaget was instrumental in our understanding that language and thought are closely related, Vygotsky (1978, 1986) showed us that language learning is a social process. Specifically, Vygotsky believed that **cognitive development,** including the development of language, is greatly affected by an individual's social interaction with others. In other words, mediators such as teachers and parents influence a child's cognitive and language skills. Thus, emergent literacy/readiness is viewed as an evolving stage, or phase, that is influenced by teachers, rather than a static stage that a learner progresses through independently.

zone of proximal development
According to Vygotsky, the zone where learners can achieve success with guidance.

One of Vygotsky's major contributions is the **zone of proximal development,** which represents the difference between what learners can do on their own and what they can accomplish with guidance. Within that zone, concepts are maturing; that is, they are being refined through social interaction but are not yet sufficiently developed to be applied without help. Vygotsky believed that learners can do more with appropriate mediation than by themselves. Thus, a teacher's actions are viewed as critical in a child's cognitive development. The instructional implications of Vygotsky's concepts include these suggested behaviors:

1. Identify the child's zone of proximal development. This area lies immediately beyond the area in which the learner can function without help.
2. Present tasks the child can do with the help of others who are able to complete the tasks on their own. The tasks should be completed through social interaction and participation. The child should not simply watch others complete the task but should actively collaborate in completing it.
3. Monitor the child's ability to complete tasks. The zone of proximal development shifts to a higher level whenever the child is able to complete tasks previously performed only with help.

MODEL LESSON

A Think-Aloud Procedure in Roberta Jerrald's Class

Roberta Jerrald's interactive beliefs guide her decisions about *what* to teach. Interactive beliefs imply that reading involves both getting meaning from the text as well as bringing meaning to the text. Her integrated beliefs guide her decisions about *how* to teach. Integrated beliefs imply that reading experiences take place in social contexts using authentic texts and that teacher-directed and learner-directed experiences are important. Thus, Roberta frequently uses the think-aloud procedure. This allows her to show how what she brings to the text interacts with what she is reading and how a reader can make decisions about what to learn, as needed.

Roberta is using a modified think-aloud procedure with the book *Ten Little Caterpillars* (Martin, 1967), which includes the following lines of text on four different pages:

> The first little caterpillar crawled into a bower.
>
> The second little caterpillar wriggled up a flower.
>
> The third little caterpillar climbed a cabbage head.
>
> The fourth little caterpillar found a melon bed. (pp. 3, 5, 7, 9)

First, she reads the title and says, "I wonder what this will tell me about the 10 caterpillars. It could tell about how they live together or about what they do." After the first line she says, "Bower. Now that's a word I haven't seen before. I wonder what it means. Maybe I can find out by looking at the picture on this page or by reading farther. If not, I might have to ask someone or look in the dictionary." After the second line she says, "This sentence tells me about the second caterpillar. I wonder if the rest of the sentences will tell me about what the other caterpillars do."

After the third line Roberta says, "It sure looks like each sentence is going to tell about a different caterpillar. How many of you think so? Thumbs up if you do, down if you don't. I have a picture in my mind of a caterpillar climbing into a cabbage head. It's easy to think of a cabbage head because I sometimes buy them in the grocery store and because they grow in my neighbor's garden. I wonder if she has caterpillars in her garden."

After the fourth line she says, "The first part of each sentence is pretty much the same. That makes it easier to read. I wonder what a melon bed looks like. The bed I sleep in is a place to lie down. A melon bed is probably a place where the melon sits in the garden."

Roberta continues in a similar fashion. At the end of the story, she wraps it up by saying, "Well, after the title I predicted that we might find out about how the caterpillars live or what they might be doing. It looks like the book is mostly about what they are doing. I never did find out the meaning of bower. I think I'll go look it up in case I see it again."

Another of the implications of Vygotsky's work is the use of modeling within social situations. The social, sharing nature of reading activity makes this an excellent time for modeling to occur, especially through a procedure known as a **think-aloud** (Davey, 1983; Fitzgerald, 1983).

A think-aloud is a method framework (detailed in chapter 9) in which the teacher reads a passage aloud and talks through the processes used to make sense of what is being read, thereby modeling the thought processes and application of background knowledge necessary to understand the text. Think-alouds should be an occasional part of oral reading activities, and can be incorporated into any shared book activity.

think-aloud A procedure whereby a reader states aloud the thought processes and decisions that occur while reading.

Oral Language Factors

The language base of beginning readers is critically important to their learning to read. A solid oral language foundation allows them to generalize from what they already do well. Children who do not have well-developed aural and oral language skills have more difficulty learning to read.

Early oral language progresses through three basic stages: babbling, holophrastic speech, and telegraphic speech. In the initial babbling stage, the infant generates random sounds. Although these sounds may not be an attempt to actively communicate, the infant appears to experiment with the vocal system. The sounds generated include, but go beyond, the sounds that will eventually make up the infant's native language. Only later, when children learn which sounds make up the language of the communicating group to which they belong, are unnecessary sounds dropped. Perhaps because of the lack of need and practice, adult speakers have great difficulty pronouncing and even hearing sounds not used in their native language.

After the babbling stage the infant appears to apply words to events, apparently using single words logically and consistently to label complete thoughts. For example, a single word such as *milk* or *doll* might be used to communicate thoughts like "I want more milk" or "Give me the doll." This stage, beginning midway to late in the first year of the infant's life, features what is called **holophrastic speech.** Early in this stage, parents might hear the child say *papa* or *mama,* even when the adult is not the father or the mother. At a certain stage of cognitive development, children do overgeneralize. In addition, it appears that early sound combinations are the ones farthest apart in the vocal tract. Thus, it seems easy to rock back and forth between the two sounds of *mama* or *papa:* both the *m* and the *p* are formed at the front of the **vocal tract** with the mouth closed, whereas the *a* sound is formed at the back with the tract open.

Soon after the holophrastic stage, the child begins to string two or three words together in **telegraphic speech.** Examples of such utterances are "Milk here," "All gone milk," or "Baby milk." The child's speech is not yet in the form of complete sentences, yet thoughts seem to be grouped in sentence form. One problem with interpreting an expression like "Milk here" is that we really have no way of knowing whether the child means "Bring the milk here," "The milk has spilled over here," "Here is the milk," or something quite different. In many instances, what adults think a child means is not, in fact, the intended meaning. This problem also applies to the speech of kindergarten and first-grade students; teachers must be careful not to impose their adult interpretation on what their young students say.

Parents and teachers should provide many opportunities for oral expression. Storytelling by children is a beneficial activity, as is the recapping or retelling of a story that has been told to them. Structured oral language activities should form an ongoing part of an emergent literacy/readiness instructional program. Such activities can range from dictating a story to the teacher to explaining or describing an event to planning a class play. Teachers should also provide opportunities for children to build conversational skills such as turn-taking, listening, and **intonation.**

Perceptual Factors

Perception deals with the senses and is divided into visual (seeing), auditory (hearing), tactile (touching), olfactory (smelling), and tasting categories. In traditional readiness programs, emphasis was placed on **visual and auditory discrimination** because readers depend on vision to differentiate between letters (Braille readers depend on tactile perception instead) and because hearing is instrumental in differentiating the sounds associated with different letters. In more child-centered programs, perceptual and discrimination activities are de-emphasized in favor of more integrated reading and writing activities. Four terms are important to remember in a discussion of perceptual factors:

1. *Acuity.* The "strength of the signal." Related questions include: "How well does the child hear?" and "How good are the child's eyes?"
2. *Discrimination.* The ability to notice similarities and differences.
3. *Recognition.* Awareness that something experienced is the same as something previously experienced. Visually recognizing a word signals an awareness that the word has been seen before.
4. *Identification.* Deals specifically with identifying, or grasping, meaning.

These definitions are consistent with those found in *A Dictionary of Reading and Related Terms* (Harris & Hodges, 1981) and *The Literacy Dictionary* (Harris & Hodges, 1995).

holophrastic speech
A stage of early language acquisition when a child uses a single word to express a thought.

vocal tract   Speech organs used to make sounds.

telegraphic speech
A stage of oral language development when all but essential words are omitted.

intonation   The rise, fall, and stress in a voice and the pauses in speaking.

visual and auditory discrimination   The ability to see (visual) and hear (auditory) likenesses and differences.

PRACTICAL TEACHING STRATEGIES

Supporting the Development of Oral Expression

Picture/Sequencing Story. Show a picture or a sequence of two or three pictures and have children tell a story about what is shown.

Expressing Emotions. Have children pretend they are certain animals or objects in a given situation and talk about their feelings.

Activity Sequence. Have children think of a specific sequential activity such as getting ready for school in the morning, going home from school, or getting from the classroom to the library. Then have them tell a partner or a group the specific directions to follow to perform the activity. If the activity has not been stated, other children can try to guess it from the set of directions.

Relating Intonation and Mood. Tell a story to your students, then tell it again, varying your tone of voice and general expression. Discuss how the different readings make the story seem scarier, happier, and so on. Have the children try to vary their own expression on sentences they repeat after you. Other children can guess the moods that are expressed.

Build a Story. Have children sit in a circle. Begin a story with one sentence and have each child add another sentence until the story gets back around to you. If the session is tape-recorded, transcribe the whole story while the children watch. Later, let them illustrate the story and post it on the classroom bulletin board.

Show and Tell. Ask children to bring something special with them from home. Let them show the item and talk about it (that is, show and tell).

Visual and Auditory Discrimination.   While the ability to discriminate letters and sounds is important for reading, discrimination is often confused with perception. Basically, **visual perception** is the ability to notice lines and squiggles on a page. Normal reading is impossible in total darkness because visual perception is impossible, but light intensity can vary widely without affecting reading. Can you think of the variety of lighting conditions under which you have managed to read over the years? The more important aspect of the visual factor is discrimination, which allows readers to recognize differences between printed letters, words, and so on.

> **visual perception** In reading, the ability to see the characteristics of such things as letters, words, or lines of print.

Some kindergarten programs attempt to enhance students' concepts of "same" and "different" by using discrimination activities closely linked to stories children are reading or writing, while more traditional programs might attempt to do so by having children match words, letters, or combinations of words and letters in different sizes, shapes, and colors. However, because the goal of early literacy programs is to facilitate later fluent reading, it is best to provide activities that bridge to more authentic, realistic texts. For example, if you wish to reinforce the importance of noticing that even small differences in letters are significant, you might point out that the letters *m* and *n* both appear in a recently completed language experience story. Then, carefully clarify the similarities and differences, as demonstrated in this short exercise with *m* and *n*.

Look at [or trace] *m* and *n*. Are they the same?

Do both have straight lines? Where? How many?

Do both have curved lines? Where? How many?

Such specific questioning can help children differentiate between particular features of letters and allows them to examine the details that make up overall configurations.

Similarly, auditory perception is basically the ability to notice the presence of sound. More important for reading, however, is the ability to discriminate between the sounds of various letters, syllables, and words. Controversy continues to surround what should be taught in the auditory discrimination component of emergent literacy/readiness reading programs. For example, according to Gibson and Levin (1980):

> Auditory perceptual analysis of words is an important skill for learning to read, and training in it helps and does show transfer, at least in the initial stages of learning to read. . . . Clapping for each unit, marking (with dashes), deleting sounds, producing omitted sounds, and substituting sounds are successive stages of training, with apparently successful results in kindergarten and first grade. (p. 260)

However, Aulls (1982) is less definite about the value of such activities, citing a number of studies that support his conclusion:

> Emphasizing reading tasks such as sounding out words or emphasizing phonics may be a waste of time for many kindergartners. . . . [although] there does appear to be justification for teaching auditory segmentation to those children who have naturally begun to sound out words and who have already begun to read. (p. 99)

One benefit of auditory discrimination activities is that they provide a common terminology for both teacher and student, as has been clearly demonstrated in teacher's guides for some time:

> The purpose of giving practice in listening for beginning sounds is not to teach children to "hear" sounds or to distinguish sounds from one another. Children who understand and reproduce their language do this automatically. However, many pupils in kindergarten or first grade have trouble with the concept that a word has a beginning because they think of a word as one undifferentiated sound. Since children will be taught in a later lesson that one sound to use in decoding is the sound "at the beginning of a word," they need to know exactly what this expression means. (*Getting Ready to Read,* 1979, p. 21)

As in visual discrimination, later transfer to print is better when auditory discrimination tasks center around reading-related materials. The suggested activities that follow on page 165 include print-based auditory and visual discrimination activities that can also refine emerging concepts of "same" and "different."

auditory/visual integration   The linking or association of sound and sight.

Auditory/Visual Integration.   Beginning readers are learning that oral language can be represented in symbolic form, that sounds and symbols are linked, and that the purpose of reading is to acquire meaning. Activities that build these concepts relate to **auditory/visual integration.** In traditional readiness programs, children are presented with both the visual text and the sound(s) represented. They must see and hear both at the same time, perhaps naming an item aloud, in chorus with the teacher, while they look at it.

Thus, activities to promote auditory/visual integration differ somewhat from those that target visual and auditory discrimination. For example, whereas a purely auditory activity might ask children to repeat the beginning sound in *baby,* a corresponding auditory/visual integration activity would present the visual image of the word while the teacher pronounced it. Children might be asked to repeat the beginning sound or point to the part of the word that has the *b* sound as they say the letter-sound with the teacher. Traditionally, such activities focus on the association between specific sounds and specific parts of a word and are used with sounds in beginning, medial, and ending positions, as well as with whole words and phrases.

Although some kindergarten programs will implement specific auditory/visual integration activities in their curriculum, such activities are de-emphasized in child-centered programs. Within a child-centered environment, children learn to integrate the auditory and visual aspects of reading as they participate in real reading acts—for example, as teachers use big books and run their hands under the words while children watch or read along, or by reading predictable, repetitive books.

Affective Factors

We have all experienced tasks that seemed to be completed in record time, whereas others dragged on and on. Think back to tasks of both types. Did you discover that the tasks

---

PRACTICAL TEACHING STRATEGIES

Discrimination Activities That Teach the Concepts of "Same" and "Different"

Word-Matching Games. Divide a piece of poster board into large rectangles. Print a word in each rectangle. Make a matching set of rectangular word cards, then have students cover the words on the paper with the appropriate word cards. You can turn this activity into a "bingo game" by having students, perhaps in pairs, cover the words that you point to on your "bingo card." You might also make labels for objects around the classroom and attach an envelope below the label on each item. Give children a set of word cards that include the labeled items and have them place their word cards in the envelopes under the appropriate labels. If children's names are on their word cards, you will have a quick check of who is having difficulty matching cards to labels.

Letter-Matching Games. Using plastic or paper letters, arrange groups of letters that are the same except for one that is obviously different.

C C X C C   F S F F F

Ask children to replace the one that is different so that all the letters are the same. Gradually increase the similarity of the letters.

C C O C C   F F E F F

Discriminating Letter Features. Help children perceive the difference among letters by discussing and pointing out the features of letters—curved lines, straight lines, and height. Present two letters with color on the parts that make them different.

Discriminating Word Features. Ask children to discriminate between similar words, drawing a circle around the part(s) that are different (e.g., *near/rear, rat/rut, window/widow*). Also, discuss similarities and differences between words of clearly different shapes and lengths. For example, write *mow* and *motorcycle* on the board or on chart paper. Discuss how they are the same and different (e.g., one is longer, two of the letters in *mow* are in *motorcycle*, one word has a letter with a "tail," and so on).

---

you found pleasant flew by, whereas those you did not enjoy moved slowly? Your affective set—the way you felt about the tasks—influenced your motivation and performance. This principle also applies to literacy tasks. Most children come to school eager to learn to read and write, although many are already doing so at the appropriate developmental levels as they scribble and turn pages in books and magazines "pretending" to read. They come to school viewing literacy as potentially exciting (Downing et al., 1979). Much of that feeling comes from having had interesting and exciting stories read to them at home, which leads to the dual realization that their pleasure originated in books and that learning to read and write would be a real mark of independence. Hopefully, parents will continue to read to their children after they come to school. However, teachers should read to their pupils also. Reading to students is a vital part of any kindergarten literacy program that intends to foster a desire to read.

Teachers should read to children often—sometimes individually, sometimes in small groups, and sometimes in whole-class situations. In addition, it is important to allow time for a discussion of what was read, pointing out pictures and interesting drawings and thereby fostering positive attitudes as well as story comprehension. Encouraging children to talk about their personal experiences that relate to the reading selection is also highly motivational, especially with beginning readers, who often are **egocentric.**

Issues of motivation are closely tied to feelings. Is a specific activity liked or disliked? Our response is called **attitude.** A closely related term is **interest,** which indicates the importance we place on pursuing a given topic or activity. To illustrate how these two affective factors interact, consider, for example, that you dislike something but are interested in finding out more about it. You may have an intensely negative attitude

egocentric Describing the self-centeredness of children, who are unable to take another's point of view.

attitude The way a person feels about something.

interest Intentional focusing of attention on something as a result of motivation.

PRACTICAL TEACHING STRATEGIES

Developing Recognition and Discrimination of Beginning and Ending Sounds of Words

Picture–Sound Match. Provide students magazines and blunt scissors. Have students find and cut out pictures of objects with names beginning with the same sounds the students' own names begin with, then have them say the names of the pictures they have cut out and let the other students determine whether the beginning sounds are the same.

Keyword Banks. Take cut-out pictures and place them in a box. Provide containers that are labeled, each with a single word. Have students take the pictures out of the box and place each in a container that has a label beginning with the same sound as that particular picture. Children can also add individual words to a computer file, saved under their own names, through age-appropriate word processing software.

Tongue Twister Sounds. Find or make up simple tongue twisters (for example, "Six silly sheep saw a slippery snake"). Have students repeat the twisters after you, first slowly, then slightly faster. Put several twisters into a box, and have students choose ones for you to say. Then have them suggest other words that might make each tongue twister longer (for example, "Saw a slippery snake sliding").

Keyword Spaceship. On a large piece of poster board, draw a spaceship on Earth, aimed toward the moon. Present a target word and have children provide words or pictures with a sound similar to that of the target word. For every three correct words, move the ship closer to the moon. Dividing the students into teams makes this a motivational game.

Keyword Match. Present key words that begin or end with a specific sound. Provide students with other words and ask them to decide where the sounds are the same.

toward snakes but have a strong interest in finding out more about them—perhaps where they are most likely to be found in order to avoid them! Conversely, it is possible to feel very positive about something but have no interest in studying it further. Perhaps you find Gothic architecture visually pleasing but have no interest in studying its history or specific characteristics. In literacy instruction, teachers need to be aware of both the interests and the attitudes of their students. Often children's attitudes toward learning to read and write may be positive, but their interest in performing specific instructional tasks may be quite low. To generate interest in required activities, teachers must foster a positive attitude toward the task being performed. And for young children, long-term goals do not provide strong motivation. Telling children they need to complete a task so they will eventually become good readers is not conceptually relevant for them. The immediate task must be motivational.

A short attitude survey can help you choose instructional tasks and materials to motivate your students. Heathington (1976) has developed attitude scales for use in both primary and intermediate grades. The answer sheets for the Heathington primary scale ask students to show how they feel about various things by marking a set of faces that range from smiles to frowns. The scales provide a variety of pertinent questions—for example, "How do you feel when you go to the library?"—but teachers sometimes supplement these with their own questions about students' attitudes and interests: "What do you like to do most? What are your favorite TV shows? Do you have (want) any pets? Your favorite story is . . . ? The best day of the week is . . . ? When you grow up, you'd like to be . . . ?" (Further discussion and more examples of attitude and interest assessment are included in chapter 11.)

Even though an attitude/interest inventory can be a valuable tool, you should keep in mind that young children have short attention spans and their interests can change fairly quickly. Consequently, it is important to talk to young children often to keep abreast of their current interests. Furthermore, with children who have somewhat poor attitudes toward reading, you will need to make special efforts to identify motivational materials. Such children benefit from stories likely to be of high interest as well as the extra time spent reading to them and discussing their interest in the stories.

The Home Environment

Before children come to school, they have had vast learning experiences. They have learned how to communicate and have **internalized** a set of language rules, in addition to acquiring a sophisticated awareness of the behaviors necessary for effective communication (for example, turn taking, intonation, gestures, and facial expressions). During those formative years, several home environment factors are highly **correlated** to reading achievement.

internalized Made a part of one's existing knowledge.

correlated Showing a relationship to something else.

Through interviews with parents of early readers, Durkin (1966, 1974–1975) has identified these common elements:

▶ Parents of early readers spend much time in conversation with their children.
▶ Early readers ask many questions, and their parents take the time to answer those questions.
▶ A frequently asked question by early readers is, "What's that word?"

The importance of home environment and parental involvement has also been noted by the Commission on Reading (Anderson, Hiebert, Scott, & Wilkinson, 1985; see also Mason, 1980):

> Parents play a role of inestimable importance in laying the foundations for learning to read. Parents should informally teach preschool children about reading and writing by reading aloud to them, discussing stories and events, encouraging them to learn letters and words and teaching them about the world around them. These practices help prepare children for success in reading. (p. 57)

Other factors related to children's later reading success include:

▶ The value that adults in the home place on literacy.
▶ The amount of reading done by adults in the home (modeling).
▶ The amount of reading material available in the home.
▶ The number of language-based games and activities in the home.
▶ The availability of personal reading materials for the child.

There are literally thousands of books available for the preschool child, ranging from colorful picture books, with and without story lines, to fairly complex stories. One type of book popular with young children contains highly predictable patterns of language—perhaps rhyming patterns, repeated words and phrases, or predictable concepts. Such books are highly motivational because they allow children to quickly begin to read along with a parent or teacher, using prior knowledge to predict and thus aid understanding, just as mature readers do. An example of a predictable text is *Ten Little Caterpillars*, which was cited and excerpted in the model lesson on page 161. Other predictable texts are included in the more extensive discussion of such books in chapter 6.

Reading to children from an early age plays such an important role in establishing later success in reading that parents often ask their children's kindergarten or first-grade teacher to suggest appropriate reading materials. Numerous reference sources provide titles, critiques, or suggestions for parents about reading to their children at home. For example:

Literature and the Child, B. E. Cullinan & L. Galda, (1997), New York: Harcourt Brace College Publishers.

Magazines for Kids and Teens, D. R. Stoll (Ed.), (1997), Newark, DE: International Reading Association.

Hey! Listen to This. Stories to Read Aloud, J. Trelease (Ed.), (1992), Newark, DE: International Reading Association.

The Read-Aloud Handbook (5th edition), J. Trelease, (2001), New York: Penguin Books.

Additionally, the International Reading Association (800 Barksdale Road, Newark, DE 19711) publishes informational material for parents, including Children's Choices and Teacher's Choices, which are annual compilations of children's and teachers' favorite books.

MODEL LESSON

Fostering Discourse Knowledge and Predicting Outcomes in Meyung Kim's Class

Meyung Kim is guided in her decisions about *what* to teach by her reader-based beliefs, which lead her to value what readers bring to a text and imply that readers' expectations play a large part in constructing meaning. She also has integrated beliefs that influence her decisions about *how* to teach. In the lesson below, we see that Meyung is using a procedure that shows children that their predictions and expectations for what will occur in upcoming text are important, and that the activity is occurring in context, using an authentic text. Children are, however, expected to check the text to show how their predictions are supported by what appears in what they have read.

To help beginning readers get an initial sense of the role of prediction in understanding what they read, Meyung uses the following simple strategy.

Choose an interesting story to read, and divide it into two parts. Have paper or a chalkboard available.

Read the first part of the story and discuss it, asking for suggestions about what might come next; that is, what might happen in the rest of the story. Record responses. Ask for reasons to support the predictions. Be ready to help clarify the information in the text that provides the basis for the predictions.

Read the next section of the story.

Go back to the predictions and discuss them. Talk about why some predictions may not have appeared in the story.

Meyung tries to use this procedure every few days. Sometimes she chooses the selection that will be read; at other times she asks the children for their suggestions. She finds that the children enjoy this activity and often transfer "predicting" to other activities.

Good reading habits are built when children are read to with appropriate intonation and evident pleasure and when their attention is drawn to the reading material. Reading a wide variety of materials helps children build their discourse knowledge and use syntax and context. As parents use specialized reading vocabulary (for example, "Let's turn the page" or "Isn't that a funny title?"), children learn terms that will serve them well in reading tasks.

Beyond actual reading, many games and activities allow young children to classify ("Let's put all the blocks with the big letters together"); to match items ("Let's see if this puzzle piece will fit into this slot"); to discriminate ("Let's see if we can find what's wrong in this picture"); or to build concepts of *same* and *different* ("Let's see if we can find a word that looks the same"). A guessing game like "I Spy" allows children to play with language ("I spy something with a color that rhymes with *bed*"). All of these activities can be done at home, and all aid in the successful completion of future reading tasks.

Assessment in Kindergarten Literacy Programs

Teachers are decision makers who continually make instructional choices based on the information around them. To make instructional decisions for beginning readers, information is gathered in three ways: (1) observations of children's behavior and abilities, (2) information from parents and children, and (3) formal and informal tests. The characteristics of formal and informal tests are discussed in chapter 11, as are assessment procedures appropriate across grade levels. The discussion here looks at assessment, specifically in the context of emergent literacy/readiness classrooms, and includes special considerations for teachers who assess literacy development in young children.

Observational and Informal Data

A school environment provides a wealth of opportunity for the observant teacher to informally assess student abilities, interests, attitudes, and social skills. Assignments, oral responses to questions, student-initiated questions, attention span, speed of task completion, and patterns of responses all provide data on which to base instructional deci-

Informal observations of children's interaction with print (here, with a big book) are informative and are an important part of an assessment program

sions. In addition to specific, individual reading- and writing-related tasks, group activities and observation of playground behavior can also provide valuable information. Is the child an active participant in games? Does the child take leadership or passive roles? In what kinds of activities? Is the child shy or more of a bully? How do other students react to the child? Does the child participate in group or individual play that includes activities such as labeling, naming, and so on? Answers to such questions provide valuable insights. Informal observations should be recorded along with other data, for together these pieces of information will enable you to plan instructional activities according to children's needs. The structured observation of students to make instructional decisions has been called "kidwatching," a term often attributed to Ken and Yetta Goodman (see Pike, Compain, & Mumper, 1994).

If observation is to play a significant role in instructional decision making, it is important to be systematic in your observations. All children will need to be observed. You will need to guard against focusing on certain children over others—something that is easy to do. Thus, before beginning systematic observations, plan to set aside a portion of the day to watching your students. Ensure that each day has a certain number of children designated as "targets" for observation. Also, be aware that observation is an informal procedure. It need not require that you stay away from the children's activities and merely listen and observe in a "hands off" manner. Although this might occur at times, you are a member of the class and thus your observations will often take place while you participate with children in classroom activities. Such activities can include discussions, shared reading and writing experiences, conferences, question–answer dialogues, and play. When these occur during designated observational time, feel free to participate but be sure to record your observations in an organized record-keeping system.

Observations can be recorded on checklists, in notebooks, on file cards, or in any way that allows easy access and a consistent way to summarize data. Many publishers

FIGURE 5-11

Informal checklist of behaviors and abilities

Student's name: _____   Date: _____

Age: Years: _____   Months: _____

Use the following scale in the decision column: 1 = yes, 2 = somewhat, 3 = no.
Comments should be added whenever possible, especially if the decision is "somewhat."

	Decision	Comments
1. Knows the alphabet (can say it with little or no help)	_____	
2. Can write the alphabet	_____	
3. Can distinguish between upper- and lowercase letters	_____	
4. Recognizes written letters by name	_____	
5. Can rhyme words	_____	
6. Can count to 20	_____	
7. Can state numbers from written form	_____	
8. Can write numbers	_____	
9. Recognizes and matches items that are the same	_____	
10. Knows relational words (*before, after, back, front, under, above, until*)	_____	
11. Can describe (tell) a picture-based story	_____	
12. Can appropriately order a simple picture-story (i.e., a cartoon strip)	_____	
13. Can read common words (*stop, dog, run*)	_____	
14. Can read own name when written by a teacher	_____	
15. Can write own name	_____	
16. Knows own age	_____	
17. Can repeat sequence of events in a simple story	_____	
18. Speaks in sentences rather than in words or phrases	_____	
19. Knows simple reading terms (*page, word, story*)	_____	

General comments (e.g., attentiveness, concentration, ability to follow directions, shyness, pronunciation of words/sounds, general verbal fluency):

_____

_____

_____

offer commercial checklists, and schools or school districts often have suggested checklists for teachers' use. One simple checklist is presented in Figure 5-11 and can help draw attention to specific behaviors and abilities. Some of the items can be deduced by observation; others require input from parents or children. Such a checklist can suggest activities or items that might be motivational and can identify children who might need a little special consideration. As with any informal evaluation instrument, you should feel free to modify checklist items to fit your particular instructional situations.

SUSAN'S

COMMENTS FROM THE CLASSROOM

There is little in teaching that equals the excitement of watching a reader "emerge." The child's realization that he or she is, indeed, reading produces a glow of success that is electrifying. It was, for me, the greatest joy of teaching first grade—and it lasted throughout the year. It seemed that there was always at least one child who was in the process of "popping out," ready to demonstrate newfound learning.

Phase One: I organized group instruction (loosely) on elements of a Reading Recovery lesson. We began each lesson with a reread of known texts. Each of my four reading groups had a tub that held books we'd already read together. After each child had reread two or three books, we'd put the reread tub away and begin the next phase of the lesson.

Phase Two: New Book. Each first-grade classroom in our school has multiple copies of leveled books. The books progress in difficulty from prereading to the fluent reading level. One book was usually presented each day. During book presentation, the title was read, a brief summary of the story recounted, and then all children opened their books and began to look through the pictures, discussing what might be happening. The last stage of book presentation was locating words that were repeated frequently in the book, were crucial to its meaning, or that might have been difficult in a first reading. Once each child had located the given words (using initial letters to help in the search), children were off and reading. Each child read separately so that each was completely engaged in the initial reading. On to Phase Three.

Phase Three: Writing. We would then agree upon a sentence that somehow related to the new book. After generally strong-arming the group into a decision, we would write the sentence together, saying the words slowly so that the sounds in each word were heard and those sounds were represented with the appropriate letters. This was a setting as well for repeated practice of writing sight words in sentence context.

Phase Four: Word Work. Beside my seat at the reading table I had a collection of 1-inch tiles on which were printed lowercase letters of the alphabet. I would give each child a set of letters and they would use them to form words. These were always words that were phonetically regular and usually belonged in large part to the same "word-family." For example, they'd form *bat, fat, hat,* and then try *had* to promote flexibility in identifying the location of the word's altered sound.

End Phase: Sign-Off Sheet. Each child had a sign-off sheet that had space for me to write the date and the title of the book. The sheet and the new book (and any rereads the child requested) went into a plastic baggie and then directly into the child's backpack. There was then space for the child's parent or guardian to sign his/her name. In this way, I could keep track of who was reading at night with an adult. That ended the lesson and cleared the table for me to call the next group.

Parental Input

Informal discussions with parents can prove to be very productive, providing valuable information about the children in your class. Through parent conferences, parent-teacher association (PTA) meetings, and notes or questionnaires sent to parents, teachers can learn about students' siblings, motivating factors, attitudes toward school, and home reading environments. Parents can also be a tremendous help in specific instructional aspects of an emergent literacy/readiness program. Usually, parents are aware of the value and importance of good reading abilities and are willing to help in whatever way they can. Having parents function as storytellers, give demonstrations, or help with class activities can provide valuable assistance and can extend regular classroom learning, especially when that parental involvement is used as a base for oral, written, or art experiences. In addition, young children typically are proud when their parents visit their classes and thus try hard to do their best. Parental involvement often helps foster a positive student attitude and motivation.

Working parents who are unable to come to class during school hours might be able to arrange an interesting field trip to their business or place of work, or perhaps they have a hobby that can be brought to school and left for the teacher and children to discuss whenever it is appropriate. This can serve as a background for language experience lessons and tasks such as brainstorming with the children about what to write in a journal, a letter of invitation, or a thank-you note. These types of parental involvement can form the basis for highly motivating lessons that build experiential background, oral language, and vocabulary, and allow children to feel proud even though their parent(s) are not physically present.

Formal Tests

Four areas appear to predict success in reading: knowledge of letter names, general oral vocabulary knowledge, recognition of whole words, and visual discrimination ability (Barrett, 1965; Bond & Dykstra, 1967; Loban, 1963; Richek, 1977–1978; Silvaroli, 1965). Although some studies have failed to show that these four areas are predictive of later reading ability (Calfee, Chapman, & Venezky, 1972; Olson & Johnson, 1970; Samuels, 1972), they generally are included in formal emergent literacy/readiness tests. Such tests usually measure the following abilities:

auditory perception	awareness of left-right sequence
auditory discrimination	letter identification and recognition
visual perception	oral sentence or short passage
visual discrimination	comprehension
auditory/visual integration	word identification and recognition
concepts of *same, different,*	motor skills
over, and *under*	

Formal tests intended for beginning readers range from paper-and-pencil tests given to groups of students to individually administered tests. Traditional, formal reading readiness tests often require that students match pictures, words, letters, or shapes to either visual or auditory stimuli. For example, children might be asked to listen to or look at an item and then find that item in a series of choices, or they might complete an item to match a stimulus. There have been several criticisms and cautions raised with regard to these traditional tests.

One caution has to do with children clearly understanding what they are expected to do and whether or not they view the task as important. Even with seemingly simple tasks, you will need to be sure that young children clearly understand test directions, for beginning readers easily confuse test items and may be unable to grasp certain types of instructions (for example, "From the pictures on the right, mark the one that is the same as the one on the left"). In addition, you will need to ensure that a test clearly relates to what is being measured. For example, it should not evaluate a student's ability to follow directions unless that is the specific objective of the test.

Celebrating Diversity

Assessing for Information about Diversity

Assessment, whether formal or informal, provides much information about the diverse nature of your students. Although assessment information, in terms of student diversity, is usually linked to their relative abilities or scores on an assessment tool, other information about the diversity found in your class also becomes readily apparent. As a teacher, you will be able to use assessment to learn about your students and to use what you learn to create appropriate learning opportunities for them.

In kindergarten as well as in other elementary grades, observations are especially helpful in learning about children. For example, observations can tell you whether or not children of similar backgrounds or cultures are extending their circle of influence beyond children of their own background or culture. If not, try—through flexible grouping or through show-and-tell activities that allow others to learn about a particular child's culture or interest—to provide opportunities for these children to interact meaningfully with all of the children in the class. Similarly, an assessment of interests and attitudes often indicates these are grounded within a particular child's cultural background; you can use this information to choose particularly appropriate materials for given children.

Finally, home environments will also differ widely with students in any class. These different environments will be more or less supportive of school, of literacy, and of you as a child's teacher. You will need to consider and plan for how different home environments and values will influence your teaching of literacy and how you can use diverse home environments to support your literacy instruction.

Another caution regarding the testing of young children relates to their attention spans. A kindergarten or first-grade student is often a bundle of energy, unused to sitting still and focusing his or her attention for extended periods. Most formal tests contain timelines, beyond which rest periods or other activities are suggested. Such instructions should never be ignored.

Before choosing a formal test, you should answer the following questions:

- What exactly do I want to measure, and why?
- What exactly does this test measure, and how?
- Does the test measure what it says it is measuring?
- Is there a close relationship between what I want to measure and what the test measures?

To answer these questions, you will need to become familiar with a particular test, taking the time to examine it carefully and to read the test manual completely. A test manual contains valuable information on administration procedures and the intent of the test. With that information you should decide whether to spend potential instructional time on testing. If the test is mandated, requiring its administration, you should follow the test's directions and consider its results carefully, keeping in mind what you know about the children and their literacy behavior in more authentic situations.

Formal reading readiness tests were mainly developed from the 1920s to the 1950s, with periodic revisions and updates through the present date. They have become less popular in recent times, partly because studies have shown that the predictive power of such tests is fairly low. In other words, a good score on a formal emergent literacy/readiness test does not always predict with a high degree of certainty how well a student will learn to read. For this reason, many now advocate using more informal and observational measures at this level (Durkin, 1987; Goodman, Goodman, & Hood, 1989; Sulzby, 1990).

Teachers in child-centered programs may have special difficulty assessing students with traditional, formal tests (Valencia, Hiebert, & Afflerbach, 1994; see also Stallman & Pearson, 1990, for a discussion of formal readiness tests and their incompatibility with

FIGURE 5-12

Sample page from Clay's *Stones: The Concepts about Print Test*

Instructions for administration are found in Clay's (1993) *An Observation Survey of Early Literacy Achievement.* Auckland, New Zealand: Reed Publishing. Notice that the test pages shown below come from a real book. Children are asked to make decisions and choices within this real-book context.

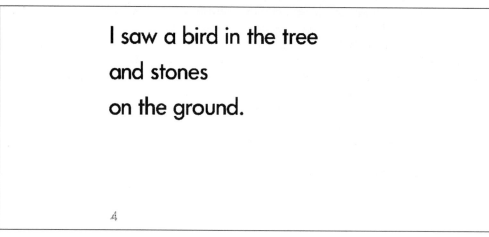

shifting views of literacy development). Because child-centered programs generally do not structure teaching within skill units, formal assessment instruments (which usually measure independent or isolated skills) are often viewed as less appropriate. In keeping with beliefs that literacy develops through interaction with more authentic reading and writing tasks, students in child-centered programs may be better assessed through observational and informal measures during more genuine literacy tasks and through an ongoing compilation of student work. Such compilations, or portfolios, can be extremely useful in documenting students' progress. In addition, tests such as *Sand: The Concepts about Print Test* and *Stones: The Concepts about Print Test* (Clay, 1985a, 1985b, 1993, see Figure 5-12) measure more global aspects of literacy—aspects learned through interaction with print rather than through direct teaching of isolated skills (Clay, 1980a, 1980b). Thus, such tools may be more compatible with child-centered programs than traditional tests and more closely match the instructional situation and environment.

Using a Literacy Framework to Guide Emergent Literacy

The way you implement emergent literacy/readiness instruction will be guided by your literacy framework. If reader-based beliefs influence you in terms of *what* to teach, you tend to feel that what the reader brings to the text is a major influence on constructing meaning and that readers sample text to confirm or reject their predictions. However, if you have text-based beliefs about what to teach, you tend to believe that reading begins with decoding and takes place through exact pronunciation of what is written. Thus, you may stress perceptual, discrimination activities in your program. Such an approach has as its goal the direct teaching of sound–symbol relationships, and you would provide many activities aimed at helping students understand that letters and sounds are related. Thus, you may stress activities that require readers to be explicit about their background knowledge as you lead them through a text.

Beliefs about the nature of emergent literacy programs—and about how they should be constructed—vary. Some advocate a focus on sound–symbol relationships and decoding processes (Chall, 1979, 1989; Liberman & Shankwiler, 1980). Others think that decoding is not central to reading and imply that emergent literacy/readiness programs should focus on meaning (Carbo, 1988; Goodman & Goodman, 1979; Smith, 1996). A third view holds that reading is an interactive process between text and reader and that a reader's initial focus therefore depends on factors such as overall reading ability, the reader's purpose for reading, and the difficulty of the text (Danks & Fears, 1979; Fredericksen, 1982). Thus, interactive beliefs about what to teach would lead to teaching that emphasizes decoding as well as elements of prior knowledge. Table 5-4 summarizes how various beliefs can influence *what* to teach.

TABLE 5-4

A summary of how a literacy framework can be used to inform decisions about what to teach

Issues and Beliefs in a Literacy Framework That Inform This Issue	Instructional Decisions That Are Informed by Your Beliefs
Issue 1. What Should I Teach? Meaning exists more in what the reader brings to a text and reading is a result of expectations. Reading begins with elements of prior knowledge. (Reader-based beliefs)	Developing strategic use of context and contextual strategies. Predicting meanings and relating texts in all activities to already-known concepts would be stressed.
Meaning exists more in the text and reading is translating the text or extracting the meaning from the text. Reading begins with decoding. (Text-based beliefs)	Developing decoding skills would be stressed, as would discrimination tasks that relate to letters and sounds.
Meaning exists both in the text and the reader. Reading is both translation and expectation. All of the knowledge sources can be used simultaneously. (Interactive language learning beliefs)	Developing each of the knowledge sources is given equal time. Relating new meanings to old, the importance of prior knowledge, and teaching decoding lessons would all occur.

TABLE 5-5

A summary of how a literacy framework can be used to inform instructional decisions about how to teach

Issues and Beliefs in a Literacy Framework That Inform This Issue	Instructional Decisions That Are Informed by Your Beliefs
Issue 2: How Should I Teach? Students direct much of their own learning, and inductive learning is emphasized. (Holistic language learning beliefs)	Common method frameworks include the language experience approach, shared book experience, morning message, journal writing, and think-alouds. Published reading programs and skill sheets typically are not used. Big books, much of children's literature and other print material, and children's oral and written language form the basis for most instruction. Informal assessment, with an emphasis on observation and "kidwatching," typically is used to evaluate students' progress.
Teacher-directed reading activities and deductive learning are emphasized. Specific skills, often organized in terms of difficulty, are frequently taught. (Specific skills beliefs)	Common method frameworks include deductive instruction that targets specific skills such as left-to-right sequencing, concepts of "same" and "different," letter and sound discrimination, and auditory/visual integration, often based on a scope and sequence suggested in a published program. Evaluation is generally formal; when informal, it focuses on specific skills.
Both student-directed and teacher-directed experiences are used. Both inductive and deductive learning are used. Reading experiences take place in the contexts of authentic social contexts and with authentic reading materials. Specific skills are taught when needed. (Integrated beliefs)	Common method frameworks include the language experience approach, shared book experience, morning message, journal writing, think-alouds and, as needed, inductive and deductive instruction in skills such as left-to-right sequencing, concepts of "same" and "different," letter and sound discrimination, and auditory/visual integration. Evaluation includes both formal as well as informal and observation practices.

Use the self-test questions on http://www.prenhall. com/leukinzer to assess how prepared you are for the exam over the content of this chapter.

Your beliefs also guide your decisions about *how* to teach. If you have specific skills beliefs, then you value teacher-directed activities and deductive learning. Teacher-directed think-alouds and auditory/visual decoding activities are used. If you have holistic language learning beliefs, then you feel that students should direct their own learning as much as possible. Thus, published reading programs that are prescriptive would not be as valued as children's choices in big book activities or in language experience approaches. If you have integrated beliefs that guide your decisions about how to teach, both student-directed and teacher-directed learning are valued and all of the approaches discussed in this chapter would be used as appropriate to meet your students' needs. Table 5-5 summarizes the influence of literacy frameworks on decisions about *how* to teach.

Ms. Tonningsen

Ms. Tonningsen's first-grade class in Portland, Oregon has a fascinating home page at http://www.riverdale.k12.or.us/~ktonning/. If you visit, you will see links to places outside Ms. Tonningsen's classroom as well as links to her children's work, their book projects, and their newsletter. There are photographs of children at work in their first-grade classroom, and discussion of how they are accomplishing their goals of becoming readers and writers.

The images of classroom activities, especially on the Newsletter pages, demonstrate clearly how children's experiences are used as a bridge to reading and writing activities, and how these activities can be used to integrate instruction across the many areas encompassed in the primary-grade curriculum. You will also see that Ms. Tonningsen and her class make wonderful use of the Internet to help their learning, to share their work with others, and to help others who wish to learn about the potential of the Internet to support young children's development. Ms. Tonningsen's home page is shown in Figure 5-13.

FIGURE 5-13

The home page for Ms. Tonningsen's first-grade class in Portland, Oregon (http://www.riverdale.k12.or.us/~ktonning/)

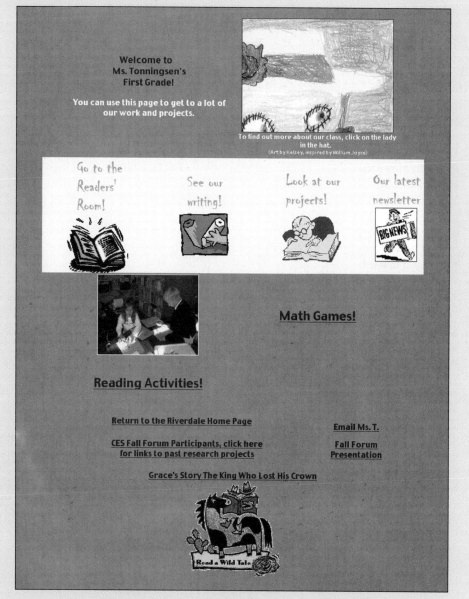

Major Points

▶ Beginning readers should be read to often, allowed to use their oral language skills, and provided with many chances to experiment with print.

▶ Kindergarten programs based on emergent literacy viewpoints teach traditional readiness aspects in a more integrated manner, using inductive methods and functional reading and writing experiences.

▶ Internet experiences are appropriate for young children and can enhance their literacy learning.

▶ Traditional readiness programs for beginning readers stress auditory and visual discrimination, emphasize the relationship of sounds and symbols, and build an understanding of reading-related concepts. Deductive methods are common, as is the teaching of specific skills.

▶ A number of factors interact to affect literacy development: cognitive development, oral language, perceptual factors, affective factors, and home environment.

▶ Emergent literacy/readiness activities for beginning readers are most effective when they deal specifically with print-related items (for example, letters, letter groups, words, sentences, stories, and concepts such as "page").

▶ Informal measures and observational data, in addition to more formal emergent literacy/readiness tests, are used to assess beginning readers' literacy development.

Making Instructional Decisions

1. Make a list of what you think a child entering first grade might already know that would help in learning to read. Tell how the things you have identified relate to reading. How would you capitalize on what the child already knows in your emergent literacy/readiness program?

2. Differentiate between attitude and interest. How do you think the terms are related? How do they differ? How might aspects of both affect your emergent literacy/readiness instruction?

3. If possible, visit two kindergarten classrooms to observe what is taking place. Discuss with each teacher how activities are planned, which seem to be most appropriate for the students, and why. Then write down your impressions of each classroom and how you might modify what you see in each situation to more closely reflect your own beliefs.

4. An ongoing debate in early childhood education centers around the curricular content of kindergarten programs. Some educators believe kindergarten should prepare children for later schooling by focusing on the social skills and curricular background necessary for instruction in first grade. According to this view, kindergarten should provide children with opportunities to scribble, draw, look at picture books, and explore literacy as their interests dictate. Others believe kindergarten should more formally teach some basic decoding content, usually with regard to letter names, letter-sounds, and discrimination of both upper- and lowercase letters, within a designated curriculum. What do you think kindergarten instruction should accomplish? How does your literacy framework relate to this debate?

5. Go back to any three of the Internet sites mentioned in this chapter. Explore them and write a lesson plan incorporating what you find into an experience appropriate for young children.

6. Examine a formal and an informal readiness test. What similarities and differences do you see, both in terms of structure and focus of evaluation? How would you use the information from each in an emergent literacy/readiness program?

Further Reading

Bromley, K. (2000). Teaching young children to be writers. In D. S. Strickland, & L. M. Morrow, (Eds.), *Beginning reading and writing* (pp. 111–120). New York: Teachers College Press.

A short chapter that relates reading and writing in early grades and summarizes what teachers can do to foster young children's writing development.

Kinzer, C. K., & Leu, D. J. (1997). The challenge of change: Exploring literacy and learning in electronic environments. *Language Arts, 74*(2), 126–136.

> *An article that uses examples to discuss the possibilities for literacy learning that is supported by electronic learning environments.*

Lass, B. (1982). Portrait of my son as an early reader. *The Reading Teacher, 36*, 20–28.

> *Provides a brief overview of research on characteristics of early readers and provides a timeline of emerging reading behaviors.*

McGee, L. M., & Richgels, D. J. (1989). "K is Kristen's": Learning the alphabet from a child's perspective. *The Reading Teacher, 43*, 216–225.

> *Discusses case studies of children's and parent's dialogues and games that lead to the development of children's alphabet knowledge. Provides guidelines for classroom adaptations.*

Morrow, L. M., Burks, S. P., & Rand, M. K. (Eds.). (1992). *Resources in early literacy development: An annotated bibliography.* Newark, DE: International Reading Association.

> *An annotated bibliography that provides reference sources on topics such as the home environment, oral language, writing and drawing, children's literature, developing comprehension, and learning about print, play, television, computers, and assessment.*

Slaughter, J. P. (1993). *Beyond storybooks: The shared book experience.* Newark, DE: International Reading Association.

> *A very readable paperback that describes the shared book experience and is filled with a wealth of ideas for using this experience to address specific reading tasks within meaningful book experiences.*

Wagstaff, J. (1998). Building practical knowledge of letter-sound correspondences: A beginner's word wall and beyond. *The Reading Teacher, 51*(4), 298–304.

> *Presents a teacher's experience in developing children's awareness of letter-sound relationships through the use of word walls, shared reading of predictable books, and other techniques that do not focus on "letter of the week" procedures.*

References

Aaron, I. E., Chall, J. S., Durkin, D., Goodman, K., & Strickland, D. S. (1990). The past, present, and future of literacy education: Comments from a panel of distinguished educators, Part I. *The Reading Teacher, 43*, 302–311.

Allen, R. V., & Allen, C. (1976). *Language experience activities.* Boston, MA: Houghton Mifflin.

Almy, M., Chittenden, E., & Miller, P. (1966). *Young children's thinking: Studies of some aspects of Piaget's theory.* New York: Teachers College Press.

Anderson, R. C., & Freebody, P. (1985). Vocabulary knowledge. In H. Singer & R. B. Ruddell (Eds.), *Theoretical models and processes of reading* (3rd ed., pp. 343–371). Newark, DE: International Reading Association.

Anderson, R. C., Hiebert, E. H., Scott, J. A., & Wilkinson, I. A. G. (1985). *Becoming a nation of readers: The report of the commission on reading.* Washington, DC: National Institute of Education.

Ashton-Warner, S. (1963). *Teacher.* New York: Simon & Schuster.

Ashton-Warner, S. (1972). *Spearpoint.* New York: Knopf.

Aulls, M. W. (1982). *Developing readers in today's elementary schools.* Boston, MA: Allyn & Bacon.

Barrett, T. C. (1965). Visual discrimination tasks as predictors of first grade reading achievement. *The Reading Teacher, 18*, 276–282.

Bond, G. L., & Dykstra, R. (1967). The cooperative research program in first grade reading instruction. *Reading Research Quarterly, 2*, 5–142.

Bransford, J. D. (1988, August). Personal communication.

Bybee, R. W., & Sund, R. B. (1982). *Piaget for educators.* Columbus, OH: Merrill.

Calfee, R., Chapman, R., & Venezky, R. (1972). How a child needs to think to learn to read. In L. Gregg (Ed.), *Cognition in learning and memory* (pp. 139–182). New York: John Wiley & Sons.

Calkins, L. M. (1983). *Lessons from a child. On the teaching and learning of writing.* New York: Heinemann.

Carbo, M. (1988). Debunking the great phonics myth. *Phi Delta Kappan, 70*, 226–237.

Catterson, J. (1989). Reflections: An interview with Jane Catterson. *Reading-Canada-Lecture, 7*, 40–49.

Chall, J. S. (1979). The great debate: Ten years later, with a modest proposal for reading stages. In L. B. Resnick & P. A. Weaver (Eds.), *Theory and practice of early reading* (Vol. 1, pp. 29–55). Hillsdale, NJ: Lawrence Erlbaum Associates.

Chall, J. S. (1989). Learning to read: The great debate 20 years later—A response to "Debunking the great phonics myth." *Phi Delta Kappan, 70*, 521–538.

Clay, M. M. (1980a). *The early detection of reading difficulties: A diagnostic survey* (2nd ed.). New York: Heinemann Educational Books.

Clay, M. M. (1980b). *Reading: The patterning of complex behavior* (2nd ed.). New York: Heinemann Educational Books.

Clay, M. M. (1985a). *Sand: The concepts about print test.* Exeter, NH: Heinemann Educational Books.

Clay, M. M. (1985b). *Stones: The concepts about print test.* Exeter, NH: Heinemann Educational Books.

Clay, M. M. (1993). *An observation survey of early literacy achievement.* Auckland, New Zealand: Hienemann.

Dale, E. (1965). Vocabulary measurement: Techniques and major findings. *Elementary English, 42*, 895–901, 948.

Danks, J., & Fears, R. (1979). Oral reading: Does it reflect decoding or comprehension? In L. B. Resnick & P. A. Weaver (Eds.), *Theory and practice of early reading* (Vol. 3). Hillsdale, NJ: Lawrence Erlbaum Associates.

Davey, B. (1983). Think-aloud—Modeling the cognitive processes of reading comprehension. *Journal of Reading, 27*, 44–47.

Davidson, S., Stickney, C. P., & Weil, R. (1980). *Intermediate accounting concepts: Methods and uses.* Hinsdale, IL: Dryden Press.

DeFord, D. E. (1986). Classroom contexts for literacy learning. In T. E. Raphael & R. E. Reynolds (Eds.), *The contexts of school-based learning* (pp. 163–190). New York: Random House.

Downing, J., Dwyer, C. A., Feitelson, D., Jansen, M., Kemppainen, R., Matihaldi, H., Reggi, D. R., Sakamoto, T., Taylor, H., Thakary, D. V., & Thomson, D. (1979). A cross-national survey of cultural expectations and sex-role standards in reading. *Journal of Research in Reading, 2,* 8–23.

Durkin, D. (1966). *Children who read early: Two longitudinal studies.* New York: Columbia University, Teachers College Press.

Durkin, D. (1974–1975). A six-year study of children who learned to read in school at the age of four. *Reading Research Quarterly, 10,* 9–61.

Durkin, D. (1987). *Teaching young children to read* (4th ed.). Boston, MA: Allyn & Bacon.

Durkin, D. (1989). *Teaching them to read* (5th ed.). Boston, MA: Allyn & Bacon.

Education Week on the Web. November 10, 1997.

Fitzgerald, J. (1983). Helping readers gain self-control. *The Reading Teacher, 37,* 249–253.

Fredericksen, J. R. (1982). *A componential theory of reading skills and their interaction* (Tech. Rep. No. 242). Champaign, IL: University of Illinois, Center for the Study of Reading.

Galda, L. (1988). Readers, texts, and contexts: A response-based view of literature in the classroom. *New Advocate, 1,* 92–102.

Getting Ready to Read (Teacher's ed.). (1979). Boston, MA: Houghton Mifflin.

Gibson, E. J., & Levin, H. (1980). *The psychology of reading* (3rd ed.). Cambridge, MA: MIT Press.

Goodman, J. R. (1990). A naturalistic study of the relationship between literacy development and sociodramatic play in five-year-old children. Unpublished doctoral dissertation, Peabody College of Vanderbilt University, Nashville, TN.

Goodman, K. S., & Goodman, Y. M. (1979). Learning to read is natural. In L. B. Resnick & P. A. Weaver (Eds.), *Theory and practice of early reading* (Vol. 1, pp. 137–154). Hillsdale, NJ: Lawrence Erlbaum Associates.

Goodman, K. S., Goodman, Y. M., & Hood, W. J. (Eds.). (1989). *The whole language evaluation book.* Portsmouth, NH: Heinemann.

Graves, D. H. (1983). *Writing: Teachers and children at work.* Exeter, NH: Heinemann.

Harris, A. J., & Sipay, E. R. (1990). *How to increase reading ability* (9th ed.). White Plains, NY: Longman Publishing Group.

Harris, T. L., & Hodges, R. E. (Eds.). (1981). *A dictionary of reading and related terms.* Newark, DE: International Reading Association.

Harris, T. L., & Hodges, R. E. (Eds.). (1995). *The literacy dictionary: The vocabulary of reading and writing.* Newark, DE: International Reading Association.

Harste, J. C., Woodward, V. A., & Burke, C. L. (1984). *Language stories and literacy lessons.* Portsmouth, NH: Heinemann.

Heathington, B. S. (1976). *Scales for measuring attitudes.* In J. E. Alexander & R. C. Filler (Eds.), *Attitudes and reading* (pp. 27–32). Newark, DE: International Reading Association.

Hoffman, J. V., McCarthy, S. J., Abbott, J., Christian, C., Corman, L., Curry, C., Dressman, M., Elliott, B., Matherne, D., & Stahle, D. (1994). So what's new in the new basals? A focus on first grade. *Journal of Reading Behavior, 26,* 47–73.

Holdaway, D. (1979). *The foundations of literacy.* Exeter, NH: Heinemann.

Inhelder, B., & Piaget, J. (1964). *The early growth of logic in the child.* New York: Norton.

Kawakami-Arakaki, A. J., Oshiro, M. E., & Farran, D. C. (1989). Research into practice: Integrating reading and writing in a kindergarten curriculum. In J. M. Mason (Ed.), *Reading and writing connections* (pp. 199–218). Boston, MA: Allyn & Bacon.

Leu, D. J., & Leu, D. D. (2000). *Teaching with the Internet: Lessons from the classroom* (3rd ed.). Norwood, MA: Christopher-Gordon Publishers, Inc.

Liberman, I. Y., & Shankwiler, D. (1980). Speech, the alphabet, and teaching to read. In L. B. Resnick & P. A. Weaver (Eds.), *Theory and practice of early reading, 2.* Hillsdale, NJ: Lawrence Erlbaum Associates.

Loban, W. D. (1963). *The language of elementary school children.* Urbana, IL: National Council of Teachers of English.

Luria, A. R. (1976). *Cognitive development: Its cultural and social foundations.* Cambridge, MA: Harvard University Press.

Martin, J. B., Jr. (1967). *Ten Little Caterpillars.* New York: Holt Rinehart & Winston.

Mason, J. M. (Ed.). (1989). *Reading and writing connections.* Boston, MA: Allyn & Bacon.

Mason, J. M. (1980). When do children learn to read: An exploration of four-year-old children's letter and word reading competencies. *Reading Research Quarterly, 15,* 203–223.

McCallum, R. D. (1988). Don't throw out the basal with the bathwater. *The Reading Teacher, 42,* 204–209.

McGee, L. M., & Richgels, D. J. (1990). *Literacy's beginnings: Supporting young readers and writers.* Boston, MA: Allyn & Bacon.

McKenna, M. C., Robinson, R. D., & Miller, J. W. (1993). Whole language and research: The case for caution. In D. J. Leu & C. K. Kinzer (Eds.), *Examining central issues in literacy research, theory, and practice* (pp. 141–152). Chicago, IL: National Reading Conference.

McKenna, M. C., Stahl, S., & Reinking, D. (1994). A critical commentary on research, politics, and whole language. *Journal of Reading Behavior, 26(2),* 211–333.

Morphett, M. V., & Washburn, C. (1931). When should children begin to read? *Elementary School Journal, 31,* 496–503.

Nessel, D., & Jones, M. (1981). *The language experience approach to reading.* New York: Teachers College Press.

Olson, A. V., & Johnson, C. (1970). Structure and predictive validity of the Frostig Development Test of Visual Perception in grades one and three. *Journal of Special Education, 4,* 49–52.

Piaget, J. (1963). *The origins of intelligence in children.* New York: Norton (Original edition by International Universities Press, 1952).

Pike, K., Compain, R., & Mumper, J. (1994). *New connections: An integrated approach to literacy.* New York: HarperCollins College Publishers.

Richek, M. A. (1977–1978). Readiness skills that predict initial word learning using two different methods of instruction. *Reading Research Quarterly, 13,* 209–221.

Robeck, M. C., & Wallace, R. R. (1990). *The psychology of reading: An interdisciplinary approach* (2nd ed.). Hillsdale, NJ: Lawrence Erlbaum Associates.

Rosenblatt, L. M. (1988). *Writing and reading: The transactional theory.* (Tech. Rep. No. 416). Urbana, IL: Center for the Study of Reading.

Rowe, D. W. (1989). Author/audience interaction in the preschool: The role of social interaction in literacy learning. *Journal of Reading Behavior, 21,* 311–350.

Rowe, D. W. (1994). *Preschoolers as authors: Literacy learning in the social world of the classroom.* Cresskill, NJ: Hampton Press.

Rowe, D. W. (1998). The literate potentials of book-related dramatic play. *Reading Research Quarterly, 33*(1), 10–25.

Rowe, D. W., & Harste, J. C. (1990). Learning how to write. In R. Tierney, S. Greene, & N. Spivey (Eds.), *Writing, learning and knowing: Social-cognitive perspectives.* Unpublished manuscript.

Samuels, S. J. (1972). The effect of letter-name knowledge on learning to read. *American Educational Research Journal, 9,* 65–74.

Shanahan, T. (Ed.). (1990). *Reading and writing together: New perspectives for the classroom.* Norwood, MA: Christopher-Gordon.

Silvaroli, N. J. (1965). Factors in predicting children's success in first grade reading. In J. A. Figure (Ed.), *Reading inquiry international* (Vol. 10, pp. 296–298). Newark, DE: International Reading Association.

Slaughter, J. P. (1993). *Beyond storybooks: The shared book experience.* Newark, DE: International Reading Association.

Smith, C. B. (Moderator). (1994). *Whole language: The debate.* Bloomington, IN: ERIC Clearinghouse on Reading, English and Communication.

Smith, F. (1996). *Reading without nonsense,* 3rd ed. New York: Teachers College Press.

Stahl, S. A., & Miller, P. D. (1989). Whole language and language experience approaches for beginning reading: A quantitative research synthesis. *Review of Educational Research, 59,* 87–116.

Stallman, A. C., & Pearson, P. D. (1990). Formal measures of early literacy. In L. M. Morrow & J. K. Smith (Eds.), *Assessment for instruction in early literacy* (pp. 7–44). Englewood Cliffs, NJ: Prentice Hall.

Stauffer, R. (1980). *The language experience approach to the teaching of reading* (2nd ed.). New York: Harper & Row.

Sulzby, E. (1990). Assessment of emergent writing and children's language while writing. In L. M. Morrow & J. K. Smith (Eds.), *Assessment for instruction in early literacy* (pp. 83–109). Englewood Cliffs, NJ: Prentice Hall.

Teale, W. H., & Sulzby, E. (Eds.). (1986). *Emergent literacy: Writing and reading.* Norwood, NJ: Ablex.

Teale, W. H., & Sulzby, E. (1989). Emergent literacy: New perspectives. In D. S. Strickland & L. M. Morrow (Eds.), *Emerging literacy: Young children learn to read and write* (pp. 1–15). Newark, DE: International Reading Association.

Teale, W. H., & Yokota, J. (2000). Beginning reading and writing: Perspectives on instruction. In D. S. Strickland & L. M. Morrow (Eds.), *Beginning reading and writing* (pp. 3–21). Newark, DE: International Reading Association.

Valencia, S. W., Hiebert, E. H., & Afflerbach, P. P. (1994). Definitions and perspectives. In S. W. Valencia, E. H. Hiebert, & P. P. Afflerbach (Eds.), *Authentic reading assessment: Practices and possibilities* (pp. 6–21). Newark, DE: International Reading Association.

Vygotsky, L. S. (1978). *Mind in society.* Cambridge, MA: Harvard University Press.

Vygotsky, L. S. (1986). *Thought and language.* (A. Kozulin, Ed. & Trans.). Cambridge, MA: MIT Press (Originally published 1962).

Waller, G. T. (1977). *Think first, read later! Piagetian prerequisites for reading.* Newark, DE: International Reading Association.

Wells, G. (1986). *The meaning makers: Children learning language and using language to learn.* Portsmouth, NH: Heinemann.

Willinsky, J. (1988). Recalling the moral force of literature in education. *Journal of Educational Thought, 22,* 118–132.

Yaden, D. B., Rowe, D. W., & MacGillivray, L. (2000). Emergent literacy: A matter of polyphony. In M. L. Kamil, P. Mosenthal, P. D. Pearson, & R. Barr (Eds.), *Handbook of reading research, Volume III* (pp. 425–454). Mahwah, NJ: Lawrence Erlbaum Associates.

CHAPTER 6

The Important Role of Children's Literature

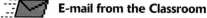

E-mail from the Classroom

Subject: My Favorite Children's Literature Selection
From: Christina M. Ianno, cmianno@FREESIDE.SCSD.K12.NY.US

My all time favorite book is *The Math Curse*. It's written by John Scieszka and illustrated by Lane Smith.

It's an excellent book to use with third graders or older children. I have started my last two years' math classes with it. I know—you're wondering what children's literature has to do with math—but good books can be used in any content area. *The Math Curse* begins with a student describing his anxiety over math. The teacher explains that almost everything can be thought of as a math problem. The situations are turned into riddles, which are then turned into math problems—one on each page. Half the fun is trying to figure out how to solve the riddles or problems.

Using it in class, I first read the entire book and have the students just listen. Then, I read each page and the students try to figure out what the problem is and write it down. I then go back and read the book again, helping students who need assistance to write down each problem. Once the students have each problem written out, their homework is to try to solve each one. Some are really easy, and some are kind of hard. It is a nice introduction to the year to get students' attention when it comes to math. Also, students at this age seem to really like brain teasers.

Christi
Sixth Grade Teacher
Syracuse, NY

Key Concepts

aesthetic stance

Caldecott Medal

culturally conscious literature

directed reading–thinking activity

Drop Everything And Read (DEAR)

efferent stance

grand conversations

literature discussion groups

narrative discourse structure

Newbery Medal

read-aloud session

readers theater

text sets

thematic units on diversity

After reading this chapter, you should be able to:

1. Use children's literature to meet the individual needs in your classroom.

2. Explain why children's literature is important for your classroom literacy program.

3. Help children become independent readers by using at least three different instructional strategies.

4. Use literature to help children understand the diversity of the human experience with at least two instructional strategies.

5. Use keypal response partners, read-aloud response journal activities, grand conversations, literature discussion groups, and text sets to increase the variety and depth of children's reading responses.

6. Explain how your literacy framework informs decisions about the use of literature in your classroom, considering issues such as "What to teach" and "How to teach."

Use Exceptional Works of Literature: A Principle of Effective Literacy Instruction

This chapter explores a fourth, research-based principle of effective literacy instruction.

4. **Use exceptional works of literature and other text types.** Exceptional children's literature, including a variety of text types, is essential to include in an effective literacy program (Anderson, Hiebert, Scott, & Wilkinson, 1985; Galda, Ash, & Cullinan, 2000; Snow, Burns, & Griffin, 1998). A story is an important tool for you to use as you seek to support each child's literacy development in your classroom.

Christi Ianno's message illustrates this important point: A good story may be used for many instructional purposes, even the teaching of math (Anderson, Fielding, & Wilson, 1988; Galda, Ash, & Cullinan, 2000; Tompkins & McGee, 1993; Tunnell & Jacobs, 1989). Moreover, reading or listening to a good book often leaves a lasting impression about reading. Think about the books you read in childhood, books such as *The Snowy Day, Babar, Green Eggs and Ham, Where the Wild Things Are, Stevie, Little House in the Big Woods, Charlotte's Web,* or *The Velveteen Rabbit.* Titles like these usually bring back warm and pleasant memories about reading, and your ability to retain those memories reflects the profound effect literature exerts on young children. As teachers, we need to ensure that our children have similarly positive experiences with literature. Children's literature should be at the center of every classroom literacy program.

literature Often a story, but comprises a variety of text types, including fiction, nonfiction, and poetry.

When we use the term **literature,** we include many different types of writing: fiction, nonfiction, and poetry. At its core, though, literature often represents a powerful story—the story of individuals who celebrate life as they struggle with its challenges.

It is easy to learn many things from a good story. This is why literature is so helpful for teaching. Every culture uses stories to pass important information on to future generations. Clearly, a story is an important vehicle for learning that has been used as long as humans have had the power of language.

Another reason why literature is such a powerful vehicle for literacy learning is because its positive effects reach into every component of literacy you encountered in chapter 3: social aspects, affective aspects, emergent literacy, automaticity, metacognitive knowledge, discourse knowledge, syntactic knowledge, vocabulary knowledge, and decoding knowledge. With the exception of writing experiences, no other tool at your disposal has such a profound and pervasive impact on literacy development. Knowing how literature contributes to each component will help you understand why it is so important to literacy instruction and how you can use these insights in a classroom literacy program.

Developing Social Aspects through Literature

The literature choices you make establish an important social context for your classroom. The stories you choose and the way you use them say much about the potentials you imagine for reading: increasing multicultural understanding, developing critical thinking and analysis, learning about life, or simply the pleasure of enjoying a good tale. In addition, the enthusiasm you bring to works of literature tells your children what you think is exciting and important. And the efforts you make to ensure positive literature experiences at home for your students profoundly affect their life each day after school. There is nothing more important to your literacy program than the literature experiences you make available to children.

Developing Affective Aspects through Literature

Literature has a powerful effect on three important affective aspects: interest, motivation, and emotional response. Good literature captures children's interest and motivates them. Interested readers invest more of themselves in reading experiences and thus take more away from those experiences. They are willing to work harder to recognize difficult words, guess the meaning of unfamiliar words, and think critically about what they have read. Interested readers are motivated readers who quickly learn many things from their reading experiences.

Literature is also useful for children who are struggling to understand the realities of life. Children find emotional support in stories about an issue they are trying to understand—death, love, fear, personal relationships, or self-respect. Literature shows children they are not alone in their emotions, and it often provides solutions to issues of personal concern (Harris & Sipay, 1990).

Developing Emergent Literacy through Literature

Literature is important for developing emergent literacy both at home and at school. Parents who read to their children are preparing them for later reading experiences at school (Taylor & Strickland, 1986). In fact, many suggest that reading aloud to children on a regular basis is the most important thing parents can do to support their children's literacy development. Young children develop important insights from having a parent read to them: reading is enjoyable, print progresses from left to right, written words are related to spoken language, stories have a predictable structure, letters are used to form words, words are used to form sentences, and many other important insights (Clay, 1989; Cochran-Smith, 1984; Trelease, 2001). Similar experiences with literature in preschool and elementary school classrooms continue this development (Tunnell & Jacobs, 1989). Teachers can assist the transition to literacy by encouraging parents to read frequently to their children and by making literature experiences the center of emergent literacy programs at school.

Developing Automaticity through Literature

It is common to hear reading teachers say, "The more you read, the better you read." There are many important truths in this simple statement. Perhaps the most important truth is this: As we read, we continually practice all of the many aspects of this complex process. Reading exciting works of children's literature makes your children better readers as they recognize new words, make new inferences, develop new and more efficient reading strategies, and anticipate new outcomes—all while they are enjoying a wonderful tale. Good literature encourages the reading of more good literature and directly leads to better reading ability. Clearly, "The more you read, the better you read."

Developing Metacognitive Knowledge through Literature

The rich contexts of literature also support the development of metacognitive knowledge, enabling readers to develop effective reading strategies. When readers are entranced by a story, they often discover useful reading strategies on their own as they seek to discover how a story unfolds. Interested readers look for new ways to decode a word, novel approaches to determining word meanings, and different methods of making inferences. These experiences lead to new types of reading strategies; literature is very useful in helping children develop effective reading strategies.

Developing Discourse Knowledge through Literature

Literature helps children develop a clear sense of how stories are structured. They learn that stories have certain types of beginnings and recognize that stories usually contain problems faced by main characters, problems that often are resolved through a series of episodes. Children also discover that different types of stories have different types of structures; for example, a fable differs from a mystery or a work of science fiction. Knowing the structure of different forms of writing helps develop both reading and writing in important ways.

Developing Syntactic Knowledge through Literature

Literature helps young readers enrich their syntactic knowledge. The work of the best writers provides excellent models of language use. Young children already are familiar with the sentence patterns of oral language; reading frequently to them introduces the more complex syntactic patterns found in written language. This is one reason why reading to children before they come to school is so helpful. Familiarity with the more complex patterns of written language is important as children encounter increasingly more complex sentence patterns in content areas such as social studies, science, and math.

Developing Vocabulary Knowledge through Literature

Literature increases vocabulary knowledge as it captures, entertains, and enriches the lives of readers with vivid experiences that are impossible to create in a classroom. Literature lets you travel to the top of Mount Everest or to the bottom of the sea; to the edge of the galaxy or to the center of Earth; to the time of King Arthur or to the time of space traders—all without leaving a comfortable chair. Participating in these experiences, if only vicariously, enriches a child's vocabulary knowledge. What better way is there to understand words such as *Nazi, Europe, terror,* and *diary* than to read *Number the Stars* or *The Diary of Anne Frank?* What better way to visualize the words, *prairie, head cheese, journey, pioneer, hearth, covered wagon, fiddle, threshing,* or *harvest* than to discover the *Little House* series by Laura Ingalls Wilder? Good literature teaches word meanings in a powerful and entrancing fashion.

Developing Decoding Knowledge through Literature

A major goal for younger readers is to develop automatic decoding skills, or fluency with reading. Because automatic decoding permits readers to focus their attention on a text's meaning and on their response, both comprehension and response increase with the development of automatic decoding (Snow, Burns, & Griffin, 1998). Literature provides opportunities for children to develop this automaticity (Rasinski, 1989). Good literature engages young readers, drawing them into a favorite book again and again. These repeated reading experiences lead children to discover many important elements of decoding knowledge as they pause and consider the print on the pages of a favorite book: letter–sound relationships, the sound of a favorite word, or how to use the context of a sentence to guess an unfamiliar word. We seek to get our younger readers "hooked on books" (Fader, 1976) so that they read and reread their favorite literary experiences. Once hooked, they have greater opportunities to recognize words and, as a result, to develop automatic decoding skills.

Check your ongoing understanding of chapter concepts by using the guided review for this chapter on http://www.prenhall.com/leukinzer

Using Literature to Develop Independent Readers

You can see that literature is a powerful vehicle for learning, enabling children to develop each component important to reading and response. These instructional benefits clearly are essential to consider. Nevertheless, as important as it is to teach children how to read, this is not the most important goal of any reading program. Surprised? You shouldn't be.

The most important goal of everyone who works to support reading is to develop **independent readers.** Independent readers are those who not only know how to read, but choose to read for pleasure, information, and personal growth. Independent readers read at home, not just at school. They regularly visit a local library. Independent readers are often children who sneak a flashlight under the covers at night to find out how a story ends. Independent readers are children who are likely to read a book in the evening instead of watch television. Because these children choose to read independently, they have additional opportunities to develop their reading ability beyond the limited time available at school. As a result, they become better readers (Anderson, Fielding, & Wilson, 1988). Independent readers are lifelong learners who

independent readers Readers who know how to read and actually choose to read for pleasure, information, and personal growth.

E-mail from the Classroom

From: Bonnie Olinto, 102474.3544@COMPUSERVE.COM
To: RTEACHER@BOOKMARK.READING.ORG (A discussion group for the
   journal, *The Reading Teacher*)
Subject: Read-Alouds for Third Grade

Dear Friends,

I am going to be teaching third grade and would love some advice on great read-alouds!
Anyone have any suggestions? This is my first year teaching and I want the children to love
to read!!

Thanks,
Bonnie
Fairfax County, Virginia

know how to read and use this ability to improve their own lives as well as the society in which they live.

Teaching our children to read without also developing their desire to read independently is wasted effort (Fuhler, 1990). We do not want our students to read only while they are with us at school. We want them to seek out reading experiences after they have left us so they continue to develop into thoughtful and informed citizens. We need to keep this point in mind as we plan learning experiences for our students.

All of us should make the development of independent readers the most important goal of our reading program. If we wish to cultivate independent readers in our classroom community through children's literature, we must: (1) become familiar with popular children's literature, (2) identify our students' reading interests, and (3) put children and books together in pleasurable settings. Let's look at how to accomplish each of these goals.

Becoming Familiar with Popular Children's Literature

There are so many ways to become familiar with popular children's literature. You can begin by looking at books awarded the Newbery or Caldecott medals. The **Newbery Medal** is awarded annually to the author of the "most distinguished contribution to American literature for children published during the preceding year." The **Caldecott Medal** is awarded annually to the artist of the "most distinguished American picture book for children published in the United States during the preceding year." Newbery and Caldecott medal winners are selected by adults, using adult criteria. Although medal-winning books meet the highest standards of the two associations that select them, they do not always meet the unique needs of children. Newbery and Caldecott medal winners are listed in Appendices A and B for your use. You may find some of your childhood favorites in these lists.

As the messages on this page and the next from the RTEACHER mailing list demonstrate, teachers like Bonnie Olinto also become familiar with popular children's literature through the Internet. Posting a question to a mailing list like RTEACHER is a great way to obtain book recommendations from other teachers. Often teachers will share instructional ideas, too.

Another mailing list to help you become more familiar with children's literature is **KIDLIT-L,** where approximately 3,000 members share their insights about literature for children and young adults. Many are librarians. To subscribe to this list, send a subscription request to the administrative address for **KIDLIT-L** (listserv@bingvmb.cc.binghamton.edu) as described in Chapter 3.

You can also become familiar with children's literature by exploring a central site for children's literature on the Internet. One of the best is **The Children's Literature Web**

Newbery Medal An annual award given to the author of the "most distinguished contribution to American literature for children."

Caldecott Medal An annual award given to the artist of the "most distinguished American picture book published in the United States."

E-mail from the Classroom

Subject: Re: Read-Alouds for Third Grade
From: Mellony Spinelli, dspinell@BORG.COM
**To: RTEACHER@BOOKMARK.READING.ORG (A discussion group for the
journal, *The Reading Teacher*)**

Bonnie,
    There are so many great books for children at this level. Some of my favorites are these. I know others on our list will share their favorites, too:

So You Want to be President by Judith St. George. Illustrated by David Small. Philomel, 2001.

Click, Clack, Moo: Cows that Type by Doreen Cronin. Illustrated by Betsy Lewin. Simon & Schuster, 2001.

Two Bad Ants by Chris Van Allsburg. Houghton Mifflin, 1988.

Koala Lou by Mem Fox. Illustrated by Pamela Lofts. Harcourt Brace, 1989.

Wilfrid Gordon McDonald Partridge by Mem Fox. Kane/Miller Book Pub., 1990.

Muggie Maggie by Beverly Cleary. Illustrated by Kay Life. William Morrow & Co., 1990. (A third grader learns about cursive writing.)

Ruby by Rosa Guy. Laureleaf, 1992.

Be Good to Eddie Lee by Virginia Fleming. Illustrated by Floyd Cooper. Philomel, 1993. (Learning about children who are different.)

Mean Soup by Betsy Everitt. Harcourt Brace, 1992. (Learning about feelings.)

Aunt Isabel Tells a Good One by Kate Duke. Dutton, 1992. (Learning about the elements of a story.)

The Christmas Miracle of Jonathan Toomey by Susan Wojciechowski. Illustrated by Patrick James Lynch. Candlewick, 1995.

    Did you know there are about 5,000 new children's books every year? There are some very good ones. The ones you should choose are the ones which make you feel some emotion—kids know. As you progress in your year and find topics you are covering in social studies or science, you could go to the library and ask for additional books for your read-alouds. These are just a few of my favorites—the list could go on and on. . . . Happy reading!!!!

Mellony Spinelli, Reading Recovery/Reading Teacher
DeWitt Clinton Elementary School
Rome, New York

Guide (http://www.acs.ucalgary.ca/~dkbrown/index.html). This location (see Figure 6-1) contains the most extensive set of links to children's literature resources available on the WWW. It is a tremendous resource. Another central site for children's literature is found at **The Reading Zone of the Internet Public Library** (http://www.ipl. org/youth/lapage.html). This location will be useful for both you and your students. Each of these central sites contains links to literature resources that will keep you fascinated for days. You should take a little time to explore them.

    You might also look at books selected as either Children's Choices or Teacher's Choices by the International Reading Association and the Children's Book Council. Each year, a joint committee from these two organizations coordinates a selection process involving thousands of children who read new books and vote for their favorites. Another, similar process, exists for Teacher's Choices. Both lists are available at http://

FIGURE 6-1

The home page for **The Children's Literature Web Guide**
(http://www.acs.ucalgary.ca/~dkbrown/index.html), a central site for children's literature
on the WWW

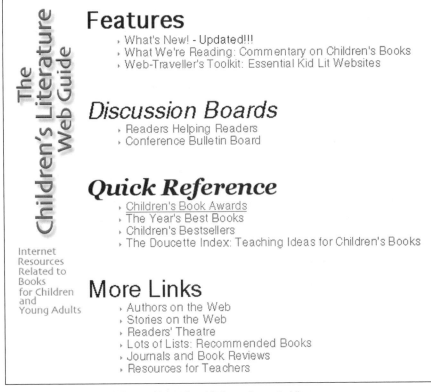

The Children's Literature Web Guide

Internet Resources Related to Books for Children and Young Adults

Features
> What's New! - Updated!!!
> What We're Reading: Commentary on Children's Books
> Web-Traveller's Toolkit: Essential Kid Lit Websites

Discussion Boards
> Readers Helping Readers
> Conference Bulletin Board

Quick Reference
> Children's Book Awards
> The Year's Best Books
> Children's Bestsellers
> The Doucette Index: Teaching Ideas for Children's Books

More Links
> Authors on the Web
> Stories on the Web
> Readers' Theatre
> Lots of Lists: Recommended Books
> Journals and Book Reviews
> Resources for Teachers

Note: Courtesy of David K. Brown, University of Calgary, Doucette Library.

www.reading.org/choices/choices_download.html. Directions appear at this page to purchase copies in bulk. Many teachers enclose copies of these lists in letters mailed out to parents at the beginning of the year. You may also wish to explore the extensive set of award-winning books located at the WWW site **Children's Book Awards** (http://www.acs.ucalgary.ca/dkbrown/awards.html).

Simply talking to children and other teachers at school about their favorite books is also useful. Children provide useful information about what their peers like to read. A school librarian can identify books which are popular at your school. Grade-level colleagues can share their experiences with popular literature selections.

It is also possible to become familiar with popular children's literature by consulting a comprehensive annotated bibliography. General bibliographies of children's literature are found in *Association for Library Service to Children, Notable Children's Books* (Chicago: American Library Association, annual) and *The Horn Book Guide to Children's and Young Adult Books* (Boston: Horn Book Inc., annual). Each is considered by experts to be a valuable resource for exploring the world of children's literature. Your library will probably have a copy of each. In addition, don't overlook your local bookstore as a source of great information about children's reading tastes. Bookstore owners will often share their knowledge of popular authors and book titles.

All of these methods can help you become more familiar with children's literature. However, none takes the place of actually reading children's literature regularly. Personal familiarity enables you to make appropriate choices as you work to build a classroom library and as you make suggestions to individual children.

As you begin to rediscover the world of children's literature, you should develop an easy-to-access database for books you have read. It takes just a few minutes after reading each book to jot down bibliographic information, a synopsis of the story, and several

FIGURE 6-2

A sample entry in a database of children's literature selections

Steptoe, John   *Mufaro's Beautiful Daughters*   30 pages
New York: Lothrop, Lee & Shepard Books, 1987

Synopsis: An African folktale originally collected near the ruins of an ancient city in Zimbabwe, this story tells a tale of good and evil. Nyasha ("mercy") and Manyara ("ashamed") are two sisters who have been invited to appear before the king, who will marry one of them. Manyara, true to her wicked ways, secretly leaves the village first so that she can become queen. Along the way, she ignores a starving boy and a wise woman. Nyasha follows in her footsteps but feeds the starving boy and helps the wise woman. Guess who becomes the queen? Beautiful illustrations! A wonderful tale!

Discussion Questions:

1. How did you feel when Manyara left the village ahead of her sister? Why?

2. What would you have done first if you were the queen or king in this story?

3. How is this tale similar to Cinderella? How is it different?

4. There is a lot of useful information about this story that did not appear in the story itself. Where does this information appear and what did you learn from reading it?

questions you might use to begin a discussion. You should write this information in a consistent format on index cards or on disk, using database management software. You will find your growing file a useful aid in selecting books. It will also be useful during discussions with children about the books they have read. A sample entry in a database is illustrated in Figure 6-2.

Becoming Familiar with Children's Interests

In addition to becoming familiar with children's literature, you need to determine the unique interests of your students, especially those who are reluctant readers. Knowing your students' interests will help you recommend exciting selections to them.

How can you determine your students' interests? Although many methods are available, the most common is an **interest inventory.** Interest inventories contain questions for children to answer about things they enjoy. You can review each student's response to develop a better understanding of individual reading interests. Interest inventories are especially useful in putting together reluctant readers and interesting books. An example of an interest inventory is shown in Figure 6-3 on page 191. You could use this example to develop your own. Chapter 11 also discusses interest and attitude measures.

Additional information can be collected informally as you interact with individual children during the day. Information about favorite activities, hobbies, games, or sports is often revealed during classroom discussions. During the year, you can discover much about your students through these informal discussions.

interest inventory A form used by teachers to gather information about student interests.

Putting Children and Books Together in Pleasurable Settings

If you are familiar with popular children's literature and know your students' interests, you will be able to create a classroom environment rich in literature and help each individual student meet his or her individual needs. You will start many children on the road to becoming independent readers who are able to read, and who also choose to read, on their own. Others, however, will still be reluctant to select and complete a book on their own, telling you they find books boring and uninteresting. Despite your

FIGURE 6-3

An interest inventory used in grades 3–8

WHAT ARE YOUR INTERESTS?

Name: _____ Date: _____

Books

1. What are the titles of the last two books you read?
   _____
   _____

2. Do you have a favorite author? Who is it?
   _____
   _____

3. If you were going on vacation tomorrow and could only take one book with you, what would it be about?
   _____
   _____

4. Where do you get the books that you read?
   _____
   _____

5. Which book would you most like to read again?
   _____
   _____

6. What is your favorite type of book? Fiction? Nonfiction? Science fiction? Romance? Adventure? Biography? Fantasy? Folk tale? Historical fiction?
   _____
   _____
   _____

After School

1. Do you have any hobbies? What are they?
   _____
   _____

2. What do you like to do in your spare time?
   _____
   _____

3. If you had a day in which you could do anything and go anywhere you wanted, what would you do and where would you go?
   _____
   _____

4. Do you have any pets? What are they?
   _____
   _____

5. Do you read any magazines at home? If yes, which ones?
   _____
   _____

6. Do you like sports? Which ones do you like best?
   _____
   _____

7. What are your favorite TV programs?
   _____
   _____
   _____

best intentions and concerted efforts, some children will read a book only if it is required for an assignment.

What can you do about these reluctant readers? You will need to actively seek out ways to put these children together with books in pleasurable settings. Fortunately, there are many ways to combine children and books in pleasurable settings (Hiebert & Colt,

Rocking chairs and pillows are favorite places for children to have pleasurable reading experiences.

1989; Zarrillo, 1989). Some methods, such as read-aloud response journals and individualized reading activities, have already been described in previous chapters; others are described here.

Read-Aloud Sessions.   One of the best ways to bring children and books together in a pleasurable setting is relatively simple: Demonstrate the pleasure of reading a good book in a **read-aloud session** each day (Barrentine, 1996). A read-aloud session is a method framework often used by teachers to develop independent readers. Although teachers conduct read-alouds in a variety of ways, many follow these suggestions (Trelease, 2001):

read-aloud session   A method framework used to develop independent readers; involves choosing a book, practicing reading it, creating a comfortable atmosphere, reading the selection expressively, discussing unfamiliar words, and supporting the children's response.

1. Choose a book with both your students and yourself in mind.
2. Practice reading the book.
3. Create a comfortable atmosphere for reading aloud.
4. Read the selection with feeling and expression.
5. Discuss the meanings of unfamiliar words.
6. Support children's responses to what you have read.

It is especially important to select a book that both you and your students will enjoy. Your students will not listen for long if the story is not interesting, and you will not be able to be an effective model if you are not interested in what you are reading. A set of good books for read-aloud sessions is listed in Figure 6-4. You will discover many others as you explore the world of children's literature.

After you have selected an interesting book, you should practice reading it. Prepare for the intonation patterns in unusual or exciting scenes; perhaps try out different voices for each of the main characters. When you are ready, create a comfortable atmosphere for reading aloud. If possible, gather the children in front of you in a cozy part of the room where

FIGURE 6-4

Great books to read aloud to your students

Wordless Books for Very Young Readers
Amanda and the Mysterious Carpet by Fernando Krahn
The Creepy Thing by Fernando Krahn
Frog on His Own by Mercer Mayer
The Hunter and the Animals by Tomie dePaola
Shopping Trip by Helen Oxenbury
Shrewbetinna's Birthday by John Goodall
Up a Tree by Ed Young

For Young Readers
Alexander and the Terrible, Horrible, No Good, Very Bad Day by Judith Viorst
Brown Bear, Brown Bear, What Do You See? by Bill Martin, Jr.
The Giving Tree by Shel Silverstein
Hey, Al by Arthur Yorinks
Joseph Had a Little Overcoat by Simms Taback
Julian, Dream Doctor by Ann Cameron
Miss Nelson Is Missing by Harry Allard
Miss Rumphius by Barbara Cooney
Mufaro's Beautiful Daughters by John Steptoe
Rapunze by Paul O. Zelinsky
So You Want to Be President? by Judith St. George
Sky Dogs by Jane Yolen
The Ox-Cart Man by Donald Hall
The Polar Express by Chris Van Allsburg
The People Could Fly: American Black Folktales by Verna Aardema
The Velveteen Rabbit by Margery Williams
The Very Hungry Caterpillar by Eric Carle
The Year of the Panda by Miriam Schlein

For Older Readers
A White Romance by Virginia Hamilton
Bridge to Terabithia by Katherine Paterson
Journey of the Sparrows by Fran Leeper Bus
Dear Mr. Henshaw by Beverly Cleary
Dogsong by Gary Paulson
Faithful Elephants by Yukio Tsuchiya
Fast Sam, Cool Clyde and Stuff by Walter Dean Myers
Grandfather's Journey by Allen Say
Maniac Magee by Jerry Spinelli
My Life by Earvin Johnson
Oh, The Places You'll Go by Dr. Seuss
Nobody Nowhere: The Extraordinary Autobiography of an Autistic by Donna Williams
Number the Stars by Lois Lowry
Roll of Thunder, Hear My Cry by Mildred Taylor
Skin Deep by Toecky Jones
Taking Sides by Gary Soto
The Diary of Anne Frank by Anne Frank
The Lion, The Witch and the Wardrobe by C. S. Lewis

---

they can get comfortable. Be sure that children can see the story's pictures. Many teachers bring in a rocking chair for themselves and a rug for the children to sit on.

When everyone is settled, read the selection with feeling and expression. Let your voice create the mood. If the story is scary, you might want to read slowly and carefully. If the story is humorous, stop and enjoy the humor with your students. If the story is sad,

MODEL LESSON

Conducting a Read-Aloud Session in Katie Brown's Class

Katie Brown is a first-grade teacher who wants to help her students develop greater independence in reading. Few children in her class will read an entire book until they are confident they can do so. Katie has used language experience stories, message of the day activities, and many big books to develop her students' familiarity with high-frequency sight words such as *see, can, what, you, me,* and *I.* She also had her students listen to Space ABC's (http://buckman.pps.k12.or.us/room100/ABCspace/spaceabc.html), an alphabet book developed by the first-grade children at Buckman Elementary School in Portland, Oregon. Her students listened and followed along as the children in Oregon read each of their pages in this book, using RealAudio technology on the Internet. Her students are becoming familiar with using context to predict upcoming words, yet many think they cannot read until they are able to read their first book, as they say, "All by myself!" This is something many have not yet been able to do. Until they do so, many will not even try to read a book independently. Katie has a balanced literacy framework but tends to value the meaning that readers bring to a text more than the meaning in a text. As a result, she tends to favor prediction strategies for children who are unable to recognize a word.

Choose a Book with Both Your Students and Yourself in Mind. Katie spoke with Nancy Hamm, the school librarian, about her needs. Nancy suggested that Katie look at several predictable texts (stories with a repeated phrase, sentence, or episode). Katie selected *Brown Bear, Brown Bear* by Bill Martin, Jr. This story looked easy to read because it repeated a three-sentence pattern over and over, changing only the name and color of the animal that appeared in each picture: "Brown bear, brown bear. What do you see? I see a redbird looking at me. Redbird, redbird. What do you see? I see a yellow duck looking at me. Yellow duck, yellow duck. What do you see? I see a blue horse looking at me. . . ." The book also contained many common words her students could recognize. Katie liked the simple illustrations that went with each page because they cued readers about the next animal in the sentence pattern. This enabled children to predict each upcoming sentence.

Practice Reading the Book. Katie read the book to herself that night. She decided to help her students read some of the predictable patterns on their own after she introduced a sentence pattern and showed them the picture for each new animal.

Create a Comfortable Atmosphere for Reading Aloud. After lunch, Katie had her students sit on the rug in front of her rocking chair and get comfortable.

Read the Selection with Feeling and Expression. Katie introduced the book by telling her class she had found a book they could all read by the end of the day. She then started reading the book to her class. After several repe-

let your feelings show. If the story contains a predictable sentence or phrase that repeats itself, stop and have your students say it for you. Share the pleasure of the reading experience through your voice and intonation.

Read-aloud time provides opportunities to develop an understanding of new word meanings. As you encounter words that may be unfamiliar to your students, briefly explain their meanings. However, do not excessively disrupt the story for this purpose.

Finally, be sure to give children an opportunity to respond to what you have read. This step may be accomplished in a brief discussion of listeners' reactions or in a writing experience that follows the story. If children liked the book, be sure to mention other titles by the same author and let them know where those books can be found. You might even want to bring in a few to share at the end of your read-aloud session.

Many teachers have a read-aloud session each day after lunch. Having it after lunch provides a transition from the relatively unstructured lunchtime activities to the more focused activities in the classroom. For younger children, you might read a single short book each day. For older children, you might read one or two chapters each day from a longer selection.

Read-aloud sessions are a powerful way to bring children and books together in a pleasurable setting. They allow you to share your enthusiasm for literature—and this titions of the pattern, she encouraged her students to read the third sentence in the pattern aloud each time it appeared. Thus, Katie would read, "Yellow duck, yellow duck. What do you see?" She would then turn the page so that her students could see the next animal (a blue horse) and note its color. The children would then read the next sentence on their own, "I see a blue horse looking at me." The children really enjoyed reading their part of the pattern. When she reached the end of the story where all of the animals were listed, Katie pointed to each word and had the class read the appropriate color and animal name that appeared under each picture (brown bear, red bird, yellow duck, and so on).

Discuss the Meanings of Unfamiliar Words. Because all of the words in this story were familiar, Katie did not discuss any new word meanings. However, she did encourage children to talk about the different animals in the story.

Support Children's Responses. As the class talked about the different animals in the story, Katie encouraged the children to share what they knew about each one. She learned a lot about her students from what they said. Afterward, the children wanted to read the book again. Katie helped them to use the repeated sentence pattern and the pictures to figure out each sentence. Because nearly all of the sentences followed the same pattern, the children were able to read the entire story. Katie told her students how impressed she was that they had read the book all by themselves. She then put the book on the table in the reading corner and encouraged them to read it whenever they had a free moment. Many of her students were surprised to discover they could read an entire book when it contained such predictable sentences. Katie could see an immediate difference in the way they approached other books, too. They began to explore books they wouldn't even open before. She encouraged her students to take the book home to read to their parents and show them what good readers they were becoming. Each child signed up for one evening to share the book at home. The experience was so positive Katie decided to bring in more predictable texts for her class.

In this lesson, Katie Brown used a read-aloud activity to show her students they could use context to predict upcoming words and sentences. This supported her children as they brought meaning to the text. Her reader-based beliefs informed this decision. Other teachers, though, will use a read-aloud activity for different purposes. Teachers with text-based beliefs about how one reads, for example, might use a read-aloud activity to increase affective aspects such as interest and motivation. They would be less interested in using predictable texts since these types of stories encourage the use of prediction strategies rather than careful analysis of letter-sound relationships. Like all teachers, however, teachers with text-based beliefs understand the importance of bringing children and books together in pleasurable settings. Read-alouds show children how important it is to enjoy a good book together.

enthusiasm is contagious. If children see you appear interested and enthusiastic about literature, they will be more interested in reading themselves. Read-aloud sessions can also be used as a springboard for many other learning experiences. You can see how one teacher used a read-aloud session in the model lesson above.

Readers Theater. Another way to put children and books together in pleasurable settings is to use **readers theater.** Readers theater activities engage a group of children in a dramatic presentation of a short script they have adapted from a shared reading selection. As a method framework, readers theater often follows these steps.

readers theater A method framework used to develop independent readers in four steps: reading, writing a short script, practicing, and performing.

1. Choose and read a literary selection.
2. Write a short script.
3. Practice reading the script.
4. Orally perform the script for the class.

In the first step, a small group of children chooses and reads a literary or nonfiction selection. It may be a piece that one member of the group has discovered or a selection that the teacher suggests. In either case, the first step is to read the passage and become familiar with it. Then the group writes a short script, which usually comes from one of

Activities for Read-Aloud Sessions

Counting Books and Alphabet Books. Use counting books to develop number concepts with preschool and kindergarten children. Use alphabet books to develop letter concepts. Consider using one of these:

Animalia by Graeme Base

Anno's Counting Book by Misumasa Anno

My First Counting Book by Lillian Moore

The Very Hungry Caterpillar by Eric Carle

A, B, C's: The American Indian Way by Richard Red Hawk

Ashanti to Zulu: African Traditions by Margaret Musgrove

After reading a counting book aloud, encourage children to write their own. Provide blank pages and help them draw numbered sets of objects on each page (one pencil, two bikes, and so on). Then write their words at the bottom as they dictate to you. Staple the pages together, and don't forget to have children number the pages in their books. Do a similar activity with alphabet books.

Recipe Reading. Use books related to food to provide an experience with recipe reading. Consider using one of these:

Kwanzaa: An African-American Celebration of Culture and Cooking by Eric Copage

Everybody Cooks Rice by Norah Doley

Cranberry Thanksgiving by Wende and Harry Devlin

The Gingerbread Man by Ed Arno

Stone Soup by Marcia Brown

Rain Makes Applesauce by Julian Scheer

After reading these books, have children read and follow a recipe to make the food described in the book. You may want to do this in the school kitchen with parent helpers. Duplicate the recipe and send it home with children to share with their families.

---

the more exciting episodes in the story. In this process the group turns the narrative into a script for a dramatic presentation.

The next step is to practice reading the various parts in the script with intonation, expression, and eye or hand movements. Children should try different ways of reading each line and try out different parts until agreement is reached about who will read each part and how it will be read. Practice should continue until the group feels ready to perform the script for the class.

A readers theater performance usually is given without props and with readers sitting on chairs in the front of the room. This is different from a play in that the message is usually communicated solely through the voices of the readers—their rhythm, intonation, and pace—rather than through the appearance and movement of actors. Some teachers and students, however, prefer to stage more elaborate readers theaters in which props and moving actors are used.

Initially, readers theater may require teacher direction and guidance, perhaps even teacher-developed scripts to be used as examples. Free scripts for readers theater may be downloaded from the Internet at the page for **Readers Theater Editions** (http://www.aaronshep.com/rt/RTE.html) or **Readers Theater Scripts** (http://www.geocities.com/rtscripts/index.html). Additional resources for readers theater activities, including a listserv for people using readers theater in the classroom, may

Celebrating Diversity

Using Readers Theater to Support Limited English Proficiency Students

Readers theater is a wonderful method framework for all children, especially for those whose first language is not English (Wolf, 1993). During a readers theater experience, children have multiple opportunities to read and discuss the selection with their friends. This will take place, for example, as children prepare a script and practice reading it several times for their presentation. This is very supportive for Limited English Proficiency (LEP) students, especially if they have an opportunity to work in a group with more-proficient English speakers. The experience can be even more supportive if the work of literature comes from the same culture as an LEP student. This will broaden everyone's understanding of cultural differences as it connects reading and writing and provides for individual differences in your classroom.

be located on the Internet at **Other Resources** (http://www.aaronshep.com/rt/other.html#Scripts).

After children have had several opportunities to participate in a readers theater presentation, they will be eager to select their own pieces, write their own scripts, and determine their own performances. In the model lesson that follows (p. 198), Bob Catney's fifth graders have already completed several readers theater activities with prepared scripts. Now he wants them to read a literature selection and prepare their own script, which they will then practice and perform.

Reading Corners. If you are committed to putting children and books together in pleasurable settings, it is essential to establish a **reading corner** in your classroom, where children can interact with books and other reading materials in a comfortable fashion. In addition to many different types of reading materials, a reading corner often contains a bookshelf, magazine rack, newspaper rack, carpet, comfortable chairs, pillows, and a display table. A reading corner should be designed to help children become independent readers.

reading corner Portion of a classroom devoted solely to reading and used to develop independent readers.

With the cooperation of the school library or media center, you might establish a small classroom library in your reading corner. You could develop a rotating series of displays, highlighting particular authors or categories of books. Over time, you could acquire your own classroom collection of books. Classroom libraries can be started without great expense by using paperback editions of children's literature, which publishers make available at reasonable prices.

Publishers of paperback books for children often manage book clubs for classrooms. Classrooms receive monthly listings of available titles, and students may place orders through the teacher. Teachers and children are under no obligation to purchase books at any time, but teachers usually receive free books for their classroom libraries if a purchase is made. Several have online locations. These are listed below:

Scholastic Book Services (http://teacher.scholastic.com/clubs/)

Troll Communications (http://www.troll.com/index.html)

You might also decide to place a computer connected to the Internet in your reading corner. Set bookmarks to a variety of magazines on the Internet developed specifically for children. On-line magazines for children include:

Magazines (http://www.yahooligans.com/School_Bell/Language_Arts/Magazines/)—A central site for online kids' magazines.

MODEL LESSON

Readers Theater in Bob Catney's Class

Bob Catney has a balanced literacy framework. He has interactive beliefs about the first issue: *What* should I teach? He believes all components of the reading process are important to teach. Bob likes readers theater because it does a wonderful job of meeting individual needs. As they develop a readers theater presentation, children learn about different components of the reading process, depending on their individual needs. Children who are weak at decoding knowledge receive opportunities to practice this skill as they practice reading and rereading their script aloud before performing it. These students find additional learning opportunities as they discuss the meanings of vocabulary, debate the feelings of a character and how a certain part should be read, and as they develop and edit the spelling of scripts.

Bob has integrated beliefs about the second issue: *How* should I teach? He believes children learn best when they direct their own learning and when they receive more teacher-directed lessons. His readers theater activities are one of several more student-directed learning activities he includes in his program.

Choose and Read a Literary Selection. One group of children has been reading *Maniac McGee* by Jerry Spinelli in a literature discussion group. Bob suggests the children prepare a readers theater presentation based on an episode in the book and then share it with the class. The children discuss different portions of the story and finally settle on an episode from one of the chapters near the end.

Write a Short Script. The group sets off to draft a script. Jinny writes a preliminary draft that afternoon on the classroom computer. As the children read it together the next day, they make suggestions for several changes. Tomás then takes those ideas and revises the script on disk and prints out copies for everyone. The next day the group makes final editing changes and then agrees that the script is ready. The children print out final copies for everyone on the classroom printer.

Practice Reading the Script. The following day is spent reading the parts orally and practicing for the performance. Children try out different parts and different ways of reading each character's voice. They discuss how each character is feeling and why, often referring to passages in the book as evidence for their ideas about how people should read their parts. They eventually settle on the way the piece should be read and they practice it several more times.

Orally Perform the Script for the Class. Every Friday morning, Bob sets time aside for children to share the reading experiences they have had during the week. Jinny and Tomás's group presents its oral reading of *Maniac McGee* in front of the room; the performance is polished and entertaining. Afterward, the group shares the book with the entire class in case other children want to read it. Bob notices several children jotting the title and author down, and later that day he sees them looking for the book when the class visits the school library.

Readers theater can be used by teachers with all types of literacy frameworks. Consider, for example, your beliefs in relation to the first issue: What should I teach? Teachers with text-based beliefs (i.e., meaning is more in the text) will emphasize aspects of decoding knowledge, stressing accurate spelling as students develop their script and focus attention on accurate oral reading as students perform their script. Teachers with reader-based beliefs (i.e., meaning is more in what readers bring to a text) will emphasize prior knowledge components, stressing interpretive elements in the production such as intonation and gestures based on children's understanding of how people feel in different situations.

Consider the second issue of a literacy framework: *How* should I teach? Teachers who believe that children learn best with teacher-directed activities will select the story, provide the script, and direct the practice sessions. Teachers who believe that children learn best when they direct their own learning will allow students to select their own story, develop their own script, and make their own decisions about elements in the performance.

You can see how your literacy framework provides you with important insights and informs the manner in which you use readers theater to support literacy learning. That is the most important function of a literacy framework. It helps you to develop richer insights about why you do what you do in the classroom.

PRACTICAL TEACHING STRATEGIES

Making Your Reading Corner Come Alive

Internet Book Reviews. Set a bookmark on your classroom computer for **World of Reading** (http://www.worldreading.org/). This resource contains book reviews written by children. This allows your students to select books that sound appealing to them. Also invite your students to post their own book reviews at this location.

Great Reads on the Net. Next to your Internet computer, place a bulletin board or a piece of heavy poster board. Invite students to post short descriptions of great stories they find on the Internet. Many wonderful reading experiences are beginning to appear. You might have children begin their explorations by visiting **Children's Writing** (http://www.acs.ucalgary.ca/~dkbrown/writings.html). Encourage them to write the title, location, and a short summary of the contents. Have them also set a bookmark. Other students can use this information to guide their own online reading experiences.

Book Swapping. Set up a swap table in your reading corner, where each student who contributes a book to the table is entitled to take one. Invite children to bring in two books for every one they take. You can then use the extra book in your classroom library.

Book Talks. Each week, introduce new additions to your classroom library in a book talk. Tell your children a few things about each author and book, and then read a short paragraph from the book to interest them. When you are finished, place the books on the display table in your reading corner.

Author of the Week. Make an author-of-the-week bulletin board for your reading corner and have each child be responsible for the board for one week. The child should research a favorite author and create the display, which might contain a short biography, the titles of the author's important books, and a photograph. Invite them to use the extensive links to prominent authors located at **Authors and Illustrators on the Web** (http://www.acs.ucalgary.ca/~dkbrown/authors.html). If children select their authors early in the year, they could write or e-mail them, telling them about their selection for the display. Some authors will respond, and the responses could be displayed.

National Geographic Kids (http://www.nationalgeographic.com/kids/)—One of the best magazines for children to use to explore the world around them.

National Geographic (http://www.nationalgeographic.com/media/ngm/)—The main magazine, designed for both kids and adults.

HiPMag Online (http://www.hipmag.org/)—An online magazine for deaf and hard-of-hearing kids and their pals.

Zuzu (http://www.zuzu.org/)—A hip magazine made for kids with poetry, artwork, recipes, and mystery pictures.

CyberKids (http://www.cyberkids.com/)—Art, stories, and puzzles, all contributed by kids.

Alternatively, you might subscribe your class to one of several hard copy magazines devoted to children. If you do, be sure to announce each issue as it arrives and display it prominently in your reading corner. Popular children's magazines include the following:

Cricket (Cricket Magazine, P.O. Box 51144, Boulder, CO 80321–1144)—Stories, poetry, and informational articles.

Ebony, Jr. (Johnson Publishing Company, 820 South Michigan Avenue, Chicago, IL 60605)—Articles, poetry, and stories about famous African-Americans.

Kids (Kids Publishing, Incorporated, 777 Third Avenue, New York, NY 10017)—A magazine written by children for children.

National Geographic World (National Geographic World, P.O. Box 2330, Washington, DC 20077-9955)—Material from National Geographic written for primary-grade students.

During Drop Everything And Read (DEAR) time, everyone reads a self-selected item silently, without interruption.

Ranger Rick (National Wildlife Federation, Membership Services, 8925 Leesburg Pike, Vienna, VA 22180-0001)—Articles and stories on wildlife and conservation with color photographs.

A reading corner can become an important location for developing independent readers. You can develop many creative strategies to use in such a spot, some of which are described on page 199.

Drop Everything And Read (DEAR).   Another way to bring children and books together is to provide regular time for **Drop Everything And Read (DEAR).** DEAR, sometimes referred to as sustained silent reading, is a method framework providing uninterrupted time for both students and teachers to read self-selected materials (McCracken, 1971). Regardless of the label you use, this method framework consists of three procedural steps:

Drop Everything And Read (DEAR) A method framework used to develop independent readers by providing time for them to read self-selected materials; involves introducing the process, ensuring that everyone has something to read, and reading silently without interruptions.

1. Introduce the purpose and procedures.
2. Be sure everyone has something to read.
3. Everyone reads silently without interruption.

It is important that you introduce the purpose and procedures of this activity before beginning. Several days ahead you should explain what children will be expected to do during DEAR. Tell them this will be a time to read self-selected materials silently without interruption. It is especially important that children understand they will need something to read each day during DEAR. It is best to schedule the activity on a regular basis so that children are always prepared with reading materials.

On the day you begin, have children take out the books they have chosen and start the reading session. Be sure to have several extra reading selections to share with children who may have forgotten to bring their own. It is important that you, too, read something for pleasure during this period. Completing homework assignments, grading papers, and similar activities are not allowed. This is a time for everyone to read something for pleasure.

MODEL LESSON

Drop Everything and Read in Liza Pease's Class

Liza Pease teaches sixth grade. She has a text-based belief about what to teach and a specific skills belief about how to teach. Recently she has been concerned that her students were seldom choosing to read on their own outside of class. Increasingly, she has noticed her students talking about TV, movies, and sports. Seldom does she hear them talk about what they have read. Liza decides to set time aside every Thursday for DEAR to help her students become more independent readers—readers who choose to read on their own.

Introduce the Purpose and Procedures. On Monday, Liza announces they will begin DEAR on Thursday. She tells her class a 10-minute session each Thursday will be devoted to reading whatever anyone chooses to read. She explains the two rules for this activity: (1) everybody must read, and (2) there will be no interruptions. She says they will need to have something to read during each session, beginning on Thursday. One student asks whether he may read a comic book. Liza explains they may read anything they wish, including comics, magazines, and newspapers.

Be Sure Everyone Has Something to Read. On Thursday afternoon, Liza announces that it is time to begin Drop Everything And Read. She reminds her students of the two basic rules and tells them to begin reading the selection they brought. Two children have forgotten to bring something. Liza takes out several magazines she brought for this purpose and has the children choose something to read from these materials. Then, Liza begins reading the book she brought to read, John F. Kennedy's *Profiles in Courage*.

Read Silently without Interruptions. When several children begin whispering, Liza reminds them of the second rule for Drop Everything And Read. The remainder of the period goes quietly. After 10 minutes, Liza announces the time for DEAR is over. She discusses the activity with her students; everyone seemed to enjoy it. Liza announces that the class will engage in Drop Everything And Read every Thursday and that everyone should bring something to read. She tells them she will increase the amount of time to 20 minutes as they become familiar with the activity.

DEAR may be used by teachers to develop independent readers, regardless of the type of literacy framework they possess. This is because all teachers, regardless of their literacy frameworks, should seek to develop independent readers—those who choose to read something for pleasure, information, or self-improvement.

Initially, schedule DEAR for short periods but gradually increase the time set aside as children are able to read for longer periods. Do not allow interruptions during DEAR sessions. Questions, comments, and other conversation should wait to be held until after the silent reading period has been concluded. In addition, children should not be asked to report on what they have read. DEAR must be truly free reading for pleasure if you hope to develop independent readers.

DEAR often involves an entire school—children, teachers, and even the school secretary and custodian may be reading at this time. In the model lesson that follows, Liza Pease has decided to use DEAR in her sixth-grade class to provide more independent reading experiences for her students.

The School Library or Media Center. When considering pleasurable settings in which to bring children and books together, you should not limit your students to the four walls of your classroom. The school library or media center should be at the center of the schools' efforts to develop independent readers. Reserve time for a visit to this special place at least once a week and coordinate the literature experiences you and the school librarian provide. Be sure to share what you are doing in the classroom and find out what the librarian is doing as well. In addition, ask about useful books on themes you are developing in class—these can be borrowed, introduced in a book talk, and placed in your reading corner.

E-mail from the Classroom

From: Karen West, krwest@flash.net
Re: Involving Parents

Dear Readers,

I think one of the most powerful things we can do is involve parents in our classroom program and our professional growth. Here are some things I do at my school:

- Fall pot-luck—you can invite families, and welcome them into your program. Explain your classroom routines. Be prepared to explain what you teach and why, based on your experience, knowledge, and beliefs.
- Develop a program for parent volunteers in the classroom. Find out how they want to participate. Encourage working with learners, not only preparing materials, stapling, cutting, and so on. They could read to a group of students, listen to a student reader, learn to hold individual writing conferences, and more.
- Develop a portfolio system. Perhaps use anecdotal records for evaluation, to inform instruction, and to share documents at conferences.
- Provide some resources that are available for parents to check out which support your views on literacy development.
- Have an open door policy, where parents and colleagues are always welcome.

Best wishes on your journey!

Sincerely,
Karen West, First-Grade Teacher
Tucson, AZ

Your school library is also the perfect place to obtain books for read-aloud sessions, DEAR, or readers theater. When children enjoy a particular story you have read aloud, remind them that it came from the library. Then provide them with a list of related titles by the same author or on the same topic. Ask the librarian to assist you with this task. Pass out the lists just before your regular class visit to the school library. Encourage children to locate books on the list and check them out.

If your school library is well stocked, take full advantage of it. If you do not have a good library, advocate among your colleagues, principal, and parents to improve it. A good school library is important if children are to develop into independent readers.

The Home Environment.   There is a well-known saying from Africa, "It takes an entire village to raise a child." This important insight could also apply to the development of independent readers. Karen West, a first-grade teacher in Arizona, recognizes the importance of inviting parents into her reading program.

As a teacher, you need to enlist the support of all of the important people in the lives of your students. If you are committed to developing independent readers, you must consider ways to extend pleasurable reading situations to children's homes. To do so, you should actively seek the assistance of parents. Parents are almost always willing to help you in these efforts but sometimes do not know what to do. This will require you to regularly communicate the importance of a home environment that supports reading and to provide clear examples of what parents can do to accomplish this. Enlist parents as an important part of your team at Open Houses, Back-to-School Nights, and report card conferences. Send home a letter listing specific ways in which they can help their children become better readers. Use a letter like the one in Figure 6-5. Feel free to copy or edit this letter if it will help you in your work. If you have a home page on the Inter-

FIGURE 6-5

A sample letter sent home to parents at the beginning of the school year

September 4

Dear Parents,

The beginning of school is such an exciting time for everyone. It is a time of new beginnings, new friends, and wonderful new experiences. It is also the time when I receive many questions from parents. Many wish to know how they can help their child with reading, the heart of our school program.

Here are six things you can do to ensure success for your child. Each is easy to do, and each will make an important difference in your child's development:

1. *Set aside a regular time every day to read with your child.* Sharing a good book at bedtime is an enjoyable way to end the day. Reading together for 15 minutes each day is the single most important thing you can do to help your child at school.
2. *Take your child to the local library each week.* Help him or her obtain a library card.
3. *Help your child establish a personal library.* Books can be acquired as birthday and holiday presents.
4. *Create a quiet place in the home where your child can read without being interrupted—away from family traffic and television.* Join your child in this place during a regular reading time.
5. *Model your own reading habits for your child.* When you come across something of interest as you read, show it to your child. Also, involve your child when you search for information in a phone book, TV guide, dictionary, or repair manual. Explain to your child what you are doing.
6. *Encourage the members of your family to give books as holiday and birthday presents.* Giving a book as a present tells your child how important reading is. If you need help selecting a good title, I would be happy to help, as would our school librarian.

If you have an Internet computer, good ideas for parents are available from the International Reading Association at http://www.reading.org/publications/brochures/brochures.html

If you have any further questions about how you can help your child, please call me. I welcome the opportunity to talk with you.

Cordially,

Marcia Teitlebaum

net for your class or school, you may wish to include a link with suggestions for what parents can do at home to help their children with reading.

Other Activities Promoting an Environment Rich in Literature.   As you spend time in schools, you will encounter many new and exciting instructional activities, bulletin board ideas, reading-center tasks, and other means of developing a classroom environment rich in literature. Some ideas will come from colleagues at your school, others will come from professional journals, and still others will come from people you meet on Internet mailing lists. It will be helpful for you to keep track of these ideas, regardless of their source.

You should begin now to collect and organize ideas you find useful. Some teachers keep a notebook for literature ideas; others keep their ideas on separate 3 × 5 cards, organized in a file box. Still others organize this information on a computer, using database management software. However you choose to record and organize your ideas, you might want to include some of the suggestions on page 204.

PRACTICAL TEACHING STRATEGIES

Creating a Classroom Rich in Literature Experiences

CyberGuide for Literature. One of the best resources we have found for using children's literature in combination with the Internet is **CyberGuides** (http://www.sdcoe.k12.ca.us/score/cyberguide.html). Here you will find an extensive set of links to outstanding works of children's literature organized by grade level. Each link contains lesson plans, instructional ideas, links to other web resources, and suggestions for how to use those resources. This location should be familiar to every teacher with an Internet connection in the classroom. Set a bookmark!

Pourquoi Tales: A Multicultural Internet Project. Pourquoi tales are explanatory myths that exist in every culture around the world (e.g., "Why the sun rises every day," "Why the tides rise and fall," and so on). *Anansi, Paul Bunyon,* and *Pecos Bill* stories are also examples. Read several pourquoi tales in class. You may start with Virginia Hamilton's *In the Beginning: Creation Stories from Around the World* or perhaps have students read and then share stories from **Creation Stories** (http://www.internet-at-work.com/hos_mcgrane/creation/cstorymenu.html) during Internet Workshop. Post an invitation for other classrooms around the world to collect and share pourquoi tales from their part of the world. You may wish to post the description of your Internet Project and advertise for collaborating classrooms at any of the sites for Internet Project listed in chapter 2. Exchange these stories by e-mail or at a classroom home page. You may wish to see how **Ms. Hos-McGrane's Grade Six Class** in the Netherlands completed their Internet Project on creation myths (http://www.internet-at-work.com/hos_mcgrane/creation/cstorymenu.html). This project will open up the wider world to your students, help them to develop a better understanding of different cultural contexts, and engage them in wonderful adventures with literature.

Stories from Australia for Young Children. Set a bookmark for **Alex's Scribbles** (http://www.scribbles.com.au/max/bookmain.html) and have your primary-grade students enjoy a wonderful series of adventures about Max the koala and his friends. These stories have been written and illustrated by Alex, a 5-year-old boy, and his father, Scott. They are accompanied by delightful music and interactive animations. Over 250,000 children have traveled to this computer site in Australia to explore these great adventures. Alex, it appears, is quickly becoming the most widely read 5-year-old author in the world.

Book Cover Doors. Turn your classroom door into a book cover each month and use that opportunity to announce to the rest of the school what you are reading aloud to your class. In the lower grades, let your students vote on their favorite read-aloud book from the past month. In the upper grades, have your students design and construct the book cover for the book you are reading aloud at that time.

RIF. Visit RIF (**Reading Is FUNdamental**) at http://www.rif.org/. RIF coordinates a nationwide program to provide each child with three free books. RIF will provide 75 percent of the cost if local groups provide 25 percent. Explore current procedures for including your students in this program.

Book Fairs. Encourage your school's parent-teacher organization to sponsor a book fair. Invite book dealers to display and sell their new books each year in the school auditorium or cafeteria.

A Final Note

It is important that children leave your classroom at the end of the year as better readers. It is equally important, however, that they leave your classroom as independent readers. Becoming familiar with popular children's literature, identifying your students' reading interests, and putting children and books together in pleasurable settings are the tools of an effective independent reading program. As you refine your strategies for developing independent readers, you will start to see children taking home books to find out how a story ends. You will also see children having a hard time putting a book down as your class goes off to lunch, and you will notice more and more of your students spending time in the enriching world of children's literature. These patterns will tell you that you have succeeded in helping the children in your class become independent readers.

NIKKI'S
COMMENTS FROM THE CLASSROOM

Each year, early in the spring, our school celebrates Right-to-Read Week. Classes abandon normally scheduled activities to participate in a variety of reading adventures using children's literature. Each day a new adventure begins, and teachers and students get very creative! Last year the first graders celebrated Dr. Seuss Day and made Cat-in-the-Hat hats and ate green eggs and ham. (I was personally thankful that I was teaching sixth grade.)

During Right-to-Read Week, we try our best to involve the whole school community in some capacity. Parents, grandparents, neighborhood businesspeople, the superintendent, and a host of others are invited to share a story or favorite chapter from a book with whole classes or small groups of children. Each class brainstorms several weeks ahead who they will invite. They mail out invitations, and schedules are then coordinated around available times for our guest readers.

My students' favorite day of our Right-to-Read Week last year was READ-A-THON DAY. All the students and teachers in the school lugged cozy comforters or lumpy sleeping bags and fluffy pillows to school to take part in a reading marathon. It was on this day that we spent most of our time engrossed in good books. Late in the school day, however, everyone in the school put on a costume of their favorite book character and marched in an all-school READ-A-THON parade. Much to the delight of our students, even the office and cafeteria personnel joined us in the parade.

No prizes for costumes were awarded but everyone wrote a few lines about their favorite book, telling why they felt that book ranks as number one. These book testimonials were collected and compiled by PTO (Parent Teacher Organization) members in an all-school book review categorized by title, author, and subject. Every classroom, and the library, then got a copy of the review. After that, before students made a trip to the library or while they were in the library, they checked the recommendations for good books written by their friends.

The best part about our week celebrating reading is that we walk our talk. We tell children how important reading is and how much fun it can be. We show them how reading plays a role in everyone's life no matter who they are or what they do. I am thankful that our school system now uses children's literature for our core reading instruction. It allows reading to play a more natural role in our curriculum. But I am equally glad that our school system makes an extra effort to highlight reading in such a special way as Right-to-Read Week. The spirit of unity—sharing in the value of literature and reading—permeates our hallways and surrounds our school and our students with a contagious desire to find a good book and curl up and read!

Source: Nikki Robinson has been teaching for 23 years in a variety of grade levels but is currently assigned to a sixth-grade classroom in a large suburban elementary school in Columbus, Ohio. She explains that continually seeking formal education and practicing the strategies she learns has refined her teaching techniques. She feels that the longer she spends time in the classroom, the more insightful her decisions become.

Using Literature to Help Children Understand the Diversity of the Human Experience

There are other reasons why literature should be at the center of your reading program. One of the most important is that literature is a tremendous tool for helping children understand the diversity of the human experience. As members of a democratic and increasingly multicultural society, each of us needs to understand the unique perspectives of many different individuals, each with a special set of cultural, linguistic, and historical experiences. The nature of our democracy depends on our ability to understand and value these different experiences. Learning about other cultural experiences makes each of us a more sensitive, more knowledgeable, and more valuable member of society. Literature can be an important ally in accomplishing this goal.

Fortunately we are able to draw upon an increasingly rich collection of what Harris (1992) refers to as **multicultural literature** to assist us in these important tasks. According to Harris, multicultural literature focuses on groups that have traditionally existed in a subordinate status relative to the dominant, mainstream culture of our country. This includes literature with people of color (such as African Americans, Hispanic Americans, Native Americans, and Asian Americans); regional cultural groups (such as Appalachian, Cajun, and French-Canadian); religious minorities (such as the Amish, Jewish, or Islamic members of society); people with exceptionalities; the aged; and literature that describes women and girls in nonstereotypical roles. Au (1993) and Yokota (1993) point out that the best multicultural literature is **culturally conscious literature,** which accurately represents a group's values, culture, history, and language with characters who are complex and not stereotyped. Examples of literature selections most would recognize as culturally conscious can be seen in Table 6-1.

Strategies for Using Literature to Celebrate Diversity

Rasinski and Padak (1990) describe four basic approaches to using multicultural and multiethnic literature in the classroom. Some teachers use a **contributions approach.** With a contributions approach, lessons on diversity and related literature selections usually enter the classroom because of their relationship to the calendar. Cinco de Mayo, for example, might be a time when Hispanic literature is used to develop greater awareness of Hispanic Americans and their contributions to our country. Black History Month might be a time to engage children in reading literature selections about the contributions of African Americans. Such an approach suffers from two important problems, however. First, it implicitly tells children that we should only think about issues of diversity when the calendar tells us it is important. It would be more useful to engage children in thinking about the diversity of the human experience throughout the school year. Second, a contributions approach tends to limit the extent to which any single culture may be studied. As a result, we increase opportunities for developing a shallow, stereotypical understanding of cultural, ethnic, and national groups.

Other teachers take an **additive approach** to diversity. In this approach, content and concepts about diversity are added to the basic curriculum. Instead of being relegated to calendar celebrations, an additive approach includes multicultural and multiethnic literature within instructional units; however, these selections are more closely related to the core curriculum than to issues of diversity. So, alphabet books like *Ashanti to Zulu: African Traditions* by Margaret Musgrove and *A, B, C's: The American Indian Way* by Richard Red Hawk might be incorporated into a unit on alphabet books for young readers without a central focus on their cultural or historical significance. Here, children are exposed to greater diversity in their literature experiences but relationships between dominant and subordinant groups are usually not addressed. In addition, the basic content of the curriculum does not change to address issues of diversity in the human experience.

Still other teachers take a **transformation approach.** In this approach, the nature of the curriculum is transformed to include the perspective of subordinate cultures to concepts, historical events, and issues. For example, a teacher planning a unit in social

multicultural literature
Literature focusing on groups that have traditionally existed in a subordinate status relative to the dominant, mainstream culture of our country.

culturally conscious literature Literature that accurately represents a group's values, culture, history, and language with complex, nonstereotyped characters.

contributions approach
An approach to diversity where culturally conscious literature selections enter the classroom because of their relationship to the calendar.

additive approach An approach to diversity where culturally conscious literature is used to add content and concepts about diversity within instructional units related to the core curriculum rather than to issues of diversity.

transformation approach An approach to diversity where culturally conscious literature is used to include the perspective of subordinate cultures to concepts, historical events, and issues.

TABLE 6-1
Culturally conscious literature selections

Celebrating Diversity in the Human Condition

The Alfred Summer by Jan Slepian
All Together Now by Sue Ellen Bridgers
Blabber Mouth by Morris Gleitzman
Eclipse by Kristine L. Franklin
George by E. L. Konigsburg
Getting Him by Dennis Hasely
Mine for Keeps by Jean Little
Only My Mouth Is Smiling by Jocelyn Riley
On My Honor by Marion Dane Bauer
Risk 'n Roses by Jan Slepian
Sticky Beak by Morris Gleitzman
The Summer of the Swans by Betsy Byars
Take Wing by Jean Little
The Moves Make the Man by Bruce Brooks

Celebrating African-American Experiences

Anansi the Spider by Gerald MacDermott
Ashanti to Zulu by Margaret Musgrove
Cornrows by Camille Yarbrough
The Dark Way by Virginia Hamilton
Fast Sam, Cool Clyde and Stuff by Walter Dean Myers
The Hundred Penny Box by S. B. Mathis
Jambo Means Hello: Swahili Alphabet Book by Muriel
   Feelings
John Henry by Ezra Jack Keats
Mufaro's Beautiful Daughters by John Steptoe
Moja Means One: Swahili Counting Book by Muriel
   Feelings
More Stories Julian Tells by Ann Cameron
Roll of Thunder, Hear My Cry by Mildred Taylor
Tailypo! by Jan Wahl
Tar Beach by Faith Ringgold
Shaka: King of the Zulus by Diane Stanley
Some of the Days of Everett Anderson by Lucille
   Clifton
A Story: An African Tale by Gail Haley
Traveling to Tondo: A Tale of the Nkundo of Zaire by
   Verna Aardema

Celebrating Hispanic Experiences

. . . And Now Miguel by Joseph Krumgold
Baseball in April by Gary Soto
Benito by Clyde Bulla
The Black Pearl by Scott O'Dell
Dreams by Ezra Jack Keats
Flecha al Sol by Gerald McDermott
Friday Night Is Papa Night by Ruth Sonneborn
Gilberto and the Wind by Marie Hall Ets
The Girl from Puerto Rico by Hila Colman
Louie by Ezra Jack Keats
Mira! Mira! by Dawn Thomas

Nine Days to Christmas by Marie Hall Ets
Taking Sides by Gary Soto
Three Stalks of Corn by Leo Politi
Viva Chicano by Frank Bonham

Celebrating Asian Experiences

Child of the Owl by Laurence Yep
Dragonwings by Laurence Yep
Dreamcatcher by Audrey Osofsky
Faithful Elephants by Yukio Tsuchiya
Farewell to Manzanar by Jeanne Wakatski Houston
First Snow by Helen Courant
Hello, My Name Is Scrambled Eggs by Jamie Gilson
A Jar of Dreams by Yoshiko Uchida
Lon Po Po by Ed Young
The Journey: Japanese Americans, Racism, and
   Renewal by Sheila Hamanaka
The Star Fisher by Laurence Yep
Tales from the Gold Mountain by Paul Yee
Tet: The New Year by Kim-Lan Tran
Yeh-Shen: A Cinderella Story from China by Ai Ling Louie

Celebrating Native-American Experiences

Brother Eagle, Sister Sky by Susan Jeffers
High Elk's Treasure by Virginia Driving Hawk Sneve
Island of the Blue Dolphins by Scott O'Dell
Lone Bull's Horse Raid by Paul Gobel
Our Cup Is Broken by Florence Crannell Means
Pueblo Storyteller by Diane Hoyt-Goldsmith
Red Hawk's Account of Custer's Last Battle
   by Paul and Dorothy Gobel
The Desert Is Theirs by Byrd Baylor
The Girl Who Loved Wild Horses by Paul Gobel
The Sacred Path: Spells, Prayers, and Power Songs
   of the American Indians by John Bierhorst
The Sign of the Beaver by Elizabeth George Speare
Whirlwind Is a Ghost Dancing by Leo and Diane Dillon

Celebrating Many Additional Cultural Experiences

The Amish by Michael Erkel
Babushka's Doll by Patricia Polacco
Balancing Girl by Berniece Rabe
Stay Away from Simon! by Carol Carrick
Cowboy by Bernard Wolf
Here I Am! An Anthology of Poems Written by Young
   People in Some of America's Minority Groups by
   Virginia Baron
Number the Stars by Lois Lowry
Dicey's Song by Cynthia Voight
How Could You Do It, Diane? by Stella Pevsner
Watch the Stars Come Out by Riki Levinson
Nadia the Willful by Sue Alexander

studies on the westward migration of European Americans might also include literature selections about this experience from the Native-American perspective. In addition to historical information from a European-American perspective, children might read selections such as dePaola's *The Legend of the Bluebonnet* and learn how the Plains Indians valued living in harmony with nature. And they might also read Baker's *Where the Buffaloes Begin* and Gobel's *Buffalo Woman* to understand the close relationship that existed between the Plains Indians and the buffalo. Finally, they might read *Culleton's Spirit of the White Bison* to learn about the slaughter of the primary food supply by European Americans and how this disrupted much of the culture of the Plains Indians. One advantage of this type of approach is that it presents children with a culturally diverse explanation of historical change. In addition, children from different cultural groups find value from including their culture's perspective into the curriculum. There are also challenges with this approach: it requires substantial revision of the traditional curriculum, greater preparation on issues of diversity for teachers, and access to a wide body of children's literature.

decision-making and social action approach An approach to diversity where children define an important social issue, gather the appropriate information related to the issue, use this information to clarify their assumptions, make decisions about the social issue, and then take action to address the issue.

A final approach described by Rasinski and Padak (1990) is a **decision-making and social action approach.** In this approach, children define an important social issue, gather the appropriate information related to the issue, use this information to clarify their assumptions, make decisions about the social issue, and then take action to address the issue. When teachers take a decision-making and social action approach, literature is used as the entry point into a social issue of importance. For example, *Martin Luther King, Jr. and the Freedom Movement* by Lillie Patterson might be used to begin a unit on human rights. This could be followed by reading related works such as *Frederick Douglass and the Fight for Freedom* by Douglas Miller, *Rosa Parks* by Eloise Greenfield, and *Anthony Burns: The Defeat and Triumph of a Fugitive Slave* by Virginia Hamilton. Reading experiences such as these could lead to discussions about equal rights humans should guarantee to one another, which could be developed and listed by the class. This discussion could lead to gathering additional information about human rights as defined in the U.S. and Canadian Constitutions, the Declaration of Human Rights from the United Nations, and other political documents, followed by collaborative writing and decision-making experiences in which children could define their own list of human rights guaranteed to each member of the class by other members. A unit such as this could be especially useful at the beginning of the year to define the rights and responsibilities of citizenship in your classroom as well as citizenship in our larger society. Au (1993) points out that children learn an important lesson with this approach that transcends the literature itself—they can make a difference in the society in which they live. This type of approach, however, requires extensive planning and organization by teachers.

thematic units on diversity An approach to diversity that looks intensively into a single cultural and/or ethnic experience as children explore different forms of literature within that experience.

A different way of using literature to understand the diversity of the human experience has been proposed by Norton (1990). This approach uses **thematic units on diversity** that look intensively into a single cultural and/or ethnic experience as children explore different forms of literature within that experience. Norton suggests that units begin by broadly exploring a culture's themes through traditional literature such as folktales, myths, and legends. This first phase allows children to discover themes and issues that have traditionally been important to a culture.

In the second phase, teachers and children can explore this traditional literature with a more focused lens, perhaps by looking at a single type of traditional tale within the culture or by looking at traditional tales from one subgroup within the larger cultural unit.

During the third phase, factual accounts such as autobiographies, biographies, and historical nonfiction can be used to understand how individuals from this cultural group have responded to the historical challenges of life. During this phase, the beliefs, values, and themes discovered in the earlier exploration of the culture's traditional literature are employed to better understand the lives of historical figures.

Historical fiction is then used in the fourth phase to explore how authors describe the response of fictional characters within this culture. Comparisons might be made between the works of authors who come from the culture and works by authors who do not come from the culture.

Celebrating Diversity

Using Literature to Experience the Diversity of the Human Condition

Children's literature provides special opportunities for understanding how people endeavor to fit into a society that wants to include all its citizens but struggles with how this should be done (Walker-Dalhouse, 1992). There simply is no other set of materials as rich in potential for celebrating diversity and for helping your students to understand what it is like to walk in someone else's shoes. Children's literature allows you to bring into the classroom a complete range of human experiences and cultural backgrounds, experiences that do not always exist in even the most diverse classroom (Norton, 1990). Bringing these works into your classroom sends an important message to your students about the respect and dignity each of us needs to accord every human experience. Your literature choices, your responses, and your approach to this issue are central to accomplishing this most important goal. Au (1993) has described several other important reasons for using literature that portrays a variety of cultural experiences. First, children feel pride in themselves and in their culture when they see their backgrounds valued in classroom reading experiences. Second, children develop a richer appreciation of the historical forces that have shaped American society and the contributions made by different cultural groups. Finally, a literature of diversity enables all children to explore issues of social justice. Exploring issues of social justice is essential to preparing children for citizenship in a diverse society where these issues are fundamental to our collective well being.

To locate additional literature to help children understand the diversity of the human experience, you can find many useful resources on the Internet. One of the better locations is **Multicultural Resources for Children** (http://falcon.jmu.edu/~ramseyil/multipub.htm). Here you will find many great resources. It is a real treasure for teachers serious about multicultural literature.

The use of contemporary fiction, biography, and poetry can help children understand contemporary expressions of this cultural viewpoint during the fifth phase. At each phase, connections with the reading selections from previous phases become points of focus. In this way, children become aware of the major themes that emanate from any single culture and the sources of these themes in the literature of a culture. The five phases of Norton's (1990) sequence are described in Figure 6-6 (p. 210), along with literature selections that might be used in a thematic unit on the Native-American experience. Similar units could be developed for other cultural groups.

A useful feature of Norton's approach is that children are encouraged to discover connections between their various reading experiences. As children read contemporary fiction about a particular cultural group, for example, they are encouraged to draw on information gathered from earlier reading experiences with traditional tales, biographies, and historical fiction. These experiences are thought to be especially useful to children because they allow children to discover additional meaning in a single selection by thinking about it in relation to other selections (Short, 1993).

Supporting Children's Responses to Literature

As we think about the role of literature in our reading programs, we should also consider ways to increase the variety of responses children have to their reading experiences (Purves, 1993). Increasing children's response patterns increases their ability to think critically about what they have read. This, in turn, increases learning.

There are at least two ways of thinking about how children might read and respond to a work of literature. One way is to read a work for its factual information. Rosenblatt (1978, 1985) refers to this as reading from an **efferent stance.** When you read from an

efferent stance
Reading a work for the factual information contained within it.

FIGURE 6-6

A unit on the Native-American experience using Norton's sequence for multicultural literature study (adapted from Norton, 1990)

Phase I: Traditional literature (generalizations and broad views)
Selections: *Raven's Light* by Susan and Robert Shetterly, *The Eye of the Needle* by Teri Sloat, *The Legend of the Bluebonnet* by dePaola, *Legend Days* by Highwater, *The Star Maiden* by Esbensen, *The Fire Bringer* by Baylor.

A. Identify distinctions among a folktale, fable, myth, and legend.
B. Identify ancient stories with commonalities that are found in many regions.
C. Identify types of stories that dominate the subject.
D. Summarize the nature of oral language, the role of traditional literature, the role of audience, and literary style.

Phase II: Traditional tales from one or several areas (narrower views)
Selections: *The Ring in the Prairie: A Shawnee Legend* by Bierhorst, *Buffalo Woman* by Gobel, *The Girl Who Loved Horses* by Gobel, *Star Boy* by Gobel, *The Whistling Skeleton* by Grinnell, *Iktomi and the Boulder* by Gobel.

A. Analyze traditional stories and compare with the Phase I findings.
B. Analyze and identify beliefs and themes in the traditional tales of one region.

Phase III: Autobiographies, biographies, and historical nonfiction
Selections: *Chief Sarah: Sarah Winnemucca's Fight for Indian Rights* by Morrison, *War Clouds in the West: Indians & Cavalrymen, 1800–1890* by Marrin, *Buffalo Hunt* by Freedman.

A. Analyze for the values, beliefs, and themes identified in traditional literature.
B. Compare information in historical documents, biographies, and autobiographies.

Phase IV: Historical fiction
Selections: *Sweetgrass* by Hudson, *Lost in the Barrens* by Mowat.

A. Evaluate according to the authenticity of setting, beliefs, values, and language.
B. Search for the role of traditional literature in historical fiction.
C. Compare with autobiographies, biographies, and historical nonfiction.

Phase V: Contemporary fiction, biography, and poetry
Selections: *Moonsong Lullaby* by Highwater, *Thirteen Moons on Turtles Back* by Bruchac and London, *Hiawatha* by Susan Jeffers, *In My Mother's House* by Nolan Clark, *High Elk's Treasure* by Sneve, *Jimmy Yellow Hawk* by Sneve, *When Thunder Spoke* by Sneve, *Ceremony—In the Circle of Life* by White Deer of Autumn.

A. Analyze appearance of beliefs found in preceding phases.
B. Analyze characterizations and conflicts for authenticity.
C. Analyze themes and look for similarities with other phases.

efferent stance, you read to find out what all characters did, why they did it, when they did it, and other factual aspects of a story.

Too often children are asked to only read and respond to works of literature from an efferent stance. This happens when a teacher asks factual questions about a story to determine how much everyone has understood. Used every day, such an approach really limits children's thinking. It leads children to believe the only way to respond to a work of literature is by answering others' questions about narrow slices of information unconnected to their own lives. Because modeling influences the kinds of questions readers ask of themselves, such an approach to reading and response severely limits children's opportunities for critical thinking and learning.

A second way to read a work of literature is to enter the world created by the author, experience the events vicariously, and return to your own world with new knowledge and a new perspective on life. Rosenblatt (1978, 1985) refers to this as reading from an **aesthetic stance.** When you read a work from an aesthetic stance, you vicariously live through the experiences in the world the author has created; you share in the feelings,

aesthetic stance
Reading a work to live vicariously through the experiences in the world the author has created.

Celebrating Diversity

Seeking Greater Understanding through the Internet

Understanding the diversity of the human experience should not be limited to our national borders. Our world is quickly shrinking in response to powerful social forces and technological innovations, bringing each of us into closer contact with people who have had cultural experiences different from our own. As citizens of our increasingly interdependent world, we have to rely on one another for our survival and well being. Understanding the diversity of the global human experience is central to achieving the type of life that we all seek on this Earth. Sensitive works about the experience of people in other countries are important for this purpose. For example, *Sami and the Time of Troubles* by Florence Parry Heide and Judith Heide Guilliland concerns the struggle of people in Lebanon for peace in a time of strife; the French story *You Be Me, I'll Be You* by Pili Mandelbaum focuses on skin color in a mixed-race family; and *Faithful Elephants: A True Story of Animals, People, and War* by Japanese author Yukio Tsuchiya shares a touching story about the consequences of war. Read works such as these about other cultural experiences around the world and then communicate with a classroom from that part of the world, sharing your students' written responses. Invite the other classroom to share their responses about the work you read or to a work of American literature. To find a classroom to exchange responses with, visit **Intercultural E-mail Classroom Connections** (http://www.iecc.org/) or **Web66: International WWW Schools Registry** (http://web66.coled.umn.edu/schools.html).

Reading allows children to experience both efferent and aesthetic responses.

problems, and thoughts of characters. Then, as a result of your "lived through" experience, you see your own world and yourself in a new and different way.

As you read a piece of literature, for example, you might visualize the situations in the story, worry about the imminent death of a character, wonder how an author develops such rich ideas, think about a similar experience in your past, or notice how an author's style includes a wonderful talent for dialogue. These are just some of the richer types of responses that are possible as you read a work of literature from an aesthetic

PRACTICAL TEACHING STRATEGIES

Increasing Aesthetic Response Patterns

Keypal Response Partners. Match up your students with children in other classrooms around the world to share their responses to literature experiences through weekly e-mail messages. Have students print out the messages they send and those they receive; keep these in a response folder. Share these folders with parents at Open House Night. For all the information you need to begin a keypal project, visit a great resource developed by a school in Canada, **Keypals** (http://sesd.sk.ca/teacherresource/KeyPal/keypals.htm).

Diaries. As you read *The Diary of Anne Frank, A Hand Full of Stars* by Rafik Schami, or *Dear Mr. Henshaw* by Beverly Cleary to upper-grade students, have them make and keep their own diaries as one of the characters in the story. Encourage children to make an entry each day. You may want to make the diaries private, or you may choose to collect students' diaries once a week and write a private response to each individual.

Book Parties. Have a short book party several times during the year. Children can dress up as their favorite characters from books they have read in the previous month. Have children wear name tags showing their characters' names and the titles of their books. This activity is an excellent way to generate interest in, and conversations about, good books for future reading experiences.

Literature Logs. Encourage children to keep and maintain literature logs by writing short reactions to each new book they read. Periodically collect, read, and react to students' comments in their logs.

Taking Another Perspective. As you discuss issues in social studies, have children consider how some of the characters in literature selections would view the issue. Have children also explain why they think their characters would look at events in this way.

---

stance. Clearly each leads to a deeper and more thoughtful experience with the work of literature. We want to encourage the widest possible range of response patterns with our children so they gain from the many critical thinking experiences that are possible with literature. Supporting a variety of response patterns enables children to learn more from their reading experiences.

The best way to support children in developing a wide variety of response patterns is to keep in mind the distinction between an efferent and aesthetic stance. There will be times, of course, when you will want to focus children's attention on the factual elements of a story. At the same time we engage in these activities, though, we also should think about expanding children's responses to what they have read. To do this, we encourage their reading of a work of literature from an aesthetic stance—supporting their ability to have a "lived through" experience during the reading and then reflecting on this experience in relation to their own life. You will find many ways to accomplish this if you keep in mind the distinction between an efferent and an aesthetic stance.

In addition, three method frameworks may be especially useful as you seek to develop a wider range of response patterns among your students: read-aloud response journals, "grand conversations," and literary study circles.

Read-Aloud Response Journals

We encountered the use of read-aloud response journals in chapter 2. This method framework contains five steps: read a selection aloud, share a writing task related to the reading selection, have children write their responses in their journals, share the responses, and encourage children to expand some of their earlier entries into larger writing projects.

The model lesson that follows shows how teacher Tim Dunbar uses a read-aloud response journal activity to support aesthetic responses among his students. Tim is following Norton's outline to develop a better understanding of the African-American

MODEL LESSON

A Read-Aloud Response Journal Activity in Tim Dunbar's Class

The unit Tim developed has been going well but the discussions and responses his students generate focus on the factual aspects of the African-American experience. This concerns Tim because he has a reader-based belief about which components of reading are most important. What does he want his students to learn? He wants his students to bring their meanings to these texts and engage in more aesthetic—not efferent—responses. Tim wants his students to engage in a "lived through" experience today, putting them in touch with what they imagine were the feelings, fears, hopes, and dreams of African Americans who had been enslaved. To do this, he has decided to engage his students in a read-aloud response journal experience with Deborah Hopkinson's *Sweet Clara and the Freedom Quilt,* a biographical story of how an African-American woman used a quilt to record the route north to freedom.

How does Tim believe children learn best? Tim's beliefs fall between holistic language learning beliefs and integrated beliefs. He believes in student-directed learning opportunities but sometimes he likes to construct these learning environments himself. As a result, Tim has selected the book they will use today but he will have his students select their own writing topic, after brainstorming several together.

Read a Selection Aloud. Tim has decided to read *Sweet Clara and the Freedom Quilt* to his class today. This is a story of how Sweet Clara is separated from her own family and learns to make quilts for the slave master's family. Over time, she gathers information about her family's location and the route north across the Ohio River to freedom. Each new piece of information is added to the quilt—which is actually a secret map of the way north. When all the information is recorded, Sweet Clara slips away, locates her family, and takes them to freedom. She leaves the quilt behind so that others may follow.

Engage Children in a Related Writing Task. After reading *Sweet Clara and the Freedom Quilt,* Tim has the class brainstorm possible writing topics, all related to the feelings the characters in this story must have had. He writes these ideas on the chalkboard as they are generated. Children are encouraged to use these ideas or to respond to the story in their own fashion in their read-aloud response journal.

Write Responses in Journals. Children are given about 15 minutes to complete their entry. As Tim circulates around the room during this time, he notes the categories of responses children are making in their journals. Toward the end, Tim tells students that writing time is drawing to a close. This reminds children to wrap up their entry.

Share the Responses. Tim writes several categories of responses on the board: "Feelings," "The Injustice of Slavery," "Connections with My Own Life," and "Other Types of Responses." He lets the children decide the category that best fits their responses and then forms groups around these categories. In groups, children share their responses aloud. After an entry is shared, the other children are encouraged to respond with positive comments. Afterward, Tim engages children in a discussion about their feelings as they listened to this story of freedom lovingly sought and found.

Expand Entries into Larger Writing Projects. Tim requires the children to develop two writing ideas during this 4-week unit into larger works of writing that are revised, edited, and published. He reminds children they may choose to develop one or several ideas from their read-aloud response journals. He also reminds them to have a conference with him by the end of the week to plan their first writing project.

In this lesson, Tim used a read-aloud response journal activity to develop aesthetic or "lived through" responses. His reader-based beliefs informed this decision about the first issue in a literacy framework: What should I teach? Teachers with text-based beliefs about what should be taught would have encouraged efferent, or factual, responses. Efferent responses reflect meanings in the text. Teachers with text-based beliefs would have sought additional factual types of responses, perhaps by asking students to write about the facts in this story, not about how students would have felt had they been in this situation.

Tim also considered his beliefs in relation to the second issue of a literacy framework: How should I teach? He constructed the nature of this lesson in a manner consistent with his beliefs between a holistic language learning explanation and an integrated explanation. While Tim structured the activity, his students directed much of their learning. Teachers with specific skills beliefs would have had students write about a teacher-directed topic, probably related to a skill the teacher was trying to develop.

experience among his fifth-grade students. They have read and discussed a number of traditional African tales to develop a broad understanding of traditional themes, beliefs, and values. While they were reading, they shared their responses with children at Uthongathi, a school in South Africa. Tim established this connection through **Intercultural E-mail Classroom Connections** (http://www.teaching.com/iecc/). The communication enriched their experiences with traditional African literature.

Tim's class has also read and discussed a number of traditional tales from the African-American experience in the southeastern United States. As they read, they compared these stories to traditional tales from Africa. Now they are reading and studying several biographies of famous African Americans: Hamilton's *Anthony Burns: The Defeat and Triumph of a Fugitive Slave*, Ferris's *Go Free or Die: A Story of Harriet Tubman*, and Miller's *Frederick Douglass and the Fight for Freedom*.

Grand Conversations

grand conversations
A method framework that helps children develop wider response patterns to their reading; involves reading, reminding children of the guidelines, engaging children in a conversation they direct, and asking one interpretive or literary question.

Having **grand conversations** after reading a selection together is another great way to help children develop wider response patterns to their reading. The term "grand conversations" was initially used by Mary Ann Eeds (Eeds & Wells, 1989; Peterson & Eeds, 1990) to describe a special way of discussing a story that contrasted with what she called the more common "gentle inquisitions" that took place in many classrooms. During gentle inquisitions, teachers ask children to recall specific factual information after reading a story ("How did Sweet Clara record the information she gathered about the route north?"). This, of course, encourages narrower efferent responses instead of more diverse aesthetic responses. Having a grand conversation refers to talking about a book as adults might discuss a book in the evening after dinner. Here everyone has the opportunity to contribute their responses without one person calling on others to answer factual questions about the story. Eeds and Wells (1989) have shown that a grand conversation approach to discussion increases the variety of response patterns and that children as young as first graders can benefit from engaging in grand conversation discussions. As a method framework, grand conversations usually contain four procedural steps:

1. Read a work of literature together with your students.
2. Remind children of the guidelines for grand conversations.
3. Engage children in a conversation about the work that the children themselves direct.
4. Ask one interpretive or literary question to further children's responses and thinking.

During the first step, read a selection with your students. For younger children, this may mean that you read the work to them aloud. For older children, this might take place by each student silently reading the work.

In the second step, teachers take a moment to remind children of the guidelines for grand conversations. Over time, you will develop your own list but you might wish to begin with a list like the following:

▶ Only one person talks at a time.
▶ Listen carefully so you can tell when someone has finished speaking.
▶ Take turns speaking.
▶ Everyone should share at least one idea.
▶ No one should share more than two ideas until everyone has shared something.
▶ Stay on the topic.

During the third step, children share their own responses to the reading experience. This is the real heart of the grand conversation experience. Teachers often begin this step with a nondirective question in the same way an adult might begin this conversation with another adult: "So what did you think about this story?" Children are then encouraged to share their individual responses to the reading experience as long as they stay on topic. During a grand conversation, the teacher's role is to support the exchange of responses. Tompkins and McGee (1993) note that, while children need to control this conversation, teachers should facilitate their efforts by encouraging children to elaborate on their responses when something is not clear: "I'm not quite clear about what you mean. Can you explain that again?"

The fourth step takes place after you sense that children have shared all of the responses they are likely to share. As this occurs, teachers sometimes ask a single literary or interpretive question to help children see the work of literature in an entirely different way: "I wonder how Sweet Clara would think about how Cinderella was treated?" This question might help children discover a special literary technique or help them to interpret the work from a different perspective.

Literature Discussion Groups or Book Clubs

Another way to encourage a wider pattern of responses is to engage children in **literature discussion groups.** These groups are sometimes referred to as book clubs (McMahon, Raphael, Goatley, & Pardo, 1997). Although literature discussion groups are defined in a variety of ways, they often provide opportunities for small groups of children to read a single work of literature on their own and then come together to have a grand conversation. Afterward the group will develop a project, allowing the members to share the work and their responses with the rest of the class. Teachers who use literature discussion groups frequently follow a six-step sequence:

literature discussion groups A method framework where small groups of children read a single work of literature and then come together to have a grand conversation, develop a project, and share their work with the rest of the class.

1. The teacher introduces three to five different books to the class, each with multiple copies.
2. Children determine which book they want to read and form groups based on this book.
3. Children read the literature selection for their group independently.
4. The teacher and each group have a grand conversation about the work.
5. A project is developed to extend children's response and understanding of the work.
6. The results of the project are shared with the other groups.

To begin the use of literature discussion groups, first collect multiple copies of several literature selections and introduce each work of literature to the class. During this introduction, share information about the book and author to whet the reading appetites of your students.

After all of the books have been introduced, provide an opportunity for children to pick the one book that each will read during the time set aside for this experience. As a result of this self-selection process, several different groups are formed, each with a different book to read.

During the third step, allow children in each group to silently read their work without interruptions. Depending on the age of your students and the amount of reading they need to complete, this time might range from 15 minutes to as much as an hour each day.

After the children in a group have completed their reading, or after they have read only the first portion of a longer book, get together with them to have a grand conversation. Follow the procedures described earlier to support a broad range of responses and allow children to direct the conversation around their responses to the work.

When a group completes its discussion, it is time to think about a project that would be interesting to complete and useful for extending children's response and comprehension. It often helps to have a preliminary brainstorming session and a list of different alternatives for the project before having the group choose one to complete. The projects might be related to a literary aspect of the work they have read: "Describe our feelings at one point in the story. Explain the techniques this author used to make us feel this way. Share our results with the class." Or "Find three different techniques the author uses for dialogue and describe why we think each technique is used. We will then share our ideas with the class in a bulletin board display." Alternatively, the project might focus on some content aspect of the work: "Conduct a readers theater presentation of an exciting episode in the book we have just read." "Collect and read three more *Anansi the Spider* tales. Make a presentation of these works for the rest of the class."

The final step in the use of literature discussion groups is to share the results of each group's reading activity with the rest of the class. Each group's presentation will provide children with the opportunity to share their ideas in public and inform other children about an exciting reading experience.

Text Sets

text sets A variation of literature discussion groups where members of each group do not read a single book but instead read multiple books related in some way.

There are many variations for conducting literature discussion groups. One proposed by Short and her colleagues (Harste, Short, & Burke, 1988; Short, 1993) is referred to as **text sets.** With this approach, members of each group do not read a single book; instead, each group receives 5 to 15 conceptually related books, which are usually shorter selections or picture books. Members of the group read different books and then get together to share what they have read. This approach is especially useful when you do not have multiple copies of books available for all of the members of a group.

Children do not read every book in each text set before discussing their reading experience. Instead, individual children will read several books of their own choice from the set and then get together to share their responses, discussing similarities between the books, exploring differences they have found, and discovering other books in the set to read next.

The use of text sets usually involves multiple discussions over a longer period of time. Children get together three or four times, after each student has read several books. Over time this provides each student with an opportunity to read and respond to many of the books in the set.

Text sets have been found especially useful in providing children with opportunities to see connections between their reading experiences and to share those connections with others (Hartman & Hartman, 1993). Examples of several text sets can be seen in Figure 6-7.

FIGURE 6-7

Examples of text sets used at different grade levels

Text Sets for Third Graders

Award-winning picture books

Hey, Al by Arthur Yorinks
Song and Dance Man by Karen Ackerman
Lon Po Po: A Chinese Red Riding Hood Tale by Ed Young
The Polar Express by Chris Van Allsburg
St. George and the Dragon by Margaret Hodges
Owl Moon by Jane Yolen

Fables by Arnold Lobel
Shadow by Blaise Cendrars
Jumanji by Chris Van Allsburg
Ox-Cart Man by Donald Hall

The Cinderella Cycle (Cinderella Tales from Different Cultures and Points of View)

The Egyptian Cinderella by S. Climo
Cinderella by A. Ehrlich
Yeh-Shen: A Cinderella Story from China
    by A. LouieHooks

Mufaro's Beautiful Daughters by J. Steptoe
Prince Cinders by B. Cole
Moss Gown by W. Hook
Cinderella: The Untold Story by R. Shorto

Text Sets for Sixth Graders

Biography bonanza

The Many Lives of Benjamin Franklin by Aliki
Lincoln: A Photobiography by R. Freedman
Stonewall by J. Fritz
Can't You Make Them Behave, King George? by J. Fritz
Susanna of the Alamo by J. Jakes

Deborah Sampson by H. Felton
The Wright Brothers by R. Freedman
The Double Life of Pocahontas by J. Fritz
Peter the Great by D. Stanley

Chris Van Allsburg: Illustrator Extraordinaire

The Garden of Abdul Gasazi by C. V. Allsburg
Ben's Dream by C. V. Allsburg
The Wreck of the Zephyr by C. V. Allsburg

Jumanji by C. V. Allsburg
The Mysteries of Harris Burdick by C. V. Allsburg
The Polar Express by C. V. Allsburg

Developing Familiarity with Narrative Discourse Structure

A final aspect of children's literature should not be overlooked. Literature can help young children develop an important type of discourse knowledge—knowledge about **narrative discourse structure.** Narrative discourse structure refers to the structural organization common to most stories and narratives and includes the special structural characteristics common to particular types of narratives such as fairy tales, mysteries, science fiction, fables, and fantasies.

Knowledge of narrative discourse structure assists with comprehension in several ways (Spiegel & Fitzgerald, 1986). First, knowing the structure of narratives helps readers develop appropriate expectations for upcoming meaning. Do you remember the expectations you had in chapter 3 when you read the first sentence of a story that began, "Once upon a time . . ."? You immediately knew the story was not true, and you knew it took place in a kingdom long ago and far away. You also expected to see a prince and princess as characters, and you knew a problem would appear that would require a solution. In addition, you expected a happy ending. You can see how knowing the structure of narratives makes reading easier—it helps readers develop expectations to guide their construction of meaning.

Knowing the structure of narratives is important because it allows a reader to infer structural information omitted by an author. For example, sometimes an episode in a narrative is left out because an author assumes the reader will correctly infer what took place. The knowledge that narratives contain episodic structure makes it easier for a reader to infer the missing information.

It is clear that knowing the structural organization of narratives helps us to understand how children read stories. But exactly how are stories structured?

Knowledge of the General Structure Common to All Narratives

Most researchers believe that narratives contain three basic structural elements: setting information, an initiating episode that establishes a problem to be resolved in the story, and succeeding episodes that explain how the problem gets resolved. Narratives typically contain a structure similar to the following:

I. Setting information
   A. Time information
   B. Character information
   C. Location information
II. Initiating episode (story problem)
   A. Initiating event
   B. Goal formation
III. Succeeding episodes (including the final resolution)
   A. Attempt
   B. Outcome
   C. Reaction

Setting information usually appears at the beginning of a narrative. It includes information about the time when the story takes place, the character(s) in the story, and the location where the action occurs. Setting information often appears in the first few sentences of a story.

> *Time:* Once upon a time,
>
> *Character:* there was a little girl with a red hood
>
> *Location:* who lived near the edge of a dark forest.

Not every story contains all three elements at the beginning—one or more may be missing. Nevertheless, readers who know character, location, and time information

narrative discourse structure The organizational structure common to all stories; includes setting information, a problem, and episodes that describe attempts to resolve the problem.

setting information An element of narrative discourse structure found at the beginning of stories; includes information about the character(s), location, and time.

Various discourse structures are learned as children interact with print.

should be at the beginning of a narrative will use available clues in the rest of the story to infer this information when it is missing.

initiating episode One element of narrative discourse structure; usually the first organized sequence of actions that describe the problem to be resolved in the story.

An **initiating episode** usually is found in the first episode of a narrative. It specifies the problem that must be resolved in the story and describes an initiating event and the formation of a goal by one or more characters.

Initiating event: One day, Little Red Riding Hood's mother gave her a basket of bread and jam.

Goal formation: She told Little Red Riding Hood to take the food to her grandmother's house in the woods.

Initiating events and goals are not always stated in a story; however, readers familiar with narrative structure infer this information when it is missing by using surrounding clues in the rest of the story.

succeeding episodes The element of narrative discourse structure that tells how the character attempts to solve the problem established in the initiating episode.

Succeeding episodes, including the final episode, describe how the character attempts to solve the problem established in the initiating episode. Succeeding episodes typically contain an attempt to solve the problem, the outcome of that attempt, and a reaction to that outcome. Succeeding episodes may also result in characters establishing new problems to be solved in the course of the story.

Attempt: Little Red Riding Hood walked all day on the trail to her grandmother's house.

Outcome: When she arrived, they sat down immediately and feasted on the home-baked bread and strawberry jam.

Reaction: They were so content that they didn't even think about the wolf that had bothered them the week before.

Readers use their knowledge of narrative discourse structure to infer the missing structural elements in a story. When a structural element is not explicitly stated, knowledgeable readers will infer it by using clues provided in the rest of the story. However, not all children are aware of narrative discourse structure, especially those who are quite young and those who have not listened to enough stories to become familiar with their structure.

FIGURE 6-8

A dictated story from a 4-year-old that illustrates the consequences of not understanding the problem–resolution structure of stories

Time Goes

One bright sunny morning there were polar bears outside New York. And then Katie and Sarah went out to play in Sarah's new sled. And then they came in for a nice glass of hot chocolate. And then Katie had nice ten marshmallows. And then they went back outside. And then they went outside to come and make a snowman. And his name was Frosty the Snowman. And then they came down in the basement to play. And then on their new boats, Katie hopped on and Sarah hopped on one by one with their new animals. Then they went out to the part of the ghosts. And then they saw Count and Big Bird from Sesame. And then they saw themselves walking in the snow. And then they went to the ghost's house.

The End

You can tell if children are familiar with story structure by listening to their own stories. If children are familiar with typical story structure, their oral stories will be well formed and contain all of the important structural features: setting information, a problem, and a series of episodes that attempt to resolve the problem. If a child is unfamiliar with the structure of stories, some of these elements will be missing.

Figure 6-8 shows a story dictated by a 4-year-old child. Notice how the story contains some structural elements, such as a title and setting information. The story appears to wander, though, because the child did not include a problem in the story that gets resolved by the characters. This child appears to lack an understanding of the problem–resolution features that characterize a well-formed story. She is likely to miss these elements during a reading or listening experience, especially if the story requires her to infer them.

Shanahan and Shanahan (1997) suggested it is also important to look at the structure of narratives from the perspectives of several characters in a story. Stories are not structured around one character's problem; each character often has a different perspective on the problem in a story and how best to solve it. Creating separate graphic story maps from each character's perspective is likely to result in engaging discussions with your students. Looking at narrative structure in this fashion may lead to a richer, more complex understanding of stories by supporting interpretation as well as comprehension.

Knowledge of Specific Types of Narrative Structure

In addition to the common structural characteristics of all narratives, a variety of narrative forms have unique characteristics. Science fiction, for example, varies from contemporary fiction because of differences in the time information presented at the beginning of the story. Knowledge of those unique characteristics is important for effective comprehension of particular narrative types. For example, if we don't know that we are reading a fable, we may not infer an unstated moral or message. Table 6-2 on page 220 lists the major narrative forms and their defining characteristics. These defining characteristics of different story forms are usually learned by children in the elementary grades.

Using a Directed Reading–Thinking Activity

It is possible to develop narrative discourse knowledge by using a method framework often referred to as a **directed reading–thinking activity (DRTA),** which includes three procedural steps—predicting, reading, and proving—that are repeated as children read and discuss a selection.

directed reading–thinking activity (DRTA) A method framework used to assist children in predicting outcomes and drawing conclusions; includes predicting, reading, and proving.

TABLE 6-2

Major narrative forms and their defining characteristics

Narrative Form	Setting Information	Episodes	Examples
Fiction			
Historical fiction	Characters: fictional and historical Time: in the past	Fictional characters enacting historically accurate episodes	Island of the Blue Dolphin, The Courage of Sarah Noble
Modern realistic fiction	Characters: realistic Time: contemporary	Realistic episodes revolving around contemporary issues	Maniac Magee, On My Honor
Folktales	Characters: average citizens or animals Location: countryside Time: long ago	Fantastic actions with animals talking, witches casting spells, and so on	The People Could Fly: Black American Folktales
Fairy tales	Characters: royalty Location: castle or kingdom Time: long ago	Magical or fantastic actions, with animals talking, witches casting spells, and so on	Mufaro's Beautiful Daughters, Yeh-Shen: A Cinderella Story from China
Fables	Characters: usually animals Location: countryside Time: long ago	Magical or fantastic actions with animals talking with human characteristics and a moral, often at the end	Doctor Coyote: A Native American, Aesop's Fables, Frederick's Fables
Myths	Characters: cultural hero(ine)	Hero(ine) demonstrates courage, bravery, and skill in resolving a serious challenge	John Henry: An American Legend, Iktomi and the Boulder
Modern fantasies	Characters: realistic Time: contemporary	Magical or fantastic actions	Jumanji
Science fiction	Characters: usually realistic Location: often outer space Time: future	Fantastic actions logically predicted when the story was written	A Wrinkle in Time, Interstellar Pig
Nonfiction			
Biography	Character: historically important individuals	Factual account of an individual's life	Lincoln: A Photobiography
Autobiography	Character: historically important individual	Factual account of the author's life	The Land I Lost: Adventures of a Boy in Vietnam

During the first step, predicting, ask children to share what they think will happen in the story. If you use a DRTA to develop knowledge of narrative discourse structure, guide children in making predictions about structural elements found in stories. At the beginning, this would mean that you would ask children to make predictions about setting information. Here you might guide predictions about the time, characters, or location by asking, "Let's look at the title. When do you think this story took place?

Who do you think might be the characters in this story? Where do you think this story takes place?"

After children make predictions about setting information, invite them to read the beginning of the story where this information is likely to be found. This is the second step of a DRTA, reading. After reading the beginning, engage students in a discussion about the evidence they found that helps them become familiar with the time, characters, and location of the story. This is the third step of a DRTA, proving.

The procedural steps of a DRTA can be used several times as you read a story together. For example, you might repeat the first step and guide predictions about the problem in the story. This could be done by asking, "Now what do you think is going to be the main problem in this story? Who do you think is going to have this problem?"

After children make predictions about the problem in the story, invite them to read the next section of the story to discover if their guesses were correct. Then, after reading this section, engage them in another discussion about the evidence they found that specifies the problem.

Finally, guide predictions about the resolution of the problem by asking, for example: "Okay, how do you think this problem is going to be solved? Who do you think will solve the problem? How will they do this?" After reading the final section of the story, engage children in a discussion about the evidence in the story describing how the problem in the story is resolved.

Throughout this conversation you should follow the three steps of a DRTA: predict, read, and prove. At each point, your questions focus children's attention on the major elements of a story such as the setting, the story's problem, and the solution to the problem.

Using a DRTA helps children discover the structural characteristics of narratives in an inductive manner; they gradually come to discover that stories have certain structural characteristics from the predictions and discussions that follow. Because of the inductive nature of learning, this method framework is consistent with more integrated and holistic language learning beliefs as you consider the second issue of a literacy framework: How should I teach?

Deductive Instruction

If you have specific skills beliefs about how you should teach, you would probably choose a different method framework for helping children become familiar with the structure of narratives. **Deductive instruction,** described in chapter 2, is a teacher-directed method framework where you:

1. State the skill or rule.
2. Provide examples of the skill or rule.
3. Provide guided practice.
4. Provide independent practice.

deductive instruction
A method framework containing four steps: state the skill or rule, provide examples, provide guided practice, and provide independent practice.

When deductive instruction is used, the teacher defines the structural characteristics of a particular literary form for children, often listing these features on the chalkboard. When teaching the structural characteristics of a fable, for example, the teacher might explain that a fable usually has four distinguishing features: (1) it is a story that is not true, (2) animals are usually main characters, (3) animals usually take on human characteristics, and (4) an explicit lesson, or moral, is often stated at the end.

During the second procedural step, the class reads an example of the form and discusses how the story reflects the defining characteristics of the form. During the next several days they might read and discuss other examples of that narrative form in guided and independent reading experiences. Often children conclude their study with a writing experience, perhaps producing their own fable and then sharing their work with others in the class.

In the model lesson on page 222, Melissa Burns has decided to introduce several students to fables and the structural characteristics of that narrative form.

MODEL LESSON

Using Deductive Instruction to Teach the Structural Characteristics of a Fable

Melissa Burns teaches second grade. She believes discourse knowledge is important because she has a reader-based belief about the first issue in a literacy framework: "What should I teach?" When she considers the second issue in a literacy framework, "How should I teach?" Melissa takes an integrated stance. She provides both student-directed and teacher-directed experiences for her students, depending on their individual needs. As a result, she organizes her reading program around reading workshops where she can provide mini-lessons for students who learn best with more support from her.

Next week, she is going to add several text set activities to her program. One of the text sets includes a great collection of fables from the school library. She will also include several excellent fables located on the Internet at **Folklore, Myth, and Legend** (http://www.acs.ucalgary.ca/~dkbrown/storfolk.html). She has noticed several students are having difficulty with comprehension even though they decode words accurately. She thinks part of the problem may be a lack of discourse knowledge; they do not always understand how stories are structured and this makes it difficult to understand what is happening in a story. She invites these students to a mini-lesson on fables. She selects a deductive method framework for the mini-lesson because most of these students have learned quickly when things were more structured and teacher-directed.

State the Skill or Rule. Melissa begins by telling her students they will be reading a special type of story called a fable. She tells them that a long time ago a man called Aesop told many fables to teach people how they should act. Melissa writes the word *fable* on the chalkboard and asks whether anyone has ever read or heard a fable before. Several children respond, saying they think a fable has animals in it. One says that he has read a book of fables at home. After children respond, Melissa lists the four characteristics on the chalkboard under the word *fable* and explains each one.

1. It is not true.
2. Animals are the main characters.
3. The animals act like humans.
4. A lesson, or moral, is often stated at the end of the story.

Provide Examples of the Skill or Rule. Melissa has her students read *The Hare and the Tortoise* by Paul Galdone. She tells them to read the story to themselves and see whether they think it is a fable.

Provide Guided Practice. Everyone thinks the story is a fable. Melissa initiates a discussion about why children came to that conclusion. She directs their attention to the list of characteristics on the board, and children explain how each feature was contained in the story.

Provide Independent Practice. Melissa tells this group they should each choose a fable to read from **Folklore, Myth, and Legend** (http://www.acs.ucalgary.ca/~dkbrown/storfolk.html), the location she bookmarked on one of the Internet computers in the reading corner. She asks them to choose a fable, read it, and then share the story with the group the next day during a follow-up mini-lesson. This lesson will review the organization of fables as students retell the stories they have read.

Deductive instruction is useful if you wish to provide teacher-directed experiences for your students on specific aspects of literacy learning. However, if you believe students will learn better when they direct their own learning a bit more, you might wish to switch the first two steps in a deductive method. Instead of stating the principle and then providing examples, you could provide examples of several fables, perhaps through read-alouds, and have children discover the defining characteristics of this form by asking them what all of the stories have in common. This approach changes a deductive method framework to one more consistent with holistic language learning beliefs, including more student-directed learning. Chapter 4 referred to this approach as an inductive method framework.

TABLE 6-3

What should I teach? A summary of how a literacy framework can be used to inform decisions about what to teach with children's literature

Beliefs about How One Reads	Related Assumptions	Most Important Components	Probable Focus of Literature Use
Reader-based	Meaning exists more in what the reader brings to the text. Reading is a result of expectations. Reading begins with elements of prior knowledge.	Prior knowledge components: metacognitive, discourse, syntactic, and vocabulary knowledge.	Developing aesthetic responses. Developing metacognitive, discourse, syntactic, and vocabulary knowledge.
Text-based	Meaning exists more in the text. Reading is translation. Reading begins with decoding.	Decoding knowledge.	Developing efferent responses. Developing fluency and automaticity of decoding.
Interactive	Meaning exists in both the text and the reader. Reading is both translation and expectation. Reading uses each knowledge source simultaneously.	All knowledge sources: decoding, metacognitive, discourse, syntactic, and vocabulary knowledge, depending on individual needs.	Developing both efferent and aesthetic responses, depending on individual needs. Developing each of the knowledge sources important for literacy, depending on individual needs.

Using a Literacy Framework to Inform Instructional Decisions

An important part of your preparation as a teacher is to develop a comprehensive understanding of children's literature. Knowing about children's literature will enable you to implement our fourth principle of effective instruction:

4. Use exceptional works of literature and other text types.

Your use of children's literature will become even more effective, however, as you combine this knowledge with your literacy framework to meet the unique needs each child has. A literacy framework empowers you by informing two important types of decisions: "What should I teach with children's literature?" and "How should I teach it?"

Developing Insights about What to Teach

As you consider the use of children's literature in your classroom, you will need to decide what you will teach using children's literature. To help with this aspect of decision making, think for a moment about how you believe people read. Your belief will inform your decisions about what you will teach with children's literature. Table 6-3 summarizes the relationship between this portion of your literacy framework and decisions about using children's literature.

Teachers with a reader-based perspective emphasize the prior knowledge readers bring to a text. These teachers find literature important for developing richer aesthetic responses to their reading; they see literature as an important opportunity for their children to have a "lived through" experience with their reading. Literature is viewed as a means to travel to Africa to experience tribal life on the Serengeti, to visit King Arthur's court and live the code of honor among knights, or to see ancient China and feel the respect granted to elders. In addition, they value literature because it helps develop vocabulary, syntactic, discourse, and metacognitive knowledge, each of which is a prior knowledge component.

Teachers who follow a text-based explanation of how a person reads emphasize the meaning in a text. As a result, these teachers find literature crucial for developing efferent responses to their reading; they see literature as an important opportunity for their students to acquire factual information about cultures, people, and times. These teachers tend not to use literature for developing those elements commonly associated with what readers bring to a text: vocabulary, syntactic, discourse, and metacognitive knowledge. Instead, they emphasize the importance of decoding knowledge in their teaching. These teachers value literature because it helps develop fluency and automaticity in decoding, which, in turn, provides access to the meanings in a text.

Teachers with an interactive perspective find literature a powerful vehicle for developing both aesthetic and efferent responses. They also value the use of literature to develop both decoding components and prior knowledge components, depending on the needs of individual students.

Areas of agreement exist among all three types of teachers. Regardless of your beliefs about how one reads, it is likely that you will find literature a useful vehicle in which to develop social aspects; most teachers seek to communicate the value they have for multicultural understanding and the diversity of the human experience through the choices they make with literature for classroom activities. Also, regardless of your beliefs, it is likely that you will find literature a useful vehicle in which to develop affective aspects. All teachers want their children to be interested in reading. As a result, all teachers should support their children in becoming independent readers who not only can read but also choose to read on their own for pleasure, information, and personal growth. Most teachers, too, will find literature the most powerful tool for developing emergent reading abilities. Most would agree that reading aloud and other early literacy activities help young children develop important early insights about literacy.

Developing Insights about How to Teach

As you consider the use of literature in your classroom, you will also need to decide how to use children's literature to support literacy learning. Your conclusion about how children learn to read can be used to inform decisions about which method frameworks to use. Table 6-4 on page 225 summarizes the relationship between this portion of your literacy framework and the method frameworks you would probably favor.

Teachers with holistic language learning beliefs feel reading is learned inductively as children engage in self-directed, functional, purposeful, holistic experiences with authentic literature. Thus, they use activities and method frameworks that provide children with greater ownership of the reading and learning experience. Reading workshop is a popular method framework, as is the use of cooperative learning groups. In addition, grand conversations, literature discussion groups, and text sets are often used. Directed reading–thinking activities and read-aloud response journal activities are also used by teachers with holistic language learning beliefs. Each of these method frameworks allows children to direct much of their learning experience with literature. Internet Workshop, Internet Inquiry, and Internet Project are also used, perhaps as children explore information about the topics of their stories or their authors.

Teachers with specific skill beliefs about how reading ability develops favor deductive instruction. They find this method framework more consistent with their concerns about directly teaching important aspects of children's literature. Deductive instruction

TABLE 6-4

How should I teach? A summary of how a literacy framework can be used to inform decisions about how to teach with children's literature

Beliefs about How One Reads	Related Assumptions	Favored Method Frameworks and Instructional Activities
Holistic language learning	Children learn best in an inductive fashion as they direct their own learning and reading experiences. Children learn best during holistic, meaningful, and functional experiences with authentic literature.	Reading workshop Cooperative learning groups Grand conversations Literature discussion groups Text sets Directed reading–thinking activities Read-aloud sessions Internet Workshop Internet Inquiry Internet Project
Specific skills	Children learn best when taught directly by the teacher in a deductive fashion. Children learn best when they master specific reading skills.	Deductive instruction Directed Reading Activities
Integrated	Children learn best as a result of both student-directed, inductive experiences and teacher-directed, deductive experiences, depending on individual needs. Children learn best when they engage in meaningful, functional, and holistic experiences with authentic texts and when they acquire specific reading skills, depending on individual needs.	Reading workshop Cooperative learning groups Grand conversations Literature discussion groups Text sets Directed reading–thinking activities Read-aloud sessions Deductive instruction Directed reading activities Internet Inquiry Internet Workshop Internet Project

is likely to be used, for example, to teach the structure of narrative forms. In addition, Directed Reading Activities would also be used. Each of these approaches was described in chapter 2.

Teachers with an integrated explanation of how reading develops believe that children learn best when exposed to authentic and holistic experiences with print and receive instruction in important skill areas, depending on their individual needs. Thus, these teachers use all of the method frameworks described in this chapter. All three types of Internet method frameworks are also used: Internet Inquiry, Internet Project, and Internet Workshop.

There are areas of agreement among all three types of teachers, largely because each type of teacher values literature activities for developing independent readers. Read-alouds, readers theater, reading corners, and Drop Everything And Read are popular method frameworks for developing independent readers and are used by all teachers. Similarly, because learning about the diversity of the human experience is valued by all teachers, the model presented in Figure 6-6 for developing units about this topic will probably be used by teachers regardless of their beliefs about how reading ability develops. Teachers with a holistic language learning belief, though, use student-directed experiences throughout these units, while those with a specific skills view tend to use teacher-directed experiences. Teachers with integrated beliefs use both types of experiences to support their students as they learn about diversity through children's literature.

Use the self-test questions on http://www.prenhall.com/leukinzer to review the material presented in this chapter.

Featured Teacher

Mr. Sangiuliano and Miss Surreira

Mr. Sangiuliano and Miss Surreira team teach a mixed-grade, elementary classroom at the Sowams School in Barrington, Rhode Island. They have created an exceptional model for using literature in the classroom. If you explore their classroom home page in Figure 6-9 (http://booksontapeforkids.org/class/) you will discover their project called "Books on Tape." Businesses in their town contribute small amounts to this project, enabling the class to purchase library-bound copies of award-winning children's literature. Small groups then work together to develop an oral reading of the book. Each group practices very hard to read their work as the characters in the story, with each student reading a character's part and one student reading the narration. They develop appropriate sound effects to include, too. After practicing their reading of the story many times to get it just right, they record their reading on tape. They then each write short autobiographies of the readers (using first names only for child safety purposes) and package the entire set of storybook, tape, and autobiographies together and mail it to a children's hospital in the United States. Their goal is to present a set of books, autobiographies, and tapes to two children's hospitals in each state. This is a wonderful social service project that helps students to see the importance of making our world a better place.

Importantly, these teachers have found the project especially helpful for developing fluency and automaticity among their weakest readers. Rereading their part over and over again appears to especially support these children in developing fluency.

FIGURE 6-9

The home page for Mr. Sangiuliano and Miss Surreira's mixed-grade classroom in Barrington, Rhode Island (http://booksontapeforkids.org/class/)

Major Points

▶ Experiences with literature are important to every classroom literacy program.

▶ Literature's effects on reading comprehension and response are all-encompassing; using literature develops every component of literacy and supports the development of independent readers.

▶ To develop independent readers through children's literature, teachers must become familiar with popular children's literature, identify their students' reading interests, and put children and books together in pleasurable settings. Many method frameworks can help develop independent readers: read-aloud sessions, Drop Everything And Read, and readers theater.

▶ Many useful resources for children's literature appear on the WWW. Children's literature experiences and technology support one another.

▶ Literature is a tremendous tool for helping children understand the diversity of the human experience. Culturally sensitive literature should be an important part of your literacy program.

▶ Literature is useful to increase the variety of responses children have to their reading experiences. Developing aesthetic as well as efferent responses increases children's ability to think critically about what they have read. This, in turn, increases learning.

▶ A literacy framework can guide decisions about the use of children's literature. Your beliefs about how children read can help determine what to teach and emphasize through children's literature. Your beliefs about how children's reading ability develops can help determine which method frameworks you will find most useful.

Making Instructional Decisions

1. Briefly define your current literacy framework by identifying your beliefs about how children read and how children learn to read. Then explain how you will use children's literature in your classroom reading program. Be sure to describe what you will teach and how you will teach it. Discuss the connection between your literacy framework and these two sets of instructional decisions.

2. What instructional issue about children's literature seemed most important to you as you read this chapter: How do I develop independent readers? What is the best way to develop decoding knowledge with literature? How do I develop multicultural units with literature? What are the best books for third/first/sixth grade? Join the mailing lists LITERACY or RTEACHER. Raise your question and seek advice from colleagues.

3. This chapter described the importance of developing independent readers. Identify a grade level and then describe the ways in which you will go about helping your students achieve this.

4. Learning about the diversity of the human experience should be a goal for all teachers as they think about the role of literature. Explain how you will accomplish this important goal by integrating experiences with children's literature and the Internet.

5. Select an interesting piece of children's literature for a read-aloud session. Practice reading it aloud until you have a clear sense of how you want it to sound. Then read your selection to a class of children or to your peers. Follow the procedural steps listed on page 192. Evaluate yourself after completing this experience. What pleased you about the experience? What decisions would you change next time?

Further Reading

Giorgis, C., & Johnson, N. (2001). Finding a place. *The Reading Teacher, 55*, 304–309.

Reviews an extensive set of children's literature selections that could be used in literature discussion groups or text sets for a unit on finding one's sense of place. Also provides a number of useful literature strategies for use in your classroom.

Martinez, M. (1993). Motivating dramatic story reenactments. *The Reading Teacher, 46* (8), 682–688.

Describes how dramatic story reenactments can be used successfully in a kindergarten classroom to enhance children's responses and understanding of literature as well as develop knowledge of narrative discourse structure.

McMahon, S. I., Raphael, T. E., Goatley, V. J., & Pardo, L. S. (Eds.). (1997). *The book club connection.* New York: Teachers College Press.

A wonderful book providing a comprehensive description and analysis of how to develop a book club approach to the use of literature in your classroom.

Shanahan, T., & Shanahan, S. (1997). Character perspective charting: Helping children to develop a more com-plete conception of story. *The Reading Teacher, 50* (8), 668–677.

Shows how charting the narrative discourse structure of a story from the perspective of different characters leads to a richer understanding and interpretation. The article provides several examples of this technique.

Yokota, J. (1993). Issues in selecting multicultural litera-ture. *Language Arts, 70* (3), 156–167.

Describes trends in multicultural literature and criteria to keep in mind when selecting multicultural literature. Also provides a list of culturally conscious multicultural literature.

References

Anderson, R., Fielding, L., & Wilson, P. (1988). Growth in reading and how children spend their time outside of school. *Reading Research Quarterly, 23,* 285–303.

Anderson, R. C., Hiebert, E. H., Scott, J. A., & Wilkinson, I. A. G. (1985). *Becoming a nation of readers: The report of the commission on reading.* Washington, DC: National Academy of Education.

Au, K. H. (1993). *Literacy instruction in multicultural settings.* Fort Worth, TX: Holt, Rinehart and Winston.

Barrentine, S. J. (1996). Engaging with reading through in-teractive read alouds. *The Reading Teacher, 50* (1), 36–43.

Clay, M. M. (1989). Concepts about print in English and other languages. *The Reading Teacher, 42* (4), 268–277.

Cochran-Smith, M. (1984). *The making of a reader.* Norwood, NJ: Ablex.

Eeds, M., & Wells, D. (1989). Grand conversations: An ex-ploration of meaning construction in literature study groups. *Research in the Teaching of English, 23,* 4–29.

Fader, D. N. (1976). *The new hooked on books.* New York: Put-nam.

Fuhler, C. J. (1990). Commentary: Let's move toward literature-based reading instruction. *The Reading Teacher, 43* (4), 312–315.

Galda, L., Ash, G. E., & Cullinan, B. E. (2000). Children's lit-erature. In M. L. Kamil, P. Mosenthal, P. D. Pearson, & R. Barr (Eds.), *Handbook of reading research, Volume III* (pp. 361–380). Mahwah, NJ: Lawrence Erlbaum Asso-ciates.

Harris, A. J., & Sipay, E. R. (1990). *How to increase reading ability* (9th ed.). New York: Longman Publishing Group.

Harris, V. J. (1992). Multiethnic children's literature. In K. D. Wood & A. Moss (Eds.), *Exploring literature in the classroom: Content and methods* (169–201). Norwood, MA: Christopher-Gordon.

Harste, J., Short, K., & Burke, C. (1988). *Creating classrooms for authors.* Portsmouth, NH: Heinemann.

Hartman, D. K., & Hartman, J. A. (1993). Reading across texts: Expanding the role of the reader. *The Reading Teacher, 47* (3), 202–211.

Hiebert, E. H., & Colt, J. (1989). Patterns of literature-based reading instruction. *The Reading Teacher, 43* (1), 14–21.

McCracken, R. A. (1971). Initiating Drop Everything And Read. *Journal of Reading, 14,* 521–524, 582–583.

McMahon, S. I., Raphael, T. E., Goatley, V. J., & Pardo, L. S. (Eds.). (1997). *The book club connection.* New York: Teachers College Press.

Norton, D. E. (1990). Teaching multicultural literature in the reading curriculum. *The Reading Teacher, 44* (1), 28–40.

Peterson, R., & Eeds, M. (1990). *Grand conversations: Litera-ture groups in action.* Toronto, Ontario: Scholastic-TAB.

Purves, A. C. (1993). Toward a reevaluation of reader re-sponse and school literature. *Language Arts, 70* (5), 348–361.

Rasinski, T. V. (1989). Fluency for everyone: Incorporating fluency instruction in the classroom. *The Reading Teacher, 42* (9), 690–693.

Rasinski, T. V., & Padak, N. V. (1990). Multicultural learn-ing through children's literature. *Language Arts, 67* (6), 576–580.

Rosenblatt, L. (1978). *The reader, the text, the poem: The trans-actional theory of literary work.* Carbondale, IL: Southern Illinois University Press.

Rosenblatt, L. (1985). Viewpoints: Transaction versus inter-action—A terminological rescue operation. *Research in the Teaching of English, 19,* 98–107.

Shanahan, T., & Shanahan, S. (1997). Character perspective charting: Helping children to develop a more com-plete conception of story. *The Reading Teacher, 50* (8), 668–677.

Short, K. (1993). Intertextuality: Searching for patterns that connect. In D. J. Leu & C. K. Kinzer (Eds.), *Literacy re-search, theory, and practice: Views from many perspectives. Forty-first yearbook of the National Reading Conference.* Chicago: National Reading Conference.

Snow, C. E., Burns, S., & Griffin, P. (1998). *Preventing read-ing difficulties in young children.* Washington, DC: Na-tional Academy Press.

Spiegel, D. L., & Fitzgerald, J. (1986). Improving reading comprehension through instruction about story parts. *The Reading Teacher, 39* (7), 676–683.

Taylor, D., & Strickland, D. S. (1986). *Family storybook read-ing.* Portsmouth, NH: Heinemann.

Tompkins, G. E., & McGee, I. M. (1993). *Teaching reading with literature: Case studies to action plans.* Upper Saddle River, NJ: Merrill/Prentice Hall.

Trelease, J. (2001). *The read-aloud handbook* (5th ed.). New York: Penguin Books.

Tunnell, M. O., & Jacobs, J. S. (1989). Using "real" books: Research findings on literature-based reading instruction. *The Reading Teacher, 42* (7), 470–477.

Walker-Dalhouse, D. (1992). Using African-American literature to increase ethnic understanding. *The Reading Teacher, 45,* 416–422.

Wolf, S. A. (1993). What's in a name? Labels and literacy in readers theatre. *The Reading Teacher, 46* (7), 540–545.

Yokota, J. (1993). Issues in selecting multicultural literature. *Language Arts, 70* (3), 156–167.

Young, T. A., & Vardell, S. (1993). Weaving readers theatre and nonfiction into the curriculum. *The Reading Teacher, 46* (5), 396–406.

Zarrillo, J. (1989). Teachers' interpretations of literature-based reading. *The Reading Teacher, 42* (9), 22–29.

CHAPTER 7

Connecting Reading and Writing

 E-mail from the Classroom

Subject: Connecting Reading and Writing with E-mail
From: Linda Shearin, lshearin@bellsouth.net

Engaging young elementary students in an e-mail project is an exciting new way to connect reading and writing! This spring I worked with two kindergarten and three first-grade students who were reading at a level well above their peers. They participated in e-mail discussions about what they were reading with three students in Dr. Leu's course at the University of Connecticut.

Pairing a college student with a younger student provided both with unique opportunities. The younger student benefited by having a consistent and thoughtful correspondent. The college student had an opportunity to gain insights about the child's response to literature as well as answer questions posed by the younger student. The college students were reading the same books as the younger students.

Composing their own e-mail messages, the younger students also gained word processing and editing experience as well as telecommunication skills with e-mail.

E-mail enables us to connect reading and writing in ways that otherwise would not have been possible.

Key Concepts

author's chair	predictable texts
central Internet sites	prewriting
dialogue journal	process writing approaches
drafting	publishing
editing	reader response journal
Internet Projects	reading/writing center
journal writing	revising
keypals	style study
pattern stories	thematic units
peer conferences	writing workshop

After reading this chapter, you should be able to:

1. Explain why writing is important to the development of reading proficiency.
2. Identify four important insights to guide the connection between reading and writing.
3. Connect reading and writing experiences by integrating the Internet into your classroom.
4. Use a variety of method frameworks to make the reading–writing connection in your classroom.
5. Understand how a literacy framework informs decisions about connecting reading and writing.

Integrate Reading and Writing: A Principle of Effective Literacy Instruction

As you learn about reading instruction, you will increasingly see many writing experiences integrated within the reading curriculum. This reflects a fifth principle of effective literacy instruction:

5. **Integrate reading and writing experiences.** It is important to integrate writing with reading experiences to support children's literacy development (Calkins, 2000; Gavelek, Raphael, Biondo, & Wang, 2000; Yaden, Rowe, & MacGillivray, 2000).

Effective teachers regularly integrate writing with reading experiences in their classrooms. They find that connecting reading and writing is an important part of their literacy programs. Consequently, they develop method frameworks to integrate the two within their classrooms. Many, like Linda Shearin, also find the Internet provides new opportunities in this area. As Internet connections appear in schools, you can support literacy learning in many ways by connecting reading and writing experiences with this important new tool.

There are at least four reasons why it is important to connect reading and writing in your classroom. First, connecting reading and writing experiences makes literacy learning come alive for your students; learning about reading and writing becomes a natural part of nearly any activity. When you integrate reading and writing into classroom projects, your students will become excited about their work, so excited that many will not realize the new literacy skills they are acquiring. A fourth-grade student said it best at the end of the year: "I didn't know I was learning so much about reading and writing. I was just having fun!"

Second, by combining writing with reading experiences, you maximize learning during a busy instructional day. Instead of treating reading and writing as separate subjects, you combine these experiences to make the most effective use of limited instructional time. This is increasingly important as school districts and states mandate new curricular programs and you find yourself with less and less time during the day for traditional subject areas. By integrating reading and writing experiences, often in conjunction with other subject areas, you can take maximum advantage of every learning opportunity to support literacy.

Third, writing may be used to develop every aspect of reading comprehension and response. It is one of the most important tools to help children become literate and may be used to develop social aspects, affective aspects, emergent literacy aspects, decoding knowledge, vocabulary knowledge, syntactic knowledge, discourse knowledge, and metacognitive knowledge. As you saw in chapter 3, each of these is central to becoming literate. Knowing how to connect reading and writing experiences is one of the most important things you can learn as a teacher because it allows you to support literacy for so many curricular goals.

Finally, connecting reading and writing prepares your students for the world that awaits them. When your students enter the world of work in an electronic information age, much of their success will be determined by their ability to quickly obtain information, use this information to solve important problems, and communicate solutions to others (Leu, 1997). Reading and writing tasks will be tightly connected in your students' futures. Often this will take place through networked electronic environments as they effortlessly shift from reading, to writing, to reading, and back to writing. Connecting reading and writing in your classroom rather than conducting lessons in these areas separately will best prepare your students for their electronic futures (Kinzer & Leu, 1997).

Check your ongoing understanding of chapter concepts by using the guided review for this chapter on http://www.prenhall.com/leukinzer

Developing Insights about Writing

If writing is so important to developing reading ability, how should you provide appropriate writing experiences for your students? During the past several decades, much research has focused on this question. Four major conclusions from this research should inform your work with students:

1. Writing is a process.
2. Writing experiences should serve an authentic communicative purpose.

PRACTICAL TEACHING STRATEGIES

Prewriting Activities

Brainstorm Writing Ideas. Before children begin writing, ask them to brainstorm possible writing ideas. As students generate their ideas, record these on the chalkboard. Having a list of possible writing ideas and listening to others' ideas about a writing project provides support for students who have a difficult time coming up with a starting point for their own writing.

Prewriting Read-Alouds. Before asking students to write in a particular genre, read aloud at least one selection that uses this form of writing. This can be used to scaffold students' learning in supportive ways. If, for example, you wish to have students keep a diary during a unit, begin by reading aloud selections in which the main character keeps a diary so that students can become familiar with how diary entries are written. Consider these examples:

Anne Frank: Diary of a Young Girl by Anne Frank

Diary of a Rabbit by Lilo Hess

Penny Pollard's Diary by Robin Klein

Tell your students that they, too, will have an opportunity to keep a diary. Brainstorm together topics that students might write about in a diary. Display the list of ideas where students can refer to it. After sufficient discussion, give each student a small spiral notebook to use as a diary. Allow students to decorate their diaries in any way they wish before making their first entries.

---

3. Writing experiences are most valuable when they create complete, extended texts.

4. Reading and writing are similar types of processes.

Writing Is a Process

Traditionally schools simply assigned writing tasks to students and then evaluated their products (Applebee, 1981). Teachers would assign a writing task, students would complete the assignment, and teachers would correct it. By focusing on the outcome, traditional approaches treated writing as a product; this may be how you encountered writing instruction in school. One of the most important conclusions from recent research work is that writing should be viewed as a process, not a product (Calkins, 2000; Graves, 1983; Smith, 1982). **Process writing approaches** have replaced product approaches to writing.

> **process writing approaches** An approach to writing instruction where students are supported during each element of the writing process: prewriting, drafting, revising, editing, and publishing.

Teachers who take a process approach to writing do more than simply assign writing tasks and evaluate the results. Instead they focus their attention on the process of writing and look for ways to support students during each phase of this process:

- Prewriting
- Drafting
- Revising
- Editing
- Publishing

Recognizing writing as a process leads teachers to support each of these elements as they design appropriate writing experiences for their students.

Prewriting experiences generate potential topics and writing ideas by helping students explore personal knowledge related to their writing task. We all write better when we think about what we know before we begin. Examples of prewriting activities include reading material related to a topic, brainstorming ideas, mapping relationships among ideas, listing sources of information, and even talking to a friend about various ideas. Appropriate prewriting experiences support students in this often-difficult beginning phase of the writing process.

> **prewriting** One element of the writing process during which writers generate potential topics and writing ideas.

PRACTICAL TEACHING STRATEGIES

Drafting Activities

Writing Folders on Your Classroom Computer. Make separate writing folders for each child on your classroom computer. Show children how to save their drafts in their folder, and then show them how to print out their drafts. Having a hard copy of their draft will be necessary for revision conferences, where peers make suggestions for revisions.

Timed Draft Writing. Sometimes you will find your students have a topic but just can't seem to get started with their drafts. If this is the case, timed draft writing activities are sometimes useful. Tell your students they will have only 5 minutes (or another short period of time) to complete as much as they can of their first draft. Sometimes setting a time limit is a useful strategy to help students overcome the difficulty of beginning a writing project. Writing that first sentence is sometimes the hardest part of writing.

Co-authored Writing. Periodically encourage pairs of students to work on a co-authored paper in a cooperative learning group activity. After a prewriting activity, they might want to work together on one draft, talking and making decisions as they go. Or, after making preliminary decisions about topic and structure, they might wish to write separate drafts and then compare and combine their ideas. Students often learn much from working with others and seeing how someone else writes. This is especially true when you match a proficient writer with a less-proficient writer.

Several considerations should influence prewriting activities. It is important for students to explore a wide range of potential writing ideas during prewriting. Such exploration allows students to select their own topics from several possibilities and work on a writing task that is personally important and engaging. It is also important to provide sufficient time for this phase of the writing process. In a survey of U.S. classrooms, Applebee (1981) concluded that students have, on average, 3 minutes to think of a topic during a typical writing lesson. More recent classroom practice demonstrates that this has increased, but much more time is needed if students are to have sufficient opportunity to explore all possibilities. Finally, prewriting should be viewed as an opportunity for students to discover what it is they have to say about a topic. Prewriting gets ideas to flow; it is a time of beginnings. It is not a time when the final structure of a text must be decided. You can see examples of prewriting strategies on page 233.

drafting One element of the writing process during which writers capture preliminary ideas.

The second element of the writing process is **drafting,** which consists of initial attempts to capture ideas in writing. All of us write better if we know we don't have to worry about getting everything written perfectly in the first draft. Drafting is often messy, as writers erase, rewrite, or even start over. The goal is to simply get the writer's first attempt down on paper or disk. There will be plenty of time later for revising. Strategies to support the drafting phase are described above.

revising One element of the writing process during which writers consider what they have written and make changes in the content.

Revising is the third component of the writing process. As writers revise, they read their work, consider what they have written, and make changes in the content of their writing. Revising is an important but difficult part of the writing process. It is important because it holds great potential for developing insight into written language as students consider alternatives to their initial choices about words, sentence structures, discourse patterns, and other elements of writing. Revising is difficult for writers, though. Younger writers want to focus their attention on spelling and the appearance of their writing much more than its content. They need to look carefully at word choices, sentence structure, and other elements from their reader's perspective. And writers of any age are often too close to their work to notice sections that are unclear.

peer conferences A strategy used to support student writing. One student reads another student's work and makes suggestions for improvement.

To help students understand how to improve the content of their writing, teachers often use **peer conferences** during which another student reads a writer's work and makes suggestions for improvement. It helps writers of all ages to have someone else read and react to their writing before they revise it. Readers can provide writers with the best suggestions for making writing clearer. Suggestions for conducting peer conferences appear on the next page.

PRACTICAL TEACHING STRATEGIES

Ideas for Conducting Peer Conferences to Support the Revision Phase of the Writing Process

Internet Peer Conferences. Visit the **Keypals** site (http://sesd.sk.ca/teacherresource/KeyPal/keypals.html) and connect with another classroom at your grade level that wishes to engage in revision conferences over the Internet. Send drafts of student work over the Internet and seek suggestions from your partner class for improving student work.

Peer Revision Conferences. Using a volunteer, demonstrate to your class how to conduct a peer revision conference. As you complete each step, write it on the chalkboard for all to see. First the author reads his or her work aloud to the listener (you) so that both you and the author can hear it. You should then provide three types of comments: praise (things you liked about the writing), question (meaning that was not clear in the writing), and polish (suggestions to make the paper better). After the demonstration, have a pair of students model the process again. Then divide the class into pairs and attempt peer conferences. Remind each pair to follow the list of procedures you wrote on the chalkboard. Afterward, get together as a class and share your ideas for helping authors improve their work.

Monitoring Revision Conferences. As students use peer conferences for revision, monitor these conferences by asking the person who engaged in the revision conference to initial the first draft in the upper right-hand corner. Some teachers require each draft to have at least two sets of initials before it is revised. Encourage students to have their parents/guardians engage in one of the revision conferences. This keeps parents/guardians informed about the work their children are doing at school.

PRACTICAL TEACHING STRATEGIES

Supporting the Editing Phase of the Writing Process

Peer Editing Conferences. Using an overhead projector, demonstrate to your class how to conduct a peer editing conference. As you complete each step, write it on the chalkboard for all to see. First, the editor reads the work aloud to the author so that both can hear it. As you read, mark each spelling, punctuation, and other change with the appropriate editing mark. Finally, explain each suggestion for a change to the author. Remember that the author has the right to accept or reject each change that you suggest. After the demonstration, pass out a copy with editing marks (below), have your class divide into pairs, and attempt peer editing conferences. Remind each pair to follow the list of procedures you wrote on the chalkboard. Afterward, get together as a class and share your ideas for making editing conferences useful to authors.

Editorial Boards. Use an editorial board for large writing projects in class. Appoint board members and have students bring their work to a member of the editorial board for final editing. Regularly rotate members of the board so every student in your class has an opportunity to participate in this important experience.

Editing Marks. Conduct a short writer's workshop session on the use of common editing marks, shown below. Show students how you use these marks when you edit your own work and encourage them to use the same marks during editing conferences.

capitalize	≡	delete something	
use a period	⊙	check the spelling of this word	
insert something	∧	begin a new paragraph	
add a comma	∧	transpose	

The fourth aspect of the writing process is **editing.** During editing, the writer should attend to the surface characteristics of writing, including spelling, capitalization, punctuation, and usage. Editing takes place near the end of the process so that attention has first been directed to the content of the piece during prewriting, drafting, and revising. Strategies you can use to support the editing phase of the writing process appear above.

editing One element of the writing process during which writers make changes in the spelling, punctuation, and other surface characteristics of their work.

PRACTICAL TEACHING STRATEGIES

Supporting the Publishing Phase of the Writing Process

Publishing Student Work on the WWW. Students may publish reviews of their favorite books at the commercial site **Amazon.com** (http://www.amazon.com) after teacher review. Have them do a search to locate a book at this site, then follow the directions for posting a review. You may also publish articles, stories, and poems in a class or school newspaper at your classroom's home page on the WWW. Send the hard copy home to your students' parents and invite them to visit your classroom home page if they have Internet access.

Author's Chair. Have a special author's chair from which children read their completed works to the class. (Place this chair in a prominent place in your classroom.) After authors have shared their writing, invite classmates to share their positive comments about the aspects of the work they liked best. This will make each author feel very special.

publishing One element of the writing process during which writers formally share their writing with others and receive recognition for their work.

The final element in the writing process is **publishing,** when writers formally share their writing with a wider audience and receive recognition for their work. Sometimes publishing involves binding students' work and making it available for others to read. This is not the only way to publish a work, though. Other strategies for formally sharing a finished work are described above.

An Example of Process Writing in the Classroom

Focusing on writing as a process means that we provide support to students during each phase of the writing process. The writing project described in the model lesson on page 237 shows how a teacher provides support during each of these phases. However, two important points need to be made. First, it is important that teachers not require students to go through each phase of the writing process for every writing assignment. For example, some writing tasks, such as an entry in a journal or a diary, do not require careful editing

Peer feedback and editing is a helpful strategy in process writing.

MODEL LESSON

A Process Writing Activity in Bianca Marsella's Class

Bianca Marsella has reader-based beliefs about *what* to teach; prior knowledge components are more important to her than decoding. She developed a thematic unit to develop many aspects of prior knowledge, especially the discourse structure of pourquoi tales—the "why" stories used by each culture to explain the origin of things. In addition, Bianca has a perspective about *how* to teach that falls somewhere between holistic language learning beliefs and integrated beliefs; she believes that most students learn best through directing their own learning experiences but that others may require direct instructional support from her.

Prewriting. Bianca's third-grade class has been hard at work on their thematic unit. The children have listened to, read, and discussed pourquoi tales from many different cultures, including:

How the Rhinoceros Got His Skin by Leonard Weisgard

The Fire Bringer by Margaret Hodges

Just So Stories by Rudyard Kipling

They have also visited **Creation Stories and Myths** (http://www.internet-at-work.com/hos_mcgrane/creation/cstorymenu.html) and read many other pourquoi tales from around the world. Bianca tells her students that they will have a chance to create their own pourquoi tales and publish these in a book entitled *Just Our Stories* (with apologies to Rudyard Kipling). The book will be posted at their classroom home page for other classes to read and enjoy. A hard copy will also be placed in the local library for the community to enjoy before being returned to the class.

Bianca begins with a brainstorming activity. Students share possible titles for their pourquoi tales: "How the Snake Lost Its Legs," "How Ms. Marsella Got Her Smile," "How San Francisco Got the Bay," and "How the Eagle Got Its Wings." As each title is shared, Bianca writes it on the board and a few moments are spent brainstorming explanations that might be included in the story. Once a list of titles is developed, she encourages students to decide on their own titles and begin drafting their pourquoi tales.

Drafting. Bianca circulates around the room, providing assistance and encouragement. When she notices interesting ideas that are being developed, she has students share them with the class. Nonetheless, several students are having difficulty getting started. She calls these students together for additional brainstorming and discussion about possible stories. As each possibility is brainstormed, Bianca maps out the story's setting, problem, and resolution on the board. This support provides each student with the necessary structure to get started. At the end of each day's work, students who are writing on paper return drafts to their individual writing folders, which are located in the writing center of the classroom. Students working on the four classroom computers store their work in their individual file folders. During the week, all students have a chance to compose their first draft on one of the computers.

Revising. As students finish their drafts, Bianca invites them to ask someone in the room to conduct a peer conference with them. She has students share their work in two separate peer conferences so that they can obtain different reactions to their writing. She gives both writer and listener a paper with these procedures listed for conducting effective peer conferences.

1. Read the draft aloud.
2. Share your response to each of the following questions:
   a. Praise (What did you like?)
   b. Question (What did you not understand?)
   c. Polish (What will make the writing better?)

After receiving comments from two listeners, students begin to revise their work in a second draft.

Editing. Bianca requires each tale to be read and edited by at least two people. The editors sign the front page of the second draft so that a list of their names can be compiled for inclusion in the final book. After two people have read and edited each story, students complete a third and final draft, taking into consideration their editors' suggestions.

(continues on next page)

Publishing. After each story is completed, Bianca invites the author to sit in the author's chair and read the tale to the entire class. She has students "turn in" their electronic copies by placing them in her folder on the computer. This allows her to quickly transfer them to the classroom's home page and display them for the world to read. She takes the hard copies, with illustrated covers, to the local library for display.

How might teachers with alternative beliefs teach this lesson? A teacher with text-based beliefs about *what* to teach would have used this activity to focus on correct spelling and punctuation. Because these teachers are most concerned about meaning in the text, accurate spelling and punctuation become central literacy goals. Editing conferences would have received the most attention because this aspect of the writing process supports accurate spelling and punctuation.

A teacher with specific skills beliefs about *how* to teach would have provided less opportunity for students to direct their own learning in this activity. Writing topics would have been identified by the teacher, conference partners would have been selected by the teacher, and students would have been asked to include several skills in their stories that were recently introduced in class. Writing process activities often are seen by teachers with specific skills beliefs as opportunities to practice skills.

and are rarely published or shared publicly. Teachers may want to allow their students to decide which of their many writing projects require the steps described above or are developed all the way to publishing.

Second, it is important to recognize that the writing process is more recursive than linear. In other words, writing does not always follow a strict sequential process of prewriting, followed by drafting, revising, editing, and publishing. When drafting an article, writers may also revise portions of it or they may go back and edit word choices and spelling. They may even make plans to have their writing published. Writers appear to develop their own style during the writing process. Graves (1983) points out that writing is not easily packaged into a sequence of steps. Teachers who want to support their students throughout the writing process should not expect a neat linear sequence of procedural steps.

Writing Experiences Should Serve an Authentic Communicative Purpose

A second insight to guide instruction is that writing experiences are most appropriate when they serve an authentic communicative purpose. This seems like common sense, doesn't it? Who would want children to write something with no purpose? Nonetheless, the only purpose of some classroom writing tasks is simply to record that something was completed (Moffett, 1985). For example, writing a book report, which is turned in to the teacher and passed back with a grade, communicates only that the child has completed reading a book. However, a book review written to guide other children in making a reading selection would serve a more useful communicative purpose. The review might be read aloud to the class and then included in a collection of other reviews organized by title, topic, or author for later reference on the classroom's home page, or it might be sent to one of many locations on the WWW that accept students' reviews of books.

Writing experiences that serve an authentic communicative purpose are both personal and meaningful for students. They are personal because students recognize they are sharing a part of themselves with their readers. They are meaningful because the writing exists to communicate important information. When writing is both personal and meaningful, students invest considerable energy and attention. They are more careful because they realize they are sharing something important about themselves with their readers; as a result, they gain more from the experience.

As teachers, we need to create contexts in which students have authentic reasons for writing. A classroom should be viewed as a literacy community, where students use writing to communicate, satisfy needs, present information, express personal thoughts and opinions, record information, and interact with others. Internet experiences are especially valuable here, but one must always keep in mind issues of child safety. We discuss these issues in chapter 14. Examples of activities that use writing for authentic communication appear on page 240.

E-mail from the Classroom

Subject: Writer's Workshop
From: Diane J. Stern, dianestern1@juno.com

Writer's Workshop is a great way to accomplish a lot in the classroom. I begin with a pre-writing activity. Many children will say they have nothing to write about if you just sit them down and ask them to start writing. I have found that children realize they have a lot to write about if you ask them the right questions. In fact, the children in my classes have a list of questions in the back of their writers' notebooks that they can refer to when developing a list of topics for themselves. The questions revolve around their own interests, abilities, talents, etc. You may also model other methods of prewriting such as brainstorming, list-making, storymapping, outlining, etc.

From there, my children engage in drafting. The children should be encouraged to "get their thoughts out" during the drafting phase and not be hampered by concerns about spelling and mechanics. The ideas that are in their heads are of the utmost importance. Rough drafts are followed by revising, editing, and publishing.

I have found that it is helpful to have the children brainstorm revision and editing questions to ask themselves, based on their beliefs in what good writing looks and sounds like. These questions can be posted at the writing center so the children can consult them when they reach these stages in their writing. Peer conferences, conferences with the teacher, and author's chair, when the children share their writing for various purposes, are all additional parts of the workshop. When the children choose to read a piece from our author's chair, the excitement is almost palpable!

Benefits for the teacher include a class full of interested students, an activity that easily integrates with the rest of the curriculum, a strong reinforcement for the act of reading, and a valuable diagnostic tool.

One last hint. Teachers must write too. Children take their writing more seriously, and teachers learn much about the writing process themselves.

Diane Stern

Classroom computers can be used to publish children's work and facilitate the revision process.

PRACTICAL TEACHING STRATEGIES

Writing Activities for Authentic Communication

Send E-mail to Experts. After students have begun Internet Inquiry, have them e-mail questions to experts when they require important information. Several locations have lists of experts your students may contact by e-mail. These include **Ask an Expert** (http://www.askanexpert.com/) and the **Mad Scientist Network** (http://www.madsci.org/). Students should not bother these people with general questions about where to find information. Require your students to only ask very specific questions they cannot answer by other means.

Get Well Cards and Letters. Have students create get well cards and letters whenever a classmate is ill and absent from school for more than a few days. Keep a set of markers and white construction paper in your writing center for this purpose. Encourage students to describe what is taking place at school so the absent student keeps posted on what is happening. Collect the letters at the end of the day and ask one student to deliver them. If the student has e-mail access at home, send these letters via e-mail. Twenty or thirty letters from friends always brighten someone's day. Moreover, it fosters the feeling of community that is so important to every classroom.

Suggestion Box. Create a classroom suggestion box. Encourage students to share their ideas for making the classroom a better place in which to learn. Regularly post suggestions on a bulletin board and encourage students to write their reactions to the ideas. Post student responses as well. This might also be done on your classroom home page by having students e-mail their suggestions to you. You could post these and invite comments.

PRACTICAL TEACHING STRATEGIES

Writing Activities that Create Complete, Extended Texts

Social Studies Journals. Have students keep a social studies journal. Have them use it to ask questions, record interesting information, and summarize what they have read. Encourage students to use the journals to review information they have covered. Other writing activities related to social studies can also be recorded in these journals.

Self-Evaluations. Have students write descriptive self-evaluations of their work at the end of each marking period. Include these with their report cards to parents and use them during parent conference meetings.

Writing Experiences Are Most Valuable When They Create Complete, Extended Texts

Writing experiences are most appropriate when they require students to create complete, extended texts such as letters, stories, or articles. Too often the writing experiences in our schools only require students to fill in a blank or complete a sentence. In an analysis of language arts textbooks used in the elementary grades, DeGroff and Leu (1987) found that, on average, students were expected to write only one piece per week that was longer than a single sentence. That level of involvement in writing simply is not enough to develop proficient readers and writers.

Complete, extended texts offer numerous benefits. First, extended writing experiences promote the development of all components of the comprehension and response processes. More limited writing experiences make more limited contributions. For example, a task requiring students to write single-word answers demands attention only to spelling and vocabulary elements. Single sentences require only spelling, vocabulary, and syntactic knowledge; however, writing a letter, article, or story requires students to attend to all of the components associated with comprehension or composition. Thus, extended writing experiences hold greater potential for students to learn about written language.

In addition, writing a complete, extended text has much greater potential to develop critical thinking and reasoning abilities. We certainly cannot expect students to argue persuasively or explain their reasoning in a single word or sentence. Writing a complete,

Projects that include reports or other extended writing experiences can be shared with an audience, posted, and read by others.

extended text also provides more reading opportunities at every phase of the process. Single words or sentences limit the rereading that students must do, especially during revision and editing. Finally, extended texts usually serve a greater communicative purpose than single words or sentences can. A single word or sentence typically reflects a student's understanding or completion of a reading assignment. Complete texts, however, permit purposeful communication. Examples of writing activities that create complete, extended texts and support critical thinking appear on the previous page.

Reading and Writing Are Similar Processes

It is important to keep in mind that reading and writing are similar types of processes. They have been compared by various authors as being two sides of the same coin, two wings of the same bird, or a mirror into which reader and writer peer from different sides. Each of these metaphors helps us understand how closely reading and writing are related.

In both reading and writing, meaning is composed. Writers compose meaning as they construct a message for their readers. Readers then compose meaning as they reconstruct the author's message. Furthermore, Tierney and Pearson (1983) pointed out that both writers and readers plan, draft, align, revise, and monitor as they compose meaning.

To begin, both writers and readers plan. Writers plan their messages, taking into account their goals and their audiences. Readers plan as they consider their purposes for reading, their knowledge about the topics, and the authors of the messages.

Similarly, both writers and readers engage in drafting. Writers create drafts as they initially craft the messages they wish to communicate. Readers create drafts as they acquire the meaning that they draw from the texts. They may create one draft before they start, a second as they read and refine their initial expectations, and yet another draft after they finish reading and have thought about the text more carefully. Readers continually draft new interpretations of what they are reading, just as authors develop new drafts of what they are writing.

The process of aligning refers to the stance that writers take toward their readers and that readers take toward writers. How each views the other influences how each performs the writing or reading task. Clearly, both readers and writers align themselves with the other.

In addition, both writers and readers revise their work. Writers revise as they attempt to make meaning clearer for their audiences. Readers revise as they attempt to reconstruct the meaning the authors intended. We probably notice this process most clearly when we finish a story with a surprise ending and we are forced to revise our interpretations of the story.

Finally, both writers and readers monitor their work. Writers monitor their work as they create it, deciding when and where it needs to be revised, when and where it should be edited, and when it is complete. Readers also monitor, deciding when something makes sense, what to do when something does not make sense, and when their comprehension of a text is complete. Both writers and readers use their metacognitive knowledge during this process.

Because reading and writing are such similar types of processes, it is important for teachers to make as many connections as possible between reading and writing experiences. Reading can assist the development of writing proficiency and writing can assist the development of reading proficiency.

Connecting Reading and Writing on the Internet

The Internet provides exciting opportunities for you and your students to connect reading, writing, and support literacy learning (Leu & Leu, 2000). Many teachers are discovering new and powerful ways to support literacy learning in their classrooms. You will, too. As you explore the potential of the Internet to support literacy learning, consider at least three useful strategies:

1. Using Internet Project to connect reading and writing.
2. Engaging in keypal activities.
3. Publishing your students' work on the WWW.

Using Internet Project to Connect Reading and Writing

Internet Project
Collaborative learning experiences between classrooms that take place on the Internet.

Increasingly, teachers are using **Internet Project** to connect reading, writing, and support literacy learning of important curricular goals (Leu, 2001). There are two types of locations for Internet Project: permanent site locations and temporary site locations. Permanent Internet Projects provide a meeting ground for classrooms and students to exchange information about a common topic or project activity. One of the best examples for primary grade students is **The Mind's Eye Monster Exchange Project** (http://www.monster exchange.org/). This location pairs your classroom with another participating classroom. Students in each classroom draw a picture of a monster and write descriptions of what it looks like. Paired classes exchange descriptions of their monsters and attempt to draw a picture of how they think the other students' monsters look. Finally, the images of all monsters are posted so that students may compare the originals with the written descriptions. The location also includes many lesson plans and extension activities. This is a wonderful project for younger children (see Figure 7-1).

Other Internet Projects are regularly posted at central locations by teachers who are seeking classes to join them in a collaborative project. These almost always include opportunities to connect reading and writing experiences over the Internet and are an important source of curricular activities for your class. Central sites for Internet Project include:

▸ **Global SchoolNet's Internet Project Registry** (http://www.gsn.org/pr/index.html)
▸ **SchoolNet's Grassroots Project Gallery** (http://www.schoolnet.ca/grassroots/e/project.centre/search-projects.html)
▸ **Australian Curriculum Projects Registry** (http://rite.ed.qut.edu.au/oz-teacher-net/registry/index.html)

An example of a project posted by a teacher looking for collaborating classes is shown in Figure 7-2.

FIGURE 7-1

The Mind's Eye Monster Exchange Project: An Internet Project site for connecting reading and writing in the primary grades (http://www.monsterexchange.org/)

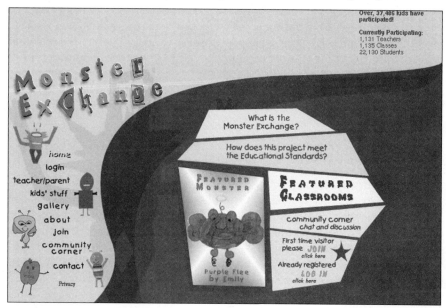

Note: Courtesy of WinStar for Education.

FIGURE 7-2

An example of an Internet Project posted by a teacher seeking to collaborate with other classrooms

---

THE GINGERBREAD MAN PROJECT

Project Information

Project Title: The Gingerbread Man
Project Start & End Dates: 1/01/03 to 5/30/03
Project Summary:

Read and compare several versions of the Gingerbread Man, then have students write and illustrate their own version. Submit it to this website along with an illustration to be posted and then communicate by e-mail with other classrooms.

Project Level: Basic
Curriculum Fit: Arts, Language
Technologies Used: E-mail
Project E-mail Address: mbryant@pc.collegestation.isd.tenet.edu
Registration Instructions:

E-mail the sponsor of your desire to participate and give your school, location, and the projected completion date of your story/ illustration. Then submit your story and illustration through e-mail within a week of your completion date.

Number of Classrooms: 10
Age Range: 5 to 7 years
Target Audience: Anyone
Project URL: http://pc.collegestation.isd.tenet.edu/melanieweb/gingerbread.html

Project Contact Information
Melanie Winslow Bryant—mbryant@pc.collegestation.isd.tenet.edu
Kindergarten Teacher—Pebble Creek Elementary—College Station ISD
http://pc.collegestation.isd.tenet.edu/melanieweb/bryant.html
College Station, Texas, U.S.

Using Keypals in the Classroom

keypals The online equivalent of penpals. Keypals exchange e-mail messages.

Teachers have traditionally used penpal experiences to connect reading and writing and to provide important learning experiences for students. On the Internet, penpals become **keypals.** What is especially exciting about keypal experiences is that students can immediately receive messages from their partners. Students come into class in the morning excited to discover if they have received messages from their keypals in various parts of the world. Important new friendships may develop between your students and those from different cultural and linguistic backgrounds as they practice a second language, find out about life in another part of the world, work on joint projects, share useful websites, and even help one another with homework. Central sites for connecting your students with keypals are listed in Table 7-1.

Publishing Student Work on the Internet

Another important way to connect reading and writing is to publish your students' work on the Internet. Many teachers are publishing their students' writing at a classroom or school home page (chapter 14 provides guidance about how to do this). By publishing your students' work at your classroom home page, you make it available for the entire world to read. As your students develop connections with keypals, you will find them proudly directing their new friends to the work they have written and published on the Internet. Moreover, students can show proud parents their writing, published for the world to read on the Internet.

TABLE 7-1

Central sites for developing keypal contacts

Keypals (http://sesd.sk.ca/teacherresource/KeyPal/keypals.html)—This site contains one of the most extensive sets of contact locations for connecting with keypals. It provides you with directions for using keypals in your classroom, it contains links to keypal sites, and it has a master list of mailing lists (listservs) from different organizations. The mailing lists link teachers to teachers, students to students, and classes to classes.

Intercultural E-mail Classroom Connections (http://www.teaching.com/iecc/)—This is a good location for developing keypals from different countries. It contains several mailing lists (listservs) for teachers looking for partner classrooms. You may subscribe to these directly from the web page.

epals (http://www.epals.com/index.html)—A useful resource for locating classrooms that want to host a keypals project.

Celebrating Diversity

Developing Keypal Relationships around the World

Forming keypals with students in other parts of the world immediately helps students to understand and respect the diverse nature of our global society. Have students make keypals with classrooms in several different parts of the world using the locations identified in Table 7-1. At the beginning of their correspondence, ask students to share and seek information with their keypals about common areas: How do you spend a typical day? What types of stories do you enjoy the most? How do you spend your free time? What are your favorite foods? What type of clothing do you like most? Later have students share their perspectives about local as well as international issues or books they have read. Have students in your room share the results during Internet Workshop and compare the important insights about different cultural experiences your students are developing.

Publishing on the Internet and receiving positive feedback from faraway places can be one of the most effective ways to develop many important aspects of your classroom curriculum. Some classrooms keep a map of the world above their computer. Teachers and students pin pieces of yarn from their location to all of the places they have received e-mail from to provide meaningful lessons in geography.

Connecting Reading and Writing in Traditional Ways

Although the Internet provides many new and exciting opportunities to connect reading and writing, many other opportunities support the development of reading through writing experiences outside of the Internet. Ideas range from simple (having very young students read their writing to you each day) to complex (integrating reading and writing activities within a thematically organized instructional unit). There is probably no limit to the ways in which creative teachers can make the reading–writing connection in their classrooms. Creating new and productive learning experiences for children is one of the great satisfactions of teaching.

Using Reader Response Journals

One of the best ways to connect reading and writing is by encouraging journal writing activities. One type of journal often used for this purpose is a **reader response journal.** Reader response journals are used in a variety of ways. The most common procedural steps in this method framework usually consist of the following:

reader response journal A type of journal and a method framework in which students record their ideas and feelings about what they have read.

1. Read a section of a literary work.
2. Write a response to what was read.
3. Use some of your responses as beginning ideas for larger writing projects.

Students use a reader response journal to record their ideas and feelings about what they have read. Reader response journals can be used in conjunction with independent reading selections as well as with teacher-selected reading assignments. A sample entry from a reader response journal is shown in Figure 7-3 on page 246.

Reader response journals allow students to assume control of their responses to reading assignments (Hancock, 1993b; Kelly, 1990). They support readers in their aesthetic experiences with text, helping them to have a more complex "lived through" experience (Rosenblatt, 1985). Entries in reader response journals also find their way into more extended writing pieces. This happens when teachers encourage students to go back into their reader response journals and look for writing ideas that might be elaborated on into larger written works.

An interesting variation of a reader response journal is to encourage students to write a character journal (Hancock, 1993a). In a character journal, students assume the role of one of the main characters and make entries in the response journal as that person. Character journals encourage a wider range of response patterns, help students develop more aesthetic or "lived through" experiences, and help them to better understand the perspective of a major character.

Teachers sometimes choose to devote a regular 10- or 15-minute period each day to writing in reader response journals. During this time, all students write about the selections they have been reading; they may write anything they wish, but they must write. In many ways this activity can be considered the writing equivalent of DEAR, a method framework described in chapter 6.

Students should be supported in determining how they wish to respond to any reading experience. Sometimes, though, your students may need direction about how to make a response to their reading, especially when you begin this activity for the first time. Journal starters like those in the following list provide guidance for students who may be uncertain about what to write in their journals (Youngblood, 1985).

The character I like best in this story is . . . because . . .

This character reminds me of somebody I know because . . .

FIGURE 7-3

A sample entry from a reader response journal

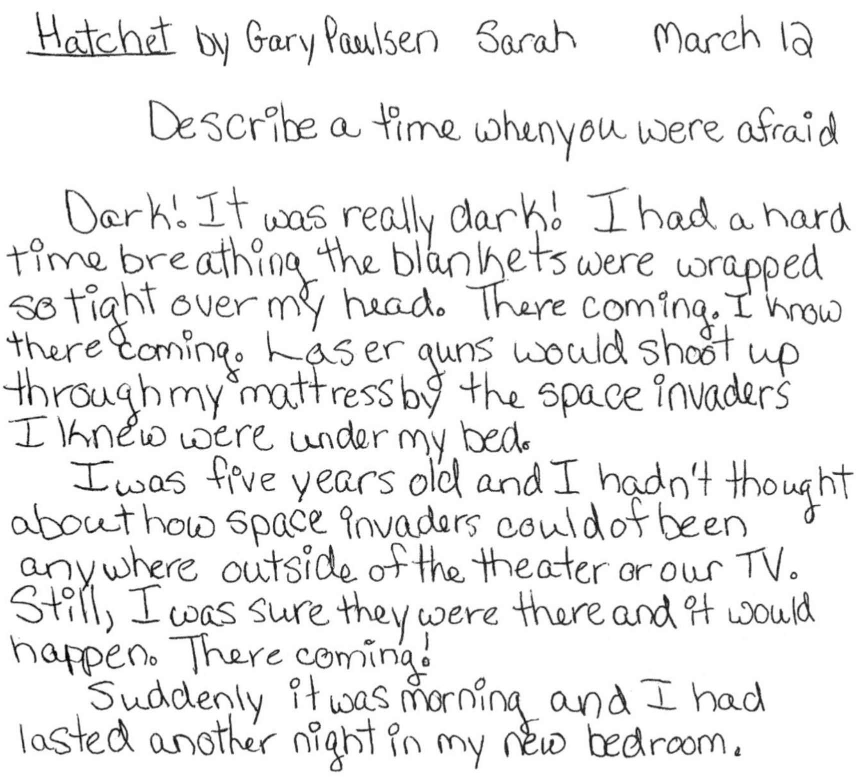

<u>Hatchet</u> by Gary Paulsen   Sarah   March 12

Describe a time when you were afraid

Dark! It was really dark! I had a hard time breathing the blankets were wrapped so tight over my head. There coming. I know there coming. Laser guns would shoot up through my mattress by the space invaders I knew were under my bed.

I was five years old and I hadn't thought about how space invaders could of been anywhere outside of the theater or our TV. Still, I was sure they were there and it would happen. There coming!

Suddenly it was morning and I had lasted another night in my new bedroom.

This character reminds me of myself because . . .

This section makes me think about . . . because . . .

This episode reminds me of a situation in my own life. It happened when . . .

If I were . . . at this point I would . . .

Using Dialogue Journals

dialogue journal   A type of journal and a method framework through which students engage in a written conversation with their teachers.

A **dialogue journal** gives teachers another method framework for connecting reading and writing. Dialogue journals can be used in many ways; the most common procedural steps in this method framework include the following:

1. Students make entries in their individual dialogue journals.
2. The teacher collects the journals at the end of the day.
3. The teacher reads and writes responses in each of the journals and returns them to students the following day.

The first step in using dialogue journals is usually to have students make entries in their individual journals about any topic they choose. Students often write about what they are reading, events that have happened during the day, problems they are experiencing with other students, or important experiences they have had at home. It is important to allow students to select topics of personal importance to create authentic writing (and reading) experiences for them and to increase interest and motivation.

The second step is to collect the students' journals. Some teachers require students to make regular entries and turn in their journals each day. Other teachers have students turn in their journals only when they have made new entries, and still other teachers have students write in their journals whenever they choose but turn them in once a week. A useful strategy is to divide your class into five groups and then collect a differ-

FIGURE 7-4

A dialogue journal entry by a second-grade student

> Oct. 4
> My whole class is
> working on a book, Cald
> Corduroy goes to hawaii.
> We are going to ilasterat
> it. Some are going to do it
> alone. Some a are going to
> it with a parner. I am going to
> work with a parner. My parner is
> Ian.
>
> I cant wait to see
> your illustrations and get
> our book published. It was
> such fun writing it.

ent group's journals each evening. This reduces the number of responses you need to make during any single day so that you can thoughtfully respond to each student.

During the final step of the process, the teacher reads through the students' entries and writes a response to each student. These responses may include process questions. Process questions require students to elaborate on their writing and extend the writing process; for example: "Tell me more about . . .", "Can you explain why . . .", "What are you going to do now?", and "How did that make you feel?"

Dialogue journals provide opportunities for students to solve personal difficulties and give teachers useful insights about their students (Bode, 1989; Gambrell, 1985). In practice, dialogue journals prompt "written conversation between two persons on a functional, continued basis, about topics of . . . interest" (Staton, 1988).

Fuhler (1994) has suggested that teachers encourage parents to become involved in both dialogue and reader response journals. By involving both parents and teachers in reading and responding to children's journals, important conversations take place that inevitably assist the literacy development of each child. These experiences also provide useful information to both teachers and parents as they read each other's responses. An example of a dialogue journal entry between a second-grade student and her teacher is shown in Figure 7-4.

Using Buddy Journals

buddy journal A type of journal and a method framework through which pairs of students engage in written conversations.

The use of **buddy journals** is a method framework quite similar to that of dialogue journals. Buddy journals are kept by pairs of students who write back and forth and maintain a written conversation about topics of mutual interest (D'Angelo Bromley, 1989). Buddy journals provide an authentic means of connecting reading and writing in the classroom. These journals involve three procedural steps:

1. Buddy journal partners are selected.
2. Students make entries in their journals.
3. Students exchange journals, read their partner's entry, and write a response.

The selection of partners for the buddy journal experience is important. Sometimes teachers assign buddy journal partners, accepting the possibility that some students may be uncomfortable with the partners selected for them. To minimize the discomfort, teachers might limit buddy journal teams to a period of only two weeks and then assign new partners. Other strategies are to assign partners by selecting names out of a hat or to let students select their own partners. Letting students help determine the method used is often useful. Regardless of the method chosen, however, the teacher should be prepared to serve as a buddy journal partner if there is an uneven number of students in the class.

The second step in the process is to have students make entries in their own journals. Generally, students should be encouraged to write about topics of their own choosing to provide ownership and increase interest and motivation. At times, however, buddy journals can be used in conjunction with specific reading selections. Under those circumstances the teacher should encourage students to converse with each other about any topics related to their reading selections. This approach increases the connection between reading and writing and provides a unique means of discussing reading experiences.

The final step is to have students exchange their buddy journals, read their partner's entry, and write a response. This step gets the written conversation started. Several entries from a buddy journal are shown in Figure 7-5 on page 249.

Conducting a Style Study

style study A method framework where students develop insight about writing by looking closely at how authors use different language patterns and then try to emulate those patterns.

Another way to connect reading and writing is to conduct a **style study.** This method framework allows students to develop greater insight into an author's craft by looking closely at how authors use different language patterns. Afterward, students are encouraged to try out these techniques in their own writing. A style study is a wonderful way to cultivate a deeper sensitivity to an author's craft through rich literary and writing experiences. By carefully examining the writing of professionals, students begin to read an author like a writer (Bearse, 1992; Lancia, 1997). This is important because it means that students will begin to see new writing patterns and then try out these patterns in their own written work. As a method framework, a style study contains the following procedural steps:

1. Read a passage from children's literature together.
2. Identify several stylistic patterns used by this author.
3. Discuss why the author probably chose to use these patterns.
4. Provide students with a writing task where they are asked to try out at least one of the patterns they have seen.
5. Share the results.

A style study can be used whenever you read a common work of literature with your students. Because you will want students to look through the text for stylistic elements characteristic of a particular author, it is usually best when each student has his or her own copy of a work.

After you have read the passage together, draw students' attention to several stylistic features used by an author. You should have several examples identified in advance; however, with experienced students, it is often useful to have them locate these features by themselves. These features might consist of a grammatical element like a sequence of par-

FIGURE 7-5

Buddy journal entries

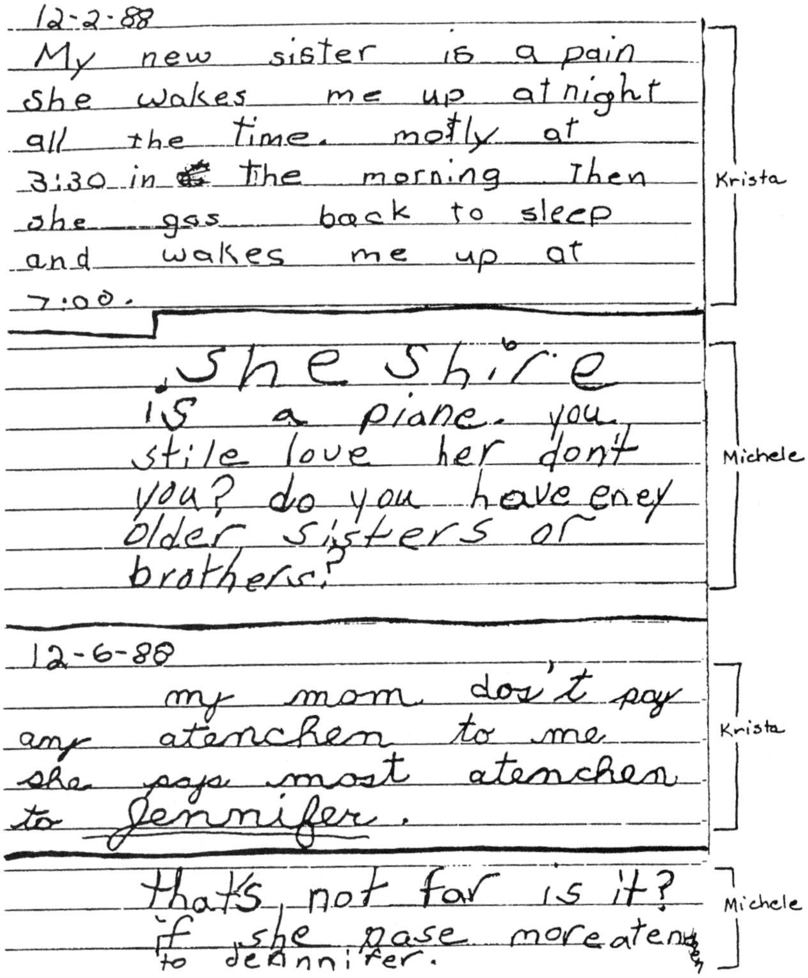

> 12-2-88
> My new sister is a pain
> she wakes me up at night
> all the time. motly at
> 3:30 in the morning Then
> she gss back to sleep
> and wakes me up at
> 7:00.
> — Krista
>
> She shire
> is a piane. you
> stile love her don't
> you? do you have eney
> older sisters or
> brothers?
> — Michele
>
> 12-6-88
> my mom dos't pay
> any atenchen to me
> she pas most atenchen
> to Jennifer.
> — Krista
>
> thats not far is it?
> if she pase more ateny
> to Jennifer.
> — Michele

Source: From K. D'Angelo Bromley, "Buddy Journals Make the Reading-Writing Connection," *The Reading Teacher,* 43 (1989), p. 128. Reprinted by permission.

ticipial phrases. (He jogged along slowly, singing a tune, thinking of his plan, and contemplating the marvelous catastrophe that was about to occur.) It might also include a special technique during dialogue sequences such as using very short sentences to communicate the desperation of a situation ("Now?" "Yes!" "Should I do it quickly?" "Yes. Just do it!"). After a while you will notice that each author excels at certain aspects of writing. Some are exceptional at dialogue, others at descriptions, and others at communicating mood.

After identifying each feature, engage children in a short discussion about why that feature was used by an author. This is important because it shows children why authors choose to write in certain ways. Later, they may wish to make similar choices.

Next you should provide students with a short writing task where they get to "try on" the author's stylistic technique and see if they can use it effectively in their own writing. If you noticed, for example, that the author uses short sentences in dialogue sequences when the characters are in a desperate situation, you might brainstorm several similar situations and then ask students to write a short dialogue sequence with this technique.

Have students share their attempts at using this stylistic feature in their own writing. You will find that students can quickly adapt these techniques to their own writing. You will also begin to see these elements appear during other classroom writing activities as students pick up the tricks they find each author using. In addition, students often begin

MODEL LESSON

Conducting a Style Study in Gerry Aaronson's Class

It is early in the school year and Gerry Aaronson wants to increase his students' awareness of the syntactic conventions authors use in their writing. He believes that introducing this idea to his fourth-grade class now will help them to see many other stylistic features during the course of the year. These syntactic elements of prior knowledge that readers bring to a text are important to Gerry because he has reader-based beliefs about *what* to teach. Gerry's literacy framework also includes integrated beliefs about *how* to teach. He combines student-directed and teacher-directed activities in his classroom. Gerry has been reading *James and the Giant Peach* by Roald Dahl aloud to his class each day after lunch. Today he has brought in multiple copies of this work so that each pair of students has a copy to share.

Read a Passage from Children's Literature Together. Instead of reading the next chapter in *James and the Giant Peach* aloud to his class, Gerry asks them to read this chapter silently.

Identify Several Stylistic Features Used by This Author. After students complete their reading of the chapter, Gerry asks his class if they noticed any special aspects to this author's writing style. He points out that Roald Dahl is especially known for his use of dialogue. The students find two different stylistic features. One student notices that the author uses the word "and" a lot during dialogue but isn't certain why the author does this. Gerry writes several examples children found on the board:

"They will eat up the peach and then there'll be nothing left for us to stand on and they'll start on us." (p. 56)

"I'm going to take a long silk string," James went on, "and I'm going to loop one end of it around a seagull's neck. And then I'm going to tie the other end to the stem of the peach." (p. 61)

The class also notices that Roald Dahl often uses a sequence of descriptive adjectives when he paints a word picture:

"Their eyes waited upon him, tense, anxious, pathetically hopeful." (p. 56)

"Seagulls love worms, didn't you know that? And luckily for us, we have here the biggest, fattest, pinkest, juiciest Earthworm in the world." (p. 60)

Discuss Why the Author Probably Chose to Use These Features. The discussion leads the class to realize that the author uses the word *and* during dialogue because it makes the language sound more like the way we actually speak in conversation. This is one of the tricks Dahl uses to make his writing more realistic. The class also notices that descriptive sequences of adjectives are a powerful way of describing feelings and appearances with a minimum number of words.

Provide Students with a Writing Task. Gerry lets his students pick from one of several different writing tasks. They can write a dialogue between two individuals using *and* to connect ideas and make the dialogue sound more like oral language or they can describe something in the classroom using a sequence of descriptive adjectives. If students wish to develop another writing idea, Gerry invites them to do so.

Share the Results. Afterward, Gerry's students share their results in small groups. As he circulates around the room, he praises their work. He senses his students have picked up new techniques they will soon use in their own writing projects.

This activity focused on syntactic structures, an element of prior knowledge. Gerry selected this aspect of literacy because he has reader-based beliefs about *what* to teach. Teachers with a text-based perspective about *what* to teach would use an author style study to teach children about punctuation, an aspect of language related to meaning that exists in a text.

Consistent with his integrated perspective, Gerry combined teacher-directed and student-directed learning experiences in this author style study. Teachers with holistic language learning beliefs about *how* to teach would allow students to direct their own learning, perhaps by sharing stylistic aspects of an author and a work they have chosen to read. Teachers with specific skills beliefs would direct even more of this activity than Gerry did. These teachers would identify the stylistic aspects in the lesson rather than inviting students to identify them. These teachers would also provide only a single writing activity and require all students to complete it.

reading literary works very differently, noticing stylistic decisions and thinking about why the author chose a particular technique in a situation. A style study often leads to many new insights about reading and writing. The model lesson on the previous page shows how one teacher used a style study to connect reading and writing.

Developing Reading/Writing Centers

A **reading/writing center** is a location in the classroom where children can participate in a series of independent, self-guided, teacher-designed activities that connect reading and writing. These centers take many forms but usually share several characteristics.

reading/writing center A classroom location in which students participate in a series of independent activities that connect reading and writing.

First, reading/writing centers contain all the reading and writing materials that students require to complete the activities. For example, the following materials were available for one reading/writing center activity at the third-grade level:

1. Ten articles about exotic animals from the nature magazine *Ranger Rick*. Each had been separated from the magazine and stapled into construction-paper covers.
2. Duplicated copies of a fact sheet—an outline with major headings such as the name of your animal, size, appearance, home, food, family, and unusual facts. Students had previously learned how to use this form for recording information about animals in a science project.
3. Writing paper and felt-tip pens.
4. Students' writing folders.

Reading/writing centers also contain clear directions for completing particular learning activities. The directions are usually written in procedural steps that students should follow (see Figure 7-6). These centers contain students' writing folders in which they keep drafts of their writing projects. Students can take their folders as they need them and return them at the end of the day. Finally, reading/writing centers have a place to display completed work. Often this consists of a bulletin board where students may post their work, providing examples for other students.

FIGURE 7-6

An example of a reading/writing center activity

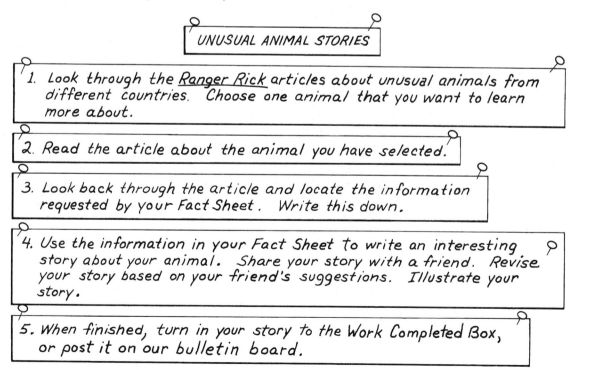

UNUSUAL ANIMAL STORIES

1. Look through the *Ranger Rick* articles about unusual animals from different countries. Choose one animal that you want to learn more about.

2. Read the article about the animal you have selected.

3. Look back through the article and locate the information requested by your Fact Sheet. Write this down.

4. Use the information in your Fact Sheet to write an interesting story about your animal. Share your story with a friend. Revise your story based on your friend's suggestions. Illustrate your story.

5. When finished, turn in your story to the Work Completed Box, or post it on our bulletin board.

Children's writing may be bound, made into a book, and placed into the classroom library.

Integrating Writing Activities within Thematic Units

thematic units
Multiple learning experiences integrated around a topic, an author, or a genre.

An increasingly common way of making the reading–writing connection is to integrate reading and writing experiences within **thematic units.** Thematic units consist of multiple learning experiences integrated around a single topic ("Nature Is a Part of All Our Lives," "The Time of the Dinosaurs," "Making and Keeping Friends"), author (Laura Ingalls Wilder, Katherine Paterson, Arnold Lobel), or genre (biography, science fiction, mysteries). Thematic approaches to instruction have been prompted by a concern that school learning is too often fragmented, unconnected, and, as a result, not especially meaningful (Routman, 2000). By connecting learning in several areas around a thematic unit, teachers attempt to provide a meaningful focus for students' experiences. This makes both learning and teaching more of a meaningful enterprise. Thematic units have other advantages, too. They make it more likely that knowledge learned in one area will transfer to other areas. They allow students to read and think deeply about a single issue. Finally, thematic units appear to increase positive attitudes about reading and writing since these tasks always take place within authentic contexts.

integrated language arts unit   A thematic unit where reading, writing, speaking, and listening experiences are organized around a topic, author, or genre to provide focus for teaching and learning in language arts.

There are two different ways in which teachers organize thematic units. Sometimes teachers will organize a thematic unit to integrate instruction in the language arts: reading, writing, speaking, and listening. This type of thematic unit is sometimes referred to as an **integrated language arts unit.** Here reading, writing, speaking, and listening experiences are organized around a topic, author, or genre in an attempt to focus teaching and learning in the language arts. At other times, teachers will organize a thematic unit in an attempt to integrate instruction in at least two different content areas, one of which usually is language arts. This type of thematic unit is sometimes referred to as a **cross-curricular unit.** Here a topic is used to focus teaching and learning on language arts and at least one of the other traditional subject areas: math, science, social studies, art, and physical education. An example of how a cross-curricular thematic unit was organized in one fourth-grade class can be seen in the overview of this unit in Figure 7-7. Here the

cross-curricular unit   A thematic unit using a topic to focus teaching and learning on language arts and at least one of the other traditional subject areas: math, science, social studies, art, or physical education.

FIGURE 7-7

FIGURE 7-7

A thematic unit overview: Life in the Desert Southwest

Whole Class Reading Experiences

The Skirt by Gary Soto
The Moon of the Wild Pigs by Jean Craighead George

SOCIAL STUDIES

Goals/Concepts

▶ Develop an understanding of the cultures of the Southwest

READ-ALOUD RESPONSE JOURNAL ACTIVITIES

▶ *Dreamplace* by George Ella Layton
▶ *The Great Change* by Carol Grigg
▶ *Antelope Woman* by Michael Lacapa

Additional Activities

▶ Reading and discussion from the chapter on "Cultures of the Southwest" in our social studies textbook
▶ Readers theater presentation from one of the books in class where the story depicts a cultural group from the Southwest (small groups)

SCIENCE

Goals/Concepts

▶ Understand the weather cycles of the Sonoran Desert
▶ Understand the major life-forms in the desert
▶ Understand the interrelationships between animals and plants in the desert

READ-ALOUDS

▶ *Cactus* by Carol Lerner
▶ *A Desert Year* by Carol Lerner
▶ *Desert Animals* by Luise Woelflein
▶ *Cactus* by Jason Cooper
▶ *Cactus Hotel* by Brenda Guiberson

Additional Activities

▶ Text set activities with informational books about animal and plant life in the Southwest desert from the school library
▶ Develop a report on one of the animals of the Southwest desert
▶ Create a shoebox diorama illustrating the environment of this animal

LANGUAGE ARTS

Goals/Concepts

▶ Develop an understanding of Byrd Baylor's poetry
▶ Write poetry about life in the desert
▶ Maintain a reader journal during whole class reading experiences
▶ Develop report writing skills

READ-ALOUD RESPONSE JOURNAL ACTIVITIES

▶ *The Desert Is Theirs* by Byrd Baylor
▶ *Desert Voices* by Byrd Baylor
▶ *The Other Way to Listen* by Byrd Baylor

Additional Activities

▶ Style study of Byrd Baylor
▶ Literature discussion groups
  ▶ *Mystery of the Navaho Moon* by Timothy Green
  ▶ *A Brand Is Forever* by Ann Herbert Scott
  ▶ *Local News* by Gary Soto
  ▶ *Ten Mile Day* by Mary Ann Faser

ART

Goals/Concepts

▶ Develop an understanding of some of the art of the Southwest

READ-ALOUDS

▶ *The Goat in the Rug* by Charles Blood and Martin Link
▶ *Diego Rivera: Artist of the People* by Anne Neimark
▶ *Children of Clay* by Rina Swentzell

Additional Activities

▶ Dyeing wool with natural dyes
▶ Weaving with pocket looms
▶ Make God's eyes
▶ Make and decorate clay pots
▶ Visit art exhibition

unit theme of "Life in the Desert Southwest" is used to integrate language arts with experiences in social studies, science, and art.

To develop a thematic unit, it is often helpful to create an overview like that in Figure 7-7. This will help you keep the larger picture in mind before you develop daily lesson plans. To develop an overview, you may wish to follow the following procedures:

1. Identify a thematic topic, author, or genre that will allow you to integrate multiple curricular goals.
2. Identify reading selections to accomplish your curricular goals.

3. Develop reading, writing, listening, and speaking experiences to meet your curricular goals.
4. Identify a major project to be completed by the end of the unit.

The first step is to identify a thematic topic, author, or genre that will allow you to integrate multiple curricular goals. As you identify a theme, avoid what Routman (2000) has referred to as "themes of convenience." These are themes like circus, bears, or monsters that are easy to develop but do not deal with "powerful ideas" or issues of substance. The point of thematic instruction is to engage students in thinking about issues with depth in an effort to integrate learning in several areas. This is hard to do with superficial themes.

As you identify the theme for your unit, begin by looking closely at your curricular goals. Several authors (Routman, 2000) have pointed out that curricular goals are often sacrificed for entertaining thematic topics or activities that have little to do with the curriculum of a school. Since the purpose of thematic instruction is to increase learning across several areas, be very clear about your goals for the unit. Curricular goals should determine themes and activities—themes and activities should not determine curricular goals.

If you are planning an integrated language arts unit, there are three types of themes to consider: topical themes, author themes, or genre themes. However, if you are planning a cross-curricular unit, you will probably want to consider only topical themes. Topical themes provide more opportunities to make connections with content in math, science, social studies, or art.

The second step in planning an overview for a thematic unit is to identify reading selections that will allow you to accomplish your curricular goals. This is a challenging task, especially if you are not familiar with children's literature. One way to approach this phase is to seek assistance from your school or local librarian. You may also wish to consult some of the sources described in chapter 6. You may also wish to consult the extensive monthly reviews of children's literature that appear at the end of each issue of *The Reading Teacher*. As you review each work of literature, do some preliminary thinking about how you wish to use it. Is it best used as a read-aloud to prompt a journal response? Is it best used as a text set activity or a whole class reading experience? Or is it best used as a reference work for students as they develop their projects? Thinking about how it will be used as you review and collect materials will save time later.

The third step in planning an overview for a thematic unit is to develop reading, writing, listening, and speaking experiences to meet your curricular goals. Here you should think about the different method frameworks described in this text and how they might be used in your unit: cooperative learning groups, deductive instruction, inductive instruction, read-aloud response journals, reader response journals, literature discussion groups, grand conversations, readers theater, directed reading–thinking activities, sustained silent reading, and many others. Develop a plan for using these experiences to connect reading and writing as your students learn important concepts.

Finally, you may wish to have each student complete some type of project during the unit. For older students, this is likely to be some type of written project. For younger students, it might be a dramatic presentation to another class or a sequence of smaller writing projects that are kept in a portfolio. Often it is useful to present several different projects to students and allow them to select the activity they wish to complete during the course of the unit. Older students who have worked in thematic units may wish to propose their own projects at the beginning of the unit. A brainstorming session is useful to generate a list of possibilities for students.

Conducting Writing Workshop

writing workshop A learning session devoted to supporting student learning in writing.

Writing workshop is a whole class session or a small group mini-lesson on writing. It is frequently orchestrated by the teacher to assist students with their writing (Loback, 1995). Writing workshop can be used for a variety of purposes: to introduce writing-process strategies, such as brainstorming or peer conferencing; to explain strategies writers use to solve common writing problems; and to provide a time when students get together to read

JUDY'S

COMMENTS FROM THE CLASSROOM

One of the best ways for young children to understand the concept that words express meaning and that letters develop into words is to write language experience stories. Language experience stories are a big part of connecting reading and writing in the first grade.

I do a preliminary activity to prepare for each LES activity. We write the topic of the experience on a large sheet of chart paper. Then I make two columns—the first to list what we already know about that topic and the second to predict what we think we will learn. I feel I can help students make more sense of what they are about to see or do if I find out what they already know. And predicting the outcome of our learning makes a great directed reading-thinking activity.

After we complete our special class project, I ask a number of questions: "Did you see what you thought you would see?" "Did you learn (or do) what you thought you would?" "What happened that surprised you?" In a third column of our chart, we fill in a "What did we learn?" list. We add words we learned and identify things that we did or saw. I find that if I write the children's names beside their responses, they take ownership of that information. Then when we write our class story about our experience, each child is apt to volunteer the same information again, reading it from our chart.

One language experience story brought a community member to our class to show how to spin wool into yarn with her spinning wheel. She went through the step-by-step process of turning raw wool into yarn. Her visit was a big hit. (Of course the lamb that visited with her was as well!) Our language experience story then became a flowchart describing the process of turning wool into yarn. I was still able to model proper capitalization, correct punctuation, and complete sentences. And later, we used the Internet connection in our classroom to find out more things about wool. We even made friends with a class in New Zealand who told us about their lives on sheep ranches.

After we write language experience stories as a class, the children then write letters home to their parents to tell them about the experience. They have the words, thoughts, and ideas readily available that help them to be very successful in their writing. And they love reading their letters out loud before they send them.

FIGURE 7-8

Examples of topics for writing workshop sessions

Writing Process Strategies

Brainstorming techniques when you are on your own.
How to map writing ideas during the drafting phase.
How to outline writing ideas.
Successful peer conference strategies.
Revision strategies that work.
Using editing marks.
Using illustrations at just the right location.

Strategies to Overcome Common Problems

Using your response journal for great writing ideas.
Working through writer's block.
Writing patterns used by great writers.
Making your meaning clear.
Letting a draft "sit" so you approach it as a reader would.
Using headings and subheadings to organize informational articles.
Using questions (and answers) to present information.
Ending a story effectively.
Developing great titles.
Strategies for successful spelling.

their work and help each other solve common writing problems. Examples of topics that might be covered during writing workshop sessions are listed in Figure 7-8 above.

Teachers organize writing workshops in several ways, depending on their literacy framework and their goal for the session. Some teachers rely on a deductive method framework to teach specific strategies. Others use an inductive method framework to organize the workshop lessons. Still others use a writing workshop as a time to allow students to raise their own concerns and seek solutions for their individual writing problems.

In the model lesson on page 257, Emily Dodson's third-grade class has been working in an integrated language arts unit called "The Time of the Dinosaurs." She created the unit by combining one selection in the published reading program with several additional reading and read-aloud experiences, including:

Dinosaur Time by Peggy Parish

Patrick's Dinosaur by Carol Carrick

In the Days of the Dinosaurs by Roy Chapman Andrews

Digging up Dinosaurs by Aliki

Dinosaurs, Asteroids, and Superstars: Why the Dinosaurs Disappeared by Franklyn Branley

The Illustrated Dinosaur Dictionary by Helen Roney Sattler

Using Pattern Stories

pattern story activities A method framework where one story is used as a pattern for students to follow when writing their own, similar story.

predictable text A story containing repeated sentences, phrases, rhymes, or structural elements that makes reading the story very predictable and easy for beginning readers.

Writing experiences can be especially helpful in developing an understanding of reading/writing patterns. As students think about what to write, they must reflect on the structural characteristics of a particular form. As a result, students acquire new insight into the structural characteristics of written language, which helps them with both reading and writing. One useful technique is to engage students in **pattern story activities.**

For younger children, pattern story activities often begin by reading a **predictable text,** a story containing a repeated pattern that makes reading the story easy because it is very predictable. *Brown Bear, Brown Bear, What Do You See?* and *Fire! Fire! Said Mrs. McGuire,* both by Bill Martin, Jr., are popular examples of predictable texts. This type of

MODEL LESSON

Inductive Instruction during Writing Workshop in Emily Dodson's Class

Emily likes to use writer's workshop in her class. She has an integrated perspective about how to teach.

To connect reading and writing, students are preparing written reports on their favorite type of dinosaur. They are also working with the art teacher to create fired clay models. The librarian wants to display the reports and models in the school library. Students have collected their information on an outline fact sheet that Emily prepared and are currently using that information to draft their reports. Each child works individually during the writer's workshop sessions. Emily has noticed, however, that some students are having difficulty presenting and organizing their information. Consequently, she has scheduled a mini-lesson to show these children two different approaches: topic headings (size, appearance, favorite location) or question headings ("How Big Is a Brontosaurus?" "What Did a Brontosaurus Look Like?" "Where Did Brontosauruses Live?").

Provide Examples of the Skill or Rule. Emily duplicated two pages of text for students in her mini-lesson. The first comes from one of their reading selections on dinosaurs. It uses topical section headings to organize and present information: "Plant-Eaters," "Meat-Eaters," "Dinosaur Birds," and "The Dinosaurs Disappear." The other is from the book *Sharks* by Carl Green. It uses question headings to organize and present information: "How Long Do Sharks Live?" "Do Sharks Sleep?" "What Do Sharks Eat?" She reads both pages aloud and has her students follow along, paying attention to the way each author writes.

Help Students Discover the Skill or Rule. Emily asks questions to help students notice the two writing styles: "What is the same about the way these two authors wrote their articles? Yes, they both wrote facts. But how did they organize those facts? Right—in parts or sections. Now, what is at the beginning of each section? Yes, a title. We call these little titles headings. They tell you what each section is about. Now look and see if you notice anything different about how these two authors wrote their headings. That's right—one author used what we call a topic heading and the other used a question heading." Then Emily shares several other examples of these two organizational patterns in other books and has one student summarize the two ways writers can organize their facts.

Provide Guided Practice. Emily writes these two organizational methods on the blackboard: "Topic Headings" and "Question Headings." Then she asks students to brainstorm what they might choose for headings if they used the first method in their own papers. They quickly notice that each heading on their fact sheet ("Size," "Appearance," "Favorite Location," "Type of Food," and "Unusual Facts") could be used as a topic heading. Emily writes those headings on the board under "Topic Headings." Then she asks students to brainstorm questions that might be used in place of those words and writes them on the board under "Question Headings": "What Size Was the Brontosaurus?" "What Did the Brontosaurus Look Like?" "What Was Its Favorite Location?" "What Type of Food Did It Eat?" "What Are Some Unusual Facts About the Brontosaurus?" Emily and the class talk briefly about how students might use each type of section heading to organize their reports.

Provide Independent Practice. After the mini-lesson, children return to their work and use one of the two types of headings to organize their information. Emily circulates through the class, helping students who need her assistance. She notices that one student has combined the two patterns by using a topic heading ("Size") while beginning her paragraph with the related question ("How big was the Tyrannosaurus?"). Emily has this student read her draft aloud to the class so they can see this third pattern to use. Several students pick up on this idea and use it in their own work.

Teachers with holistic language learning beliefs about *how* to teach might use writer's workshop sessions to allow students to raise their own concerns and seek solutions for their individual writing problems. Students would define their own writing activities and seek assistance as they needed it. Teachers with specific skills beliefs about *how* to teach would rely on a deductive method framework to teach specific strategies to all children during the writer's workshop session. You can see how your beliefs about *how* to teach will inform the way in which you would use this method.

story may be used as a pattern for students to follow when writing their own, similar story. Pattern stories are especially useful with very young students, who often focus their attention on letters and sounds and not on higher-level aspects of written language organization. Pattern stories help these children understand that stories contain a regular structure, which is helpful to both readers and writers (Rhodes, 1981).

Beginning readers and writers enjoy writing pattern stories after reading counting books such as *Moja Means One: Swahili Counting Book* by Muriel Feelings, or alphabet books such as *The Folks in the Valley: A Pennsylvania Dutch ABC* by John Aylesworth. They

FIGURE 7-9

Examples of pattern books for readers and writers

For Younger Readers

Polar Bear, Polar Bear, What Do You Hear? by Bill Martin, Jr. (1991). New York: Henry Holt and Co.

 This is a variation of *Brown Bear, Brown Bear, What Do You See?* by Bill Martin, Jr. In this story, students visit the zoo and hear the sounds made by animals.

Jack's Garden by Henry Cole (1995). New York: Greenwillow.

 Using a cumulative, repetitive structure similar to *This Is the House that Jack Built*, this story describes Jack's garden.

What Would You Do If You Lived at the Zoo? by Nancy White Carlstrom (1994). New York: Scholastic.

 A book in question-answer format with cutout shapes. Great fun!

Hunky Dory Found It by Katie Evans (1994). New York: Dutton.

 A story about a dog who finds and collects objects dropped by its friends. Each page ends with "Hunky Dory found it."

Miss Mabel's Table by Deborah Chandra (1994). San Diego, CA: Browndeer.

 A counting and rhyme book describing the ingredients Miss Mabel requires to make pancakes for 10 people who come to her restaurant.

Night Becomes Day by Richard McGuire (1994). New York: Viking.

 This book shows how objects turn into other objects (e.g., "Tree becomes paper and paper becomes news").

For Older Readers

The Principal's New Clothes by Stephie Calmenson (1989). New York: Scholastic.

 This is a variation of *The Emperor's New Clothes.* Here, the principal is vain and ends up wearing only his underwear.

The Chocolate Touch by Patrick Catling (1981). New York: Bantam.

 John Midas loves chocolate, not gold. In this story, everything he touches turns to chocolate—even his mother—until he learns his lesson.

Prince Cinders by Babette Cole (1989). London: Collins.

 A variation of the Cinderella tale, only here it is a boy who loses his suspenders at the ball.

Ruby by Michael Emberly (1989). Boston: Little Brown.

 A modern version of *Little Red Riding Hood* played by a mouse and a cat.

Chicken Little by Stephen Kellog (1988). London: Beaver Books.

 A modern version of this classic tale.

The Paper Bag Princess by Robert Munsch (1980). Toronto: Annick Press.

 In this version of the traditional "prince rescues a princess" tale, the princess rescues the prince through her keen intelligence.

Sleeping Ugly by Jane Yolen (1981). New York: Coward-McCann.

 A version of the classic *Sleeping Beauty.*

also enjoy writing pattern stories after reading narratives with a repeated sentence or episodic pattern such as *Too Much Noise* by Ann McGovern.

 With older students, nearly any familiar story can be used as a pattern (Sipe, 1993). Variations can be created in many different ways; for example, by writing the same story told by another character, by changing the time in which the tale takes place, or by changing the solution to a problem. Recently, children's author John Scieszka published several marvelous examples you may wish to share with students as examples of pattern stories, including *The True Story of the Three Little Pigs, The Frog Prince Continued,* and *The Stinky Cheese Man.* Other works of children's literature you may wish to share with students as examples of pattern books are listed in Figure 7-9.

Celebrating Diversity

Using Pourquoi Tales to Develop Insights into Different Cultural Experiences

Pourquoi tales, or stories that explain natural phenomena such as the origin of fire, how the leopard got its spots, or why the sun always rises in the East, are excellent vehicles for pattern stories. At the same time, pourquoi tales are wonderful vehicles for studying the similarities and differences between cultures. All cultures develop their own explanatory myths, but each culture develops explanations for natural elements important to its own individual culture.

Whenever you develop a thematic unit on diversity, consider adding several pourquoi tales from this culture and using them to develop insight into the culture you study. Remember, too, to use these for pattern story activities. You may also develop a separate thematic unit on pourquoi tales from many cultures and use these to study the similarities and differences between cultural experiences.

Using a Literacy Framework to Guide the Connection of Reading and Writing

What Should I Teach?

As you consider the issue of what to teach through connecting reading and writing experiences, your beliefs about *how* one reads can be used to inform your decisions about *what* to teach. For example, with a text-based belief, you connect reading and writing to develop decoding knowledge. Writing is seen as a useful tool for developing spelling and automatic decoding skills. Practices like peer conferences are important because students can practice their decoding skills as they read their work aloud. Keypal experiences are viewed as opportunities to practice correct spelling.

If you have a reader-based belief, however, writing is considered a useful tool for developing the prior knowledge important for reading, not decoding skills. Reading and writing are connected to provide students with opportunities to learn about new concepts (vocabulary knowledge); try out different word order patterns (syntactic knowledge); learn about new discourse structures (discourse knowledge); and acquire effective reading and writing strategies (metacognitive knowledge). Keypal experiences are viewed as excellent opportunities to communicate the prior knowledge students possess and to develop new understandings about the world around them.

An interactive belief leads you to connect reading and writing to develop both decoding skills and the elements of prior knowledge. Reading and writing are connected to provide some students with useful opportunities for developing spelling and automatic decoding skills and other students with useful opportunities for developing important aspects of prior knowledge.

How Should I Teach?

As you consider the issue of how to teach through connecting reading and writing experiences, your beliefs about how children learn to read can be used to inform your decisions. For example, if you have a specific skills belief, you see writing experiences as an opportunity to practice important reading skills. In addition, you favor the use of deductive instructional methods, especially during writing workshop sessions. And you are more likely to make connections between reading and writing within Internet Workshop where specific reading skills were practiced.

Featured Teacher

David Leahy

David Leahy, a fourth-grade teacher at Jacob Wismer Elementary School in Beaverton, Oregon, is another exceptional teacher who can teach us all important lessons about effective literacy instruction. Pay a visit to his classroom home page (http://www.beavton.k12.or.us/jacob_wismer/leahy/leahy.htm) and you will see many exceptional ideas for integrating reading and writing into your own classroom. Follow the link to "Featured Pages" (http://www.beavton.k12.or.us/jacob_wismer/leahy/featured.htm) and you will discover a wonderful model for publishing student work on the Internet to create a curriculum that other classrooms may then use. One example is his class project on a Virtual Underground Railroad Quilt.

Each student developed a written inquiry project on one aspect of the Underground Railroad. David posted these on the Internet, with images from their project, in the form of a quilt. Each image links to the student's research project, explaining important aspects of the Underground Railroad: the routes north, ways to escape, code words, stations, and so on. This resource is now being used by many classrooms around the world who are studying about the Underground Railroad. Many teachers use this for an Internet Workshop assignment, with each student bringing back to the workshop session information about one aspect of the Underground Railroad he or she obtained from this location. Be certain to pay a visit!

FIGURE 7-10

The home page for David Leahy's fourth-grade classroom in Beaverton, Oregon (http://www.beavton.k12.or.us/jacob_wismer/leahy/leahy.htm)

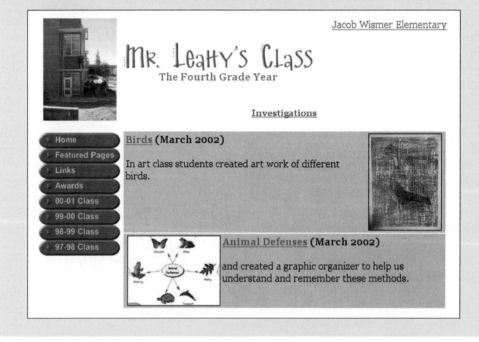

If you have a holistic language belief about how children learn to read, you see writing as the perfect opportunity to create authentic learning environments for children. Internet Workshop, Internet Project, and Internet Inquiry are important, functional opportunities for students to discover central aspects of reading and writing. You view writing as a means to learn insights important to reading, not as a means to practice specific reading skills. Several method frameworks are also useful: reader response journals, dialogue journals, buddy journals, pattern story writing, and thematic reading and writing experiences. Each uses writing in authentic ways to develop important insights about reading.

If you have an integrated belief, you see writing as both an opportunity to practice and to learn important insights about reading. All of the method frameworks described in this chapter are used.

Use the self-test questions on http://www.prenhall. com/leukinzer to review the material presented in this chapter.

Major Points

▶ Connecting reading and writing during instruction is important for many reasons: it excites students about their learning; it allows you to make the most effective use of limited instructional time; it allows you to develop every aspect of reading, writing, and response; and it prepares students for the electronic world that awaits them.

▶ Recent research has provided four major insights that should guide our attempts to connect reading and writing: (1) writing is a process; (2) writing experiences are most appropriate when they serve an authentic communicative purpose; (3) writing experiences are most appropriate when they require students to create complete, extended texts; and (4) reading and writing are similar types of processes.

▶ You can use the Internet to connect reading and writing by using central sites to locate useful resources, developing collaborative Internet Projects, integrating keypal activities, and publishing student work on the WWW.

▶ There are many ways to connect reading and writing in a classroom: reader response journals, dialogue journals, buddy journals, style studies, reading/writing centers, thematic units, writer's workshops, and pattern story activities.

▶ A literacy framework assists teachers in making the reading–writing connection. Your beliefs inform decisions about two main issues: *What* should I teach? and *How* should I teach?

Making Instructional Decisions

1. This chapter suggests that appropriate writing experiences can be used to develop each of the components of reading comprehension and response. If you were most interested in developing syntactic knowledge among your students, which of the method frameworks described in this chapter would you most likely use? Why?
2. Consider the learning experience in the model lesson on process writing (page 237). Explain how this experience does or does not take into consideration each of the four major insights that should guide our attempts to connect reading and writing. Given your evaluation, do you think this learning experience could be improved? If yes, how? If no, why not?
3. Describe how you would use the Internet to connect reading and writing in your classroom. Identify several locations on the Internet you would find useful for your classroom.
4. Define your own literacy framework, then list the instructional practices described in this chapter that are consistent with your framework. Also, list any instructional practices described here that are inconsistent with your framework. Explain why you have identified each practice as you have.

Further Reading

Calkins, L. M. (2000). *The art of teaching reading.* New York: Longman Publishing Group.

A very practical treatment of reading instruction which focuses on the integration of writing with reading instruction in the classroom.

Iannone, P. V. (1998). Just beyond the horizon: Writing-centered literacy activities for traditional and electronic contexts. *The Reading Teacher, 52,* 438–443.

Explains how the Internet may be used to support writing experiences in classrooms and lists many useful locations on the web that support writing.

Lancia, P. J. (1997). Literary borrowing: The effects of literature on children's writing. *The Reading Teacher, 50*(6), 470–475.

Shows how connecting reading and writing experiences contributes to more powerful writing styles among elementary students.

Leu, D. J., Jr. (2001). Internet Project: Preparing students for new literacies in a global village. *The Reading Teacher, 54,* 568–585. Also available at *Reading Online.* [Online Serial]. Available: http://www.readingonline.org/electronic/elec_index.asp?HREF=/electronic/RT/3–01_Column/index.html

Explains how to use Internet Project in your classroom to support literacy learning. It lists many useful Internet locations for this method and provides online examples.

References

Applebee, A. N. (1981). Looking at writing. *Educational Leadership, 38,* 458–462.

Bearse, C. I. (1992). The fairy tale connection in children's stories: Cinderella meets Sleeping Beauty. *The Reading Teacher, 45,* 688–695.

Bode, B. A. (1989). Dialogue journal writing. *The Reading Teacher, 42,* 568–571.

Calkins, L. M. (2000). *The art of teaching reading.* New York: Longman Publishing Group.

Chaney, J. H. (1993). Alphabet books: Resources for learning. *The Reading Teacher, 47,* 96–104.

Chomsky, C. (1971). Write first, read later. *Childhood Education, 47,* 296–299.

Clay, M. (1986). Constructive processes: Talking, reading, writing, art, and craft. *The Reading Teacher, 39,* 764–770.

Crowhurst, M. (1979). The writing workshop: An experiment in peer response to writing. *Language Arts, 56,* 757–762.

D'Angelo Bromley, K. (1989). Buddy journals make the reading-writing connection. *The Reading Teacher, 43,* 122–129.

DeGroff, L. C., & Leu, D. J. (1987). An analysis of writing activities: A study of language arts textbooks. *Written Communication, 4,* 253–268.

Fowler, G. F. (1982). Developing comprehension skills in primary students through the use of story frames. *The Reading Teacher, 36,* 176–179.

Fuhler, C. J. (1994). Response journals: Just one more time with feeling. *Journal of Reading, 37,* 400–405.

Gambrell, L. B. (1985). Dialogue journals: Reading-writing interaction. *The Reading Teacher, 38,* 512–515.

Gavelek, J. R., Raphael, T. E., Biondo, S. M., & Wang, D. (2000). Integrated literacy instruction. In M. L. Kamil, P. Mosenthal, P. D. Pearson, & R. Barr (Eds.), *Handbook of reading research, Volume* III (pp. 361–380). Mahwah, NJ: Lawrence Erlbaum Associates.

Graves, D. (1983). *Writing: Teachers and children at work.* Exeter, NH: Heinemann.

Hancock, M. R. (1993a). Character journals: Initiating involvement and identification through literature. *The Journal of Reading, 37,* 42–50.

Hancock, M. R. (1993b). Exploring and extending personal response through literature journals. *The Reading Teacher, 46,* 466–474.

Hynds, S. (1989). Bringing life to literature and literature to life: Social constructs and context for adolescent readers. *Research in the Teaching of English, 23,* 30–61.

Kelly, P. R. (1990). Guiding young students' response to literature. *The Reading Teacher, 43,* 464–470.

Kinzer, C. K., & Leu, D. J., Jr. (1997). The challenge of change: Exploring literacy and learning in electronic environments. *Language Arts, 74* (2), 126–136.

Lancia, P. J. (1997). Literary borrowing: The effects of literature on children's writing. *The Reading Teacher, 50* (6), 470–475.

Leu, D. J., Jr. (1997). Caity's secret: Literacy as deixis on the Internet. *The Reading Teacher, 51* (1), 62–67.

Leu, D. J., Jr. (2001). Internet Project: Preparing students for new literacies in a global village. *The Reading Teacher, 54,* 568–585. Also available at *Reading Online.* [Online Serial]. Available: http://www.readingonline.org/electronic/elec_index.asp?HREF=/electronic/RT/3–01_Column/index.html

Leu, D. J., Jr., & Leu, D. D. (2000). *Teaching with the Internet: Lessons from the classroom* (2nd ed.). Norwood, MA: Christopher-Gordon Publishers, Inc.

Loback, M. R. (1995). Kids explore heritage through writer's workshop and professional publication. *The Reading Teacher, 48,* 522–525.

McGee, L. M., & Richgels, D. J. (1990). *Literacy's beginnings: Supporting young readers and writers.* Boston, MA: Allyn & Bacon.

Moffett, J. (1985). Hidden impediments to improving English teaching. *Phi Delta Kappan, 67,* 50–55.

Noyce, R. M., & Christie, J. F. (1989). *Integrating reading and writing instruction in grades K–8.* Boston, MA: Allyn & Bacon.

Raphael, T. E., & Englert, C. S. (1990). Writing and reading: Partners in constructing meaning. *The Reading Teacher, 43,* 388–400.

Read, C. (1971). Preschool children's knowledge of English phonology. *Harvard Educational Review, 41,* 1–34.

Rhodes, L. K. (1981). I can read! Predictable books as resources for reading and writing instruction. *The Reading Teacher, 34,* 511–517.

Rosenblatt, L. (1985). Viewpoints: Transaction versus interaction—a terminological rescue operation. *Research in the Teaching of English, 19,* 96–107.

Routman, R. (2000). *The art of teaching reading.* Portsmouth, NH: Heinemann.

Russell, C. (1983). Putting research into practice: Conferencing with young writers. *Language Arts, 60,* 333–340.

Sipe, L. R. (1993). Using transformations of traditional stories: Making the reading-writing connection. *The Reading Teacher, 47,* 18–26.

Smith, F. (1982). *Writing and the writer.* New York: Holt, Rinehart & Winston.

Smith, F. (1983). Reading like a writer. *Language Arts, 60,* 558–567.

Staton, J. (1988). Dialogue journals in the classroom context. In M. Farr (Ed.), *Interactive writing in dialogue journals: Practitioner, linguistic, social, and cognitive views.* Norwood, NJ: Ablex.

Tierney, R. J., & Pearson, P. D. (1983). Toward a composing model of reading. *Language Arts, 60,* 568–580.

Yaden, D. B., Rowe, D. W., & MacGillivray, L. (2000). Emergent literacy: A matter of polyphony. In M. L. Kamil, P. Mosenthal, P. D. Pearson, & R. Barr (Eds.), *Handbook of reading research, Volume III* (pp. 425–454). Mahwah, NJ: Lawrence Erlbaum Associates.

Youngblood, E. (1985). Reading, thinking and writing using the reading journal. *English Journal, 74,* 46–48.

8

Vocabulary and Literacy

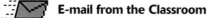 **E-mail from the Classroom**

Subject: Student Teachers and Vocabulary Lessons
From: Manfred Herndon, Mherndon@aol.com

I always tell my student teachers to listen carefully to children's speech. The words they use say a lot about how they feel, where they come from, and what they think. I once heard on a radio commercial: "We think about people based on the words they use." I also remember reading that vocabulary knowledge is highly related to success in reading. Of course, that makes sense, because knowing what the words mean helps us understand what's being read. And I like playing with language and learning new words myself. My student teachers are usually fascinated with the wide variety of language and vocabulary used by my students. And teaching vocabulary, which is really concept development, always seems to end up among their favorite lessons.

Some Internet sites that focus on human languages are really helpful. Some have audio clips that let me show my students how people with different languages say things that my class knows in English. There are also lists of words that show words adapted from other languages that are used in English everyday. The children in my class (and my student teachers) really like exploring these sites! Vocabulary lessons seem to be great motivators!

Manfred Herndon (Third Grade Teacher)

After reading this chapter, you should be able to:

1. Use effective strategies to teach vocabulary in your literacy program.
2. Discuss the role of concept development in teaching and learning new vocabulary.
3. Integrate the Internet into your vocabulary instruction.
4. Explain how pronunciation and meaning are determined in reading.

Vocabulary Knowledge Helps Comprehension: A Principle of Effective Literacy Instruction

Over the years, research has consistently found that vocabulary knowledge is closely related to a person's reading comprehension abilities. Partly because of such results, the following was listed in chapter 1 as a principle of effective literacy instruction:

6. **Vocabulary knowledge helps comprehension.** Vocabulary knowledge is closely related to reading comprehension, and vocabulary instruction can help build background knowledge and word attack strategies that lead to increased reading achievement (Anderson & Freebody, 1981; Nagy, 1988; Nagy & Scott, 2000; Smith, 1997).

Fluent reading of words and understanding the concepts they represent results from effective instruction and concept development linked to word recognition. Chapter 8 explores effective techniques you will be able to use in your classroom to help your students learn the meanings of unfamiliar words and to recognize these words fluently.

Vocabulary knowledge is closely related to conceptual knowledge—the words we use represent concepts that we know and use to communicate with others. Linking words to concepts, and developing new concepts that can be thought of as new vocabulary knowledge, is an important part of being a teacher of reading and writing. Thus, this chapter presents the knowledge you will need to teach vocabulary in ways that will enhance your students' reading comprehension.

The Meanings of Words

Good language users almost unconsciously select the appropriate meanings of words from a large number of possibilities. Even the simplest words often have more than one meaning, as well as many shades or gradations of meaning. Look at these examples:

1. Copper is a good *conductor* of electricity.
   Give your ticket to the *conductor*.
   The orchestra *conductor* was quite young.
2. She wanted to *staple* the three pages together.
   Corn was a *staple* in some Native Americans' diets.
3. The *frog* jumped into the pool.
   He started coughing because he had a *frog* in his throat.
4. She played a classical *guitar* piece with the symphony orchestra.
   She played rhythm *guitar* in a rock band.

The first three sets of examples show that words can have more than one meaning; the last set demonstrates that a word can have multiple shades of meaning, too. Did you visualize a different guitar in each of the last two sentences, even though you thought of a guitar in each case? Almost all words in our language have multiple meanings, yet we use most of them appropriately from a very young age. In fact, we usually are not even aware of our own skill in distinguishing among the possible variations. Think of the common word *up:*

Look *up* at the moon.

Look *up* the word in the dictionary.

Lock *up* the car.

The drain is stopped *up.*

Sam said he's tied *up* and can't come.

To help children develop and expand their vocabularies, it is important to understand how words and their meanings are learned. It is also important to understand how concepts are stored in memory and how they are accessed for use in appropriate situations.

The Relationship of Words and Concepts

Words can be thought of as labels for concepts. When we read, we attempt to match a printed label to a concept in memory. Think of the word-label as a trigger to access the concept. Thus, a concept must be present before a word for that concept should be taught.

This line of reasoning raises several questions: Can we know something without a language label? For example, can we have a concept for a chair and can we access that concept without using a language label? Is it possible to have an internalized concept in memory without thinking of it in language-related terms? Such questions are important and have led to perspectives that advocate teaching word-labels and concepts together, as opposed to learning the concept first and later attaching a label to it.

Have you ever had the experience of trying to say something and not being able to, even though you knew clearly what you were trying to say? Often we say that something is on the tip of our tongue even though we are unable to verbalize it at that moment. This **tip-of-the-tongue phenomenon** supports the belief that we have internalized representations of concepts that can be assessed, or triggered, by language (Brown & McNeil, 1966). Thus, the implication is that we can and do know things without a labeling term being accessible at all times.

tip-of-the-tongue phenomenon Having a concept and a word in memory, but being unable to access that knowledge at that time.

Primary and Intermediate Grade Level Concerns. Vocabulary knowledge changes throughout our lives, with new concepts learned and others increasingly refined. In the primary grades children usually have a concept in their speaking vocabulary before they are taught its printed form. Because beginning readers have not yet learned to use decoding strategies, they are still attempting to understand what the "squiggles" on the page represent, and oral vocabulary can be a bridge between written words and concepts. For this reason, vocabulary in traditional published reading programs was controlled to focus on the speaking vocabulary of young children. However, this led to texts that were artificial when compared to authentic language; published reading programs no longer focus to the same extent on controlling the vocabulary found in reading selections (Hoffman et al., 1994). This makes it important to know whether or not the concept is in the child's speaking vocabulary before teaching it in print. Although some would argue that such lessons are an exercise in word recognition (as teaching concepts isn't the stated goal), most teachers and published reading programs call them "vocabulary lessons," because new (written) words are introduced for concepts accessed through a child's spoken words.

In later grades, children are relatively competent decoders and are confronted with new concepts as well as new word-labels for those concepts, especially in subject areas such as social studies, mathematics, and science. In the intermediate grades and beyond, therefore, teachers must more often teach the new concept in addition to forging the link between the written word and its concept. Figure 8-1 on p. 268 illustrates the differences between vocabulary lessons in primary and higher grades.

Factors in the Communication of Meaning

What is it that allows people within a culture to communicate with each other? It is the commonality of shared experiences within a culture or a social group that allows communication to take place. In other words, individuals communicate by referring to their overlapping, common experiences. When society or a group accepts a word-label to refer to a particular experience or concept, everyone familiar with that word is then able to access that concept. However, if a social or cultural group has not agreed on a word-label, then communication about that concept is difficult or impossible. In addition, if the experiences of different groups cause an underlying concept to be differently perceived, then even a shared word-label may cause confusion! Listen to children talk to each other on the playground, your school's hallway, and in class—even in school, children develop their own shared labels, or jargon, which often is difficult for teachers to understand.

You may find students in your classroom who have difficulty with vocabulary for any of these reasons: (1) they may not have the relevant concept as part of their background knowledge, (2) they may have a different label for the targeted concept, or

FIGURE 8-1

A representation of the basic difference in vocabulary instruction in primary grades (concept known) and intermediate grades (concept unknown)

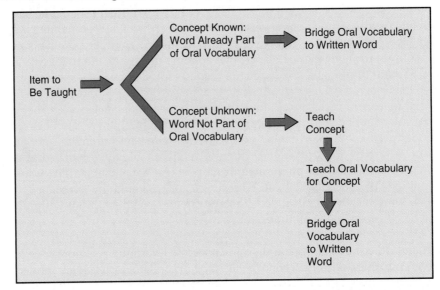

Celebrating Diversity

Exploring Language Differences in Your Classroom

Cultural and social groups have common vocabularies; communication occurs without difficulty between members of a given group. Communication across these groups might be difficult, however, partly because of differences in word-labels for common concepts. Your classroom will probably include students who speak a language other than English or who live in close communities that have developed their own word-labels. For example, African American or Latino/Latina students may have different labels for the same concepts, which might also differ from those used by other students or by a teacher.

In general, children are fascinated with how others speak. Use the children's language as a way to broaden their understanding and vocabulary knowledge. The vocabulary differences among the children in your class will prove a rich place to start. Ask them to provide different word-labels for pictures of items and post these around your classroom. After completing language experience stories, allow students to restate the story in their own, unique words and post both. Have a child or a group of children perform a brief skit, using their "everyday" language, and allow other students to interpret what certain words mean. Allow the performing group to explain the vocabulary. Have fun using these and other activities to celebrate differences while drawing the classroom community closer together.

(3) they may have a somewhat different meaning for the label. Effective teachers must be aware of the diversity in their students' backgrounds and must ensure that vocabulary lessons are related to students' prior knowledge and shared experiences.

Thus, when communication fails, any of several factors may be responsible. For example, someone from France attempting to communicate with someone from the United States about a furry domestic animal that meows may not understand for one or more of these reasons:

1. There may be no shared experience with such an animal.
2. The two societies or cultures may have evolved a different word-label for such an animal.
3. The same word-label may represent different concepts in the different societies.

PRACTICAL TEACHING STRATEGIES

Using Internet Inquiry to Build Awareness of Language Differences

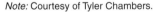 Several Internet sites provide interesting information about the world's languages and can be used to give your students insights into different vocabulary. You might want to suggest that children explore sites such as these:

The Human Languages Page (http://www.june29.com/HLP/)—A site that contains over 1,600 links to language resources. These include translations of words and phrases between languages useful for children who are curious about the differences between languages (see Figure 8-2).

Say Hello to the World Project (http://www.ipl.org/youth/hello/)—A listing of the world's languages with audioclips allowing children to listen to "hello" in each language. It also shows a list of English words that have been borrowed from each language and provides resources for teaching and learning the respective language (see Figure 8-3, p. 270).

Youth Division of the Internet Public Library (http://www.ipl.org/youth/)—This is a site with many links and much information for children and teachers. The "Say Hello to the World Project" is part of this site. The "reading" branch of this library has several activities appropriate for vocabulary learning.

FIGURE 8-2

A screen from **iLoveLanguages** (http://www.ilovelanguages.com/)

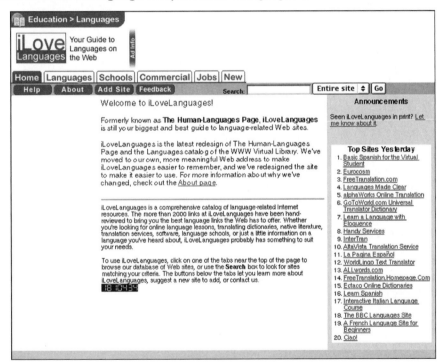

Note: Courtesy of Tyler Chambers.

In this case, the second reason is the most likely explanation, since we know that people in France also keep cats as pets and people in the two countries do speak different languages. In France, such a creature is called *le chat*. Thus, because the two individuals do not share the same word-label for the same concept, communication is difficult, if not impossible.

Check your ongoing understanding of chapter concepts by using the guided review for this chapter on http://www.prenhall.com/leukinzer

Building Concepts

The Importance of Examples

When teaching new vocabulary concepts, it is important to provide examples. Examples can take many forms and allow students to experience and clarify meaning and integrate it into existing knowledge (Duffelmeyer, 1985). Concrete examples should be used whenever

FIGURE 8-3

Sample screen from the **Say Hello to the World** (http://www.ipl.org/youth/hello/) project, where phrases from other languages can be found and related to words and phrases in English

Internet Public Library

Say Hello to the World

If you wanted to say hello to everybody in the world, how many people would that be? And how many languages would you have to learn?

You would have to learn at least 2,796 languages and say hello to 5,720,000,000 people!

That's a lot of work, so let's get started! Choose any language:

- Arabic
- French
- Hindi
- Korean
- Russian
- Tagalog
- Cherokee
- German
- Hungarian
- Mayan
- Spanish
- Thai
- Chinese
- Greek
- Indonesian
- Mohawk
- Swahili
- Turkish
- Czech
- Hawaiian
- Italian
- Portuguese
- Swedish
- Welsh
- Finnish
- Hebrew
- Japanese
- Romanian
- And many more!

Non-Verbal Languages: • Braille • Sign Language

Learn more about the Say Hello Project.
Send us e-mail!

Back to the IPL Youth Page
the Internet Public Library – = – http://www.ipl.org/ – = – youth@ipl.org

Note: Courtesy of Lorri Mon.

possible and appropriate, providing the opportunity for students to see, touch, smell, and otherwise experience the meanings of words during concept development. For abstract concepts such as "*truth*" or "*beauty*," concrete examples are difficult to provide. In such cases, teachers often let character actions from literature serve as examples. A discussion about how a character felt or acted in certain situations or about how other characters felt about the main character can clarify concepts such as "heroism," "justice," or other abstract notions that do not lend themselves to concrete examples.

Experience.   Experience is the most concrete way of teaching a new concept. Teachers often take their classes on field trips and point out things that will form the basis of a vocabulary lesson when the class returns to school. A field trip need not be an expensive outing; it can be a walk around the block. Direct experience can also be provided by bringing an object into the classroom. It is critical, however, to focus the students' attention. They must actively perceive the object, not simply look at it. Children should also be helped to identify features that link the new concept to a familiar one.

Facsimile.   It often is not possible to provide hands-on experience when developing a new concept. In such cases, a facsimile can be effective. Common facsimiles are drawings, photographs, filmstrips, videotapes, audiotapes, and computer simulations related to the object or concept under discussion. You must remember, however, to build the concept actively and not to allow students to be passive observers.

Discussion.   Although less concrete than experience or a facsimile, a purposeful discussion can lead to the understanding and acquisition of a new concept. The discussion must relate to things that are already a part of children's knowledge, while focusing on the unique features of the new concept. For example, to teach the concept "gorilla," you might begin by asking whether anyone knew of an animal that lived in trees in the jungle. If children suggested a monkey, you might build on that knowledge in further questions: What is a monkey like? What makes a monkey a monkey and not an elephant? The class could then discuss the similarities between monkeys and gorillas, and could conclude by establishing the similarities and differences between gorillas and other animals.

Feature Analysis

As infants interact with the world, they encounter many new things, and each new experience adds to their conceptual understanding and memory. Initially, however, such concepts may be overgeneralized. If you have had experience with a young child, you may have noticed that, for a little while, all furry, four-legged animals might be called "doggie." The child may have seen a particular furry, four-legged animal that was called "doggie" and may have generalized that set of features to include any furry, four-legged animal. Later, as the child gained experience with different kinds of animals and focused on finer discriminations, features such as barking, having a cold nose, and chewing bones may have been added, and "doggie" came to include only the appropriate animals.

To see how we use features to discriminate among related items, let's work through a sample exercise. In the blank to the right of each feature, write all possible choices from the word list.

dog   cat   horse   poodle   stuffed toy dog

Has four legs: _____

Is alive: _____

Eats meat: _____

Barks: _____

Has a long nose and often is trimmed to
have a ball of fur at the end of its tail: _____

This example is not a completely accurate representation of how we identify perceived items, but it illustrates that features can provide a basis for classification. As more features of an item are identified, classes of objects become more narrowly defined. This same process is what enables infants to make fewer overgeneralization errors and narrow the use of "doggie" to the appropriate animals.

What you did in the preceding example is a type of **feature analysis.** When linguists analyze words to determine differences in meaning, they often use feature analysis, employing plus and minus signs to indicate the presence or absence of a given feature (Katz, 1972; Leech, 1974; Lyons, 1977; Pittelman, Heimlich, Berglund, & French, 1991).

> **feature analysis** A linguistic method that specifies differences between concepts, which can aid in the understanding of new vocabulary concepts.

Boy	**Man**	**Girl**
+alive	+alive	+alive
−female	+male	+female
−adult	+adult	−adult

A feature analysis chart, developed in a class discussion, often aids children's understanding of a new concept by relating it to concepts they already know. Anders and Bos (1986) point out that feature analysis can be effectively used in content-area reading with content-specific concepts. Using this approach at various stages (before, during, and after reading) allows students to relate their already-acquired knowledge to new concepts and increases their interest in the selection.

To use feature analysis effectively, provide clear examples that focus on important features of the concept to be acquired. Activities should include both positive and negative examples of the concept to help define its boundaries and show how it is both similar to, and different from, already-known concepts. For example, if the concept "goblet" is to be learned, you might show and discuss several kinds of drinking vessels and show things similar to, but different from, goblets—perhaps drinking glasses and bowls. A discussion of common and different features of goblets, drinking glasses, and bowls will help your students build knowledge about goblets. Such a discussion will also help your students to place the concept of "goblet" within already-known items related to "containers that hold liquid and that you can drink from." In addition, you should be aware that concepts are continually refined as features are identified and clarified; they are not learned on a one-shot basis. Thus, revisiting concepts in different contexts is important to learning vocabulary.

MODEL LESSON

Discussion of Features in Linda Amato's Class

Linda Amato is preteaching some of the vocabulary she feels is important for her second graders to know before they read a story. She has reader-based beliefs about what to teach—believing that meaning and prior knowledge are most important—and so she does not include decoding or word analysis as part of her vocabulary lessons. Linda also has integrated beliefs about how to teach, believing that children learn best through a combination of direct instruction while providing children with opportunities to self-direct their learning. In this case, she had the class read a page of the story and write down words they wanted some help with. We join her as she teaches the word *canoe* to her students:

1. Linda shows the class a picture of a rowboat. Pointing to the rowboat, she asks, "Who can tell me what this is?" She writes the students' response on the chalkboard: "boat."
2. Pointing to a picture of a canoe, she says, "Raise your hand if you know what this is called." Three of the eight children in the instructional group raise their hands.
3. Linda asks one of the children to name the item and receives the response: "canoe." She writes "canoe" on the chalkboard beside "boat."
4. She shows the children a picture of a sailboat and asks whether this is also a boat. With a little guidance, the children decide that the original word (*boat*) is not specific enough. They should have called the first boat a rowboat, and this one a sailboat. Linda erases "boat" from the chalkboard and replaces it with "rowboat."
5. Linda says, "Let's list how a rowboat and a canoe are the same and how they're different. Tell me how they're the same."
6. As the children provide responses, Linda writes them on the chalkboard in the appropriate columns.

Near the end of the discussion, Linda writes "sailboat" to the right of the other two words and asks which of the features already identified apply to the sailboat.

7. The children generate sentences using the word *canoe*. The sentences reflect the word's meaning and are specific enough that a reader would not confuse it with another kind of boat.

Use of Context

If we keep in mind that the goal of literacy instruction is the comprehension of text, then to-be-learned words and concepts should always be linked to larger contexts. This is done either through using the words and concepts in reading materials and conversations or through links to already-known concepts. Children need to see that vocabulary is useful; moreover, using new vocabulary in meaningful contexts teaches students that words have particular shades of meaning and play different roles depending on how they are used in sentences. This is easily seen in the following sentences:

> The *ball* was kicked hard into the net.
>
> The *ball* was caught in the outfield.
>
> She putted the *ball* and her score remained at par.
>
> The racket hit the *ball* with a resounding "thwack!"
>
> He shot the *ball* from the free-throw line.

As you read through the above sentences, you probably pictured a soccer ball, baseball, golf ball, tennis ball, and basketball even though the type of ball was not specified. This shows the importance of context and your own background knowledge. Without context, or with only generic context (such as "The ball was round"), it is difficult to develop or refine concepts. Context is a powerful tool to help readers derive meanings for unfamiliar words. Nevertheless, we must not assume that all children will understand new concepts simply because they have been used in a written context. An effective teacher provides or makes explicit appropriate background information before students are expected to use the context clues embedded in a sentence or story.

PRACTICAL TEACHING STRATEGIES

Use of Concrete Examples and Context

Experiencing New Concepts

▶ Have students see, touch, smell, taste, and use an item as appropriate, and then discuss the name and the features of the item being experienced.

▶ Have students walk around the school yard with you. Stop periodically to write a word on a notepad, and discuss it before moving on. Follow-up by using these words in language-related classroom activities. (This activity can be done as part of any field trip.)

Using Facsimiles

▶ Using a picture, videotape, movie, audiotape, Internet site, or other source, have children focus on the features of the target item. Discuss its size, looks, possible uses, relationship to similar items, and so on.

Using Context

▶ During discussion of a new vocabulary item, have students close their eyes. Present a detailed, verbal picture of the concept. Then, have students open their eyes and link the concept to the written form by showing them the word. Finally, present sentences with the target word omitted, and let students supply the word to practice its use in sentence context.

▶ The Internet is a wonderful resource for contextualizing vocabulary concepts. Because of the graphics, animations, videoclips, audio, and textual capabilities of the Internet, rich contexts are possible. For example, sites such as **The Science Learning Network** (http://www.sln.org) provide pictures and descriptions that contextualize many science-related concepts. Look for sites that can help provide context for your vocabulary curriculum. The youth section of the **Internet Public Library** (http://www.ipl.org/youth/) is a good place to find links to such sites (see Figure 8-4).

▶ Provide for free reading time. Ask children to write down three words they feel are particularly interesting or that they would like to know more about. Use these words as the basis for refining knowledge by referring back to the context in which they were used. This activity not only allows children to choose words of interest, but facilitates their use of words in longer, more authentic contexts.

FIGURE 8-4

Sample screen from the youth section of the **Internet Public Library** (www.ipl.org/youth/), showing buttons that lead to links in several areas

The Internet Public Library Youth Division

Reference
Dictionaries | Encyclopedias | Biography | Homework Help ...

Reading Zone
Picture Books | Story Hour | Books & Authors | Fables ...

Fun Stuff
Arts & Crafts | Toys | Pre-Schoolers | Games ...

Our World
Religion | Languages | History | Geography & Culture ...

USA
Presidents | 50 States | Government ...

Art & Music
Art | Music | Museums | Buildings & Cities ...

Computers/Internet
Search Engines | Safe Surfing | Games | Computers ...

Math Whiz
Arithmetic & Basic Math | Geometry | Projects ...

Science Net
Earth Science | Animals & Insects | Dinosaurs ...

Health & Nutrition
Food & Nutrition | The Body | Exercise | Safety ...

Sports & Recreation
Baseball | Basketball | Football | Soccer ...

Teachers & Parents
Math | Reading | Science | Our World | Computers ...

Reference | Our World | USA | Reading Zone | Art, Music and Museums | Math Whiz | Science Net | Health & Nutrition | Sports & Recreation | Fun Stuff | Ask A Question | Selection Policy | Contact Us

Note: Courtesy of The Internet Public Library Youth Division.

All experiences, including reading picture books and other age-appropriate materials, increase vocabulary knowledge.

Although context is very powerful in determining a word's meaning, these examples illustrate some limitations of context:

1. A common practice, especially when the salvage value is assumed to be zero, is to apply an appropriate percentage, known as the depreciation rate, to the acquisition cost in order to calculate the annual charge (Davidson, Stickney, & Weil, 1980).
2. The giraffe, a tall animal with a long neck, lives in Africa.
3. John, the basketball player, is really quite skinny and has red hair and a fair complexion. His friend Sam, however, is corpulent.

If the concepts of "salvage value" and "depreciation rate" are not already a part of your background knowledge, it is unlikely that the context clues embedded in the first example will help you with the concept of "annual charge." If you know nothing about giraffes, you will probably need a picture to acquire the concept. Finally, in the third example there are many possible meanings for *corpulent*. The contrast might be implying that Sam is dark complexioned, does not have red hair, or is not a basketball player, in addition to the correct implication that Sam is overweight.

Despite these limitations, context is an extremely valuable aid in developing concepts. Also, context teaches something beyond a word's basic meaning: It shows the way a particular meaning is used in a sentence, thus refining a word's meaning even if a common meaning is already known. Much vocabulary is acquired "in context" simply by reading; therefore, encouraging reading in your classroom will help students develop their vocabulary knowledge. For example, Sustained Silent Reading (SSR), discussed in chapter 6, is an activity that will positively influence children's vocabularies. In addition, context helps the reader to understand how a word is used in a sentence; that is, its part of speech. Figure 8-5 presents several common activities to help students internalize a word's function in a sentence. Such activities are best used with a group of children where discussion can occur.

FIGURE 8-5

Examples of group activities that might be used to teach *clock* as a part of speech

1. Modified cloze (fill-in-the-blank) procedure:

   Instructions to students: A clock is something used to tell time. It is used in sentences in the same way that the word *boy* is used. Write the word *clock* wherever it appropriately completes the sentence.
   a. Don't touch the _____.
   b. My house is _____.
   c. Bring me the _____.
   d. Where is the _____?

2. Categorization exercises:

   Instructions to students: Circle all the words that can be used in sentences (a) and (b). Underline all the words that can be used in sentences (c) and (d).

   sit   eat   clock   jump   dog   table   go   spoon

   a. She is looking at the _____.
   b. The _____ is in the kitchen.
   c. He will _____ soon.
   d. Don't _____ in the bedroom.

3. Correcting exercises:

   Instructions to students: Put a check mark in front of each sentence in which clock is used properly. If clock is not used properly, cross it out, choose a word from the following list, and write it on the blank in front of the sentence.

   sit   jump   eat   go

   _____ a. He will clock on the chair.
   _____ b. The clock was on the table.
   _____ c. Look at the clock!
   _____ d. She wants to clock the candy.

Note that the instructions in Figure 8-5 never actually state that *clock* is a noun. Memorizing a word's part of speech does little to facilitate the proper use of a word and may be confusing and faulty if the word is later used in a different context. If the goal of instruction is the students' proper use of new vocabulary in good sentences, then practice in context will be of far more value than memorized parts-of-speech definitions. The teaching strategies on p. 276 promote the use of both concrete examples and context. Memorizing parts-of-speech definitions will not transfer easily into students' use of new vocabulary in real-world situations. Use of new words in context, however, will aid in such transfer.

Deciding What to Teach

Vocabulary can be divided into three general types: function words, content words, and content-specific words. Figure 8-6 illustrates these three categories.

Function Words

Function words are often called the glue that holds a sentence together. Frequently occurring words such as articles (*a, an, the*), conjunctions (*and, but, or*), prepositions (*at, into, over*), and auxiliary verbs (*could run, had snowed*) are function words.

Function words make a sentence cohesive, linking words and phrases so that understanding can occur. Function words are often irregular in spelling and/or pronunciation, and, if taught out of context, they can be difficult for young children to conceptualize because the concepts they represent are not concrete. Although there are times

function words Words that facilitate comprehension by connecting other words and phrases.

PRACTICAL TEACHING STRATEGIES

Use of Concrete Examples and Context

Oral Question. Who knows what _____ means? (This is perhaps the most common, yet least effective, approach because not all students typically respond.)

Oral (or Written) Expression. Say (or write) in a sentence . . . .

Matching Activity. Match the word with the meaning.

a. house _____   1. grows in the garden
b. flower _____   2. a place to live

Fill in the Blank. Using the choices provided, write the appropriate word in each sentence.

                              house   flower

a. The _____ grows in the garden.
b. The _____ has three bedrooms.

Multiple Choice. Choose the best meaning for each word.

                         house   elephant   corn

a. a place to live
b. something to eat
c. a large animal

FIGURE 8-6

Different categories of vocabulary

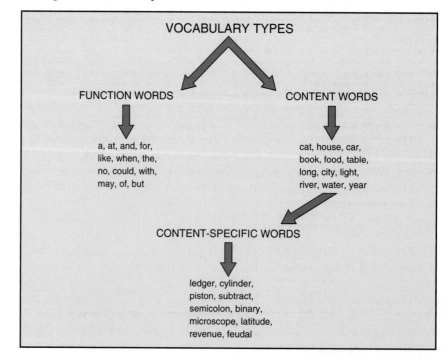

when it is appropriate to present words in isolation (for example, when discussing the "context" of a prefix), we advocate teaching all vocabulary in context. Context generally serves to clarify meaning.

Content Words

Content words such as nouns (*house, car,*) pronouns (*I, his, they*), verbs (*run, swim*), adjectives (*hot, sticky*), and adverbs (*then, neatly, suddenly*) have concrete meanings.

content words Words with definitions in general use in everyday language.

Everyday content words such as *dog* or *car* are sometimes called general vocabulary words. Nevertheless, the same word can have both general and specific meanings, depending on the context in which it is used. For example:

The *race* was run yesterday.

The Asian *race* has a long and fascinating history.

Again, vocabulary requires the context to clarify meaning, and you cannot assume that children know meanings other than those they appropriately demonstrate in context.

Content-Specific Words

Content-specific words always have specialized meanings within a particular subject area and must be learned within the context of that area.

content-specific words Words with definitions specific to a content area; words not used in everyday language.

For example, *beaker* and *isotherm* do not have general-meaning counterparts; their meanings are embedded in a subject area such as science. Especially in the middle grades, teachers should spend time teaching their students the meanings of words apt to be encountered in their reading material. In subject areas such as science, social studies, and mathematics, words often have content-specific meanings; not knowing those meanings can make comprehension impossible. Chapter 10 deals with this issue in more depth.

Selection of Vocabulary Items

In general, you will select vocabulary words from one or more of these sources:

1. Words used by children in their natural, oral language.
2. Words that children will encounter in their reading materials.
3. Graded word lists.

The first vocabulary source centers around children's use of oral language and is closely related to the language experience approach discussed in chapter 2. Have one or several children dictate a story, which you will then write down. That story then forms the basis of a vocabulary lesson. You can, for example, point out synonyms that are appropriate substitutions for some of the children's words. In addition, having the children attempt to read the dictated story may show that certain words are in their speaking, but not reading, vocabularies and should therefore be targeted for instruction. This approach is highly motivational and helps forge a link between already-known concepts and print. Nonetheless, using a child's oral language as a base for vocabulary lessons is sometimes criticized because only known concepts are used. The teaching suggestions previously shown can expand a child's vocabulary while using oral language as a foundation.

The second source of vocabulary items is based on the philosophy that vocabulary is best learned and retained when the items to be learned occur in real, meaningful situations. Consequently, vocabulary identified as critical to children's understanding of an upcoming passage or story are taught before a selection is read and revisited using context from the selection after reading. With this approach, someone must determine which words in the text are important for overall understanding of the passage. Sometimes, teacher's guides for reading selections present a list of words introduced in each unit or each story, with the expectation that teachers will focus on those new and important words.

One possible disadvantage of teaching vocabulary based on words suggested by a teacher's guide within a published reading program is that not all reading materials introduce the same vocabulary at identical grade levels. Harris and Jacobson (1982)

Expanding a Child's Vocabulary through Oral Language

Logical Cloze. Transcribe a story provided by a student. Then present logical replacements for some of the content words, teach and discuss the new words, and ask the children to place them in the appropriate blanks. For example, the new words to be taught might be *morning, cape, previous,* and *annoyed* (to replace the words in bold).

The girl was on her way to school. It was a rainy **day** _____, and she had her **raincoat** _____ and her umbrella with her. She hoped that she wouldn't forget her umbrella at school like she did the **last** _____ time. Her mother was **upset** _____ with her when she didn't bring the umbrella home.

Thesaurus Detective. After children have mastered the skills necessary to use a thesaurus, cut pages out of a newspaper and have them work in pairs. Within each pair, have one child circle five familiar words that the other child is to replace with words found in the thesaurus. Then have children read the words to each other one at a time, with the listener trying to provide the meaning of the synonym and matching it to the original word.

---

showed that words introduced in different basal readers can vary by as much as five grade levels. Because the vocabulary in published reading programs is becoming less controlled than when Harris and Jacobson did their study and is increasingly based on selections of children's literature, the variance in vocabulary across published reading programs is increasing. In our highly mobile society, where a significant number of children change school districts and instructional materials from one year to the next, differences in the vocabulary suggested by different teacher's guides can easily occur. Thus, you will need to remember that children will have used a variety of materials and will not have been exposed to a similar or core set of vocabulary.

The third way you might select vocabulary is from graded word lists. There are many published word lists available that indicate the frequency of words encountered by students at specific grade levels. These lists usually are developed from an analysis of reading materials, including textbooks, that children are expected to read in each grade. Teachers who systematically use such a list generally construct pretests and then teach the specific words that students do not know. Some common lists are identified here:

Dale, E., & O'Rourke, J. (1976). *Living word vocabulary: The words we know.* Elgin, IL: Dome.

Fry, E. B., Kress, J. E., & Fountoukidis, D. L. (2000). *The reading teacher's book of lists* (4th ed.). Englewood Cliffs, NJ: Prentice-Hall.

Harris, A. J., & Jacobson, M. D. (1982). *Basic reading vocabularies.* New York: Macmillan.

Marzano, R. J., & Marzano, J. S. (1988). *A cluster approach to elementary vocabulary instruction.* Newark, DE: International Reading Association.

Word lists can provide useful information, such as the number of students at a given grade level who do not know a specific word or a frequency ordering of words encountered by students in elementary reading materials. There are also lists of roots, prefixes, suffixes, synonyms, antonyms, homophones, commonly misspelled words, and so on. Such lists can provide words that are conceptually or semantically related (for example, Marzano & Marzano's list) as well as words that might be specific to regional or cultural areas (for example, Gunderson, 1984). Systematic teaching from a list, however, means that the words taught may not match the words students find in their reading, so you will have to provide contextualized examples for these words in your lessons.

Pretesting

Children do not have identical needs when it comes to vocabulary instruction. A quick and informal pretest of new or necessary terms may help identify those students who will benefit from instruction. Although it is good practice to revisit, reinforce, and use previously taught vocabulary in real text, it is not a good use of time or resources to teach already-known words. Thus, pretesting makes teaching more effective, interesting, and relevant. It also helps to prevent student boredom or frustration. The previous suggestions provide several ways to test students' vocabulary knowledge quickly.

After pretest results are known, you will need to group children for instruction. One student may not know any of the words to be taught, another may know all but three, and still another may know all but a different three. Logistically, it is impractical to teach individualized vocabulary lessons to each student, but groups can be formed to minimize the ratio of known to unknown words. For example, let's imagine that five words are to be taught (1, 2, 3, 4, 5) to a group of five students (A, B, C, D, E) and that you have given a brief pretest. After the pretest you decide on this arrangement:

Student	Unknown Words	Group Placement
A	1, 2	1
B	4, 5	2
C	1, 2, 3	1
D	1, 3, 5	2
E	4	1

With this grouping, children in group 1 are exposed to a maximum of two already-known words; those in group 2, only one. Teaching the five students as one group would have resulted in exposure to as many as four already-known words (for student E).

This example shows that pretesting does not result in perfect matches, but can help target vocabulary instruction. The example may seem unrealistic because of the relatively low number of already-known words included in the grouping arrangements. But in reality, when more words are presented to a greater number of students, grouping for vocabulary activities substantially reduces the number of already-known words that are taught. Teaching specific words to a targeted group occurs easily during the day when using a flexible grouping arrangement (see chapter 13), which allows time for small group activities.

Deciding How to Teach

General Principles

Some general principles apply to all vocabulary instruction, regardless of grade level. Nagy (1988) points out that effective vocabulary instruction has three components:

1. *Integration.* Teaching strategies must use methods that integrate the concept to be learned with existing knowledge.
2. *Repetition.* Teaching strategies should provide sufficient practice so that meaning is accessed automatically, without the need to decode the word during reading. This level of familiarity requires many encounters with a new word—certainly far more than the number of repetitions necessary just to learn a definition.
3. *Meaningful use.* Teaching strategies should provide opportunities for children to use a new concept and word in context rather than in isolation. This approach facilitates inferencing and allows for repetitive practice that is interesting and motivational.

Other common strategies include revisiting words learned over a period of time. Although words receive the greatest attention during the initial teaching phase, children need to revisit them periodically. This task is simplified if children collect vocabulary words as they are learned. For example, children might maintain a **word bank,** a special section of a notebook, or a personal database of words and meanings on the classroom's computer.

Periodically, then, you would remind students to review and use words from their collection in their writing or in other meaningful activities.

word bank A place to organize word cards and a means to help develop decoding and vocabulary knowledge.

Allowing access to books and providing free reading time has a positive influence on vocabulary growth.

Beck, McKeown, and Omanson (1987); Beck, McKeown, and Kucan (2002) also point out that vocabulary should be specifically taught and describe a rich vocabulary program with the following features:

1. Students should manipulate words in varied ways, perhaps by describing how they relate to other words and to students' experiences.
2. Activities should involve a great deal of discussion and students should justify the associations and relationships they make.
3. Words should be encountered many times.
4. Students should be encouraged and supported in their efforts to use new vocabulary words outside of the vocabulary lesson.
5. Children should make their thinking explicit and teachers should model this process.

Beck and her colleagues also note that extensive reading and exposure to environments where oral presentations use unfamiliar words help to develop children's vocabulary. In addition, systematic vocabulary instruction promotes curiosity about words and their meanings, and independence in word analysis (Anderson & Nagy, 1993). Anderson and Nagy also point out that wide, ongoing reading will result in vocabulary growth and that even a slight amount of daily reading can lead to gains of several thousand words per year, especially when multiple meanings and nuances of meanings are considered.

Environmental Print and Vocabulary Development

Children learn a great deal about literacy from the print they see around them. Partly because of this, chapter 5 pointed out the importance and benefits of labeling known items in kindergarten classrooms. Even at higher grade levels, teachers with holistic language perspectives often present vocabulary instruction as an **incidental learning** experience, consciously using new vocabulary during morning message and story reading, Internet Inquiry projects, classroom conversations, or functional writing activities.

Within these activities, students' attention is drawn to the new words, and follow-up activities—writing tasks, dictation, and other literacy activities—allow students to

incidental learning
Learning that takes place without direct instruction, often as part of everyday routines.

practice writing, seeing, and hearing the words in context (see Noyce & Christie, 1989, for a discussion of the value of copying and dictation activities). Such activities, which result in discussion and examination of a word and its use, and which focus on letters and parts of words, are important and valuable.

It is the discussion, however, and not merely the exposure to print that is important to word use and acquisition. In fact, there is evidence that simple exposure to print in the child's environment is not the critical factor in word recognition and print-vocabulary development. Among others, Stahl and Murray (1993); Gough, Juel, and Griffith (1992); and Masonheimer, Drum, and Ehri (1984) have found that children do not seem to develop word-recognition knowledge from simple exposure to environmental print. In studies that examined children's ability to read print embedded in logos used by fast-food companies, cereals, sneakers, and so on, children who did not already have some knowledge about print focused on the logo as a whole, rather than the print, and the exposure to environmental print embedded within a logo accounted for little word learning. Stahl and Murray (1993, p. 232) state that "Children seem not to attend to the words in logos unless they are already reading words. The print in the logos . . . seems not to be salient for emergent readers and does not seem to be a significant source of word meaning." What appears most important is to develop children's knowledge about print through interactions with print, through interactions with adults about and around print, and through subsequent discussions of new words in context.

Conceptual Links

Research indicates that certain concepts are closely linked with each other (Adams & Collins, 1979; Anderson, Reynolds, Schallert, & Goetz, 1977). For example, if people are asked to say the first word that comes to mind when they are presented with list A, most will respond with the words in list B:

List A	List B
mother	father
boy	girl
man	woman
dog	cat
day	night

Moreover, research in **schema theory** implies that there are sets, or networks, of concepts that appear to help trigger each other (Anderson, 1994; Anderson & Pearson, 1984). For instance, a person given the stimulus word *restaurant* is more apt to respond with *menu*, *food*, or *waiter* than with *car* or *television*.

schema theory A theory about knowledge that says objects and their relationships form a network in memory.

Notice that although the words in the lists are opposites, they are in the same domain; that is, each pair deals with parents, children, pets, and so on. This supports the notion that associated concepts might be stored in memory as being related, and that accessing one concept in a linked network helps to access others associated with it. Thus, instructional practices that attempt to link words into meaningful networks rather than teach each word separately are advocated (Nagy & Scott, 1990). This can be done in a variety of ways, but one common option is teaching in thematic units, as discussed below.

Thematic Clusters. The fact that one concept seems to facilitate access to related concepts implies that vocabulary might be effectively presented in **thematic clusters.**

thematic clusters Instruction that organizes vocabulary instruction around thematically related words and concepts.

Instructional materials intended for children in kindergarten or beginning first grade often take advantage of this—for example, crossword and find-a-word puzzles often use thematically related words. Thematic vocabulary clusters can also be drawn from thematic literature units (see chapter 6).

Children in kindergarten or beginning first grade are often provided "puzzles," after which they write the word in the puzzle. Such activities allow children to match

282 CHAPTER 8 Vocabulary and Literacy

MODEL LESSON

Linking Vocabulary in Thematic Contexts in Jean Marie Clayton's Classroom

Jean Marie Clayton has interactive beliefs that guide her decisions about what to teach, and integrated language learning beliefs that guide her decisions about how to teach. Her interactive beliefs result in her emphasizing all knowledge sources equally. Although this doesn't mean that she teaches everything all of the time, she usually tries to address several knowledge sources in her lessons. For example, she targets vocabulary as well as syntactic knowledge by placing vocabulary words in a paragraph. Her integrated language learning beliefs lead to a mixture of teacher-led and student-led approaches. As you will see below, Jean Marie leads the discussion, but the children provide the examples and are responsible for creating the story that embeds the vocabulary items. As Jean Marie and her students brainstormed together, the children began to get a sense of how the relationship of one word to another can develop an appropriate context:

1. Jean Marie discussed the following words with the children, focusing on the words' meanings, how the words might be related to each other, and so on:

   barn   difficult   handle   horse   cheerful   beautiful

2. The children next wrote a brief story, in small groups, that used the target words. The example included here was suggested by a group of four first-grade students. As each child presented the teacher with an oral sentence, the teacher wrote it on the chalkboard, and the children copied it in their notebooks. The last sentence was provided by the teacher; a title was determined after the story was completed.

   There was a cheerful horse who lived in a barn. The horse was cheerful because he got to live in a big barn and had lots to eat. There was a big handle on the door of the barn. It was difficult to turn. The horse was cheerful because his barn was beautiful.

3. The children underlined the vocabulary words in the story, and then Jean Marie led a discussion of each word's appropriate contextual use and how the words help the story "fit" together and make sense.

---

word-labels and picture clues, and also provide opportunities for each child to write the words. Young children often enjoy beginning crossword or find-a-word puzzles, but it is important to contextualize words in such puzzles within sentences and stories. The model lesson above presents one popular and effective way of teaching vocabulary by linking meanings within a coherent context.

Concept Webs. Webs of related concepts can also be used to present vocabulary. For example, restaurant terms might be diagrammed as a web, with the central component being the most general or generic concept and outlying components representing increasing detail or specificity. The amount of detail in such a concept, or semantic, web varies according to the age and level of students. The semantic web shown on page 284 is reasonably complex.

Semantic webs are most effective when discussion specifically relates to students' background knowledge, explains the concepts behind the words used, and corrects students' misunderstandings (Stahl & Vancil, 1986). In addition, a concept web can contain both known and new concepts, allowing connections to be highlighted between the two (Johnson, Pittelman, & Heimlich, 1986). Marzano and Marzano (1988) have organized more than 7,000 words into semantically related clusters and they present a number of webbing approaches to the teaching of those words. Additional approaches to semantic webbing have been provided by Heimlich and Pittelman (1986).

NIKKI'S

COMMENTS FROM THE CLASSROOM

Because older students have had more life experiences—read more books, visited more places (including Internet sites), and yes, watched more television—I try to build on these experiences and create opportunities for students to attach new words and concepts to their existing knowledge. Angie Davis, a fifth-grade teacher, says she imagines students wearing a velcro suit that represents what they already know. Angie and I try to get new words to "stick" to those "suits," to expand students' existing schema by adding more layers. We use a variety of strategies to get new words to "stick" in students' minds.

We try to use more meaning-centered variations of the "look the new words up in the dictionary or glossary" study strategy. While sometimes the dictionary seems the most efficient way to find out what a list of words mean, merely writing down the meaning often doesn't allow the word to "stick."

My students like to work in pairs. The partners read the word in context, create a new sentence using the word, write their definition, draw a picture of the word (nouns, pronouns, adjectives), perform a demonstration of the word (verbs, adverbs), find a rhyming word, find a word that means the opposite, and create an analogy using the word or describe the situation in which they may have heard the word before or could use the word in the future. At that point, the partners compare their work with the dictionary definition. The partners share their new understanding orally with the rest of the class, or sometimes, if the vocabulary is basic to a thematic unit, the partners place their vocabulary work on a bulletin board—a variation on a word wall. That way, the words are accessible for future writing assignments.

We don't always take time to do each of those things, but if the vocabulary is key to understanding a story or theme, then taking the time to build the foundation is worth it. I have discovered that because the meanings are attached to what the students already know, they seem to have a deeper understanding. Anytime a student has drawn a picture or demonstrated the meaning of the word, it really "sticks"—they don't forget it. An interesting by-product is that students seem to also absorb the correct spelling of a word learned in a more meaning-based way.

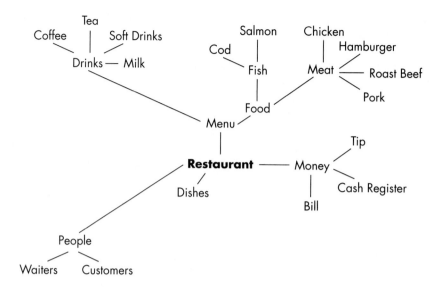

Synonyms.   We know individuals use their interpretive abilities to remember things not specifically stated in what they read. For example, look at the following sentences:

1. The woman was outstanding in the theater.
2. He pounded the nail into the board.

Readers presented with these sentences often believe the words *actress* or *hammer* were used in the respective sentences. Their response suggests that readers remember the essence of what they have read, not the particular words. The process of remembering the key idea as it fits the context is called **instantiation** (Anderson, Pichert, Goetz, Schallert, Stevens, & Trollip, 1976).

Related research has provided a rationale for using synonyms—in addition to appropriate, logically related examples—in vocabulary instruction. If you were teaching the word *hammer,* for instance, you might say something like this:

He hit the nail with a _____.

What word fits in the blank? What other words could be used? Which is most appropriate? Why? What do all the words have in common? You might also approach it this way:

He hit the nail with a *hammer.*

What other words could be used instead of *hammer* (for example, rock, wrench, and so on)? Why could we use those other words? Why might hammer be the best choice? Where might a hammer be found? Such discussion methods use children's prior knowledge and help them place the new concept into a network of similar items (for example, tools, or items used to hammer), thus facilitating learning.

Analogies and Continuums.   Analogies and continuums use known concepts to build new ones, implying that knowledge is organized in a series of related, linked concepts. Using analogies to teach students new words and their uses is appropriate at all grade levels. For example, if students are learning *conductor* and *foal,* they can be presented with items such as these:

Pipe is to water as *conductor* is to electricity.

Dog is to puppy as horse is to *foal.*

Used with discussion, analogies foster concept development because they show the relationship between known items and incorporate the unknown item in a way that helps children to infer the unknown meaning. In this approach, be sure all other words

instantiation
Remembering what the reader perceives to be the most important information in the material that was read.

in the analogy are known and focus the discussion on the relationship within the familiar half of the analogy. Questions about the relationship on the other side of the analogy should then follow naturally.

Continuums, which include meanings that are known as well as one or more to be taught, also facilitate vocabulary development by using prior knowledge. For example, students might be shown the following:

scream   shout   speak   *murmur*   whisper

Discussion of the change in gradation of meaning from left to right presents a scheme in which students can fit the new term—in this case, *murmur.*

Use of Word Parts

Although knowledge of word parts aids in word recognition, it also helps readers discover the meanings of words, which thus expands their vocabularies. Nagy et al. (1992) point out that implicit instruction of word parts, or structural analysis, can help students with word meanings and vocabulary acquisition. They note that instruction in such strategies should take place in sentence context and include discussion about when structural analysis works. Structural analysis should be used together with the other strategies discussed earlier.

When readers use word parts as clues to meaning, they are using their knowledge about affixes (prefixes and suffixes) and root words. **Morphemes,** the smallest meaningful parts of language, include prefixes, suffixes, and root words.

morphemes Prefixes, suffixes, and root words.

For example, these words each contain one morpheme:

play   run   cow

These words contain two morphemes each:

playful   rerun   cows

Knowing the meanings of common prefixes and suffixes can help determine word meanings. For instance, knowing that the prefix *non-* means "not" or "no" helps a reader understand words like *nonprofit, nonsense,* and *nonstop.*

Prefixes, suffixes, and roots often are taught as vocabulary items in literacy instruction. Although teaching all affixes and roots is impossible, teaching the most common ones is worthwhile. Many published lists contain the most useful morphemes—for example, Fry, Kress, and Fountoukidis's *The Reading Teacher's Book of Lists,* 4th ed. (Englewood Cliffs, NJ: Prentice Hall, 2000). In addition, you will be able to use activities such as those shown on page 286 to teach affixes and roots.

Dictionaries

Although dictionary definitions are of relatively minor importance in teaching word meanings, dictionaries can be used to create vocabulary learning experiences. They are also reference sources for students during independent literacy-related activities. Dictionaries can be used at all grade levels: there are many attractive and useful dictionaries for elementary-aged students, beginning with picture dictionaries. Such dictionaries make effective use of color, drawings, photos, and other visual aids to explain and define concepts. Popular primary dictionaries include:

American Heritage First Dictionary: A to Z. (1997). New York: Houghton Mifflin Co.

Costello, R. B. (Ed). (2001). *Macmillan Dictionary For Children.* New York: Simon and Schuster. [This is most appropriate for children aged 9 and up.]

My First Dictionary: Four thousand words and their meanings for young readers. (1991). New York: HarperCollins, Inc.

My First Picture Dictionary. (1993). Richmond Hill, Ontario, Canada: Scholastic.

Scholastic First Dictionary. (1998). New York: Scholastic, Inc.

PRACTICAL TEACHING STRATEGIES

Teaching Affixes and Roots

Affix Deletion. Write several sentences containing words with the same affix:

1. He had to <u>reheat</u> the food because it had cooled down.
2. After she used the towel, Mary had to <u>refold</u> it.
3. Because the color came out of his shirt when it was washed, Sam had to <u>redye</u> it.

Have children state the meaning of each underlined word. Then cross out the affix and discuss how the meaning of the word has changed. Finally, agree on the meaning of the affix.

Affix Addition. Change the previous activity by using the key words without the affixes and asking the children to add them. Present the activity like this:

Re- is a prefix that means "again." Use it to change the meaning of the sentences. (You will have to add it to one of the underlined words and take out the other.)

1. He had to <u>heat</u> the food <u>again</u> because it had cooled down.
2. After she used the towel, Mary had to <u>fold</u> it <u>again</u>.
3. Because the color came out of his shirt when it was washed, Sam had to <u>dye</u> it <u>again</u>.

Discuss with the children that the prefix *un-* means "not" and can have a strong influence on meaning. Present this example:

They were welcome at the picnic.

Then tell children to add *un-* to *welcome* in the sentence and discuss what happens to the meaning of the entire sentence.

Root Word Addition. Write affixes on the chalkboard and have students supply the root words.

-less (without)	-en (like)
care(less)	wool(en)
thought(less)	gold(en)
hope(less)	wood(en)

Affix and Root Word Hunt. Have children look through a reading selection and circle certain prefixes, suffixes, and/or root words. Then have children present their findings, exploring how the meanings of the words would have been different if the prefix or suffix had not been used.

However, we need to remember that using a dictionary to look up an unknown word's meaning requires a number of skills. For example, a child must (1) be able to alphabetize by at least the first letter of a word; (2) be able to locate a word without turning every page of the dictionary; (3) be able to associate a word and its meaning; (4) be aware that a word often has more than one meaning; and (5) use context to select one meaning from alternatives. If these skills are present, the dictionary can be a useful tool, especially as students encounter unfamiliar words in content-area subjects. However, dictionary definitions need to be discussed, used in meaningful examples, and related to students' prior knowledge.

To teach your students the value of using a dictionary, model its use and draw their attention to the reason the dictionary is being consulted (see the previous suggestions for examples). Modeling the use of a thesaurus and a glossary is also effective. Modeling can result in children using these tools independently when they find new words in reading assignments. Certainly, a dictionary and other reference sources, written at an appropriate level, should be available for student use in every classroom.

Teachers support children's vocabulary development in many different ways.

PRACTICAL TEACHING STRATEGIES

Facilitating Dictionary Use as an Aid to Acquiring Word Meanings

Modeling.   Pick an interesting, unknown word and use it incidentally during the day. Say something like this: "Yesterday I heard someone say that he really doesn't like canines. I'd like you to help me look that word up in the dictionary and see what *canine* means." Then have children help you find the word in the dictionary, read the meaning, and relate it to their previous knowledge.

Finding Correct Meanings.   Present sentences like, "She put the fish on the <u>scale</u> to find out how heavy it was" and "Her wedding dress had a long <u>train.</u>" Have children find the underlined words in the dictionary and decide which of the listed meanings make sense in the sentence context.

Learning Centers

A **learning center** is an area in a classroom that contains a variety of instructional materials dealing with a specific goal or objective.

Because it is often used independently by students, provisions are usually made for self-evaluation. Such a center lends itself to vocabulary instruction, whether in thematic units or not. Included in a vocabulary-learning center can be activities related to any of the methods outlined in this chapter. Students can work in pairs or small groups to complete analogy or continuum exercises, create and discuss webs, self-select vocabulary to be learned, revisit (or add to) words in their word banks, and so on.

A learning center, sometimes called an activity center or a learning station, contains a set of activities to support students' learning. Because students work independently, they must be aware of acceptable behavior at the center and must be aware of the goal of the activities. Careful planning is required to create an effective learning center. Huff

learning center A classroom location where instructional materials are used independently by students.

(1983) and Sherfey and Huff (1976) suggest the following steps be considered in planning a learning center:

1. Clearly define the center's purposes.
2. Consider the characteristics and the needs of students who will be using the center.
3. Define the concepts and skills to be developed in the center.
4. Outline expected learning outcomes.
5. Select appropriate activities and materials.
6. Evaluate the center.
7. Implement needed changes.

Children can use learning centers individually or in small groups and should spend about 15 minutes there at one time. The center should be sturdy enough to withstand classroom use and should include a variety of activities focused on the targeted concept. A learning center can contain many things, ranging from teacher-made poster board items to a microcomputer and software. The critical component is how the center is related to overall instructional goals. When well-planned and carefully implemented, learning centers represent an efficient use of classroom time.

Response Cards

response cards   Cards that provide a teacher with immediate information about a child's response.

Another useful and efficient activity in vocabulary instruction and evaluation uses true-false and A-B-C **response cards.**

For this activity, print one to three vocabulary words on cards, along with a response choice as shown in Figure 8-7. The single-word cards are used with true-false responses; the multiple-word cards prompt a response of A, B, or C. The single-word card can also be used as a vocabulary flash card. In addition, children can also perform response-card activities in pairs, using words from their word banks. The following procedural steps are used in response card activities.

1. Ask children to tear a piece of paper into either two (for true-false activities) or three (for A-B-C activities) parts and write either true and false or A, B, and C on their papers.
2. Check your vocabulary cards to be sure that the statements or clues appear on the backs of the cards. The process will flow more smoothly if you don't have to think of sentences or definitions "on the fly."
3. For the true-false activity, hold up a single-word vocabulary card and provide a statement or phrase about the word that is either true or false. For example, for the word *smoke* you might say, "Something that usually is present with a fire" or "Something we eat." Have children hold up their true or false paper in response to each spoken sentence.

FIGURE 8-7

Response cards for use in a vocabulary lesson

4. For the A-B-C word-choice activity, hold up a multi-word vocabulary card and provide context clues to help students choose the appropriate word from the card. Have students hold up their A, B, or C paper to match the letter under the word they think is correct.

This simple procedure can be modified easily, yet it remains valuable for several reasons:

▶ Children are not self-conscious about responding. As the response is not oral and all students face the teacher, other students cannot see an incorrect response.
▶ Teachers do not spend time grading papers or worksheets but gain an overview of student comprehension. With a class list of names handy, you can quickly note the students who show problems with certain words and need individual help.
▶ The cards are inexpensive, easy to make, and simple for students to copy for their word banks.
▶ The activity provides a quick way to review and reinforce previously presented vocabulary.

🖳 Two Special Cases: Homonyms and Referential Terms

Homonyms

Often there is confusion in terminology about what to call words that sound the same. Because a difference exists between words identical in sound and spelling and words that sound the same but are spelled differently, you should learn the following precise terms. Calling them all homonyms is inaccurate and can lead to instructional confusion. Learning the precise terms will help when you encounter them in teacher's guides and in professional reading.

Homophones: Words that sound alike, are spelled differently, and mean different things (for example, "He *led* his horse." "The metal looked like *lead*.").

Homographs: Words that do not sound alike, are spelled alike, and mean different things (for example, "He *read* the book." "He will *read* the book.").

Homonyms: Words that sound alike, are spelled alike, and mean different things (for example, "the bathroom *scale*"; "the fish *scale*").

homophones Words with the same pronunciation but different spellings and meanings.

homographs Words with the same spellings but different pronunciation and meanings.

homonyms Words with the same pronunciation and spelling but different meanings.

Homonyms present an interesting methodological challenge to the teacher. As neither the written nor the oral form of a homonym changes between meanings, young children sometimes become confused when the two meanings are presented together, especially when a teacher focuses attention on the known meaning and then tells students to learn the new meaning (Kinzer, 1982). As students mature, it is appropriate to teach new meanings for homonyms by relating each new meaning to both its word-label and an already-known meaning. But with children in the primary grades, teachers must tread carefully. If the goal is to teach a new meaning for a homonym, then learning the meaning is more important than realizing that the word is a homonym. Thus, teachers in the lower grades should teach new meanings of homonyms in the same way they teach normal words with single meanings.

The suggestion here is not that young students cannot use words in more than one way or with more than one meaning. Children know at an early age that an airplane can *fly* and that a *fly* is a sometimes-bothersome insect. The confusion results when young children are asked to become consciously aware that the label for two separate concepts is the same. Young students seem to believe instead that the two words are separate items even though they sound the same. This ability to see similarity and difference across several dimensions at the same time appears to be unavailable until children can comprehend membership in multiple classes. As young children mature, the ability to perceive multiple meanings with similar labels develops naturally.

Referential Terms

referential properties
Word characteristics requiring readers or listeners to use background to determine what item is being mentioned.

Certain vocabulary terms have **referential properties** and can be fully understood only through experiential knowledge (Murphy, 1986).

In other words, experiences with language clarify certain references not explicitly stated. Consider the following examples and try to decide where Steve is physically located:

1. On the telephone, Steve says, "Come to my house tonight."
2. On the telephone, Steve says, "Go to my house tonight."

Now try to decide where the food is physically located:

3. Sally, Bill, and Tom are sitting at a table. Sally says to Tom, "He has the food."
4. Sally, Bill, and Tom are sitting at a table. Sally says to Tom, "The food is over here."
5. Sally, Bill, and Tom are sitting at a table. Sally says to Tom, "The food is over there."

You probably decided correctly that Steve was at home while on the telephone in the first example and not at home in the second. In example 3, Bill had the food; in example 4, it was near Sally; and in example 5, it was not near Sally. Your ability to specify the locations in these examples indicates your facility with one kind of reference—place reference. Other forms of reference and their effects on the comprehension of text are discussed in chapter 9.

Referential terms can cause great difficulty for young children, and teachers must be aware that vocabulary items often have referential meanings that go beyond the words' literal use. With such terms it is not enough to explain word meanings. Discussion must develop the students' understanding of the referential nature of the terms and should include several examples of their use. Examples of such activities are shown below.

Part of the difficulty children have in understanding referential terms is related to their cognitive level and to the differences between oral and written language. We know that children's understanding of time and place does not develop fully until about third grade (Bybee & Sund, 1990; Lowery, 1981). In addition, written language loses the physical clarifiers of oral communication. For example, in speech the sentence "The food is

PRACTICAL TEACHING STRATEGIES

Teaching the Referential Nature of Pronouns

Pronoun Examples. Use examples to teach pronoun reference in different sentence structures. Use sentence pairs similar to these:

1. a. The teacher gave both Sue and Tabitha erasers, even though the girls didn't need them.
   b. Even though the girls didn't need them, the teacher gave both Sue and Tabitha erasers.
2. a. Chris wanted a drink of water because she was thirsty.
   b. Because she was thirsty, Chris wanted a drink of water.
3. a. Bill said the bike was new, but Tipp didn't believe it.
   b. Tipp didn't believe it, but Bill said the bike was new.

Discuss with the children that some referential terms can refer to items in front of them or behind them. Also, draw attention to the fact that referential terms can refer to one or more words, a phrase, a clause, or a sentence.

Extending Sentences. Present a gradual sentence expansion, leading ultimately to the replacement of one or more parts of the sentence with a referential term(s):

Susie and Willy eat lunch.

They eat lunch.

Susie and Willy eat *it.*

They eat *it.*

over there" or "He has the food" usually is accompanied by some form of head motion or gesture (such as pointing), which clarifies the meaning and makes it more concrete. Saying that print is speech written down is an inaccurate simplification. In text, for instance, quotation marks are intended to aid meaning but can also cause confusion. Try to locate the food in this example:

Sally said, "Tom said, 'The food is here.'"

Thus, cognitive development and differences between oral and written language combine to produce confusion when children are asked to comprehend referential vocabulary terms in text.

Using a Literacy Framework to Inform Your Decisions about Vocabulary Instruction

Your literacy framework will serve as a guide as you decide both what to teach and how to teach vocabulary knowledge to your students. Table 8-1 summarizes how a literacy framework can be used to guide instructional decisions about *what* aspects of vocabulary knowledge to teach.

What to Teach and Emphasize

Teachers who have reader-based beliefs feel that reading consists largely of predicting, or of setting expectations for upcoming words. Thus, they believe that prior knowledge is important to successful reading because readers are able to use this knowledge to accurately predict the meanings of words and, as a result, vocabulary knowledge becomes important. Therefore, they would probably spend little time teaching isolated words or structural analysis that examines the components of words. Instead, they would encourage children to use contextual strategies such as thematic units, concept webs, analogies, and so on.

Teachers who have text-based beliefs feel that reading consists largely of translating words and word parts into sounds and blending these sounds together to form words. Relatively speaking, vocabulary knowledge is not viewed as important when compared to people who hold reader-based beliefs. Thus, they would probably emphasize word parts (prefixes, roots, and suffixes) and activities that analyze how parts join together to

TABLE 8-1

A summary of how a literacy framework can be used to inform decisions about what to teach regarding vocabulary

Issues and Beliefs in a Literacy Framework That Inform This Issue	Instructional Decisions Informed by Your Beliefs
Issue 1. What Should I Teach?	
Meaning exists in what the reader brings to a text, and reading is a result of expectations. Reading begins with elements of prior knowledge. (Reader-based beliefs)	Developing strategic use of context and contextual strategies. Vocabulary as a knowledge source and as part of predicting meanings and relating new vocabulary to already-known concepts would be stressed.
Meaning exists in the text, and reading is translating the text or extracting the meaning from the text. Reading begins with decoding. (Text-based beliefs)	Developing structural analysis skills. Vocabulary would receive emphasis largely as it relates to decoding.
Meaning exists both in the text and the reader. Reading is both translation and expectation. All of the knowledge sources can be used simultaneously. (Interactive language learning beliefs)	Developing each of the knowledge sources is given equal time. Relating new meanings to old, the importance of prior knowledge, and teaching vocabulary within decoding lessons would all occur.

TABLE 8-2

A summary of how a literacy framework can be used to inform decisions about how to teach vocabulary knowledge

Issues and Beliefs in a Literacy Framework That Inform This Issue	Instructional Decisions Informed by Your Beliefs
Issue 2. How Should I Teach?	
Students direct much of their own learning, and inductive learning is emphasized. (Holistic language learning beliefs)	Common method frameworks include contextualized approaches, usually within the language experience approach, shared book experience, Internet method frameworks, morning message, and writing activities. Word lists and skill sheets are not typically used. Big books, children's literature, and oral language form the basis for most vocabulary instruction. Children often are allowed to self-select or indicate which words should be a part of the vocabulary lesson.
Teacher-directed reading activities and deductive learning are emphasized. Specific skills, often organized in terms of difficulty, are frequently taught. (Specific skills beliefs)	Common method frameworks include deductive instruction that targets specific skills such as structural analysis and dictionary knowledge. Instruction often is based on word lists or suggested vocabulary lists from published reading programs.
Both student-directed and teacher-directed experiences are used. Both inductive and deductive learning are used. Reading experiences take place in the contexts of authentic social contexts and with authentic reading materials. Specific skills are taught when needed. (Integrated beliefs)	Common method frameworks include inductive and deductive instruction in skills such as structural analysis and dictionary use as well as contextualized activities such as semantic webs, wide reading, and Internet method frameworks. Words to be taught are both teacher-provided and student-selected.

form meanings. They might also use the dictionary in vocabulary lessons, as it includes word meanings as well as aids to decoding and structural analysis.

Teachers who have interactive language learning beliefs feel that reading consists of both expectations for upcoming word meanings and strong decoding and structural analysis skills, which combine to help students discover and learn word meanings. These teachers would view vocabulary knowledge as equally important as the other knowledge sources that readers use and, as a result, they would probably spend an average amount of time on vocabulary instruction (about the same amount of time as they would spend on the other knowledge sources associated with reading comprehension) and would likely use both context and structural analysis in their vocabulary lessons.

How to Develop Vocabulary Knowledge

Table 8-2 summarizes beliefs about *how* children learn to read and how these beliefs can be used to guide instructional decisions about which method framework to use in vocabulary instruction.

Teachers with holistic language learning beliefs favor learning experiences that are inductive in nature. Thus, they would probably use inductive methods to teach words in context and would integrate vocabulary development into daily classroom activities such as language experience activities, Internet Inquiry, Internet Project, and Internet Workshop, as well as content lessons in mathematics, science, social studies, and so on. They would almost certainly use word banks and encourage children to read widely and interact with print to extend their vocabularies.

Teachers with specific skills beliefs favor learning experiences that are deductive and that focus on specific skills. Thus, they would likely use deductive methods and or-

Featured Teacher

Lisa Brannan

Lisa Brannan is a third-grade teacher at Forest Creek Elementary School in Round Rock, Texas. Her classroom website (http://www.teacherweb.com/TX/ForestCreekElementary/LisaBrannan/index.html; see Figure 8-8) is used as a learning experience for her students and as an informational/outreach tool for her students' parents and on-line visitors. Lisa Brannan uses her website to inform children and their parents about vocabulary assignments that she takes from lists. As is quickly seen from her students' work and her description of classroom activities, vocabulary is also built through writing assignments and a wealth of experiences that she provides.

FIGURE 8-8

Lisa Brannan's classroom web page (http://www.teacherweb.com/TX/ForestCreek Elementary/LisaBrannan/index.html)

ganize vocabulary instruction around word lists such as those discussed on page 278 and target specific skills in vocabulary lessons, such as structural knowledge of words, dictionary use, and so on.

Teachers with integrated beliefs would use both deductive and inductive methods to develop vocabulary knowledge. They would combine all of the approaches discussed in this chapter and would select the words they think should be taught, as well as allow their students to self-select words they feel they need to learn.

Use the self-test questions on http://www.prenhall.com/leukinzer to review the material presented in this chapter.

Major Points

▶ In the primary grades, teachers generally teach the words for already-known concepts. In intermediate grades and beyond, teachers generally teach both concepts and their word-labels.

▶ Before presenting an unknown word, teachers should teach the concept represented by the word.

▶ Vocabulary may be explicitly taught. Lessons can be based on word lists, reading materials, Internet searches, children's oral language, or any combination of these sources.

▶ When teaching vocabulary, teachers should, whenever possible, give concrete examples that are grounded in rich contexts. It is also helpful to compare the features of the unknown items to those of similar, known items.

▶ Vocabulary activities should include many varied examples of the unknown concept in context. Vocabulary words should be revisited often.

▶ The Internet, because of its color and multimedia capabilities, can be a rich source for contextualizing vocabulary teaching and learning.

▶ Homonyms and referential terms can be difficult for children in lower elementary grades to learn.

▶ Vocabulary growth continues throughout life, as known concepts are refined and new concepts are added.

Making Instructional Decisions

1. The following words can be categorized as function (list A); content (list B); and content-specific (list C) words.

is	car	cat	at
shelf	that	cumulus	molecule
beaker	table	microchip	and

Two examples in each list have already been provided, one of which comes from the words presented here. Place each of the remaining words into one of the three lists. Then explain how you might teach the words from each list differently and why.

List A	List B	List C
on	door	ledger
is	shelf	beaker
_____	_____	_____
_____	_____	_____
_____	_____	_____

2. Go to an Internet site such as the **Science Learning Network** (http://www.sln.org) and explore some of the links you find there. Explain how you might use what you find to provide a contextualized vocabulary lesson for third-grade children.

3. Imagine that you need to teach the following new terms to primary-grade students, who already know the meanings given in the second column. Describe your lesson.

To Be Learned	Already Known
fish _scale_	weighing _scale_
human _race_	run a _race_
pig _pen_	_pen_ to write with

4. How might vocabulary teaching differ in primary and intermediate grades? Why? The words in item 3, above, reflect one source of difference, but there are others.

5. Look at two different levels of a published reading program. Examine the introductory material to see how new vocabulary is identified and introduced. How are in-

structional strategies presented in the teacher's guide? Which strategies would you use? Which would you modify or reject? Why?

6. Some people believe that incidental learning is very effective, especially as practiced in whole language classrooms. However, others suggest that direct instruction in word meanings should be combined with such approaches (Jenkins, Matlock, & Slocum, 1989). Will you merge these two findings to teach vocabulary in your classroom? How? As you determine your response, consider your beliefs about how to teach literacy and the implications of these beliefs to vocabulary development.

Further Reading

Beck, I., & McKeown, M. G. (1983). Learning words well—A program to enhance vocabulary and comprehension. *The Reading Teacher, 36,* 622–625.

Describes a program of varied methods to teach vocabulary to fourth-grade students. Involves cognitive, physical, and affective elements.

Gaskins, I. W., Ehri, L. C., Cress, C., O'Hara, C., & Donnelly, K. (1997). Procedures for word learning: Making discoveries about words. *The Reading Teacher, 50* (4), 312–327.

Presents a procedure for helping children to learn words, focusing on structural analysis and spelling patterns as well as word meaning.

Koskinen, P. S., Wilson, R. M., Gambrell, L. B., & Neuman, S. B. (1994). Captioned video and vocabulary learning: An innovative practice in literacy instruction. *The Reading Teacher, 47,* 36–43.

Presents strategies for using captioned video to increase vocabulary learning, especially among lower-ability students.

Nagy, W. E. (1988). *Teaching vocabulary to improve reading comprehension.* Newark, DE: International Reading Association.

A short monograph that presents reasons for the failure of certain types of vocabulary instruction as well as practical suggestions for improving that instruction.

Rasinski, T. V., Nancy, D., Padak, N. P., Church, B. W., Fawcett, G., Hendershot, J., Henry, J. M., Moss, B. G., Peck, J. K., Pryor, E., & Roskos, K. A. (Eds.). (2000). *Teaching word recognition, spelling, and vocabulary: Strategies from* The Reading Teacher. Newark, DE: International Reading Association.

This book includes 17 articles on such topics as word analogy instruction, decoding, phonemic awareness, read-alouds, flashcards, psycholinguistics, spelling development, vocabulary development, scaffolding, and context use. It also includes IRA position statements on early literacy instruction.

Stallman, A. C., Commeyras, M., Kerr, B., Reimer, K., Jiminez, R., Hartman, D. D., & Pearson, P. D. (1990). Are "new" words really new? *Reading Research and Instruction, 29,* 12–29.

A research-based article that examines whether second- and fifth-grade children already know the meanings of vocabulary to be taught in basal readers. It points out the various reasons for including vocabulary lessons in published reading programs and how direct instruction can account for only a small part of the words children learn.

References

Adams, M. J., & Collins, A. M. (1979). A schema-theoretic view of reading. In R. O. Freedle (Ed.), *Discourse processing: Multidisciplinary perspectives.* Norwood, NJ: Ablex.

Allen, J. (1999). *Words, words, words: Teaching vocabulary in grades 4–12.* Portland, ME: Stenhouse Publishers.

Anders, P. L., & Bos, C. S. (1986). Semantic feature analysis: An interactive strategy for vocabulary development and text comprehension. *Journal of Reading, 29,* 610–616.

Anderson, R. C. (1994). Role of the reader's schema in comprehension, learning, and memory. In R. B. Ruddell, M. R. Ruddell, & H. Singer (Eds.), *Theoretical models and processes of reading* (4th ed.), pp. 469–482. Newark, DE: International Reading Association.

Anderson, R. C., & Freebody, P. (1981). Vocabulary knowledge. In J. T. Guthrie (Ed.), *Comprehension and teaching: Research reviews* (pp. 77–117). Newark, DE: International Reading Association.

Anderson, R. C., & Nagy, W. E. (1993). *The vocabulary conundrum.* (Report No. 570). Urbana, IL: University of Illinois, Center for the Study of Reading (ERIC Document Reproduction Service No. ED 354 489).

Anderson, R. C., & Ortony, A. (1975). On putting apples into bottles—A problem of polysemy. *Cognitive Psychology, 7,* 176–180.

Anderson, R. C., & Pearson, P. D. (1984). A schema-theoretic view of basic processes in reading. In P. D. Pearson (Ed.), *Handbook of reading research* (pp. 255–317). New York: Longman Publishing Group.

Anderson, R. C., Pichert, J. W., Goetz, E. T., Schallert, D. L., Stevens, K. V., & Trollip, S. R. (1976). Instantiation of general terms. *Journal of Verbal Learning and Verbal Behavior, 15,* 667–679.

Anderson, R. C., Reynolds, R. E., Schallert, D. L., & Goetz, E. T. (1977). Frameworks for comprehending discourse. *American Educational Research Journal, 14,* 367–381.

Anderson, R. C., Spiro, R. J., & Anderson, M. C. (1978). Schemata as scaffolding for the representation of information in discourse. *American Educational Research Journal, 15,* 433–440.

Beck, I. L., McKeown, M. G., & Kucan, L. (2002). *Bringing words to life: Robust vocabulary instruction.* New York: Guilford Publications.

Beck, I. L., McKeown, M. G., & Omanson, R. C. (1987). The effects and uses of diverse vocabulary instructional techniques. In M. C. McKeown & M. E. Curtis (Eds.), *The nature of vocabulary acquisition* (pp. 147–164). Hillsdale, NJ: Lawrence Erlbaum Associates.

Blachowicz, C. L., & Fisher, P. (2001). *Teaching vocabulary in all classrooms.* Merrill/Prentice Hall.

Bolinger, D. L. (1961). Verbal evocation. *Lingua, 10,* 113–127.

Brown, R., & McNeil, D. (1966). The tip-of-the-tongue phenomenon. *Journal of Verbal Learning and Verbal Behavior, 5,* 325–337.

Bybee, R. W., & Sund, R. B. (1990). *Piaget for educators* (2nd ed.). Prospect Heights, IL: Waveland Press.

Dale, E., O'Rourke, J., & Bamman, H. A. (1971). *Techniques of teaching vocabulary.* Palo Alto, CA: Field Enterprises.

Davidson, S., Stickney, C. P., & Weil, R. L. (1980). *Intermediate accounting concepts, methods and uses.* Hinsdale, IL: The Dryden Press.

Duffelmeyer, F. A. (1985). Teaching word meanings from an experience base. *The Reading Teacher, 39,* 6–9.

Eeds, M. (1985). Bookwords: Using a beginning word list of high-frequency words from children's literature K–3. *The Reading Teacher, 38,* 418–423.

Elley, W. B. (1989). Vocabulary acquisition from listening to stories. *Reading Research Quarterly, 24,* 174–187.

Fry, E., & Sakiey, E. (1986). Common words not taught in basal reading series. *The Reading Teacher, 39,* 395–398.

Gipe, J. (1978–1979). Investigating techniques for teaching word meanings. *Reading Research Quarterly, 14,* 624–644.

Gold, Y. (1981). Helping students discover the origins of words. *The Reading Teacher, 35,* 350–351.

Gough, P. B., Juel, C., & Griffith, P. L. (1992). Reading, spelling, and the orthographic cipher. In P. B. Gough, L. C. Ehri, & R. Treiman (Eds.), *Reading acquisition* (pp. 35–48). Hillsdale, NJ: Lawrence Erlbaum Associates.

Gunderson, L. (1984). One last word list. *Alberta Journal of Educational Research, 30,* 259–269.

Halff, H. M., Ortony, A., & Anderson, R. C. (1976). A context-sensitive representation of word meaning. *Memory and Cognition, 4,* 378–383.

Harris, A. J., & Jacobson, M. D. (1982). *Basic reading vocabularies.* New York: Macmillan.

Heimlich, J. E., & Pittelman, S. D. (1986). *Semantic mapping: Classroom applications.* Newark, DE: International Reading Association.

Hirsch, E. D., Jr. (1989). *First dictionary of cultural literacy.* Boston, MA: Houghton Mifflin.

Hoffman, J. V., McCarthy, S. J., Abbott, J., Christian, C., Corman, L., Curry, C., Dressman, M., Elliott, B., Matherne, D., & Stahle, D. (1994). So what's new in the new basals? A focus on first grade. *Journal of Reading Behavior, 26,* 47–73.

Huff, P. (1983). Classroom organization. In E. Alexander (Ed.), *Teaching reading* (2nd ed., pp. 450–468). Boston, MA: Little, Brown.

Jenkins, J. R., Matlock, B., & Slocum, T. A. (1989). Two approaches to vocabulary instruction: The teaching of individual word meanings and practice in deriving word meanings. *Reading Research Quarterly, 24,* 215–235.

Johnson, D. D., & Pearson, P. D. (1984). *Teaching reading vocabulary* (2nd ed.). New York: Holt, Rinehart & Winston.

Johnson, D. E., Pittelman, S. D., & Heimlich, J. E. (1986). Semantic mapping. *The Reading Teacher, 39,* 778–783.

Katz, J. J. (1972). *Semantic theory.* New York: Harper & Row.

Kinzer, C. K. (1981). Regular vs. mixed meaning's effects on second and sixth graders' learning of multiple meaning words. Unpublished doctoral dissertation, University of California, Berkeley.

Kinzer, C. K. (1982). *Interference effects of known meanings on vocabulary learning: Encountering the unexpected during the reading process.* Paper presented at the annual meeting of the International Reading Association, Chicago, IL.

Kurth, R. (1980). Building a conceptual base for vocabulary development. *Reading Psychology, 1,* 115–120.

Labov, W. (1973). The boundaries of words and their meanings. In J. N. Bailey & R. W. Shuy (Eds.), *New ways of analyzing variations in English.* Washington, DC: Georgetown University Press.

Leech, G. (1974). *Semantics.* New York: Penguin.

Lenneberg, E. H. (1967). *Biological foundations of language.* New York: John Wiley & Sons.

Lowery, L. (1981). *Learning about learning: Classification abilities.* Berkeley: University of California, Berkeley, PDARC Department of Education Publication.

Lyons, J. (1977). *Semantics* (2 vols.). Cambridge, MA: Cambridge University Press.

Marzano, R. J., & Marzano, J. S. (1988). A cluster approach to vocabulary acquisition. Newark, DE: International Reading Association.

Mason, J., Kniseley, E., & Kendall, J. (1979). Effects of polysemous words on sentence comprehension. *Reading Research Quarterly, 15,* 49–65.

Masonheimer, P. E., Drum, P. A., & Ehri, L. C. (1984). Does environmental print identification lead children into word reading? *Journal of Reading Behavior, 16,* 257–271.

Murphy, S. (1986). Children's comprehension of deictic categories in oral and written language. *Reading Research Quarterly, 21,* 118–131.

Nagy, W. E. (1988). *Teaching vocabulary to improve reading comprehension.* Newark, DE: International Reading Association.

Nagy, W. E., et al. (1992). *Guidelines for instruction in structural analysis.* (Report No. 554). Urbana, IL: University of Illinois, Center for the Study of Reading (ERIC Document Reproduction Service No. ED 345 207).

Nagy, W. E., & Scott, J. A. (1990). Word schemas: Expectations about the form and meaning of new words. *Cognition and Instruction, 7,* 105–127.

Nagy, W. E., & Scott, J. A. (2000). Vocabulary processes. In M. L. Kamil, P. Mosenthal, P. D. Pearson, & R. Barr (Eds.), *Handbook of reading research, Volume III* (pp. 269–284). Mahwah, NJ: Lawrence Erlbaum Associates.

Noyce, R. M., & Christie, J. F. (1989). *Integrating reading and writing instruction.* Needham Heights, MA: Allyn & Bacon.

Pittelman, S. D., Heimlich, J. E., Berglund, J. E., & French, M. P. (1991). *Semantic feature analysis: Classroom applications*. Newark, DE: International Reading Association.

Rosch, E. H. (1978). Principles of categorization. In E. H. Rosch & B. B. Lloyd (Eds.), *Cognition and categorization* (pp. 27–48). New York: Lawrence Erlbaum Associates.

Shapiro, J., & Gunderson, L. (1988). A comparison of vocabulary generated by grade 1 students in whole language classrooms and basal reader vocabulary. *Reading Research and Instruction, 27*, 40–46.

Sherfey, G., & Huff, P. (1976). Designing the science learning center. *Science and Children, 14*, 11–12.

Smith, C. B. (1997). Vocabulary and Reading Comprehension. ERIC Clearinghouse on Reading, English, and Communication Digest #126. Available Online. [Accessed 12/29/01]. http:www.indiana.edu/~eric-rec/ieo/digests/d126.html.

Stahl, S. A., & Kapinus, B. (2001). *Word power: What every educator needs to know about teaching vocabulary*. Washington, DC: National Education Association.

Stahl, S. A., & Murray, B. A. (1993). Environmental print, phonemic awareness, letter recognition, and word recognition. In D. J. Leu & C. K. Kinzer (Eds.), *Examining central issues in literacy research, theory, and practice* (pp. 227–233). Chicago, IL: National Reading Conference.

Stahl, S. A., & Vancil, S. J. (1986). Discussion is what makes semantic maps work in reading instruction. *The Reading Teacher, 40*, 62–67.

Vygotsky, L. S. (1962). *Thought and language*. (E. Haufman & G. Vokow, Trans.). Cambridge, MA: MIT Press.

Woodson, M. I. C. E. (1974). Seven aspects of teaching concepts. *Journal of Educational Psychology, 66*, 184–188.

CHAPTER 9

Reading Comprehension: The Construction of Meaning

 E-mail from the Classroom

Subject: Canada Comes Alive
From: Linda Shearin, lshearin@bellsouth.net

The Internet is a great tool for supporting reading comprehension, which makes up the heart of my reading program. In North Carolina, our fifth-grade students engaged in a comparative study of peoples and regions of Canada.

I used the site **Canadiana,** where I located Canadian school home pages. I then e-mailed these schools to contact classes for a collaborative project. Our fifth-grade classes brainstormed questions they wanted to have answered about the Canadian communities.

The first year we did this, our students assumed Canadians still lived in log cabins and cooked over open fires. What a wonderful opportunity this presented to correct some misconceptions about their lifestyle. This worked both ways, because our students were amazed at the Canadian students asking if all our students were "wanded" for weapons before entering school. A great discussion ensued about how the Canadians developed this impression.

When the responses arrived from the Canadian students, our fifth graders were surprised to find out that there were many similarities between themselves and their Canadian counterparts. Our questions piqued the interest of the Canadian students, prompting them to request the same information from us.

Simple but effective communication made our neighbors to the north more real to us, and us to them.

After reading this chapter, you should be able to:

1. Use Internet Workshop, Internet Project, and Internet Inquiry to help children become more proficient at meaning construction.

2. Teach metacognitive strategies important for comprehension by using reciprocal questioning and reciprocal teaching.

3. Teach syntactic aspects of reading comprehension by using author style studies, language experience sentences, and language experience stories.

4. Use appropriate teaching strategies to support the comprehension needs of Limited English Proficiency students in your classroom.

5. Use a literacy framework to inform decisions about what to teach and how to teach reading comprehension.

Teach Reading Comprehension: A Principle of Effective Literacy Instruction

As Linda Shearin's e-mail message points out, reading comprehension is at the center of an effective literacy program. This reflects our next principle:

7. **Teach reading comprehension.** An effective literacy program should integrate systematic instruction in reading comprehension (Anderson, Hiebert, Scott, & Wilkinson, 1985; National Reading Panel, 2000; Snow, Burns, & Griffin, 1998). We should not assume all children will naturally develop effective reading comprehension strategies.

Reading comprehension is a funny thing. We all do it, we all want our children to do it, but few of us know how we do it. How would you explain what you did as you constructed meaning in the preceding paragraph? It's difficult, isn't it? Explaining the comprehension process to someone else is not easy. And yet, in our roles as teachers of reading, this is exactly what we must do. We seek to explain to children how to do something—comprehend information in print—that is very difficult to explain. Most other teaching duties are not nearly so difficult. Two-digit by two-digit multiplication, for example, is something you could easily explain to someone else. Reading comprehension is another matter entirely.

In this book, we describe the nature of literacy processes so you are in a better position to assist children. Discovering how you read and write allows you to become more insightful in helping children perform these activities. Now it is time to focus specifically on reading comprehension and make this important area as clear as possible.

Before getting into the substance of this chapter, let's preview three important concepts at the center of any discussion about how we construct meaning from print: inferential reasoning, using Internet resources to support comprehension, and the nature of reading comprehension instruction. Each is central to understanding this chapter.

One important concept in this chapter is the role inferences play during reading comprehension. Inferences take place as we "read between the lines," filling in missing information not explicitly stated in text. As you will see, much of the meaning we construct from text is not actually in the words themselves. Instead, meaning often is in the connections we make between elements in a text and in the meanings we bring to the text from our different backgrounds. Consider, for example, the meanings Linda Shearin's class initially brought to their communication about Canada and how this made them think of Canadians as "living in log cabins and cooking over open fires." In addition, consider the meanings the Canadian students brought to their communication about the United States and how this made them think of "wands," handguns, and violence.

The meanings you bring to a text contribute to the inferences you make while reading. Understanding this aspect of inferential reasoning informs your teaching in important ways; it allows you to see clearly the source of many comprehension problems and it enables you to help individual children who have difficulties with comprehension.

A second concept is also important in this chapter: knowing how to effectively use the rich information resources on the Internet to support reading comprehension. The Internet and other networked technologies will be central to your students' success at seizing life's opportunities. It is essential to know how to effectively use the Internet to support comprehension. Linda Shearin has provided us with a wonderful model for how this might be done. Her message shows us how children can teach one another about the world around them so that we might all understand one another a little better.

Finally, there is a third concept important to this chapter: Comprehension instruction consists of making visible the many "hidden" strategies we use to construct meaning from text. As young children watch us read silently and comprehend information, it must seem like a mystery to them. They see our eyes move and pages turn, but they never see how we construct meaning from print. All of this is hidden from them.

Every teaching strategy used in comprehension instruction seeks to make visible these invisible strategies of meaning construction. When children hear us explain what we do, they learn much about this complex process. When we hear children explain what they do, we also learn much: We learn what they know, and what they still have to learn, about this "hidden" world of reading comprehension. As you will see, each method framework used to support reading comprehension seeks to make the nature of this process more visible to children so they better understand how to do it themselves.

Let's take a closer look at each of these important ideas about reading comprehension.

How Do Inferences Contribute to Comprehension and Response?

Understanding the nature of inferential reasoning is central to any discussion of reading comprehension. Some refer to inferential reasoning as reading between the lines (Beck, 1989). Strictly speaking, an **inference** is a reasoned assumption about meaning not directly stated in the text. Readers make inferences whenever they add meaning to the explicit, or stated, meaning of a text. You do this with nearly every sentence you read.

There are two basic types of inferences: slot-filling and text-connecting. A **slot-filling inference** occurs when you add background knowledge to a text, thereby filling in missing "slots" of meaning. As you read the next two sentences, for example, you will make many slot-filling inferences, probably without even realizing it.

Mary had a little lamb. Its fleece was as white as snow.

First, you inferred that *Mary* was a little girl. You could have inferred that *Mary* was a ewe. Second, you inferred *had* meant *owned*. You could have inferred that *had* meant *gave birth to* (that is, Mary the ewe gave birth to a little lamb). You could have also inferred that *had* meant *ate* (that is, Mary the girl had a little bit of lamb for her entrée). Finally, you inferred *lamb* referred to a live baby sheep. You could have inferred that *lamb* referred to a stuffed animal. You could also have inferred that *lamb* referred to a type of meat. You can see how slot-filling inferences happen frequently as we read and bring our background knowledge to text.

This is what happened with the U. S. and Canadian students who participated in Linda Shearin's Internet Project. Each group made slot-filling inferences, bringing their prior knowledge about the other students' culture to their initial communication experiences. The Internet Project helped each group to alter their background knowledge about the other's culture. As a result, comprehension of material about the other country was fundamentally changed through this Internet experience.

The second type of inference is a **text-connecting inference,** which occurs when you connect two different pieces of information in a text. Consider again the couplet above. You probably inferred that *its* referred to the lamb. You could have inferred that *its* referred to Mary, the ewe giving birth to the baby lamb. You could have also inferred that *its* referred to the lamb which was eaten by Mary (that is, Mary had a little bit of lamb for her entrée. Its fleece had once been as white as snow).

Reading is very much an inferential process. We use inferences all the time to construct meanings from texts, usually without being aware of the many inferences we make. As teachers, we need to show children how inferences happen and help them to reason effectively with the information they read. This chapter will show you how to do this. Several strategies that take advantage of this insight are described on page 303.

Check your ongoing understanding of chapter concepts by using the guided review for this chapter on http://www. prenhall.com/leukinzer

inference A reasoned assumption about meaning that is not explicitly stated in the text.

slot-filling inference An inference that occurs when a reader uses background knowledge to add meaning to a text.

text-connecting inference An inference that occurs when a reader connects two pieces of textual information to make a reasoned assumption about meaning.

Celebrating Diversity

Using the Internet to Develop Multicultural Understandings

Misunderstandings about different cultural contexts usually result from a lack of background knowledge. Stereotypes and faulty inferences result from a lack of understanding, not something inherent in the human condition. Increase your children's understanding of many different cultural groups by visiting one of several outstanding multicultural resources on the Internet to locate useful resources and gather ideas for classroom use. One of the best central sites we have found in this area is **Multicultural Pavilion** (http://curry.edschool.Virginia.EDU/go/multicultural/). Others include:

The African American Mosaic
(http://www.loc.gov/exhibits/african/intro.html)

Kwanzaa Information Center
(http://www.melanet.com/kwanzaa/)

Multicultural Resources Page
(http://www.ss.uno.edu/SS/Links/McRes.html)

Jewish Culture and History
(http://www.igc.apc.org/ddickerson/judaica.html)

Native American Indian Resources
(http://www.kstrom.net/isk/mainmenu.html)

Kids Web Japan
(http://www.jinjapan.org/kidsweb/)

Supporting Comprehension with Internet Experiences

Reading comprehension will be critical to our children's success in seeking life's opportunities. In a short time, we have moved from an agrarian, to an industrial, to an information age with intense global competition. It is no longer land, labor, or capital that define one's life opportunities in the information age in which we live. Instead, reading comprehension, problem solving, information access, and communication are essential to success. The Internet and other networked technologies will become increasingly important to enable individuals to access the best information in the shortest time as they solve important problems. The Internet will also become important to communicate solutions. Comprehension will be central to these activities.

Experiences with the Internet and other networked technologies will be critical in the instructional program you develop with other resources to support reading comprehension. Internet experiences provide authentic contexts for engaging in information activities, experiences that will increasingly define our children's futures. Internet experiences will not replace traditional comprehension instruction. However, for teachers who are fortunate enough to have Internet access in their classroom, Internet experiences nicely complement the other parts of their comprehension program.

As we consider how to use the Internet to support comprehension, it is helpful to recall the three method frameworks initially described in chapter 2:

- Internet Workshop
- Internet Project
- Internet Inquiry

Internet Workshop, Internet Project, and Internet Inquiry provide wonderful opportunities to develop new comprehension strategies and make these more visible to all your students. During these instructional activities, students have authentic experiences

PRACTICAL TEACHING STRATEGIES

Supporting Inferential Reasoning during Reading

Reading Koala Stories from Australia. Have pairs of primary-grade children visit **Alex's Scribbles** (http://www.scribbles.com.au/max/bookmain.html), a wonderful site in Australia with stories about koalas, kangaroos, and platypuses developed by a young boy, Alex, and his dad. In order to move to the next page, the children must make an inference and click on the correct element in the illustration. This is a wonderful location to help very young children with the challenging task of reading comprehension. Set a bookmark!

Developing Background Knowledge on the Internet. Before you begin an instructional unit or literature selection, develop background knowledge with Internet Workshop, using a WWW page related to the topic. Before a unit on Benjamin Franklin, for example, have your children visit **The World of Benjamin Franklin** (http://sln.fi.edu/franklin/rotten.html); before a unit on the Civil War, have your children visit **Selected Civil War Photographs Home Page** (http://rs6.loc.gov/cwphome.html). Have children explore the location and share information they discover during the workshop session. Using Internet Workshop like this develops important background knowledge so that children are more likely to make appropriate inferences.

Always Ask "How Did You Figure that Out?" When you discuss a story selection, always ask children how they figured out the meanings they constructed. This results in children explaining their inferential thinking to other children, which is always a useful activity as you seek to make these hidden processes more visible.

with information resources as they engage in critical thinking, analysis, and synthesis. This section will explore the potential of each method framework to support the comprehension program in your classroom.

Using Internet Workshop to Support Reading Comprehension

Internet Workshop should be the centerpiece for effective Internet use in your classroom, especially if you also use Internet Project or Internet Inquiry. Internet Workshop may be combined with each of these method frameworks, providing children with opportunities to share their discoveries and sharpen their critical thinking skills.

You will recall **Internet Workshop** is usually defined around these steps:

1. Locate a site(s) on the Internet with content related to a classroom unit of instruction and set a bookmark for the location(s).
2. Develop an activity requiring students to use the site(s).
3. Assign this activity to be completed during the week.
4. Have students share their work, questions, and new insights at the end of the week during Internet Workshop.

> **Internet Workshop** A method framework containing these steps: locate a site with content related to instruction, develop an activity requiring the use of this site, assign the activity, and have students share their work.

Internet Workshop can support several aspects of your comprehension program. First, it is useful for developing background knowledge central to thematic units of study. Second, it enables you to share comprehension strategies effective in navigating Internet resources. Making "hidden" strategies more explicit in these conversations provides important support to children struggling with how to construct meaning from the complex information resources on the Internet. In addition, it permits you to develop the critical literacies so essential to information evaluation today. Finally, it permits you to develop the new comprehension strategies important to reading and communication on the Internet.

Many teachers use Internet Workshop at the beginning of a cross-curricular thematic unit, seeking to develop important prior knowledge and critical thinking useful to students during the upcoming unit of study. As students complete an activity designed by a teacher, they encounter concepts and resources on the Internet that will be useful in

FIGURE 9-1

A portion of the screen at **Kids Web Japan** (http://www.jinjapan.org/kidsweb/), the location used by Diane Thorton to develop background knowledge before beginning a unit on Japan

Note: Courtesy of Kids Web Japan.

their unit. This allows students to share the background knowledge they develop. It also provides important opportunities to discuss navigation, critical thinking, and comprehension strategies students found useful as they completed the activity. Each type of experience supports comprehension in important ways.

Figure 9-2 illustrates an Internet Workshop developed to introduce sixth-grade students to a thematic unit on Japan. Diane Thorton, the teacher who developed this activity, based it on the many resources available at **Kids Web Japan** (http://www.jinjapan.org/kidsweb/), a site appearing in Figure 9-1. After completing the activity, she had her students share the information they located during Internet Workshop. They also shared how they found the information so that others could learn from their discoveries. The model lesson on page 307 that describes how this took place.

Using Internet Project with Internet Workshop to Support Reading Comprehension

Internet Project A method framework with these steps: develop a collaborative project, post a description on the Internet, arrange collaboration details with participating teachers, and complete the project.

You will recall from chapter 2 that **Internet Project** usually follows these procedures:

1. Develop a collaborative project with a summary of the project, a clear list of learning goals, expectations you have for collaborating classrooms, and a projected timeline for beginning and ending the project.
2. Post the project description and timeline several months in advance at one or several locations, seeking collaborative classroom partners.
3. Arrange collaboration details with teachers in other classrooms who agree to participate.
4. Complete the project, exchanging information with your collaborating classrooms.

Perhaps the best way to illustrate the potential of this approach for supporting reading comprehension is to review one of the best examples of Internet Project we have seen. It was posted by a teacher in Boston to the **KIDLIT-L** mailing list as she sought other classrooms to join her class with this project. Take a careful look at the

FIGURE 9-2

An Internet activity page developed by Diane Thorton to introduce a unit on Japan

---

EXPLORING JAPAN

Internet Researcher: _____   Date: _____

<u>Objectives</u>

This Internet Workshop will introduce you to our unit on Japan. You will have an opportunity to explore an important resource on the Internet for our unit. You will also learn about recent news events from Japan and learn to think more critically about what you read on the Internet.

<u>News about Japan</u>

1. Go to the bookmark I have set for **Kid's Web Japan** (http://www.jinjapan.org/kidsweb/) and scroll down to the bottom of this page. Now click on the button "Monthly News" (http://www.jinjapan.org/kidsweb/news.html) and read several recent news stories from Japan. Choose ones of interest to you. Find out what is happening in Japan and be ready to share this during Internet Workshop.

   _____
   _____
   _____
   _____

<u>Critical Thinking</u>

2. Be a detective. What clues can you find at **Kid's Web Japan** (http://www.jinjapn.org/kidsweb/) to indicate the information at this site comes from the government of Japan? Write them down and bring these clues to Internet Workshop. How did you find them? Write down the strategies you used.

   _____
   _____
   _____
   _____

3. If the information at this location comes from the government of Japan, how might this shape the news stories presented in "Monthly News" (http://www.jinjapan.org/kidsweb/news/html)? Write down your ideas and bring them to Internet Workshop.

   _____
   _____
   _____
   _____

Continued

Looney Lobsters Love Regional Literature project description in Marjorie Duby's e-mail message on page 308.

You can see how this one project has tremendous potential for supporting reading comprehension. By reading regional literature selections from around the country, children develop important background knowledge about the world around them. Moreover, the discussions that take place will provide important opportunities for learning about comprehension as classes plan their activities, read messages from other classrooms, compose messages describing their experiences, read literature selections in class, share these stories with "reading buddies" in younger grades, and engage in many other experiences arising out of this project. Internet Project is an exciting vehicle for supporting reading comprehension.

FIGURE 9-2

Continued

<u>Your Choice</u>

4. Visit at least one of the many other locations at **Kids Web Japan.** You decide where to go! Write down notes of what you discovered and share your special discoveries with all of us during Internet Workshop.

_____

_____

_____

_____

_____

_____

_____

_____

<u>Evaluation Rubric:</u>

8 points—You recorded important information for each item (4 × 2 = 8 points).
2 points—You effectively shared important information with us during our workshop
        session, helping each of us to learn about Japan.
10 points—Total

If you engage in Internet Project with other classes around the world, Internet Workshop takes on a special quality. It becomes an opportunity to read messages together arriving from project classrooms, discuss plans for project participation, share activities related to the project, compose new messages to project partners, and complete other tasks related to the project. Sometimes these activities will be completed by individuals or by groups who then report to the entire class. Internet Workshop becomes the focal point for participation and planning activities with Internet Project. As a result, discussion naturally focuses on new strategies for comprehending information as these are shared during Internet Workshop.

Using Internet Inquiry with Internet Workshop to Support Reading Comprehension

Internet Inquiry A method framework with these phases: question, search, analyze, compose, and share.

Internet Inquiry is a method framework that allows individuals or groups to identify an important question and gather information as they seek answers to their question. Internet Inquiry is a student-directed activity since it turns over much of the responsibility for learning to students who explore issues important to them. You will recall from chapter 2 that Internet Inquiry includes five phases:

1. Question
2. Search
3. Analyze
4. Compose
5. Share

Opportunities exist during each phase to support the development of reading comprehension. Often this will take place during Internet Workshop sessions. During the question phase, for example, different questions may be brainstormed by children and recorded on the chalkboard. The discussion about each question often helps children to clarify what they know and what they need to know related to each topic. Exchanging information about these topics during conversations helps develop important background knowledge before children begin their research.

MODEL LESSON

Using Internet Workshop to Support Reading Comprehension

Diane Thorton is starting a cross-curricular thematic unit on Japan in her sixth-grade class. The unit will include reading, writing, social studies, and spelling. Diane has reader-based beliefs about *what* to teach; prior knowledge components are more important to her than decoding. In addition, she has an integrated perspective about *how* to teach, believing that some students learn best through direct instruction but that most of her students learn best when they direct their own learning activities or learn collaboratively from one another. She designed this Internet Workshop activity for three purposes: to build prior knowledge about Japan before she begins her unit, to develop critical thinking strategies, and to develop navigation strategies at an important location on the WWW she plans to include in her unit.

Locate a Content-Related Internet Site and Set a Bookmark. Searching for a central site for Japan, Diane visited **Yahooligans!** (http://www.yahooligans.com), a location with links checked for child safety. Then she went to the "Countries" location, looking for links to sites in Japan. She discovered a wonderful location, sponsored by the Japanese government, for kids around the world: **Kids Web Japan** (http://www.jinjapan.org/kidsweb/). She set a bookmark on the single Internet computer in her classroom.

Develop an Activity Requiring Students to Use the Site(s). Diane spent about 15 minutes simultaneously exploring the information at **Kids Web Japan** and developing the activity in Figure 9-2. She switched back and forth from the word-processing program on her computer to her Internet browser to create the activity page. When she was done, she printed out copies of the activity page for the entire class.

Assign this Activity to Be Completed during the Week. On Monday, Diane briefly introduced the activity and the activity page to her students. She told her students they should complete their work during the two half-hour sessions each student had available that week on the Internet. Diane told her class to bring all of the great information they discovered about Japan to Internet Workshop on Friday.

Have Students Share during Internet Workshop. On Friday afternoon, Diane has her class gather their chairs into a circle for Internet Workshop. She reminds them to bring their activity page with their notes. She invites children to share what they learned and to ask questions about their experiences. The discussion is a rich one, with many wonderful discoveries shared with the class. Strategies about using good locations at the site are also shared; these will be useful in upcoming weeks when students will be asked to complete Internet Inquiry. In addition, they discussed the importance of critically thinking about who created the information at this Internet site and how this might shape the information presented here. At the end of the 30-minute session, Diane is certain this experience has provided her students with a wonderful opportunity to develop background knowledge and critical thinking, as well as to prepare them for the reading and writing experiences next week when they begin their unit on Japan.

Because she has reader-based beliefs in her literacy framework, Diane was concerned about developing background knowledge students could bring to upcoming reading experiences about Japan. She also wanted to develop navigation strategies at this WWW site for her students, which is another aspect of prior knowledge readers bring to texts. Notice, for example, how Diane created open-ended tasks on her activity sheet. A teacher with text-based beliefs would have asked students to find the same, specific information at the website (e.g., How many people live in Japan? Who is the prime minister of Japan? What is fall like in Japan?).

Diane also has integrated beliefs about how to teach. Consistent with specific skills beliefs, Diane designed the activity sheet for students to complete rather than allow children to determine their own experiences at this site. Consistent with holistic language learning beliefs, however, she developed each question to allow individuals to explore the information they wanted to learn more about. Then, at the workshop session, individuals shared their discoveries with their colleagues. A teacher with specific skills beliefs would have limited children to only visit locations at the site he or she wanted them to visit and probably would not have included Internet Workshop to share learning experiences. Students would simply complete the task as the teacher directed. There would be little opportunity for children to direct their own learning experiences.

E-mail from the Classroom

From: Marjorie Duby, mduby
Subject: Looney Lobster Loves Regional Literature

Hello to all!

My fifth-grade class in Boston, Massachusetts, and I are in the planning stages to begin the second year of the travels of Looney Larry and Looney Lester Lobster. For this school year the project title will be "Looney Lobsters Love Regional Literature." If any of you have an elementary school class and are interested in the project, let me know.

PROJECT BACKGROUND

Last year our traveling stuffed crustaceans, Looney Larry and Looney Lester of Boston, Massachusetts, accepted the gracious hospitality of elementary school classrooms across the United States for one school week and then were mailed to another classroom, eventually returning to Boston.

They received cuddles, pets, and tours of local sites. They learned of local customs and culture. As we kept in touch with them and others through the Internet via electronic mail and our **Looney Lobster on the Loose** website at http://bps.boston.k12.ma.us/rc328sb/looney.html, we learned much virtually.

Our Looneys enjoyed traveling and learning so much that they would like to again travel the United States learning about local regional literature.

OUR PROJECT ANNOUNCEMENT

Would you be willing to show hospitality in your elementary school classroom for one school week to our traveling Looney? During Looney's visit, would you be willing to read aloud picture books based on local lore—a folktale, a custom, a happening, or a regionally identifiable daily life story?

What we will send

A small box which will include:

1. A small pouch with Looney Lobster, a small, cuddly, stuffed crustacean.
2. A photo album showing our class members—on our travels around Boston and in our classroom.
3. Looney Lobster's itinerary.
4. A single-use camera.
5. A pouch of SASE envelopes.

What we will ask that you do

1. In your message of interest, identify the title and author of a picture book(s) based on your local lore—a folktale, a custom, a happening, or a regionally identifiable daily life story—which your class will read aloud to Looney during his visit to your school.
2. Immediately after being notified of your acceptance into the project, arrange to send a photo of your class (digitized, photocopy of a photo, or original photo), possibly holding a copy of the regional book they will read aloud during your school week.
3. Once they are accepted into the project and the "Looney Lobsters Love Regional Literature" book list is created, begin to locate the book list entries at your local library for read-aloud use during the scheduled school weeks.
4. Subscribe to our Looney Lobster Listserv (mailing list) which will network participants, allowing students to converse about the literature and the daily experiences of Looney.
5. Send electronic mail messages related to Looney's visit to the Looney mailing list.
6. If possible, create a school-based web page of Looney's travels and experiences linked to our **Looney Lobsters Love Regional Literature** web page.

E-mail from the Classroom

Continued

7. With the single-use camera, take a close-up picture of your state's license plate and two other pictures of your choice.
8. Remove one of the SASE from the box. Inside the envelope, place the front page of your local newspaper.
9. Following Looney Lobster's scheduled visit to your school, immediately send him to his next scheduled site, allowing a minimum of 4 days for Priority Mail travel.

What we will be doing

1. Calculating the accumulated mileage for our Looney Lobsters.
2. Locating the latitude and longitude of each city that our Looneys visit.
3. Becoming aware of the daily time zones for each school that Looney Lobster visits.
4. Observing the daily weather of Looney's host school and comparing it to our weather.
5. Obtaining from our local library the regional literature suggested by participants for each scheduled Looney visit.
6. Reading aloud the weekly book list suggestion to our lower grade reading buddies.
7. Reacting to the read-aloud selections with other participant students through the mailing list.
8. Receiving the SASE information that is sent to us as our Looneys move to the next school site.

How we will let you know about Looney's travels:

1. We will have a web page that will include Looney's itinerary, the regional literature book list, and the daily adventures of Looney.
2. Our group will telecommunicate using our Looney Lobsters mailing list and individual electronic mail messages.
3. We will gather and distribute, prior to the beginning of the project, a "Looney Loves Regional Literature Participant Handbook" featuring the itinerary, the book list resources, and the pictures of participant school classes.

If you are interested in hosting Looney Lobster and participating in this project, please respond to: mduby@boston.k12.ma.us

Our project announcement resides at: http://bps.boston.k12.ma.us/rc328sb/rlit.shtml.

========================

Marjorie Duby, Grade 5
Joseph Lee School, Boston, Massachusetts
"The Home of Looney Lobster"
http://bps.boston.k12.ma.us/rc328sb/looney.html

Visit our home page at
http://bps.boston.k12.ma.us/rc328sb/D4.html

During the search phase, children often find it useful to exchange research strategies. Calling children together for short workshop sessions to exchange library resources, WWW locations, and strategies for finding information can be important to children unfamiliar with independent inquiry.

During the analyze phase, help children determine the accuracy of information they locate on the Internet. Literacy on the Internet requires new forms of critical thinking and reasoning about the information that appears in this venue. Anyone may publish anything on the Internet. Traditional forces, guaranteeing some degree of control over

Research reports in all content areas are enhanced by using the Internet, and these activities support background knowledge and reading comprehension as well.

the accuracy of information in published books, do not exist. As a result, children may sometimes encounter web pages created by people with political, religious, or philosophical stances that distort the nature of the information they present to others. Sometimes, a person simply gets the facts wrong on a web page. This requires us to help our students become "healthy skeptics" about the accuracy of information they encounter. Such skills have not always been central in classrooms, where textbooks and other traditional information resources often are assumed to be correct.

You can help to accomplish this important skill by requiring children to provide at least two references for each important piece of information gathered from the Internet and inviting children to bring instances of contradictory information to Internet Workshop for discussion. Both strategies begin to sensitize students to the important issue of information accuracy on the Internet.

The compose phase of Internet Inquiry often relies on writing process stages (see chapter 7). Peer revision conferences often are helpful in assisting authors to become sensitive to the comprehension needs of their readers. These conversations can lead to important insights about reading comprehension and comprehension strategies.

The share phase of Internet Inquiry may also be used to heighten awareness about useful comprehension strategies. As students share their work, direct the audience to share what they found especially useful as a listener or reader. Discussion about these elements often leads to important insights about comprehension and composing strategies. The next page shows a model lesson of Internet Inquiry with Internet Workshop.

Supporting Reading Comprehension in Traditional Texts

As we indicated at the beginning of this chapter, comprehension instruction seeks to make visible the many "hidden" strategies we use to understand written information. While comprehension takes place within every component of the reading process, the following sections will focus our attention on supporting comprehension within metacognitive, discourse, and syntactic components.

MODEL LESSON

Using Internet Inquiry with Internet Workshop to Support Reading Comprehension

Diane Thorton is concluding her cross-curricular thematic unit on Japan. She decides to spend a portion of the final two weeks on this unit using Internet Inquiry. Diane has reader-based beliefs about *what* to teach and an integrated perspective about *how* to teach. Each activity has supported the meaning children bring with them to their reading experiences. Diane developed each activity to focus on areas she thought were important, but it also permitted students to direct their own learning.

Diane chooses to use Internet Workshop in conjunction with Internet Inquiry. She tells her students their inquiry project will be developed to explore a question of Japanese culture, history, or geography important to them. They use the first session of Internet Workshop to brainstorm research questions.

As students and small groups explore their questions, they get together again in Internet Workshop sessions to exchange research strategies, navigation strategies, resources they have discovered in the library, and web locations.

She also directed a workshop session, showing students how to cite Internet resources in their projects. She found useful information about this issue at several locations:

> ▶ **The Learning Page of the Library of Congress: Citing Electronic Sources**
>   (http://lcweb2.loc.gov/ammem/ndlpedu/resources/cite/)
> ▶ **Citing Electronic Resources** (http//www.ipl.org/ref/QUE/FARQ/netciteFARQ.html)
> ▶ **Citing Internet Resources** (http://www.classroom.com/community/connection/howto/
>   citeresources.jhtml)

At the end of the 2-week inquiry period, Diane's students share their research in a "Social Studies Fair." Each student or small group prepares a short written report as well as a poster board presentation. Students from the other sixth-grade classes visit their presentations during one afternoon. As students visit, they are asked to read each brief report and complete a form, identifying two aspects about the report they liked, making it easy to understand. These comments are then used in a final workshop session after the fair. Students share their comments and engage in conversation about useful strategies for comprehending and composing informational writing.

Diane's decisions about what to teach were informed by her reader-based beliefs about how children read. You can see how she focused more on prior knowledge elements, especially metacognitive knowledge and the important strategies used to locate and evaluate information.

Teachers with a text-based belief about what to teach would have spent less time than Diane on helping students develop strategies for reading comprehension. These teachers tend to assume that if children can decode the information they encounter, comprehension will take care of itself. They focus on the meaning in texts rather than the strategies and other knowledge children bring to these texts.

Diane's decisions about how to teach were informed by her integrated beliefs about how children learn to read. You can see how she combined student-directed and teacher-directed learning experiences.

Teachers with a specific skills belief about how to teach probably would not have selected Internet Inquiry since this is an instructional method that depends on students to direct their own learning. If teachers with specific skills beliefs used this method, they would have directed students to research topics specified by the teacher, not generated by students. Moreover, specific comprehension skills would have been taught before the unit and the unit would have been used as an opportunity to practice those skills. In addition, Internet Workshop would probably not be used to share learning experiences.

Historically, the teaching strategies described in these sections were developed for use with traditional texts. However, as you will see, they may also be used during experiences with the Internet and other electronic texts.

Developing Comprehension through Metacognitive Knowledge

Metacognitive knowledge, which includes the strategies we use during reading, contributes to reading comprehension in many important ways. As texts become more complex, new forms of strategic knowledge are required to facilitate comprehension. One

metacognitive knowledge   A type of knowledge important for reading that includes the strategies used during reading and comprehension monitoring.

MODEL LESSON

Reciprocal Questioning in Tammy Norton's Class

Tammy has an interactive belief about *what* to teach. She considers all components of the reading process important to develop. She has an integrated belief about *how* to teach. She finds some children do best when they direct their own literacy experiences. Other children do best when Tammy teaches in a more direct fashion. Tammy uses reading workshop in her combined first- and second-grade classroom. The children in the group she is working with today need support at reasoning with the information in text. Their comprehension is not always as good as it might be. Tammy thinks it is because they need support at asking themselves questions about what they are reading. She has brought multiple copies of *Nate the Great and the Snowy Trail* by Marjorie Weinman Sharmat to the mini-lesson. The story tells how Nate the Great discovers his lost birthday present by following several clues.

Teacher and Students Read. Tammy passes out a copy of the book to each student. Together they talk briefly about the author and look at the cover illustration. Tammy asks students what they think the story might be about. Several possibilities are identified. In the course of the discussion, several important story concepts emerge and are explained. Then Tammy tells her students that good readers act like detectives, asking themselves questions and looking for clues to the meaning of a story. She asks her students to read the first page silently.

Students Question Teacher

Tammy:	Now, what questions do you want to ask me about what we've read? Let's try to ask questions with answers that aren't right in the story. Let's see whether I can really use the clues in the story.
Tomás:	OK, how about this: How did Nate the Great and Sludge feel?
Tammy:	That's a good one. I think they were cold and wet. The story talks about the snow dog and the snow detective that Nate was making. That's one clue. It also says, "They were cold, and white, and wet." That's another clue that helped me. Then Nate says, "And so were we." That's another clue. I put these sentences together and figured out that Nate and Sludge were cold and wet.
Dominic:	What was Nate the Great?
Tammy:	Oh, that's easy. He was a detective. It says right there in the book, "I, Nate the Great, am a detective." Can you ask me a question with an answer that isn't right there in the book?
Dominic:	What time of year was it?

strategy many readers use is to ask questions of themselves about the meanings they are constructing as they read. To support the use of this strategy, it is important to show children how to ask themselves questions as they read. Two method frameworks are most commonly used: reciprocal questioning and reciprocal teaching. Each shows children how to ask themselves questions as they comprehend text.

Reciprocal Questioning

reciprocal questioning (ReQuest) A method framework designed to improve metacognition and comprehension; involves reading and questioning by both teacher and students, predicting, and checking predictions.

Reciprocal questioning (ReQuest) is a method framework first developed by Manzo (1969). The following steps are often used:

1. Teacher and students read.
2. Students question teacher.
3. Teacher questions students.
4. Students predict the story's outcome.
5. Teacher and students finish reading to check predictions.

Tammy Norton uses reading workshop to organize her reading program. In the model lesson above, she uses reciprocal questioning to help a small group of her students develop greater strategic knowledge, especially regarding the questioning of events taking place in a story.

Tammy: Good. I was wondering about that, too. I think it was winter. It doesn't say that anywhere, does it? But they were making a snow detective and a snow dog. Those are the clues that made me think it was winter.

Teacher Questions Students

Tammy: OK, my turn. I've got one that will really make you think. I was wondering about what kind of stories Nate likes to read.

Mike: I know. I think he likes mysteries. It says he's a detective, and detectives like to solve cases, like in *Encyclopedia Brown*.

Tammy: Well done. That was hard, but you found the clue the author left for you. Now let's read by ourselves to page 21. Try to find out what you think the problem in this story is.

Tammy repeats these three steps several times as she and the students read the story.

Students Predict the Story's Outcome. Just before the solution is revealed, Tammy asks her students what they think the birthday present will be. Answers range from a sled, to a book, to a cat. Each child explains the reasoning behind his or her prediction.

Teacher and Students Finish Reading to Check Predictions. Tammy has her students read the rest of the story. She asks them to find out what the present is and how Nate discovers it. Afterward they discuss all the clues in the story that should have told a good detective what the present was. Tammy concludes by stating that readers need to be detectives, too. Just like Nate the Great, they need to ask questions and look for clues as they are reading.

Because reciprocal questioning develops metacognitive knowledge, this method framework is used most often by teachers who seek to develop the meanings readers bring to texts, (i.e., by teachers with reader-based or interactive beliefs about the first issue in a literacy framework: What should I teach?). Teachers with text-based beliefs typically do not use reciprocal questioning. Their discussions focus on meaning explicitly stated in a text.

Teachers who take a holistic language learning stance in relation to the second issue in a literacy framework (How should I teach?) will encourage students to frequently question one another during reciprocal questioning. Teachers with a specific skills stance will believe it is more useful to have teachers question students during reciprocal questioning.

During the first step, both teacher and students read a portion of the selection silently. With beginning readers, this might be just a sentence or two. With better readers, longer portions of a story should be used—perhaps a paragraph, a page, or even several pages.

The second step has students ask the teacher questions about what they have read. During this phase, encourage students to ask challenging questions that require inferential thinking. As you answer these questions, take the opportunity to make visible the "hidden" processes used during comprehension, explaining the thought process you used to figure out the answers.

Next, ask questions of the students about the same story portion. In their answers, invite students to explain the evidence they used and the reasoning they applied to the problem. After each answer ask, "How did you figure that out?" Making the strategies used to determine an inference explicit helps everyone develop new comprehension strategies.

These three steps are then repeated with succeeding portions of the reading selection. As you work your way through the passage, ask questions of one another and share the comprehension strategies you used to understand different aspects of the story.

Whenever an important event in the story is about to occur, ask children to predict what will happen next. This fourth step is similar to the predicting step of a DRTA. Ask children what they think will take place or how they think the story will end. As a part of their answers, children should again explain their reasoning processes. Share your own prediction and explain your reasoning.

MODEL LESSON

Reciprocal Teaching in Bridget Clancy's Class

Bridget Clancy has reader-based beliefs about *what* to teach. She believes the meanings and strategies that readers bring to a text are more important than the meaning in a text. She likes using reciprocal teaching because it develops the important comprehension strategies readers bring to a text and use during the meaning construction process. Bridget also has integrated beliefs about *how* to teach. She believes students should direct their own learning, but that teachers have an important role to play, too. She likes reciprocal teaching because it allows both teachers and students to direct the learning of important strategies, making these hidden strategies more visible to everyone. Bridget has a chart on the board listing the steps for reciprocal teaching and the questions to be asked at each step. She is conducting a mini-lesson with a small group of children during reading workshop. Bridget and her students have read the first two pages of *The History of Chocolate* by James Reder. They are now reading the following portion of this informational book:

> The people of Spain didn't want other people to find out about this special drink that came from the Aztecs in Mexico. They kept it a secret for more than a hundred years.
>
> Finally, though, other people found out about the secret. They learned where the special beans came from. Then they started growing the kakahuatl tree, or cacao tree, in other parts of the world so they could get more of the special beans. Still, only the very rich people could afford the special chocolate drink because these cacao beans were so expensive.
>
> Today, cacao beans grow around the world and chocolate is not so expensive. We can eat chocolate now because so many cacao trees produce the chocolate bean.

Summarize

Bridget: Let's see. Let me look on our chart here. First, I need to summarize and ask myself, "What did I read?" Well, I read that Spain kept the secret of chocolate, but now it's not a secret, and we can all eat chocolate. I'm glad about that. I really like chocolate.

Clarify

Bridget: Now let's see. I need to ask, "Are there any parts that are not clear to me?" Yes. I'm not really clear about why there are so many cacao trees now and chocolate is not so expensive. I'd better read that part again. [Bridget reads the passage aloud.] Here it is. It says, "They learned where the special beans came from. Then they started growing the kakahuatl tree, or cacao tree, in other parts of the world so they could

---

Finally, you and your students should read to the end of the selection to check your predictions. A short discussion of the story's conclusion might be appropriate to end this step.

Reciprocal questioning is a method framework that may be used to guide the reading of a story with a group of children during a mini-lesson. It allows the discussion to focus on comprehension and the critical thinking strategies that contribute to comprehension. Reciprocal questioning can be used at all grade levels.

Once children are familiar with the reciprocal questioning process, you can ask them to follow this procedure as they work in pairs on the Internet in your classroom. Have them bring the new strategies they use to an Internet Workshop to share with others.

Reciprocal Teaching

reciprocal teaching   A method framework designed to improve metacognition and comprehension with these steps: summarize, clarify, question, and predict.

Reciprocal teaching is a second method framework often used to develop important comprehension strategies (Palincsar, 1986; Palincsar & Brown, 1984). It is especially useful in helping students develop their ability to monitor the developing understanding of a passage and to ask themselves questions about their understanding of a passage. Reciprocal teaching consists of four steps repeated by the teacher and students as they read a passage:

- ▶ Summarize
- ▶ Clarify

get more of the special beans." More and more people must have kept learning about the beans, because it also says, "Today, cacao beans grow around the world and chocolate is not so expensive."

Question

Bridget: Now I need to ask a question a teacher would ask about this portion of the passage. Let's see. Are there more cacao trees now or when the Spanish were keeping their secret?

Toni: I know. There are more now.

Bridget: Good. How did you figure that out?

Toni: I read two things in the story and put them together. First it says everyone is growing them around the world, and it also says that chocolate is not so expensive now. If we had fewer trees today, it would be more expensive, not less.

Predict

Bridget: Great! Now I need to ask, "What will probably happen next in this passage?"

Raghib: I think we're going to read about the different kinds of chocolate they make. We just read about how we all can eat chocolate. It sounds like the author is going to tell us about the different kinds they make.

Bridget: Let's read the next two pages to ourselves and find out what the author talks about next.

Bridget and her students read the next two pages silently. They discover that Raghib's guess was correct. Then Bridget guides one of her students to follow the same steps she has just modeled. When the student finishes by making a prediction about the next portion, Bridget and her students read several more pages silently. Then another student becomes the teacher and completes each of the four steps. This process is repeated until the informational selection is completed.

Reciprocal teaching often is used by teachers who take an integrated stance in relation to the issue: How should I teach? It permits both teachers and students to direct the learning through their exchanges of different strategies used to summarize, clarify, question, and predict. If a teacher dominated the conversation, it might become a bit more like specific skills in nature; if students dominated the conversation, it might become a bit more like holistic language learning.

▶ Question
▶ Predict

The goal of reciprocal teaching is to help readers internalize these steps so that they can use them independently during their own silent reading. The instructional approach is to have the teacher model the use of the procedural steps first and then have students follow the teacher's lead, all while reading a story together. Students are expected to follow the steps on their own after a number of practice sessions in the group setting.

During the first step, readers ask, "What did I read?" They should summarize the main point(s) of what they have just read. At the second step, readers ask, "Are there any parts that are not clear to me?" Then they reread the unclear portions and attempt to clarify the meaning.

When they reach the third step, readers ask, "What question would a teacher ask about this portion of the passage?" They should ask (and answer) a comprehension question related to the main point(s) of what they have just read. At the fourth step, readers ask, "What will probably happen next in this passage?" Readers then predict what they will read in the next portion. These four steps are repeated at regular intervals as readers work their way through a passage. Teachers usually model the steps first, as Bridget Clancy does in the model lesson on pages 314–315. They have students take turns modeling the steps aloud. Bridget is using reciprocal teaching to help her seventh-grade students practice monitoring what they are reading.

PRACTICAL TEACHING STRATEGIES

Developing Metacognitive Strategies

Using Mysteries to Develop Inferential Reasoning.   As a story form, mysteries are exceptional vehicles to make explicit the "hidden" strategies used to make inferences. Mysteries require you to make many text-connecting and slot-filling inferences as you try to figure out who did what to whom. Read together several mysteries with your students and exchange the strategies you and your students use to infer the "whodunnit" conclusion before you get to the end.

What clues did the children use to figure out their solution? Why did they use those clues and not others? You might want to make a bulletin board outlining the main characters and potential clues in the story as you encounter them. Then, compare the clues you posted on the bulletin board with the solution to the mystery. Great mysteries for younger children include the *Something Queer* books by Elizabeth Levy, the *Miss Mallard and Sherlock Chick* animal detective stories by Robert Quackenbush, stories by Crosby Bonsall, or the *Polka Dot Private Eye* books by Patricia Reilly Giff. Older children will enjoy the *Encyclopedia Brown* books by Donald Sobol, the *Einstein Anderson* series by Seymour Simon, *The House of Dies Drear* by Virginia Hamilton, *The Way to Sattin Shore* by Philippa Pearce, or Ellen Raskin's *The Westing Game*.

Think-Alouds.   Try reading a portion of text aloud to your students. As you read, articulate your reading and reasoning strategies, including any predictions you make, questions you pose to yourself, and inferences you make about what you are reading. Ask students to do the same. Such explicit modeling of the reading comprehension process has been shown to significantly contribute to improved metacognitive skill (Baker & Brown, 1984; Wade, 1990). Consider the periodic use of think-alouds if you have children work in pairs on the Internet. This allows wonderful discussions to take place as they use this resource.

Developing Comprehension through Syntactic Knowledge

syntactic knowledge
The knowledge that readers have of the word-order rules that determine the meaning of sentences.

Syntactic knowledge includes an understanding of the word order rules determining grammatical function, meaning, and pronunciation. Syntactic knowledge helps us distinguish the difference in meaning between sentences like *Jinny selected a kitten* and *A kitten selected Jinny*, two sentences with identical words but different word orders and, as a result, different meanings. Clearly, words have different meanings depending on how they are combined. Syntactic knowledge contributes to children's reading comprehension, and children's literature can be especially helpful in developing this knowledge.

Developing Syntactic Knowledge with Children's Literature

style study   A method framework where students develop insight about writing by looking closely at how authors use different language patterns and then try to emulate those patterns.

Children's literature can be an especially supportive environment for increasing children's knowledge of syntactic structures occurring in written language. Studying the sentence patterns used by some of our best authors allows children to closely observe the ways in which word order patterns contribute to meaning. A useful method framework for developing syntactic knowledge, especially among older children, is a **style study**. This method framework was described in chapter 7 as a means to connect reading and writing experiences. It is very useful to help children become more aware of the variety of syntactic patterns and how these serve to communicate different meanings. A style study consists of the following procedural steps:

1. Read a passage from children's literature together.
2. Identify several stylistic patterns used by this author.
3. Discuss why the author probably chose to use these patterns.
4. Provide children with a writing task and invite them to try out at least one of the patterns they have seen.
5. Share the results.

E-mail from the Classroom

Subject: Hatchet
From: John Fleischauer, jofleisc@mailbox.syr.edu

I've been reading Gary Paulsen's HATCHET and have been struck not only by the power of the narrative but also by the style employed by the author. What I find really interesting is that much of the book consists of "think-alouds" that reveal Brian's process of problem solving. While this contributes much to the power of the story (it slows down the action while it builds up the tension), it seems to me that it also presents a series of models of critical thinking procedures that would be valuable for students. It might be interesting to isolate the various instances where Brian employs critical thinking in solving a particular problem and discuss these procedures with students. It might be that a closer look at these procedures would not only be useful for improving their critical thinking skills, but application of these procedures might even help students to improve their strategies for reading comprehension.

Regardless, it's a great book!
John

Often, teachers will incorporate a style study with the reading of chapter books, by periodically looking at a chapter carefully for syntactic patterns used by a particular author and then having students use these patterns in their writing. This is an excellent chance to expose children to patterns that do not often occur in their oral language experiences, such as participial phrases at the beginning of sentences (*Having noticed the dark clouds, Louise pulled her collar up tight around her neck*) or the use of related independent clauses separated by a semicolon (*The sky was dark; it would rain before she got home*). You and your students will see many other special syntactic structures as you read exceptional works of children's literature together. As you encounter them, consider the use of a style study to help children explore their meanings and incorporate them into their own writing patterns.

A style study is effective with a wide range of syntactic elements. Sometimes, though, you should support children's use of specific syntactic features as they construct meaning during reading: punctuation, sequence relationships, or cause-and-effect relationships. Each is related to the inferences readers must make during reading.

Punctuation

A reader's ability to determine stress and intonation in written language contributes to the comprehension process (Cook-Gumperz & Gumperz, 1981). Knowledge of punctuation assists readers in determining the correct stress and intonation as they construct the meaning of a sentence.

Instruction in using punctuation takes place early in a literacy program, (usually by the end of third grade). Teachers often teach punctuation concepts by linking children's oral language to its written representation. They sometimes use a method framework referred to as **language experience sentences,** a variation of the language experience story described earlier (see chapters 2 and 5). Language experience sentences include these four procedural steps:

1. Elicit oral language containing the target punctuation.
2. Transcribe the language containing the target punctuation.
3. Read the transcribed language, modeling the use of punctuation.
4. Practice reading similar sentences.

During the first step, the teacher elicits an oral sentence containing the desired stress and intonation pattern. This task often is accomplished by asking students about something they have done or said. In step two, the teacher transcribes that sentence, usually on the chalkboard. For a more permanent copy, the sentence could be transcribed on a large sheet

language experience sentences A method framework used to develop an understanding of punctuation.

Teaching Punctuation Using Language Experience Sentences in Arlanta Brown's Class

Arlanta Brown has interactive beliefs about *what* you should teach, finding all literacy components important to share with her young children. Her beliefs about *how* one should teach fall somewhere between specific skills and integrated perspectives. She believes direct instruction is important for many things but always provides some opportunities for her students to also direct their own learning activities through reading and writing projects. Arlanta is teaching her first-grade students the stress and intonation pattern associated with a comma separating items in a list. She is using language experience sentences to teach this concept.

Elicit Oral Language Containing the Target Punctuation

Arlanta: Daria, tell us three things that you do before you come to school in the morning.

Daria: Let's see. I wake up, I eat breakfast, and I brush my teeth. That's three things.

Transcribe the Language Containing the Target Punctuation

Arlanta writes the following sentence on the blackboard:

Daria wakes up, eats breakfast, and brushes her teeth in the morning.

Read the Transcribed Language, Modeling the Use of Punctuation

Arlanta: Listen while I read this sentence. [Arlanta reads.] Do you see that I wrote this little mark between each of the things Daria does in the morning? This mark is called a comma. Can you say that word? Comma. What happens when I'm reading and I come to a comma? Listen again. [Arlanta reads.]

Sam: You kind of stop for a bit but not like at the end.

Arlanta: Right. With a comma you should stop reading for just a little bit, but not as long as you do at the end of a sentence.

Practice Reading Similar Sentences

Arlanta: Let's read some more sentences like this. Michael, what do you do when you get home after school? Tell us three or four things so we can write them down and put commas between them.

Michael: I go home. I change my clothes and have a snack, and I ride my dirt bike, and I have dinner.

Arlanta transcribes this series with commas and has children read it orally: *Michael goes home, changes his clothes, has a snack, and rides his dirt bike until dinner.* Then she repeats this activity with other students and other sentences containing commas to separate items in a series. Afterward, she invites each child to draw a picture and then use the words on the blackboard to write his or her own sentence with commas.

Language experience sentences, because they include direct teacher instruction, tend to be more consistent with specific skills or integrated beliefs about how you should teach. If you have holistic language learning beliefs about how you should teach, punctuation may be taught through the use of editing conferences and other writing process strategies. These provide opportunities for student-directed learning. The use of editing conferences was described in chapter 7.

of card stock or other heavy paper. Step three requires the teacher to model the use of punctuation while reading the transcribed sentence aloud. The stress and intonation pattern represented by the punctuation mark should be clearly expressed, the punctuation mark should be identified, and its function discussed. Finally, the teacher should elicit other sentences containing the desired stress and intonation pattern, transcribe them, and have students practice reading them. See the model lesson above.

Sequence Relationships

sequence relationship
A relationship of time between two or more events, explicitly or implicitly stated.

Sequence relationships often are expressed in syntactic patterns. A sequence relationship expresses the time relationship between two or more events. This structure is sometimes difficult for younger children to grasp. Sequence relationships can be either explicitly or implicitly stated. Implicitly stated relationships require the reader to make an inference about the time order of events.

Explicit

Events appearing in the order in which they happened.	Tom finished his work *before* he went home.
Events appearing in the opposite order from that in which they happened.	Tom went home *after* he finished his work.

Implicit

Events appearing in the order in which they happened (separate sentences).	Tom finished his work. He went home.
Events appearing in the order in which they happened (linked by a coordinating conjunction).	Tom finished his work and went home.

Explicit sequence relationships contain signal words such as *before, after, then, later, following, first, initially, earlier, afterward, next,* or *finally.* These signal words state the time relationship between the two events and thus should make such relationships easy to comprehend. Unfortunately, however, two elements of explicit sequence relationships are difficult for young children. First, the signal words for sequence relationships are not common in the oral language of young children. Consequently, they often are unfamiliar with the meanings of signal words and must learn both their meanings and their function in explicit sequence relationships.

A second difficulty is that relationships may appear in the opposite order from that in which they happened. In oral language, children are accustomed to events being stated in the order in which they occur, and they assume a similar situation exists in written language. As a result, children often interpret sentences such as "Tom went home *after* he finished his work" as "Tom went home, *and then* he finished his work." Children have the greatest difficulty comprehending explicit sequence relationships when the events appear in the opposite order from that in which they happened (Pearson & Camperell, 1981; Pearson & Johnson, 1978).

Sequence relationships can also be implicitly stated, requiring readers to make an inference (usually a text-connecting inference). Implicit sequence relationships may be indicated by sequentially ordered events in separate sentences or by the coordinating conjunction *and* within a single sentence. Such relationships require readers to infer the temporal relationship between events. This type of inference presents little difficulty for young readers because sequence relationships are expressed in the same way in oral language.

With younger readers, sequence relationships often are taught within a language experience story, which typically contains these steps:

1. Provide students with a vivid experience.
2. Elicit oral language that describes the experience.
3. Transcribe the students' oral language.
4. Help students read what was transcribed.

Throughout a language experience story, discussion should help students identify the various events and their sequence relationships. Special attention should be devoted to helping students understand the meanings of signal words and the ways in which they identify sequence relationships. Emilia Kritz demonstrates how this method framework can be used to develop an understanding of sequence relationships with young children.

Among older readers, instruction in understanding sequence relationships often takes place during the discussion of a story. Questions used to initiate a discussion about sequence relationships include these:

When did _____take place?

What happened before _____?

Did _____ happen before or after_____?

MODEL LESSON

Teaching Sequence Relationships Using a Language Experience Story in Emilia Kritz's Class

Emilia Kritz has an interactive belief about *what* to teach. She teaches both prior knowledge components and decoding components in her first-grade class. When Emilia considers the second issue in a literacy framework (*How* should I teach), she finds herself somewhere between a specific skills and an integrated perspective, leaning more toward an integrated perspective. She believes in providing direct instruction on comprehension strategies to children in her first-grade class. She always tries to place this instruction within the context of her children's experiences, though. This is why she likes language experience stories so much—they provide her with opportunities to show important comprehension strategies, but her students always get to use their experiences and interests to generate the passage.

Provide Students with a Vivid Experience. Today, Emilia is taking her first-grade class to the library. When they return to the classroom, she plans to build on this experience to discuss sequence relationships, something that causes many of her students difficulty.

Elicit Oral Language That Describes the Experience. When they return, Emilia has her class sit on the carpeted floor in front of the chalkboard. She invites her students to write a story together about their trip to the library, describing what took place in sequential order. Emilia elicits several sentences from the students, one for each event they experienced in the library.

Transcribe the Students' Oral Language. Emilia writes down each sentence on the chalkboard as the student says it:

We went to the library.

Ms. Hamm showed us the new bookshelves.

We sat in a circle.

Ms. Hamm read us a story about the ox-cart man.

We really liked the story.

We got to check out a new book.

We came back to our room.

Help Students Read What Was Transcribed. Emilia has her students read the entire sequence of sentences. Then she carries out three activities to assist her students' understanding of sequence relationships.

First, Emilia initiates a discussion, asking sequence questions such as "What happened before we sat in a circle? What happened before Ms. Hamm read us a story? What happened before we came back to our room?" She writes the students' responses next to the story they had dictated earlier.

Ms. Hamm showed us the new bookshelves *before* we sat in a circle.

We sat in a circle *before* Ms. Hamm read us a story.

We got to check out a new book *before* we came back to our room.

Then, Emilia discusses the meaning of the signal word *before* and then has students read this second set of sentences. Together they discuss the sequence of the different events and the way in which certain words like *before* are used to show that order.

Finally, Emilia has her students draw pictures of two events, one happening before the other. She walks around the classroom, helping students write a sentence containing the word *before* to describe their pictures. Afterward, students read their sentences and show their pictures in a short cooperative learning group activity.

An important distinction must be made here between using questions to test and to teach reading comprehension (Durkin, 1981). If you accept correct responses and reject incorrect responses but do nothing else, you are testing reading comprehension. You are simply determining whether students can answer the questions. If you follow sequence questions with a request for students to model their reasoning

Sequence and cause-and-effect activities are important to comprehending all genres of text.

processes, you are teaching reading comprehension. After each sequence question, for example, you might ask, "How did you figure that out?" In order to answer, students would have to model the reasoning processes they used. The suggestions below will help you teach, not test, understanding of sequence relationships during the discussion of a story:

1. Avoid playing the game called "Can-you-guess-the-answer-I-have-in-mind?" Do not ask a question merely to obtain a correct response. Follow a sequence question with a brief discussion by asking students how they determined their answer to your question. What information did they use from the text? What information did they figure out by themselves because it was missing from the text? Have they ever used such a strategy before? Is it a good one to remember? After students model their reasoning processes, model your own, and explain how you arrived at your answer. Your explanation should help students who were unable to determine the sequence relationship.

2. Pay particular attention to sequence relationships that present events in the opposite order from that in which they occurred. Those will be most difficult for young readers to understand.

3. Before reading a story with difficult sequence relationships, use a prereading question to direct students' attention to the important information. For example, say to students, "Read and see whether you can find out which happened first—X or Y."

Cause-and-Effect Relationships

A **cause-and-effect relationship** expresses the relationship between two events in which one event is the consequence of the other. Often the two events appear in the same or adjacent sentences; sometimes they appear in separate paragraphs. Cause-and-effect relationships can also be either explicitly or implicitly stated. Again, implicitly stated relationships require the reader to make an inference, this time about which event was the cause and which was the effect.

cause-and-effect relationship A causal relationship between two or more events, explicitly or implicitly stated.

TABLE 9-1

Signal words for cause-and-effect relationships

Signal Words	Examples
because	He went home *because* he was ill.
so	He was ill, and *so* he went home.
therefore	He was ill, and *therefore* went home.
hence	He was ill. *Hence,* he went home.
thus	He was ill, and *thus* went home.
since	*Since* he was ill, he went home.
as a result	He was ill and, *as a result,* went home.
consequently	He was ill, and *consequently* went home.
for this reason	He was ill. *For this reason,* he went home.
that being the case	He looked ill. *That being the case,* he went home.
on account of	*On account of* his illness, he went home.
accordingly	He looked ill, and *accordingly* went home.

Explicit cause-and-effect relationships contain signal words such as *because* and *therefore,* which clearly indicate the causal relationship between the two events. Again, we might think that such words would make these explicit relationships easy to comprehend, but unfortunately, young children often are unfamiliar with the meanings of those words. Consequently, both the meanings of signal words and their function in explicit cause-and-effect relationships are frequently taught to young children. The cause-and-effect signal words usually taught are listed in Table 9-1.

Implicit cause-and-effect relationships require readers to infer the correct relationship between two ideas in the absence of signal words. The two events are stated in separate sentences or are connected by the coordinating conjunction *and* in the same sentence. The following examples show both explicit and implicit cause-and-effect relationships.

Explicit

The hatch had just started, and *therefore* the fish began to feed.
    (cause)   (signal word)   (effect)

Implicit

The hatch had just started. The fish began to feed.
     (cause)   (effect)
The hatch had just started, and the fish began to feed.
     (cause)   (effect)

With implicit cause-and-effect relationships, readers must have the appropriate background knowledge to infer the correct meaning. Without that knowledge, readers may interpret the two events as temporally, but not causally, ordered. For example, the implicit sentences just presented might be interpreted as "First, something unrelated to the fish (maybe a bird's egg) hatched. Then the fish began to feed." In that case, the two events would not be thought of as causally related. However, appropriate background knowledge would lead to the correct inference: that it is mayflies that are hatching, and this causes the fish to begin feeding on them.

Instruction in cause-and-effect relationships often takes place during the discussion of a story. Questions that might be used to direct students' attention to cause-and-effect relationships include these:

Why did _____ take place?

MODEL LESSON

Teaching Cause-and-Effect in Bridget Clancy's Class

Bridget has reader-based beliefs about *what* to teach and integrated beliefs about *how* to teach. She is conducting another mini-lesson with a small group of children experiencing difficulty with comprehension strategies during reading workshop. She has been using the book *The Secret Soldier* (McGovern, 1975) to engage her students in discussions of cause-and-effect relationships as they read and enjoy this story about a girl who fought in the Revolutionary War. They have just finished a page that began with the following paragraph:

The trouble was getting worse. In many villages, people were getting ready for war. Groups of men and young boys began training to be soldiers. They were called minutemen because they were ready to fight at a minute's notice. (p. 19)

Bridget:	Look up at the first paragraph. Why were these soldiers called minutemen?
Marcus:	Because they could fight at a minute's notice.
Bridget:	Tell us how you know that, Marcus.
Marcus:	It says because.
Bridget:	Right! *Because* is a signal word that signals a special relationship between two ideas. It tells us why something happened. Can you find the two ideas in this sentence?
Linda:	"They were called minutemen" and "They were ready to fight at a minute's notice."
Bridget:	Good! Can anyone find the cause-and-effect statements in this sentence?
Bonnie:	I can. "They were ready to fight at a minute's notice" is the cause, and "They were called minutemen" must be the effect. Being ready to fight at a minute's notice causes them to be called minutemen.
Bridget:	Good! Now look at the first two sentences in this paragraph and read them again to yourself. Sometimes signal words are missing, yet we still have a special relationship between the two ideas. One sentence can be the cause and another sentence the effect, even without a signal word. Does one of the first two sentences describe a cause?
Joan:	I think people were getting ready for war, so the trouble was getting worse. "People were getting ready for war" is the cause.
Marcus:	But the people didn't cause the trouble. The trouble caused the people to get ready for war. I think "The trouble was getting worse" is the cause.
Bridget:	One way to test your idea is to put these two sentences together with a signal word like *because* at the beginning of each sentence. That usually tells you which one is the cause and which one is the effect.
Joan:	Because the trouble was getting worse, the people were getting ready for war. Yeah. That's what I mean. "The trouble was getting worse" must be the cause.

Teachers with integrated or holistic language learning beliefs about how to teach often will use discussions with literature selections like Bridget does to support children's understanding of cause-and-effect relationships. These allow students more control over their own learning. Teachers with specific skills beliefs might use activities such as those described on the next page.

What happened as a result of _____?

How are _____ and _____ connected?

Which words tell us that _____ happened because of _____?

As with sequence relationships, it is important to initiate discussions that teach, not test, comprehension. It is also important to direct the student's attention to the text so that concrete examples of causes, effects, and signal words can be seen. The model lesson shows how Bridget Clancy taught cause-and-effect to her seventh graders.

PRACTICAL TEACHING STRATEGIES

Developing Understanding of Cause-and-Effect Relationships from a Specific Skills Perspective

Marking Cause-and-Effect Relationships. Present cause-and-effect statements and show students how to identify each component in the relationship, marking each with an appropriate letter or symbol. Have students practice with additional examples.

                 C   E

The school bell rang for recess, *so* the children went outside.

Cause-and-Effect Cloze Tasks. Teach the meaning of new signal words, such as *therefore*, by using any of the methods described for vocabulary instruction in chapter 8. Then have students complete sentences like the following, either independently or in a cooperative learning group:

1. The wind was too strong for our sailboat, and therefore _____.

2. _____, and therefore we were late for dinner.

To reduce the difficulty level of the task, you might provide suggested answers at the bottom of the page:

                      we forgot the time   it tipped over

⌨ Developing Comprehension through Discourse Knowledge

discourse knowledge
The knowledge that readers have of the language organization that determines meaning beyond the single sentence level.

Discourse knowledge contributes to comprehension (Beck, McKeown, Omanson, & Pople, 1984) because it includes the knowledge of language organization that helps us understand entire texts. Whereas syntactic knowledge allows us to determine meaningful relationships among words, discourse knowledge allows us to determine meaningful relationships among sentences. At least three aspects of discourse knowledge are important for young readers to acquire: pronoun and adverbial references, drawing conclusions, and predicting outcomes. Each is related to oral and written language differences and to the inferences that readers are required to make as they comprehend a text.

Pronoun and Adverbial References

pronoun references
Words that are substituted for nouns or noun phrases.

adverbial references
Words that are substituted for specific time or location designations.

Pronoun references are words substituted for nouns or noun phrases; they include words like *I, you,* and *she.* **Adverbial references** are words substituted for specific designations of time or location; they include words such as *here, today, now, last week,* and *last month.* Both pronoun and adverbial references are very common, as we can see in the following example:

> Heather and *her* friend were determined to see the solar eclipse in *their* viewing box. *They* struggled with the box to get *it* right. First the hole was not big enough. Then *it* was too big. Finally, by putting tape across the hole and then poking a tiny hole in *it* with a toothpick, Heather was able to get the light to shine. "*We* can see *it* here now," *she* said.

Readers must infer the meanings of pronoun and adverbial references by imagining a situation they cannot see. This task is easy for mature readers who are familiar with the demands of written texts. It is much more difficult for young readers (Anderson & Shifrin, 1980; Rubin, 1980) who are accustomed to seeing, not imagining, the meanings of such words in oral language contexts.

Pronoun and adverbial references require either a text-connecting or a slot-filling inference. For example, the word *they* in the example paragraph requires a text-connecting inference. It requires readers to understand its logical connection to its referent in the

MODEL LESSON

Using Deductive Instruction to Teach Text-Connecting Inferences with Pronoun and Adverbial References in Bob Nobilo's Class

Bob's beliefs about *how* to teach fall somewhere between an integrated perspective and a holistic language learning perspective. Students in his third-grade class often direct their own learning within literature discussion groups. He also uses reading workshop a lot. Bob doesn't often use a deductive method framework but today he has decided to use it with six students who are really having difficulty with comprehension, especially keeping track of who is referred to with pronoun references. He has developed a short mini-lesson to provide them with support about this aspect of comprehension. They have responded favorably in the past to direct instruction like this as long as they are able to immediately use the skill within an engaging literature selection immediately after the lesson.

Before beginning the lesson, Bob writes the following sentences on the chalkboard:

Peter was talking to Joan on the phone about Hal. He said, "I didn't see Hal at work today. I thought maybe he stayed at home. Is he there with you, Joan?"

Joan said, "No. He isn't here. And Mark isn't here either. Do you know where he is? Maybe they are together somewhere."

State the Skill or Rule. Bob begins by pointing to the sentences on the blackboard and saying, "Sometimes when you read, one word will take the place of another word or phrase. Both will mean the same thing. Look at these sentences on the board. Can you read them for us, Matt?" Matt reads the sentences aloud.

Provide Examples of the Skill or Rule. Bob shows that pronoun and adverbial references are logically connected to their referents. He circles the first *He* on the board and draws an arrow back to its referent, *Peter.* Bob does the same thing with *I* and draws the arrow back to *Peter.* Then he circles the second *he* and draws an arrow back to *Hal.* While he does all of this, Bob explains that certain words often mean the same thing as other words in a story.

Provide Guided Practice. Bob then asks the students to look at the second sentence on the board and find similar kinds of words that mean the same thing as other words. He asks individuals to come to the board and circle each pronoun or adverb and then draw arrows back to its referent. Students follow this procedure for *he* (Hal); *here* (at work); and *they* (Hal, Mark). Bob has the students explain their decisions to the group.

Provide Independent Practice. Bob gives each student a copy of a page from *James and the Giant Peach* by Roald Dahl. He directs them to read the page while looking for pronouns and their referents. Each student is to circle the pronoun and draw an arrow back to its referent. Then they are to get together in pairs to check their answers. When they are finished, the groups get together with Bob and compare their answers.

Deductive instruction is sometimes changed by teachers with holistic or integrated beliefs into an inductive lesson, allowing students to develop the strategy from the examples. In this case, a teacher might want to use a classroom reading experience with literature to generate the examples. Discussion with children would be used to share the strategies they use to infer the pronoun reference. Guided practice and independent practice could then be used after the reading of the literature selection to ensure children had acquired the strategy for inferring pronoun and adverbial references.

passage: the words *Heather and her friend.* Other examples of references that require a text-connecting inference in this paragraph include *her* (Heather); *their* (Heather and her friend); *it* (the box); *it* (the hole); *it* (the tape); *We* (Heather and her friend); *it* (the eclipse); and *she* (Heather).

When pronoun or adverbial references do not have an explicit referent in the text, they require readers to make a slot-filling inference. The word *here* in the example paragraph requires a slot-filling inference, in which readers must understand the logical connection between *here* and its unstated referent—the inside wall of the box. When pronoun or adverbial references require a slot-filling inference, readers must have the appropriate background knowledge to fill in the missing meaning. Slot-filling inferences with pronoun or adverbial references are especially difficult for young readers to make.

The ability to infer the meanings of pronoun and adverbial references is developed early in most instructional programs, usually during the first two grades, for two reasons.

First, pronoun and adverbial references are among the most common words in our language. Second, imagining the referents for pronoun and adverbial references in written language is a new task for young children who are used to seeing these relationships in oral language contexts.

Instruction in making text-connecting inferences for pronoun and adverbial references usually precedes instruction in making slot-filling inferences. It is easier to show students in a concrete way the connections between references and their referents. Those connections often are demonstrated by circling the references and drawing lines back to their referents. Both text-connecting and slot-filling inferences can be taught inductively but are more often taught deductively, as in the model lesson by Bob Nobilo on page 325.

Predicting Outcomes and Drawing Conclusions

procedural knowledge
Knowledge of common event sequences.

Predicting outcomes and drawing conclusions both rely on **procedural knowledge,** or knowledge of common event sequences. Your own procedural knowledge is probably extensive. For example, you have procedural knowledge about the first day of class in a university course, and you can use that knowledge to make inferences, either when you experience that first day yourself or when you read about the experiences of someone else during his or her first day of class. The first event in your procedural knowledge includes your arrival. Within that sequence you probably have a location where you prefer to sit, based on previous experiences. Some students look to the front row, others to the back row, and still others to an aisle seat. Your knowledge probably includes the meanings associated with sitting in each of those locations. People often sit in the front to make an impression, sit in the back to avoid making an impression, and sit next to the aisle to make a quick exit. All of this knowledge is a part of the initial event in your procedural knowledge of the first day of class.

Your second event probably includes the professor's arrival. It may include the fact that professors are likely to be carrying a stack of syllabi, which they set down on the table or lectern at the front of the room. It may also include your professor writing the title of the course and his or her name on the chalkboard. Your procedural knowledge for the first day of class probably contains a number of other events that define your expectations for the remainder of that first period: Passing out the syllabus, going over the syllabus, finding out where the text may be purchased, and hearing why this course is the most important course in your college career.

You possess thousands of procedural schemata such as this in your prior knowledge, each containing event sequences. You have, no doubt, a procedural schema for eating at a restaurant, driving home, eating dinner at home, flying on an airplane, and many other events. Throughout the day you use this knowledge to make inferences about what is happening or what you are reading.

The following passage and its related question show how procedural knowledge is used to make inferences during reading:

> The two boys were across the street from José's house when they saw the ominous line of clouds approaching and heard the thunder. They were playing under a tall eucalyptus tree at the time and could see the lightning flash all along the storm front as it came closer. "Hurry," said José.

What do you think the two boys will do?

If you have a procedural schema for what to do in a lightning storm, you are familiar with the common event sequences that accompany such a storm: getting away from trees, staying away from metal objects, heading for cover, and so on. Based on the information in the passage and your own procedural knowledge, you probably inferred that the two boys would head for shelter inside Jose's house.

predicting outcomes
A comprehension task requiring the reader to use appropriate procedural knowledge to infer a future effect from a stated cause; a forward inference.

Your inference illustrates a comprehension task referred to as **predicting outcomes,** which requires the reader to infer future effects from a stated cause. The inference in such a task is always projected into the future; it is usually a slot-filling inference about a future effect.

SUSAN'S

COMMENTS FROM THE CLASSROOM

Modeling is the first technique that comes to my mind when thinking about comprehension instruction. I use the morning read-aloud, a perfect opportunity to share the pictures brought to mind by an author's words. Rare is the day that my descriptions are not followed by voluntary descriptions of the children's visualizations.

It's also an easy format for establishing those links children should be making to the printed word—links to other texts. . . "That's just like what happened in the book we read last week!". . . and links to self. . . "That reminds me of the time that I. . .".

Shared writing is another setting for comprehension instruction. As authors, we discuss the scenes we can depict in our readers' heads. Verbalizing the differences when picturing "walking down the hall" as opposed to "running wildly through the school" helps us decide as a group on our word choices during shared writing. It also gives us a basis for critiquing and appreciating word choices in the books we read.

The opportunities to model reading comprehension are as numerous as the literacy settings within your classroom, and not all demonstrations need to be didactic or dry. Take, for instance, daily Drop Everything And Read (DEAR) time. While sprawled out on an oversized pillow, I might let out a loudly whispered "Oh, no!" or a short burst of laughter followed by a sincere apology for disturbing the peace. After quiet reading is over, I would then explain the horrific/wildly amusing incident that occurred in my book and the subsequent pictures that popped into my head while I was reading the excerpt.

Then there's always the comprehension instruction within reading group. I don't think there is any method more productive than having children pose their own

questions for the books we are reading. Each child is responsible for posing one question per day on his or her reading, while having a clear understanding that the best questions are the ones that either cannot be answered or have more than one answer.

The basic setup is this: Children are assigned a book chapter or set of pages for the evening. As the children do their nightly reading, they write their question on a sticky note and post it on the page where the question arose. The next day we meet for guided reading groups and begin to read the assigned chapter aloud. Each child poses his or her question to the group after we've read the page where it's been posted. All answers and challenges to answers must be supported with the ideas from the book that led to the response. I've been amazed at the book discussions I've heard from second-grade children using this method. They far surpass any discussion that's taken place when I am the only one asking the questions. I keep the answered sticky notes in a large notebook and, every once in awhile, we go over the questions that we answered, the ones we couldn't agree upon, and the ones that could only be answered after we had read further into the book.

Drawing conclusions and predicting outcomes are a part of subject-area reading materials as well as narratives. Age-appropriate books, including history books, are available in all content areas.

drawing conclusions
A comprehension task requiring a reader to infer an unstated cause from a stated effect; a backward inference.

A related comprehension task, **drawing conclusions,** requires the reader to infer an unstated cause from a stated effect. In this case, the inference is always backward to what has been read in the text. Drawing a conclusion usually requires readers to use their procedural knowledge to make a slot-filling inference about a previous cause. Let's look at the following passage and related question to see how this process takes place:

> The team raced to the far end of the court to cut the net down. The captain climbed up to the hoop, cut the net, put it around his neck, and let out a yell. The crowd was going crazy with excitement!
>
> Why was everyone so excited?

Were you able to infer backward from the stated effects in the passage to determine the unstated cause—that a basketball team had just won a tournament? If so, you relied on the information in the text and your procedural knowledge of the events commonly associated with winning a basketball tournament to make a slot-filling inference and draw a conclusion.

One of the most common method frameworks used to help children predict outcomes and draw conclusions is a **directed reading-thinking activity (DRTA).** A DRTA consists of three procedural steps, which are repeated as students read and discuss a selection:

directed reading-thinking activity (DRTA)   A method framework used to assist students in predicting outcomes and drawing conclusions; involves predicting, reading, and proving.

1. Predicting
2. Reading
3. Proving

During the predicting step, ask students to predict the outcome and explain their inferential reasoning. At the beginning of a story, use questions like these to initiate responses:

What will a story with this title be about? Why do you think so?

Who do you think will be in a story with a title like this? Why?

Where do you think this story will take place? Why?

PRACTICAL TEACHING STRATEGIES

Predicting Outcomes and Drawing Conclusions

Riddle Reading and Riddle Writing.   Reading riddles provides opportunities to practice drawing conclusions in an engaging fashion. You may want to write a riddle on the board each day and then, at the end of the day, see who has figured out the answer. Older students might enjoy writing and sharing their own riddles. You could then develop a class riddle book to share with other classes in your school.

Thematic Units.   New experiences develop procedural knowledge for students, especially when they are integrated into other subject areas. For this reason, thematic units across subject areas are very helpful. Organize reading experiences around specific themes. Plan experiences in other subject areas around those themes. Chapter 6 described how thematic units can be developed.

Reading Mysteries.   Mysteries are especially valuable for providing practice in predicting outcomes and drawing conclusions. Be sure to select mysteries for read-aloud sessions. Have students predict outcomes, draw conclusions, and then explain their reasoning at various points in the story. You may wish to build the student's experiences with the following books:

> *The Case of the Cat's Meow* by Crosby Bonsall
>
> *Encyclopedia Brown Saves the Day* by Donald Sobol
>
> *Encyclopedia Brown: Boy Detective* by Donald Sobol
>
> *Mystery at the Edge of Two Worlds* by Christie Harris
>
> *Something Queer Is Going On* by Elizabeth Levy
>
> *The House of Dies Drear* by Virginia Hamilton

Each student is expected to make a prediction and support it with a reasonable explanation. Encourage different predictions as long as students can justify them logically.

The second procedural step in a DRTA is to have students read. Ask students to read silently up to a predetermined point, at which time students' earlier predictions should be checked. Directions like these might be given:

> Now that you have all told me what you think this story is going to be about, I want you to read and see if you were correct. Read up to the end of page 4, please.

The third procedural step is proving. During this step, ask students to draw conclusions and explain their reasoning process. In discussion, students are asked to evaluate the evidence in relation to their predictions. They see whether they were correct or incorrect and, most importantly, why they were correct or incorrect. Questions like the following can be used to begin the discussion:

> Was your guess correct? Why or why not?
>
> What do you think now? Why?
>
> Why do you think X happened?
>
> Why did A (a character) do X (an action)?
>
> What do you think will happen next?

At the end of this discussion, the three-step procedure is repeated, beginning with making predictions about the next outcome. This type of method framework can be used whenever children read a story together. It encourages them to continually think about what they have read and what is likely to happen next. Other instructional strategies can also be used, however, to develop the ability to predict outcomes and draw conclusions. Several are described above.

⌨ Supporting the Comprehension Needs of Students with Limited English Proficiency

Limited English Proficiency (LEP) students   Students whose first language is not English and who have not yet developed fluency in English.

It has been estimated that at least 2.2 million school-aged children in the United States, or 5.7 percent, are **Limited English Proficiency (LEP) students** (U.S. Department of Education, 1991). These are children whose first language is not English and who have not yet developed fluency in the English language. LEP students come from a variety of linguistic backgrounds: Spanish, Cajun, Vietnamese, Cambodian, Haitian, Korean, Cantonese, Mandarin, or one of several Native American languages. At least one public school district on the West Coast has students who speak more than 80 different primary languages.

It is important for teachers to understand the comprehension needs of these students. It is also important for teachers to develop instructional practices to meet their special needs. Although many of these students are provided with outside educational services, many LEP students still receive most of their instruction from the regular classroom teacher (Grant & Gomez, 1996).

Challenges Faced by LEP Students

Two important challenges are faced by LEP students. First, LEP students lack the knowledge of spoken English necessary to comprehend what they read. Acquiring the ability to speak English, therefore, is crucial to their developing reading proficiency. Time must be devoted to helping these students learn to communicate orally in English.

The second challenge faced by these students is that differences between English and another language often impede comprehension. Thus, it is important to become familiar with the differences between English and a student's native language. To understand the differences between other languages and English, you might seek information from three sources: (1) a speaker of the other language who also speaks English, (2) your local or state coordinator of bilingual education services, and (3) either the **Center for Applied Linguistics** (http://www.cal.org/), 1611 North Kent Street, Arlington, VA 22209 or the **National Clearing house for English Language Acquisition & Language Instruction Educational Programs** (http://www.ncbe.gwu.edu/), George Washington University, Graduate School of Education and Human Development, Washington DC 20037.

Instruction

immersion approaches   An instructional practice that challenges LEP students to learn English as rapidly as they can without special intervention.

ESL approaches   An instructional practice that teaches LEP students oral English in structured lessons before they learn how to read and write in English.

bilingual approaches   An instructional practice through which LEP students learn reading and writing in their native language concurrently with instruction in oral English.

Research into literacy instruction with LEP children is still in its infancy, and consistent findings are limited. Nevertheless, several instructional approaches are commonly found in schools: immersion; English as a Second Language (ESL); and bilingual approaches. **Immersion approaches** make no special provision for LEP children. Children are expected to pick up as much as they can, as fast as they can, during regular classroom lessons. This practice assumes that immersion in English will contribute to learning. Although this has been the traditional form of instruction for LEP children in the United States, it is not necessarily the most effective.

ESL approaches teach LEP children oral English skills before their reading instruction begins. Special ESL teachers work with children, usually in structured oral drills and usually outside the regular classroom, to develop fluency in oral English. Reading instruction in the regular classroom begins only after children have established an understanding of oral English.

Bilingual approaches teach reading and writing skills in a child's native language at the same time that they teach oral language skills in English. Reading instruction in English begins only after children have learned to read and write in their own language and have acquired fluency in oral English. Bilingual approaches often involve teachers who are fluent in the native language of their children.

Regardless of the approach, you should keep the following suggestions in mind as you work with children who are just learning to speak English:

Celebrating Diversity

Using Culturally Sensitive Works of Literature

Raphael and Brock (1993) studied the literacy development of a Vietnamese LEP student, Mei, as she engaged in literaturé discussion group activities. (See chapter 6 for a description of this method framework.) In addition to substantial gains in comprehension, they found Mei increased the amount of her participation in discussions and gained substantially in self-confidence. These differences were especially noticeable when the discussion group read and discussed a book about life in Vietnam. The book allowed Mei to take advantage of her background knowledge during reading and discussions. It also allowed her to help other students understand the story about life in Vietnam. This study suggests that it is important to include culturally sensitive works of literature in your classroom to support the literacy learning of LEP students. Including culturally sensitive works of literature also allows your other students to develop a wider appreciation of different cultural experiences. Everyone gains when we include culturally sensitive works of literature in our classrooms.

1. Encourage discussion among all your students, but especially between LEP children and others. Speaking and listening experiences develop important prerequisites for reading and writing. Thus, LEP children need a language-rich environment to develop greater proficiency in English (Krashen & Terrell, 1983).
2. Make frequent use of cooperative learning group activities. This method framework provides a supportive environment for LEP children—a group learning situation with extensive use of oral English. LEP children are able to participate successfully in cooperative learning groups, thereby increasing their self-perceptions.
3. Try to reduce the anxiety level of LEP children as much as possible. These children appear to learn best in classrooms in which anxiety levels are reduced (Dulay, Burt, & Krashen, 1982).
4. Pay less attention at the beginning to your students' pronunciation and accent. Concentrate on meaning and communication.
5. Understand the difficulty your students face in learning a second language, and help your other students to appreciate this challenge. LEP children may require as many as 5 to 7 years of instruction in English before they can read English textbooks effectively (Cummins, 1981).
6. Select books for read-aloud sessions that are culturally appropriate for your LEP students. Use those opportunities to encourage their participation in oral discussions.
7. Respect your students' linguistic and cultural heritage. Work those aspects of diversity into your classroom activities (Au, 1993).
8. Use language experience activities as much as possible to teach beginning reading skills. Language experience activities allow LEP children to simultaneously improve their oral and written English language skills. They also allow children to use their background knowledge to maximum advantage.

Several additional strategies are described on page 332.

Using Questioning Strategies to Develop Reading Comprehension and Response

It is important for both readers and teachers to ask questions about what they are reading. For readers, questions serve to monitor comprehension, focus attention on puzzling aspects of the text, and guide the search for answers. Questions are an essential part of the comprehension process. For teachers, questions serve a variety of functions:

Modeling the reasoning process. Questions, along with answers and explanations of how answers were derived, can be used to model the reasoning processes important for comprehension.

PRACTICAL TEACHING STRATEGIES

Supporting the Comprehension Needs of LEP Children

Bilingual Internet Projects   Set up an Internet Project using e-mail with a school where students use the language of your LEP student(s) as their first language. Use **Intercultural E-Mail Classroom Connections** (http:www.sto-laf.edu/network/iecc/) or **Web66: International WWW Schools Registry** (http://web66.coled.umn.edu/schools.html). Then, have your LEP student work with a group of students to translate all incoming and outgoing messages. This will demonstrate the value of the LEP student's language and teach your other students something about this language.

Picture Dictionaries.   Have your LEP children write and publish a picture dictionary. Include common school objects and activities. Have other students help them in this task. If they are available, have children use a scanner and printer.

Using Dave's ESL Cafe.   One of the best locations on the Internet for LEP children is **Dave's ESL Cafe** (http://www.pacificnet.net/~sperling/eslcafe.html). You will find many great resources for your students here, including locations to chat with other LEP children and share experiences, a graffiti wall for posting writing, an idiom page for help with this difficult area, and many more exciting resources. There are also many useful resources for teachers, including a location to share your questions and seek answers from other teachers. Set a bookmark!

Peer Tutoring.   Have native-speaking children regularly work with each LEP child in your classroom. They can complete many enjoyable and productive tasks together:

- Reading a storybook together and talking about the pictures
- Writing and illustrating a story together
- Writing buddy journals (see chapter 7)
- Playing Simon Says

Celebrating Diversity

Using Mailing Lists and Bulletin Boards

Sharing experiences and questions about the learning needs of LEP children on a bulletin board, chat location, or mailing list can usually put you in touch with many wonderful ideas to assist your students. You might wish to participate in scheduled chat sessions with educational experts at the **Center for Applied Linguistics Chat Online** (http://www.cal.org/chat/). You might also use one of the search engines for mailing lists to find a mailing list to meet your exact needs:

Liszt Select
(http://www.liszt.com)

TileNet
(http://www.tile.net/tile/listserv/index.html)

Pitsco's Launch to Lists
(http://www.pitsco.com/p/listservs.html)

Initiating a discussion. Questions can be used to trigger a discussion of central information before a passage is read, thus increasing the background knowledge readers bring to a text. Questions can also be used to initiate a discussion about what has happened or is likely to happen.

Guiding students' reasoning. Questions can be used to guide children's thinking. Teachers can use questions to help children replicate the reasoning strategies of proficient readers.

Focusing attention. Questions can be used to focus attention on a specific portion of text for subsequent instructional purposes.

Providing practice in specific comprehension tasks. Questions can be used to engage children in specific types of inferential tasks, such as cause-and-effect, sequence, pronoun and adverbial references, predicting outcomes, or drawing conclusions.

Assessment. Questions can be used to monitor students' understanding of a passage they have read.

Comprehension Questions

There are a variety of ways to organize the questions that teachers use during reading instruction. The traditional approach identifies the levels of comprehension addressed by the questions.

A levels approach organizes comprehension questions according to the type of information a reader must contribute to the answer. Three levels are specified: literal, inferential, and evaluative.

Literal-level questions ask for information directly from the text. Readers can answer literal-level questions by relying on the literal, word-for-word meaning of a passage; they must contribute little, if any, information to respond to literal-level questions because the answer is explicitly stated in the text.

Inferential-level questions ask for information not explicitly stated in the text. Readers must use their background knowledge in conjunction with text information and read between the lines. Inferential-level questions require readers to make either text-connecting or slot-filling inferences.

Evaluative-level questions ask readers to make a critical judgment about information in the text. To answer such questions, readers must evaluate textual information in relation to their own values and experiences. Examples of each type of question can be seen in Figure 9-3.

literal-level questions Questions asking for information explicitly stated in the text.

inferential-level questions Questions asking for information that requires a reader to use background knowledge in conjunction with information explicitly stated in the text.

evaluative-level questions Questions asking readers to make critical judgments about information in the text, using previous experiences or values.

FIGURE 9-3

Examples of literal, inferential, and evaluative questions

Text

Bob and Claire wanted to go out to eat, so Bob called to make a reservation. They drove to the restaurant, but when they arrived, no one was there. The door was locked, and a sign said "Closed on Mondays."

"What's going on?" Bob asked. "I just reserved a table over the phone."

Claire answered, "Are you sure you called the Steak House?"

"Uh, oh," said Bob apologetically. "I think I may have called the Steak Place."

Literal Questions
1. Who wanted to go out to eat? (Bob and Claire)
2. Why did Bob call? (to make a reservation)

Inferential Questions
1. When did Bob and Claire drive to the restaurant? (after Bob made the reservation)
2. On what day did this story take place? (Monday)
3. At what restaurant did Bob make a reservation? (the Steak Place)
4. Where did Bob and Claire go? (the Steak House)

Evaluative Questions
1. What would you have done next in this situation? (All logical answers are acceptable.)
2. What do you think Bob and Claire should have done differently? (All logical answers are acceptable.)

question-answer relations (QARs) A taxonomy of relationships between questions and answers.

right-there QARs One type of in-the-book QAR; questions with answers that are explicitly stated in the text.

putting-it-together QARs One type of in-the-book QAR requiring readers to make a text-connecting inference.

author-and-you QARs One type of in-my-head QAR requiring readers to connect background knowledge to information in the text.

on-your-own QARs One type of in-my-head QAR calling for answers that are not in the text but that depend on the reader's own experiences.

Raphael (1982, 1986) has suggested it is appropriate to consider questions and their answers together. By doing so, we can be more precise in our use of questions and our understanding of why students have difficulty with certain questions. Based on an initial taxonomy developed by Pearson and Johnson (1978), Raphael has developed a system referred to as **question-answer relations (QAR).**

A QAR approach organizes questions into two basic groups: questions that are "in the book" and questions that are "in my head." In-the-book questions have answers that can be found in the text. These questions come in two types: "right there" and "putting it together." **Right-there QARs** are similar to literal-level questions. They require literal recall of explicitly stated information. In other words, the answer is right there in the text. **Putting-it-together QARs** require readers to connect information stated in two or more locations; thus, they require a text-connecting inference.

The second major category includes in-my-head question-answer relationships. These questions also come in two types: "author and you" and "on your own."

Author-and-you QARs require readers to connect information in the text with information they bring to it. The answer is not explicitly stated but requires readers to make a slot-filling inference. **On-your-own QARs** feature answers that are not in the text. Readers rely entirely on their own experiences and can even answer on-your-own QARs without reading the text. Examples of each type of question-answer relationship can be seen in Figure 9-4.

Guidelines for Using Questions

Questioning occurs frequently during classroom reading lessons. Therefore, it is important for you to think about how you will use questions in your own classroom. The suggestions on page 335 should help.

FIGURE 9-4

Examples of in-the-book and in-my-head questions

Text

Bob and Claire wanted to go out to eat, so Bob called to make a reservation. They drove to the restaurant, but when they arrived, no one was there. The door was locked, and a sign said "Closed on Mondays."

"What's going on?" Bob asked. "I just reserved a table over the phone."

Claire answered, "Are you sure you called the Steak House?"

"Uh, oh" said Bob apologetically. "I think I may have called the Steak Place."

In-the-Book Questions

Right There

1. Who wanted to go out to eat? (Bob and Claire)
2. Why did Bob call? (to make a reservation)

Putting It Together

1. When did Bob and Claire drive to the restaurant? (after Bob made the reservation)
2. At what restaurant did Bob make a reservation? (the Steak Place)

In-My-Head Questions

Author and You

1. At what restaurant were Bob and Claire? (the Steak House)
2. On what day did this story take place? (Monday)

On Your Own

1. How would you feel if you took a friend to dinner and the restaurant was closed? (All logical answers are acceptable.)

Questions should be asked at all levels and should not be used only to test comprehension.

1. *Do Not Use Questions Solely to Test Comprehension.* Durkin (1979, 1981) found that teachers use questions largely to test, not teach, reading comprehension. As mentioned earlier, when teachers play the guess-the-answer-I-have-in-my-head game with students, they are testing, not teaching. To teach reading comprehension, model your own reasoning processes aloud to children and ask them to explain their reasoning processes as well. This procedure is sometimes referred to as a "think-aloud" (Davey, 1983; Fitzgerald, 1983). For example, you might follow up each comprehension question with "Can you tell us how you figured out that answer?" Making reasoning processes explicit is especially helpful for less-proficient students and provides important insights to teachers about their students' comprehension processes (Wade, 1990).

2. *Help Students Understand that Answers May Come from the Text or from Knowledge about the World They Bring to a Text.* Students are not always aware of this distinction. Some research suggests that knowing the distinction between in-the-book and in-my-head QARs facilitates comprehension (Raphael, 1982, 1986). This can also be developed through the effective use of Internet Workshop as you discuss information students have discovered on the Internet.

3. *Ask Higher-Level Questions.* If you take a levels approach to questions, higher-level questions are more appropriate than lower-level questions because the former provide more reasoning opportunities for readers. For example, to answer an evaluative-level question, readers must consider information at the literal, inferential, and evaluative levels. To answer an inferential-level question, readers must consider information at both literal and inferential levels. However, to answer a literal-level question, readers need to consider only information at the literal level. Higher-level questions also provide greater opportunities to model reasoning processes.

4. *If Children Are Unable to Answer a Higher-Level Question, Ask a Related Lower-Level Question.* Breaking down the reasoning task into easier elements provides a supporting scaffold, or foundation, on which children can make an inference.

5. *Accept Greater Variation in Responses as You Ask Higher-Level Questions.* Answers to literal-level questions or in-the-book QARs are either correct or incorrect: The answers are explicitly stated in the text. However, answers to inferential-level questions, evaluative-level questions, or in-my-head QARs rely on background knowledge, which differs among individuals. As a result, higher-level questions usually have more than one acceptable answer.

6. *Ask Questions Before Children Read a Story.* This approach helps students attend to the important background knowledge required to comprehend a passage. For example, ask children whether they have ever experienced a problem like the one in the story they are about to read. Then have a short discussion about how they solved their problem. Hansen and Pearson (1980) found this strategy especially helpful for children because it builds an instructional scaffold that supports children's comprehension. Evaluative-level questions and on-my-own QARs are especially appropriate for prereading activities.

7. *Plan Discussion Questions in Advance.* Devising questions as you discuss a story with children will result in many literal-level questions or in-the-book QARs. It is nearly impossible to generate more complex questions without advance planning. Thus, before discussing a story, you should be sure that you have thought about the types of questions you will ask.

8. *Provide Sufficient "Wait Time."* It is important after asking a question to wait sufficiently long for an answer. Often, you will find yourself wanting to say something if no one is responding to your question. Just wait. It is important to allow children an opportunity to think about the question you have asked.

9. *Provide All Students with Equal Opportunities to Respond to Questions.* Be certain all of your students have opportunities to share their thinking with others. Sometimes teachers find themselves asking more questions of boys than girls. Monitor who gets called on in class to ensure all children receive equal opportunities.

Using a Literacy Framework to Inform Instruction in Reading Comprehension

There are two basic decisions to consider related to reading comprehension, and your literacy framework can assist you with both. First, you will need to decide what to teach and emphasize. Should you try to develop syntactic, discourse, and metacognitive knowledge? How much should you emphasize these types of knowledge? Your beliefs about the most important components will guide you in these decisions.

Second, you will need to decide how you will teach reading comprehension. Should you favor deductive or inductive learning experiences? Should you follow a hierarchical sequence of comprehension skills, or should you engage students in experiences where they will develop their own comprehension strategies? Should questions be used to practice and assess comprehension or should they be used more to develop comprehension through modeling experiences? Which method frameworks should you use to teach comprehension? Your beliefs about how children learn best will assist you in these decisions.

What Should I Teach and Emphasize?

To guide you in deciding what you will teach and emphasize, you need to consider your beliefs about the most important components in the reading process. Table 9-2 summarizes how that portion of your framework can be used to guide decision making about comprehension instruction.

Reader-Based Beliefs. Teachers who have reader-based beliefs about the most important components spend the most time developing syntactic, discourse, and metacognitive knowledge because they believe that meaning exists more in what a reader brings to a text than in the text itself. Inferences are especially important to these teachers; therefore, predicting outcomes and drawing conclusions are encouraged since they involve inferences, either looking forward toward upcoming information or looking backward toward previous information. Implicit cause-and-effect and sequence relationships requiring readers to make inferences are also emphasized. This is true because teachers with reader-based beliefs are most concerned with developing readers' abilities to bring prior knowledge to a text; this is especially true of implicit relationships. In addition, inferential- and evaluative-level questions and in-my-head QARs are used more than other types of questions because they rely on meanings readers bring to a text.

TABLE 9-2

A summary of how a literacy framework can be used to inform decisions about what to teach about comprehension

Beliefs about How One Reads	Related Assumptions	What Should I Teach?
Reader-based	Meaning exists more in what the reader brings to the text.	I should teach prior knowledge components of reading comprehension, especially comprehension strategies, inferential reasoning, predicting outcomes, drawing conclusions, inferential- and evaluative-level questions, and in-my-head QARs.
	Reading is a result of expectations.	
	Reading begins with elements of prior knowledge.	
Text-based	Meaning exists more in the text than in the reader.	I should teach elements that help children determine the meaning in a text: explicitly signaled relationships, signal words, literal-level questions, in-the-text QARs.
	Reading is translation.	
	Reading begins with decoding.	
Interactive	Meaning exists in both the text and the reader.	I should teach both prior knowledge and textual meaning elements, depending on individual needs.
	Reading is both translation and expectation.	
	Reading uses each knowledge source simultaneously and interactively.	

Text-Based Beliefs. Teachers who hold text-based beliefs about the most important components of reading spend the least amount of time developing syntactic, discourse, and metacognitive knowledge. Because they believe that meaning exists more in the text than in the prior knowledge a reader brings to that text, they spend more time developing decoding knowledge. When these teachers do teach elements related to the comprehension of extended text, they focus instructional time on elements that help readers comprehend the meaning that exists in the text: punctuation, explicitly signaled sequence relationships, explicitly signaled cause-and-effect relationships, signal words, literal-level questions, and in-the-book QARs. These teachers spend less time teaching elements that help readers bring meaning to a text, such as predicting outcomes or drawing conclusions.

Punctuation, explicitly signaled cause-and-effect relationships, explicitly signaled sequence relationships, and signal words are all taught because they are elements of meaning in a text. Implicit relationships that require readers to make an inference and contribute meaning to a text are not emphasized. Literal-level questions and in-the-book QARs are used more than other types of questions, again, because they help a reader comprehend the meaning that already exists in a text.

Interactive Beliefs. Teachers who have interactive beliefs about the most important components of reading spend a moderate amount of time developing syntactic, discourse, and metacognitive knowledge. But even as they develop those elements associated with what a reader brings to a text, they are also developing decoding knowledge wherever necessary, a component associated with the meaning that is already in a text. These teachers help youngsters draw conclusions and predict outcomes. They help students with punctuation, key words, and explicit cause-and-effect and sequence relationships, as well as with the inferences required in implicit cause-and-effect and sequence relationships. These teachers use the complete range of questions to develop reading comprehension: literal, inferential, and evaluative questions, in addition to in-the-book and in-my-head QARs.

How Should I Teach?

You will also need to make decisions about how to teach the comprehension of extended text. Your beliefs about how children learn best should guide you in those

TABLE 9-3

A summary of how a literacy framework can be used to inform decisions about how to teach reading comprehension

Beliefs about How One Reads	Related Assumptions	How Should I Teach?
Holistic language learning	Students learn to read best in an inductive fashion as they direct their own reading experiences.	I should emphasize student-directed reading experiences and inductive learning. Reading experiences always take place in the context of authentic social contexts and always with authentic reading materials. Popular method frameworks include those that allow for much student direction during learning experiences: Internet Inquiry, Internet Project, Internet Workshop, style studies, inductive instruction, and cooperative learning groups.
Specific skills	Students learn best when they are taught specific skills directly by the teacher in a deductive fashion.	I should teach specific skills with direct instructional practices. Popular method frameworks include directed reading activities, deductive instruction, and language experience sentences.
Integrated	Students learn best as a result of both student-directed, inductive experiences and teacher-directed, deductive experiences.	I should create authentic learning environments for children to explore their own literacy insights and directly teach specific skills, depending on individual needs. All method frameworks described in this chapter are used, depending on individual needs.

decisions. Table 9-3 summarizes how that portion of your framework can be used in decision making.

Holistic Language Learning Beliefs.   Teachers with holistic language learning beliefs find that reading ability develops as students direct their learning with print. As a result, inductive experiences are favored and comprehension instruction always takes place, as needed, within the context of student-directed reading experiences. Questions are used more for modeling than for practice and assessment, and the most common method frameworks include Internet Inquiry, style studies, inductive instruction, and cooperative learning groups. In addition, method frameworks from other chapters also based on inductive learning often are used, such as text sets and literature discussion groups (see chapter 6).

Specific Skills Beliefs.   Teachers with specific skills beliefs find that reading ability develops as students learn specific reading skills, which should be taught in teacher-directed, deductive lessons. As a result, deductive experiences are favored and a hierarchy of specific comprehension skills are apt to guide instruction. Questions are used mainly to practice and assess students' developing skills, and the most common method frameworks include deductive instruction, directed reading activities (DRAs), and language experience sentences.

Integrated Beliefs.   Teachers with integrated beliefs find that both specific skills and holistic perspectives are important. All of the method frameworks described in this chapter are used, depending on individual needs. All Internet methods are used, including Internet Inquiry, Internet Project, and Internet Workshop.

Use the self-test questions on http://www.prenhall.com/leukinzer to review the material presented in this chapter.

Featured Teacher

Fred Roemer

Pay a visit to the classroom of Fred Roemer, a fifth-grade teacher in Florida. Fred's classroom web page, **Mr. Roemer's Fifth Grade Polar Bears** (http://www.pb5th.com/index.shtml; see Figure 9-5), is one of the most sophisticated classroom web pages available. There are many lessons to be learned by exploring this classroom web page, but there are two lessons, in particular, that we wish to draw your attention to. First, notice how Fred uses this site to build community. The class is always referred to as the Polar Bears. You will see this throughout the web page, and you sense that Fred uses this label to build a common sense of community. Developing solidarity and community is important for you to consider. As you work to build a group cohesiveness and identity for your classroom, you will discover how important this is throughout the year as you work to have each student in your classroom support other students.

Fred also has developed a daily log section at his web page. Each day, a student is assigned to write a description, and commentary, of what took place that day. The entry usually contains at least one photo from their digital camera. The daily log is read by many students in the classroom to see what is being said about the events of that day. In addition, grandparents and parents like to read these commentaries to see what took place that day. Take a look at Fred's classroom web page to discover many other ways in which this talented teacher integrates the Internet into his classroom community.

FIGURE 9-5

The home page for Fred Roemer's fifth-grade classroom in Florida

Major Points

▶ An inference is a reasoned assumption about meaning not explicitly stated in the text. Readers make inferences by using their background knowledge to connect different pieces of information in a text and to fill in missing information. Inferential reasoning is sometimes referred to as reading between the lines.

▶ Experiences with the Internet and other networked technologies can be very useful to support reading comprehension. Internet experiences provide authentic contexts for engaging in information activities, experiences that will increasingly define our children's futures. Common method frameworks include Internet Workshop, Internet Project, and Internet Inquiry.

▶ Comprehension instruction seeks to make visible the many "hidden" strategies we use to understand written information.

▶ There are many ways to develop the metacognitive strategies important during comprehension. The most common method frameworks include reciprocal questioning and reciprocal teaching.

▶ There are many ways to develop important syntactic aspects of comprehension: style studies, language experience sentences, language experience stories, and discussions with children's literature.

▶ There are many ways to develop important discourse aspects of comprehension: deductive instruction, directed reading-thinking activities (DRTAs), and discussions about children's literature.

▶ Questioning strategies can be used to teach aspects of reading comprehension. Traditional approaches use different levels of questions. More recent approaches use a taxonomy based on question-answer relationships.

▶ A literacy framework assists with decisions about what to teach and how to teach it.

Making Instructional Decisions

1. Identify at least four inferences a reader must make to comprehend the following passage. Specify whether each is a text-connecting or a slot-filling inference.

   It was raining, and they were inside the old barn. They unloaded their rifles and climbed the ladder to the loft. The hay was warm and dry. Craig and Bill sat swapping tales of their adventures with grouse and waiting for a chance to get back outside. They both enjoyed the chance to stretch the truth a bit. Finally the rain stopped, and Bill said, "Let's get going. We have to bring something home for dinner." Craig noticed, though, that it was already dark outside.

2. Develop an Internet Workshop page you could use to introduce a thematic unit. Find a central site related to this unit on the Internet and develop a page useful to establish prior knowledge about the topic.

3. Some teachers believe you cannot teach children how to comprehend. They argue children develop comprehension abilities on their own as a result of extensive reading, thinking, and discussion. These teachers provide many opportunities for students to read, think, and discuss what they have read. They believe each child will acquire his or her own insights about comprehension as a result of these experiences. Others believe comprehension processes can be taught. These teachers teach specific comprehension strategies to their students. They believe too many children are missing basic comprehension strategies and need direct instruction in this area. Still other teachers combine these two beliefs—they believe children learn best when they have extensive reading, thinking, and discussion opportunities combined with specific instruction in comprehension strategies when necessary.

   How do you believe reading comprehension develops? Should you teach children specific comprehension strategies? Should you assume these will develop most appropriately as long as you provide extensive reading, thinking, and discussion opportunities? As you think about this question, consider your beliefs about the second issue in a literacy framework: How should I teach? How might this aspect of your literacy framework inform your initial thoughts about comprehension instruction?

4. Plan a lesson using a language experience story to teach either sequence or cause-and-effect relationships. Identify which experience you will provide, how you will elicit oral language, and what you will do to teach sequence or cause-and-effect relationships.

5. Define one question each that you might use to assess comprehension of the passage in item 1 on a literal, inferential, and evaluative level. Then develop right-there, putting-it-together, author-and-you, and on-your-own QARs for the same passage.

Further Reading

Baumann, J. F., Jones, L. A., & Seifert-Kessell, N. (1993). Using think-alouds to enhance children's comprehension monitoring abilities. *The Reading Teacher, 47,* 184–193.

> *Describes how the use of think-alouds can be used to support children's comprehension by helping them to monitor their own comprehension processes. Describes many useful classroom activities that can be used with think-alouds to support comprehension.*

Commeyras, M. (1993). Promoting critical thinking through dialogical-thinking reading lessons. *The Reading Teacher, 46,* 486–494.

> *Describes a method framework, called dialogical-thinking reading lessons (D-TRL), that engages students in discussion and thinking about a story-specific issue. The process helps students to understand strategies and reasoning processes central to reading comprehension from their discussions about how they interpreted a story.*

Dugan, J. (1997). Transactional literature discussions: Engaging students in the appreciation and understanding of literature. *The Reading Teacher, 51,* 86–96.

> *This article describes a method for integrating reading, writing, and discussion to help make more explicit the meaning-making process. These useful strategies support reading comprehension and response in your classroom.*

Guillaume, A. M. (1998). Learning with text in the primary grades. *The Reading Teacher, 51,* 476–486.

> *Are you looking for great ideas to help younger children construct meaning as they read and write about informational texts? This article shares many useful strategies.*

Swift, K. (1993). Try reading workshop in your classroom. *The Reading Teacher, 46,* 366–371.

> *Describes a yearlong project conducted by a teacher to study the effects of a reading workshop approach. The approach uses many writing and journal experiences along with discussion and group instruction to support reading comprehension and response.*

References

Anderson, R. C., Hiebert, E. H., Scott, J. A., & Wilkinson, I. A. G. (1985). *Becoming a nation of readers: The report of the commission on reading.* Washington, DC: National Institute of Education.

Anderson, R. C., & Shifrin, Z. (1980). The meaning of words in context. In R. J. Spiro, B. C. Bruce, & W. F. Brewer (Eds.), *Theoretical issues in reading comprehension.* Hillsdale, NJ: Lawrence Erlbaum Associates.

Au, K. H. (1993). *Literacy instruction in multicultural settings.* Fort Worth: Harcourt Brace Jovanovich.

Baker, L., & Brown, A. L. (1984). Cognitive monitoring in reading. In J. Flood (Ed.), *Understanding reading comprehension.* Newark, DE: International Reading Association.

Beck, I. (1989). Reading and reasoning. *The Reading Teacher, 42,* 676–682.

Beck, I. L., McKeown, M. G., Omanson, R. C., & Pople, M. T. (1984). Improving the comprehensibility of stories: The effects of revisions that improve coherence. *Reading Research Quarterly, 19*(3), 263–277.

Cook-Gumperz, J., & Gumperz, J. (1981). From oral to written culture: The transition to literacy. In M. F. Whiteman (Ed.), *Writing: The nature, development, and teaching of written communication.* Hillsdale, NJ: Lawrence Erlbaum Associates.

Cummins, J. (1981). Four misconceptions about language proficiency in bilingual education. *NABE Journal, 5,* 31–45.

Davey, B. (1983). Think-aloud: Modeling the cognitive processes of reading comprehension. *Journal of Reading, 27,* 44–47.

Durkin, D. (1979). Reading comprehension instruction in five basal reading series. *Reading Research Quarterly, 14,* 481–533.

Durkin, D. (1981). Reading methodology textbooks: Are they helping teachers teach comprehension? *The Reading Teacher, 39*(5), 410–417.

Dulay, H., Burt, M., & Krashen, S. (1982). *Language two.* Oxford: Oxford University Press.

Fitzgerald, J. (1983). Helping readers gain self-control. *The Reading Teacher, 37,* 249–253.

Grant, C. A., & Gomez, M. L. (1996). *Making schooling multicultural: Campus and classroom.* Upper Saddle River, NJ: Merrill/Prentice Hall.

Hansen, J., & Pearson, P. D. (1980). *The effects of inference training and practice on young children's comprehension* (Tech. Rep. No. 166). Urbana, IL: University of Illinois, Center for the Study of Reading.

Krashen, S., & Terrell, T. D. (1983). *The natural approach.* New York: Pergamon.

Leu, D. J., Jr. (1982). Differences between oral and written discourse and the acquisition of reading proficiency. *Journal of Reading Behavior, 14*(2), 111–125.

Manzo, A. V. (1969). The request procedure. *Journal of Reading, 11,* 123–126.

McGee, L. M., & Richgels, D. J. (1990). *Literacy beginnings.* Boston, MA: Allyn & Bacon.

McGovern, A. (1975). *The secret soldier.* New York: Scholastic Books.

Michaels, S., & Cook-Gumperz, J. (1979). A study of sharing time with first grade students: Discourse narratives in the classroom. *Proceedings of the Berkeley Linguistic Society, 5,* 87–103.

Murphy, S. (1985). Children's comprehension of deictic categories in oral and written language. *Reading Research Quarterly, 21,* 118–131.

National Reading Panel (2000). *Teaching children to read.* Washington, D.C.: National Institute of Health.

Palincsar, A. S. (1986). The role of dialogue in providing scaffolded instruction. *Educational Psychologist, 21,* 73–98.

Palincsar, A. S., & Brown, A. L. (1984). Reciprocal teaching of comprehension-fostering and monitoring activities. *Cognition and Instruction, 1,* 117–175.

Pearson, P. D., & Camperell, K. (1981). Comprehension of text structures. In J. T. Guthrie (Ed.), *Comprehension and teaching.* Newark, DE: International Reading Association.

Pearson, P. D., & Johnson, D. D. (1978). *Teaching reading comprehension.* New York: Holt, Rinehart & Winston.

Purcell-Gates, V. (1989). What oral/written language differences can tell us about beginning instruction. *The Reading Teacher, 42*(4), 290–295.

Raphael, T. E. (1982). Teaching children question-answering strategies. *The Reading Teacher, 36,* 186–191.

Raphael, T. E. (1986). Teaching question-answer relationships, revisited. *The Reading Teacher, 39,* 516–522.

Raphael, T. E., & Brock, C. H. (1993). Mei: Learning the literacy culture in an urban elementary school. In D. J. Leu & C. K. Kinzer (Eds.), *Examining central issues in literacy research, theory, and practice: The forty-second yearbook of the National Reading Conference.* Chicago, IL: National Reading Conference.

Rubin, A. (1980). A theoretical taxonomy of the differences between oral and written language. In R. J. Spiro, B. C. Bruce, & W. F. Brewer (Eds.), *Theoretical issues in reading comprehension.* Hillsdale, NJ: Lawrence Erlbaum Associates.

Snow, C., Burns, M., & Griffin, P. (Eds.) (1998). *Preventing reading difficulties in young children.* Washington, DC: National Academy Press.

Stauffer, R. G. (1976). *Teaching reading as a thinking process.* New York: Harper & Row.

Sulzby, E. (1982). Oral and written mode adaptations in stories by kindergarten children. *Journal of Reading Behavior, 14*(2), 51–60.

Teale, W. H., & Sulzby, E. (Eds.). (1986). *Emergent literacy: Writing and reading.* Norwood, NJ: Ablex.

U. S. Department of Education. (1991). *The condition of bilingual education in the nation: A report to the Congress and the president.* Washington, DC: U. S. Department of Education, Office of the Secretary.

Wade, S. E. (1990). Using think-alouds to assess comprehension. *The Reading Teacher, 43,* 442–451.

Content-Area Reading and Study Skills

 E-mail from the Classroom

Subject: Re: Our Recollections
From: Andi Markinson, amark@vanderbilt.edu

Hello Everyone!

This is a response to an interesting question posed on our class discussion list: "Would you be a better reader today if your reading teachers would have spent a bit more time on how to read things in addition to children's stories?"

In primary grades, I learned how to read stories. It seems like my teachers didn't use many other materials. So I guess I learned how to read stories, and I loved reading them. But starting in middle grades, I had to read more and more textbooks, and now I have to read articles and other things that aren't stories. And in talking to my parents (who still love reading novels), most of the reading they do in everyday life is business-related and job-related material—memos, letters, instruction manuals, maps, and so on. So, I guess I was taught to read using stories, but in real life we read other things.

So I do wonder if I'd be a better reader today if my reading teachers would have spent a bit more time on how to read things in addition to stories. The literature I read while learning to read was great. It made me want to read, it taught me lots of important things, and it made me look forward to reading. But I'm not sure that it helped me figure out how to learn things by reading other kinds of books. I do have to say, though, that reading is what I like to do when I need to relax!

After reading this chapter, you should be able to:

1. Teach children about strategies that will help them read the many different kinds of material they will encounter in various academic subject areas.
2. Choose techniques to help children better read and study required reading material in content-area subjects.
3. Teach children about the different structures of reading materials in social studies, mathematics, and science, and how these will affect comprehension.
4. Teach child-centered research and study skills such as I-Search and K-W-L.
5. Use computers and the Internet to help children with reading and studying in the content areas.

Teach Reading Using Different Kinds of Texts: A Principle of Effective Literacy Instruction

As children move through the grade levels, they are required to read a variety of materials, from stories to textbooks and other items that are unique to various subject areas. Because different types of reading materials have different structures, they place different demands on readers, who need to apply different strategies to effectively comprehend those texts. Thus, chapter 1 noted the following principle of effective literacy instruction:

8. **Teach reading using different kinds of texts.** Different strategies are required for reading different kinds of texts; teaching strategies that are most appropriate for texts in the various content areas will result in more effective comprehension of materials that do not rely on narrative text patterns (Bean, 2000).

Check your ongoing understanding of chapter concepts by using the guided review for this chapter on http://www. prenhall.com/leukinzer

This chapter presents the differences in reading demands across content areas and provides strategies that can be taught to readers to make their reading more effective. Beginning to teach content-area reading strategies to young readers and continuing to refine these throughout the elementary grades is an important part of being an effective teacher of reading and writing.

Changes in Reading throughout the Grades

Andi's reflective e-mail shows clearly that there is a difference between the reading materials usually used in early reading instruction and the reading demands on children as they mature. Teaching children skills related to research and study is an important part of reading instruction. By about third grade, instruction specifically related to reading tapers off and more emphasis is placed on learning content in academic subject areas. In fact, the whole school experience often is restructured as a child moves from the primary to intermediate grades. Where there was only one classroom and one teacher, there now may be different teachers and different classrooms for various subjects. And where there was previously a great deal of stability, there now may be a continually changing instructional environment—one that will continue to change throughout the intermediate grades, with even more pronounced changes in the secondary grades.

Along with different subject areas come varied demands on readers. The phrase "reading to learn versus learning to read" is commonly used to describe these changing demands. The kinds of activities and strategies most common in kindergarten through third grade are targeted at children's learning to read. Activities tied to informational material or to the textbooks most common above second grade facilitate children's reading to learn. Some subject-specific reading demands are easily seen. For example, in science children are required to understand and manipulate various formulas and to learn many new, content-specific terms. In mathematics they must read many self-contained units (such as word problems) and comprehend many numerical examples and rules in the form of theorems and laws. In all subject areas, different types of texts demand different strategies from the reader in terms of approach and interpretation as well as background knowledge and recognition of text structure. For example, readers unaware that a text is designed to persuade may interpret it as fact and use it incorrectly.

genres Categories of literary compositions, each having a special style, form, or content.

Differences in text styles seem fairly easy for people to recognize within narrative writing **genres**. After all, poetry is clearly different from dramatic scripts and both differ from stories, even in visible ways.

expository Designed to explain or present.

However, the general differences between **expository** texts and narratives, and the concept that expository texts in different subject areas make different demands on readers, seem somewhat more difficult to recognize. Nonetheless, knowing these differences and understanding how readers comprehend different text types will make you a more effective teacher and better able to prepare your students to read the wide range of materials ahead of them.

PRACTICAL TEACHING STRATEGIES

Helping Children Understand Organizing Structures in Reading Materials

Table of Contents.   Using a book's table of contents, have children predict what specific information might be found in various chapters, sections, and subsections. Write their predictions on the chalkboard. Then have children go to the appropriate pages to check their predictions.

   Provide a list of specific items of information found in a book's various chapters, sections, and subsections. Allow children to match the items on the list with the titles in the table of contents. Have them explain and discuss the reasons for their matches and check to see whether the match-ups are correct.

Copyright Differences.   Examine several copyright pages and tables of contents from books in one subject area but with copyright dates spanning 15 years (for example, science books). Have children use the tables of contents to compare the topics, then have them use the copyright pages and attempt to match copyright pages to tables of contents. Be ready to provide some guidance with this activity, pointing out which topics are relatively recent and thus would not have been included in earlier books.

Glossary and Index Activities.   Discuss the difference between a glossary and a dictionary: A glossary contains definitions only for words that appear in that particular book, whereas a dictionary includes many other words. Find sentences that contain content-specific vocabulary in a book with a glossary and have children look up the meanings of the specialized words in the glossary. Then read the paragraphs that contain the terms to see whether the definitions are appropriate.

   Compare the pages of an index and a glossary of a book. Have children identify the differences and write these on the chalkboard (for example, a glossary contains definitions, an index contains page numbers, and so on). Discuss the purposes of each and the ways in which the differences help to meet those purposes.

The Role of Organizing Structures in Reading Materials

Organizing structures help readers anticipate upcoming content, provide shortcuts to finding information, or help readers understand the importance or accuracy of information by knowing its source and authors. Such structures include the title and headings, copyright page, preface, table of contents, reference list/bibliography, index, and glossary. Understanding the use and importance of these organizing structures helps a reader comprehend what is presented.

   For example, a copyright page can tell us whether information is out of date or whether the item was published by a special-interest group and, therefore, might be biased. A preface can point out the author's purpose for writing the material, and a table of contents presents an outline of what information is included and helps set up readers' expectations about what will be presented. Each organizing structure contains important information that can help the reader. However, it is not only related to books. For example, World Wide Web home pages on the Internet often contain copyright information, buttons, and links similar to a table of contents. Knowing who (or what organization) is maintaining a website can help users to recognize potential biases, and the "look and feel" (including headings and graphics) of a website can influence children's perceptions and expectations for what will be found. Thus, discussions of various organizing structures should be related to both electronic and nonelectronic reading and research materials. The strategies previously listed can help teach this aspect of literacy.

Recognizing Differences in Text Organization

Text structure is also an important factor in the reading process. The major structural difference between narrative and expository text is that narratives usually are written along a time sequence; exposition is organized according to **superordinate** and **subordinate** concepts.

superordinate concept
Part of the organizational pattern in expository text; a major unit supported by subunits.

subordinate concept
Part of the organizational pattern in expository text; a subunit that supports a larger unit.

This difference is easy to see, even in the partial tables of contents shown below. The example on the left comes from a mathematics textbook (Bassler, Kolb, Craighead, & Gray, 1981); the example on the right comes from a fictional narrative (Defoe, 1967).

Table of Contents
Addition and subtraction—whole numbers

Rounding numbers through hundred thousands

Finding sums and differences through 6 digits

Estimating sums and differences by rounding

Checking addition and subtraction

Multiplication and division—whole numbers

Multiplying by 1- and 2-digit factors

Estimating products by rounding

Solving multiple-step problems

Table of Contents
I Go to Sea

On the Island

We Plan to Leave the Island

The English Ship

Home!

These examples clearly show the conceptual organization of exposition and the sequential arrangement of narratives.

Several organizational patterns are found in content-area texts, with certain patterns more common in certain subject areas. For example, the following passage demonstrates the time-order sequence usually found in the narrative materials of language arts. See if you can find the cues that tell the reader the organizational pattern is a time sequence:

> Tracy knew she would not be able to sleep. But her mother had told her to brush her teeth and put on her nightgown anyway, and Tracy did as she was told.
>
> Just as she got into her nightgown, a loud crack of thunder filled the air! Tracy jumped into bed and pulled the covers over her head. When Meg peeked into the room, Tracy wailed, "The last time we had a storm like this, I stayed awake all night!"
>
> Meg sat beside Tracy and tucked her little sister in. Then she started to hum softly. It was one of Tracy's favorite songs.
>
> As the song went on, Meg noticed that Tracy's eyes had closed. Meg turned off the bedroom light as she tiptoed out of the room. Tracy didn't hear the next clap of thunder as the storm continued into the night. (Carson, 1990)

Background knowledge tells children that brushing one's teeth happens before getting into bed, getting tucked in, and going to sleep. In addition, conjunctions such as *and* can indicate sequential order, as can specific references such as *last time, then,* and *next.* Children have less difficulty with this type of text than with other organizational patterns.

The following passage, taken from a social studies textbook, demonstrates how number order is used as an organizational pattern. In this case, the structure of the passage outlines its content. The organizational cues lie in the enumeration of points—first, second—and in the two-part activity that relates to and balances the two factual statements that precede it:

> Look at the map above. It shows you two things. First, it tells you the periods in which early Islam spread. Second, it shows the areas into which Islam spread. Islam began in the cities of Mecca and Medina. Use the map key to find the name of the area in which these two cities are found. Use the map key to find the territory that Muslims had conquered by Muhammed's death in 632. (Myers & Wilk, 1983, p. 272)

Can you pick out the cues indicating that the next passage, taken from a science textbook, is organized in a comparison/contrast pattern? Notice the comparisons between radio and television and the implicit assumption that the reader's background knowledge will incorporate this new information:

> Television is the most popular form of communication in the world today. Television is very similar to radio. In radio, sound energy is changed to radio wave energy. Radio wave energy is sent through space. In television, both sound and light are changed to in-

visible waves. Television sets change the invisible waves back to light and sound. (Sund, Adams, & Hackett, 1980, p. 275)

The last organizational pattern presented here is one of cause and effect. Often, events happen because of other events. This can be noticed most frequently in history textbooks, for example, where the causal relationships between historical events are a primary focus. Cause-and-effect relationships can also be subtle, as in the following example from an elementary mathematics textbook (Bassler, Kolb, Craighead, & Gray, 1981). Notice that the passage implies that a plane boundary is dependent on a plane region; therefore, the plane region can be considered the cause of the plane boundary:

A closed plane figure together with its inside is called a plane region. The figure around the plane region is called its boundary. Plane regions are named for their boundaries.

This is a circle.   This is a circular region.

You should not assume that children who can read one kind of text structure can read another with similar ease. Suggested activities to build children's awareness of the different structures through a discussion of how authors use language to signal the type of organization are shown on page 350.

Vacca and Vacca (1986, p. 33; see also 2002) provide a representative list of signal words for the four organizational patterns discussed here. Obviously, not all of the words are found at all elementary grade levels. Teachers should preview the material their students will be reading and then discuss the signal words they will encounter.

Time	Enumeration	Comparison/Contrast	Cause-Effect
on (date)	to begin with	however	because
not long after	first	but	since
now	second	as well as	therefore
as	next	on the other hand	consequently
before	then	not only/but also	as a result
after	finally	either . . . or	this led to
when	most important	while	so that
	also	although	nevertheless
	in fact	unless	accordingly
	for instance	similarly	if . . . then
	for example	yet	thus

Adapting Reading Rates

Reading rate depends on a number of factors, among them the reader's purpose for reading. For instance, a mathematics word problem requires a different reading rate from that required by a story read for entertainment. Within some content-area texts, it is vital not to miss even one word; the directions for a science experiment are just one example. Many suggest that reading rates be consciously changed to meet the demands of each reading task (Farr & Roser, 1979; Shepherd, 1982). To build the idea that reading speed varies and that reading materials need not always be read from beginning to end, teachers can use activities designed to enhance skimming and scanning abilities.

Skimming.   Many content-area reading techniques discussed in this chapter require that a student first preview the reading material. Usually this step entails **skimming,** a quick movement through a text to discover its key concepts and main ideas.

skimming Reading rapidly to get a general idea of material that will be reread in detail.

PRACTICAL TEACHING STRATEGIES

Facilitating Children's Understanding of Various Text Structures

Signal Word Search.   Choose a paragraph or page in a future reading assignment that demonstrates the overall structure of the selection. Tell children about the structure being used, including the signal words appropriate to such a structure. On a copy of the chosen paragraph or page, have children mark any signal words they find. Then discuss how each of the marked words specifically indicates the pattern in the passage.

Sequence Completion.   Create an ordered list of the steps in a selection with a time-sequenced or a numbered, step-by-step organization. Then delete some of the steps in the sequence, give the list to children before they read the selection, and discuss the concept of a sequenced organizational pattern. Have children check the steps on the list as they meet them in their reading and add those that are missing.

Sequence Reorder.   For a similar activity, create an out-of-order list of the steps in a sequence. Before children read the selection, discuss the concept of an ordered sequence and have children decide how to reorder the list so that it makes logical, sequential sense. Then have children read to see whether their reordered sequence holds true, and discuss again the concept of sequence.

Predicting in Categories.   For a superordinate–subordinate structure, discuss the pattern and list the major categories found within a given selection. Have children predict what might be found under each category. Then have children read to see whether their predictions were accurate. In a post-reading discussion, examine which of the predictions are on target and discuss why some were not.

Skimming gives the reader an idea of what to expect upon more detailed reading; the process is aided by an awareness of headings and subheadings.

There are many reasons for skimming. We may skim a newspaper to decide what to read in depth. We may skim an encyclopedia entry or a web page to decide whether any or all of it needs careful attention. Or we may skim a journal article to determine whether it contains information relevant to a particular assignment. Skimming can save valuable time, and children need to develop that ability.

scanning   Reading rapidly to find specific information.

Scanning.   **Scanning** is rapid movement through a reading selection to find specific information. It is another skill that mature readers use daily.

Looking through a telephone directory to find a specific telephone number is just one example. Teachers need to foster this skill by giving their students the opportunity to practice it.

Using Research Materials

Especially in higher grades, children are required to study more informational material and are expected to use the library to find background or supplementary material. To perform effectively, they must use card catalogs, encyclopedias, almanacs, newspapers, books on related topics, atlases, and abstracts. Each of these must be mastered both in their traditional as well as electronic formats. Research abilities are important in content-area subjects and require skills such as organizing, alphabetizing, and summarizing, in addition to knowing about reference tools and sources, their contents, and their proper use.

The use of reference materials such as encyclopedias, and tools such as the card catalog, is usually included in a language arts program before specific content-area textbooks are encountered. Trips to the library and a discussion of what the library contains should begin early in the primary grades. In addition, picture encyclopedias specifically

PRACTICAL TEACHING STRATEGIES

Helping Children Acquire Skimming Abilities

Newspaper Page Skim. Provide children with the front page of a newspaper and allow only enough time for them to skim the page. Then, from a list of topics, have children identify those that were on the page. Follow up with a discussion of which topics are of most interest to them.

World Wide Web Page Skim. Provide a printed version of a web page such as **Beret's Best Sites for Children** at http://www.beritsbest.com/ and follow a procedure similar to that previously described. Allow only enough time for children to skim the printout, have them recall topics and links that were on the page, and follow up with a discussion of topics of interest and what might be found if specific links were followed.

Skim for Sequence. Provide a passage with a sequenced organizational pattern. As a prereading activity, discuss which words signal sequence. Then have children skim the passage to determine the sequence.

Skim for Main Ideas. Provide a paragraph or passage and direct children to find the main idea. Set a time limit that allows only rapid skimming, not careful reading. After they have skimmed, have them write down the main idea and then go back and read the selection carefully, writing down supporting details.

PRACTICAL TEACHING STRATEGIES

Helping Children Develop Their Scanning Abilities

Scanning for Information. Ask children to scan to find the following:

1. A particular date in a history selection.
2. The murderer's name in a short mystery story.
3. A specific heading in a science chapter.
4. A specific ingredient in a recipe.
5. Answers to questions like "Who wrote _____?" (to be found in a list of titles and authors).

designed for young children should be used early to teach young readers that information sources are available for numerous topics.

Research Skills and the Internet

The Internet has provided a powerful way to access information that is current and useful for student assignments and teacher preparation in every subject area. You need to discuss with children how to use computers to access appropriate sites and the strategies that are helpful when searching the Internet. Sites such as **B. J. Pinchbeck's Homework Helper** (http://school.discovery.com/homeworkhelp/bjpinchbeck/index.html) include many links to on-line reference sources and specialized resources categorized by subject area. Your discussion with students will need to include appropriate ways to cite Internet resources in their work. Information about citing electronic resources is found at the **American Psycholologlical Association's** on-line site at http://www.apastyle.org/elecref.html and at the **Internet Public Library** (http://www.ipl.org/ref/QUE/FARQ/netciteFARQ.html).

Chapter 14 presents a discussion of browsers and other tools for searching the Internet as well as a discussion of child safety issues, copyright concerns, and so on. Here, we simply note that you have to determine your student's sophistication with

PRACTICAL TEACHING STRATEGIES

Developing Reference-Use Abilities

Library Hunts.   Each week, post a question that requires children to use reference skills in the school library. Ask older children questions like, "What is a book published by Paul Zelinsky in 1997?" or "Who illustrated *Where the Sidewalk Ends?*" For younger children, ask questions like, "Where would you find a book by Ezra Jack Keats?" or "What are the titles of one fiction book and one nonfiction book?" Put the question up on the chalkboard just before library period, and see who can return with an answer. Below the question, place a box in which children can submit their answers. Before the end of the day, write several of the correct responses below the question and discuss how the answers were found.

Reference Match.   After a discussion and demonstration of various types of reference materials, provide a list of reference materials and a separate list of information found in those materials. Have children match the information to the source. For example:

Atlas	_____	a. Map
Encyclopedia	_____	b. Information about famous people
Thesaurus	_____	c. Use to find out which rivers flow through California
		d. Use to find out how the telephone was invented and how it works
		e. Use to find synonyms

Topic Sort.   Place several topics in a box. On the chalkboard, show an illustration of the spines of an encyclopedia set. Have children choose a topic and state which volume they would use to find information on that topic.

1	2	3	4	5	6	7	8	9	10	11	12	13	14	15	16	17	18	19	20	21
A	B	C-Ch	Ci-Cz	D	E	F	G	H	I	J-K	L	M	N-O	P	Q-R	S-Sn	So-Sz	T	U-V	WX YZ

Index cards and card catalogs have been replaced by computerized search capabilities in many libraries and classrooms.

Newspaper Fact Hunt. After a discussion of the general purpose of an index, provide newspapers to familiarize children with newspaper parts and a newspaper index. Have children use the index to find answers to questions like these: Where would you look for information about football scores? Where would you find out which movies are in town and when they are being shown? What page contains the comics? On what page would you find the weather forecast and yesterday's highest and lowest temperatures in the United States?

Internet Search Practice Activity. Divide children into groups of four and assign each group a list of several topics from which to choose. Groups should decide what they wish to know about the topic and what words and phrases to use to search for relevant information. Searches can be run throughout the day as each group cycles through computer time. Search results can be printed and critiqued by the group, as well as the class.

Dictionary Keys. Discuss the concept of key words in dictionaries, asking children how they know which words are on any given page of a dictionary. Write on the chalkboard the key words for a dictionary page, as well as words that would and would not appear on that page. Have children place the words in alphabetical order, stating whether or not they would be found on the page indicated by the key words.

Atlas Information. Have children use an atlas to find information such as which state borders another, which is the longest river in a particular area, which two cities are farther apart from another two, which of two European countries is farthest north, and so on.

Card Catalog Search. Visit the library and discuss the card catalog, its function, and the three types of cards it contains (author cards, subject cards, and title cards). Then present one list with the information desired and another with the three types of cards. Have children match the two columns. Also, have children use the card catalog to find out how many books by a particular author are owned by the library, how many books written on a given subject in the past two years are in the library, and so on. As more and more school libraries are also placing card catalogs on computer databases, children will also have to be taught how to find library information on the library's computer as well as in its card catalog. Notice, however, that the research and search strategies will not change—computerized card catalogs still use author, title, and subject (key word) categories to categorize information. Key word searches are also used to find information on the Internet.

regard to computer use and adjust your instruction as needed. An increasing number of children have computers and Internet access at home and know how to access the Internet and search for information. Others need to be shown how to use your classroom computer and how to connect to the Internet. All will benefit from lessons and examples about the use of key words, how to narrow a search using "and" and "or" qualifiers, and how to judge the accuracy of information. Also, you need to show your class examples of searches and how these can be influenced by the choice of key words. If you do not have a computer in your classroom, such discussions should occur using printed examples of searches.

The following central sites are useful across subject areas—they are valuable to teachers and students because they have links to information in a variety of areas:

Girl Tech (http://www.girltech.com/index.html)—A commercial site especially appropriate for girls that includes free links and information in all subject areas as well as chat rooms and fun activities (a sample web page appears in Figure 10-1).

Berit's Best Sites for Children (http://www.beritsbest.com/)—A site that includes links to places and activities about art, astronomy, the environment, government, health and safety, history, science and mathematics, and world travel. All sites are selected and reviewed along posted guidelines.

Canada School Net (http://www.schoolnet.ca)—A site that includes information and links to a wide variety of material across subject and interest areas, sorted by age and grade level.

FIGURE 10-1

An excerpt from the **GirlTech Internet Site** (http://www.girltech.com/index.html)

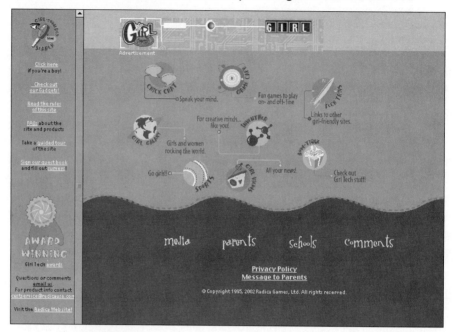

Note: Courtesy of GirlTech.

Teaching Approaches for Content-Area Literacy

Although the general teaching strategies discussed throughout this text apply to both narrative and expository materials, the method frameworks discussed in this chapter are specifically appropriate to content-area literacy instruction. Even though all literacy educators should use both narrative and expository materials, the particular approaches described here are especially important for middle-school teachers, whose children encounter predominantly expository texts. Ideally, a separate course in content-area literacy should be a part of your teacher preparation. However, as an introduction some representative, readable texts in this area are listed at the end of this chapter.

The I-Search Strategy

The I-Search strategy is an interdisciplinary, student-centered inquiry process that highlights children's conscious participation and ownership in planning and carrying out research. It also recognizes that children need to work together and that they should gain experience in sharing their findings with others in a variety of formats (MacRorie, 1988; Zorfass & Copel, 1995). There are four basics steps to the I-Search instructional framework:

1. Allow children to choose a motivating theme.
2. Allow children to formulate their own research plans.
3. Allow children to follow and revise their plans as they gather information.
4. Allow children to prepare papers as a foundation to sharing their findings through oral reports, skits, posters, experiments, or presentations using computer software.

Throughout these steps, you have to support and guide the children in their preparation and implementation of their research plans and presentations. Often, this means working with groups of children who critique each other's drafts, or allowing children who have discovered research sources to share those sources with the class. Also, brainstorming various sources (dictionaries, encyclopedias, appropriate computer software and databanks, Internet sites, library resources, newspaper archives, interviews, or let-

Celebrating Diversity

Teaching library research and reference skills provides many opportunities to celebrate diversity in our society. Many of the activities described that involve using the card catalog, encyclopedia, Internet, newspaper, and other sources can be targeted toward finding information about diverse cultures, races, languages, customs, and so on. Such activities build children's reference skills as well as provide natural bridges and links to issues about diversity.

E-mail from the Classroom

Subject: I-Search and the Internet
From: Jan Barth, wex018@mail.connect.more.net

Hello Teachers,

I would like to share an idea for classroom Internet use with you. As part of an I-Search unit on the conservation of resources, some of my 8th grade classes used the Net to research an environmental disaster, the Exxon Valdez oil spill in Alaska on March 24, 1989. Students prepared a report about how the spill occurred, the impact it had on plant and animal life and the food chain, and the methods of cleanup used after the spill. They used all their accumulated information about the spill and cleanup efforts to devise a way to clean up a simulated oil spill in the classroom. Teams of 3 children worked cooperatively to determine the best way to clean up the spill. They were to consider the cost of the materials and time for the cleanup. If you desire, you can hold a competition between teams to determine winners. Be sure to have a scoring guide in place before the teams begin their planning and the actual competition takes place. That way, students know what they are working toward.

A good site to start with is a site maintained by the **Exxon Valdez Oil Spill Trustee Council** (http://www.oilspill.state.ak.us/index.html). The children loved researching about the oil spill on the Net. They found pictures, great information about how the spill occurred, and information about the cleanup and the effect of the spills on the living organisms. The great thing about researching this particular spill is that there are follow-up research projects that are collecting data about the long-term effects on the ecosystem. Science and technology issues can be combined in a reflective essay where children think about the future of this ecosystem and the demand for oil, which ultimately was responsible for the ecosystem's destruction.

I hope I have given you some useful ideas about how to use the Internet—I really found it to be a great resource within an I-Search strategy! Good luck!

Sincerely, Jan Barth
Brookfield Middle School
Brookfield, Missouri 64628
wex018@mail.connect.more.net

ters to appropriate individuals) from which children can choose those most appropriate for their time frames and topics is an important first step. Because research and presentation is a part of working in all content areas, the I-Search strategy is valuable in all subject areas. Teachers from various areas often get together to plan an I-Search unit that cuts across subject areas to help children understand that what they are learning can apply in more than one subject. Above, Jan Barth shares her children's experience with an I-Search unit that incorporated the use of the Internet in addition to other resources the children had identified as appropriate.

TABLE 10-1

TABLE 10-1

A check sheet to monitor use of think-aloud strategies

	How Often I Did It			
What I Did	**Not Very Often**	**A Little Bit**	**Much of the Time**	**All of the Time**
Making predictions				
Forming pictures				
Using *like* (analogies)				
Finding problems				
Using fix-ups				

Think-Alouds

think-aloud A method to show children the thoughts that occur as people read; requires teachers to read a text and tell what they are thinking as they read.

The **think-aloud** method (Davey, 1983) is a procedure that takes advantage of the benefits of modeling, in which you would read a passage and talk through your thought processes for your students.

Specifically, you would focus on the use of predictions, imagery (creating a mental picture of what is being read), links between background knowledge and the text (that is, creating analogies to something already known), monitoring to see whether understanding is taking place, and fix-up strategies to address problem areas. You would model not only how to read, but also when and why to use certain strategies. After your students become familiar with the think-aloud approach, they can practice it with partners and then try to apply the think-aloud strategies in their silent reading. To keep them conscious of think-aloud strategies, Davey suggests that students complete a check sheet similar to the one shown in Table 10-1 after reading a passage. The model lesson on page 357 demonstrates the use of a think-aloud approach with a social studies passage (Myers & Wilk, 1983).

Other chapters have pointed out the benefit of having teachers model reading behaviors and processes (for example, chapter 9 discusses the ReQuest procedure). In particular, the modeling of questioning strategies can result in children transferring those behaviors to their own reading practices. Modeling is especially valuable in content-area reading, where different strategies are required because of the different text structures and the demands of subject-specific reading material. Thus, modeling helps children acquire appropriate strategies to use with specific kinds of text.

Questioning the Author (QtA)

Questioning the Author (QtA) A procedure specifically designed to facilitate children's comprehension and engagement with content-area materials.

Questioning the Author (QtA) is a popular method that incorporates features of think-aloud and cooperative learning method frameworks.

QtA is designed to help children comprehend content-area materials by having them query the author's words and ideas. This develops strategies that are important during reading (Beck, McKeown, Hamilton, & Kucan, 1997; Beck, McKeown, Worthy, Sandora, & Kucan, 1996). To initiate a QtA lesson, follow these steps:

1. Tell children that authors are real people who aren't perfect and sometimes have trouble explaining things in their writing. As readers, therefore, our job is to figure out what the author is trying to explain.
2. Tell children one or two reasons why texts are sometimes hard to understand. For example, readers sometimes don't know enough about the topic being discussed, which can make a text seem confusing.

MODEL LESSON

Think-Aloud with Content-Area Material in Tom Eckert's Class

Tom Eckert's interactive beliefs guide his decisions about *what* to teach; his integrated beliefs guide his decisions about *how* to teach. Because interactive beliefs imply that meaning exists both in the text and in what the reader brings to the text, Tom enjoys using think-alouds to show how his experiences and questions interact with what is written. His use of think-alouds is also guided by his integrated beliefs, leading to modeling activities that are teacher-led as well as student-led, using authentic texts. Below is an example of a think-aloud based on the following passage from *Herders and Nomads of the Steppe* (Myers & Wilk, 1983):

> Thousands of years ago, nomads traveled the grasslands of Europe and Asia. Skilled at riding horses, they became warriors feared for their raids on settled communities. During the time of the Romans, some rode out of the north and east to attack cities of the empire. (p. 237)

Introduction. Tom tells the class they will soon be reading an informational selection called *Herders and Nomads of the Steppe*. First, however, he wants them to listen as he thinks aloud about his own reading of the first part of the selection.

The Think-Aloud. Tom reads the title, *Herders and Nomads of the Steppe*. He says, "I know about herders. They're like shepherds—people who take care of animals. And I know that a nomad is a wanderer, but I'm not sure about *steppe*. I can probably use the context to find out. The words 'of the' in the title probably mean that the steppe is where the herders do their wandering. But that doesn't really tell me what the steppe is. I'll have to look for clues as I read on, but I might need to use a dictionary or ask someone about this word. Based on the title, I predict the passage will tell me about what kind of animals the herders kept, where they wandered, and what a steppe is."

After reading the first sentence, ("Thousands of years ago") Tom says, "This tells me the passage is not about what is going on now. But maybe there are things going on now that relate to what happened thousands of years ago. I'll probably have to make these connections myself, based on what I know." After reading the second sentence, Tom notes, "Now I know where this takes place—in Europe and Asia. I went to Italy last summer (that's in Europe!) and saw lots of grassland. I wonder if that's where these nomads roamed thousands of years ago."

After reading "During the time of the Romans, some rode out," he says, "This is confusing to me. Does the 'some' who rode out refer to the Romans or the nomads? I'll look back and see. Since it says that the nomads were good at riding horses, I'll guess *some* refers to the nomads, but I'll have to change my prediction if other things don't fit."

Purpose Setting. After the first paragraph, Tom reminds the class to try to think-aloud as they read silently and to complete their check sheets every half page.

Reading and Follow-Up. Children read and complete their check sheets. Tom then discusses the passage and allows children to share their check sheets. He also allows some children to think-aloud about other paragraphs in the selection they have just read.

3. The teacher models reading a text using a think-aloud, as discussed in the previous section. The process that is modeled should be organized around thinking about the author's message.

4. After the think-aloud, discuss the questions asked as well as items in the text that might cause a reader to look for more information.

Beck and her colleagues call the questions used in the QtA strategy "queries." For content-area materials, two types of queries are suggested: initiating queries and follow-up queries. Initiating queries are of the type: What is the author's message? What is he or she talking about? Follow-up queries are of the type: What does the author mean here? How does this connect with what the author told us before? Why do you think the author tells us this now? Queries should focus attention on what the author has done and how this affects understanding.

QtA lessons are planned by the teacher to stop at appropriate points in the text material (the places that relate to the major understandings that students are to come away with) when query-based discussion is initiated. Thus, discussion occurs during reading as opposed to at the end of reading selections. Also, QtA lessons should encourage interaction and collaboration to find out information that leads to increased understanding.

Jigsaw Grouping

Jigsaw grouping is a method framework developed to encourage active participation in cooperative group learning situations. Originally developed by Aronson and his colleagues (e.g., see Aronson, Blaney, Stephin, Sikes, & Snapp, 1978) it has been modified by Slavin (Slavin, 1989; 1994) into Jigsaw II and is especially valuable in facilitating participation by children of diverse cultural and ethnic backgrounds. Both Jigsaw and Jigsaw II are based on features of a jigsaw puzzle, where pieces fit together and form a whole. Children are divided into groups, with the number of groups equal to the number of children in each group. Before reading an assigned text, each child in a group is assigned a topic on which to become "expert," with the topics related to the main idea of the reading so that understanding each topic enhances understanding of the central issue or concept.

After reading, each child does appropriate research and additional reading activities to explore the assigned topic. Then the children with common topics from all groups meet in "expert groups" to discuss and further refine their answers, and go back to their originally assigned groups to teach each other their topics. Finally, a culminating group project or product is developed, in which knowledge of all of the topics is useful. The Jigsaw and Jigsaw II procedures are beneficial in facilitating discussion and can be incorporated into any subject area.

Directed Reading Activity

directed reading activity (DRA) A method framework containing the following steps: preparation, guided reading, skill development and practice, and enrichment.

Directed reading activity (DRA) is commonly associated with a formal reading program but is also applicable to content-area reading.

Of the four basic steps in a traditional DRA, steps 1, 2, and 4 are emphasized slightly more in expository texts than they are in narrative texts:

1. *Preparation.* This step involves providing needed background, preteaching necessary vocabulary (especially important in content-area reading), and providing motivation for reading.
2. *Guided reading.* With questions or outlines, readers' attention is directed as they proceed through the material. This step aids in the retention and comprehension of what is read.
3. *Skill development and practice.* Direct instruction in comprehension or other areas is provided, as are opportunities to practice what is taught.
4. *Enrichment.* Activities based on the reading selection often allow children to pursue topics more specifically related to their own interests.

We know that background knowledge influences the comprehension process and that interaction is especially important with content-area material. The preparation stage, therefore, is critical. Shortly before assigning reading material, you must carefully read the selection with your students in mind. Prereading discussion can then center around concepts covered in the reading, with background knowledge provided as needed. You should also deal with unknown vocabulary and provide children with a clear and definite purpose for reading the assigned text.

With content-area material, the second DRA step requires an awareness that textbooks are to be used as instructional tools, and teacher guidance is expected. A study guide or outline, periodic help with vocabulary and concepts, and other support must be available as children read. As readability and other analyses have consistently shown, most content-area textbooks are more difficult for children than narrative materials intended for comparable grade levels.

In content-area reading, the skill-development and practice step of a DRA can provide practice with difficult vocabulary terms and concepts. Each child might keep an informal

JUDY'S

COMMENTS FROM THE CLASSROOM

Because my first graders live in a rural community, it is a challenge to help them develop literacy because of their age and somewhat limited experiences.

Although we live in Maine, many children live at least 200 miles from the ocean, so one of the themes I like teaching is "All About the Ocean." It's difficult for my students to develop a deep understanding of what the ocean is like from a picture; therefore, we study sea creatures, do activities that involve ocean projects, read a number of related "information" books, and explore relevant websites, such as the **Gulf of Maine Aquarium** (http://octopus.gma.org/). I integrate as many subject areas as possible to help children make important connections between them.

I usually start my ocean unit by having the children listen to a tape of ocean sounds. Then I play it again and have them draw what they think might be making the sounds. Next, after sharing *There's a Sea in My Bedroom* by Margaret Wild, I put a large conch shell on the writing center table. I include paper with a story starter that says, "There's a sea in my classroom." Children pick up the shell and "listen" for the sound of the ocean. They really get excited by writing their stories and sharing them with the rest of the class.

We also do research on the creatures that would live in the ocean as opposed to those who live in our nearby lakes and streams. In the art center, children read and follow directions to create ocean creatures that we hang around our room. In our math center, we have a box of seashells for counting and sorting. After handling these smooth and rough shells, children write about the differences and describe how it feels to touch them.

The children also think of various ways to classify the shells into groups. After sorting them, they invite other class members to try to guess what their classification technique is. This is my favorite way to connect math and science.

After a culminating activity, we take a field trip to the southeastern part of the state. There, we spend part of a day at a Maine museum and the remainder of the day at the shore. Both the children and parents who have not had the opportunity to visit the ocean love it. Before we go to the ocean we brainstorm a list of things we expect to see there. After returning from our trip, we go over our list. We write a language experience story, adding or deleting whatever information we gained in our study. Finally, I replay the tape of ocean sounds. It is amazing to see their new knowledge show up in their drawings as they make more detailed and accurate pictures.

MODEL LESSON

Directed Reading Activity in Elizabeth Alejandro's Class

Interactive beliefs guide Elizabeth Alejandro's decisions about *what* to teach; specific skills beliefs guide her decisions about *how* to teach. In the following directed reading activity, you will see that she accesses her students' background knowledge and relates ideas from the passage to their experiences. Her specific skills beliefs, however, lead her to teach skills directly as she provides a study guide that focuses their attention on specific vocabulary in the text, as well as teaching about main ideas contained in the text.

Preparation. Elizabeth tells her class they will be reading about different ways of growing food. She notes that the popular belief is that food can best (or perhaps can only) be grown in soil, and asks why that belief is popular. Elizabeth also asks the children if they know of any methods of growing food, other than in soil, and if they would like to share any experiences they have about farming. In addition, Elizabeth sets a purpose for reading: to find out why alternative ways of growing food are becoming more important.

Guided Reading. Elizabeth provides a study guide for the children to use while reading. During the reading she walks around and helps children who need it, asking individual questions periodically. When the reading and study guide activity have been completed, Elizabeth leads a class discussion that addresses children's understanding of the selection and reviews main ideas as well as their relationship to children's general knowledge.

Skill Development and Practice. Elizabeth decides to combine a lesson on scanning with additional attention to the vocabulary and concepts introduced earlier. Children are directed to scan certain pages to find vocabulary items. They then discuss how each word is used and what it means in this specific selection. The class also discusses the potential benefits of scanning and the different types of materials in which scanning might be useful. Thereafter, children practice using the vocabulary items and concepts, and they use telephone books and newspapers for further scanning activities.

Enrichment. Elizabeth provides a list of three items and asks children which they are most interested in: (1) finding out about more ways to feed the world's increasing population, (2) finding out about how foods grown by hydroponics are being received by consumers, or (3) finding out about the effects of fertilizer on soil. The children divide into groups and go to the library to research their interests. Each group prepares a brief report and later presents it to the rest of the class.

list of difficult or unknown items encountered while reading. Class discussion can then teach the needed vocabulary as well as review main ideas and supporting details. You should periodically check children's understanding of the selection and point out relationships to previous work and knowledge, thereby setting up the enrichment step of the DRA. As in other types of reading lessons, the enrichment stage in a content-area DRA should provide activities that allow children to apply new knowledge and go beyond the text.

Several authors have addressed the application of DRA to content areas (Rubin, 1983; Thomas & Alexander, 1982). They note that, as in all teaching, the activity must take into account the special demands of the appropriate subject area and individual differences among children. A model of a content-area DRA appears above.

Vocabulary and Concept Development

One of the major barriers to comprehension in content-area reading is the high number of new concepts presented. When reading in science, mathematics, or social studies, children encounter words that are familiar in everyday use but that have unfamiliar meanings within the particular subject area. They are also confronted with new words and concepts that are subject specific. Consequently, content-area teachers must identify and teach the vocabulary and concepts required for their subject areas. Because children learn vocabulary best when it occurs in meaningful situations, content-specific vocabulary should be presented as part of a reading assignment. Both content-specific vocabulary and concept development are discussed in chapter 8.

MODEL LESSON

Study Guides in Judith Lee's Class

Judith Lee has interactive beliefs about *what* to teach and integrated beliefs about *how* to teach. Her interactive beliefs have led her to provide her students with a study guide that includes questions that point to meaning in the text (literal level questions) as well as higher-level questions that require readers to use their prior knowledge. Her integrated beliefs lead her to use study guides as a modeling procedure because the use of such guides serves as a way for students to understand what they should do (in terms of setting their own questions) while reading. Thus, the teacher-directed study guide has as its primary goal a transfer to student-directed learning. Using *Food for the Future* (Buggey, 1983), a social studies passage discussing how food might be grown to feed the world's increasing population, Judith wants the children to learn about different ways of growing food and has constructed the following three-level guide. The parenthetical information was included because she felt that the children needed additional help in some areas.

Level I [literal level]

Why will we need more food in the future?

Why will we not be able to use more land? (p. 213, par. 1)

What three methods of growing food other than using farmland are discussed? (Look at subheadings.)

Why are conditions inside greenhouses "perfect for growing crops"? (p. 232, par. 2)

What does hydroponics mean? (p. 233, par. 2)

Will plants grow closer together in water or in soil? (p. 233, par. 2)

Level II [inferential level]

Why does the author say that greenhouses can be used in many places where crops usually cannot grow? (p. 232, par. 2)

How does irrigation in deserts allow crops to grow? (p. 232, par. 1)

How are insects and weeds kept from getting inside a greenhouse?

What is the major difference between greenhousing and hydroponics?

Level III [evaluative level]

Why do you think plants grown in water don't need as many roots as plants grown in soil?

How might greenhouses control growing conditions?

Do you think it would be better to irrigate in deserts instead of using greenhouses? Explain. (p. 232, par. 1 & 2)

The **vocabulary self-selection strategy** (VSS) is appropriate to aid children in acquiring and retaining content-area vocabulary (Ruddell, 1993).

In this approach, children are asked to nominate one or more words from a selection or passage they have read. Words nominated for discussion are written on the board, and the student or group that has nominated the word explains the context in which the word was found (perhaps by reading the sentence as part of this explanation). The children then explain what they think the word means in that context and why it might be important for the class to learn the word. The teacher also nominates a word. The entire class then discusses the words chosen for study, which is always done with a focus on each word's meaning within the context in which it was found. Words studied by the class are then defined, discussed, related to children's backgrounds, and placed in vocabulary journals or word banks.

vocabulary self-selection strategy (VSS) An instructional procedure that uses words selected by children as its base.

Study Guides

Study guides help children comprehend and remember what they have read. Some guides are referred to during reading; others are used after the selection has been read.

A teacher should incorporate into a guide the important content of a reading selection and the organizational structure of the material. As noted by Herber (1978);

study guides Teacher-designed aids that assist children in reading text.

Herber and Herber (1993); Tierney, Readence, and Dishner (1990); and Tierney & Readence (2000), a study or "levels" guide should have three levels, each corresponding to one of the three general levels of comprehension questions—literal, inferential, and evaluative. Also, the study guide must be easy to read. The guide may include specific page and paragraph references or other aids, depending on the teacher's assessment of children's abilities. Study guides are not intended to stand alone but should be used as part of an overall lesson, (for example, within a directed reading or an I-Search activity).

Marginal Glosses

marginal glosses Teacher-constructed margin notes that aid students' comprehension by emphasizing and clarifying concepts, noting relationships, and modeling.

Another technique applicable to reading in all content areas is glossing. It provides a system of marginal notes designed to explain concepts, point out relationships, and otherwise clarify the text as the child reads. **Marginal glosses** are constructed by the teacher and are provided for the child when a passage is assigned.

In effect, the marginal glosses reflect your presence, providing a guide for the reader while demonstrating the kinds of questions to be asked during reading. Just as questioning strategies provide a model for children to follow when reading independently, glosses also model what should take place when children read on their own.

Singer and Donlan (1989) suggest the following steps to use in preparing a relevant and useful gloss. As an alternative, more-able readers can prepare the glosses for (or together with) less-able readers.

1. *Preview.* The teacher identifies vocabulary or other material to emphasize or clarify.
2. *Create the gloss.* The teacher writes the marginal notes on copies of the original passage, which appears in Figure 10-2. Glosses can be used for all or part of a selection.
3. *Hand out the gloss.* The teacher gives copies of the passage with glosses to children to insert in the appropriate places in their texts, so that they may refer to them as they read.

Figure 10-2 on page 363 shows how glosses can clarify vocabulary, point out relationships, direct attention, and emphasize important points.

Advance Organizers

advance organizers Aids that enhance comprehension by explaining concepts, encouraging prediction, or establishing background knowledge.

independent reading level The level at which children can read by themselves with few word recognition problems and excellent comprehension.

Although **advance organizers** technically are any prereading guide or aid that clarifies concepts, sets up expectations, or builds background, they usually are thought of as specific, brief selections or outlines that children read before a main reading assignment is attempted.

Advance organizers require that teachers present a brief outline related to the assigned reading and written at the students' **independent reading level.** Organizers should always foster comprehension and, thus, should never be difficult to read. An advance organizer appropriate to a science textbook passage on the measurement of electricity is shown in Figure 10-3 on page 363. Advance organizers do not always appear in written form (although that is usual)—specific prediscussion or visuals that begin a reading selection can also be considered advance organizers.

Mapping and Other Schematic Overviews

A number of techniques can visually relate important concepts in a reading selection, thereby enhancing retention and providing a study guide. Most often, these techniques expect the reader to identify main ideas and important concepts, together with their supporting details. Because less-able readers have difficulty identifying main ideas and relationships, teachers must not only teach the techniques but must also discuss why certain concepts are identified as important and why a particular item is related to another, perhaps in a subordinate way. Children then need to practice the techniques, while at the same time identifying main ideas and supporting details.

FIGURE 10-2

Text with marginal glosses

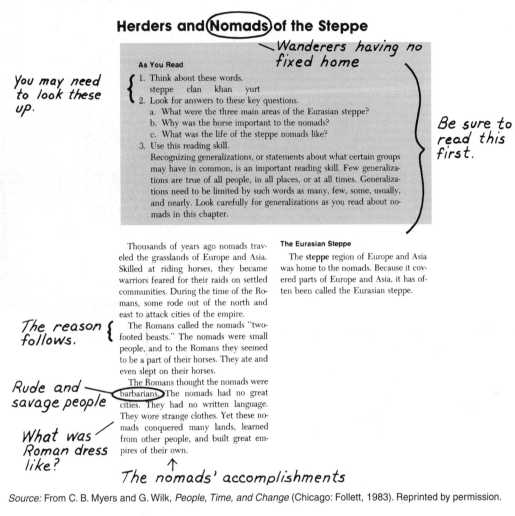

Herders and Nomads of the Steppe

Wanderers having no fixed home

You may need to look these up.

As You Read

1. Think about these words.
   steppe   clan   khan   yurt
2. Look for answers to these key questions.
   a. What were the three main areas of the Eurasian steppe?
   b. Why was the horse important to the nomads?
   c. What was the life of the steppe nomads like?
3. Use this reading skill.
   Recognizing generalizations, or statements about what certain groups may have in common, is an important reading skill. Few generalizations are true of all people, in all places, or at all times. Generalizations need to be limited by such words as many, few, some, usually, and nearly. Look carefully for generalizations as you read about nomads in this chapter.

Be sure to read this first.

Thousands of years ago nomads traveled the grasslands of Europe and Asia. Skilled at riding horses, they became warriors feared for their raids on settled communities. During the time of the Romans, some rode out of the north and east to attack cities of the empire.

The reason follows.

The Romans called the nomads "two-footed beasts." The nomads were small people, and to the Romans they seemed to be a part of their horses. They ate and even slept on their horses.

Rude and savage people

The Romans thought the nomads were barbarians. The nomads had no great cities. They had no written language. They wore strange clothes. Yet these nomads conquered many lands, learned from other people, and built great empires of their own.

What was Roman dress like?

The Eurasian Steppe

The **steppe** region of Europe and Asia was home to the nomads. Because it covered parts of Europe and Asia, it has often been called the Eurasian steppe.

↑
The nomads' accomplishments

Source: From C. B. Myers and G. Wilk, *People, Time, and Change* (Chicago: Follett, 1983). Reprinted by permission.

FIGURE 10-3

An advance organizer

You will be reading about measuring electricity. The unit you will read has three parts. The first part will tell you about one way of measuring electricity, using a unit of measurement called VOLTS. The other two parts in the reading will tell you about measuring electricity with units called AMPERES and WATTS.

When you read, try to find out why there are three different units to measure electricity. What is the purpose of each unit of measurement? Do you think we need three ways, or units, to measure electricity?

Before you start reading, write down a sentence or two about what you think you might find out by reading the unit on measuring electricity.

_____

_____

_____

FIGURE 10-4

An example of a semantic map

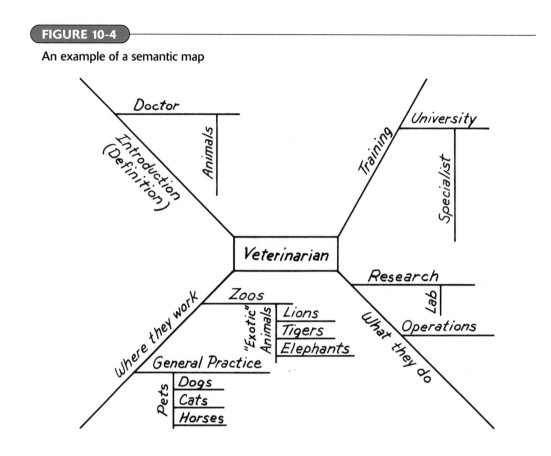

Semantic Mapping. Hanf (1971; see also Johnson & Pearson, 1984) has suggested semantic mapping as a method of organizing ideas to enhance note-taking and as a recall and study technique (see Ruddell & Boyle, 1989, for research with older children; also Garner, 1987). The strategy consists of identifying and recording main ideas and related supporting details in visual, graphic form. Semantic mapping requires these two steps:

1. Record the title or main idea anywhere on a piece of paper, leaving enough room so that additional information (the supporting details) can be added around the central idea.
2. Place the secondary, related ideas around the main idea in an organized pattern. Plan the placement of the secondary ideas so that their proximity to the main idea reflects the strength of the relationship.

A semantic map can be a small-group, whole-class, or individual activity. As a prereading activity, you might provide a list of the main ideas and supporting details. Through guided discussion, children should decide which item is the main—or superordinate—idea and rank the supporting details by importance. Based on the discussion, create the map on the chalkboard or chart paper and have children copy it to use as an aid for study, discussion, or recall. Then reading takes place. It is also possible for students to generate the map during reading, noting ideas as they arise, or to create the map as a postreading activity. Figure 10-4 presents a sample semantic map. Novak and Gowan (1984) present and discuss a concept map, which differs slightly from a semantic map in its stronger emphasis on linking the chosen words to concepts.

Structured Concept Outlines. A structured outline schematically represents the relationships among concepts in reading material. This technique requires that concepts be ordered into superordinate, coordinate, and subordinate categories. For example, the outline on page 365 might apply to a selection about growing tomatoes.

FIGURE 10-5

Marginal gloss combined with a structured concept outline

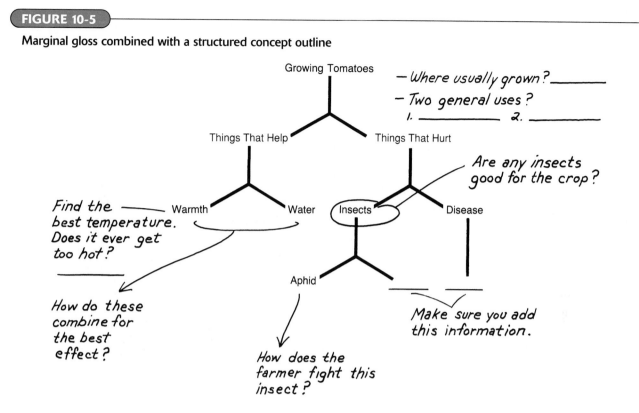

Such an outline may serve the function of an advance organizer or may be used as an aid for post-reading activities. In either case, it is important for teachers to point out what relationships exist and to discuss with students how and why the various concepts are related. A structured outline is similar to the herringbone technique (Tierney, Readence, & Dishner, 1990), which tells who, what, where, when, why, and how in a schematic format that provides structure for recall and study. Figure 10-5 presents an example of a structured concept outline.

SQ3R

Originally developed by Robinson (1961) as a study strategy for college students, SQ3R is also taught as a study tool for secondary and upper elementary-grade students. SQ3R stands for these actions:

Survey	Quickly skim through the material. Focus on headings and titles to get a general feel for what the material covers.
Question	Based on the survey just completed, identify questions the material will probably answer.
Read	Read the material to answer the questions previously identified.
Recite	Orally or in writing attempt to answer the identified questions.
Review	Reread portions of the material to verify the answers previously given.

Although SQ3R has been shown to be an effective study strategy when used as described, it is rarely used spontaneously by students (Cheek & Cheek, 1983) and needs to be taught and reinforced. Some (Vacca, 1981) believe that children need more structure than is provided by SQ3R. Pauk (1984), for example, suggests a more structured method of presenting the technique and stresses setting purposes at each step. In addition, he has added "record" after "reading," thus making his technique SQ4R.

Activities in different content areas, such in science, can provide valuable experiences on which to base reading and writing activities.

PRACTICAL TEACHING STRATEGIES

Illustrating the Use of Structured Concept Outlines

Concept Outline Discussion.   Prepare, duplicate, and distribute a structured concept outline. Use it as the basis for discussion with children prior to their reading the selection.

Concept Outline Completion.   Omit certain parts of an outline and tell children to complete it as they read. This activity provides a purpose for reading and allows children to make active choices while they read.

Combined Glosses and Structured Concept Outlines.   Combine a structured concept outline with marginal glosses, leaving adequate space for children to write their responses. Instruct them to make notes or otherwise complete the outline as requested by the gloss (see Figure 10-5 on page 365).

Pauk believes children should record succinct margin notes of ideas, facts, and details from their reading, thus establishing cues for immediate and future reviews.

Connecting Writing and Content-Area Reading

Writing activities should be used in all types of classrooms, ranging from more traditional to whole language, to help build children's comprehension of content-area, or expository, texts. Teachers should provide practice with different text structures and should ensure that the classroom environment includes books of many types—from children's literature to expository materials. Teachers should also ensure that writing activities move beyond stories. Flood, Lapp, and Farnan (1986) suggest a three-step procedure that links reading and writing:

1. *Prewriting.* Children choose a topic and brainstorm what they already know about it, listing the ideas generated. Children are then directed to gather additional information about the topic from reference sources, interviews, or a targeted expository

MODEL LESSON

SQ3R in Ann Dodds' Class

Ann Dodds has text-based beliefs about *what* to teach. Thus, she uses an SQ3R procedure to help students find information within a text. She is also guided in her use of SQ3R by her holistic language learning beliefs for *how* to teach. Thus, children are encouraged to pose their own questions and direct their learning as they move through the passage. Ann begins with a discussion of SQ3R, reminding the class of the steps involved.

Survey. Children are asked to survey a science passage about the invention of the telephone, quickly skimming the headings and overall content. A short period of time is allowed, and then they are asked to identify the title of the passage and the three subheadings.

Question. Ann lists on the board the title and subheadings that children provide and asks what questions might be answered in each subsection. Children generate these questions:

The Telephone: A Useful Invention
    Q: Why is the telephone useful?
    Q: What makes the telephone useful?
    Q: How was it invented?

Before the Telephone
    Q: How did people talk to each other before the telephone?

The Invention
    Q: Who invented the telephone?
    Q: When was it invented?
    Q: How was it invented?

After the Invention
    Q: What happened after the invention?
    Q: How did the telephone change people's lives?

Read. The class is asked to read the selection, keeping the questions in mind.

Recite. Children actively but silently recite or write down the answers to the questions as the information is learned.

Review. When finished reading, children review their answers—in a large group with Ann, in pairs or small groups, or individually. The parts of the passage that provide answers are reread and the passage as a whole is discussed.

selection. After they have gathered the information, students list the facts they learned about the topic.

2. *Writing.* Children select the most important topic (the most all-encompassing) from the two lists created during the prewriting stage and list supporting details or subtopics under that main idea. Following their main topic-subtopic outline, the children then write a short expository paragraph.

3. *Feedback and editing.* Partners or groups can read each other's paragraphs to determine whether a main idea and its supporting details are included. Feedback or further information can be provided, which the original author can use to rewrite and strengthen the paragraph.

The language experience approach (LEA) can also be used to build familiarity with expository text structures (Kinney, 1985). The language experience is provided by the teacher, who might use a feature analysis to compare ideas or vocabulary terms or might list headings and subheadings from a text and allow children to brainstorm what might be found in the selection. Children then dictate a story or description to the teacher, based on the brainstorming or information session. The teacher can guide the students, perhaps asking for information that might fit under a specific heading or asking for a

MODEL LESSON

K-W-L in Gwen Percy's Class

Gwen Percy has reader-based beliefs about *what* to teach. These beliefs are well suited to her use of K-W-L because this procedure allows children to brainstorm and to access their own ideas and knowledge. Gwen also has holistic language learning beliefs about *how* to teach. Again, K-W-L, which allows children to specify what they need to know and thus to take an active part in directing their learning, is an appropriate match. Here is a typical example of Gwen's use of K-W-L in her fourth-grade classroom.

Before Reading (Know). Gwen models and then facilitates discussion and activity in four areas:

1. *Brainstorming.* Gwen asks the class to brainstorm what they know about a topic and writes their responses on the chalkboard or chart paper. As conflicts or uncertainty about the appropriateness of a response arise, questions are noted (for example, Is _____ a part of the topic?). The questions become part of what needs to be found out.
2. *Categorizing.* She encourages students to categorize items generated during brainstorming. If the children have trouble with this task, she models the categorizing process, using a think-aloud procedure. Another strategy is to write similar items closer together in the beginning, as they are generated.
3. *Anticipating.* Gwen facilitates discussion about what readers may discover when they read about the categorized topics.
4. *Questioning.* Gwen helps children specify certain questions to be answered during and after reading. It is important that such questions be specific.

During Reading (Want to Know). The class is asked to read and actively look for new information and ideas, which are noted on a worksheet/table like the one shown here. (Longer or more difficult reading assignments should be broken into manageable chunks.)

What We Know	What We Want to Find Out	What We Learned

After Reading (Learn). As a class activity, Gwen compiles the information that the children learned and helps them relate it to what they previously knew and what they needed to find out. During discussion, both Gwen and the children add additional information to the worksheet/table, which can then be used to generate a written summary. Gwen and her students find that using the Internet is very helpful during this step in the K-W-L process.

contrast or comparison sentence at some point. After the dictation is completed, children can read and discuss their writing, copy it into their notebooks, and read the target selection. An interesting follow-up to reading is a discussion that compares the dictated story to the actual selection from which the headings came.

The K-W-L Strategy

K-W-L A method framework with three steps: know, want to know, and learn.

The **K-W-L** method framework (Ogle, 1989) includes both writing and reading and requires brainstorming, categorizing, and information-gathering notetaking activities.

K-W-L stands for know, want to know, and learn. The procedure begins with discussion about what children already know about the topic. That information is then organized into categories, after which children raise questions that might need to be answered. During and after reading, children record what they are learning and what they

PRACTICAL TEACHING STRATEGIES

Developing Summarizing and Notetaking Abilities

Summary Statements. Have children listen to a story or expository reading. Ask them to restate or paraphrase the main idea of the selection. At another time children might be asked to provide a one- or two-sentence written statement.

Note taking Contrasts. Model and then allow children to practice taking notes in various forms: listing points, summarizing paragraphs, and outlining. Use a short reading selection, film, audiotape, or website as the basis for the notetaking activity. Be sure to discuss the children's work, focusing on reasons for including (and not including) certain information.

Outline Completion. Provide headings and subheadings in outline form, but leave the outline incomplete. Then read a selection that pertains to the outline and have children complete it. This activity enhances both notetaking and summarizing skills.

Picture Categories. For young children, compile a set of pictures that includes items in two categories. Mix up the pictures and have children tell which belong together. Alternatively, identify a category and have children tell which pictures do not belong.

still want to know. The K-W-L procedure recognizes the importance of prior knowledge, group learning, writing, and a personalized learning experience. When extended to use semantic mapping, as discussed in chapter 8, the process is called K-W-L Plus (Carr & Ogle, 1987).

Summarizing, Note Taking, and Organizing

Many of the strategies and techniques discussed in this chapter require that information be summarized or organized, often in written form. These skills can be developed from the earliest stages of schooling. When children are asked to restate or paraphrase a story, their summarizing ability is enhanced, as are their notetaking skills when summary statements or main points are compiled in written form. When children are asked to categorize similar items, they develop categorizing skills that help in organizing information.

Brown, Campione, and Day (1981; see also Brown & Day, 1983) identify the following actions as helpful in summarizing:

- Deleting nonessential information
- Deleting repetitive information
- Using blanket terms to replace lists of simpler items (for example, pets to replace "dogs, cats, hamsters, and goldfish")
- Selecting topic sentences or, if there are none, creating topic sentences

Tei and Stewart (1985) suggest that the first two of these actions are the most appropriate for middle school children. However, with teacher guidance and modeling, children can use all of them to write summary paragraphs.

Reading in Specific Content Areas

The techniques presented earlier in this chapter can be used in any subject area. In addition, there are method frameworks appropriate for use with texts in specific subject areas. The discussion that follows presents some of the specific demands faced by readers in social studies, science, mathematics, and language arts, and describes method frameworks that specifically address reading in those subjects. Those areas are not in any way superior to others, but all four use reading material as a major instructional component.

Social Studies

Organizational Differences.   Children who have difficulty reading mathematics and science texts may have less difficulty reading language arts and social studies materials. This difference may result from patterns of text organization. The majority of reading materials within language arts are narrative texts organized along a time sequence. Science and mathematics texts, however, are usually organized hierarchically. Social studies texts can be organized along either of these patterns, although history—one particular component of social studies—usually is presented in a time-sequenced format. We can usually determine a book's general organization from its title and the headings included in the table of contents. Can you see the hierarchical organization in the following example?

Climates of the World

Arid climatic regions
Arid climate defined
   Arid regions
   African continent
   European continent
   American continents
Desert climatic regions
   Desert climate defined
   Desert regions
      African continent
      Asian continent
      American continents

However, a title such as *Decline of the Dinosaurs* would imply a time-sequenced organization, moving from the evolution of dinosaurs through their most prolific period to their decline and eventual extinction. Organizational structures can also have a mixed organization, like the time sequence within a hierarchical pattern illustrated here:

Government in the United States

Government at the federal level
   Evolution of federal government
      The pre-revolutionary period
      The post-revolutionary period
Government at the state level
   Evolution of state legislatures

Thus, in social studies material, children often are required to contend with different organizational structures within one reading selection, and they need to be aware of that possibility.

Graphic Elements.   Social studies readers also see graphic elements—maps, charts, and graphs—that normally are not used in narrative texts. Although other content areas include such material, the graphs and charts in social studies can incorporate fairly unique symbols. The examples in Figure 10-6 typify the graphics children encounter in their social studies textbooks in addition to more normal photographs, graphs, and charts. Even good readers may have difficulty interpreting graphic information and may be unable to move back and forth between textual material and graphics without losing their place. Interpretation of maps and graphs rarely is taught as a specific skill, even though the complexity of such reading has been noted (Summers, 1965; Vacca, 1981).

Fry (1981) presents a taxonomy of graphs with six main subdivisions, although combinations across these types are often used.

1. *Lineal graphs,* showing sequential data (simple timelines, parallel timelines, and flow charts).

FIGURE 10-6

Graphic material from a representative third-grade social studies text

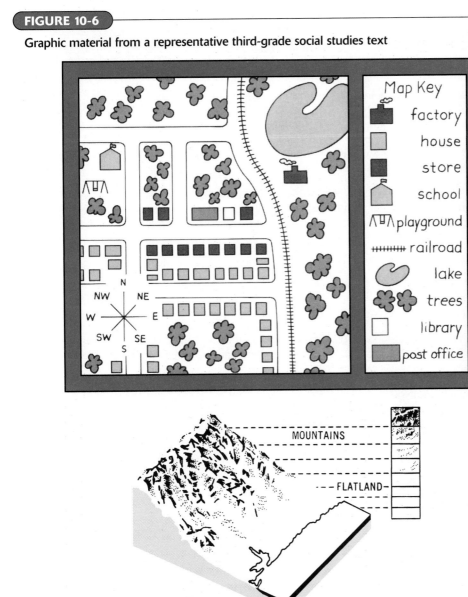

Source: From J. Buggey, *Our Communities* (Chicago: Follett, 1983), pp. 18, 94. Reprinted by permission.

2. *Quantitative graphs,* used for numerical data (growth curves, bar graphs, pie graphs, and multiple variable graphs).
3. *Spatial graphs,* representing area and location (two-dimensional road maps and three-dimensional contour maps).
4. *Pictorial graphs,* depicting visual concepts (realistic drawings, schematic drawings, and abstracted representations).
5. *Hypothetical graphs,* demonstrating an interrelationship of ideas (sentence diagrams or semantic maps).
6. *Intentional omissions from the taxonomy of graphs: high verbal figures* (posters and advertisements); *high numerical tables* (statistical tables); *symbols* (word equivalents like the outline of a man on a restroom door); and *decorative designs* (designs whose main purpose is decorative rather than conceptual or informative).

Summers (1965) has pointed out differences between what he calls map readers and **map thinkers.** A map reader can locate information but cannot interpret the presented

map thinkers Students who are able to locate information on a map and interpret it.

PRACTICAL TEACHING STRATEGIES

Relating Literacy Instruction and Social Studies

Map Information Hunt.   After a discussion of the information found in various parts of a map, provide a list of questions children should answer while referring to a specific map.

Map Drawing.   Provide a summary of information in paragraph or list form. Then have children use that information to draw a map or create a graph. Discuss the advantages of the information in graphic form (for example, better overview, visual summary, and ease of seeing relationships).

Fact and Opinion Statements.   Find statements of fact and opinion in newspapers, or create statements that would fit into those categories. Present the statements in pairs, and have children discuss and explain which are fact and which are opinion.

Factual Statement	**Opinion Statement**
1. American Airlines and Northwest Airlines both reported losses during the first quarter.	The airlines will close down if they lose money in the next quarter.
2. All land and buildings in Davidson County will be reassessed before the next taxation year.	All taxes on real estate in Davidson County will go up next year.

Cause-and-Effect Statements.   Follow the same initial procedure as that in the previous activity. Then delete either a cause or an effect, and direct children to supply the deleted item. Have children present and explain their answers.

Cause	**Effect**
1. There have been several airplane accidents recently.	Fewer people want to travel by airplane nowadays.
2. Fewer people want to travel by airplane nowadays.	The airlines are making less money.
3. All land and buildings in Davidson County will be reassessed before the next taxation year.	The county clerk needs to hire more staff to update Davidson County's tax records.
4. The county clerk needs to hire more staff to update Davidson County's tax records.	_____
	_____

These examples show that causes and effects can be transposed; that is, the effect of one cause may be the cause of a different effect. Such transpositions serve to focus attention on the differences between causes and effects.

Central Internet Sites for Social Studies.   Sites such as the following can help children learn to find information, and navigate the Internet to find information, relevant to topics in their social studies textbooks. You might also want to use online encyclopedia sites (see http://school.discovery.com/homeworkhelp/bjpinchbeck/bjreference.html for a listing of encyclopedias and other reference sources) to compare search strategies in on-line and paper-copy versions of similar research materials. Central social studies sites include:

Thomas Legislative Information on the Internet (http://thomas.loc.gov)—This site contains the text for historical documents such as the Declaration of Independence, the Federalist Papers, and the Constitution in a searchable database (look for the "historical documents" link). It also provides information about these documents, lists pending legislation, and includes the e-mail addresses for members of Congress.

The White House for Kids (http://www.whitehouse.gov/kids/; see also http://www.whitehouse.gov/kids/index2.html)—This link, a subset of the general White House site, is geared for children and provides information about the president and his family as well as a newsletter and information about historical events. Children can leave messages for the president and take a tour of the White House through photographs.

HyperHistory Online (http://www.hyperhistory.com/online_n2/History_n2/a.html)—This site contains many links to useful historical resources and is a great starting point for studying a range of topics from Native American history through current events.

History/Social Studies Web Site for K–12 Teachers (http://www.execpc.com/~dboals/boals.html)—A large listing of WWW locations, documents, facts, and timelines that support social studies learning, organized by topic. A very valuable resource site for teachers; contains over 2,000 files covering major themes and aspects of world history across civilizations.

Celebrating Diversity

Finding Opportunities to Celebrate Diversity in the Social Studies Content Area

The traditional areas of social studies—history, geography, civics, culture, and so on—provide many opportunities to study aspects related to multiculturalism, segregation, the economic condition, and other topics that can directly relate to children in your class and are vital for all students to know. Aspects of social studies can also provide opportunities for all children and their parents to share their expertise in show-and-tell sessions and oral (or written) histories of their families. Studying maps and charts can be used to find information in activities that address issues of diversity and to summarize and present children's research findings to the class. In short, children can use the strategies that enhance reading in social studies, including map-reading and map-thinking skills, in contexts that celebrate diversity.

information, much as a child might be able to locate literal information in text yet be unable to assimilate that information into existing knowledge structures or interpret it in the general context of the text as a whole.

A teacher's goal is to move children beyond the realm of map readers and mold them into map thinkers. According to Summers, a map thinker must be aware of these six elements:

1. *Map title.* Similar to a book title, this tells what the map depicts; it provides an introduction to the map and its features. Discussion of the title and other activities similar to those associated with a book or story title are appropriate.

2. *Legend.* Often compared to the table of contents in a book, the legend indicates what the map symbols stand for and provides other information, such as the map scale. The legend usually appears in a box within the map or graph. Children should try to focus on each item in the legend and visualize whatever it represents. For example, a map thinker should try to imagine the vast oceans that a legend might equate with the color blue.

3. *Direction.* The top of a map usually—but not always—indicates north. Children must be taught to realize that north is not just a direction; it is also a concept with related understandings of true and magnetic north, intermediate distances, and polar regions.

4. *Distance scale.* Three types of scales are common: graphic, statement, and fractional scales. The scale enables a reader to tell how far or how big something is. A small-scale map depicts a large area made smaller; a large-scale map depicts a small area made larger.

5. *Location.* This usually is depicted by a grid system that segments maps, most often with horizontal and vertical lines. Township range lines and marginal letters and numbers are common grid systems, as are parallels and meridians that locate places by latitude and longitude.

6. *Types of maps.* Major map types include land, elevation, climate, vegetation and water features, political, economic, and population. Combinations of these types often are found on one map.

Miscellaneous Concerns. In addition to changes in structure and different kinds of graphic information that must be actively incorporated into the text, social studies readers face other challenges:

▶ Vocabulary terms involve a larger-than-normal proportion of words with Latin and Greek roots, prefixes, or suffixes.

▶ Social studies vocabulary and concepts reflect a variety of disciplines: anthropology, sociology, economics, political science, and more.

> Many social studies textbooks focus on details to such an extent that important major issues may be difficult to grasp. History segments often stress many details without drawing clear relationships to the larger picture.
> In our world of rapid change, the material in social studies textbooks can become rapidly dated; It is sometimes obsolete or even false. As a result, children who have seen more recent or correct information in newspapers, on news broadcasts, or on the World Wide Web may be confused.
> Differentiating fact, opinion, and propaganda can be difficult.
> Some younger children may have trouble grasping time-dependent concepts. Children at certain lower **cognitive levels** have problems understanding concepts involving time, space, and distance relationships, all of which are important to social studies and appear in various kinds of maps.

cognitive levels Stages of intellectual development.

Instructional Strategies.   The teaching procedures noted earlier in this chapter apply to social studies material as well as to other content areas. Building children's backgrounds, providing prereading activities, and implementing other techniques discussed throughout this text are important activities for teaching social studies material. Children will benefit from cloze and **maze procedures,** both of which emphasize context clues to aid comprehension. Cause-and-effect activities should also be emphasized, along with activities to build concepts and vocabulary.

maze procedure A fill-in-the-blank activity to support comprehension.

All of these techniques have been discussed in previous chapters. The suggestions below include several strategies that relate to teaching map-thinking, fact/opinion, and cause-and-effect within social studies material, as well as central sites that are useful as you teach content-area reading using social studies materials.

Mathematics

Differences in Content and Approach.   The exercises in Figure 10-7 on page 375 are representative of reading demands in mathematics. You can see that mathematics passages contain numerous items not generally found in narrative texts. Perhaps the most obvious are the numeric symbols. Just as a set of letters represents a concept, numbers and other symbols also represent meaning. For example, the number 50 represents a quantity of items totaling a certain amount, which could be expressed as "2 more than 48" or in innumerable other ways. Thus, just as readers must learn the specific concepts represented by letter combinations, so must they also learn the concepts for other symbol sets. Look again at Figure 10-7 and notice the other numeric arrangements and process symbols generally not used in narrative texts: decimals (5.1, 6.5), fractions ($\frac{3}{8}, \frac{1}{4}$), and mathematical symbols ($+, -, =$).

In addition to different symbol sets, other differences are associated with reading mathematics materials:

> Specialized vocabulary that is content specific—for example, *division, quotient, digit, multiplication, product,* and *numeral.*
> Specific shapes and diagrams—for example, triangle, rectangle, and parallelogram.
> A slower rate of reading than is necessary in narrative texts and in some other expository texts such as history books. Word problems and theorems must be carefully read (and read more than once).
> Eye movements that deviate from the expected left-to-right sequence, as in this problem: $3 + 2(6 + 1) = 17$. Mathematical rules require that $6 + 1$ be computed and the sum multiplied by 2 before that product is added to 3. Eye movements also go from up to down and from down to up in addition and division problems, as well as diagonally in the multiplication of fractions.
> A different approach to comprehension. For example, word problems such as the following require attention to parts of the text which are not normally thought important:

John was going to the store. On the way, he stopped at Mary's house. Mary lived 2 blocks from John. John and Mary went to the store together. The store was 2 blocks past Mary's house. How far did John go to get to the store?

FIGURE 10-7

A sample mathematics page from an elementary text

PRACTICE

Add or subtract. Write each answer in lowest terms.

1. $3\frac{2}{5}$
$-2\frac{1}{5}$

2. $6\frac{2}{6}$
$+3\frac{2}{6}$

3. $5\frac{2}{3}$
$-1\frac{1}{3}$

4. $6\frac{1}{4}$
$+2\frac{1}{4}$

5. $8\frac{7}{8}$
$-\frac{2}{8}$

6. $5\frac{1}{6}$
$+3\frac{1}{6}$

7. $9\frac{3}{4}$
$-1\frac{3}{4}$

8. $3\frac{3}{8}$
$+3\frac{1}{8}$

9. $8\frac{5}{12}$
$+\frac{3}{12}$

10. $3\frac{4}{9}$
$+1\frac{2}{9}$

11. $6\frac{5}{7}$
$-\frac{2}{7}$

12. $4\frac{2}{5}$
$-2\frac{1}{5}$

13. $7\frac{5}{9} + 3\frac{2}{9} = \square$ 14. $5\frac{1}{2} - 2\frac{1}{2} = \square$

*15. $(3 - 2\frac{1}{2}) - 1\frac{1}{2} = \square$

Follow the rule to complete.

Rule: Add $1\frac{2}{7}$

	Input	Output
16.	$3\frac{4}{7}$	
17.	$1\frac{1}{7}$	
18.	$2\frac{3}{7}$	

Rule: Subtract $1\frac{1}{8}$

	Input	Output
19.	$1\frac{2}{8}$	
20.	$2\frac{3}{8}$	
21.	$5\frac{5}{8}$	

APPLICATION

22. Ralph filled $7\frac{3}{4}$ bags with leaves. Rudy filled $5\frac{1}{4}$ bags with leaves. How many more bags of leaves did Ralph fill?

*23. Rosa wants to knit 2 scarves. She needs $4\frac{1}{2}$ packages of yarn for one, and $3\frac{1}{2}$ packages for the other. She has $9\frac{1}{2}$ packages. After making the scarves, how much yarn will she have left?

Mixed Practice

1. $5.1 + 6.5 = \square$

2. $4.64 + 3.81 = \square$

3. $82.1 - 49.6 = \square$

4. $3.6 - 2.9 = \square$

5. 99.62
$+ 48.43$

6. 137.72
$- 48.36$

7. 362
$\times\ 38$

8. $17 - 2.58 = \square$

9. $48 \times 97 = \square$

10. $386 \div 25 = \square$

11. $42\overline{)847}$

12. $\$6.38$
$\times\ \ 81$

13. $52.4 + 3.73 = \square$

14. $178.6 - 5.2 = \square$

15. $50 \times \$6.71 = \square$

16. $36\overline{)\$7.20}$

17. $32\overline{)946}$

18. $4.26 - 3.8 = \square$

Source: From L. J. Orfan and B. R. Vogeli, *Mathematics* (Morristown, NJ: Silver Burdett, 1987), p. 331. Reprinted by permission.

Normally, children would read to find out who the people in the story were or what the action was. However, such information is unimportant for this problem. With mathematics problems, children who focus on the types of questions asked with narrative materials may attend to inappropriate items. In fact, reading difficulties may account for as much as 35 percent of student errors on mathematics achievement tests (O'Mara, 1981).

Instructional Strategies.   Fay (1965) suggests a strategy called **SQRQCQ** be used to solve word problems.

SQRQCQ   A study strategy for reading math word problems: survey, question, read, question, compute, and question.

Survey	Read the problem rapidly, skimming to determine its nature.
Question	Decide what is being asked—in other words, what is the problem?
Read	Read for details and interrelationships.
Question	Decide which processes and strategies should be used to address the problem.
Compute	Carry out the necessary computations.

FIGURE 10-8

Adaptation of the cloze procedure for mathematics

Following is a brief passage that could occur in a mathematics book written for upper elementary or middle school children. To the right is a cloze test constructed for the passage on the left. In actual practice, longer passages are used so that more blanks are obtained.

Divide 20 by 5. Now, multiply 20 by 1/5. Is dividing by 5 the same as multiplying by 1/5? Are these sentences true?

Divide 20 by ___. Now multiply 20 by ___. Is _____ by 5 the same _____ multiplying by 1/_____? Are these sentences true?

$36 \div 18 = 36 \times 1/18$

_____ $6 \div 18$ _____ 36×1 _____ 18

$72 \div 8 = 72 \times 1/8$

72 _____ $8 = 72$ _____ $1/8$

Here are some observations you should note concerning the cloze test:

1. Both word tokens (i.e., words) and math tokens (i.e., numerical digits or process symbols) are counted in this procedure.
2. Every fifth token is deleted, starting with the fifth token.
3. Deleted tokens are replaced by blanks of two sizes. The shorter blanks are used for math tokens.
4. Tokens are ordered according to the words used to read them. For example, 1/5 can be thought of as one, process symbol, five. Therefore, these tokens would be ordered as 1, /, 5. It is important that the translation to words be consistent within a passage.

Source: From R. B. Kane, M. A. Byrne, and M. A. Hater, *Helping Children Read Mathematics* (New York: American Book, 1974), pp. 18–19. Adapted by permission.

Question   Ask whether the answer seems correct. Check computations against the facts presented in the problem and against basic arithmetic facts.

Kane, Byrne, and Hater (1974) suggest a modification of the traditional cloze technique for mathematics. Their **modified cloze procedure** specifies areas of student difficulty in textual aspects of mathematics material and in the comprehension of mathematical concepts.

modified cloze procedure A comprehension assessment procedure that departs from the traditional routine of deleting every fifth word.

The modification is then completed as a joint activity among students, or among the teacher and students. The exercise should be accompanied by a discussion that focuses children's attention on pertinent information that helps fill in the blanks. As you model the thought processes necessary to replace the deletions, children can learn the reasoning specific to mathematics. An example of a mathematics cloze passage is shown in Figure 10-8.

It is also necessary to teach children the specialized symbolic vocabulary of mathematics. All of the process symbols have the same properties as letter- and word-based vocabulary. For example, the various multiplication and division signs shown below represent the same concept and can be considered synonyms.

$$3 \times 2 \qquad 3 \cdot 2 \qquad 3(2)$$
$$3 \overline{)2} \qquad 3 \div 2 \qquad 3/2$$

These symbols can be taught with the same procedures used to teach word synonyms. Any symbols that stand for concepts can be considered vocabulary items and can be taught with the techniques presented in chapter 8.

Although mathematics and language arts seem intuitively distant, Evans, Leija, and Falkner (2001) point out that there are many ways to relate literature and mathematics. They have presented suggestions and strategies for teaching the National Council for Teachers of Mathematics Standards through children's literature. Their suggestions are based on patterns and structures that children can incorporate in reading activities while enhancing their mathematics abilities.

MODEL LESSON

SQRQCQ in Sarah Jackson's Class

Sarah Jackson's text-based beliefs guide her decisions about *what* to teach, and her specific skills beliefs guide her decisions about *how* to teach. These beliefs are especially influential in content areas such as mathematics, where careful attention to the precise meaning and demands of word problems are central to children's understanding. Sarah thus uses the SQRQCQ strategy to teach the importance of carefully attending to the text in the problem. Deductive learning is emphasized.

Sarah knows three main things that can prevent a child from correctly completing a word problem: (a) reading the problem incorrectly and thus not finding the appropriate information, (b) not performing the appropriate computation (for example, subtracting when addition is needed), and (c) not performing the computation correctly (for example, multiplying incorrectly). She has decided to address the first point by teaching her children SQRQCQ. She first explains that SQRQCQ will help them better understand their mathematics problems. She then explains what the letters stand for and demonstrates how to read a mathematics problem (written on the chalkboard) using the SQRQCQ technique.

After Sarah is sure her students know what SQRQCQ requires a reader to do, she tells them they will practice the technique together. She hands out a sheet of simple word problems and instructs the class not to begin reading until she says to. After all the children have sheets, she asks several children to describe the first step in SQRQCQ. Then she directs the children to skim the first problem rapidly and to turn their papers over when they have finished skimming.

When the children are finished, Sarah discusses with them what the problem is generally about. She then reminds them of the next step in the procedure, suggests they write down what is being asked, and again instructs them to turn over their papers when they are finished.

Sarah continues this process, discussing each step of the SQRQCQ procedure both before and after it is attempted. She has the children practice several of the problems on the sheet in this way and reinforces the technique several times during the next week and periodically thereafter.

Central WWW Sites Related to the Mathematics Content Area. WWW sites such as the following can provide content in which to apply the reading and study skills related to mathematics:

Math Magic (http://mathforum.org/mathmagic/what.html)—Provides projects where teams of children can apply problem-solving skills.

Eisenhower National Center for Mathematics and Science Education (http://www.enc.org/)—Contains a selection of resources and activities as well as links to mathematics and science sites. Includes a selection of award-winning sites in science and mathematics that change monthly (look under the "Web Links" section).

Math Archives (http://archives.math.utk.edu/newindex.html)—The teaching materials section of this site contains K–12 materials. This site includes resources and software that can be downloaded for use in mathematics instruction and that can be used to practice skills in reading mathematics content.

Science

Technical Reading. The following passage from an elementary science textbook (Sund, Adams, & Hackett, 1980) illustrates some of the reading demands in this content area:

The chart below shows several common compounds. It also shows the chemical formula and the phase of the compound.

Compound	Formula	Phase of Matter
carbon dioxide	CO_2	gas
water	H_2O	liquid
ammonia	NH_3	gas
salt	$NaCL$	solid

Study and note taking strategies are an important part of content-area reading instruction.

There are simple rules for writing chemical formulas. The formula for water is H_2O. The small subscripted number 2 means that a water molecule has two hydrogen atoms. The O has no number after it. No number means there is only one atom of oxygen; the number 1 is not written in chemical formulas. A molecule of water has 2 atoms of hydrogen and 1 atom of oxygen. CO_2 is the formula for carbon dioxide. What elements make up carbon dioxide? How many atoms of each element are in a molecule of carbon dioxide? (p. 90)

Science texts often seem more technical than other content-area texts. For example, the above explanation of the rules for writing formulas is specific and reflects technical writing. It must be carefully read or the concept may not be grasped. The passage also includes several terms specific to science: *element, molecule, compound, atom, dioxide,* and *formula.* And, like mathematics and social studies, science uses several symbol sets. The chemical symbols and the numerical subscripts in the formulas must all be mastered to understand this science passage correctly.

Like social studies, science draws on several disciplines for its knowledge base. In fact, science materials show some overlap with social studies materials; units on space exploration, weather, and climate are examples. Thus, the previous discussion of maps and charts applies to science as well. And science, too, has a great many words with Latin and Greek **morphemes.**

morphemes The smallest meaningful linguistic units.

A further distinction in the vocabulary found in science materials is the high number of words with a meaning specific to science; that is, words not found in everyday speech. Social studies and mathematics include many words with both general and content-specific meanings; science, however, has a large number of words with only content-specific meanings. Thus, teachers may need to preteach specific science concepts before children see the terms in text. Even though context often helps, we cannot assume unknown words will become clear through reading alone.

A key component in understanding science material is reading to follow directions, particularly in laboratory exercises, where even the slightest departure can result in a failed experiment. In addition, science experiments follow a structure different from that of other textual materials:

1. Problem
2. Hypothesis

MODEL LESSON

PQRST in William Hernandez's Room

William Hernandez, a fourth-grade teacher, is guided by interactive beliefs about *what* to teach. Thus, he often uses PQRST with his students because this procedure allows him to encourage them to apply their own experiences and knowledge when predicting during the preview step of PQRST. However, it also encourages students to be precise about the generalization stated or implied in the text. His integrated beliefs about *how* to teach also guide him toward the use of PQRST because this procedure allows both teacher- and student-directed learning within the various procedural steps. Here is an example of how he teaches PQRST to his students.

First, William explains that science textbooks are often structured so that a generalization or theory is stated near the beginning of a selection, the generalization is expanded and supported throughout the rest of the selection, and a summary statement of the generalization or theory is usually presented at the end. He has the class look at a section in their science textbooks that demonstrates this structure.

William then explains that a technique called PQRST helps readers consciously identify the generalization or theory and become more aware of the supporting details. He reminds the class that they should be active readers who anticipate what may come next, based on what has come before and based on their own prior knowledge. He then presents each of the steps in PQRST, demonstrates what a reader might do at each step, and questions a number of children to make sure they know what should be done at each step.

Preview. William asks the class to open their books to a specific selection that has not been read before. He tells them to preview the selection, jotting down a note about the generalization or theory. When all are finished, he asks what they think the generalization is and has several children supply the reasons for their decision.

Question. William tells the class to write down questions they might have about the generalization or theory and questions they think might be answered as they read through the selection. He tells the children not to refer to their books at this stage.

Read. William knows a different class might need to continue this lesson on another day, but he thinks this class can go ahead. He tells the class to keep their questions in mind and to read the selection, writing down brief notes that might help them answer their questions.

Summarize. He also reminds the children about the need to summarize. William suggests they group relevant facts and attempt to specifically answer their own questions, using their notes as a place to start.

Test. Because William wants to do this final step as a group activity, he has five or six children read their summaries aloud while the other students silently compare their own to those that are read. Children then discuss the accuracy of the summary statements and the answers to the questions identified earlier. During this process, children are encouraged to use the selection as a reference to justify their conclusions. William reinforces the use of PQRST on a continuing basis.

3. Procedure
4. Observation
5. Collection of data (results)
6. Conclusions

If children are unfamiliar with this structure, it must be taught.

Instructional Strategies. PQRST is an effective study technique specific to science (Spache, 1963; Spache & Berg, 1966).

It recommends that children reading science materials follow a five-step sequence:

Preview	Rapidly skim the selection. The reader should not move on until the generalization or theory of the passage has been identified.
Question	Raise questions for study purposes.

PQRST A science study technique that stresses previewing, questioning, reading, summarizing, and testing.

Read	With questions in mind, read the selection and answer the questions. Sometimes experiments need to be done before the questions can be answered.
Summarize	Organize and summarize the information gathered through reading. Group relevant facts and summarize answers to each question. This step is best done in writing.
Test	Go back to the reading selection and check the summary statement for accuracy. Can the generalization or theory identified in the first step be supported through the answers and summaries?

Forgan and Mangrum (1985) note that the difference between SQ3R and PQRST is "more than semantic" and agree with Fay (1965) that PQRST, rather than SQ3R, should be used with science material.

Central WWW Sites Related to the Science Content Area.   WWW sites such as the following can provide the content in which to apply reading and study skills related to science:

> **Eisenhower National Center for Mathematics and Science Education** (http://www.enc.org/weblinks/math/ and http://www.enc.org/weblinks/science/)—Contains a selection of resources and activities as well as links to mathematics and science sites. Includes a selection of award-winning sites in science and mathematics that change monthly.

> **Boston Museum of Science** (www.mos.org/)—Organized by category, this site includes links as well as an in-depth focus related to exhibits and activities sponsored by the museum (see Figure 10-9).

FIGURE 10-9

The teacher resources page (http://www.mos.org/learn_more/ed_res/index.html) from the Boston Museum of Science (www.mos.org/)

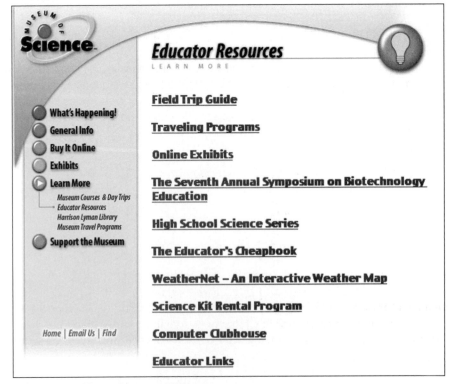

Note: Courtesy of Boston Museum of Science.

Web Earth Science for Teachers (http://www.usatoday.com/weather/wteach. htm)—Part of the *USA Today* site, this site is especially valuable for interdisciplinary studies that link to science because resources and activities often relate science to current events, weather-related news, and so on.

Language Arts

In some ways, the reading task in a language arts or English classroom can be the most demanding of all. Although the various subject areas make specific demands on a reader, a language arts reading assignment can include any or all of the demands and text structures previously discussed. Although the general reading requirements in language arts revolve around narrative text structures, once children are able to read on their own, they are required to read everything from autobiographies to historical fiction. As a result, the reading requirements are varied and complex.

Part of the structure of a mathematics text may appear within the context of a biography of a mathematician, or that of a history text may appear in a historically based novel. In language arts reading materials, children must cope with different structures in various genres and with specialized concepts such as mood, setting, imagery, characterization, plot, foreshadowing, and other literary techniques. In addition, a literary selection may combine vocabulary from other content areas with its own, unique vocabulary demands. Thus, a wide range of vocabulary concepts can be encountered in literature, including vocabulary and language structures that are archaic or unfamiliar, as in the following passage:

> "Say, Tom, let me whitewash a little."
> Tom considered, was about to consent; but he altered his mind.
> "No-no-I reckon it wouldn't hardly do, Ben. You see, Aunt Polly's awful particular about this fence—right here on the street, you know—but if it was the back fence I wouldn't mind and she wouldn't. Yes, she's awful particular about this fence; it's got to be done very careful; I reckon there ain't one boy in a thousand, maybe two thousand, that can do it the way it's got to be done."
> "No—is that so? Oh come, now—lemme just try. Only just a little—I'd let you, if you was me, Tom." (Twain, 1982, p. 25)

The various demands of language arts materials require prereading attention to concepts and textual organization. Teachers should give particular care to literary techniques, as well as to visual imagery. The specific teaching suggestions presented in chapter 4 are appropriate for the various genres found in language arts reading.

Central WWW Sites Related to the Language Arts Content Area. Websites such as the following can provide the content in which to apply reading and study skills related to language arts:

MidLink Magazine (http://longwood.cs.ucf.edu/~MidLink/)—Allows children to write and present news stories and other writing; has the benefit of requiring the application of research skills that help in submitted writing.

Kidlink (http://www.kidlink.org/)—Provides a forum for children (ages 10–15) to communicate with each other worldwide. Language translation services are available, as are locations for student-to-student and classroom-to-classroom contact.

Sites for Children: Language and Literature (http://www.ala.org/parentspage/ greatsites/lit.html)—Compiled by the Children and Technology Committee of the Association for Library Service to Children, a division of the American Library Association, this site contains links to favorite children's stories, to authors and illustrators, to classic children's literature, to sites that provide reference resources, to sites that contain writing by children, and to sites that provide children's book awards. A very comprehensive listing!

Featured Teacher

Kathi Mitchell

Kathi Mitchell is a fifth-grade teacher at Kimball School in Concord, New Hampshire. Her classroom website (http://www.concord.k12.nh.us/schools/kimball/Classes/MITCHELL/index.html; see Figure 10-10) is a wonderful blend of links and activities across all content areas. It provides information for her students and their parents while being helpful to other teachers as well. As you will see if you visit her site, there is a link back to her school, which is also exemplary in its construction and information. Other teachers' classroom pages at Kimball School can be accessed through http://www.concord.k12.nh.us/schools/kimball/index.html.

FIGURE 10-10

The home page for Kathi Mitchell's fifth-grade class at Kimball School (http://www.concord.k12.nh.us/schools/kimball/Classes/MITCHELL/index.html)

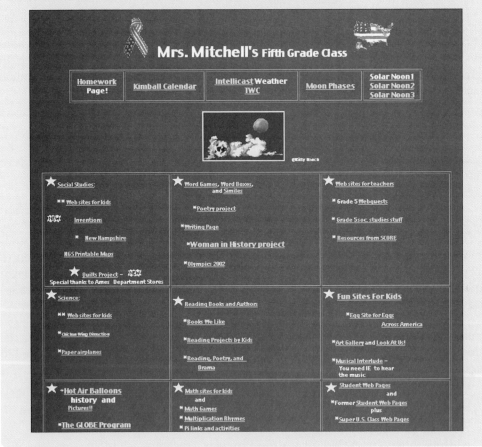

The Relationship of a Literacy Framework to Content-Area Instruction

In previous chapters we discussed that a balanced literacy framework includes integrated beliefs about how children learn to read. With a balanced literacy framework, you choose instructional methods and modify procedural steps depending on your children's needs. The method frameworks included in this chapter can be used within the various explanations that teachers might have for two important questions pertaining to literacy frameworks (What should I teach? and How should I teach?). However, the second question is more relevant to the content-area reading strategies presented in this chapter. This is because there is little debate about what to teach: organizing and text structures, study and research skills, summarizing and notetaking are all important aspects of content-area reading. *How* to teach these aspects of reading, however, depends on whether you lean toward a holistic language learning or a specific skills perspective.

If you have a holistic language learning perspective, you probably will be most comfortable with the I-Search, K-W-L, and jigsaw method frameworks. These frameworks place great importance on children's control of research and reporting of findings. If you have a specific skills perspective, you probably will be most comfortable with directed reading activity (DRA) and study strategies such as SQ3R. However, a balanced literacy framework allows you to choose and modify the procedural steps within each of these frameworks, depending on children's needs.

For example, if children are struggling in the use of a table of contents within an I-Search activity, you might quickly conduct a mini-lesson on this aspect of research. Alternatively, you might want to provide additional time for the enrichment phase of a DRA, allowing children to pursue their own interests. In general, your balanced framework will allow you to choose a more student-directed or teacher-directed method framework as you get to know the individual strengths and needs of the children in your classroom. Regardless of your literacy framework, however, all teachers recognize the importance of teaching appropriate reading and study strategies, even as they emphasize different procedural steps within those strategies. Teachers are also increasingly acknowledging the important part that the Internet has to play in content-area reading and related activities.

Use the self-test questions on http://www.prenhall.com/leukinzer to review the material presented in this chapter.

Major Points

▶ Reading and content-area teachers who expect children to read texts in specific subjects must provide children with reading instruction connected to the specific reading-related skills associated with that subject area.

▶ Knowledge of book parts and general research skills helps children's comprehension and should be a part of reading instruction.

▶ The organization of narrative texts, which are generally used to teach reading, and expository texts, which children are required to read in subject areas, differs greatly. Textual organization also differs among subject areas.

▶ Reading rate depends largely on the purpose for reading. Flexibility in reading rates needs to be taught.

▶ Method frameworks used in content-area reading include frameworks that can be used in any subject as well as frameworks specific to one subject.

▶ Most effective reading and study strategies are based on an interactive explanation of how a person reads.

▶ Research strategies using the Internet are a part of teaching research and study skills. Internet sites also provide subject-matter content where appropriate reading and study skills strategies can be applied and practiced.

Making Instructional Decisions

1. List and discuss the specific reading demands of social studies, mathematics, science, and language arts materials. Identify general differences in organizational patterns and reading requirements. Find an elementary school textbook for each subject area, provide specific examples of the items on your list, and devise a lesson using at least two of the method frameworks in this chapter.

2. Content-area textbooks and expository texts in general, which permit the reader to discover new ideas or perhaps to reinforce and extend already-known concepts, form most of the reading children are required to do beyond the primary grades. Thus, it might be argued that expository material should be an early focus, allowing children to learn to read using materials like those they will encounter later. Do you

agree with this argument? Would it present any difficulty for a teacher who strongly believes in using children's literature to teach reading? Relate your response to beliefs about what to teach and how to teach literacy.

3. Find a reading unit in any content-area subject and construct a directed reading activity for a reading selection. Then construct a three-level study guide and a set of marginal glosses for the same material.

4. If possible, practice using the SQ3R technique with an elementary school student. Otherwise, practice guiding a classmate through SQ3R or use it yourself in your own reading.

5. How does a map reader differ from a map thinker? How might your instructional practices foster the development of map thinkers?

6. How can the Internet be used together with children's subject-matter textbooks and within the method frameworks discussed in this chapter?

Further Reading

Bulgren, J., & Scanlon, D. (1998). Instructional routines and learning strategies that promote understanding of content area relationships. *Journal of Adolescent and Adult Literacy, 41*(4), 292–302.

Discusses the demands of middle and secondary schools and how they may contribute to learning difficulties. Presents several approaches for the comprehension of content-area concepts.

Dillner, M. (1994). Using hypermedia to enhance content-area instruction. *Journal of Reading, 37,* 260–270.

Discusses the procedures and decisions a teacher makes to create a hypermedia lesson and gives some examples of how children use that lesson. Incorporates interesting ideas for developing lessons using hypermedia.

Duffelmeyer, F. A. (1994). Effective anticipation guide statements for learning from expository prose. *Journal of Reading, 37,* 452–457.

Provides guidelines for writing anticipation guides, as well as examples of effective and ineffective statements with respect to such guides.

Egan, M. (1994). Capitalizing on the reader's strengths: An activity using schema. *Journal of Reading, 37,* 636–641.

Provides techniques that allow readers to use their prior knowledge to interact with print.

Hadaway, N. L., & Young, T. A. (1994). Content literacy and language learning: Instructional decisions. *The Reading Teacher, 47,* 522–527.

Discusses the use of teacher modeling and interaction with textbooks in ways that help children integrate literacy processes and help diverse learners. Part of a themed issue dealing with literacy in the content areas.

Horowitz, R. (Ed.). (1994). A themed issue about classroom talk about text: What teenagers and teachers come to know about the world through talk about text. *Journal of Reading, 37,* 628–714.

A themed issue that includes articles about facilitating student-to-student discussion, authentic discussion about texts, learning in science, inviting multiple perspectives, the role of student-led discussions, and the role of discourse diversity.

Ruddell, M. R. (2000). *Teaching content reading and writing* (3rd ed.). New York: John Wiley & Sons.

A readable textbook that deals with content-area reading. Although its focus is on middle and secondary grades, the strategies discussed can be easily adapted for younger children.

Wood, K. D., & Harmon, J. M. (2001). *Strategies for integrating reading and writing in middle and high school classrooms.* Newark, DE: International Reading Association.

A short, readable paperback that contains strategies and examples for improving students' performance and interest in various subject areas.

References

Aronson, E., Blaney, N., Stephin, C., Sikes, J., & Snapp, M. (1978) *The jigsaw classroom.* Beverly Hills, CA: Sage Publishing Company.

Baker, L., & Brown, A. C. (1983). Metacognition and the reading process. In P. D. Pearson (Ed.), *Handbook of reading research.* New York: Plenum Press.

Bassler, O. C., Kolb, J. R., Craighead, M. S., & Gray, W. L. (1981). *Succeeding in mathematics* (revised). Austin, TX: SteckVaughn.

Bean, T. W. (2000). Reading in the content areas: Social constructivism dimensions. In M. L. Kamil, P. Mosenthal, P. D. Pearson, & R. Barr (Eds.), *Handbook of reading research, Volume III* (pp. 629–644). Mahwah, NJ: Lawrence Erlbaum Associates.

Beck, I. L., McKeown, M. G., Hamilton, R. L., & Kucan, L. (1997). *Questioning the author: An approach for enhancing student engagement with text.* Newark, DE: International Reading Association.

Beck, I. L., McKeown, M. G., Worthy, J., Sandora, C. A., & Kucan, L. (1996). Questioning the author: A year-long classroom implementation to engage students with text. *The Elementary School Journal, 96*(4), 365–414.

Brown, A. L., Campione, J. C., & Day, J. D. (1981). Learning to learn: On training students to learn from texts. *Educational Researcher, 10,* 14–21.

Brown, A. L., & Day, J. D. (1983). Macrorules for summarizing texts: The development of expertise. *Journal of Verbal Learning and Verbal Behavior, 22,* 1–8.

Buggey, J. (1983). *Our communities.* Chicago, IL: Follett.

Carr, B., & Ogle, D. M. (1987). K-W-L Plus: A strategy for comprehension and summarization. *Journal of Reading, 30,* 626–631.

Carson, J. (1990). Unpublished manuscript.

Cheek, E. J., Jr., & Cheek, M. C. (1983). *Reading instruction through content teaching.* Columbus, OH: Merrill.

Davey, B. (1983). Think-aloud—Modeling the cognitive processes of reading comprehension. *Journal of Reading, 27,* 44–47.

Defoe, D. (1967). *Robinson Crusoe* (abridged and adapted by Ron King). Belmont, CA: Fearon.

Dupuis, M. M. (Ed.). (1984). *Reading in the content areas: Research for teachers.* Newark, DE: International Reading Association.

Evans, C. W., Leija, A. J., & Falkner, T. R. (2001). *Math links: Teaching the NCTM 2000 standards through children's literature.* Newark, DE: International Reading Association.

Farr, R., & Roser, N. (1979). *Teaching a child to read.* New York: Harcourt Brace Jovanovich.

Fay, L. (1965). Reading study skills: Math and science. In J. A. Figure (Ed.), *Reading and inquiry* (pp. 93–94). Newark, DE: International Reading Association.

Flood, J., Lapp, D., & Farnan, N. (1986). A reading-writing procedure that teaches expository paragraph structure. *The Reading Teacher, 29,* 556–562.

Forgan, H. W., & Mangrum II, C. T. (1985). *Teaching content area reading skills* (3rd ed.). Columbus, OH: Merrill.

Fry, E. (1981). Graphical literacy. *Journal of Reading, 24,* 383–389.

Garner, R. (1987). Strategies for reading and studying expository text. *Educational Psychologist, 22,* 299–312.

Hanf, M. B. (1971). Mapping: A technique for translating reading into thinking. *Journal of Reading, 13,* 225–230.

Herber, H. (1978). *Teaching reading in content areas* (2nd ed.). Englewood Cliffs, NJ: Prentice-Hall.

Herber, H. L., & Herber, J. N. (1993). *Teaching in content areas with reading, writing, and reasoning.* Needham Heights, MA: Allyn & Bacon.

Johnson, D. D., & Pearson, P. D. (1984). *Teaching reading vocabulary* (and ed.). New York: Holt, Rinehart & Winston.

Kane, R. B., Byrne, M. A., & Hater, M. A. (1974). *Helping children read mathematics.* New York: American Book.

Kinney, M. A. (1985). A language experience approach to teaching expository text structure. *The Reading Teacher, 38,* 854–856.

MacRorie, K. (1988). *The I-Search paper.* Portsmouth, NH: Boynton-Cool.

Manzo, A. V. (1969). The ReQuest procedure. *Journal of Reading, 11,* 123–126.

Manzo, A. V. (1985). Expansion modules for the ReQuest, CAT, GRP, and REAP reading/study procedures. *Journal of Reading, 28,* 498–503.

Markham, E. M. (1981). *Comprehension monitoring in children's oral communication skills.* New York: Academic Press.

Myers, C. B., & Wilk, G. (1983). *People, time, and change.* Chicago: Follett.

Novak, J. D., & Gowan, D. B. (1984). *Learning how to learn.* Cambridge, MA: Cambridge University Press.

Ogle, D. M. (1989). The know, want to know, learn strategy. In K. D. Muth (Ed.), *Children's comprehension of text* (pp. 205–223). Newark, DE: International Reading Association.

O'Mara, D. A. (1981). The process of reading mathematics. *Journal of Reading, 25,* 22–30.

Pauk, W. (1984). The new SQ4R. *Reading World, 23,* 274–275.

Robinson, F. P. (1961). *Effective study.* New York: Harper & Row.

Rubin, D. (1983). *Teaching reading and study skills in content areas.* New York: Holt, Rinehart & Winston.

Ruddell, M. R. (1992). Integrated content and long-term vocabulary learning with the Vocabulary Self-Collection Strategy (VSS). In E. K. Dishner, T. W. Bean, J. E. Readence, & D. W. Moore (Eds.), *Reading in the content areas: Improving classroom instruction* (3rd ed., 190–196). Dubuque, IA: Kendall Hunt.

Ruddell, M. R. (1993). *Teaching content reading and writing.* Needham Heights, MA: Allyn & Bacon.

Ruddell, R. B., & Boyle, O. F. (1989). A study of cognitive mapping as a means to improve summarization and comprehension of expository text. *Reading Research and Instruction, 29,* 12–22.

Shepherd, D. L. (1982). *Comprehensive high school reading methods.* Columbus, OH: Merrill.

Singer, H., & Donlan, D. (1989). *Reading and learning* (2nd ed.). Hillsdale, NJ: Lawrence Erlbaum Associates.

Slavin, R. E. (1989). A Cooperative learning approach to reading in content areas: Jigsaw Teaching: In D. Lapp, J. Flood & N. Farnan, (Eds.), *Instructional theory and practice for content area reading and learning.* Englewood Cliffs, NJ: Prentice-Hall.

Slavin, R. E. (1994). *Cooperative learning: Theory, research and practice,* 2nd ed. Boston: Allyn & Bacon.

Spache, G. D. (1963). *Toward better reading.* Champaign, IL: Garrard Press.

Spache, G. D., & Berg, P. C. (1966). *The art of efficient reading.* New York: Macmillan.

Summers, E. G. (1965). Utilizing visual aids in reading materials for effective reading. In H. L. Herber (Ed.), *Developing study skills in secondary schools.* Newark, DE: International Reading Association.

Sund, R. B., Adams, D. K., & Hackett, J. K. (1980). *Accent on science* (Level 6). Columbus, OH: Merrill.

Tei, E., & Stewart, O. (1985). Effective studying from text: Applying metacognitive strategies. *Forum for Reading, 27,* 36–43.

Thomas, E. L., & Alexander, H. A. (1982). *Improving reading in every class* (abridged 3rd ed.). Boston, MA: Allyn & Bacon.

Tierney, H. J., & Readence, J. E. (2000). *Reading strategies and practices: A compendium* (5th ed.). Boston, MA: Allyn & Bacon.

Tierney, H. J., Readence, J. E., & Dishner, B. K. (1990). *Reading strategies and practices: A compendium* (3rd ed.). Boston, MA: Allyn & Bacon.

Twain, M. (1982). *The adventures of Tom Sawyer.* New York: Wanderer Books.

Vacca, R. (1981). *Content area reading.* Boston, MA: Little, Brown.

Vacca, R. T., & Vacca, J. L. (1986). *Content area reading* (2nd ed.). Boston, MA: Little, Brown.

Vacca, R. T., & Vacca, J. A. (2002). *Content area reading: Literacy and learning across the curriculum* (7th ed.). Boston, MA: Allyn & Bacon.

Zorfass, J., & Copel, H. (1995). The I-Search: Guiding students toward relevant research. *Educational Leadership, 53*(1), 48–51.

Assessment and Instructional Needs

CHAPTER 11

Supporting Literacy through Assessment

 **E-mail from the Classroom**

Sender: Bill MacWinie, BillyMac@AOL.com
Subject: Thoughts about Testing

Lately, there's been a lot about testing discussed on the radio and in our local paper. Also, I remember recently that Congress passed a requirement that all students through eighth grade would be tested every year to check their reading progress. Seems like there's a lot of testing going on all around! This was also true when I was in school—there sure seemed to be a lot of tests! There were written tests, oral tests, spelling tests, tests with answer sheets, and homework that sure seemed a lot like more tests!

I'm happy to hear that there is a move toward what people are calling "alternative tests." I'm not sure what these do yet, but maybe they'll help teachers see how much children are learning without testing so often, or at least using them together with traditional tests to give them some balance. I think it's going to be really important for me to know about lots of different ways to judge my students' progress. I know that I'll be held accountable for their learning and, because I plan to be a great teacher, that's just fine!

Bill MacWinie

After reading this chapter, you should be able to:

1. Use formal, informal, and teacher-made assessment tools in your literacy program and explain the assessment results to parents.
2. Explain general issues in assessment and their importance to teachers of literacy.
3. Implement appropriate tools to assess readers, reading materials, and the interaction between reading and reading materials.
4. Integrate assessment information with your literacy framework to guide instructional decisions.

Good Assessment Strategies Help Teachers Teach: A Principle of Effective Literacy Instruction

Effective teachers base their instruction on students' needs. Thus, being knowledgeable about each child's needs and progress is an important part of effective literacy instruction, as stated in the following instructional principle:

9. Good assessment strategies help teachers teach. Monitoring children's success in reading enhances the probability of providing appropriate, individualized instruction for all readers (Pellegrino, Chudowsky, & Glaser, 2001; P.L.107-110 (H.R.1), 2002).

Becoming a teacher who is knowledgeable about children's needs and progress means understanding the many and varied means of assessment that are used by reading and writing teachers. These assessments range from day-to-day informal observations to using regular homework assignments as diagnostic tools, to understanding the nature of alternative assessments such as the use of portfolios. It also means understanding the more traditional forms of assessment that are used by school district personnel and others to make instructional decisions that will affect your teaching.

This chapter will provide you with the basic knowledge needed to use informal, formal, and teacher-made assessment tools in your classroom. It presents both alternative and traditional assessment in a way that will help you integrate assessment into your literacy framework. It will also help you to use assessment to provide instruction for the children in your classroom based on your understanding of their strengths, as well as their needs and progress.

Check your ongoing understanding of chapter concepts by using the guided review for this chapter on http://www. prenhall.com/leukinzer

General Issues in Assessment

Tests and testing are topics under much discussion. Some teachers, administrators, and parents feel that far too much time is spent in testing, and they are equally dissatisfied with the tests traditionally used in schools. Other teachers, administrators, and parents feel that traditional, formal tests are needed to ensure a continuous evaluation of students' performance.

The debate about testing often includes terms like *alternative assessment*, which implies there are alternatives to traditional measures and that these are better than the tests used in the past. Nevertheless, although many school districts are moving toward alternative assessment, you will be required to administer traditional measures as well. Thus, this chapter discusses both forms of assessment and presents the benefits and potential difficulties of each.

Instructional Decision Making: Clarifying the Goals of Assessment

In chapter 1 we discussed the modification of instructional frameworks and instructional decisions (see Figure 1-3 on page 17). Teachers generally modify their instruction based on the outcomes of their instructional decisions, as seen through observations of children's classroom performance or their performance on a more formal measure. Assessment, whether formal or informal, plays a large role in teachers' decision making, and knowledge about assessment tools makes you better able to modify your instruction to suit your students' needs. The International Reading Association (IRA), together with the National Council for Teachers of English (NCTE) (1994), provide the following goals and implementation procedures regarding the assessment of literacy:

Goals

1. The interests of the students are paramount in assessment.
2. The primary purpose of assessment is to improve teaching and learning.
3. Assessment must reflect and allow for critical inquiry into curriculum and instruction.

4. Assessments must recognize and reflect the intellectually and socially complex nature of reading and writing and the important roles of school, home, and society in literacy development.
5. Assessment must be fair and equitable.
6. The consequence of an assessment procedure is the first—and most important—consideration in establishing the validity of the assessment.

Implementation

7. The teacher is the most important agent of assessment.
8. The assessment process should involve multiple perspectives and sources of data.
9. Assessments must be based in the school community.
10. All members of the educational community—students, parents, teachers, administrators, policymakers, and the public—must have a voice in the development, interpretation, and reporting of assessment.
11. Parents must be involved as active, essential participants in the assessment process.

As you read these guidelines, you probably noticed the emphasis on the teacher's role and on the goal of assessment to improve learning. Indeed, the role of the teacher as a decision maker who uses multiple sources of data to make instructional choices cannot be overemphasized. However, assessment should also recognize that all students have areas of strength, and these areas can be effectively used as a basis for addressing areas of need; assessment should also identify areas of strength (IRA, 2000).

Issues of standards, both nationally and locally, are also closely linked to assessment. Policy statements about standards in literacy have been jointly published and endorsed by the International Reading Association and the National Council for Teachers of English. These professional associations also have taken positions on the issue of high-stakes testing. The following documents inform designers of national tests, curriculum designers, and teachers. These publications are available from the IRA and NCTE:

International Reading Association. (1999). *High-stakes assessments in reading* (a position statement of the International Reading Association). Newark, DE: International Reading Association.

International Reading Association and the National Council for Teachers of English. (1996). *Standards for the English language arts.* Newark, DE:International Reading Association. (Jointly published and available from Urbana, IL:National Council for Teachers of English.)

Smagorinsky, P. (1996). *Standards in practice: Grades 9–12.* Urbana, IL:National Council for Teachers of English.

Wilhelm, J. (1996). *Standards in practice: Grades 6–8.* Urbana, IL:National Council for Teachers of English.

The discussion of standards is ongoing, and testing at a national level is a continual process. Internet sites such as **The National Center for Education Statistics** (http://nces.ed.gov/indihome.asp) and the **National Assessment of Educational Progress** (http://nces.ed.gov/naep/) provide information about government-mandated, nationwide assessments and provide access to data from those assessments (see Figure 11-1 on page 392). This discussion of standards is often linked to high-stakes assessment—assessment practices that place often unintended, but harmful, labels on teachers, schools, and students—especially when many assessment tools might not completely reflect what we know about how children learn (Hoffman, Assaf, & Paris, 2001; Pellegrino et. al, 2001).

Assessment can demand substantial amounts of a teacher's time, whether traditional or alternative approaches are used. Traditional assessment tools require time not only for test administration but also for the preparation, scoring, and interpretation of completed tests. Alternative assessment procedures require time for close examination of individual students' work, recordkeeping procedures, and individual conferencing

Home page for the **National Assessment of Educational Progress** (http://nces.ed.gov/naep/)

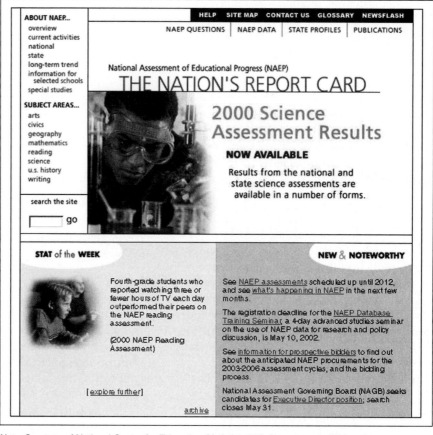

Note: Courtesy of National Center for Education Statistics, U.S. Department of Education.

standardized testing
Evaluation using standardized materials and standardized procedures for administration and scoring.

assessment program
Systematic evaluation of students' progress by various testing methods consistent with a teacher's or school district's goals.

and interviews. Some time for assessment will be used for the yearly **standardized testing** required by nearly all school districts to compare their students' progress to the progress of students in other districts or previous years. Detailed recordkeeping by teachers is usually required as part of a management system.

A management system specifies what students should learn and requires a continual **assessment program** to document progress; it is required of all teachers.

Choosing an Assessment Strategy

Because it is important to use instructional time in the best possible way, choosing assessment instruments to match specific measurement objectives is critical. The choice of an assessment tool is largely determined by the reasons for testing, as there are many purposes for administering various kinds of measures in school. In addition to teachers, assessment results are used by many people: district staff, superintendents, school board members, curriculum committees, principals, and others. Each has slightly different goals and purposes, all of which influence instructional decisions and the selection of measurement tools. Certain measures assess specific skills and are closely tied to individual children's instructional situations, while others assess children's progress as seen in their actual reading or writing. Some measures provide only group or survey data, which cannot easily be used for specific diagnostic purposes; other measures are specific to children's individual portfolios. There are also measures appropriate for comparing different sets of instructional materials, perhaps before purchasing decisions are made.

Teachers of literacy commonly use assessment tools for a variety of reasons:

1. To find a child's reading and writing competency.
2. To be able to infer strategies and processes used by a child during reading and writing.
3. To see whether one book is more difficult than another.
4. To identify motivational material for a student or class (that is, to find out students' interests and attitudes).
5. To match a child with appropriate materials.
6. To find out whether a child has mastered a desired goal.
7. To see if a child is making progress over time.

Can you see that these **targets of assessment** differ? For example, goals 1, 2, 4, 6, and 7 are student centered; that is, the student is the target and the assessment relates directly to the child.

Goal 4 differs slightly from goals 1, 2, 6, and 7 in that it measures an affective response rather than reading ability or processes, but it still deals with the reader. Goal 3 does not relate specifically to a student; instead, it assesses the difficulty of reading material, perhaps through an analysis of factors such as print size or density of ideas. Goal 5 combines two categories; it measures both the materials and the student in combination.

Thus, assessment can focus on the child, the materials, or the child and the materials together. The target and goal of assessment jointly determine the type of measurement tool needed. Several additional considerations can help you to further define the choice of an assessment tool:

1. Do I want or need to assess more than one child at a time? **Group tests** are administered to several children at the same time. Such tests result in overall time savings when a class or an entire school of students needs to be evaluated. Traditional measures include standardized tests designed for this purpose; alternative assessments include informal measures such as cloze tests, which are discussed later in this chapter.
2. Do I want or need to assess one child at a time? **Individual tests** are administered in one-on-one situations. Such tests allow more controlled conditions and permit closer observation of student behavior. Traditional measures include standardized tests designed for this purpose; alternative assessments include interviews, observations, or examination of a child's portfolio.
3. Do I want to assess general reading (or writing) ability? **Survey tests** provide indications of general ability. Reading tests that indicate general reading level (but not specific strengths and weaknesses) fall into this category. Traditional measures include standardized tests designed for this purpose; alternative assessments include portfolios and think-alouds.
4. Do I want to diagnose specific literacy needs? **Diagnostic tests** assess specific abilities and can provide information leading to specific instructional practices. Traditional measures include standardized tests and can be either group tests (for example, *Stanford Diagnostic Reading Test*) or individual tests (for example, *Durrell Analysis of Reading Difficulty; Woodcock Reading Mastery Test*), but not survey tests. Alternative assessments include retellings, running records, informal reading inventories, and miscue analyses.
5. Do I want to focus on formal assessment or do I want to see how a child or a group of children perform in realistic reading situations? This question interacts with the previous ones. The answer to this question will help you decide whether your purposes can be served through one or more of the previous tools, or whether less-formal observation of students' behavior while reading and writing are the most appropriate.

Process versus Product Assessment.   Assessment that looks mainly at the outcomes of student performance is called **product assessment.** Assessment that attempts to interpret performance in an effort to evaluate underlying strategies, actions, or behaviors is called **process assessment.**

targets of assessment
Who or what is being assessed; may include the student, the text, or the student and the text together.

group tests   Assessment instruments administered to more than one person at the same time.

individual tests
Assessment instruments administered to one person at a time.

survey tests
Assessment instruments that evaluate general ability in a certain area.

diagnostic tests
Assessment instruments that evaluate specific product and process characteristics so that instructional decisions can be made.

product assessment
Assessment that primarily evaluates the outcomes of student performance.

process assessment
Assessment that primarily evaluates the strategies, actions, or behaviors underlying the products of student performance.

Individual conferences about children's reading and writing, including feedback, should be a part of an assessment program.

Wittrock (1987) points out that most formal assessment instruments can answer questions about how well students do but cannot answer questions such as, "What strategies does this child use to construct main ideas?" or "How does this child relate prior knowledge and experiences to the text?" (p. 734). Despite the fact that process measures might be more important to teachers in making individual instructional decisions, all types of tests can be useful if they are closely tied to the purposes of testing. Nevertheless, standardized tests, especially multiple-choice tests, have been increasingly criticized as being harmful to minorities, as contributing to an over-reliance on testing, and as hindering educational reforms (Gifford, 1990; see also Pellegrino et al., 2001). If this is true, why are traditional product measures still so heavily used?

The assessment of products is easier to conduct than the assessment of processes. To assess products, a teacher needs only to follow the specific guidelines that come with a formal, published test, or to grade a student's work only on its observable, surface features. Process assessments, however, require reasoned decisions about a reader's underlying reading processes. In a product assessment, for example, a child might be asked to read a passage and answer a question. The result (the answer) is assumed to indicate whether the passage was understood. In process assessment, however, a teacher must attempt to find out how the answer was arrived at and what strategies were used and/or rejected by the reader.

Process assessment has received increasing attention because of an emphasis on higher-order thought processes such as critical thinking and problem solving (for example, see Bransford, Brown, & Cocking, 2000; CTGV, 1993; Nickerson, 1989; Siegler, 1989). One difficulty associated with process assessment is that there are usually multiple paths to solving a problem and individuals may process information differently. This flexibility makes it inappropriate to interpret the results of process measures in terms of a single strategy (Gardner & Hatch, 1989; Siegler, 1989). Consequently, teachers who use process-based assessments must consider multiple paths to an answer, thereby making assessment and interpretation more difficult. Such assessment is more student-centered, however, as children are not automatically penalized for answers that differ from an expected response. Thus, with a process measure, a teacher must determine whether the test can accurately infer a reader's processes and whether that inference is reflected in scoring and interpretation. The assessment tools and procedures discussed throughout this chapter include both process and product measures.

TABLE 11-1

Characteristics common to alternative and traditional assessment procedures

Usual Alternative Assessment Procedures	Usual Traditional Assessment Procedures
▶ Require students to perform, create, or produce something	▶ Require students to respond to fairly narrow, specific tasks or questions
▶ Focus on higher-level thinking and problem solving	▶ Focus on lower-level, literal knowledge
▶ Require tasks based on meaningful instructional activities	▶ Require tasks that are out of context and are often unrelated to specific instruction
▶ Have close linkages to real-world applications	▶ Include activities created specifically for the assessment that may not be grounded in real-world applications
▶ Require people to do scoring, using human judgment	▶ Require people or machines to do the scoring, often with answer keys that minimize human judgment
▶ Suggest new assessment roles for teachers	▶ Imply a continuum of past assessment roles for teachers

Traditional versus Alternative Assessment. Traditional measures include a wide variety of tools, from formal, multiple-choice tests with computer-scored answer sheets to teacher-made comprehension questions asked of students at the end of a reading selection. As perspectives about the value of these measures have shifted, alternatives have become more prevalent and include portfolio assessment, performance assessment, and outcome-based assessment. Herman, Aschbacher, and Winters (1992; see also Tierney, Johnson, Moore, & Valencia, 2000) present several characteristics as common to alternative assessments. Table 11-1 presents these characteristics and juxtaposes them with characteristics of traditional measurement.

One aspect of alternative assessment is "authentic assessment," which means that the tasks and procedures used in evaluation are closely related to: (a) tasks found in the real world, (b) tasks found in instructional situations, and (c) tasks as similar as possible to real literacy tasks. The following items often are used during alternative assessment:

portfolios	journals and self-reports
interviews	think-alouds
informal measures	documented observations
performance, including presentations	demonstration projects

In contrast, the following often are used during traditional assessment:

standardized, machine-scored tests	assessment of specific skills
low-level, literal questions	multiple choice tests

What Makes a Good Assessment Tool?

Assessment instruments range from formal, standardized tests purchased from test publishers, to questions constructed by individual teachers, to samples of students' ongoing work. Nonetheless, certain factors are common to all assessment tools and determine whether a measurement tool is good or bad. Understanding these factors will help you choose a test or an overall assessment program to best meet your measurement objectives. Many people define a good assessment tool like this:

▶ It is **valid.** It measures what it is supposed to measure. Sometimes a test claims to measure a particular skill or ability, but an examination of the actual test items, procedures, or testing tasks shows that it does not. At other times, a valid test might be used in a manner not intended by its authors. For example, a survey test providing

validity The ability of a test to measure what it claims to measure.

information about one's general reading ability might be inappropriately used to infer areas of specific reading disability, or a portfolio containing only samples of a student's writing might be claimed to reflect a student's reading progress.

▶ It is **reliable.** It gives consistent results, not random or changing results over time. If a test is given to a child over and over again and yields the same score each time, then it is extremely reliable. In fact, if the scores are identical each time, the test is 100 percent reliable. In reality, tests are not 100 percent reliable; differences in children's learning and in affective, physical, or environmental factors all influence the test/retest results of any given child. An instructor's manual or a technical manual will provide information about a test's reliability, stated in terms of a reliability coefficient. In education, a reliability coefficient above 0.80 is considered acceptable.

reliability The ability of a test to provide consistent information.

▶ It has a low **standard error of measurement.** Because tests are not 100 percent reliable, teachers must know how widely children's scores can vary by chance. The standard error of measurement specifies exactly how much a score must increase or decrease before the difference is attributed to something other than chance. Such information can be viewed in plus and minus terms. For example, if a child scored 17 on a 20-item test and the test had a standard error of measurement of 2, then that child's score would really be 17 plus or minus 2. In other words, it would fall between 15 and 19. Thus, if the child was tested again and received a score of 19, it would not be appropriate to assume that improvement had been shown because the two scores are both within the range of the standard error of measurement. That is, they are within two points of each other, and the difference could be due to chance. Standard error of measurement applies more to traditional, formal tests than to alternative or informal assessment, although a child's performance on an informal assessment tool will also differ even in back-to-back administrations. Thus, it may be thought of as including a standard error of measurement.

standard error of measurement A statistic that indicates how much a score must increase or decrease before the difference is attributed to something other than chance.

▶ It is manageable in terms of administration time. There is always a tradeoff concerning the time taken away from instruction for assessment. If you have a choice, consider carefully the benefits to your instructional program that will result from the assessment information and try to balance the value of the information you receive with the instructional time lost.

▶ It is easy to score and interpret. This is related to reporting procedures and teacher knowledge. Formal, standardized tests often will report results in a variety of ways; you will have to decide if the type(s) of scores are appropriate for your needs. Similarly, the types of information placed in a portfolio and your knowledge of the reading process are critical to interpreting the information a portfolio can provide.

All of the above aspects should be considered when choosing an assessment strategy. All depend heavily on your knowledge of the reading process. For example, when considering validity, it is appropriate to examine test items and procedures carefully to determine whether a test does what it claims to do and whether it measures appropriate reading skills. In other words, does it have **content validity?**

content validity One of several types of validity; assesses whether a test measures skills appropriate to the subject area.

In addition, classroom teachers are in the best position to determine whether an assessment tool has **curricular validity;** that is, whether it measures what children have been taught. Other aspects, such as a test's reliability, are also important because teachers need to be able to assume that any assessment provides consistent information. Then, if differences across time are found, you can more confidently attribute changes in student performance to learning rather than to chance.

curricular validity One of several types of validity; assesses whether a test measures what children have been taught.

⌨ Tests and Test Scores

Types and Uses of Tests

The three general categories of traditional tests are informal, teacher-made, and formal. Because all tests can be useful, it is important to know the strengths and weaknesses of each type and the circumstances surrounding their appropriate use.

FIGURE 11-2

A framework of test types and targets of assessment

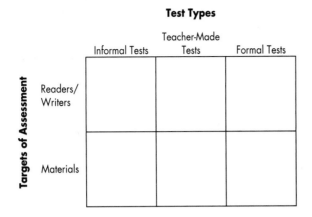

Informal Tests.   These tests allow for teacher judgment in their administration, scoring, and interpretation. They may be purchased as stand-alone items, included as part of a larger set of materials, or based on regular instructional material you will use with your students. Although tests in this category have general procedures to be followed, your judgment is critical within those procedures. For example, an informal test might indicate that testing should stop when a student becomes frustrated, or require you to look for patterns within a child's work or performance to make decisions about that child's abilities and needs. Clearly, your judgment plays a major part in determining when frustration occurred or in deciding on the occurrence of a pattern. When people talk about "alternative assessment," they generally are talking about informal tests.

Teacher-Made Tests.   These tests are made and used by teachers to assess their students' knowledge or performance, usually within a particular instructional unit or lesson. For this category of test, you alone determine the administration and scoring procedures. Teacher-made tests often are a part of popular assessment tools such as portfolios.

Formal Tests.   These tests have strict guidelines for their administration, scoring, and interpretation. They are purchased from test publishers and often are called standardized tests. When people talk about "traditional assessment," they generally are talking about formal tests.

The types of tests and the targets of assessment together provide a framework (see Figure 11-2) within which assessment tools can be analyzed and chosen. Whichever types of tests are used, they must not be used indiscriminately. You should observe children in your classroom and proceed with formal and/or informal assessments to discover or confirm areas of need so that instructional decisions can be made more reliably.

Types and Uses of Scores

Children's scores on traditional reading tests are commonly reported in five ways:

1. Raw scores
2. Percentage scores
3. Percentile scores
4. Stanine scores
5. Grade-equivalent scores

Each of these reporting methods yields different information and can be misleading if not used properly. Percentile and stanine scores are applicable only to traditional, formal measures; raw scores, percentage scores, and grade-equivalent scores are also used in informal assessments such as cloze procedures, think-alouds, running records, or informal reading inventories.

raw scores The number of correct responses on a test.

Raw scores are determined by simply adding up the number of correct responses, regardless of the total number of items on a test. A child who gets eight items right has a raw score of 8. When a single test is given to a child or group of children, the scores can be valuable because all children are taking the same test and there are no variations in how long the test is or what the test is assessing. However, many formal, published tests consist of a series of subtests, which usually measure different reading components and have different numbers of items. For example, a comprehension subtest might include 25 items, whereas a vocabulary subtest might include 40 items. Thus, a raw score of 20 on each of the subtests would not indicate relative ability in the subtest areas.

percentage scores The percentage of correct responses on a test.

Percentage scores are one way to deal with some of the shortcomings of raw scores. Percentages are calculated by dividing the number of correct responses by the total number of responses possible and then multiplying the result by 100. This process yields a theoretical score out of 100 regardless of the length of the test, thus allowing more representative comparisons. In the earlier example, a raw score of 20 on both the 25-item comprehension subtest and the 40-item vocabulary subtest would produce percentage scores of 80 and 50, respectively. Thus, percentage scores allow clearer comparisons.

percentile scores Ratings that indicate the percent of the norm population scoring below a student's score.

Percentile scores indicate the percent of the norm population scoring below individual students' scores, thereby reflecting the relative standing of those students within the norm group. In other words, a percentile score of 80 says that 80 percent of the norm group scored below that child's raw score. In our example, the raw score of 20 (or 80 percent) on the 25-item comprehension subtest probably seems fairly good. However, if the child's peer group averaged 24 (or 95 percent), then the 20 was below average when compared to children of similar ability. Unlike percentage scores, which mask an individual's rank within the peer group, percentile scores provide information about relative standing.

Normal curve equivalents (NCEs) are sometimes confused with percentiles because they are constructed so that only values of 1 through 99 are assigned as scores, and because percentile and NCE scores of 1 and 99 are equivalent. NCE scores often are used in evaluation reports; more school districts are moving toward using them. A discussion of NCEs is beyond the scope of this text; you should pursue this topic in an assessment course or in a measurement text if necessary.

stanine scores Scores related to consistent bands on a normal curve, ranging from 1 to 9.

normal curve A bell-shaped curve that, if based on enough cases, represents a naturally occurring distribution.

Stanine scores also allow a comparison of relative standing. Stanines indicate where a specific score lies in the overall distribution of scores, assuming the total distribution of scores fall into a **normal curve.** The curve is then divided into nine bands, numbered 1 through 9, which correspond to the predetermined percentages of scores falling into each band. A score in the fifth stanine would fall in the middle of the normal curve; scores of 4, 5, or 6 are considered average. Thus, in addition to relative standing, stanine scores indicate the relation of a child's score to the overall distribution of scores.

grade-equivalent scores A measure of relative standing that compares a student's raw score to average scores across grade levels.

Grade-equivalent scores are also commonly used to provide information about relative standing. For example, if a child receives a grade-equivalent score of 7.0, that child's raw score is equivalent to the average score of beginning seventh graders in the norm population. Unfortunately, grade-equivalent scores can be deceptive and can inadvertently label students. Consequently, the International Reading Association is opposed to grade-equivalent scores, and test publishers have moved away from providing them.

⌨ Evaluating Readers and Writers

The Portfolio

Teachers in more holistic, and in traditional, classrooms have turned toward portfolios to supplement or replace traditional measures. Portfolio assessment involves collecting children's work on an ongoing basis and examining it for evidence of growth in literacy.

Rather than an evaluation based on norms or externally imposed criteria, portfolio assessment allows a teacher to see—and to show children, parents, and administrators—what students have done over time.

Lapp and Flood (1989) point out the difficulty of helping parents understand that a child who achieves at the 50th percentile every year is making average and expected progress from grade to grade. They suggest that teachers place a variety of items in children's portfolios that can be shared with parents and others as appropriate. Their suggestions are similar to the recommendations of others (for example, see Farris, 1989; Glazer & Brown, 1993; Jongsma, 1989; Pikulski, 1989) and are included in the following list:

- Formal norm- and criterion-referenced test scores.
- Informal measures such as informal reading inventories, think-alouds, running records, and retellings in response to reading.
- Dated writing samples.
- Dated titles of books read voluntarily (for example, during free-reading time).
- Dated samples of what children have read (photocopied pages).
- Dated self-evaluations of reading ability and comments on feelings toward reading and writing.
- Dated photographs, audiotapes, and videotapes of reading, writing, and other classroom activities.

There is increasing recognition that teachers are the experts with regard to their students and are in the best position to judge progress on a day-to-day basis (Harp, 1989; Johnston, 1987). Several checklists and specific forms have been suggested that can be used to summarize children's progress, which can then be inserted into their portfolios. For example, Eeds (1988) has adapted suggestions by Gentry (1982) to aid teachers in documenting their students' development in early writing (see Figure 11-3 on page 400). Such forms can facilitate formal reporting to parents and the transfer of specific information to management forms, as required by many school districts.

Although it is not necessary to use any particular form—and we encourage you to create your own evaluation summaries—it is important to document and summarize children's work periodically. To be effective at lower grade levels, portfolios require children's samples or teacher's comments every 2 to 3 weeks across all areas of literacy. Figure 11-4 on page 401 illustrates the considerable growth in Tanisha's writing in only 4-1/2 months. Note the longer sentences, more complete punctuation, improvement in capitalization, greater number of words, and better-formed letters.

All of these features should be noted on a summary form inserted regularly into Tanisha's portfolio. Summary forms for children at various grade levels and for different assessment procedures across reading, writing, speaking, and listening may be found in many publications, including those by Courtney and Abodeeb (2001); Farr and Tone (1998); Glazer and Brown (1993); Johnston (1992); Leslie, Jett-Simpson, and the Wisconsin Reading Association (1997); Tierney, Carter, and Desai (1991); and Traill (1993).

In addition to writing samples and summary sheets, portfolios should include photocopied pages from materials that children are fluently reading. Growth in reading can be easily shown when material read at the beginning of first grade (characterized by short sentences, single-syllable words, large print, many pictures, and short selections) is compared to material read in the middle of first grade. Children like to be able to look back at their progress, and parents enjoy seeing how far their children have come.

Self-reports by children—either through interviews or, in higher grades, through writing—should also be part of a portfolio. Wixson, Bosky, Yochum, and Alvermann (1984) have noted that self-assessment interviews can provide much valuable information. Such reports can indicate what is read, what reactions children have toward reading and writing, what strategies they use when they come to a hard word, how they select reading materials, what they think they are learning, how well they think they are doing, where help might be appreciated, and so on. Self-reports should be completed on a regular schedule, either in oral form that you can write down or in

FIGURE 11-3

Checklist for developmental stages in early writing

Name _____ Age _____ Grade _____

	I	II	III	IV
Precommunicative Stage Date				
1. Produces letters or letter-like forms to represent a message.				
2. Demonstrates left-to-right concept.				
3. Demonstrates top-bottom concept.				
4. Repeats known letters and numbers.				
5. Uses many letters and/or numbers.				
6. Mixes upper and lowercase letters.				
7. Indicates preference for uppercase forms.				
The Semiphonetic Stage Date				
1. Realizes letters represent sounds.				
2. Represents whole words with one or more letters.				
3. Evidence of letter name strategy.				
4. Demonstrates left-to-right sequences of letters.				
5. Puts spaces between words.				
The Phonetic Stage Date				
1. Represents every sound heard.				
2. Assigns letters based on sounds as child hears them (invented spellings).				
3. Puts spaces between words.				
4. Masters letter formation.				
The Transitional Stage Date				
1. Utilizes conventional spellings.				
2. Vowels appear in every syllable.				
3. Evidence of visual as opposed to phonetic strategy.				
4. Reverses some letters in words.				

Comments _____

_____

_____

_____

Source: From M. Eeds, "Holistic assessment of coding ability," in S. M. Glazer, L. W. Searfoss, and L. M. Gentile (Eds.), *Reexamining reading diagnosis: New trends and procedures* (Newark, DE: International Reading Association, 1988), p. 56. Reprinted by permission.

writing by the children. To facilitate self-reporting, summary forms that ask children to comment on these items should be made available.

Self-assessment and self-reports can be done in a number of ways. Perhaps the most common is during a portfolio conference, where children can be asked about their perceptions of their progress and needs. Portfolio conferences should be cyclical in nature, with the beginning of the conference focusing initially on what has occurred since the last conference, and the end of the conference allowing the student to articulate and/or write down his or her goals during the time before the next conference.

Self-assessment also takes place when:

▶ Children are asked to select pieces of their work that they think show their growth and to state why they have made their selections.

FIGURE 11-4

Writing samples from Tanisha's first-grade portfolio: (a) September 9th ("I like to help my daddy, Leon. He's building! I like Nintendos!"); (b) January 31st

(a)
Tanisho
ILIKEToHELPmYdadcLEon
HisBuilcLin9!

ILiKEninTEndoc!

(b)
My Favorite Animal
By Tanisha   Jan. 31
    I like monkeys because
they are good at tricks.
I mean tricks! They are
better then a poodle.

▶ Children keep a "learning log" and update their thoughts on their progress and needs on an ongoing basis.

▶ Children work in cooperative groups and discuss their thoughts about their needs in relation to their assignments.

▶ Children are asked to talk about what they are reading and writing, with a focus on their thoughts and interests with regard to the respective selection.

▶ Children have the opportunity to revise their work, discuss their revision process, and talk about how the revision makes their work better.

▶ Children are asked to "think aloud" as they read or write.

Many of the above can be done in writing, or you, as a teacher, can make notes during discussion. These notes should be included in each child's portfolio and on cumulative checklists or summary sheets as appropriate.

It is important that children feel ownership of their portfolio; try to make sure they view it as their property, not yours. Portfolios change over time because of all that goes into them; children's access needs to be encouraged, especially to revise work or to add information about reading and writing. Furthermore, children should develop pride in their portfolios and be encouraged to share them with others. Peer input, in turn, may prompt effective writing revision and book selection. You must be careful, however, to structure peer sharing experiences so that they are purposeful and helpful, not derogatory.

Children should always know how their portfolios will be used, especially if they will be used in grading decisions at the end of a formal reporting period. In such cases, children should be given the opportunity to revise or add to their work. Portfolios can also serve an important function during child-teacher conferences and can be a place through which you and your students can communicate with each other. For example, your comments in a portfolio might include any or all of these:

⯈ The names of children who are reading or writing about similar topics and suggestions for a sharing session.
⯈ Book titles with themes similar to a book currently being read.
⯈ Information that might be included in a piece of writing.
⯈ A television show that might relate to an area of interest.
⯈ Supportive comments about progress.
⯈ Expression of personal interest in a particular topic, piece of writing, or book read by the child.

Thus, a portfolio is not simply a repository of work waiting to be graded. It is a dynamic entity that is continually modified and clearly reflects ongoing progress. Although some argue that, strictly speaking, portfolios are a means of communicating about student growth and development—not a form of assessment—portfolio assessment has, through general usage in the literacy field, become a significant term within alternative assessment. This usage is seen, for example, in highly regarded books about literacy assessment—books with titles such as *Portfolio Assessment in the Reading-Writing Classroom* (Tierney, Carter, & Desai, 1991), *Literacy Portfolios: Using Assessment to Guide Instruction* (Wiener & Cohen, 1997), and *Portfolio Practices: Lessons from Schools, Districts, and States* (Murphy & Underwood, 2001). Such publications point out that any assessment tool or procedure, including those described in this text, can provide data for inclusion in a student's portfolio. Through the inclusion of multiple pieces of data, portfolios can be viewed as a whole to indicate student growth and progress as well as student needs at any point in time.

Many of the items considered in portfolio assessment (particularly those that do not rely only on children's written products) may be considered as part of "kidwatching" (see chapter 5 for a discussion of this aspect of assessment in emergent literacy programs). Noticing what children do in real reading and writing tasks and using this observational data on summary sheets that lead to instructional decision making are critical aspects of informal assessment. In its broader usage, most of the informal and alternative assessment procedures discussed in this chapter—including the use of think-alouds, retellings, informal reading inventories, and so on—will depend on your observations and interpretation of children's reading and writing behavior.

The Informal Reading Inventory

informal reading inventories (IRIs) Individualized tests that use a graded word list and passages to determine a student's reading ability and provide diagnostic information.

Informal reading inventories (IRIs) allow a teacher to match students and materials. They provide information that will help you place children at appropriate instructional levels within a set of graded materials. The information is obtained by having children read increasingly difficult passages until they come to a passage that is too difficult, at which point they stop. The child's patterns of errors indicate materials that could be used appropriately with a particular student. IRIs are included as a part of most published reading programs, can be purchased as stand-alone items, or can be teacher-developed.

An informal reading inventory must be administered individually to children and requires some expertise to score and interpret. It thus requires somewhat more time to administer than some other measures, but it provides information that can be of great value in instructional decision making. Teachers typically use IRIs near the beginning of a school year as one information source to help determine instructional groupings and appropriate levels of materials for students. IRIs are also used when more information about a child's observed reading behavior is desired. IRIs describe the functioning level of a reader, indicating that student's independent, instructional, and frustration reading levels. These are important concepts you will often encounter.

⯈ *Independent reading level.* At this level, children can read on their own without teacher assistance. Their reading is fluent and free of undue hesitations. Intonation is appropriate for the punctuation and phrasing of the material.

▶ *Instructional reading level.* At this level, children can read if support and instruction are provided. Material at this level is challenging but not frustrating to read.

▶ *Frustration reading level.* At this level, children have great difficulty, even with teacher guidance and instruction. In effect, they are unable to read the selection even with support.

An IRI typically provides three scores, each corresponding to one of these three general levels of reading. For example, an IRI might determine that a child's independent reading level is at approximately the third-grade level, whereas that child's instructional and frustration levels might be at about the fourth and fifth grades. These scores indicate the difficulty of materials appropriate for instruction, practice, and free reading.

Published informal reading inventories usually include two copies of each reading selection. The teacher's copy usually is double spaced to allow for written comments and space to note children's **miscues,** and includes suggested comprehension questions with space to record responses. After each IRI passage is read, different kinds of comprehension questions are asked; for example, questions that deal with vocabulary, details, inferences, and main ideas.

miscues Oral reading responses that deviate from the text.

Although IRIs generally have been praised for including a range of questions, Duffelmeyer and Duffelmeyer (1989) have noted that approximately 50 percent of the main idea questions in IRIs might be inappropriate because the IRI passages may not have had an explicitly stated main idea or a unified passage focus. This condition was especially prevalent among narrative passages. Thus, Duffelmeyer and Duffelmeyer (1989) note that a child's poor performance on main idea questions is "as likely to be a reflection of ill suited passages as of the student's inability to comprehend main ideas" (p. 363). As a result, you should be cautious when scoring children's responses to main idea questions in IRIs. Likewise, the questions should be carefully examined.

Deciding Where to Start Testing. An IRI includes passages with varying difficulty levels. Thus, you must decide at what level to begin the test. Published IRIs usually provide entry to the oral reading passages through a set of graded word lists. Beginning with the list suggested by the IRI being used, a child reads successive lists until a certain number of errors occur within a given list. Most IRIs suggest that the child begin reading the passage that corresponds to the highest level list that was read perfectly, or perhaps the passage one level below that list. The word lists come in two forms: one for the teacher and one for the student. Miscues made while reading the list should be noted.

Noting Student Miscues on an IRI. The marking system in Figure 11-5 can be used to indicate reading behavior on the word lists as well as on subsequently administered passages. Different IRIs use different symbols or methods to mark reading miscues and other behaviors. Nevertheless, because the miscue types are well accepted, the particular marking system is not important. It is important, though, to choose one system and use it consistently. Once you become familiar with such a marking system, you will find it useful to note children's reading behaviors in many situations in your classroom.

The scoring system in Figure 11-5 can be used to mark all reading behaviors; noting all miscues allows patterns to be more easily observed. In addition to simply marking miscues, however, you will have to decide whether a miscue is significant. IRIs such as the *Classroom Reading Inventory* (Silvaroli, 1997; Silvaroli & Wheelock, 2001) suggest that "insignificant" miscues be noted but not necessarily counted.

Significant miscues are those that interfere with fluency or change the meaning of what was written. The following examples illustrate the difference between significant and insignificant miscues:

Text: The boy likes the kitten. Ask him where it is.
Child 1:   The boy likes the cat. Ask him where it is.
Child 2:   The boy likes the kitchen. Ask him where it is.
Child 3:   The boy like da kitt'n. Ax him where it is.
Child 4:   The boy likes the kitten let's ask where she is.
Child 5:   The boy likes the kitten. Ask him to go where it is.

FIGURE 11-5

Informal reading inventory marking system

Miscue/Behavior	Mark	Example
Miscues That Are Usually Significant (Always Counted)		
Omission Not reading something in the text (e.g., part or whole word, phrase, punctuation)	Circle the omission.	He likes the big (yellow) car.
Insertion Adding something not originally present in the text	Use caret (∧) and add insertion.	*and blue* He likes the big yellow ∧ car.
Substitution Replacing something in the text with something else (e.g., *this* for *the*)	Cross out original and add substitution.	*takes* He ~~likes~~ the big yellow car.
No response Substantial pause indicating inability to read the word, resulting in the teacher's pronouncing the word	Write *P* over teacher-pronounced items.	P He likes the big yellow car.
Miscues That Are Usually Not Significant (Always Marked, Sometimes Counted)		
Repetition Repeated reading of a word or group of words	Put dome over repeated items.	He likes the big yellow car.
Hesitation Pause that interrupts the flow or pattern of reading	Put check mark at point of hesitation.	✓ He likes the big yellow car.
Transposition Reversing order of letters in words or words in sentences	Put reverse *S* around transposed items.	He likes the big yellow car.
Mispronunciation Pronunciation clearly different from normal (e.g., *k* in *knife* or *w* in *sword*)	Write phonetic pronunciation or use diacritical marks.	*likĕs* He ~~likes~~ the big yellow car.
Self-correction Corrected by the student without teacher help	Write *C* above the miscue.	C *large* He likes the ~~big~~ yellow car.

You may have noticed that some of the miscues preserved the essential meaning of the text, whereas others did not. For example, substituting *cat* for *kitten* (child 1) or combining the two sentences (child 4) did not substantially alter the original meaning of the text, although neither child read exactly what was presented. Do you think it would be appropriate to consider those inconsistencies to be mistakes? If such reading occurred in your classroom, would you stop it and correct the mistakes immediately or allow the reader to go on? Although the children did not read exactly what was written, they did comprehend the text. Such occurrences should be noted for later analysis; however, as the miscues were semantically correct, they should not be scored as significant.

Celebrating Diversity

Recognizing Language Diversity through Assessment

Listening to children read, particularly as part of an Informal Reading Inventory, will clearly point out the diversity in your classroom. This diversity will manifest itself in differences on comprehension questions that are inferential in nature because inferential questions require children to use their background knowledge and experiences to answer these questions. Because your children will come from different backgrounds, this will result in different responses to such questions. Similarly, children from different cultural or socioeconomic groups may have speech patterns and dialects that differ from each other, leading to differences in pronunciation that will become apparent during oral reading.

These differences can form the basis for interesting classroom discussions about language and language variation, with the dialect speakers becoming the "experts" who can teach others about their own, dialect-appropriate pronunciations and vocabulary. Similarly, differences in background knowledge (consider how a new South American or European student might interpret "football" differently from other children) provide opportunities for all children to learn from each other the similarities and differences in different countries' interpretations of words common to us in the United States. Internet sites such as the **Alta Vista Translation Service/Babelfish** (http://babelfish.altavista.com/tr) provide a service that translates English text into different languages. Children often are fascinated by seeing their text change into words from other languages, and lessons built around such websites are good discussion starters for examining diversity in language and culture. Thus, while recognizing that differences in background, culture, and language will be found through testing, you should look for opportunities to use test results to celebrate children's differences in knowledge and as a basis for providing needed instruction.

What does child 2's miscue tell us? Does the substitution of *kitchen* for *kitten* indicate anything more than the fact that comprehension has not taken place? Notice that the substitution is an appropriate part of speech, even though the sentence now means something different from the original. Thus, the child has used syntactic cues effectively, correctly placing a noun where it belongs in the sentence, (that is, after an article). Notice also that the child has used many of the letters in the original word in the substitution. Indeed, the only difference between the two words is the replacement of the second *t* in kitten with a *ch*. Thus, the child is not making wild guesses about what is to be read; active and logical processing is taking place. The same may be said of child 5. Although the meaning of the original sentences has been altered, the student's miscue is not arbitrary. The **pattern of miscues** that emerges from several such instances, never from just one, permits a teacher to draw generalizations about the reader.

pattern of miscues
A group of similar miscues from which a teacher may draw generalizations about the reading process or strategies used by a reader.

But what about child 3's reading? How did you categorize that child's miscues? Did you think the child read incorrectly or simply reflected a normal dialect pattern? Some believe there are times when dialect differences should be focused on to make a child aware of more-accepted standards. Nevertheless, dialect variations usually do not impact comprehension and are not typically counted as miscues (Goodman & Buck, 1973; Harris & Sipay, 1990).

In recent years, there has been increasing recognition that IRIs focused on a subskills model of reading, categorizing children's word recognition and comprehension abilities, whereas instruction has moved to incorporate more holistic models of reading. Thus, several IRIs, including the *Classroom Reading Inventory* (Silvaroli & Wheelock, 2001) and the *Qualitative Reading Inventory-3* (Leslie & Caldwell, 2001), present forms of the IRI that include both the traditional, subskill format as well as what is called a reader response format (Silvaroli, 1997, p. 4). In a reader response format, children are not asked questions after reading, but rather are asked to predict, retell, and discuss the selections with the teacher.

MODEL LESSON

Informal Reading Inventory in Amy Chen's Class

Amy Chen has interactive beliefs that influence her decisions about *what* to teach and more integrated language learning beliefs that guide her decisions about *how* to teach. These beliefs are important to her choice of assessment tools as well as to her decisions about *what* to assess and *how* to assess. Her interactive beliefs about *what* to assess lead her to use tools that assess multiple reading behaviors at the same time. The Informal Reading Inventory—which provides indications of fluency, word attack, and comprehension—is such a tool. Her integrated beliefs suggest that testing take place using longer, authentic passages rather than using items out of context. Most recently, Amy used an IRI with a student who recently joined her class after school had already begun.

Joann joined Amy's class after school had been in session for just over one month. On Joann's first day, Amy welcomed her to the third-grade class and introduced Joann to her new classmates. To help determine Joann's reading level and to match her ability with books from the classroom library, Amy decided to administer an informal reading inventory. The IRI took place while the other children were involved in art activities under the supervision of Amy's parent-volunteer aide.

Amy uses an IRI she has created from passages contained in several books in her classroom. The books varied in difficulty, based on Amy's experiences with children, and on reading grade levels provided by the books' publishers. After administering the appropriate word lists and passages, Amy decided that Joann could probably read material just a little more difficult than that being read by the average readers in her class. However, she wanted to confirm her assessment through some regular classroom work and wanted Joann to experience success in her new situation, so Amy placed her with a group of average readers for the next group-learning activity. She made a note on her class record sheet, though, to review Joann's work after a short period of time to see whether she should be moved to more difficult material and encouraged her to self-select books from the classroom library.

Creating an Informal Reading Inventory.   There are many published IRIs readily available, and most published reading programs include one or more. Nonetheless, you may sometimes wish to create your own. For example, you might want IRI passages to come from a specific set of materials that will be used in class; such passages would have more curricular validity than a generic IRI. To create your own IRI, you will need to choose passages at various levels and will need to know scoring guidelines to establish independent, instructional, and frustration reading levels. With published IRIs, the specific number of miscues corresponding to each of the reading levels for a given passage generally is determined by the percentage of miscues within the total words read (for word recognition) or the percentage of wrong answers within the number of comprehension questions (for comprehension). However, there has been some disagreement regarding the scoring criteria for IRIs (Aulls, 1982; Betts, 1946; Cooper, 1952; Powell, 1970). We agree with those who suggest combining the criteria proposed by several researchers. You can use the results, shown here, to determine reading levels on an IRI, remembering that these percentages are only approximate guidelines (see, for example, Burns, Roe, & Ross, 1988; Johnson, Kress, & Pikulski, 1987; Powell, 1970).

Reading Level	Word Recognition Accuracy		Comprehension Accuracy
independent	99% or higher	(and)	90% or higher
instructional	85% or higher (grades 1–2)	(and)	75% or higher
	95% or higher (grades 3 and above)	(and)	75% or higher
frustration	below 90%	(or)	below 50%
listening capacity			75% or higher

The Running Record

The **running record,** initially developed by Marie Clay (1985), allows a teacher to record a child's oral reading in much the same way that is done during the oral reading phase of the IRI. Similar to the IRI, the running record provides an indication of a child's strategies during reading as well as his or her areas of difficulty; nevertheless, it differs from the IRI in that it does not require any specific passage for administration, does not require graded word lists, and does not yield a reading level score. The running record is also less formal than the IRI, as the teacher does not tape record the reading; nor is the administration procedure as specific. In fact, teachers need only a paper and pencil to conduct a running record (the passage being read is not required). It can be done at any time a child is reading and with any material being read. Johnston (1992) feels that these are advantages over the IRI and result in teachers being more willing and able to use running records on an ongoing basis with their students.

The scoring system resembles the IRI notation shown in Figure 11-5 on page 404. Omissions, insertions, substitutions, repetitions, self-corrections, attempts, and teacher-provided pronunciations are recorded during reading. However, because the teacher does not have a copy of the child's text, words read correctly are simply indicated by a check mark. On a piece of paper, you would place a check mark for each word read exactly as it appears in the text, with each line of check marks corresponding to each printed line being read. If there were five words on a line being read, then there would be a maximum of five check marks on that line of the running record.

It is important that only the child's oral reading behavior be recorded at the time of reading. Later, you will need to go back and add to the running record sheet the specific words that were omitted, substituted, and so on from the original text. The one-to-one correspondence between check marks and words per line will allow you to do so accurately. The scoring system for a running record is shown below.

Text:	Tracy knew she would not be able to sleep.
Child 1: (Correct)	Tracy knew she would not be able to sleep.
Record:	√ √ √ √ √ √ √ √ √
	Note: The nine checks indicate that all nine words were read correctly.
Child 2: (Omission)	Tracy knew she would be able to sleep.
Record:	√ √ √ √ $\overline{\text{NOT}}$ √ √ √ √
	Note: The dash above the line indicates that the 5th word ("not") was omitted; the omitted word is written below the line after the reading session.
Child 3: (Insertion)	Tracy knew that she would not be able to sleep.
Record:	√ √ THAT √ √ √ √ √ √ √
	Note: The inserted word ("that") is written above the line; a dash is written below the line to show that this is not a substitution.
Child 4: (Substitution)	Tracy felt she would not be able to sleep.
Record:	√ $\frac{\text{FELT}}{\text{KNEW}}$ √ √ √ √ √ √ √
	Note: The substituted word ("felt") is written above the line; the original word ("knew") is written below the line after the reading session.
Child 5: (Repetition)	Tracy knew she would . . . she would . . . not be able to . . . to . . . to sleep.

running record An individual, informal assessment where a teacher indicates, through a series of check marks and notes, a child's oral reading behavior. It is similar to an IRI, but is faster and can be performed on any passage; a teacher version of the passage is unnecessary.

					R				R^3

Record: ✓   ✓   ✓   ✓   ✓   ✓   ✓   ✓   ✓

Note: An "R" is written at the right-hand end of the repetition ("would") and a line is drawn back along the number of check marks that correspond to the words repeated. If something is repeated more than once, the number of repetitions is indicated beside the "R" notation.

Child 6:   Tracy k . . . now . . . knew she would not be able to sleep.
(Attempt)

Record: ✓   K|NOW| ✓   ✓   ✓   ✓   ✓   ✓   ✓   ✓
                KNEW

Note: Above the line, write each attempt, including a check mark showing that the word was ultimately correctly read; write the original word below the line after the reading session.

Child 7:   Tracy knew she wants . . . would not be able to sleep.
(Self-Correction)

Record: ✓   ✓   ✓ WANTS|SC   ✓   ✓   ✓   ✓   ✓
                       WOULD

Note: Write the miscue ("wants") above the line, the notation for self-correction (SC) to the right of the line division, and the original word below the line (after the reading session).

Child 8:   Tracy knew she [pause, teacher pronounces "would"] not be able to sleep.

(Teacher Pronounced)

Record: ✓   ✓   ✓   ⎯   ✓   ✓   ✓   ✓   ✓
                WOULD|T

Note: The dash indicates the student omitted the word, the notation for teacher pronunciation (T) is written below the line to the right of the line division, and the original word is written below the line (after the reading session).

Following the running record, a summary sheet is completed in much the same way as for an IRI. This summary sheet should then be added to the child's portfolio. Traill (1993) has stated that a running record should be done with each child at least once every 6 weeks, and that comparisons of summary sheets be used to indicate progress in both the skill and strategic aspects of reading. Summary sheets can be fairly simple and typically include the items indicated on the form in Figure 11-6.

Although the 6-week cycle recommended by Traill may be optimal, the time between running records will vary depending on the age and reading ability of your students, with older students and more-able readers being evaluated through a running record less often than younger or less-able readers. Also, when counting errors for summary purposes, Johnston's (1992) modification of Clay's (1985) categories is often used:

▶ Omissions, insertions, and multiple repetitions that are not proper nouns count as one error each time; proper nouns are counted only the first time.

▶ An omitted line counts only as one error; do not count each omitted word on the line as an error.

▶ A teacher intervention (such as "try again" or a pronunciation) counts as one error, and other errors are counted in the rereading.

▶ When in doubt about scoring, choose that which fits your interpretation of error patterns; if still in doubt, choose the lowest error count.

▶ You might end up with more errors on a line than there are words (because of insertions, and so on), but do not score more errors than there are words on a page. If this occurs, you may want to discontinue the running record and simply note how the child is creating an understanding of the text (perhaps from related pictures on the page, from prior knowledge, and so on).

FIGURE 11-6

Sample running record summary sheet

Reader: _____ Date: _____

Book title, page:

_____

Read before? (If "yes," how often?) _____

Error Rate (number of errors divided by number of words, times 100): _____ %

Accuracy Rate (Error rate minus 100%): _____ %

Number of Errors: _____ Total Self-Corrections: _____

Print-Based Self-Corrections: _____

Meaning-Based Self-Corrections: _____

Rereads often: _____ occasionally: _____ never: _____

Uses phonic analysis (provide examples): _____

Uses context (provide examples): _____

Talks about the text, background or personal experiences, and so on (explain):

_____

_____

_____

_____

The Cloze Procedure

The **cloze procedure** often is used to match readers with specific reading materials. For this purpose, it is sometimes preferred to the IRI because it allows group rather than individual administration.

> **cloze procedure** A fill-in-the-blank task used to estimate the level at which a child can read with assistance.

A cloze task also involves a child with the text, without the intervening teacher questions. Table 11-2 on page 411 outlines the major differences between cloze and IRI procedures. As described earlier, a cloze procedure presents children with a passage that has blanks in place of some of the words. Children attempt to fill in the blanks with words deleted from the original passage. The teacher uses the scoring procedure described later in this section to indicate whether the passage is at independent, instructional, or frustration level for the child and, thus, whether the material from which the passage came is appropriate.

Cloze gained widespread use after its modification by Taylor (1953). With its roots in Gestalt psychology, cloze makes use of the human drive to add closure to incomplete items. In the reading cloze procedure, this inclination has been translated into the reader's use of context to complete passages from which words have been systematically deleted. It is essentially a fill-in-the-blank task (see Jongsma, 1980; Rankin, 1974, 1978; Warwick, 1978).

Constructing a Cloze Test. To match students and materials, cloze passages can be constructed from the material children will be reading. The passages should be representative of that material and should not be broken up by illustrations or potentially distractive features. Within the chosen passages, words are systematically deleted and blanks are substituted for the deleted words. The following steps describe the construction of a cloze test in detail; Figure 11-7 on page 411 illustrates a cloze test ready for use.

1. Choose a representative passage from the beginning, middle, and end of the material (usually a book) you wish to use with your student(s). For high reliability, each passage should contain approximately 250 words, although that length may not be possible in primary-grade materials. Using a number of representative passages is strongly recommended so the results can be averaged, thereby increasing the validity and reliability of the procedure.
2. Leave the first sentence of the passage intact to provide a contextual base.
3. Beginning with the second sentence, replace every fifth word with a blank. Be sure your blanks are the same size so their length does not give a clue to the length of the deleted words. Continue until 50 words have been deleted, if possible. However, do not delete the following: proper names, dates, abbreviations, or acronyms. When such words are encountered, the next word is deleted, and the every-fifth-word-rule proceeds from that point.
4. Conclude with a complete, intact sentence without deletions.

Scoring and Interpreting a Cloze Test. A cloze test is similar to an informal reading inventory in that it provides an indication of a reader's independent, instructional, and frustration reading levels. Traditionally, cloze tests determined these levels by calculating the percentage of exact replacements of deleted words, but now synonyms usually are counted as correct. For the cloze test shown in Figure 11-7, the following replacements were provided by Lee, a third-grade student. Underlined numbers indicate exact replacements, making Lee's score 24 out of 50, or 48 percent using this criterion.

Original Deletion	Lee's Replacement	Original Deletion	Lee's Replacement
1. out	away	26. close	beside
2. and	and	27. morning	morning
3. were	sat	28. her	her
4. you	we	29. I	I
5. all	all	30. brave	alive
6. went	went	31. from	No response
7. and	and	32. have	have
8. once	No response	33. now	so
9. snarl	growl	34. what	anything
10. their	their	35. a	a
11. was	No response	36. said	said
12. plucked	No response	37. her	her
13. of	of	38. a	a
14. toward	toward	39. was	lay
15. to	to	40. at	No response
16. a	her	41. said	said
17. snarling	No response	42. low	nice
18. she	she	43. this	this
19. see	know	44. said	said
20. said	said	45. in	about
21. I	No response	46. snapped	said
22. and	then	47. the	the
23. she	she	48. for	with
24. and	and	49. said	cried
25. and	then	50. her	Petronella

TABLE 11-2

General differences between cloze and IRI procedures

	Cloze	IRI
Administration	Group or individual	Individual
	Written (or oral)	Oral
	Passages	Word lists, passages, oral questions
Uses	Match children and materials	Match children and materials
	Find a child's general reading level	Find a child's general reading level
	Provide a general readability level	Provide a general readability level
		Permit inference about children's reading progress
Type of information	Ability to use context	Word recognition score
	Comprehension score	Comprehension score
	Independent, instructional, frustration reading levels	Independent, instructional, frustration reading levels
		Listening capacity score

FIGURE 11-7

Sample cloze passage

That evening they all had dinner together in the enchanter's cozy kitchen. Then Albion took Petronella _____ to a stone building _____ unbolted its door. Inside _____ seven huge black dogs.

"_____ must watch my hounds _____ night," said he.

Petronella _____ in, and Albion closed _____ locked the door.

At _____ the hounds began to _____ and bark. They showed _____ teeth at her. But Petronella _____ a real princess. She _____ up her courage. Instead _____ backing away, she went _____ the dogs. She began _____ speak to them in _____ quiet voice. They stopped _____ and sniffed at her. _____ patted their heads.

"I _____ what it is," she _____. "You are lonely here. _____ will keep you company."

_____ so all night long, _____ sat on the floor _____ talked to the hounds _____ stroked them. They lay _____ to her.

In the _____, Albion came and let _____ out. "Ah," said he, "_____ see that you are _____. If you had run _____ the dogs, they would _____ torn you to pieces. _____ you may ask for _____ you want."

"I want _____ comb for my hair," _____ Petronella.

The enchanter gave _____ a comb carved from _____ piece of black wood.

Prince Ferdinand _____ sunning himself and working _____ a crossword puzzle. Petronella _____ to him in a _____ voice, "I am doing _____ for you."

"That's nice," _____ the prince. "What's 'selfish' _____ nine letters?"

"You are," _____ Petronella. She went to _____ enchanter. "I will work _____ you once more," she _____. That night Albion led _____ to a stable. Inside were seven huge horses.

Source: From *Petronella* by Jay Williams. Copyright © 1973 by Jay Williams. Reprinted by permission of Scholastic Inc.

Several researchers have attempted to specify the scoring criteria for interpreting cloze results (Bormuth, 1968; Rankin, 1971; Rankin & Culhane, 1969). Although we suggest the percentage bands noted by Rankin and Culhane (below), Bormuth's percentages are also noted here, as are percentages that can be used if synonym replacements are allowed. In our example, Lee's percentage of replacements was 48, placing his reading of the passage at the instructional level. Allowing 11 replacements to count as appropriate synonyms, Lee's percentage score is 70 percent, which also places Lee at the instructional level.

Reading Level	Percentage of Synonym Replacements	Percentage of Exact Replacements (Bormuth)	Percentage of Exact Replacements (Rankin & Culhane)
Independent	above 80%	above 57%	above 60%
Instructional	60% to 80%	44% to 57%	40% to 60%
Frustration	below 60%	below 44%	below 40%

Common Questions about Cloze

1. *Why do people use synonym replacements?* Synonym replacements are more consistent with many people's beliefs about how readers construct meaning. Thus, while the **exact replacement criterion** allows for more rapid scoring, synonyms that do not substantially change the meaning of a text usually are counted as correct. Others, however, feel that exact replacements do not disadvantage a reader because the percentages corresponding to the various reading levels are set at a very low level to allow for the fact that only exact replacements are counted. The previous table provides percentage bands for interpreting results using both exact replacements and synonyms.

exact replacement criterion A scoring procedure that only counts as correct responses that match the precise words deleted from the text.

2. *How accurate is the cloze procedure?* The cloze procedure is quick and easy to use and consistently provides approximate measurements. Because your judgment plays a significant part in cloze interpretation, children should be given the benefit of the doubt if their percentage scores border the bands separating the different reading levels. The test is most accurate when at least three passages are used from the material under consideration.

3. *Should there be a time limit when administering a cloze test?* No. Generally, children are given as much time as they wish to complete the cloze passage and they are allowed to go through a passage more than once.

4. *Does spelling count when scoring a student's replacements?* No. This is not a spelling test.

Other Uses of the Cloze Procedure.   The cloze test traditionally has been used to examine the match between readers and specific reading material. However, the cloze procedure can be beneficial in other ways. First, the cloze test can be used with a graded set of materials to determine a child's general reading level; this approach allows you to generalize the child's score beyond the material from which the cloze test was constructed. With this application, a set of graded passages should be used to construct a series of cloze tests. Scoring should then provide a rough guide to the child's reading level (corresponding to the grade level of the passage) at which the instructional reading level is reached. Instead of a leveled set of passages taken from a published reading program, readability formulas (discussed later in this chapter) can also be used to determine the reading grade level of the selected passages.

The other common use for cloze is as a teaching technique with several variations. For instance, you might delete specific parts of speech (for example, nouns, adjectives, or verbs) or provide choices above the blanks. As an instructional aid, however, cloze requires time for the significant discussion of replacements. It is not enough simply to grade a child's efforts; instead, children must be led to understand why given replacements are appropriate, what other options might fit, and why some replacements are not very good choices.

NIKKI'S

COMMENTS FROM THE CLASSROOM

At the beginning of the year, I use the short passages often found in informal reading inventories to help establish each child's reading level, especially the point at which they become frustrated. While I truly believe in building on a child's strengths, sometimes miscue analysis can be very revealing. Miscue analysis requires students to read longer passages (a chapter or a complete book) aloud into a tape recorder. I try to use adult volunteers to sit with the children while they read. Then I listen to the tape with a photocopy of the chapter and record each reader's miscues.

Sometimes I don't have to listen to the entire chapter before a pattern emerges. Discovering the error patterns allows me to pinpoint areas that require remediation. Grid sheets can help organize miscues into semantic (word meaning) or syntactic (grammatical structure) patterns. This method of assessment allows me to group children who share problems or pair up children with different strengths, rather than doing blanket lessons with the entire class. Then I can target groups or pairs with specific strategies that can help them. Occasionally, the analysis suggests a relatively simple strategy. For example, readers often get so caught up in decoding that they forget to look at the illustration on a page for help with its context. A quick glance at the picture can alert a child that "castle" is a more likely choice than "casting" or "candle."

As with all learning, children have fewer problems with stories for which they already have background knowledge. Once I thought a child was a much poorer reader than she was because the informal reading inventory passages were about the circus and rodeos—neither of which were part of her experiences. The interest inventory that she filled out as part of the informal reading inventory indicated that she liked birds. She chose an information book about birds for her miscue analysis. I was amazed at how she breezed through that book, even decoding some of the scientific terms with ease.

I have discovered that the lines between planning, assessment, and teaching blur as I have gained more experience. Assessing children's progress is a continuous mental activity for me. Assessment no longer means "test." Tests are now just one way for me to organize and validate my "kidwatching."

Asking children to retell what they have read or listened to can provide valuable information about their comprehension.

Retellings

retelling scores A measure of comprehension obtained by having readers tell in their own words what they have just read.

Retelling scores are derived when children are asked to read a passage and then retell in their own words what was read. Retellings are useful measures of comprehension. They have been used in informal reading inventories to supplement or, at times, to replace the comprehension questions generally asked at the end of an IRI passage. Some believe that retellings are more accurate than answers to questions because questions can sometimes be answered from general knowledge without even reading the passage. In fact, Allington, Chodos, Domaracki, and Truex (1977) have shown that approximately 30 percent of the questions asked in informal reading inventories are **passage independent.** That is, they can be answered without first reading the passage to which they refer (see also Tuinman, 1974, for a discussion of passage dependent/passage independent questions).

passage independent Describes questions that can be answered from general knowledge rather than from a reading of the text.

idea units Thought units used to determine comprehension.

To use retelling as an assessment procedure, you must first divide the original passage into units, often called **idea units** or thought units. The following example would be categorized as two idea units:

The boy ran/although his leg was hurt.

To increase the reliability of this procedure, two people should work together to segment the passage, agreeing on the segmenting of the text. Thereafter, the following procedure and scoring system can be used (Clark, 1982; Morrow, 1988):

1. Assign each unit a number from 1 through 3 in terms of its importance (1 being very important, perhaps a main idea, and 3 being of relatively little importance, perhaps an insignificant detail).
2. Make a three-columned scoring sheet with the importance ratings on the left, the units in the middle, and recording space on the right (see Figure 11-8).
3. As the child retells the passage, use the right-hand column to number the units in the order in which they are recalled.
4. Score the recall by first comparing the sequence of the recalled units with that of the original, then totaling the number of units recalled in each category of

FIGURE 11-8

Completed retelling score form

Importance	Unit	Retelling Sequence
1	Tracy	1
1	knew she would not	2
1	be able to sleep.	3
3	But her mother	
3	had told her	
2	to brush her teeth	
2	and put on her nightgown anyway,	
3	and Tracy did as she was told.	
3	Just as she	4
3	got into her nightgown,	5
1	a loud crack of thunder	6
3	filled the air!	
1	Tracy jumped into bed	7
2	and pulled the covers	
3	over her head.	
3	When Meg	12
3	peeked into the room,	13
3	Tracy wailed,	
2	"The last time	8
2	we had a storm like this,	9
2	I stayed awake	10
2	all night!"	11
2	Meg sat	14
2	beside Tracy	15
3	and tucked her little sister in.	
2	Then she started to hum softly.	16
2	It was one of Tracy's	17
2	favorite songs.	18
2	As the song went on,	
2	Meg noticed that Tracy's eyes	20
3	had closed.	21
2	Meg turned off the bedroom light	19
2	as she tiptoed	
2	out of the room,	
1	Tracy didn't hear	23
1	the next clap of thunder	
2	as the storm continued	22
3	into the night.	

	Units Recalled	Possible Units	Score (%)
Category 1:	6	6	100%
Category 2:	12	18	67%
Category 3:	5	13	38%
Total:	23	37	62%

Comments: OVER 60% MATCH IN UNITS RECALLED. FAIRLY CLOSE MATCH IN SEQUENCE ORDER. HAS A GOOD SENSE OF IMPORTANT INFORMATION. INSTRUCTIONAL LEVEL.

importance, and finally dividing that number by the total possible in each category.

Comparing the three categories allows inferences about how well the reader has understood and remembered the various levels in the passage.

Figure 11-8 shows a completed retelling measure for a passage introduced in chapter 5 (Carson, 1990). An instructional reading level was determined by the degree of consistency between the retelling and the segmented passage. Generally, a 60 to 70 per-cent match is used as the criterion for the instructional reading level. However, that determination will be influenced by your own judgment, especially as it relates to the amount and specificity of the ideas recalled and the order and fluency of the retelling. In addition, it is important that children have an opportunity to practice the retelling procedure before it is used in evaluation. Morrow (1988) points out that children un-familiar with the procedure do not know what is being asked of them and are at a dis-advantage.

Think-Alouds

Think-alouds are similar to retellings in that they are individually administered and can be used with material chosen either by the teacher or by the child. It differs, though, in that retellings occur after reading, while think-alouds occur during reading. Thus, Glazer and Brown (1993) point out that retellings are influenced by memory factors and are more closely related to the product of reading, while think-alouds are more closely related to "on-line" thinking and the in-process activity that occurs during reading. Oth-ers have suggested that oral think-alouds are excellent windows into the comprehension process; the think-aloud procedure has been used widely in classroom assessment as well as in research (for example, see Johnston, 1992; Wade, 1990.)

When performing a think-aloud, choose a passage that is not too easy or too diffi-cult for the reader. A passage that is too difficult will result in frustration and may yield frustration responses rather than insights into the reading process. Conversely, a se-lection that is too easy often results in the reader simply making comments like "That's interesting," or "That's neat!" A final consideration when using think-alouds is that readers typically are not used to stating their process or thoughts as they read. Thus, you will have to model the procedure for children and be prepared to gently prompt readers for their comments during reading. Johnston (1992) reminds us that such prompts may be necessary, as might be simple reminders that comments are expected. These reminders can be gentle statements made while reading, or subtle reminders such as clearing your throat or shifting your position to make the reader aware of you and the task at hand.

During the think-aloud, you should have a copy of the selection being read, spaced so that you can write down the child's comments and behaviors. Figure 11-9 shows such a text, together with a second-grade child's comments. After the think-aloud, take the time to complete a summary form such as that illustrated in Figure 11-10 on page 418. Notice the summary form includes patterns of responses found during the think-aloud. Both the think-aloud and the summary form should be included as part of the child's portfolio. Looking at the summary forms over time can indicate categories that appear and become stable, as well as the movement of responses from the "oc-casionally" to the "often" column. These patterns, when seen over time, can provide important evidence of a reader's progress as well as information for instruction of comprehension strategies.

Assessing Attitudes and Interests

One of the most powerful pieces of information available is an awareness of children's attitudes and interests. Informal measures can be used to discover motivational topics that can enhance instruction. Published reading programs provide assessment invento-ries; other published inventories are also available. Nevertheless, teacher-made assess-ments in this area are often more valuable than those commercially available.

Sometimes, it is easy to get so involved in teaching children how to read that enhanc-ing reading ability becomes an end in itself. This situation can result in children who are able to read but do not want to. However, when children develop a love of reading it be-comes a lifelong activity. Thus, the most effective teachers go beyond simply teaching chil-dren how to read; they show children that reading is relevant and interesting.

FIGURE 11-9

Sample think-aloud responses

Text	Response
Tracy knew she would not be able to sleep. But her mother had told her to brush her teeth and put on her nightgown anyway, and Tracy did as she was told. Just as she got into her nightgown, a loud crack of thunder filled the air! Tracy jumped into bed and pulled the covers over her head. When Meg peeked into the room, Tracy wailed, "The last time we had a storm like this, I stayed awake all night!" Meg sat beside Tracy and tucked her little sister in. Then she started to hum softly. It was one of Tracy's favorite songs. As the song went on, Meg noticed that Tracy's eyes had closed. Meg turned off the bedroom light as she tiptoed out of the room. Tracy didn't hear the next clap of thunder as the storm continued into the night.	*I wonder why?* *"Did as she was told"— I bet not always!* *Who's Meg?* —*What's this word?* *"Wailed?" – oh, well!* *So! Meg's her sister!* / *Meg or Tracy?* *I wonder what the song was?* *Thunder usually wakes me up!*

Dulin and Chester (1984; see also Dulin, 1984) imply that children's interests and attitudes should be tested across a number of areas, such as the following:

1. Comparing literacy activities to other activities; for example, by asking children to show which activity—perhaps reading a book or playing outside—they would rather do.
2. Finding out about the purposes of literacy activities; for example, by asking children the degree to which they agree with statements such as "Reading is for learning but not for enjoyment."
3. Finding out the relative desirability of various literacy activities in relation to each other; for example, by asking children to divide up 100 points across activities such as reading books, reading magazines, reading comics, writing stories, writing letters, and so on.
4. Finding out about the children's self-perception with regard to literacy tasks; for example, by asking children to rate how well—compared to other students in the class or of the student's age—they think they read.
5. Finding out how children feel about the rewards of literacy activities; for example, by asking children to rate their feelings about the value of rewards such as a grade for reading, extra credit for reading, and so on.
6. Finding out the value of things teachers can do to motivate reading; for example, by having children rate their interest in things such as having a teacher read a chapter

FIGURE 11-10

Sample of a completed think-aloud summary sheet

Reader's Name: _Jill_   Date: _11/5_   Age _7.6_

Title and page of passage read: _Tracy — teacher created story._

Summarize reader and reading characteristics during reading (e.g., tentative, willing, appropriate intonation, etc.): _good pace, fluency, and intonation._

SPECIFIC ASPECTS OF THE THINK-ALOUD:	Often	Occasionally
Evidence of Text Comprehension		
Restates text in own words		X
Restates text with words from passage		X
Adds (appropriate) own ideas to text	X	
Evidence of Comprehension Monitoring		
Comments on lack of word comprehension		X
Comments on lack of sentence comprehension		
Comments on lack of paragraph or larger-unit comprehension		
Evidence of Metalinguistic Knowledge		
Comments about personal, related experiences or background knowledge	X	
Notices and comments on text features and writing style		
Predicts, reasons, and/or evaluates ideas in the text	X	
Other summary comments		
Rereads		
Makes "backward" references to what has been read		

or excerpt from a book to the class each day, or having a teacher read and discuss the first few pages of a book that children then can choose to finish.

7. Finding out how valuable children feel various post-reading activities are; for example, by asking them to rate the value of activities such as taking an oral or written test on what they read, writing a book report, making a diorama, and so on.

These categories of items demonstrate that attitude/interest measures can examine various important aspects related to reading instruction such as how children feel about (1) reading, (2) various instructional methods and reward systems, (3) different types of materials, and (4) themselves in relationship to literacy and literacy activities. The affective information gathered through interest/attitude inventories should be added to the informal classroom records previously discussed. In addition, as children's interests and attitudes change fairly quickly, both should be assessed several times during a year, and ongoing anecdotal records of current trends, fads, and interests should be maintained.

An easily available measure of how readers feel about themselves as readers is the *Reader Self-Perception Scale* (RSPS) (Henk & Melnick, 1995). Using this scale will help you determine the children's sense of self-efficacy as readers, allowing you to target instruction in ways that will help your students become not only successful readers, but readers who feel that they are good at reading and who will want to read.

Although tests of interests and attitude are available, many teachers prefer to make their own tests in this area. An effective way to do this is to meet with peers who teach at the same grade level and decide on appropriate questions that target interest, attitude, and stress factors (see below). As a start, here are some generic questions that can be used, along with questions that you would insert based on your preliminary knowledge of the children in your classroom. You might begin by asking children:

- Do you like to read? At home? At school? For Fun? During free time?
- Do you like to read stories? Newspapers? Magazines?
- Do you like being read to? Reading on your own?
- Do you feel happy when you need to read? Frightened?
- Do you find other things to do instead of reading?
- What are some things that you like to read about?

Assessing Stress Factors in Reading

A poor attitude toward reading can indicate that a child is experiencing stress resulting from poor reading skills or from a teacher's demands to read. Gentile and McMillan (1987, 1988) point out that stress often is related to reading difficulty. They presented a scale for assessing stress reactions to reading, categorizing children's stress reactions as fight or flight responses. Fight responses manifest themselves in confrontations with the teacher and with reading material; they can be summarized as "I won't read, and you can't make me." With this response, students condemn reading, books, school, and teachers; anxiety is directed outward; and the children are confrontational. The flight reaction can be characterized as "I can't read and no one can teach me." These children condemn themselves; anxiety is directed inward; and they retreat from teachers (Gentile & McMillan, 1988, p. 21).

This stress reaction scale highlighted for teachers children's behaviors that might be seen during classroom observations during daily routines. In general, when working with fight-response children you will need to channel them away from confrontation and into reading. Flight-response children must be drawn out and interested in successful completion of reading tasks. Normally, fight reactions are more easily dealt with because they have a force behind them that can be redirected into reading. Flight reactions are generally passive, and you will have to intervene more directly to involve children and provide them with feelings of success. This might involve one-on-one intervention with reciprocal reading activities or other activities that allow the child to achieve success in easily observable ways.

Teacher-Made Tests

Teacher-made tests are perhaps the most common assessment instruments used in literacy instruction. Such measures have the advantage of being closely tied to the curriculum and program; they can be written to specifically apply to one child or a whole class. Length, type, and number of items; testing duration; and format all vary in teacher-made tests.

E-mail from the Classroom

From: Celia, cbmg@MIDWEST.NET
Subject: Re: Reading
To: RTEACHER@LISTSERV.SYR.EDU

John,

Good luck on your student teaching in the spring. I teach first grade, Title I, and one of the things I have used to help the "quiet ones" come out a little is to work through a story and then point to the inside of the back cover and ask the child, "If there were another page to this story, what do you think it would look like?"

I find this is very nonthreatening to children, because there truly is no right or wrong answer. However, it is also diagnostic because you can then tell whether or not the child has the gist of the story by what is predicted. If your child is very quiet, have him or her make a picture and then you can add the text together. Some children do not catch on to this the first time, but over time they come to anticipate your question and will oftentimes make a prediction before you can even ask the question. It is a real eye opener. Another way to help a quiet child come forth is to do some writing and/or reading with him or her and make mistakes. Then go back and, very matter-of-factly, talk yourself through your mistakes and let the child hear what you are saying and watch what you are doing. This lets the child know that adults adjust their reading and writing and it is not a "good or bad" thing; it is just part of the process.

Children may be timid because they are afraid of being wrong! Show them that there is a difference between taking risks and "being wrong."

Good luck, Celia

You will be most effective as a teacher when you are aware of the wealth of information available to you and use it in an informed manner to make your daily instructional decisions. Assignments are more than simple practice pieces for students; they are part of an overall data-gathering and decision-making process. Thus, in this context teacher-made tests go beyond quizzes or other graded items and include all the things you might ask a child to do as a part of the learning process—whether in the classroom, at home, or elsewhere. All such activities reveal children's needs and capabilities.

Effective use of incidental and teacher-initiated information requires keen observation of children's behaviors in all learning situations. Moreover, assessment is greatly facilitated by careful planning. For example, if a comprehension assignment is carefully constructed to include all levels of comprehension, then you can determine whether a child is having difficulty within a particular level(s) and can adjust your instruction accordingly.

Monitoring all aspects of children's performance requires a clear, up-to-date recordkeeping system. Maintaining such a record of children's strengths and weaknesses will allow you to be much more focused in their instruction and to target specific children's individual needs. A recordkeeping system for a vocabulary assignment might look like the one in Figure 11-11.

A part of your recordkeeping system can include the use of **rubrics,** scoring sheets that specify what must be included in a response and how to link this to specific scores. Rubrics for grading can be developed together with students and discussion can then make clear your expectations and scoring procedures. Developing scoring rubrics together with students provides them with a sense of community and takes away some stress that many students feel when they know their work will be scored (Skillings & Ferrell, 2000).

rubric   scoring sheets that specify criteria and scoring, providing clear indicators of what "poor" to "excellent" responses would include.

FIGURE 11-11

Sample class record sheet

ASSIGNMENT: *Vocabulary — write words in sentences, then use all words in story or paragraph. Words: observe, suspect, strut, elegant, modest.*

NAME	COMMENTS	DATE: 10/12
Allison	*Used words correctly. Misspelled elegant both times used "elegent"*	
Bobby	*Left out strut, modest.*	
Julio	*No problems.*	
Kathleen	*Words used correctly. Neatness and hand-writing still a problem.*	
Latisha	*modest, elegant used incorrectly*	
Wanda	*modest used incorrectly.*	

GENERAL COMMENTS: *Reteach modest. Have Kathleen recopy, grade only on neatness. See Bobby individually about this assignment. Add elegant, modest to spelling list.*

Formal, Norm-Referenced Tests

Norm-referenced tests compare an individual or a group to a **norm group** of similar individuals. These tests form the stereotype of traditional assessment. A norm-referenced test usually contains several subtests. For example, a survey reading test might include subtests in vocabulary, reading rate, general decoding, comprehension, and study skills. A diagnostic reading test might include subtests in the knowledge of word parts, blending ability, inferential and literal comprehension, identification of relationships (for example, cause and effect), oral vocabulary, and so on. Before choosing a norm-referenced test, you should carefully examine the test manual(s) to find out about the group to which your students would be compared. Determine whether your students are similar enough to the norm group for valid comparison. A manual should provide norm-group information such as the following:

norm-referenced tests Tests that compare an individual or a group to a group of other, similar individuals.

norm group The group whose test performance is used to establish levels of performance for a standardized test.

- Number of males and females
- Range of ages
- Distribution across geographic regions
- Representation of rural and urban areas
- Number of bicultural, minority, and ethnic students

> **MODEL LESSON**
>
> *Experience with a Norm-Referenced Test at Louise Henshaw's School*
>
> Louise Henshaw has reader-based beliefs about *what* to teach and test, and holistic beliefs about *how* to teach and test. Thus, while she realizes that information provided by her school's standardized testing program (in which all children are given a norm-referenced test near the end of each year) can provide some valuable information, she supplements this test with tools that assess the children's background knowledge and that focus on children's work on a daily basis. Her reader-based beliefs lead her to use interest inventories and to note observed behavior in a variety of situations, while her holistic beliefs lead her to value portfolios that include much information about all aspects of her children's performance. However, she realizes that many people rely on tests to make instructional decisions at the school district level and that standardized tests are used by many people in many ways.
>
> The goal of the standardized testing program in her school district is to compare children's achievement over several years to see how third graders perform relative to other third graders across the nation. The teachers and principal in Louise's school have agreed that the test is both reliable and valid and that the school's third-grade population adequately reflects the norm group for comparative purposes.
>
> A faculty meeting is called to discuss test administration. Everyone realizes the test instructions need to be followed to the letter. Instructions are to be read to children as stated in the test manual, a stopwatch is to be used to make sure that timed sections are accurate, subtests are to be done in order, and so on. Test booklets and answer sheets are to be collected at the end of the testing session and will be scored electronically, with the results returned to the teachers.
>
> Several months later, Louise receives those results. She notices there are several parts to the report: a section listing overall scores for her class, a section comparing her class to a norm group, a section that notes how many children missed particular items, and a section that lists her children's names along with the items each child missed. This information is clustered within question types that appeared on the test.
>
> Because the test was given late in the school year, the results will not greatly influence Louise's instruction for the children tested. However, her third graders compared favorably to their peers. She records individual children's scores on her class record sheet and on the children's official cumulative record cards. She knows that her students' next teachers will be looking at these records and will thus have an indication of general areas that might need some attention. Louise Henshaw will use other informal measures to corroborate the findings of this test. She will also share the information the following year when teachers tell each other about their classes from the year before.

Norm group scores are presented as an average or norm, making individual comparisons less reliable than comparisons of groups to the norm. For example, comparing a class average to the norm would be more accurate than comparing the scores of an individual child. The model lesson above relates the experiences of one third-grade teacher with a norm-referenced test.

Formal, Criterion-Referenced Tests

criterion-referenced test (CRT) A test that compares a child's performance to a predetermined measure of success.

A **criterion-referenced test (CRT)** does not compare a child to a norm group. Its intent is simply to provide a picture of performance by comparing it to an established criterion (Popham, 1978). Nevertheless, because criterion assessment usually is performed to judge mastery on a specific set of isolated skills such as letter-sounds, letter names, blends, main ideas, and so on, criterion assessment usually is valued by teachers who have specific-skills perspectives. Because criterion tests are relatively skill-specific in their makeup, they generally are not placed in the alternative assessment category. In contrast to norm-referenced assessment, where a child's score is compared to those of a norm group of peers, in criterion-referenced assessment a child's score is compared to a predetermined criterion of success. As Mehrens and Lehman (1984) have stated, "To polarize the distinction, we could say that the focus of a normative score is on how many of a child's peers do not perform (score) as well as he does; the focus of a criterion-referenced score is on what it is that a child can do" (p. 18).

MODEL LESSON

Experience with a Criterion-Referenced Test in Jeff Washington's Class

Jeff Washington's interactive beliefs about *what* to teach influence his assessment choices by leading him to value both process and product assessments. At times, he wants to assess how children are processing text; at other times he wants to assess how well they read. Thus, he uses a combination of think-aloud tests and tests that assess performance through specific questions about what was read. His specific skills beliefs about *how* to teach and test lead him to value criterion-referenced tests that provide information about the mastery of skills as children move through the year. He often uses the criterion-referenced test that came with the published reading program used in his classroom.

Jeff's class has just completed a lesson on cause-and-effect relationships. The lesson format came from a published reading program that includes criterion-referenced tests as part of the program. The teacher's manual suggests that the appropriate criterion-referenced test be given to see whether students have mastered the concept.

The test provided in the reading program contains 10 items, with 8 as the criterion. The teacher's guide suggests reteaching if the criterion is not met, and new lessons are provided for that purpose. An additional criterion assessment, with new items, is provided for use after reteaching.

Jeff administers the test to his students, and all but five meet the criterion. His teacher's aide works with this group of students, using the reteaching lesson, and then retests. On the retest all five students meet the criterion, and Jeff begins instruction on the next unit.

In part, the popularity of criterion-referenced assessment lies in its ability to determine whether a child has mastered a specific lesson and can be moved on to the next level of instruction. This approach has been criticized, however, because it implies that all necessary reading subskills have been correctly sequenced and identified and that a strict sequence of instruction is known to be best for all children. Unfortunately, even though much is known about reading, there is still much to learn. Even though certain skills generally are thought to be necessary in reading, they are interrelated and difficult to separate. A difficult issue to resolve in criterion-referenced measurement is the fact that the absence of any one subskill presented in a criterion reading test usually does not reflect an inability to read. A similar situation exists for most skill areas, leaving individually tested skills on a CRT open to question (see Johnston, 1983, for a discussion of holistic versus subskill theories of reading comprehension and their relationship to assessment; see also Serafini, 2001).

Nonetheless, criterion-referenced measures are included in almost every published reading program. Their advantage over norm-referenced tests traditionally has been their close tie to instruction, making them useful for a **management system.** A management system provides a detailed record of each child's progress through an instructional program and records when the mastery of specific skills occurs. Such systems are attractive to school systems concerned with accountability issues.

management system
A detailed, systematic record of a student's progress through an instructional program.

Criterion-referenced assessment can monitor a child's progress through instructional materials. For example, let's assume a reader is learning the two-letter blend *st.* The instructional program introduces the *str* blend at a more difficult level, but only after the *st* combination has been mastered. Five items testing *st* might be administered, with the criterion set at 3. When the child answers three of the five items correctly, instruction moves on to the *str* blend. Until then, more instruction is provided on *st* and the test (usually in a different form) is re-administered. This close tie to instruction is a major reason for the popularity of criterion-referenced assessment.

One misconception about the differences between norm- and criterion-referenced scores needs to be addressed here. The statement often is made that norm-referenced assessment results in a relatively arbitrary comparison of individual children to a norm group, whereas criterion assessment examines children's performance only against their own strengths. However, criterion-referenced tests also compare children's performance to an externally imposed criterion. In fact, one could argue that the criterion is more arbitrary than the norms, as norm-referenced tests provide a comprehensive and valuable discussion of the norm group and the norming procedure, whereas the rationale for a given criterion level rarely is addressed in teacher's manuals. Consequently, such questions as "How is a criterion determined?" are left unanswered.

Usually, a criterion is set at the level at which average children—average, that is, in relation to the children being tested—perform. Thus, the difference between a norm and a criterion is minimal. The major difference between criterion- and norm-referenced assessment lies in one's philosophy and in the way scores are used, rather than in any substantive difference in how appropriate performance is determined. This difference in usage is reflected in the frequency of administration of the two types of assessment. Criterion-referenced tests are used often and usually are specifically keyed to the instructional situation, whereas norm-referenced tests generally are used only once or twice a year. The previous model lesson shows how criterion-referenced tests can lead to instructional decisions.

⌨ Evaluating Materials

Readability Formulas

readability formula   A formula that indicates the difficulty of textual material in terms of a reading grade level; uses factors such as the number of syllables and sentences in a passage.

A **readability formula** provides a rough guideline for determining the difficulty level, or grade level, of reading material. Although useful, the results of a readability formula must be interpreted carefully. In fact, the International Reading Association and the National Council of Teachers of English (1984–1985) have noted that readability formulas, on their own, are insufficient for matching books with students. They suggest teachers do the following:

▶ Evaluate proposed texts based on knowledge of their children's prior information, experiences, reading abilities, and interests.
▶ Observe children using proposed texts in instructional settings to evaluate the effectiveness of the material.
▶ Use checklists for evaluating the readability of proposed materials, paying attention to variables such as children's interests, text graphics, number of ideas and concepts in the material, length of lines in the text, and other factors that contribute to the relative difficulty of textual material.

Although several readability formulas are available, all are similar in their manner of analyzing textual difficulty. Two factors usually are considered in determining difficulty level: word difficulty and sentence difficulty. To determine word difficulty, many readability formulas follow the premise that longer words are more difficult. Thus, by extension, difficult words contain more syllables than easier words. For that reason, many formulas require that the number of syllables in a given sample of text be counted. Other formulas compare the words in the sample material to a specific word list; that list guides the estimate of word difficulty.

To determine sentence difficulty, readability formulas use similar logic, reasoning that longer sentences are more difficult. Thus, many readability formulas require that the number of sentences in a given sample of material be counted. A small number suggests that the sentences are long and, thus, difficult. The relationship between the number of syllables and the number of sentences is often used to determine the approximate reading grade level (RGL) of the text being evaluated.

Readability formulas are more accurate at grade levels above second grade because most materials written for lower grade levels use a relatively limited set of words, many words of one syllable, and relatively short sentences. In addition, reading selections for young students are usually quite short. For a readability measure to be valid, however, a continuous passage of approximately 100 words should be used, and it is strongly suggested that at least three representative passages from several sections of the material be averaged to estimate the overall reading grade level. Thus, some formulas specifically state they are not intended for use below certain grade levels, whereas others may be used throughout a broad range of grades. Fry (1990) has proposed a formula for use with passages as short as 80 words, but that formula must also be used with care when evaluating beginning reading materials.

A Common Readability Measure. A popular readability measure, the *Fry Readability Scale,* is shown in Figure 11-12, along with directions for its use. The Fry scale's popularity results from its ease of use and its wide range of grade levels. Try using the Fry scale to estimate the reading grade level of the following passage (Williams, 1973). For your information, 100 words precede the double slash mark. (The answer is given at the end of this section.)

> That evening they all had dinner together in the enchanter's cozy kitchen. Then Albion took Petronella out to a stone building and unbolted its door. Inside were seven huge black dogs.
> "You must watch my hounds all night," said he.
> Petronella went in, and Albion closed and locked the door.
> At once the hounds began to snarl and bark. They showed their teeth at her. But Petronella was a real princess. She plucked up her courage. Instead of backing away, she went toward the dogs. She began to speak to them in a quiet voice. They stopped snarling and sniffed // at her.

There are, of course, other highly regarded readability formulas: for example, the formula by Spache (1953, 1976), appropriate for grades 1 through 3; by Dale and Chall (1948), for grades 4 through 6; and by Flesch (1948), for grades 5 and above. Many publishers and other private businesses offer computerized estimates of readability, based on a variety of such formulas. There is commercially available software, as well as free or inexpensive public domain (that is, without copyright) software, that can apply one or more formulas to a passage. See, for example, http://www.interventioncentral.org/htmdocs/tools/okapi/okapi.shtml, a free site that includes readability analysis information on-line. While there are many such sites, their availability can change quickly. You should use a search engine such as that found at www.google.com with the search words "readability formula" to find new sites in this area. (The reading grade level of the Petronella passage is early fourth grade.)

The Limitations of Readability Formulas. The following sentence pairs illustrate some factors that make texts more or less difficult to read. Which sentence in each pair would be easier for a second grader to understand?

1. (a) The boy ran down the street.   (b) The boy ran down the street.
2. (a) The boy ran down the street.   (b) The boy ran down the street.

3. (a) The boy ran down the street.   (b) Down the street ran the boy.
4. (a) The boy ran down the long,   (b) The boy ran down the street.
   busy street.   The street was busy. The
                                            street was long.

In each of the pairs, the first sentence is generally considered to be easier to understand than the second. Such things as print size, supportive illustrations, and word

FIGURE 11-12

The Fry Readability Scale

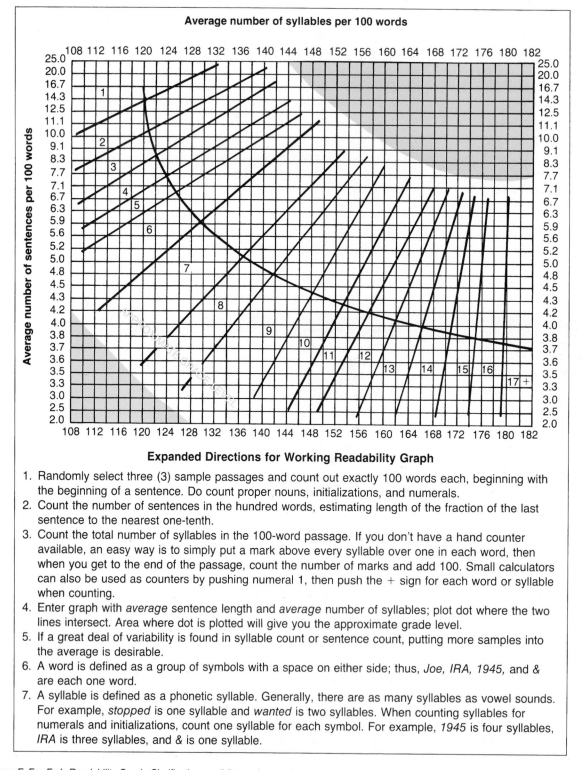

Expanded Directions for Working Readability Graph

1. Randomly select three (3) sample passages and count out exactly 100 words each, beginning with the beginning of a sentence. Do count proper nouns, initializations, and numerals.
2. Count the number of sentences in the hundred words, estimating length of the fraction of the last sentence to the nearest one-tenth.
3. Count the total number of syllables in the 100-word passage. If you don't have a hand counter available, an easy way is to simply put a mark above every syllable over one in each word, then when you get to the end of the passage, count the number of marks and add 100. Small calculators can also be used as counters by pushing numeral 1, then push the + sign for each word or syllable when counting.
4. Enter graph with *average* sentence length and *average* number of syllables; plot dot where the two lines intersect. Area where dot is plotted will give you the approximate grade level.
5. If a great deal of variability is found in syllable count or sentence count, putting more samples into the average is desirable.
6. A word is defined as a group of symbols with a space on either side; thus, *Joe, IRA, 1945,* and *&* are each one word.
7. A syllable is defined as a phonetic syllable. Generally, there are as many syllables as vowel sounds. For example, *stopped* is one syllable and *wanted* is two syllables. When counting syllables for numerals and initializations, count one syllable for each symbol. For example, *1945* is four syllables, *IRA* is three syllables, and *&* is one syllable.

Source: E. Fry, Fry's Readability Graph: Clarifications, validity, and extension to level 17, *Journal of Reading, 21* (1977), pp. 242–252.

order affect reading difficulty, yet those factors are not considered when a formula is used. In addition, short sentences do not always facilitate comprehension: 4(a) is easier for a second grader to read than 4(b) (Pearson, 1974–1975). But readability formulas usually equate length with difficulty.

Conceptual difficulty and background knowledge are other aspects of reading that formulas do not address, and misleading estimates can sometimes result. For example, because readability formulas generally assume that more syllables imply greater difficulty, a formula would consider *television* a more difficult word than *vector*, even though second graders would have much less trouble understanding *television*.

Nonetheless, readability formulas provide an easy-to-use method of estimating the relative difficulty of reading materials. If carefully and thoughtfully interpreted, readability formulas can provide an indication of the RGL of a specific piece of text. We must remember, however, that formulas can be fooled, especially at lower grade levels, where reading selections often become more difficult as the reader moves through a book. Thus, the readability of a passage at the beginning of a book might be different from that of a passage at the end—just one more reason to use multiple passages and average the results.

Additional Considerations

When evaluating materials, supplement readability formulas with other information. A form that considers readability as well as other data is presented in Figure 11-13 on pages 428 and 429. Such a form should be used with the realization that not all the items apply to every type of reading material. For example, deductive and inductive presentation methods would not apply to narrative reading material. Thus, only items that pertain to the material under consideration need to be addressed. In addition, when materials are compared, it is important they be from similar domains. For example, it is not appropriate to compare a children's literature book with a content-area textbook. The form in Figure 11-13 identifies many factors that teachers might consider important in the selection of reading materials, and it can help in decision making. Others (for example, Bell & Davey, 1994) have also provided tools and procedures for evaluating the interaction of readers and textbooks.

Observing Diversity through Assessment

Through informal assessment such as IRIs and think-alouds, and through formal, diagnostic tests that must be individually administered, you will come into close contact with all of the children in your class and will come to know each of your students' individual strengths, needs, and challenges. Whenever you use formal, informal, or teacher-made assessment tools, you will clearly notice the diversity in your classroom. Noticing diversity through assessment often results in teachers moving toward interactive beliefs that influence their decisions about what to teach and toward integrated beliefs that influence decisions about how to teach. The results of assessments emphasize that some children need more guidance in developing higher-level components of the reading process, such as prior knowledge, while others need more guidance in developing lower-level components, such as decoding or syntactic knowledge. It is difficult to take extreme positions on a literacy framework when acknowledging the diverse nature of learning and literacy highlighted through assessment. Interactive beliefs imply that all components of reading are important, and thus facilitate modifying instruction to meet individual needs.

For example, it is clear that individuals from certain cultures are disadvantaged by standardized tests, and you will need to closely examine standardized tests (a) to see if the norm group is reflective of the children being examined and (b) to see if test items

FIGURE 11-13

Material analysis form

Title _____

Author _____

Publisher _____

A. Readability
Formula used _____
Reading grade level _____, which is

(1) appropriate   5 points
(2) more than one grade off   3 points
(3) one grade off   2 points

B. Rate all appropriate items in this section using a scale of 1 through 5, with 1 being unsatisfactory and 5 being excellent.

Literary style
Use of topic sentences   _____
Use of technical terms   _____
Sentence complexity   _____
Appropriate summaries   _____

General appearance
Total selection size   _____
Print size and quality   _____
Eye appeal   _____
Durability   _____
Comments:

Content
Suitable for chosen objective   _____
Up-to-date (current and accurate)   _____
Appropriate to students' readiness   _____
Appropriate to students' interests   _____
Treatment of controversial subjects   _____
Comments:

Illustrations
Modern, generally of high quality   _____
Useful for learning and discussion   _____
Match the written text   _____
Comments:

Organization of content
Use of underlying theme   _____
Logical units, subunits   _____
Logical chapter/heading sequence   _____
Comments:

Supplementary materials/learning aids
Table of contents   _____
Appendices   _____
Glossary   _____
Suggested activities   _____
References   _____
Teacher's guide (appropriate)   _____
Teacher's guide (easy to use)   _____
Comments:

C. Presentation of content (check primary mode of presentation)
Authoritarian presentation   _____
Deductive presentation   _____
Type of text: expository   _____

Prescriptive presentation   _____
Inductive presentation   _____
Narrative   _____

are realistic in their expectations for bicultural children. If either the norm group appears inappropriate, or if a significant number of test items appear to require knowledge that would not be available to certain groups of children, then that test is inappropriate. Realistically, however, you may have little choice about mandated assessments in your school districts. If this is the case, then instructional decisions should not be made solely on test scores from these instruments. You must realize that some children will be reading at levels significantly higher than their standardized test scores.

FIGURE 11-13

Continued

D. Background knowledge demands

Note background knowledge requirements
(e.g., prior knowledge, mathematical concepts,
prerequisite coursework or reading)

_____

_____

E. Other comments

F. Overall rating

1. (a) Count the number of ratings given in Section B.   _____
   (b) Multiply by 5.   × 5 _____
   (c) Enter the result.   _____
   (d) Add 5 (from Section A).   + 5 _____
   (e) Enter the result. This is the total possible points.   _____
2. (a) Add all of the numerical ratings given in Section B.   _____
   (b) Add the appropriate points from Section A.   + _____
   (c) Enter the result. This is the raw score.   _____
3. (a) Divide 2(c) by 1(e). Enter the result.   _____
   (b) Multiply by 100.   × 100 _____
   (c) Enter the result. This percentage can be used to   _____
       compare similar materials.   _____ %

Source: From _Effective Literacy Instruction: K–8,_ Fifth Edition, by Donald J. Leu, Jr., and Charles K. Kinzer. Copyright 2003 by Pearson Education, Inc. Permission is granted by the publisher to reproduce this figure for student record-keeping purposes.

Allowing children to share their reading and their written work and listen to peer feedback is a useful, informal assessment practice.

In some ways, informal assessments are more difficult to evaluate in terms of cultural bias than are formal assessment tools. When using informal reading inventories, cloze procedures, or running records, it might be more difficult to determine the existence of cultural bias, especially in terms of background knowledge assumptions. For example, an IRI might include a passage about rodeos, with both factual and inferential

PRACTICAL TEACHING STRATEGIES

Using Internet Inquiry to Recognize Diversity in Culture and Background

You and your students are able to explore several Internet sites that will provide a good sense of cultural and linguistic diversity and that serve to highlight differences (and similarities) in background knowledge. Here are some examples:

▶ **AltaVista Translation Service/Babelfish** (http://babelfish.altavista.com/tr)—A site that can translate plain text (or web pages) into other languages. This can provide useful springboards for discussion as well as provide a vehicle to expand keypal communication throughout the world.

▶ **Say Hello to the World Project** (http://www.ipl.org/youth/hello/)—A site where audio clips of words and phrases in various languages are available, as is information about language differences and resources. (See Figure 11-14 for a sample screen from the Cherokee language page.)

▶ **Official Internet Site of the Ministry of Tourism for Egypt** (http://touregypt.net/)—Most countries have tourism sites that provide a wealth of current as well as historical information. In addition, sites such as this one usually provide a news magazine or daily paper that will provide you and your students with facts and perspectives about what is happening in other countries. Look for such sites through various search engines in your Internet browser.

---

questions asked at the end of the passage. Although factual questions often can be answered from one's knowledge of syntax or sentence structure (syntax, for example, enables you to answer "Where is the zokat?" after reading "The zokat is in the pikzet!"), children from different cultural groups or different first-language backgrounds might not be familiar with English sentence patterns. These children would have greater difficulty in answering factual questions. Spanish speakers, for example, are used to a subject-object-verb sentence structure, while subject-verb-object order is more common in English.

Similarly, inferential questions are answered using a combination of background knowledge and text information. For example, knowing that a *zokat* goes into a *pikzet* when hungry allows one to answer the inferential question, "What do you think the zokat is doing in the pikzet?" (probably eating). But students without such background knowledge would have difficulty fully comprehending such a text. To go back to the rodeo example in an IRI, children who might not have prior knowledge of rodeos, perhaps because they come from other countries or cultures that do not include rodeos, might have significant difficulty in answering the factual and/or inferential questions about a rodeo passage. Similar problems might occur in any text chosen for a cloze procedure or a running record.

Thus, teachers must be aware of equity issues, especially in informal performance assessments. However, addressing equity issues requires more than selecting culturally representative materials (Villegas, 1990). Consider Gitomer's (1993) comment that:

> There must be a fundamental understanding and respect for the ways in which members of different social groups communicate, particularly as this affects performance. For example, the reticence of one group in certain situations may be a function of social values. . . . Cultural differences may affect the ways in which one formulates a problem or develops a solution. (p. 260)

Issues of diversity in assessment might also be highlighted if your classroom includes physically challenged or learning disabled students. These children often require special arrangements in terms of environment (perhaps a quieter, less-distracting area),

FIGURE 11-14

A sample screen from the Cherokee language page at the **Say Hello to the World Project**
(http://www.ipl.org/div/kidspace/hello/cherokee.html)

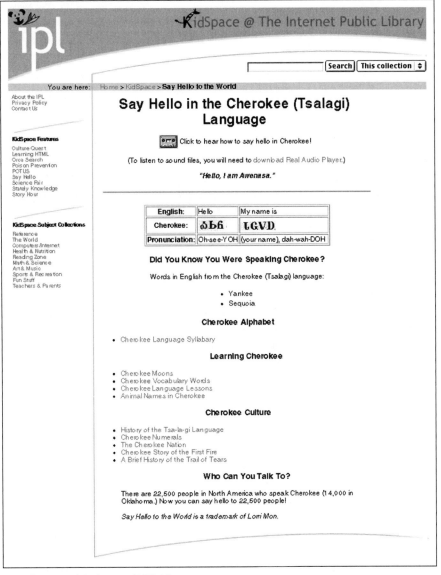

Note: Courtesy of the Internet Public Library.

TABLE 11-3

A summary of how assessment relates to a literacy framework and decisions about what to teach

Issues and Beliefs in a Literacy Framework That Inform This Issue	Instructional Decisions That Are Informed by Your Beliefs
Issue 1. What Should I Teach?	
Meaning exists in what the reader brings to a text, and reading is a result of expectations. Reading begins with elements of prior knowledge. (Reader-based beliefs)	Process assessment that examines the reader's ability to access and apply prior knowledge. Aesthetic responses are valued.
Meaning exists in the text, and reading is translating the text or extracting the meaning from the text. Reading begins with decoding. (Text-based beliefs)	Product assessment to determine knowledge of the structural components of literacy. Decoding and literal meaning are emphasized. Efferent responses are evaluated. Assessment to determine whether the reader is comprehending the text's message, together with supporting details from the text, is valued.
Meaning exists both in the text and the reader. Reading is both translation and expectation. All of the knowledge sources are used simultaneously. (Interactive beliefs)	Both process and product assessment would occur in relatively equal amounts. Both aesthetic and efferent responses are valued.

additional time to complete a task such as a writing sample or reading passage, or leeway in interpreting pronunciation when analyzing miscues. Pronunciation factors due to dialect variation, of course, have been discussed earlier and should not be counted as miscues when assessing students who speak a nonstandard dialect.

Finally, you should take advantage of the diversity you will find in your classroom in any number of ways. Your assessment program will show that each child has strengths, and using method frameworks such as jigsaw procedures within cooperative learning groups (see chapter 10) can show students that each of them can make a valuable contribution to the class and to their own learning. This is especially true for non-native speakers who can extend the background knowledge of standard-English speakers while acquiring new knowledge and skills themselves.

The Role of a Literacy Framework in Assessment

Just as your literacy framework informs decisions about what and how to teach, it can also be used to inform decisions about what and how to assess literacy in your classroom. Your belief about what to teach (and assess) informs decisions about what type of assessment information you value. If you believe meaning exists in what a reader brings to a text, you will favor a process assessment that examines children's ability to access and apply prior knowledge. You will pay particular attention to their ability to make inferences and apply information they have read. In addition, aesthetic responses will be valued. If you believe meaning exists in the text, you will favor a product assessment that examines children's ability to determine whether a child is comprehending a text's

TABLE 11-4

A summary of how assessment relates to a literacy framework and decisions about how to teach

Issues and Beliefs in a Literacy Framework That Inform This Issue	Instructional Decisions That Are Informed by Your Beliefs
Issue 2. How Should I Teach?	
Students direct much of their own learning, and inductive learning is emphasized. (Holistic language learning beliefs)	Assessment tends to focus on informal and alternative tools, particularly those grounded in authentic literacy tasks, especially think-alouds during reading and writing, IRIs, and cloze tests taken or developed from classroom reading materials. "Kidwatching," self-assessment, and assessment of interests and attitudes are valued.
Teacher-directed reading activities and deductive learning are emphasized. Specific skills, often organized in terms of difficulty, are frequently taught. (Specific skills beliefs)	Assessment tends to focus on tools that can determine subskills of reading and writing. Formal tests, either norm- or criterion-referenced tests, as well as IRIs that focus on decoding, are valued.
Both student-directed and teacher-directed experiences are used. Both inductive and deductive learning are used. Reading experiences take place in authentic social contexts and with authentic reading materials. Specific skills are taught when needed. (Integrated beliefs)	A combination of assessment procedures are used, including both formal and informal tests. Alternative assessment as well as more traditional methods are used and their information examined to make instructional decisions.

meaning. Decoding and literal meaning are especially emphasized. Efferent responses will be valued. If you have an interactive belief, you favor both process and product assessment and you look to see how children apply prior knowledge as well as how well they comprehend a text's meaning. In other words, you favor both aesthetic and efferent responses. Table 11-3 on page 432 summarizes these relationships.

A literacy framework also plays a significant role in guiding decisions about *how* to teach and how to test. Teachers with holistic beliefs about how to teach tend to be less satisfied with traditional assessment tools, especially standardized tests that use short test items and require multiple choice, fill-in-the-blank, or true/false responses. Holistic language perspectives are consistent with measures that are holistic, that present items in context, that are based on what children are reading, and that do not attempt to split reading into closely defined subskills. Teachers with specific skills beliefs tend to be more satisfied with assessment procedures that facilitate the examination of various reading subskills. Teachers with integrated language learning beliefs are likely to combine assessment approaches, using formal tests that examine specific skills as well as less-formal, holistic tools. Table 11-4, above, summarizes the influence of literacy frameworks on the issue of how to teach and test.

Regardless of your literacy framework, however, a test in and of itself is relatively meaningless, whether it be informal (teacher-made) or formal (a process or a product measure). It will be your clear understanding of your assessment goals, together with your interpretation and use of test results, that will determine the value of assessment in your instructional situation.

Use the self-test questions on http://www.prenhall.com/leukinzer to review the material presented in this chapter.

Featured Teacher

Mrs. Thomson

Mrs. Thomson teaches third grade at Ecole Victoria School, part of the Saskatoon Public School System in Saskatoon, Canada. As seen on her website (http://schools.sbe.saskatoon.sk.ca/Victo/classes/thomson/; Figure 11-15), much of what the children do incorporates the use of the Internet—from finding and using links to help class projects to using web quests that integrate a variety of subject areas with language arts and literacy. As you look through the projects and links on Mrs. Thomson's website, consider how the project-based activities in which the children participate can provide valuable information about how they are developing into effective readers and writers.

FIGURE 11-15

Mrs. Thomson's home page (http://schools.sbe.saskatoon.sk.ca/Victo/classes/thomson/)

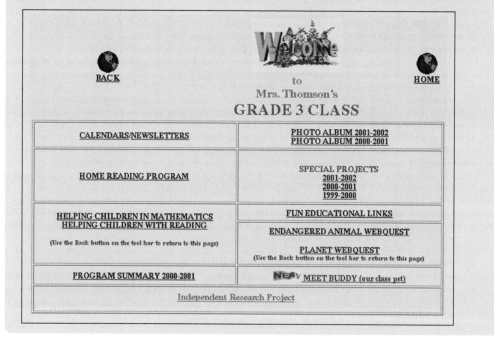

Major Points

▶ Process assessment allows teachers to infer students' underlying processes. Product assessment provides an indication of students' performance without reference to how a score was achieved.

▶ Portfolios consist of a wide variety of children's work, performance, self-evaluation, and other informal and formal items collected on a regular basis. Examining the items in a portfolio can help document a child's growth and progress as well as provide an indication of specific areas that need support.

▶ Information about issues in assessment and national assessment programs can be accessed through the Internet at sites such as **The National Center for Education Statistics** (http://nces.ed.gov/indihome.asp) and the **National Assessment of Educational Progress** (http://nces.ed.gov/naep/) and by participating in listservs and discussion groups supported by the International Reading Association and the National Council for Teachers of English.

▶ Measurement instruments can be categorized as informal (for example, IRIs, running records, think-alouds, cloze tests, retellings), teacher made, or formal (for example, standardized, norm- or criterion-referenced tests). Alternative assessment often is thought of as informal; traditional assessment often is thought of as formal.

▶ Assessment instruments are used to evaluate readers, reading materials, and the interaction between readers and materials.

▶ Assessment is a good indicator of the diversity found in a classroom and can provide guidelines to celebrate the challenges presented by different students' strengths and weaknesses.

Making Instructional Decisions

1. An increasing number of voices are being raised in favor of alternatives to traditional tests and testing methods, especially in favor of process assessment. Process measures are valuable, however, only to the extent that individual teachers understand the reading process and are able to infer students' processes based on their overt behavior. However, not all teachers understand the reading process equally or similarly and disagreement in interpreting process measures could lead to problems of accountability with parents and others. Thus, some argue that process measures can provide important knowledge about how students do what they do; others point to the difficulty of process analysis and the inconsistency of interpretation. Will you favor product measures, process measures, or a combination of both in your classroom? Relate your response to your present beliefs about teaching literacy.

2. At some point in your teaching career, you will probably be asked to recommend a reading test for use in your classroom or you may be asked to serve on a committee that will choose a test for your school or school district. What would your criteria be? What should a good test do? What would you look for in a test?

3. Interview a teacher, a parent, and a school principal. Ask them to describe how they view testing and how they use, or what they think about, test results. How do the goals and uses of testing differ among these people? What implications do these differences have for you as a future teacher?

4. Try to find a teacher who uses portfolio evaluation (you might ask a professor or a principal to recommend someone). Interview the teacher and ask how the portfolio is used in instructional decision making. Ask whether you might see a child's work. If so, try to describe that child's progress from what appears in the portfolio.

5. Interview both a primary- and an intermediate-grade teacher. Ask about the different kinds of measurement used in their classrooms. What are the purposes of each kind and how do they help in instructional decision making?

6. Choose two passages from two different published reading programs and perform a readability analysis, using the Fry scale. Compare your results with the readability information provided in the teacher's manual of each program. What are some of the reasons a mismatch might occur?

7. Using the running record scoring procedure described in this chapter, practice a running record with a second-grade and a fourth-grade student. Practice until you feel comfortable with this procedure.

8. Construct a cloze test for use with elementary students or with some of your college-age friends. Choose appropriate materials for your practice group. Administer your test. Analyze the results.

9. When discussing alternative assessments, it is more appropriate to think of validity as very high because these tasks are authentic reading and writing tasks that take place as part of the normal classroom routine, and to think of reliability in terms of the degree of agreement between two professionals, such as two teachers, who independently interpret a student's performance. Describe your thoughts about the importance of traditional notions of validity and reliability as they relate

to alternative assessment. How would teachers with different beliefs about what to teach and how to teach differ in their responses?

10. Describe your view of testing and relate it to your literacy framework. Specify how you might use assessment to make instructional decisions in your own classroom.

Further Reading

A practical guide to reading assessments (A Joint Project of the U.S. Department of Education, the International Reading Association, and HCI: The Life Issues Publisher (Health Communications, Inc.)). (2000). Newark, DE: International Reading Association.

> *Examines a wide range of assessment tools and covers the dimensions of reading outlined in the National Research Council report* Preventing Reading Difficulties in Young Children, *including concepts about print, phonological awareness, alphabetic understanding, spelling, vocabulary, and reading comprehension. Assessment tools are described on one page and include the target grade level, purpose, description, why it's important and when to use it, how to order it, administration requirements, special considerations, how to interpret the results, how to link the assessment to instruction, and whether there is a fee.*

Barrentine, S. J. (1999). *Reading assessment: Principles and practices for elementary teachers.* Newark, DE: International Reading Association.

> *A compilation of alternative assessment techniques from* The Reading Teacher.

Bell, R., & Davey, B. (1994). Assessing students' skills in using textbooks: The textbook awareness and performance profile (TAPP). *Journal of Reading, 37,* 280–286.

> *Provides a detailed tool for assessing students' use of textbooks and discusses instruction that can occur based on the findings.*

Courtney, A. M., & Abodeeb, T. L. (2001). *Journey of discovery: Building a classroom community through diagnostic-reflective portfolios.* Newark, DE: International Reading Association.

> *Provides a definition of diagnostic-reflective portfolios and why they are beneficial tools for literacy assessment and for establishing literacy learning communities in elementary classrooms. Discusses a variety of assessment tools, with an emphasis on goal setting and constructing diagnostic-*

> *reflective portfolios. Includes examples of students' reflections and development, and sample forms that can be used in students' diagnostic-reflective portfolios.*

Farr, R., & Tone, B. (1998). *Portfolio and performance assessment: Helping students evaluate their progress as readers and writers* (2nd ed.). Belmont, CA: Wadsworth Publishing Company.

> *A paperback that discusses issues surrounding portfolio and performance assessment and that provides scoring systems, checklists, and guidelines for interpreting and reporting students' progress.*

Glazer, S. M., & Brown, C. S. (1993). *Portfolios and beyond: Collaborative assessment in reading and writing.* Norwood, MA: Christopher-Gordon.

> *A short paperback that examines alternative assessment. Provides background, rationale, and guidelines for alternative assessment of reading and writing, including think-alouds, retellings, and collaborative reporting that links students, teachers, and parents.*

Harp, B. (2000). *The handbook of literacy assessment and evaluation* (2nd ed.). Norwood, MA: Christopher-Gordon.

> *Provides information on 53 traditional and informal evaluation tools. Includes tools, many accompanied by black-line masters.*

Leslie, L., Jett-Simpson, M., & the Wisconsin Reading Association. (1997). *Authentic literacy assessment: An ecological approach.* New York: Addison Wesley Educational Publishers.

> *A paperback created with input from many teachers, this book includes a wide variety of informal assessment tools and checklists that teachers will find valuable.*

Valencia, S. (1990). A portfolio approach to classroom reading assessment: The whys, whats, and hows. *The Reading Teacher, 43,* 338–340.

> *Outlines the benefit of portfolio assessment, describes what should be included, and discusses its use.*

References

Allington, R. L., Chodos, L., Domaracki, J., & Truex, S. (1977). Passage dependency: Four diagnostic oral reading tests. *The Reading Teacher, 30,* 393–395.

Aulls, M. W. (1982). *Developing readers in today's elementary schools.* Boston, MA: Allyn & Bacon.

Barrs, M., Ellis, S., Hester, H., & Thomas, A. (1989). *The primary language record: Handbook for teachers.* Portsmouth, NH: Heinemann Educational Books.

Bell, R., & Davey, B. (1994). Assessing students' skills in using textbooks: The textbook awareness and performance profile (TAPP). *Journal of Reading, 37,* 280–286.

Betts, E. A. (1946). *Foundations of reading instruction.* New York: American Book.

Bormuth, J. R. (1968). The cloze readability procedure. In J. R. Bormuth (Ed.), *Readability in 1968* (pp. 40–47). Champaign, IL: NCTE.

Bransford, J. D., Brown, A. L., & Cocking, R. R. (Eds.). (2000). *How people learn: Brain, mind, experience, and school: Expanded edition.* Washington, DC: National Academy Press.

Burns, P. C., Roe, B. D., & Ross, E. P. (1988). *Teaching reading in today's elementary schools* (4th ed.). Boston, MA: Houghton Mifflin.

Calfee, R. C. (1987). The school as a context for assessment of literacy. *The Reading Teacher, 40,* 738–743.

Carson, J. (1990). Unpublished manuscript.

Clark, C. H. (1982). Assessing free recall. *The Reading Teacher, 35,* 434–439.

Clay, M. (1985). *The early detection of reading difficulties* (3rd ed.). Portsmouth, NH: Heinemann-Boynton/Cook.

Cooper, J. L. (1952). *The effect of adjustment of basal reading materials on reading achievement.* Unpublished doctoral dissertation, Boston University.

Courtney, A. M., & Abodeeb, T. L. (2001). *Journey of discovery: Building a classroom community through diagnostic-reflective portfolios.* Newark, DE: International Reading Association.

CTGV. (1993 March). Anchored instruction and situated cognition revisited. *Educational Technology,* 52–70.

Dale, E., & Chall, J. S. (1948). A formula for predicting readability. *Educational Research Bulletin* (Ohio State University), *27,* 11–20; 28, 37–54.

Duffelmeyer, F. A., & Duffelmeyer, B. B. (1989). Are IRI passages suitable for assessing main idea comprehension? *The Reading Teacher, 42,* 358–363.

Dulin, K. L. (1984). Assessing reading interests of elementary and middle school students. In A. J. Harris & E. R. Sipay (Eds.), *Readings on reading instruction* (pp. 346–357). New York: Longman Publishing Group.

Dulin, K. L., & Chester, R. (1984). *Dulin-Chester reading attention scale/Reading interest questionnaire.* Madison: University of Wisconsin.

Eeds, M. (1988). Holistic assessment of coding ability. In S. M. Glazer, L. W. Searfoss, & L. M. Gentile (Eds.), *Reexamining reading diagnosis: New trends and procedures.* Newark, DE: International Reading Association.

Englert, C. S., & Semmel, M. I. (1981). The relationship of oral reading substitution miscues to comprehension. *The Reading Teacher, 35,* 273–280.

Farr, R., & Tone, B. (1998). *Portfolio and performance assessment; Helping students evaluate their progress as readers and writers,* 2nd ed. Belmont, CA: Wadsworth Publishing Company.

Farris, J. (1989). From basal reader to whole language: Transition tactics. *Reading Horizons, 30,* 23–28.

Flesch, R. F. (1948). A new readability yardstick. *Journal of Applied Psychology, 32,* 221–223.

Flesch, R. F. (1949). *The art of readable writing.* New York: Harper.

Fry, E. (1990). A readability formula for short passages. *The Reading Teacher, 33,* 594–597.

Gardner, H., & Hatch, T. (1989). Multiple intelligences go to school: Educational implications of the theory of multiple intelligences. *Educational Researcher, 18* (8), 4–10.

Gentile, L. M., & McMillan, M. M. (1987). *Stress and reading difficulties: Research, assessment, intervention.* Newark, DE: International Reading Association.

Gentile, L. M., & McMillan, M. M. (1988). Reexamining the role of emotional maladjustment. In S. M. Glazer, L. W. Searfoss, & L. M. Gentile (Eds.), *Reexamining reading diagnosis: New trends and procedures* (pp. 12–28). Newark, DE: International Reading Association.

Gentry, J. R. (1982). An analysis of developmental spelling in GNYS AT WRK. *The Reading Teacher, 36,* 192–200.

Gifford, B. R. (1990). *Report of the National Commission on Testing and Public Policy.* Chestnut Hill, MA: Boston College.

Gitomer, D. H. (1993). Performance assessment and educational measurement. In R. E. Bennett & W. C. Ward (Eds.), *Construction versus choice in cognitive measurement: Issues in constructed response, performance testing, and portfolio assessment* (pp. 241–260). Hillsdale, NJ: Lawrence Erlbaum Associates.

Glazer, S. M., & Brown, C. S. (1993). *Portfolios and beyond: Collaborative assessment in reading and writing.* Norwood, MA: Christopher-Gordon.

Goodman, K. S., & Buck, C. (1973). Dialect barriers to reading comprehension revisited. *The Reading Teacher, 27,* 6–12.

Harp, B. (1989). When you do whole language instruction, how will you keep track of reading and writing skills? *The Reading Teacher, 42,* 160–161.

Harris, A. J., & Sipay, E. R. (1990). *How to increase reading ability: A guide to developmental and remedial methods* (9th ed.). New York: Longman Publishing Group.

Henk, W., & Melnick, S. (1995). The reader self-perception scale (RSPS): A new tool for measuring how children feel about themselves as readers. *The Reading Teacher, 48(6),* 470–4.

Herman, J. L., Aschbacher, P. R., & Winters, L. (1992). *A practical guide to alternative assessment.* Alexandria, VA: Association for Supervision and Curriculum Development.

Hoffman, J. V., Assaf, L. C., & Paris, S. G. (2001). High-stakes testing in reading: Today in Texas, tomorrow? *The Reading Teacher,* 482–492.

IRA/NCTE Joint Task Force on Assessment. (1994). *Standards for the assessment of reading and writing.* Newark, DE: International Reading Association.

IRA, NCTE take stand on readability formulae. (December 1984–January 1985). *Reading Today, 2,* 1.

IRA Position Statement. (2000). *Making a difference means making it different: Honoring children's rights to excellent reading instruction.* Newark, DE: International Reading Association.

Johns, J. L., & Kuhn, M. K. (1983). The informal reading inventory: 1910–1980. *Reading World, 23,* 8–19.

Johnson, M. S., Kress, R. A., & Pikulski, J. J. (1987). *Informal reading inventories* (2nd ed.). Newark, DE: International Reading Association.

Johnston, P. H. (1983). *Reading comprehension assessment: A cognitive basis.* Newark, DE: International Reading Association.

Johnston, P. H. (1987). Teachers as evaluation experts. *The Reading Teacher, 40,* 744–478.

Johnston, P. H. (1992). *Constructive evaluation of literate activity.* White Plains, NY: Longman Publishing Group.

Jongsma, E. (1980). *Cloze instruction research: A second look.* Newark, DE: International Reading Association.

Jongsma, K. S. (1989). Portfolio assessment. *The Reading Teacher, 42,* 264–265.

Lapp, J., & Flood, D. (1989). Reporting reading progress: A comparison portfolio for parents. *The Reading Teacher, 42,* 508–514.

Leslie, L., & Caldwell, J. (2001). *Qualitative reading inventory-3.* Boston, MA: Allyn & Bacon.

Leslie, L., Jett-Simpson, M., & the Wisconsin Reading Association. (1997). *Authentic literacy assessment: An ecological approach.* New York: Addison Wesley Educational Publishers.

Mehrens, W. A., & Lehman, I. J. (1984). *Measurement and evaluation in education and psychology* (3rd ed.). New York: Holt, Rinehart & Winston.

Morrow, L. M. (1988). Retelling stories as a diagnostic tool. In S. M. Glazer, L. W. Searfoss, & L. M. Gentile (Eds.), *Reexamining reading diagnosis: New trends and procedures* (pp. 128–138). Newark, DE: International Reading Association.

Murphy, S., & Underwood, T. (2001). *Portfolio practices: Lessons from schools, districts, and states.* Norwood, MA: Christopher-Gordon.

Nickerson, R. W. (1989). New directions in educational assessment. *Educational Researcher, 18* (9), 3–7.

Nitko, A. J. (1980). Distinguishing the many varieties of criterion-referenced tests. *Review of Educational Research, 50,* 461–485.

Pearson, D. (1974–1975). The effects of grammatical complexity on children's comprehension, recall and conception of certain semantic relations. *Reading Research Quarterly, 10,* 155–192.

Pellegrino, J. W., Chudowsky, N., & Glaser, R. (Eds.). (2001). *Knowing what students know: The science and design of educational assessment.* Washington, DC: National Academy Press.

Pikulski, J. J. (1989). The assessment of reading: A time for change? *The Reading Teacher, 42,* 80–81.

P.L.107-110 (H.R.1). (2002). *No child left behind: Reauthorization of the elementary and secondary education act.* Available online [http://thomas.loc.gov/cgi-bin/query/z?c107:h.r.1.enr:]. Accessed 01/29/02.

Popham, W. J. (1978). *Criterion referenced measurement.* Englewood Cliffs, NJ: Prentice-Hall.

Powell, W. R. (1970). Reappraising the criteria for interpreting informal reading inventories. In J. DeBoer (Ed.), *Reading diagnosis and evaluation.* Newark, DE: International Reading Association.

Rankin, E. F. (1974). Grade level interpretations of cloze readability scores. In F. Greene (Ed.), *The right to participate.* Milwaukee, WI: National Reading Conference.

Rankin, E. F. (1978). Characteristics of the cloze procedure as a research tool in the study of language. In P. D. Pearson & J. Hanson (Eds.), *Reading: Disciplined inquiry in process and practice* (pp. 148–153). Clemson, SC: National Reading Conference.

Rankin, E. F., & Culhane, J. W. (1969). Comparable cloze and multiple choice comprehension test scores. *Journal of Reading, 13,* 193–198.

Serafini, F. (2001). Three paradigms of assessment: Measurement, procedure, and inquiry. *The Reading Teacher,* 384–393.

Siegler, R. S. (1989). Strategy diversity and cognitive assessment. *Educational Researcher, 18* (9), 15–20.

Silvaroli, N. J. (1997). *Classroom reading inventory* (8th ed.). Madison, WI: Brown & Benchmark Publishers.

Silvaroli, N. J., & Wheelock, W. H. (2001). *Classroom reading inventory* (9th ed.). New York: McGraw Hill.

Skillings, M. J., & Ferrell, R. (2000). Student-generated rubrics: Bringing students into the assessment process. *The Reading Teacher,* 452–455.

Spache, G. S. (1953). A new readability formula for primary grade reading material. *Elementary English, 53,* 410–413.

Spache, G. S. (1976). The new Spache readability formula. In *Good reading for poor readers* (pp. 195–207). Champaign, IL: Garrard.

Stiggins, R. (2001). *Student-involved classroom assessment* (3rd ed.). Upper Saddle River, NJ: Merrill/Prentice-Hall.

Taylor, W. L. (1953). Cloze procedures: A new tool for measuring readability. *Journalism Quarterly, 30,* 415–433.

Tierney, R. J., Carter, M. A., & Desai, L. E. (1991). *Portfolio assessment in the reading-writing classroom.* Norwood, MA: Christopher-Gordon.

Tierney, R. J., Johnson, P., Moore, D. W., & Valencia, S. W. (2000). How will literacy be assessed in the next millennium? *Reading Research Quarterly, 35*(2), 244–250.

Traill, L. (1993). *Highlight my strengths: Assessment and evaluation of literacy learning.* Crystal Lake, IL: Rigby Education.

Tuinman, J. J. (1974). Determining the passage-dependency of comprehension questions in 5 major tests. *Reading Research Quarterly, 9,* 207–223.

Valencia, S., & Pearson, P. D. (1987). Reading assessment: Time for a change. *The Reading Teacher, 40,* 726–735.

Villegas, A. M. (1990). *Culturally responsive pedagogy for the 1990s and beyond.* Princeton, NJ: Educational Testing Service.

Wade, S. E. (1990). Using think-alouds to assess comprehension. *The Reading Teacher, 43,* 44–53.

Warwick, G. E. (1978). Cloze procedures as applied to reading. In O. K. Buros (Ed.), *Eighth mental measurements yearbook* (vol. 2, pp. 1174–1176). Highland Park, NJ: Gryphon Press.

Wiener, R. B., & Cohen, J. H. (1997). *Literacy portfolios: Using assessment to guide instruction.* Upper Saddle River, NJ: Merrill/Prentice Hall.

Williams, J. (1973). *Petronella.* New York: Scholastic.

Wittrock, M. C. (1987). Process oriented measures of comprehension. *The Reading Teacher, 40,* 734–737.

Wixson, K. K., Bosky, A. B., Yochum, N., & Alvermann, D. E. (1984). An interview for assessing students' perceptions of classroom reading tasks. *The Reading Teacher, 37,* 346–352.

Yancey, K. B. (Ed.). (1992). *Portfolios in the writing classroom: An introduction.* Urbana, IL: National Council of Teachers of English.

Including All Children in Your Literacy Classroom

 E-mail from the Classroom

Subject: Diversity
From: Nicole Gamble, ddnrg@IX.NETCOM.COM

My students learned a very valuable lesson this week about diversity and empathy. We have been reading *Princess Pooh* by Kathleen Muldoon. It's a story about two sisters, one of whom happens to be in a wheelchair. After talking about what might be difficult about being in a wheelchair, we invited a first-grade student who uses an electric wheelchair into our classroom to demonstrate how it works. She answered a lot of our questions and the students were very interested in what she had to share. In our discussion we found out that she was unable to use a drinking fountain in school because the only wheelchair-accessible drinking fountain had been broken all year. After she left, my class asked if they could write a letter to the principal and find out about fixing the drinking fountain. They wrote the letter, took it to the principal, and the drinking fountain got fixed! The principal came into the class and told everyone that she appreciated how much they cared. It turns out that new parts for the drinking fountain had been ordered and had arrived, but the maintenance department hadn't made it a priority to fix it. What a great lesson!

Nicole

Key Concepts

book buddies

children with hearing impairments

enrichment program

giftedness

inclusive classrooms

individualized education program (IEP)

Individuals with Disabilities Education
    Act (IDEA)

language disorders

learning disability

least restrictive environment (LRE)

mainstreamed

mental retardation

PL 94–142

Reading Recovery

special education

speech disorders

visual impairment

After reading this chapter, you should be able to:

1. Explain why each child in your class is a child with special needs.
2. Adapt reading instruction to create a classroom community supportive of all children.
3. Use technology resources to support children with special needs.
4. Explain how your literacy framework informs instructional decisions as you teach children with special needs.

Meet Individual Needs, Including Children with Special Needs: A Principle of Effective Literacy Instruction

Several recent trends require literacy educators to work with a wider range of children than ever before as we witness an increasing respect for the unique needs of all children (Mercer & Mercer, 1998). Today, federal and state legislation require schools to provide a free and appropriate public education for all children, including those who are in need of special educational support. Moreover, federal legislation now insists these needs be met, to the maximum extent appropriate for the special education child, in regular classrooms. Children who were formally excluded from regular school classrooms are increasingly joining their peers in what are coming to be called "inclusive classrooms."

However, the movement is not being directed simply by federal legislation and policy debates. Increasingly, teachers themselves are finding important benefits for all children when they include youngsters who were previously excluded from regular classrooms. Consequently, it is imperative to understand the literacy needs of all types of children. Understanding these needs will allow you to take advantage of the new opportunities for meeting the needs of all students in your classroom. In this chapter, we will explore this ninth principle of effective literacy instruction:

9. **Meet individual needs, including children with special needs.** An effective literacy program should seek to meet as wide a range of individual needs as possible within the classroom, including the needs of those who are formally designated as children with special needs (Allington, 1991; Allington & Johnston, 1989; Au, 2000).

As we consider how to do this, we should be guided by three thoughts. The most important is that each of our students is a child with special needs. Each and every child has unique needs that must be acknowledged as you make instructional decisions. We must always consider each child's background and abilities as we teach reading. Nothing is more important.

The second point is related to the first: categorical designations used for pedagogical, legal, or administrative purposes must never limit our instructional decisions regarding individual children or our expectations for their achievement. Categorical designations for different populations appear in this chapter for three reasons: (1) because they are used in legal definitions for categorical aid programs, (2) because they are sometimes used for administrative purposes, and (3) because they facilitate your learning as a new teacher. However, you must never allow the use of categories by others outside your classroom to interfere with the individual learning needs of any child within your classroom. Your instructional decisions must always take into account the unique differences of each individual child. The use of labels has brought significant benefits to students whose needs have too long been ignored, but we must ensure that those labels do not blind us to the individuality each of us expresses in our daily lives.

Finally, a third thought should also guide us: Having children with special needs in our classroom provides an opportunity to celebrate and learn about diversity as we work to develop inclusive communities. Working with children with special needs provides opportunities—not an additional burden—for both us and our students. If we want to prepare students for the realities of contemporary life in a pluralistic society, we must seek out and celebrate diversity. Classrooms that celebrate diversity help each of us learn more about ourselves and our society. We can do this by including each child into the full measure of life in our classroom community. This chapter will provide instructional suggestions about how to develop a community in your classroom to support the learning of all children.

First, we will discuss support provided for children who are experiencing difficulties acquiring literacy but who have not been formally identified as exceptional. Then we will explore the situation for children with exceptionalities.

Check your ongoing understanding of chapter concepts by using the guided review for this chapter on http://www. prenhall.com/leukinzer

Children Who Are Experiencing Difficulties Acquiring Literacy

In many schools, especially in the lower grades, some children experience great difficulty in acquiring literacy. These children often receive support from special teachers in reading and writing, reading specialists, or tutors trained in one of several specific intervention programs for reading.

Local, state, and federal resources often are available to hire specially trained reading specialists to assist children in your class who experience difficulties acquiring literacy. These teachers usually have completed their master's degree in reading or literacy and received certification as a reading specialist by the state.

Assistance will be provided in either a "push-in" or a "pull-out" program. Push-in programs provide special assistance to children who require it within your classroom. The specialist will work closely with you to develop a program in your classroom to provide additional support for children who require it. Pull-out programs provide special assistance to children outside your classroom, usually in a separate room with several other children experiencing difficulty with literacy acquisition.

Regardless of which type of program your school uses, make every effort to have this extra help provided in addition to the regular reading instruction you provide. Try to avoid scheduling the assistance at the same time when reading instruction normally takes place. Children experiencing difficulty benefit when they receive this support *in addition to* their regular reading instruction, not as a replacement for it.

Some schools will provide assistance in reading through one of several intervention programs such as Reading Recovery, Success for All, Prevention of Learning Disabilities, The Wallach Tutoring Program, or Programmed Tutorial Reading (Wasik & Slavin, 1993). In various ways, these programs seek to provide special support with literacy learning. We will describe Reading Recovery since it is targeted specifically to reading.

In **Reading Recovery** lessons, specially trained teachers provide early intervention for children experiencing difficulty in their first year of reading instruction. Reading Recovery lessons take place for 30 minutes each day and usually include the following elements (Pinnell, Fried, & Estice, 1990).

Reading Recovery
One of several forms of early intervention programs for children experiencing difficulty learning to read, providing 30 minutes of intensive tutoring per day in literacy.

1. *Reading familiar stories.* The child and the teacher select a work they have read several times previously and the child reads it for fluency.
2. *Taking a running record.* The child reads a book he or she read for the first time on the previous day while the teacher takes a running record, noting his or her accuracy rate and the quality of miscues.
3. *Working with letters.* Often this takes place as the child and the teacher construct words from magnetic letters.
4. *Writing a message or story.* Each day, the child composes a short message in a special book. Usually this writing sample is one or two sentences long. These words often are then copied onto a sentence strip and used to practice word recognition.
5. *Reading a new book.* Each day, the child is introduced to a new book and reads it for the first time with assistance from the teacher.

Complete agreement does not exist about the effectiveness of each of these formally organized intervention programs, especially in relation to the costs involved (Barnes, 1997a, 1997b; Browne, Fitts, McLaughlin, McNamara, & Williams, 1997; Dudley-Marling & Murphy, 1997; Shanahan & Barr, 1995; Wasik & Slavin, 1993). Nevertheless, each tends to generally follow effective principles of good reading instruction and you are likely to see them in your school.

Understanding the History and Context of Children with Exceptionalities

children with exceptionalities
Children unable to reach their full potential without services that go beyond the requirements of the average child.

Children with exceptionalities are unable to reach their full potential without services, instructional materials, and/or facilities that go beyond the requirements of the average child. Typically, this includes those who experience a learning disability, emotional disturbance,

FIGURE 12-1

A continuum of special educational environments and services

→ Least Restrictive →

←Inclusion Models→

Most Restrictive ←

1. Classroom instruction by a regular classroom teacher, trained in both regular and special education, who is provided with special materials or who adapts existing materials to meet individual needs.
2. Classroom instruction by the regular classroom teacher in consultation with a specialist in special education.
3. Classroom instruction by a classroom team comprising the regular classroom teacher and one or more special education teachers who work together to meet the needs of all students.
4. Itinerant services provided by a special educator who regularly visits and teaches the exceptional child within the regular classroom. Itinerant teachers also make instructional suggestions to the regular classroom teacher.
5. Resource services provided by a special educator outside the classroom. Exceptional children receive instruction in a resource center for a portion of the day. The resource teacher also consults with the classroom teacher regarding instruction within the classroom.
6. Self-contained special education classrooms within the regular school for homogeneous classes of exceptional children.

hearing impairment, visual impairment, speech or language disorders, mental retardation, or giftedness. According to federal estimates, approximately 13 to 16 percent of school-age children fall into at least one of these categories (Hallahan & Kauffman, 1982; Lerner, 1985; U.S. Department of Education, 1993).

special education
Services, materials, and/or facilities provided to help exceptional children reach their full potential.

Special education encompasses the educational services, materials, and/or facilities provided to help children with exceptionalities reach their full potential. The specific nature of special education varies along a continuum ranging from the least to the most restrictive environments, as shown in Figure 12-1. The figure shows that regular classroom teachers have opportunities to work with exceptional students in more than half of the environments described. Increasingly, special educational services are provided entirely within **inclusive classrooms.** Therefore, it is important that all teachers understand special education and the needs of children with exceptionalities.

inclusive classrooms
Classrooms where exceptional students are included in the classroom community and receive their special instructional support within the regular classroom.

Federal Legislation

Historically, the most important influence in the education of exceptional children was a federal law passed in 1975—The Education for All Handicapped Children Act, or **PL (Public Law) 94–142.** For the first time, schools receiving federal funds were required to educate every child, no matter how serious the handicapping condition. The defining provision of PL 94–142 states:

PL 94–142 The first federal legislation mandating a free and appropriate public education for all children, regardless of handicap.

> In order to receive funds under the act every school system in the nation must make provision for a free, appropriate public education for every child . . . regardless of how, or how seriously, he (sic) may be handicapped.

While PL 94–142 has recently been updated, this pioneering legislation established two additional elements that currently remain as central elements in the education of exceptional children: (a) the development of individualized education programs for each child formally entered into a special education program, and (b) a principle of placing children in a least-restrictive environment and, to the maximum extent appropriate, with students who do not have disabilities.

All children, regardless of ability, benefit from experience with print.

Individualized Education Programs

Ever since PL 94–142, federal law has required that a multidisciplinary team evaluate each exceptional child and each potential exceptional child. This team submits a report to a case conference meeting at which a representative from the school, in addition to the teacher, the parents, and other appropriate individuals develop an **individualized education program (IEP).** The IEP is used to guide instruction and monitor student progress. According to current federal guidelines, an IEP must contain the following components:

individualized education program (IEP) Instructional plans for each exceptional child used to guide instruction and monitor progress.

▶ A statement of the child's present level of educational performance
▶ A statement of annual goals, including short-term instructional objectives
▶ A statement of the specific educational services to be provided
▶ An explanation of how the child's disability affects his or her involvement and progress in the general curriculum
▶ An explanation of the extent to which a child will not participate in the general education class
▶ The projected date for the beginning of special education services and modifications and their anticipated frequency, location, and duration
▶ At age 14, a statement of the child's transition service needs (Individuals with Disabilities Education Act, as amended in 1997).

The Least-Restrictive Environment

One of the most important decisions made at the case conference is the recommended instructional environment. Participants in that conference must state in the IEP the extent to which the child will be included in the regular classroom. Federal law requires that exceptional children be placed in the **least-restrictive environment (LRE)** possible, where maximum opportunity is provided for those students to engage in the full measure of school life, consistent with their educational needs. Thus, children should not be educated in a separate special education classroom if their needs can be adequately met in a regular classroom with outside instruction provided by a special educator. Other children should not leave the regular classroom for special assistance if their needs can be adequately met by the regular classroom teacher. In short, exceptional children are to be included in the mainstream of educational life and in regular classrooms wherever possible.

least-restrictive environment (LRE) A learning environment in which maximum opportunity is provided for exceptional students to engage in the full measure of school life, consistent with their educational needs. Increasingly, this is within regular classrooms.

The principle of LRE has been given a recent boost by an initiative of the federal government. This "regular education initiative" is an effort to review, coordinate, and improve mainstreaming in schools (Mercer & Mercer, 1998; Wood, 1992). Increasingly, the regular classroom is viewed as the most-appropriate and least-restrictive environment for special education students who had formerly been excluded from these settings. As a result, the education of special education students is increasingly taking place within inclusive classrooms as regular and special educators work together to develop supportive learning communities for all students.

How will this affect you as a classroom teacher of reading? Should you have the opportunity to have an exceptional child in your classroom, you will be affected in three ways. First, you will be required to attend the case conference meeting and assist in planning the student's IEP. Second, if the multidisciplinary team decides to mainstream your student for reading instruction, you will be responsible for implementing the IEP in your classroom. You may be totally responsible for reading instruction, you may work together with a special education teacher or support person in your classroom, or you may provide the instruction in consultation with a special education teacher who may advise you about materials and methods. Finally, you may be responsible for evaluating the degree to which your student has met the specified instructional objectives. With the multidisciplinary team, you will then decide on new instructional objectives.

Individuals with Disabilities Education Act (IDEA)

Individuals with Disabilities Education Act (IDEA) Legislation updating PL 94–142 providing regulations making inclusive education more of an option for students.

In 1997, federal legislation was updated by the reauthorization of the **Individuals with Disabilities Education Act (IDEA),** which has added several important new requirements for schools. These include the principle of zero rejection, the principle of nondiscriminatory evaluation, procedural due process, and parental and student participation. Each is important for you to consider as you prepare to work with children in classrooms.

The principle of zero rejection prohibits schools from excluding any student with a disability from a free and appropriate public education. Schools may not exclude any child from a free and appropriate public education no matter how severe the child's disability. Each district must provide for educating all of its students.

The principle of nondiscriminatory evaluation requires each school district to fairly evaluate students as they determine which students have a disability and which do not. Often, it has been the case that children from less-advantaged populations have been identified as children with exceptionalities with higher frequencies than children from more-advantaged populations. Often this appears to be due to cultural and/or linguistic biases that exist in many assessment instruments used to screen students into special education programs. Schools today are attempting to ensure that the assessment process does not discriminate on the basis of cultural or linguistic background.

In addition, schools are now required to provide due process to parents and children. The requirement of due process is an attempt to safeguard students and parents against any action of the school that may be harmful. Due process rights include the parents' right to sue in court in order to be certain that the appropriate services are provided for their child.

Finally, the Individuals with Disabilities Education Act requires schools to provide opportunities for parents and adolescent students to participate in designing and carrying out special education programs. Parents and adolescent students will be invited to participate in IEP conferences, and their insights will be sought during the implementation of these plans.

General Guidelines for Including All Students in Your Classroom Literacy Program

Beyond accommodating a child's particular disability, literacy instruction for children receiving special educational services does not differ substantially from the materials,

Celebrating Diversity

Using the Internet to Learn More about Inclusive Classrooms

If you have the opportunity to work with children in an inclusive classroom, you will want to bring the best insights, the best ideas, and the best materials to the children in your charge. There are many fine works of children's literature, as illustrated in Figure 12-3 on p. 449, for you to consider as part of your program. In addition, outstanding resources are appearing on the Internet to support you and your children on this journey. You may wish to visit some of these locations to discover how best to meet the needs of all children in your classroom:

Family Village (http://www.familyvillage.wisc.edu/)—This is an excellent central site for children with mental retardation and other exceptionalities. See Figure 12-2 on p. 448. Set a bookmark!

Special Education Resources on the Internet (SERI) (http://seriweb.com)—This is one of the best central sites on the Internet for special education resources. It contains a comprehensive and well-organized set of links to locations important for special education issues.

Internet Resources for Special Children (http://www.irsc.org/)—This is another central site with extensive resources on special education.

Accessibility Center (http://www-3.ibm.com/able/index.html)—If you are using Windows-based computers, this location contains links to many useful technologies, including voice input and text reader technologies.

SPECED–L (speced-1@uga.cc.uga.edu)—A useful mailing list for discussion about issues in special education.

SPEDTALK (majordomo@virginia.edu)—Another good mailing list for discussions about issues in special education.

SPEDTECH–L (listproc@ukanaix.cc.ukans.edu)—A mailing list devoted to discussions of technology and special education.

E-mail from the Classroom

Subject: Inclusion
From: Liz Mascia, emascia@jd.cnyric.org

Hi, folks!

Inclusion is not always easy, but it works and is exciting for both teachers and students. One of the most uplifting parts of my day is to walk down the hall and see all of our children making their ways to their destinations. Our school community is diverse, perhaps more diverse than our students will experience as adults since, unfortunately, people do sort themselves by all sorts of criteria once they leave the public arena. I see children being tolerant and kind to less-able peers and classmates who are different from them in some way. These are lessons that are learned by living them, not by being told about them.

Let me also add that I am already thinking about how much I will miss our listserv when our course ends. Teaching can be so isolating, and, as much as we would like it to be otherwise, days can go by without there being time to chat with a colleague about a timely issue. The listserv lets that happen.

Liz

Children can support each other and often benefit from working in pairs if teachers closely monitor the activity and if expectations are clear for each learner.

FIGURE 12-2

Family Village (http://www.familyvillage.wisc.edu/), a central site for special education and inclusion resources

Note: Courtesy of Family Village.

FIGURE 12-3

A selected bibliography of children's literature and special education selections

General

H. Bornstein (Ed.), *The Comprehensive Signed English Dictionary* (Washington, DC: Gallaudet College Press)

B. B. Osman, *No One to Play With: The Social Side of Learning Disabilities* (New York: Random House)

J. Quicke, *Disability in Modern Children's Fiction* (Cambridge, MA: Brookline Books)

Physical Disability

J. Cowen-Fletcher, *Mama Zooms* (New York: Scholastic Inc.)

C. DeFelice, *The Light on Hogback Hill* (New York: Macmillan)

P. D. Frevert, *It's OK to Look at Jamie* (Mankato, MN: Creative Education)

M. W. Froehlich, *Hide Crawford Quick* (Boston, MA: Houghton Mifflin)

L. Henriod, *Grandma's Wheelchair* (Niles, IL: Whitman)

A. G. Hines, *Gramma's Walk* (New York: Greenwillow)

R. C. Jones, *Angie and Me* (New York: Macmillan)

J. Kremetz, *How it Feels to Live with a Disability* (New York: Simon & Schuster)

B. Rabe, *The Balancing Girl* (New York: Dutton)

R. Roy, *Move Over, Wheelchairs Coming Through!* (Boston, MA: Houghton Mifflin)

M. Russo, *Alex Is My Friend* (New York: Greenwillow)

Mental Retardation

A. Baldwin, *A Little Time* (New York: Viking Press)

C. Berkus, *Charlie's Chuckle* (Rockville, MD: Woodbine House)

B. Byars, *Summer of the Swans* (New York: Viking Press)

V. Fleming, *Be Good to Eddie Lee* (New York: Philomel Books)

P. Hermes, *Who Will Take Care of Me?* (New York: Harcourt Brace Jovanovich)

N. Hopper, *Just Vernon* (New York: Dutton)

K. Kesey, *The Sea Lion* (New York: Viking Press)

H. Sobol, *My Brother Stephen Is Retarded* (New York: Macmillan)

N. H. Wilson, *The Reason for Janey* (New York: Macmillan)

J. Wood, *When Pigs Fly* (New York: G. P. Putnam's Sons)

B. R. Wright, *My Sister Is Different* (Milwaukee, WI: Raintree)

Learning Disabilities

L. Albert, *But I'm Ready to Go* (Scarsdale, NY: Bradbury Press)

J. Gilson, *Do Bananas Chew Gum?* (New York: Lathrop)

E. Hunter, *Sue Ellen* (New York: Houghton Mifflin)

J. Lasker, *He's My Brother* (Chicago, IL: Albert Whitman)

D. B. Smith, *Kelly's Creek* (New York: Crowell)

Hearing Impairment

R. Charlip and M. B. Charlip, *Hand Talk: An ABC of Finger Spelling and Sign Language* (New York: Four Winds Press)

J. M. Lee, *Silent Lotus* (New York: Farrar Straus & Giroux)

G. Maguire, *Missing Sisters* (New York: Macmillan)

J. W. Peterson, *I Have a Sister. My Sister Is Deaf* (New York: Harper & Row)

M. Riskind, *Apple Is My Sign* (Boston, MA: Houghton Mifflin)

L. Rosen, *Just Like Everyone Else* (New York: Harcourt Brace Jovanovich)

B. Wolf, *Anna's Silent World* (Philadelphia, PA: Lippincott)

FIGURE 12-3

Continued

Visual Impairment
E. Bloor, *Tangerine* (San Diego, CA: Harcourt Brace & Co.)
C. Brighton, *My Hands, My World* (New York: Macmillan)
M. Cohen, *See You Tomorrow, Charles* (New York: Greenwillow)
H. Coutant, *The Gift* (New York: Knopf)
B. D. Goldin, *Cakes and Miracles* (New York: Viking)
J. Little, *Listen for the Singing* (New York: E. P. Dutton)
P. MacLachlan, *Through Grandpa's Eyes* (New York: Harper & Row)
N. Moon, *Lucy's Picture* (New York: Dial Books)
M. Norris, *Sees Behind Trees* (New York: Hyperion Books)
J. Taylor, *Timothy of the Cay* (San Diego, CA: Harcourt Brace & Co.)
J. Yalen, *The Seeing Stick* (New York: Thomas Y. Crowell)

Speech and Language Disorders
M. Christopher, *Glue Fingers* (Toronto: Little, Brown)
P. Fleischman, *The Half-a-Moon Inn* (New York: Harper & Row)
E. B. White, *The Trumpet of the Swan* (New York: Harper & Row)

methods, and activities described in previous chapters. Good teaching is good teaching. Literacy instruction for every child requires insightful selection from the range of instructional suggestions presented in this text. Nonetheless, the following suggestions should guide you as you integrate children receiving special educational services into your classroom literacy program.

1. *Work actively to develop a sense of community in your classroom where each member is valued.* Try, whenever possible, to structure learning experiences in cooperative learning groups. In these settings, each student is supported by the experiences and knowledge that others bring to the group. Include literature selections about exceptionalities in your students' reading experiences and in your read-aloud sessions. Use these opportunities to initiate discussions about the concerns and feelings of all members of your classroom community. This focus will help your students respect the unique qualities of each member of the class. (A list of appropriate selections begins on page 449.) Finally, help students to recognize the unique contributions each member of your classroom community makes to the class.

2. *Capitalize on individual strengths.* When necessary, work around an exceptionality by taking advantage of the individual's strengths. A child with a hearing impairment, for example, may require a more visual approach than a child without one. Pictures might be needed to complement verbal definitions during vocabulary instruction.

3. *Ensure successful learning experiences.* Try to build success into your instruction by carefully considering what each child can be expected to do.

4. *Record and chart individual growth to demonstrate gains to children and parents.* Make individual growth more visible by listing individual achievements and by keeping examples of work in a portfolio. Recording growth makes it concrete and tangible.

5. *Establish an accepting and positive environment.* Praise success with enthusiasm; accept failure with tolerance. Realize that mistakes are an important part of learning. Try to compliment each child in your class each day and encourage your students to do the same.

6. *Discuss your students' progress regularly with parents, special educators, and other teachers.* It is important to keep others informed of your work. It is also important to learn from others about ideas that may work. Keep a list of the ideas others have found successful.

7. *Redefine the content of the task to match the child's background knowledge.* When a child experiences difficulty, this modification will make the task easier and will lead to initial success. Once children have been successful and understand the nature of the task, have them try it with less-familiar content.

8. *Be willing to change materials, strategies, and activities when a student has not been successful.* Do not continuously repeat unsuccessful learning experiences. Find other approaches that work and maintain them.

9. *Do not search for a single solution to literacy difficulties.* Literacy is a complicated developmental process. No single set of materials or activities will solve a literacy problem.

10. *Provide independent reading opportunities.* All children need time to read for pleasure or personal information.

11. *Use the Internet and other resources to continually upgrade your knowledge of exceptionalities.* Our knowledge in this area is expanding rapidly so be certain you are up to date with the latest information.

Supporting Children with Learning Disabilities

The term **learning disability** was first used in 1963 by Samuel Kirk to refer to children who, despite normal intelligence, had great difficulty learning in school. Since then, a variety of definitions have evolved, including these most common characteristics:

learning disability A substantial gap between expected and actual achievement levels, which cannot be attributed to mental retardation or emotional disturbance.

▶ A substantial gap between expected achievement levels (based on intelligence scores) and actual performance in at least one academic subject area

▶ An uneven achievement profile, with achievement very high in some areas and very low in others

▶ Low achievement levels that do not result from environmental factors

▶ Low achievement levels that are not due to mental retardation or emotional disturbance

The federal definition, from IDEA, is the most widely used:

> "Specific learning disability" means a disorder in one or more of the basic psychological processes involved in understanding or in using language, spoken or written, which may manifest itself in an imperfect ability to listen, think, speak, read, write, spell, or do mathematical calculations. The term includes such conditions as perceptual handicaps, brain injury, minimal brain dysfunction, dyslexia, and developmental aphasia. The term does not include children who have learning problems which are primarily the result of visual, hearing, or motor handicaps, or mental retardation or emotional disturbance, or of environmental, cultural, or economic disadvantage. (Federal Register 42, p. 65083)

Following this federal definition, most school districts require three elements to classify a child as having a learning disability:

1. A demonstrated and significant difference between a child's potential and actual achievement in at least one subject area

2. A determination that the disability is not due to other factors such as visual, hearing, or motor handicaps; mental retardation; emotional disturbance; or an environmental, cultural, or economic disadvantage

3. A demonstrated need for services

Students with learning disabilities represent 3.75 percent of all students ages 6 to 21 (U.S. Department of Education, 1992).

E-mail from the Classroom

From: Deb, John, and Daniel Nickerson, cen07606@MAIL.PC.CENTURYINTER.NET
Subject: At Risk Children, Motivation, and Inclusion

Hi,

I just completed a year of co-teaching a sixth-grade reading class with at-risk and special ed students included. The only pull-out that was done was to help complete the regular classroom assignments. After a year of this program my special ed students showed at least 1 year's growth in reading, and one more than 2 year's growth. We did a great deal of teacher reading aloud and group discussions. When we discussed, we began by having cooperative groups answer the question and then each reporter shared the answer with the big group. This way most felt that they were heard. I feel that this was the best way to adapt instruction for these kids, but it can't be done without good team teaching with time to plan together, the ability to accommodate assignments when necessary, and the ability to be flexible when it comes to pulling out.

Deb N.

Learning Characteristics

Students with learning disabilities do not all share a common set of learning characteristics because different psychological processes are impaired in different children. The most common characteristic found in children with learning disabilities is some disruption in language processing. Because reading and writing are language-based processes, children with learning disabilities frequently have extreme difficulty learning how to read and write. Consequently, their achievement in these areas may be more than 2 years behind grade level (Harris & Sipay, 1990).

Other characteristics that are likely to appear and should be accommodated during instruction include:

▸ *Perceptual-motor problems.* Students may lack both fine- and gross-motor coordination. They may appear clumsy. Writing is often labored and hard to read. Many reversals appear in letter formation (for example, *d* for *b*, *z* for *s*) and letter order (for example, *tac* for *cat*), persisting beyond the age of 7 or 8. They may often confuse similar appearing words (for example, *saw* for *was*).
▸ *Attention problems.* Students may have short attention spans. They may be easily distracted and have difficulty completing regular class assignments on time.
▸ *Lack of effective learning and problem-solving strategies.* Students may not be aware of effective strategies for learning and problem solving.

Adapting Learning Environments

At least three general categories of instructional approaches have been used to adapt reading instruction for children experiencing a learning disability: language-based approaches, multi-modality approaches, and technology approaches.

language-based approaches Instruction that provides functional reading experiences with extensive writing and oral language opportunities.

Language-based approaches often are suggested for children experiencing reading disabilities. Such approaches provide functional reading experiences in motivating and pleasurable environments, usually with children's literature and extensive writing experiences. The most practical and clear set of recommendations for classroom teachers has been provided by Ford and Ohlhausen (1988), who make the following suggestions:

▸ Focus on real, meaningful learning through the use of themes.
▸ Maximize the participation of readers by using language activities that capitalize on their strong oral language skills.

Celebrating Diversity

Considering Method Frameworks from an Inclusion Perspective

Deb Nickerson shares an important lesson in her e-mail message on page 452. She describes several accommodations in her classroom to ensure full participation in the daily learning experiences of her classroom community: read-alouds with literature so that all children can experience a common story experience and cooperative learning groups so that all children can participate in discussions and learning experiences. As you consider how to accommodate the learning needs of all the children in your classroom, many method frameworks will provide you with opportunities to help them learn from one another. These method frameworks include much social interaction and support among students as they learn together important elements of literacy. Method frameworks that inclusive classrooms find especially useful include: Internet Workshop, Internet Project, read-aloud sessions, cooperative learning groups, grand conversations, literature discussion groups, text sets, readers theater, keypals, peer conferences, and language experience activities. Each method framework provides important support for children who may require it. Each also engages your children in active consideration of one another's needs—an important component of any classroom program.

> ▶ Implement whole room activities that have built-in individualization . . . [such as] sustained silent reading (chapter 4) and journal writing.
>
> ▶ Use open-ended projects that allow students to contribute at various levels with various skills . . . [such as] the publication of a class newspaper and the production of a drama.
>
> ▶ Plan writing activities that allow individuals to respond at their own levels . . . [such as] using patterned stories and poetry. . . .
>
> ▶ Use group incentives and internal competition to motivate readers.
>
> ▶ Implement a cross-grade arrangement with a group of younger students.
>
> ▶ Organize and participate in a support group with other teachers who work with readers experiencing a learning disability. (pp. 18–22)

Students with learning disabilities typically receive additional reading instruction from a learning disability specialist or a reading specialist. The goal is to maintain the child as much as possible in a regular classroom reading program (Lerner, 1985). When an outside person and a classroom teacher are both working with a youngster, it is important that instruction be consistent (Allington & Shake, 1986; Walp & Walmsley, 1989). Otherwise children can become confused. Teacher and specialist need to communicate regularly regarding instructional approaches and materials, sharing teaching strategies that seem to be especially productive.

When **multi-modality approaches** are used, children receive information simultaneously through visual, auditory, kinesthetic, and tactile modalities (VAKT). Receiving information through multiple channels of sensory input is thought to make learning more likely.

The most common VAKT method is one originally developed by Fernald (Fernald, 1943; Tierney, Readence, & Dishner, 1985). With that method, letters and words are first taught to students by having them simultaneously see (visual), hear (auditory), and trace (kinesthetic and tactile) words with their fingers. Sometimes sandpaper letters are used to enhance tactile input. After the letters and some words are learned, children receive reading instruction based on what they write themselves, much like language experience methods. Such writing experiences provide important language input through each of the identified modalities and thus contribute to the development of reading.

Technology approaches seek to support early reading and writing acquisition through opportunities with supportive technologies. Often these include the use of

multi-modality approaches Methods of teaching reading to children through visual, auditory, kinesthetic, and tactile (VAKT) modalities.

technology approaches A strategy for assisting early reading and writing acquisition through opportunities with supportive technologies. Often these include the use of talking storybook software, word processing software, and communication experiences on the Internet.

talking storybook software, word processing software, and communication experiences on the Internet. The use of talking storybooks (see chapter 6) provides children with support in decoding, a common concern for children with learning disabilities. Clicking on an unfamiliar word in a talking storybook will provide the child with the pronunciation. Others may choose to listen to an entire sentence or the entire page. The engaging nature of these experiences helps children to rekindle an interest in reading, something that has often been lost in a task perceived as a continual struggle.

Word processing software assists children with learning disabilities in several ways. First, it reduces the frustration these children experience with awkward letter formation. Typing on a keyboard is much easier than forming letters by hand, especially since each letter appears precisely formed on the screen. Moreover, looking at letters on the keyboard may increase letter-recognition skills. Finally, word processors provide children with the opportunity to use spell checkers to improve accuracy in spelling, an area that is often difficult for children with learning disabilities.

Internet Resources for Children with Learning Disabilities

Internet communication experiences are another way to support literacy learning with children who experience learning disabilities. Keypal activities, Internet Projects, and Internet Workshop are often useful to rekindle interest in reading and writing and in providing engaging literacy experiences.

There are several useful sources of information on the Internet to support you in your work with children with learning disabilities. These include:

Learning Disabilities Association of America (http://www.ldam.org/)—This is the major organization for parents of children with learning disabilities. Many useful resources are located here.

National Information Center for Children and Youth with Disabilities (http://www.nichcy.org/)—This location contains a number of useful resources and articles on learning disabilities.

Supporting Children with Emotional Disturbances

emotionally disturbed
Individuals with normal intelligence who achieve substantially below expected levels because of chronic withdrawal, anxiety, and/or aggressive behavior.

There is no widely accepted definition of children who are **emotionally disturbed.** However, three features are found in most definitions of emotional disturbance:

1. Behavior that goes to an extreme; that is, behavior that is not just slightly different from the usual.
2. A problem that is chronic; that is, one that does not disappear.
3. Behavior that is unacceptable because of social or cultural expectations.

Approximately 3 to 5 percent of all children and adolescents have emotional or behavior disorders (Koyanagi & Gaines, 1993), but teachers are likely to encounter children who experience serious and persistent emotional and behavioral problems who have not been formally identified (Turnbull, Turnbull, Shank, & Leal, 1995).

Learning Characteristics

Children experiencing emotional disturbance have, at a minimum, a normal intellectual ability, but achieve substantially below expected levels because of withdrawal, anxiety, and/or aggressive behavior. Each of those behaviors reflects a different set of learning characteristics, often in combination, that need to be accommodated during instruction.

Withdrawal

1. May be without friends and may have difficulty working cooperatively in groups
2. Often daydreams more than is normal for a particular age group
3. May appear secretive

Anxiety

1. May cry much more frequently than is normal
2. Often appears tense and nervous; may be easily embarrassed and overly sensitive to criticism
3. May appear depressed, sad, or troubled
4. Frequently is reluctant to independently attempt new tasks
5. May be afraid of making mistakes

Aggression

1. May frequently disrupt the classroom environment
2. May frequently be involved in physical aggression
3. May intentionally destroy the property of others

Adapting Learning Environments

Several instructional approaches often are used with children experiencing emotional difficulties: contract reading, bibliotherapy, and the use of book buddies. These approaches usually complement the regular literacy program in the classroom and do not, except in extreme cases, replace it. Such approaches are not limited to students who are emotionally disturbed; they can be used with all students.

Contract reading requires both teacher and student to agree that a defined set of reading experiences will be completed in a fixed time period. A reading contract usually is written by the teacher and then signed by the student. Upon completion, it is evaluated by the teacher or by both the teacher and the student and sometimes by the parents. Reading contracts can cover a single reading period or can extend over a number of periods. Contract reading can be useful in helping aggressive students control disruptive behavior and complete work on time. It can also help anxious students meet with success or can assist withdrawn children in interacting with others to complete learning experiences. An example of a contract used in conjunction with reading workshop is shown in Figure 12-4 on page 456.

contract reading An approach in which teacher and student agree to a document defining a set of reading experiences to be completed in a fixed time period.

Bibliotherapy refers to an "attempt to promote mental and emotional health by using reading materials to fulfill needs, relieve pressure, or help an individual in his (sic) development as a person" (Harris & Sipay, 1990, p. 682). A reader might find comfort or a solution to a real-life problem by interacting with literature related to an emotional difficulty. Reading about others with similar problems and seeing how they solve their difficulties often provides important therapy (D'Alessandro, 1990).

bibliotherapy Using literature to promote mental and emotional health.

A program of bibliotherapy requires literature selections related to the emotional difficulties students are experiencing. A librarian might be able to suggest selections. Bibliotherapy also requires special care in putting children in touch with appropriate materials. Self-selection is a possibility, as is introducing a number of related books to the entire class and hoping that target children are attracted to them.

Consultation with a school psychologist should precede any program of bibliotherapy. That specialist should be informed of plans and should be encouraged to give professional guidance throughout the program. Bibliotherapy should then be followed up with discussions, retellings, journal responses, role-playing, art projects, or other activities that allow students to respond to what they have read.

The use of **book buddies** is a third approach to working with children experiencing emotional difficulties. With book buddies, older children assist younger children with literacy activities, perhaps reading stories aloud to a group of younger children, listening to their oral reading, or participating in buddy journal activities. Children experiencing emotional problems can benefit from tutoring younger children or receiving instruction from an older tutor. Children often feel special in the new roles and relationships that develop through cross-age tutoring. Nevertheless, teachers must carefully choose, train, and supervise any students who work as tutors with younger children. Clear directions regarding specific responsibilities increase their chance of success.

book buddies Involvement of older or more-proficient students in assisting younger or less-proficient students.

FIGURE 12-4

A sample reading contract used in conjunction with reading workshop

```
                          READING CONTRACT

Date:   October 5

Description of the work to be completed:

    I will read Sarah's unicorn. Then I will
make an ad for it and put it up on our
Good Books bord.



This work will be completed on:   October 8

Signed:  Michael T.          Debbie Smith


Self evaluation:   I think I did good. Maria and
Sarah liked my ad. Sarah read the book
becaus it had her name.

Teacher evaluation:  Your ad encouraged someone else
to read your book. That's the best kind
of ad. GREAT!

Parent Comments and Signature(s):  Thank you for all the
special things you do. Mike read this to us at home
and we all enjoyed it.   Bob Tanner
```

In addition to the use of contract reading, bibliotherapy, and book buddies, there are important guidelines to follow while working with children who are experiencing emotional difficulties.

1. Be sure to complete an interest inventory before beginning reading instruction; motivation and interest are critical for these children. Then use reading materials that are interesting and engaging.
2. Communicate regularly with the specialist who provides services to your student(s). Use consistent management and instructional approaches and share observations regularly.
3. Communicate regularly with the parents or guardians of your student(s). Ask that you be kept informed if problems occur at home.
4. Explain clearly the rules in your classroom. Children need to understand exactly what is expected of them.
5. Provide literacy instruction at the student's instructional level. Begin with experiences with which your students can be successful and gradually increase the difficulty of literacy tasks.

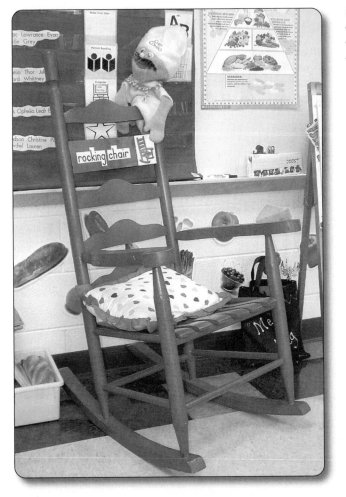

Labeling items in the classroom can help some learners make connections between concepts and words.

Celebrating Diversity

Sharing an Internet Secret

Often, children with emotional disturbances, or other children in your classroom who have not fully been appreciated by others, gain greatly from Internet use, especially when it is done appropriately. When you are about to introduce a new central site on the Internet for an upcoming unit or when you wish to introduce a new navigational strategy with the Internet, share this new information first with a student who has been less successful with school learning tasks before you share it with others. Then direct your other students to ask him or her to demonstrate the new resource or the new information. This quickly puts students who have been less successful into a privileged position—a position they have not always enjoyed. We encourage you to try this strategy. We have seen the results of this approach often enough to know that it is very promising. Children who possess important, new information on the Internet suddenly carry themselves differently in the classroom and begin to be seen with new respect by others.

6. Praise children in public. Reprimand them in private.
7. Maintain your classroom as a happy, calm, orderly, and protective environment for children. Model your concern for others and expect students to treat each other with respect.

🔲 Supporting Children with Hearing Impairments

children with hearing
impairments
Individuals with
permanently reduced
sensitivity to sounds softer
than 26 dB.

Children with hearing impairments have permanently reduced sensitivity to the sounds in their environment because of genetic factors, illness, or trauma. Usually, these children are not sensitive to sounds softer than about 26 decibels (dB). It is important for teachers to know the extent of the hearing loss. One categorization system used by the Conference of Executives of American Schools for the Deaf defines degrees of hearing impairment as follows:

> Individuals with hearing losses greater than 90 dB are usually considered deaf; those with a lesser loss are considered hard of hearing.

It is also important for teachers to know when the hearing loss took place. The earlier a loss occurs, the more likely it is that a child will have inadequately developed language. And since literacy depends on language knowledge, a child with an early hearing loss may have great difficulty acquiring higher levels of literacy, especially if the loss went undetected for a long time. Approximately 3 percent of school-age children are considered to have a mild-to-profound hearing loss (Lundeen, 1991).

Learning Characteristics

Depending on the degree of hearing loss, children compensate by using amplifying devices, speechreading (lipreading), sign language, or a combination of these methods to assist them. Teachers must realize that these students are very dependent on the visual information in a classroom, which includes facial expressions, lip movements, and writing. In addition, the following considerations should be kept in mind:

1. The language of children with a hearing impairment often is less-completely developed than the language of other children.
2. Children with a hearing impairment must concentrate very carefully on learning tasks presented orally. Fatigue can develop quickly, leading to inattentive behavior.
3. Children with amplifying devices are distracted by extraneous noises in the environment. Such devices amplify both target and background sounds.
4. Even though most schools screen children for hearing impairment, some children have mild or moderate hearing losses that go undetected. Consequently, teachers should be aware of classroom behaviors associated with hearing loss and should request a hearing evaluation for a child displaying some of the following symptoms:
   a. Frequent earaches, head colds, or sinus difficulties
   b. Difficulty following directions or frequent requests to have explanations repeated
   c. Quick fatigue during learning tasks
   d. Easy distraction by external noises
   e. Frequent mispronunciation of words
   f. Clearly immature language

Adapting Learning Environments

mainstreamed
Placement of students with
exceptionalities in inclusive
learning environments with
other students.

Children with hearing impairments are **mainstreamed** into inclusive classrooms. Of those who are mainstreamed, the majority have mild or moderate hearing losses. These children will often use adaptive technologies to increase their ability to hear sounds. Most mainstreamed children with profound or severe hearing losses have sign language interpreters who accompany them in the classroom. Teachers working with children who have hearing losses should consider these instructional suggestions:

1. Phonics instruction presents special problems to hearing-impaired children. Therefore, teachers should depend more on contextual analysis and sight word instruction and should present all new words in context.
2. Children with a hearing impairment should always sit close to the teacher, where they can clearly see the teacher's face and lips.

FIGURE 12-5

The location for **HandSpeak: A Sign Language Dictionary Online** (http://dww. deafworldweb.org/sl/), a wonderful resource for all your children to use to develop their signing abilities

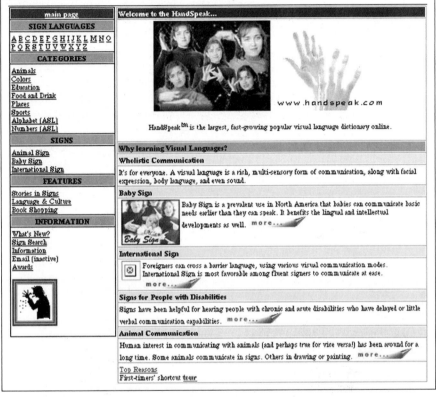

Note: Courtesy of HandSpeak.

3. Lipreading is easier for students if teachers speak normally, not with exaggerated lip movements and not too quickly or too slowly. Teachers should maintain eye contact with students and should stand still when speaking. Movement makes lipreading more difficult.

4. Because an amplifying device amplifies all sounds, teachers should attempt to limit extraneous noise in the classroom, especially during verbal instruction.

5. Periods of oral instruction should be limited. Several short sessions, separated by independent work, are better than a single long session.

6. Visual aids should be used as much as possible during vocabulary instruction and the explanation of directions.

Internet Resources for Children with Hearing Impairments

There are many wonderful websites to support children who are hearing impaired or deaf in your class. These sites should also be used to help your non-hearing impaired children learn to sign and become more familiar with the world of the deaf and hearing impaired. Here are just a few:

HandSpeak: A Sign Language Dictionary Online (http://dww.deafworldweb. org/sl/)—A great location for children to develop sign language skills. See Figure 12-5.

Hearing Impairment (http://seriweb.com/hearing.htm)—A good central site for hearing impairment with many useful links.

Interactive Finger Spelling and Braille Guide (http://www.disserv.stu. umn.edu/AltForm/)—This is a great place for non-hearing impaired children to

FIGURE 12-6

An Internet Workshop page developed by one teacher to help her children with signing and make a child with deafness feel more welcome in class

---

SIGNING

Internet Signer: _____ Date: _____

Finger Spelling

One way to sign is to spell words with your hands using the American Sign Language spelling signs. Visit the page I have bookmarked on our Internet computer for **Handspeak: A Sign Language Dictionary Online** (http://dww.deafworldweb.org/sl/). Click on the link that says "Alphabet (ASL) and be prepared during Internet Workshop to share your answers to these questions:

1. Practice making the signs for each of the letters in the alphabet. Then decide which are your six favorite letters to sign and be prepared to sign them during Internet Workshop. See if you can make a word with these letters for us to read. My favorite letters are:

   _____ _____ _____ _____

   _____ _____

2. Now practice spelling these words with ASL finger spelling. Be prepared to share them during Internet Workshop.

   Your name   A friend's name   "You're cool!"   The title of your favorite book

Signing Words

Now visit other links at **Handspeak: A Sign Language Dictionary Online** (http://dww.deafworldweb.org/sl) to learn how to sign words. I have made a bookmark for this on our computer. Watch the video for each of these words or phrases and practice signing. Be prepared to sign these items during Internet Workshop:

I	You	Come here.	What?
I love you.	Nice!	Thank you!	I know a good book.

Try to make your own sentences to share with us!

---

learn ASL finger spelling. Develop an Internet activity for this to have everyone begin to develop their signing abilities. Set a bookmark!

An example of an Internet Workshop developed by one teacher with several of these sites appears in Figure 12-6. Note how the information about signing will be shared and used during the workshop session.

Supporting Children with Visual Impairments

visual impairment
Individuals who are legally blind (20/200) or partially sighted (20/70 to 20/200), even with correction.

Students with a **visual impairment** may be legally blind or partially sighted. Individuals who are legally blind have visual acuity less than 20/200. That designation means that with their best eye those individuals can see at 20 feet (or less) what a normally sighted individual can see at 200 feet, even with correction. Partially sighted individuals have visual acuity in their best eye that falls between 20/70 and 20/200, even with correction.

Contrary to popular opinion, being legally blind does not require being totally blind. In actuality, 82 percent of those who are legally blind have some vision. Often it is enough to be able to read print in large-print books or with the aid of magnifying devices (Stephens, Blackhurst, & Magliocca, 1988). Only about one in five individuals who are legally blind depend solely on Braille for reading. More than half use large- or regular-print books for most or all of their reading. Only about 0.1 percent of school-age students have a visual disorder that interferes with learning and makes those children eligible to receive special education services (U.S. Department of Education, 1993).

Learning Characteristics

It is important for teachers to recognize behaviors that indicate visual difficulty. Vision testing usually occurs in elementary schools but does not identify all vision problems, some of which go undetected. Teachers should recommend more thorough testing for children who display these symptoms:

- Squinting
- Holding reading materials very close or very far away from their eyes
- Having red or watery eyes
- Rubbing their eyes frequently
- Covering one eye while reading
- Having crusty material around their eyes and lashes

There are several ways in which children with a visual impairment compensate: tactile sensation, listening skills, and greater attention. Some formal training may be required to take maximum advantage of each compensatory strategy.

Adapting Learning Environments

Children with a visual impairment are almost always mainstreamed into elementary classrooms. If you have the opportunity to work with a child who is visually impaired, first consult your school's specialist to learn the extent of the impairment. You should also determine the most appropriate instructional methods to use and find out which optical and mechanical devices your student may require when reading.

In your classroom try to maintain a relatively constant physical environment to help a child who is visually impaired move about. In addition, always introduce children who are visually impaired to any changes in the location of materials or furniture. Classmates can help with this task, too.

New concepts often need to be more extensively defined for children with visual impairments, taking advantage of their tactile and auditory strengths. Although students with visual impairments may have had identical background experiences, their interpretation of those experiences is different because it has been determined more by nonvisual senses. One important way to develop conceptual knowledge is to provide a rich listening environment. Tape recordings of favorite literature selections are particularly useful for younger children, and you may wish to develop a listening center for all of your students, including a central tape player and individual headphones. Most publishers make audiocassettes of popular children's literature, and books on tape can be obtained through your local public library or from Recordings for the Blind. You may contact **Recordings for the Blind** via the Internet (http://www.rfbd.org/) or their regular mail address (214 East 58th Street, New York, NY 10022).

Internet Resources for Children with Visual Impairments

Internet software is available for increasing the font size at Internet locations or for converting text on websites into audio for the visually impaired. With Apple computers, this is built into the operation system. Look for "Easy Access" to turn these features on. For Windows machines, you should visit **Accessibility** (http://www.microsoft.com/enable/). Other useful resources include:

Blindness Resource Center (http://www.nyise.org/blind.htm)—The best central site for visually impaired and blind individuals. Set a bookmark!

The National Federation of the Blind (http://www.nfb.org)—One of the more important organizations devoted to the blind. Many useful resources.

Celebrating Diversity

Considering the Accessibility of Internet Sites for All of Our Children

Information resources on the Internet are not always accessible to many children. Sometimes, for example, text-only sites are not accessible to the visually impaired. Other elements also prevent others from fully accessing various web locations. This issue is being explored now with several initiatives that seek to encourage web designers to take greater advantage of the multiple media resources, including audio, that would enable more people to access information. One initiative, called "Bobby," provides a "web accessible" symbol when a web page has been designed with exceptionalities in mind. Visit (http://www.cast.org/bobby/) to have any web page you use quickly evaluated for accessibility.

Note: Courtesy of CAST, Inc.

You may find out more about the movement to make web pages more accessible at the WWW location of the **International Program Office for the Web Accessibility Initiative** (http://www.w3.org/WAI/). Visit both of these locations to keep up with developments that make the web accessible to all of your students.

Supporting Children with Speech or Language Disorders

speech disorders
Abnormal oral language behavior due to phonological, voice, or other disorders.

Children with **speech disorders** produce oral language that is abnormal in *how* it is said, not in *what* is said. Several categories of speech disorders exist: phonological disorders, such as substituting /w/ for /r/; voice disorders, such as speaking with unusual pitch or loudness; disorders associated with abnormalities in the mouth and nose, such as orofacial clefts; and disorders of speech flow, such as stuttering. Speakers of nonstandard English dialects and children who speak English as a second (or third) language do not typically have speech disorders. Their speech needs to be compared to the speech of their language-related peers to determine whether a speech disorder exists. A speech pathologist can help make that determination.

language disorders
Difficulty expressing ideas in oral language or understanding the ideas expressed by others.

Children with **language disorders** have difficulty expressing their ideas in oral language or have difficulty understanding the ideas expressed by others. Children with language disorders may not have developed oral language capabilities or may use words in abnormal ways, perhaps echoing words spoken to them. They may also have varying degrees of delayed or interrupted language development. Children who speak nonstandard dialects or who are acquiring English as an additional language typically do not have language disorders.

According to estimates, about 5 to 10 percent of the school-age population has some type of speech or language impairment (Rossetti, 1991).

Learning Characteristics

Children with speech disorders often do quite well with literacy since their difficulty is associated with speech production, not comprehension or composition. Not surprisingly, they do especially well in silent reading, rather than in oral reading experiences. Children with language disorders often have a more difficult time with reading and writing, which are heavily dependent on adequate language proficiency.

At some time you may need to refer a child for formal speech and language assessment by a speech pathologist who will appreciate specific information about the child's speech

JUDY'S

COMMENTS FROM THE CLASSROOM

In our school we are not usually able to have multiple classrooms of one grade, so I have a variety of children with several different kinds of needs in one room. It is common to have children with physical disabilities, emotional and behavioral needs, and special learning needs in my classroom each school year. I also have one or two children who are gifted and need challenging learning experiences. My role as a teacher is not unlike a juggler doing a delicate balancing act to meet everyone's needs.

One way I accomplish meeting the needs of my diverse group of students is to enlist the help of the fifth-grade classroom. These students become our book buddies for the year. This program, now in its third year, has become extremely successful for both classes. The fifth graders get a chance to practice their oral reading and my first graders get a chance to listen to stories—something that is so necessary for beginning readers. As the program progresses, and the first graders begin to read, the partners change roles. As a positive offshoot, I often observe fifth graders sharing reading strategies for decoding, inferencing, and predicting.

At the beginning of each session, the book buddies agree on a book they will share. Once in a while I have a mystery box of books where one partner reaches in and gets a surprise book to read. But most of the time one buddy brings a book he or she likes to the paired reading session, or the buddies choose a book together from the class or school library. The school librarian is very sensitive to the needs of the students and directs partners toward books with appropriate reading levels.

At the onset of the yearly program we agree on reading goals for the book buddies. To account for books read during each session, the fifth graders take the responsibility of recording the books shared. They fill out record sheets I have prepared by writing down the book title, author's name, child's name, date the book was shared, and who did the reading. The fifth graders take this responsibility very seriously.

Additionally, after completing each book the partners fill out a segment of a bookworm with their name and the title of their book. These segments are added together and the worm begins to stretch all over the room. It becomes a visual reminder of the number of books read. When our worm begins to outgrow our room space, we add feet instead of more segments.

The added benefit of this program is that nobody worries about partners who are different in any way and become quite protective and caring toward one another. Working together, the first graders and fifth graders develop a very special friendship.

or language difficulties. Statements such as "Karen's language seems to be different" are not especially helpful. Consider the following questions before making a referral:

1. Is the child's language substantially less mature than that of peers? How does the child use vocabulary and syntax differently from peers? Can the student tell a complete story with all of the appropriate elements?
2. What sound substitutions or omissions does the child regularly make? These are some of the more common substitutions:
   a. /w/ for /r/ or /l/ as in *wead* for *read* or *lead*
   b. /b/ for /v/ as in *berry* for *very*
   c. /t/ for /k/ as in *tat* for *cat*
   d. /f/ for voiceless /th/ as in *wif* for *with*
   e. voiceless /th/ for /s/ as in *thith* for *this*
   f. /d/ for voiced /th/ as in *dis* for *this*
   g. voiced /th/ for /z/ as in *thew* for *zoo*
3. Do other students in the class often have trouble understanding what the child is saying? Why?
4. Does the child speak so fast that intelligibility suffers?
5. Does the child use normal intonation patterns?
6. Does the child experience difficulty following directions?

Adapting Learning Environments

Classrooms provide excellent opportunities for youngsters with speech and language disorders to improve their communication skills, especially when the use of oral language is encouraged, valued, and well integrated into the daily schedule. Regular sharing times, formal oral presentations, informal conversations, group discussions, and cooperative learning group tasks can all be used to foster the development of effective communication skills.

Younger students with speech disorders benefit greatly from reading experiences with predictable texts. Students can practice their rhyming or rhythmic patterns while enjoying a good story (see chapters 6 and 7). For the child who stutters, both teacher and classmates need to adhere to certain guidelines:

▸ Attend carefully to what the child has to say.
▸ Let the child finish talking before you respond or interrupt.
▸ Do not become tense or frustrated at waiting for the entire message.
▸ Do not tease or ridicule the child.

It is perfectly acceptable to talk about a disorder with a child. It helps greatly, though, if the condition is discussed in a matter-of-fact manner. For the stutterer, anxiety is likely to exaggerate the difficulty.

Internet Resources for Children with Speech or Language Disorders

Internet resources specific for children with speech or language disorders are somewhat limited. A valuable central site is **American Speech–Language–Hearing Association** (http://professional.asha.org/), the location on the website for the American Speech–Language–Hearing Association. You might also find these locations useful in your work:

Early Identification of Speech-Language Delays (http://www.kidsource.com/ ASHA/early_identification.html)—A brochure is located here that discusses issues of speech-language delays for both parents and teachers.

General Information about Speech and Language Disorders (http://www. kidsource.com/NICHCY/speech.html)—A fact sheet may be found at this location with much useful information in this area from the Office of Special Education Programs of the American Speech–Language–Hearing Association.

Questions and Answers about Child Language (http://www.kidsource.com/ASHA/child_language.html)—A useful beginning resource for parents and teachers concerned about a child with potential speech or language challenges.

Supporting Children with Mental Retardation

Mental retardation refers to significantly subaverage general intellectual functioning existing concurrently with deficits in adaptive behavior and manifested during the developmental period (Grossman, 1973, p. 11).

According to the AAMD, "Significantly subaverage general intellectual functioning" requires an IQ score of 69 or below on the most commonly used test, Wechsler Intelligence Scale for Children—Revised (WISC-R). Children with IQ scores between 70 and 85 may learn more slowly than their peers and may be called slow learners. Typically, however, they are not formally labeled as mentally retarded. Figure 12-7 illustrates the various categories of mental retardation used by the AAMD.

When "deficits in adaptive behavior" are evaluated, the AAMD suggests the age of the child be considered. In early childhood, sensorimotor, communication, self-help, and socialization skills are evaluated. In middle childhood and early adolescence, learning processes and interpersonal social skills are evaluated. According to federal estimates, students with mental retardation account for approximately 1 to 3 percent of school-age children (Turnbull, Turnbull, Shank, & Leal, 1995).

mental retardation
The condition of individuals with inadequate adaptive behavior and intellectual functioning significantly below average.

Learning Characteristics

Students with mental retardation tend to progress through the same developmental stages that normal students experience, but their rate of progress is much slower. This difference is especially evident in academic learning tasks such as reading. Other important characteristics that need to be accommodated during instruction include the following:

▶ *Short attention span.* Students may be easily distracted, especially when there are many visual and auditory signals to distract them.
▶ *Poor short-term memory.* The ability to remember words, numbers, and ideas for short periods of time is limited. Long-term memory is less of a problem.
▶ *Delayed language development.* Language development is often slower than normal, although it progresses in a sequence similar to that of most children. A higher frequency of language and speech problems can be anticipated.
▶ *Difficulty in grasping abstract ideas.* Children tend to have more difficulty with abstract concepts. They do better with concrete concepts.

Adapting Learning Environments

The most important instructional consideration with students who are mentally retarded is that their development lags behind that of other children of the same chronological age. Thus, while normally developing second graders are learning new vocabulary meanings,

FIGURE 12-7

Categories of mental retardation used by the AAMD

IQ	100	95	90	85	80	75	70	65	60	55	50	45	40	35	30	25	20	15
Categories of Mental Retardation								Mild		Moderate			Severe			Profound		

PRACTICAL TEACHING STRATEGIES

Developing Functional Reading Strategies

Reading Environmental Print.   Teach children to understand the environmental print they experience daily. Such print includes street signs, traffic signals, labels, children's names, and bus or transit signs. Include important safety words such as *Danger, Poison, Keep Out,* and *Caution.* Put each such word on a card, and use it in a sight word recognition game.

Catalog Reading.   Show children how to read a catalog to determine the name and price of items. Provide duplicate copies of the order form and have students complete it. Structure this as a cooperative learning group task.

Reading Students' Names.   Give students frequent opportunities to read the names of other children in the class. Be certain to provide opportunities to return papers that have been corrected.

Reading and Writing Personal Information.   Teach children how to read and write their names, addresses, and phone numbers. Include them in opportunities to fill out employment forms for their favorite classroom jobs.

Reading TV Directories.   Bring in TV program listings and show children how to read them. Have children make a TV viewing schedule for the week, allowing only one or two hours of television each day. This task could be effectively completed in cooperative learning groups.

the structure of various narrative and expository forms, and useful reading strategies, children of the same age who experience mental retardation might still be consolidating important emergent literacy/readiness skills. In fact, emergent literacy/readiness skills often are a major aspect of reading programs in the early elementary years for students who are mildly retarded. Acquiring oral language skills, learning letter names, listening to stories, completing language experience activities, and learning to read and write their own names might all be appropriate. Learning sight words through language experience activities might be especially useful (Raver & Dwyer, 1986).

The use of cooperative learning group experiences is also appropriate. These provide supportive environments in which children can interact with print. In addition, cooperative learning group tasks have been found to be particularly effective in increasing social acceptance and positive social behavior among children (Slavin, 1984).

functional reading strategies Reading strategies required to successfully interact with written language during daily life.

Reading instruction for children experiencing mental retardation should include, but not be limited to, **functional reading strategies,** which include the reading abilities required for daily life. Such strategies enable individuals to read signs, follow simple written directions, use the yellow pages, read and order from catalogs, read names, locate bus routes on a map, and read recipes. Examples of functional reading strategies are described above.

Internet Resources for Children with Mental Retardation

Be certain to include all children in the Internet experiences you develop in your classroom. Internet Workshop, Internet Project, and Internet Inquiry are supportive opportunities for children experiencing mental retardation. For Internet Workshop and Internet Inquiry, you may wish to pair students up with an "Internet buddy" from your class or from an older class so both may develop important insights into life and learning. In addition, you may find this resource useful:

The Arc of the United States (http://TheArc.org/)—A great central site on mental retardation. The Arc is the largest voluntary organization committed to the welfare of all children and adults with mental retardation and their families.

Hands-on activities and role-playing are valued by many educators and can extend understanding in all learners

Supporting Gifted Learners

A universally accepted definition of **giftedness** has yet to emerge. Creativity, intelligence, motivation, artistic talent, verbal ability, curiosity, and the ability to see unique relationships might all be used to define giftedness. However, each would identify a different population of students who are gifted.

Renzulli's (1978) classic definition of giftedness includes three characteristics: (1) high cognitive ability, (2) creativity, and (3) motivation. Alone or in combination, these factors sufficiently distinguish gifted children from their peers to make it possible for them to contribute something of exceptional value to society.

The federal definition is somewhat different:

> "Gifted and talented children" means children and, wherever applicable, youth, who are identified at the preschool, elementary, or secondary level as possessing demonstrated or potential abilities that give evidence of high performance capabilities in areas such as intellectual, creative, specific academic, or leadership ability, or in the performing and visual arts and who by reason thereof require services or activities not ordinarily provided by the school. (Gifted and Talented Children's Act of 1978, PL 95–561, section 902)

Given different definitions of giftedness, it is not surprising that prevalence figures vary widely. Turnbull, Turnbull, Shank, and Leal (1995) estimate the prevalence to range from 2 to 20 percent of the school-age population.

giftedness The condition of individuals with high cognitive ability, creativity, and/or motivation.

Learning Characteristics

Children who are gifted demonstrate exceptional performance with most cognitive and linguistic tasks. Indeed, a teacher's first observation of a gifted child often is to note the student's precocious language use. Children who are gifted talk about topics advanced for their ages, and the way that they talk is noticeably more mature. Some individuals believe that early reading is a mark of giftedness. Nevertheless, even though early reading often is found among gifted children, not all read at an early age.

Adapting Learning Environments

enrichment program
Learning activities provided to students who are gifted, often outside the regular classroom.

The most common form of instructional accommodation for children who are gifted is an **enrichment program,** which provides opportunities for students to pursue special interests inside and outside the regular classroom. A popular enrichment program defined by Renzulli (1978) consists of three types of activities. Type I activities are designed to help children learn about their environment and develop particular interests. Type II activities are developed around group process tasks, such as gaming and simulations. These are designed to enhance problem-solving skills, critical thinking, and creative thinking. Type III activities allow individual or group study of actual problems, such as community reaction to a new shopping center, preservation of traditional folk knowledge, or changes in the local environment. Reading and writing experiences are a natural part of each of these tasks. In addition, research skills often are developed with Type II tasks and then applied to the solution of real-life problems with Type III tasks.

A unique aspect of this enrichment program is the "revolving door" through which students enter and leave the program. Renzulli argues that children are gifted for particular tasks and at particular times. He advocates that children be included in a gifted program when they show an interest in, and talent for, the topic being covered. If they are successful and make an important contribution to the project, they may remain. If they lose interest or do not succeed in making a substantive contribution, other children are allowed to take their places. This approach opens enrichment programs to a wider population.

inquiry reading   An approach to gifted education that has students define, research, and then report on a project of personal interest.

Cassidy (1981) has described another approach for students who are gifted, one referred to as **inquiry reading.** Inquiry reading follows a week-by-week sequence of activities, allowing third through sixth graders to define, research, and then report on a project of personal interest. This method framework, which follows a procedural sequence consisting of four steps, can be used in the classroom with all students.

1. Develop a contract.
2. Research the topic.
3. Prepare the project for presentation to the class.
4. Present the project to the class.

During the first week, children learn the procedures, purposes, and goals of inquiry reading. Then they identify a topic of personal interest, locate the necessary resources, and specify a project that can be completed. All of this information is defined, along with a due date, in a contract developed by the student with assistance from the teacher.

During weeks 2 and 3, students research their topics independently or in small groups. Often this step requires independent library work and sometimes interviews with members of the community. Students read, listen, take notes, and otherwise acquire the necessary resources to complete their projects. Often the teacher sets aside time during this step to confer with students and review their progress.

The final week is spent completing the project and preparing it for presentation to the class. Students can present the results of their work in a variety of ways. They might choose an oral report, a play, a written report, an art project, a diorama, a slide show, or one of many other creative formats.

Additional strategies found to be helpful when working with gifted students can be seen on the next page.

Internet Resources for the Gifted

The Internet provides a useful way to meet the needs of children identified as gifted and talented within the context of your classroom instructional program. What is especially nice is this can be done in a manner to support the learning of all of your students. In-

---

PRACTICAL TEACHING STRATEGIES

Supporting Gifted Students

Establishing Mentor Relationships. Locate local experts in areas in which your students are interested. See whether they can contribute an hour or so each week to work on an independent project with your students. Then design a contract around the project and display the final results in your classroom.

Publishing a Classroom Magazine. Have a rotating group of students be responsible for gathering, editing, and printing articles written by members of the class. Encourage students to include stories, poetry, crossword puzzles, and other features. Use a computer since software is available for laying out and printing the results. Make arrangements to use the school's duplicating machine and produce copies for each student in the class. Suggest that they share their magazines with their parents.

Cross-age Tutoring. Involve students in tutoring situations with students in younger classes. Explain that each member of a society is obligated to contribute something of value and that tutoring younger children is one way of contributing. Help students to carefully plan and evaluate their tutoring activities.

---

ternet Project, Internet Inquiry, and Internet Workshop are all useful strategies for accomplishing this integration. In addition, you may wish to explore these resources:

National Research Center on the Gifted and Talented
(http://www.gifted.uconn.edu/nrcgt.html)—This location contains many useful resources related to the gifted and talented.

On the Right Track (http://www.assd.winnepeg.mb.ca/infozone/right track/index.htm)—This is a great central site on gifted and talented education developed by the Assiniboine South School Division in Canada.

Developing a Classroom Community That Supports All Learners

Perhaps the single most important thing you can do to support all of your students is develop a sense of community that respects the unique qualities each one of your students brings to your classroom. There is no simple prescription for how a teacher should go about developing the respect for individual differences that is such an important part of our society. More than anything else, it takes a teacher who sees the value of diversity in everyday life and brings that concern into every aspect of the classroom community.

Clearly, one way this can be accomplished is to recall the points made at the beginning of this chapter about exceptionalities. We need to recognize that each child in our classroom is an individual with special needs. We need to continually keep in mind that the categories used in this chapter should never limit our instructional decisions regarding individual children or our expectations for their achievement. And finally, we need to recall that diversity should be viewed as an opportunity, not a challenge to overcome.

Another way to accomplish this is to take maximum advantage of group learning experiences as you consider the nature of each day's literacy activities. Group learning activities allow your students to experience the advantages that come from diversity as each student makes a contribution to the completion of the learning task. You should use these activities to help your students see the advantages in diversity as they complete their learning activity. The method framework initially described in chapter 2 as cooperative group learning is especially useful, largely because it can be used in so many different learning activities. You will recall this method framework consists of four procedural steps:

1. The teacher defines a learning task.
2. The teacher assigns students to groups.

Celebrating Diversity

 Setting the Example in Your Classroom Community

In the final analysis, creating a classroom community that supports all learners can only be accomplished by the example you set and the values you bring to classroom learning. This is why it is so important to carefully consider the type of community you wish to develop in your classroom. It is also the reason why it is so important to view diversity as an opportunity for both you and your students, not as an obstacle to learning. Helping your students to see the benefits of working with peers who have different exceptionalities should be a central part of your instructional program.

3. Students complete the learning task together through cooperative group activity.
4. The results of the learning task are shared with the other groups.

While cooperative group learning may be used by itself to organize learning activities for your students, it may also be combined with a wide variety of other method frameworks during reading instruction. It could, for example, be used to organize method frameworks as diverse as readers theater (chapter 6), directed reading activities (chapter 10), read-aloud response journal activities (chapter 2), literature discussion groups (chapter 6), writing workshop (chapter 7), invented spelling (chapters 4 and 5), style studies (chapters 7 and 9), or reciprocal teaching (chapter 9).

Notice, too, how cooperative group learning can be used with method frameworks that contain very different assumptions about how children best learn to read. It could, for example, be used during the final two procedural steps of either inductive instruction (chapter 3) or deductive instruction (chapter 3), which we have defined as "provide guided practice" and "provide independent practice." You could ask students to complete the learning task you have developed in a cooperative learning group as a means of providing guided practice. Students could also be asked to complete the independent practice step and have them compare their results in a cooperative group learning task. Clearly, cooperative group learning is a method framework that can be adapted to different types of literacy frameworks and provide useful opportunities for your students to experience the advantages of diversity.

Another way to bring all students into the full measure of classroom life is through Internet experiences, especially as more sites become compliant with new standards for accessibility. Internet experiences provide a wonderful opportunity for students to share the unique discoveries each member of the class is making about the world around them. Moreover, the richness of these resources and their continually changing nature means that each student knows something that can be useful to other students. The method frameworks for Internet use described in this book (Internet Workshop, Internet Inquiry, and Internet Project) are central to fulfilling the promise inclusive education provides for all of our children.

Using a Literacy Framework to Guide Instruction of Students with Special Needs

Teaching reading to children with special needs presents the same types of instructional decisions that must be faced when you teach any child. You must still decide what you should teach and how you should teach it. As a result, you will use your literacy framework in a similar way. If, for example, you have a text-based explanation of how a person reads, you will tend to emphasize aspects such as decoding knowledge and fluent oral reading. If, however, you follow a reader-based explanation, you will emphasize aspects such as inferential reasoning, vocabulary knowledge, and other elements of prior knowledge. With a specific-skills explanation of how reading ability develops, you will

Featured Teacher

Corrie Rosetti

Corrie Rosetti teaches eighth-grade language arts and reading classes in Clarkson, Washington. He describes himself as a constructivist teacher, and looking through his amazingly extensive classroom web page (http://jawbone.clarkston.wednet.edu/Websites/Lincoln/Staff/rosetti/laonline/index.html) you can see why. Much of his class is organized around contracts that students develop and complete on an individual basis. Students assume much responsibility for their own learning but, at the same time, they are held accountable for mastery tests in specific areas. Classrooms that are organized like this provide wonderfully supportive environments for all students, no matter what their special needs might be, to develop literacy skills.

Take a look at the richness of this classroom web page (see Figure 12-8). You will find important resources for parents, the activities for that day in class, ideas for projects, a poetry forum where students publish their poetry and receive comments from other students, a discussion forum to explore controversial topics that arise in class, and much more. Be certain, too, to explore the web pages created by his students to share the research projects they completed. Corrie Rosetti has provided us with an exceptional model for us to follow as we consider how we might develop our own classroom web page to support students in literacy and learning.

FIGURE 12-8

The home page for Corrie Rosetti's eighth-grade language arts and reading classroom in Clarkson, Washington (http://jawbone.clarkston.wednet.edu/Websites/Lincoln/Staff/rosetti/laonline/index.html)

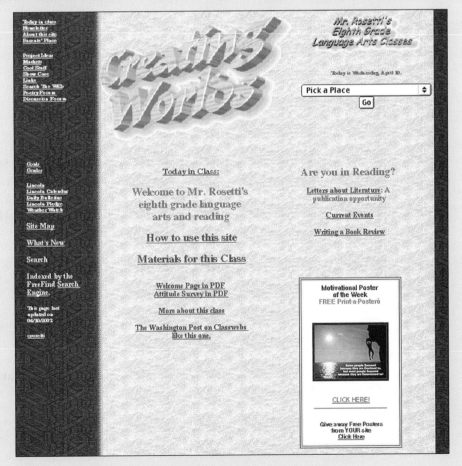

Use the self-test questions on http://www.prenhall.com/leukinzer to review the material presented in this chapter.

use more deductive instructional practices when you work with children with special needs. With a holistic language explanation, you will depend on students to learn what is important through inductive and self-selected reading experiences.

These generalizations do not mean that all children with special needs will receive identical instruction from one teacher. These children require individualized attention to their unique strengths and weaknesses. The approaches described in this chapter should be valuable resources as you accomplish this important goal.

Major Points

▶ Every child has unique needs that must be acknowledged in instructional decisions. Each student's background and abilities must be considered in reading instruction. Having children with special needs in the classroom provides opportunities to celebrate and learn about diversity.

▶ Teachers can help children with exceptionalities develop literacy proficiency by preparing other students, capitalizing on their individual strengths, ensuring successful learning experiences, building success into instruction by carefully considering what each child can be expected to do, recording and charting individual growth to demonstrate gains to students and parents, establishing an accepting and positive environment, regularly discussing student progress with others, and adjusting background knowledge to reduce the difficulty of learning tasks.

▶ To support all of your students, it is essential to develop a sense of community that respects the unique qualities that each of your students brings to your classroom.

▶ Teachers face the same types of instructional decisions with children with special needs that they face with other children. As a result, a personal literacy framework functions in a similar way as you consider each child's learning needs.

Making Instructional Decisions

1. Support for children with special needs often is provided in either a pull-out or a push-in program. Pull-out programs take children out of their regular classrooms to provide special services such as special education or remedial reading. They provide an opportunity for students and the teacher to focus on specific instructional needs outside of the hustle and bustle of the child's classroom. Push-in programs provide such services to children within their regular classrooms, working with those students and their teachers in an inclusive classroom setting. Here, children have an opportunity to always connect their learning with what takes place within the classroom community. In addition, students are likely to feel more like a full member of the classroom community, not an outsider. Which model of support services do you favor? Why? What are the likely consequences of your beliefs? What is the relationship between your beliefs on this issue and your beliefs related to the second issue in your literacy framework: *How* should I teach?

2. Read a variety of literature selections that explore issues of diversity, including cultural diversity, linguistic diversity, and the diversity of exceptionalities. Develop an outline for a thematic unit on diversity that might be used at the beginning of the year to build a supportive classroom community. See chapters 6 and 7 for suggestions about how this might be done.

3. Your school psychologist has informed you a new student will be joining your class. This student was tested for mental retardation but was not admitted into the district's special education program. The school psychologist explains that the student has below-average intellectual functioning, but it is not low enough to qualify for special assistance.

   a. Identify several learning characteristics you might look for during the first few weeks this child is in your class.

   b. Specify the major instructional consideration you will need to incorporate into your reading plans for this student.

c. Finally, describe how you will provide appropriate instruction for this student without developing expectations that are too low and thereby preventing the student from developing his or her full potential. Be certain to describe how you will use the Internet with this child.

4. Develop an Internet Workshop activity using resources identified in this chapter or others you have located. Create an activity sheet and describe how you would use Internet Workshop to consolidate this learning.

5. It is the end of the school year and you have been told you will have five exceptional children in your classroom in the fall: two children with learning disabilities, a child with emotional difficulties, a child who has been labeled as mildly mentally retarded, and a child who is visually impaired. You will be teaming with another teacher who is certified in special education during the mornings. What principles will guide your attempts to develop an inclusive classroom and, at the same time, meet the literacy needs of these children? Which Internet sites will you use to gather useful ideas?

Further Reading

Cammack, D. (2001). Two sites for teachers working with struggling or reluctant readers. *Reading Online, 4.* Available: http://www.readingonline.org/electronic/elec_index.asp? HREF-/electronic/webwatch/twosites/index.html

> *Shares two important Internet resources, useful when working with children experiencing reading difficulties.*

Cousin, P. T., Weekley, T., & Gerard, J. (1993). The functional uses of language and literacy by students with severe language and learning problems. *Language Arts, 70,* 548–557.

> *Describes the results of a collaborative project between a university professor and classroom teachers who work with exceptional youngsters. By looking at the functional uses of language and literacy for children with language and learning problems, new insights are presented about the most appropriate ways of supporting their learning needs. Presents several case studies of students in this classroom.*

Kameenui, E. J. (1993). Diverse learners and the tyranny of time: Don't fix blame; fix the leaky roof. *The Reading Teacher, 46* (5), 376–383.

> *Argues that we have spent too much time and energy searching for the "best" method to teach reading to diverse learners. Suggests that what is required is simply to use what appears to work for diverse learners. Proposes six principles to guide these efforts: do not waste instructional time; intervene and remediate early, strategically, and frequently; teach less more thoroughly; communicate reading strategies in a clear and explicit manner, especially during initial phases of instruction; guide student learning through a sequence of teacher-directed and student-directed activities; and examine the effectiveness of instructional tools.*

Speigel, D. L. (1995). A comparison of traditional remedial programs and Reading Recovery: Guidelines for success for all programs. *The Reading Teacher, 44* (4), 86–96.

> *Evaluates components in traditional remedial programs and in Reading Recovery to seek elements that appear to yield success for children struggling with literacy.*

References

Allington, R. L. (1991). Children who find learning to read difficult: School responses to diversity. In E. H. Hiebert (Ed.), *Literacy for a diverse society: Perspectives, practices, and policies* (pp. 237–252). New York: Teachers College Press.

Allington, R. L., & Johnston, P. (1989). Coordination, collaboration, and consistency: The redesign of compensatory and special education interventions. In R. Slavin, N. Karweit, & N. Madden (Eds.), *Effective programs for students at risk* (pp. 320–354). Boston, MA: Allyn & Bacon.

Allington, R. L., & Shake, M. C. (1986). Remedial reading: Achieving curricular congruence in classroom and clinic. *The Reading Teacher, 39,* 648–654.

Au, K. H. (2000). A multicultural perspective on policies for improving literacy achievement: Equity and excellence. In M. L. Kamil, P. Mosenthal, P. D. Pearson, & R. Barr (Eds.), *Handbook of reading research, Volume III* (pp. 835–851). Mahwah, NJ: Lawrence Erlbaum Associates.

Barnes, B. L. (1997a). But teacher you went right on: A perspective on Reading Recovery. *The Reading Teacher, 50* (4), 284–293.

Barnes, B. L. (1997b). Response to Browne, Fitts, McLaughlin, McNamara, and Williams. *The Reading Teacher, 50* (4), 302–303.

Browne, A., Fitts, M., McLaughlin, B., McNamara, M. J., & Williams, J. (1997). Teaching and learning in Reading Recovery: Response to "But Teacher You Went Right On." *The Reading Teacher, 50* (4), 294–301.

Cassidy, J. (1981). Inquiry reading for the gifted. *The Reading Teacher, 35,* 17–21.

D'Alessandro, M. (1990). Accommodating emotionally handicapped children through a literature-based reading program. *The Reading Teacher, 44* (4), 288–293.

Dudley-Marling, C., & Murphy, S. (1997). A political critique of remedial reading programs: The example of Reading Recovery. *The Reading Teacher, 50* (6), 460–469.

Federal Register 42, No. 250, December 29, 1977.

Fernald, G. (1943). *Remedial techniques in basic school subjects.* New York: McGraw-Hill.

Ford, M. P., & Ohlhausen, M. M. (1988). Tips from reading clinicians for coping with disabled readers in regular classrooms. *The Reading Teacher, 42* (1), 18–22.

Grossman, H. J. (Ed.). (1973). *Manual on terminology and classification in mental retardation.* Washington, DC: American Association on Mental Deficiency.

Hallahan, D. P., & Kauffman, J. M. (1982). *Exceptional children* (2nd ed.). New York: Prentice Hall.

Harris, A. J., & Sipay, E. R. (1990). *How to increase reading ability* (9th ed.). New York: Longman Publishing Group.

Kauffman, J. M. (1981). *Characteristics of children's behavior disorders* (2nd ed.). Upper Saddle River, NJ: Merrill/Prentice Hall.

Koyanagi, C., & Gaines, S. (1993). *All systems failure: An examination of the results of neglecting the needs of children with serious emotional disturbance.* Alexandria, VA: National Mental Health Association.

Lerner, J. (1985). *Learning disabilities: Theories, diagnosis, and teaching strategies* (4th ed.). Boston, MA: Houghton Mifflin.

Lundeen, C. (1991). Prevalence of hearing impairment among school children. *Language, Speech, and Hearing Services in Schools, 22,* 269–271.

Mercer, C. D., & Mercer, A. R. (1998). *Teaching students with learning problems.* Upper Saddle River, NJ: Merrill/Prentice Hall.

Pinnell, G. S., Fried, M. D., & Estice, R. M. (1990). Reading Recovery: Learning how to make a difference. *The Reading Teacher, 43* (4), 282–295.

Raver, S. A., & Dwyer, R. C. (1986). Teaching handicapped preschoolers to sight read using language training procedures. *The Reading Teacher, 40,* 314–321.

Renzulli, J. S. (1978). What makes giftedness? Re-examining a definition. *Phi Delta Kappan, 60* (3), 180–184, 261.

Rossetti, L. M. (1991). Infant-toddler assessment: A clinical perspective. *Infant-Toddler Intervention, 1* (1), 11–26.

Shanahan, T., & Barr, R. (1995). Reading Recovery: An independent evaluation of the effects of an early instructional intervention for at-risk learners. *Reading Research Quarterly, 30* (4), 958–996.

Slavin, R. E. (1984). Effects of cooperative learning and individualized instruction on mainstreamed students. *Exceptional Children, 50* (5), 434–443.

Stainback, S., & Stainback, W. (1989). Integration of students with mild and moderate handicaps. In D. Kerzner & A. Gartner (Eds.), *Beyond separate education.* Baltimore, MD: Paul H. Brookes.

Stephens, T. M., Blackhurst, A. E., & Magliocca, L. A. (1988). *Teaching mainstreamed students.* Oxford: Pergamon Press.

Sutherland, Z., & Arbuthnot, M. H. (1986). *Children and books* (7th ed.). Glenview, IL: Scott, Foresman.

Tierney, R. J., Readence, J. E., & Dishner, E. K. (1985). *Reading strategies and practices: Guide for improving instruction* (2nd ed.). Boston, MA: Allyn & Bacon.

Turnbull, A. P., Turnbull, H. R., Shank, M., & Leal, D. (1995). *Exceptional lives: Special education in today's schools.* Upper Saddle River, NJ: Merrill/Prentice Hall.

U.S. Department of Education. (1992). *To assure the free, appropriate public education of all children with disabilities: Fourteenth annual report to Congress on the implementation of the Individuals with Disabilities Education Act.* Washington, DC: Office of Special Education Programs.

U.S. Department of Education. (1993). *Fifteenth annual report to Congress on the implementation of the Individuals with Disabilities Education Act.* Washington, DC: Author.

Walp, T. P., & Walmsley, S. A. (1989). Instructional and philosophical congruence: Neglected aspects of coordination. *The Reading Teacher, 42* (6), 364–368.

Wasik, B. A., & Slavin, R. E. (1993). Preventing early reading failure with one-to-one tutoring: A review of five programs. *Reading Research Quarterly, 28* (2), 179–200.

Wood, J. W. (1992). *Adapting instruction for mainstreamed and at-risk students* (2nd ed.). Upper Saddle River, NJ: Merrill/Prentice Hall.

Instructional Patterns and Technologies

CHAPTER 13

Classroom Organization: Orchestrating Literacy Learning

E-mail from the Classroom

Subject: Classroom Organization
From: Tonie Baxter, tbaxter3@hotmail.com

I organize my classroom to meet the many individual needs I have in reading. No two students are the same; each has different skill needs and different ways that he or she learns best. Some students need more support in some of the earlier skill sets, such as phonics and fluency, while others need more support in some of the more advanced skill sets, such as critically evaluating the information they encounter while reading. Some students really do well in more independent activities and others just flounder with independent projects. That's why my organizational plan is so important to me. I use many different types of organizational patterns because my students have so many different needs. At the beginning of each year, I sit down and plan out all the organizational strategies I will use and make initial decisions about when I will use each pattern. This helps a lot, and even though I make changes in this plan as we go along, it gives me a good road map for the year. This helps me to ensure that I provide successful learning opportunities for each student.

Tonie

achievement groups

cooperative learning groups

cross-age tutoring

cross-grade grouping

departmentalized reading instruction

grand conversations

individual differences

interclass accommodations

interest groups

Internet Inquiry

intraclass organizational patterns

literature discussion groups

reading workshop

reading/writing center

strategy groups

team teaching

thematic units

tracking

yearly plan

After reading this chapter, you should be able to:

1. Accommodate individual differences through organizational decisions.
2. Organize your classroom to take advantage of individual differences in reading.
3. Use your literacy framework to inform decisions about classroom organization using individual, small group, and whole class patterns.

⌨ Organize Your Classroom to Maximize Learning: A Principle of Effective Literacy Instruction

You have acquired many important insights about effective literacy instruction as you have explored research-based principles of best practice instruction. You have also encountered many exciting activities to help you implement these principles. Now, we will explore how best to orchestrate all of these instructional ideas within the complex environment that defines a classroom.

As we seek to orchestrate learning experiences in the classroom to meet individual needs, we often look to the classroom organizational patterns we have available to us. How can we best organize our classroom for literacy instruction? Should we teach to the whole class? Alternatively, should we teach in groups, using guided reading groups, literature discussion groups, or interest groups? Perhaps we should use individualized patterns and have individuals pursue their own reading and writing workshop projects. Perhaps we should combine all of these various organizational patterns so that we have a mixture of patterns. But how should we do so?

The decisions you make about how to organize learning experiences for your students will have an important impact on their learning. Thus, we come to our next principle of effective literacy instruction:

11. **Organize your classroom to maximize learning.** Today, a teacher's ability to orchestrate instruction to meet the varying needs of individuals and groups is critical to success in the literacy classroom (Anderson, Hiebert, Scott, & Wilkinson, 1985; Snow, Burns, & Griffin, 1998).

Check your ongoing understanding of chapter concepts by using the guided review for this chapter on http://www. prenhall.com/leukinzer

In earlier times, the issue of classroom organization was an easy one to solve; everyone simply learned together as a whole class. Each year, the better students always became even better and the weaker students became even weaker. The situation is very different now. Organizational decisions have become more complex as we meet the many individual differences that exist among our students.

⌨ Individual Differences: The Challenge and the Opportunity

individual differences Ways in which students vary; in literacy, specifically background knowledge, interests, achievement levels, and skills.

As a developing professional, you are familiar with the concept of **individual differences** in educational settings. You know that each child in your classroom is unique in many ways. You also know that instruction must attempt to meet the unique needs of each student. Those individual differences within your classroom provide both challenges and opportunities. The challenge, of course, is to make instructional decisions that take into account the unique characteristics of each child in your class. The opportunity is to nurture the diversity in your classroom, modeling the respect for individual differences that are so important to our pluralistic society.

As chapter 12 pointed out, individual students differ along many dimensions. In terms of literacy instruction, however, four types of individual differences are most important:

▶ Background knowledge and experiences
▶ Interests
▶ Achievement level
▶ Skills

These are the major differences that make an important difference during literacy learning. Each contributes in an important way to a student's interaction with a text. Consequently, each needs to be recognized as you consider how best to organize for literacy learning.

Background Knowledge and Experiences

Let's look first at individual differences in background knowledge and experiences. Each child's previous experiences are unique; as a result, each has different background knowledge to assist with comprehension and composition. Often this comes from the experiences that define one's cultural traditions. If two readers are identical in every respect but background knowledge, they will still comprehend the same story in very different ways. One child might make the required inferences, while the other struggles to understand. Classroom organization needs to recognize individual differences in background knowledge and experiences.

Interests

Interests also vary among children. Some prefer to read and write narratives; others prefer exposition. Some prefer stories about animals; others prefer stories about sports. Even children with the same background knowledge would comprehend the same story differently if one was interested in the topic and the other was not. Classroom organization needs to recognize individual differences in reading and writing interests.

Achievement Level

In addition, children vary in their achievement levels. What range of reading achievement do you think a teacher might expect in an average fourth-grade class? A conservative rule of thumb is that the variation in reading achievement levels equals the grade level of the class. According to Harris and Sipay (1990), we can expect to find *at least* 4 years' difference in achievement between the highest and the lowest reader. The lowest reader might be reading at a second-grade level while the highest achieving reader is reading at a sixth-grade level. Because achievement levels vary so much within classrooms, no teacher can expect to accommodate individual differences by teaching all students with the same set of materials. Classroom organization needs to recognize these individual differences in achievement.

Skills

A final dimension of individual difference within the classroom is skills knowledge. Each child brings a unique combination of skills to instructional lessons. Some students may have comprehensive vocabulary knowledge but poorly developed decoding knowledge. Others may have comprehensive decoding knowledge but poorly developed metacognitive knowledge, or any one of many other combinations of well-developed and poorly developed knowledge sources. Multiplying the number of possible combinations by the number of students in a class helps us appreciate the importance of accommodating each child's instructional needs in this area.

Children are clearly unique in the background knowledge, reading interests, achievement levels, and specific skills each brings to literacy. The challenge is to determine how best to address that diversity to further each child's development. Schools and teachers meet this challenge through organizational decisions, attempting to accommodate the wide range of differences and provide more appropriate literacy experiences for individual children. Schools develop organizational patterns between classrooms; teachers develop organizational patterns within classrooms.

Organizational Patterns between Classrooms

Schools accommodate individual differences in literacy through organizational patterns between classrooms. Typically, these **interclass accommodations** only address differences in achievement. They do nothing to recognize differences in other areas such as background knowledge, interests, or specific-skills knowledge. Consequently, considerable variation among individuals still remains within each classroom. A variety of interclass accommodations exist and are described below. Most interclass organizational patterns are found in grades 4 and higher.

interclass accommodations Modifications in the organized patterns between classes often used to accommodate individual differences.

Homogeneous Grouping (Tracking)

Most elementary classrooms are heterogeneous; they contain children with a wide range of achievement levels. To reduce the range of achievement differences within any single class, schools sometimes form **homogeneously grouped classrooms.** For example, a

homogeneously grouped classrooms An interclass organizational pattern in which classes are formed around children similar in at least one dimension, such as achievement level.

All classrooms contain students with a variety of skill levels, interest, and backgrounds.

school with three homogeneously grouped classrooms at the fourth-grade level might have one class of high-achieving children, one class of average-achieving children, and a third class of low-achieving children. Achievement is often defined by reading level. This approach to individual differences is sometimes called **tracking** as children are placed in different educational tracks, depending on their achievement level.

tracking   An interclass organizational structure using classes homogeneously grouped according to achievement levels.

Homogeneous grouping is more frequently found in fourth through eighth grade, and seldom in kindergarten through third grade. There is not much evidence supporting its use. Low-achieving students do not do any better in such settings, although limited evidence suggests that high-achieving students do benefit from homogeneous grouping (Harp, 1989).

Departmentalized Instruction

departmentalized instruction   An interclass organizational pattern in which one teacher teaches reading while other teachers teach other subject areas.

Occasionally schools use **departmentalized instruction.** This approach makes one or several teachers solely responsible for reading and writing instruction while other teachers are responsible for other subject areas. With this arrangement—essentially a traditional high school format—students move from one subject-area classroom to another during the day, receiving instruction from each subject-area teacher. This type of interclass accommodation is almost always limited to grades 4 through 8 and is seldom found in kindergarten or grades 1 through 3.

By itself, departmentalized instruction does not meet the challenge posed by individual differences. Often, however, it is combined with some form of homogeneous grouping. For example, the teacher responsible for reading and writing at the fourth-grade level might teach reading and writing to classes that have been homogeneously grouped on the basis of reading achievement.

Team Teaching

team teaching   An interclass organizational pattern in which two or more teachers cooperate for instructional purposes, sharing ideas and students.

There are probably as many different definitions of **team teaching** as there are groups of teachers who decide to share instructional ideas and students. Team teaching usually involves several teachers who pool their students for instruction, with each teacher assuming responsibility for a specific subject area. This form of team teaching usually involves two or more teachers at the same grade level. For example, two sixth-grade teachers might decide to team-teach mathematics and literacy. Each teacher would then teach one of those subject areas to all the students in both classes. Typically, half the students would receive instruction in literacy from one teacher while the other half received instruction in mathematics from the other teacher. After that, the students would switch classrooms and receive instruction in the other subject area. Both teachers would remain responsible for teaching their own students in all other subjects.

Like departmentalized instruction, team teaching by itself does not really meet the challenge of individual differences. Again, however, team teaching usually takes place in conjunction with some form of homogeneous grouping based on achievement levels. In the previous example, the sixth graders might be grouped according to a combined achievement level in reading and mathematics. During one period, the high-achieving students would receive reading instruction while the low-achieving students received mathematics instruction. Then, the same groups would switch subjects and teachers.

Cross-Grade Grouping

Cross-grade grouping requires a school to homogeneously regroup students across several grades according to achievement levels, usually in the area of reading. Students receive instruction in all other areas within their regular classrooms. According to this scheme, children in all classes leave their regular classrooms at the same time each day to go to their assigned classrooms for reading instruction. Thus, in each classroom, reading is taught to students who are reading at about the same grade level, even though their nominal levels might be anywhere from kindergarten to sixth grade. Sometimes cross-grade grouping is referred to as the Joplin Plan, after the Missouri town where it first received notice.

cross-grade grouping An interclass organizational pattern in which a school regroups students across several grades for instruction.

Split-Half Classes

Schools that use **split-half classes** divide each classroom into groups of higher-achieving and lower-achieving children. One group comes to school an hour before the other group and receives reading and writing instruction at the beginning of the day. After that period the remaining students arrive, and the school day proceeds normally with both groups in attendance. Then, an hour before the end of school, the early arriving children leave, freeing the teacher for reading and writing instruction with the later children.

split-half classes An interclass organizational pattern in which each classroom is divided into halves based on achievement levels.

Split-half classes create scheduling problems for families with several children in school and both parents working. As children leave and return home from school at different times, busy schedules must accommodate additional juggling. In addition, split-half classes require that a school devote an additional period each day to reading and writing.

Retention and Acceleration

Retaining lower-achieving children for another year at the same grade level while accelerating higher-achieving children to a higher grade level was one of the earliest types of interclass accommodation (Harris & Sipay, 1990). In most cases of **retention and acceleration,** achievement was substantially based on reading performance. More recently, retention has found increasing favor, despite evidence that neither retention nor social promotion has been a consistently successful response to the challenge of individual differences. Whenever retention or acceleration is considered, it is important for the teacher to carefully review the child's situation with his or her parents, principal, and the school psychologist.

retention and acceleration An interclass organizational pattern in which students either repeat or skip a grade level, based on achievement.

Assistance by Reading Specialists or Special Educators

reading specialist   A teacher specially trained to diagnose and provide remedial assistance to children with reading difficulties.

In many classrooms, children who achieve at lower levels of literacy are provided with additional assistance, which is the final form of interclass accommodation. Under this arrangement, children receive remedial reading instruction from a **reading specialist** or a Reading Recovery teacher. Other children may be formally identified as students in need of special educational support and will then receive instruction from a special educator trained to work with students experiencing an exceptionality. This type of assistance was traditionally provided outside of the main classroom; students left the class and received instruction that was sensitive to their particular needs. Increasingly, this assistance is being provided today within the classroom by trained specialists.

The Weaknesses of Accommodations between Classes

Interclass accommodations of individual differences suffer from two weaknesses. First, they tend to give the false impression that achievement differences among students have ceased to exist when, in fact, significant achievement differences still remain. Teachers of homogeneously grouped classes often believe that, since all students in the class are high-, average-, or low-ability readers, they should receive identical instruction. Seldom is that response appropriate. Nearly every classroom, despite the best attempts at homogeneous grouping, will contain a range in reading achievement of at least 2 years (Harris & Sipay, 1990).

A second problem is that interclass accommodations recognize only one type of individual difference important to literacy—differences in achievement levels. None of the interclass accommodations address variations in background knowledge, interests, or skills. These differences will always exist in a classroom and are important to accommodate during literacy instruction.

⌨ Organizational Patterns within Classrooms

intraclass organizational patterns Modifications in organizational patterns within classes, designed to accommodate individual differences.

Teachers often use **intraclass organizational patterns** to accommodate additional differences within their classes. There are three types of patterns teachers use: individualized patterns, small-group patterns, and whole-class patterns.

Individualized Patterns

Individualized patterns provide an organizational framework to meet the multiple needs of students within a classroom (Staab, 1991). Such patterns can be used to accommodate all types of individual differences important to reading: background knowledge, interests, achievement levels, and skills. Because individualized patterns usually allow children to select their own reading materials, individual differences among children are easily accommodated. Children choose to read something appropriate for their own background knowledge, interests, achievement level, and skills. Individualized patterns include several different approaches. You may wish to consider several individualized patterns as you organize your class for literacy learning: reading workshop, Internet Workshop, Internet Inquiry, reading/writing centers, cross-age tutoring, and paired reading.

reading workshop   A method framework that involves sharing reading responses, providing a reading strategy mini-lesson, reviewing reading progress, engaging in self-selected reading and response, and sharing reading experiences.

Reading Workshop.   **Reading workshop** is described in chapter 2 as a method framework often used to replace or supplement a published reading program. Reading workshop uses self-selected reading experiences with children's literature, a practice that has demonstrated positive results (Tunnell & Jacobs, 1989). The process includes the following steps:

1. Sharing reading responses.
2. Providing a reading strategy mini-lesson.
3. Reviewing reading progress.

FIGURE 13-1

A sample contract used with an independent book project

Contract

I _____ will read the following book and complete my independent

book project by _____ .

Book: _____

Author: _____

My independent book project will include:

_____

_____

_____

_____

_____

Signed: _____   _____
              (Student)   (Teacher)

Date: _____

4. Engaging in self-selected reading and response.
5. Sharing reading experiences.

During reading workshop, children have an opportunity to select their own reading materials and read at their own pace. Thus, children are able to read materials consistent with their background knowledge, reading interests, achievement levels, and reading skills. As individual children read their books, you conduct mini-lessons for those who need additional assistance. You also have a conference with individuals who have completed their books to review reading progress. During this conference, you might invite a child to read a short excerpt aloud and discuss the most interesting parts of the story. Also, you might discuss how the child will share the response with the rest of the class. Often this is done through a project the child completes.

Reading workshop can be combined with reading contracts, which are helpful reminders for children of what needs to be done. A reading contract identifies the book a child selects to read, specifies the projected completion date, and defines how the book will be presented to the class in a culminating project, when appropriate. An example of a contract used with an independent book project is illustrated in Figure 13-1.

PRACTICAL TEACHING STRATEGIES

Internet Workshop and Internet Inquiry

Roll of Thunder, Hear My Cry.   Before reading aloud this wonderful work by Mildred D. Taylor, set a bookmark for a virtual tour of the **National Civil Rights Museum** in Memphis (http://www.civilrightsmuseum.org/). Invite students to take this tour and take notes about what they discover. Have them share their information during Internet Workshop. This will provide a great introduction to your reading of the book, helping children to better understand the history of the civil rights movement.

Studying Desert Plants and Animals.   After reading *The Desert Is Theirs* by Byrd Baylor, set a bookmark and invite students to visit **Desert USA—Flora** (http://www.desertusa.com/flora.html) or **Desert USA—Animals** (http://www.desertusa.com/animal.html). Have students find at least one desert plant and one animal, write down an interesting piece of information about each item, print out a picture, and share this information during Internet Workshop in a discussion about life in desert ecosystems.

Inquiry Projects in Science.   If you plan to have students do Internet Inquiry in science, set bookmarks for these excellent locations. They are great places to explore as students consider their individual inquiry projects: **Digital Dozen** (http://www.enc.org/weblinks/dd/) and **Science Learning Network: Inquiry Resources** (http://www.sln.org/resources/index.html). Give students a week for their exploration and then conduct Internet Workshop about questions students wish to explore. Use the workshop session to help children develop and refine the questions they wish to explore during Internet Inquiry.

Internet Workshop A method framework containing these steps: locate a site with content related to instruction, develop an activity requiring the use of this site, assign the activity, and have students share their work.

Internet Inquiry A method framework with these phases: question, search, analyze, compose, and share.

Internet Workshop and Internet Inquiry.   Several Internet experiences might also be organized to provide individualized patterns for learning. **Internet Workshop** and **Internet Inquiry** often provide children with opportunities to explore resources on the Internet by themselves. Each is often used in conjunction with a workshop session, though, so that individuals may share their work and benefit from the work of others. You may wish to review the description of these method frameworks in chapters 2, 9, and 14.

Designed appropriately, Internet Workshop can meet a wide range of individual differences and require little familiarity with the Internet. As a result, this instructional model often is used first by teachers before they begin to explore the use of Internet Inquiry.

Internet Inquiry requires both you and your students to have more familiarity with the Internet for it to work successfully. But the rewards often are greater with Internet Inquiry because children direct their own learning. As a result, this method is especially useful to meet the full range of individual differences in your classroom. Often, teachers will begin the year with Internet Workshop and, as everyone becomes more familiar with the use of Internet resources, will introduce Internet Inquiry later during the year.

reading/writing center A location in the classroom where children may engage in a series of independent, self-guided, teacher-designed activities that connect reading and writing.

Reading/Writing Centers.   Another way to provide individual learning experiences in literacy is with a **reading/writing center.** A reading/writing center is a location in the classroom where students may engage in a series of independent, self-guided, teacher-designed activities that connect reading and writing. Reading/writing centers take many different forms but usually share several characteristics. First, reading/writing centers usually contain all of the materials required to complete an activity. For example, the following materials were needed for one reading/writing center activity used at the third-grade level:

1. Four books containing tall tales: *Shenandoah Noah* by Jim Aylesworth, *Paul Bunyan* by Steven Kellogg, *Sally Ann Thunder and Whirlwind Crockett* by Caron Lee Cohen, and *John Henry* by Ezra Jack Keats.
2. A computer with word processing software, writing paper, pencils, and felt-tip pens.
3. Students' writing folders.
4. A box to collect students' finished work.

FIGURE 13-2

The directions for a reading/writing center activity

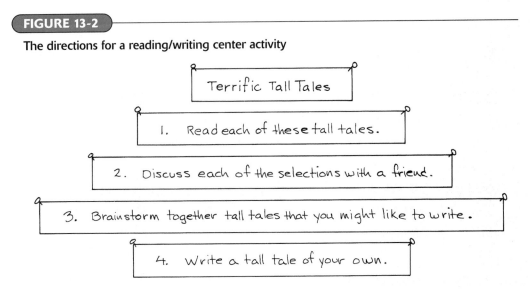

Second, reading/writing centers have clear directions detailing the procedures for completing each learning activity. These directions often are displayed prominently on a bulletin board or wall. Figure 13-2 shows the directions for the reading/writing center activity just described.

Third, reading/writing centers hold students' writing folders, where students can keep drafts of writing projects. Often, a manila folder is provided for each child and these are organized alphabetically in a small box. If you have a computer and word processing software, these may also be kept in student folders on the desktop.

Finally, reading/writing centers often have a place to turn in or display completed work. There may be a collection box and perhaps a bulletin board nearby. Displaying completed work gives other students an idea of what can be done. Usually a teacher has a single reading/writing center and rotates the activities there. Students are expected to complete center activities as they have time.

Cross-age Tutoring. Another way to provide individual learning experiences in literacy is with **cross-age tutoring** or what is sometimes referred to as book buddies. With cross-age tutoring, an older, more-proficient reader assists a younger, less-proficient reader in activities that are carefully organized by a teacher (Caserta-Henry, 1996). Cross-age tutoring provides an opportunity to individualize reading experiences and provide a supportive reading environment for students, especially those who may require additional assistance. It is usually recommended that the older child be about two grade levels beyond the younger child.

cross-age tutoring An approach using older, more-proficient students to assist younger, less-proficient students.

Cross-age tutoring is usually associated with increases in time on task, interactive learning, positive self-concepts, and positive attitudes about reading (Topping, 1989). There is also evidence that tutors gain in reading achievement at least as much as, if not more than, the children they tutor (Sharpley & Sharpley, 1981). Topping (1989) suggests that a minimum of three periods per week for at least 6 weeks duration be set aside for cross-age tutoring. Usually, each session lasts from 15 to 30 minutes.

Paired Reading. With **paired reading,** a tutor and a child read a text together. On easy sections the tutor allows the child to read out loud independently. When a mistake is made, the tutor pronounces the word correctly and has the child do the same before continuing. On more difficult sections, the two read out loud together. Then, when easier sections appear again, the child might signal the tutor to stop reading, while the child continues reading independently.

paired reading An approach in which two students read a text together.

Paired reading provides a scaffold that supports a child, especially when more challenging reading materials are encountered. It requires less training than cross-age tutoring

JUDY'S

COMMENTS FROM THE CLASSROOM

To make reading an inviting activity, I have worked to create a reading center that has become a favorite place for my students to be. Our center is often filled with children piled into beanbag chairs among the truckload of books, curled up in the rocking chair, or stretched out on some oversized stuffed animals. One frequent visitor to our reading center is a life-size granny doll we named Mrs. Minerva. She has velcroed hands, and my first graders climb into her lap and read stories to her. Children have told me that they like to read to Mrs. Minerva because she never interrupts them when they read and she never minds hearing the same story over and over again.

I work to change certain aspects of the reading center to keep children interested in using it. One technique I use is to house the books in the center in different kinds of containers. I use baskets, an empty aquarium, or specially decorated boxes. I try to match at least one container of books to a topic we are studying. For example, when we do our ocean unit I use the aquarium. I tape fish and other interesting sea creatures facing out on the inside walls. Then I tuck a few interesting shells inside and some books about the sea and animals that live there. For a study we did on plants and flowers, I placed a number of different kinds of plants and fresh cut flowers everywhere in the center and a big empty flower pot with "blooming ideas for books to read" in the middle of the center.

At different times, I have even used a big cardboard box made into a time machine, a pirate ship, or a dragon (all of which the class made while studying certain topics) to create "great escapes" and an exciting and different reading atmosphere.

The reading center is an important part of our classroom. I try to allow more individual freedom within it. Some children enjoy reading in the center with a partner while others like to browse through the books themselves. I have a few nonreaders who choose the same book much of the time as they have memorized it and can look like they are reading. That's alright for now because that is their level.

One other key to the center's popularity is having lots of predictable books in it because these books facilitate early reading success. The more successful the children feel, the more reading takes place.

Our reading center has a sign in it that says, "To be a better reader you have to read, read, read, read, read, read, read, read, read, read." Children soon take that message to heart.

Paired reading allows both children to gain from their shared reading experience.

Celebrating Diversity

Using Cross-age Tutoring with LEP Students

Cross-age tutoring is a useful approach to support the reading of children whose first language is not English. This approach supports their development in a very rich social support system. Children who work as the tutor learn, too, about a language and culture other than their own, especially if you encourage the pair to read books together about the culture of the limited English proficiency (LEP) student.

and results in similarly positive outcomes. Paired reading typically is used at frequent intervals, with each period of use lasting at least 6 weeks.

Small-Group Patterns

Small-group patterns provide an organizational framework designed to meet individual needs within a group of peers. Like individualized patterns, small-group patterns can be used to accommodate all types of individual differences important to literacy: background knowledge, interests, achievement levels, and skills. Differences in background knowledge are usually addressed by providing a group with a common task and by encouraging all group members to contribute their unique background knowledge to solving the task. Differences in interests, achievement levels, and skills usually are handled by developing groups around common interests, achievement levels, or skill needs. A variety of small-group patterns exist to meet these individual differences: guided reading groups, literature discussion groups, interest groups, cooperative learning groups, and strategy groups.

Guided Reading Groups. **Guided reading groups** (see chapter 2) are a way to organize your class according to reading level, and scaffold learning about reading at a level appropriate to different groups of children. Teachers will often have three to six different leveled groups in their class. They use reading selections for instruction that are at the level of the average student in each group. Guided reading lessons often follow these procedural steps:

1. Reread a familiar text to practice developing skills.
2. Introduce the new reading selection.
3. Read the new selection with support, when necessary.
4. Conduct a mini-lesson to teach a new strategy or review a previous strategy.

Teachers work with different guided reading groups during reading instruction. Groups who are not working with the teacher will be doing independent or small group work together. Other teachers will set up center activities and rotate students through these centers when they are not working with the teacher in their guided reading group. Sometimes, too, students will engage in paired reading, independent reading, or buddy reading during this time.

Guided reading groups are sometimes used with published school reading programs. Leveled grouping such as the type found in guided reading remains one of the most common in schools today, especially among teachers who hold more of a specific-skills belief about how to teach.

The first step in forming guided reading groups is to gather information and determine reading levels in the class. Two common sources of information include children's cumulative files and the informal assessment of reading levels completed during the first few weeks of the school year.

cumulative file A school file that contains a child's achievement and health records.

Each student has a **cumulative file,** which contains achievement and health records. Cumulative files typically are located in the school office, but classroom teachers have access to the information and often choose to review incoming children's files before the beginning of the year. At least two types of information might be useful: placement recommendations from last year's teacher and formal and informal test scores in reading.

In schools that use published reading programs, teachers are expected to record the materials each student completes by the end of the year. The next year's teacher often combines that information with additional data and places it all on a single form. Table 13-1 on pages 489–490 includes the information collected by a fourth-grade teacher from the previous year's records of two third-grade teachers. Notice how one of these teachers (Mr. Loseby) did not use a published reading program while the other teacher (Mrs. Ayre) did. The five children without such information are new students who transferred into the school at the beginning of the year.

After achievement data have been gathered, teachers must consider how many guided reading groups they want to form. The most common number is three. You should also consider how many children you want to have in each group. This decision hinges on your students' ability to work independently. Often it is best to reduce the number of children in a group that requires more individual attention. Thus, the lowest-achieving group in a classroom often is the smallest because those children frequently require more guidance and support from the teacher.

Any decisions made about placement in guided reading groups at the beginning of the year should be considered tentative and open to revision. Teachers should use the first month or two to see how well individual children fit into the organizational scheme of the classroom. In addition, teachers should be conservative when making those initial placements. Placing children in a lower-level group lets a teacher evaluate their performance and move them to a higher group at a later time. It is much harder to move children down without disturbing their confidence and motivation. As the year progresses, teachers should continuously reevaluate their grouping decisions and be prepared to accommodate children who might benefit from a change in group assignment.

If you choose to use guided reading groups, it is essential to also use alternate grouping patterns during the year—perhaps interest groups, cooperative learning groups, and any of the individualized organizational patterns described earlier. This is important if you seek to meet all of the individual differences that make a difference in your classroom organizational plan. Flexibility is important if children's individual differences are to be accommodated.

TABLE 13-1

Classroom assessment data collected at the beginning of the year by one fourth-grade teacher

Name	Level of Materials Completed Last Year	Stanine Decod/Voc/ Comp	IRI Instructional Level	Informal Observation	Interests
From Mr. Loseby					
Tomas	fourth grade	8/9/8	fifth grade	Fluent. Has read *Harry Potter*	Myths and Legends
Anne	fifth grade	9/9/9	fifth and sixth grades	Spends lunch in the library. Has read *Number the Stars*	Olympics, ballet
Tanika	fourth grade	3/9/6	fourth and fifth grades	Excellent comprehension	Poetry. African-American biographies
Sharon	fifth grade	8/4/7	fifth grade	Summer library reader	Basketball, sports
Dean	fourth grade	8/6/8	fourth grade	Summer library reader	Mysteries
Jo	fourth grade	5/5/5	fourth grade	Exposition a problem	Sports
Katie	fourth grade	6/4/5	third and fourth	A good reader	Horses, skiing
Sarah	fourth grade	7/5/5	fourth grade	Fluent reader	Science, the Internet
From Ms. Ayre					
Kathy	third grade	7/5/7	fifth grade	Excellent inferences, good vocabulary	Mysteries
Nelima	third grade	4/8/8	fifth grade	Summer library reader	The Internet
Ian	third grade	7/8/8	fifth grade	Excellent vocabulary	Sports, the Internet
Jesus	third grade	5/6/7	fifth grade	Excellent vocabulary	Basketball, poetry
Tim	third grade	4/7/7	fifth grade	Fluent, excellent vocabulary	The Internet, sports
Roberto	third grade	5/5/5	fourth grade	Weak vocabulary, exposition a problem	Mysteries, Olympics
Jessica	third grade	4/3/7	fourth grade	Good inferences, weak vocabulary	Reading, sports
Vanessa	third grade	3/4/4	third grade	Weak vocabulary	Pets, baseball
Jeff	third grade	6/3/4	third grade	Exposition a problem	Pets, the Internet
Kurt	second grade	3/4/3	third grade	Poor vocabulary, weak in exposition	Olympics
Matt	second grade	3/3/5	third grade	Weak decoding skills	Magic, travel

TABLE 13-1

Continued

Name	Level of Materials Completed Last Year	Stanine Decod/Voc/Comp	IRI Instructional Level	Informal Observation	Interests
New Students					
Erica			fifth grade	Writes a lot at home	Adventure stories
John			fourth grade	Weak vocabulary	Science fiction
Vanita			fifth grade	Excellent vocabulary	Ballet, sports
Gene			fourth grade	Lacks prefix/suffix knowledge	Dirt bikes
Daniel			first grade	Weak decoding skills, little comprehension	Hamsters, baseball

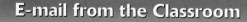

E-mail from the Classroom

Reply-To: "A Discussion Group for the Journal *The Reading Teacher*"
RTEACHER@BOOKMARK.READING.ORG
From: BobVillegma, Bvillegma@AOL.COM
Subject: Intermediate Centers

Why centers stop at the primary level has always been beyond me. Older students are so very capable of doing things on their own and need to get up and move about to get those growing bones moving. When I moved into a 6th grade position, my teammates chided me, "We can tell you were a PRIMARY teacher. You have CENTERS. We don't do centers here." I told them I'd always used centers and I'd try them out and see how they went. Needless to say, they went over very big. Other teachers even added a few "learning sites" to their rooms. I feel there are general centers that can be set up and changed easily without a lot of preparation:

Writing Center—Have a variety of paper for finished products, weird writing implements (pen with lightbulb on the end, scoliosis pen, Goofy pencil, and so on) to help release stuck thought processes, a thesaurus, picture prompts (WARNING: Just use a few, don't let them become the only source of inspiration!) in transparency boxes labeled "Setting," "Characters," etc. Calendars and ads in papers are great sources. I numbered each and put it into an acetate cover. Students using them were asked to put the number that inspired their work on the piece of writing. In addition, provide a variety of stamps: WORK IN PROGRESS stamp, Date stamp, and Student samples.

Reading Nook—This can consist of merely bookcases with lots of variety, ranging from easy picture books to tough levels. Provide comfortable seating, and a graffiti sheet where kids recommend books to one another. Reading is reading, not worksheets.

I hope this gives you some ideas. Centers are great, even for intermediate grade classrooms!

Bob

Literature Discussion Groups.   A common small-group organizational pattern is the use of **literature discussion groups.** In literature discussion groups, groups of children read the same work of children's literature on their own and then come together to have a **grand conversation** about what they have read. Afterward, the children develop a project and then share their project with the rest of the class. You will recall the procedural steps of a literature discussion group from chapter 6:

1. The teacher introduces three to five different books to the class, each with multiple copies.
2. Children determine which book they want to read and form groups based on this book.
3. Children read the literature selection for their group independently.
4. The teacher and each group have a grand conversation about the work.
5. A project is developed to extend children's response and understanding of the work.
6. The results of the project are shared with the other groups.

Literature discussion groups are used to support individual differences in each of the areas important to reading. By bringing children together to work on a common reading experience, discussion, and project, differences in background knowledge, interests, achievement levels, and skills are all supported. Sometimes, teachers will use individual contracts like that shown in Figure 13-3 on page 492 during the use of literature discussion groups to help children remember what needs to be done and when it should be completed.

Interest Groups.   It is also useful to group children by interests. Such **interest groups** allow children to explore topics that are personally interesting. For example, the sixth-grade class in one elementary school had been learning in social studies about the exploration of the western United States. Consequently, the teacher decided to let children select their favorite western state and then work with others who also selected that state. Children used Internet resources, multimedia encyclopedias, and other materials as they learned about their state. For one week, children worked in their interest groups—reading, collecting information, and finally reporting to the class about what they learned.

At the same school, the third-grade class was learning about different types of mammals in science, and the teacher decided to have children get together in groups to study their favorite mammal. This group also used the school's multimedia encyclopedias, Internet resources, and books from the school library. Each group read, collected information, and then created a bulletin board displaying their favorite mammal. Other interest groups might last longer but meet less frequently. Perhaps once a week or once a month, different interest groups might get together to share information and books about their favorite topics: sports, pets, science fiction, music, or computers. In each case, grouping decisions are based solely on children's interests.

Interest groups can serve several different purposes in a classroom reading program. You might consider it important to regularly engage children in functional reading experiences; opportunities to discover and share new information about an interesting topic can create important learning experiences. You might also want to increase interest in and motivation for reading, developing children who not only can read, but who also choose to read on their own. You might also be concerned about the negative effects on self-concept that result from the regular use of achievement groups. With interest groups, even the weakest readers have a chance to contribute to a topic that they find personally interesting.

There are several ways to form interest groups in a class. Perhaps the most common is to simply set up groups on several topics and allow children to select the area they want to pursue. Often teachers administer a reading inventory at the beginning of the school year to determine children's interests. The results of that inventory can then be used to make initial decisions about interest groups. Another approach is to ask children what areas they would like to explore that are related to a discussion topic just being completed. After children have had several experiences working in interest groups, this

literature discussion groups A method framework that helps children develop wider response patterns to their reading; small groups of students read a single work of literature on their own, come together to have a grand conversation, and then complete a shared project.

grand conversations A method framework that helps children develop wider response patterns to their reading; involves reading, reminding children of the guidelines, engaging children in a conversation they direct, and asking one interpretive or literacy question.

interest groups An intraclass organizational pattern that allows children to explore topics that are personally interesting.

FIGURE 13-3

A sample contract used in one class for literature discussion groups

---

A Contract with Ms. Clark

I _____ plan to read the following book as a part of my literature discussion group experience and complete each of the activities our group has decided upon as listed below:

Our book: _____.

Other members of my literature discussion group include:

_____   _____
_____   _____
_____   _____
_____   _____

Activities that I will complete as a member of my literature discussion group:

1. _____
_____
_____

2. _____
_____
_____

3. _____
_____
_____

4. _____
_____
_____

Signed: _____   _____
    (Student)   (Teacher)

Date: _____

---

strategy can be an effective method of turning control over to children and developing greater independence in reading.

What is your role once interest groups are functioning? Instead of providing direct instruction, you should guide students, providing resources for and direction to their reading and writing. You might circulate around the room, listening to ideas, offering suggestions, and helping children implement their own plans by directing them to the appropriate resources.

cooperative learning groups An intraclass organizational pattern that uses small groups and a cooperative learning method framework.

Cooperative Learning Groups. A third type of small-group pattern is the use of **cooperative learning groups,** described in chapters 2 and 10. Cooperative learning groups provide learning experiences for children in a supportive, collaborative environment as small groups of children work together to gather information and complete a learning task. Cooperative learning groups often follow these steps:

1. The teacher defines a learning task.
2. The teacher assigns children to groups.

Many teachers organize their rooms so there is space for a classroom reading center.

3. Children complete the learning task together.
4. The results of the learning task are shared with the entire class.

The model lesson on page 494 reviews those steps in operation.

Strategy Groups.   **Strategy groups** also attempt to meet individual differences. You may often find it useful to organize your classroom for short periods of time on the basis of specific strategy needs. Often these strategy groups will be used with reading and writing workshop. While most children are reading books they have chosen or are working on their own writing projects, you might provide instruction to a small group on inferencing strategies, the use of contextual information during reading, how to conduct peer revision conferences, or any of the numerous strategies known to be useful during reading or writing. This type of grouping is appropriate when skill and strategy needs cut across established achievement groups in your class or when several children display similar skill or strategy needs. In such situations you might regroup children temporarily on the basis of strategy needs or you might pull together certain children for a short workshop on particular reading or writing strategies.

Decisions about how many groups to use and how many children to have in each group closely parallel the decisions made with achievement groups. The number of groups will depend on children's previous experience with group work, your experience, and the amount and quality of supplemental materials available. The number of children in each group will be determined by the number of children with similar skills or strategy needs.

Despite these similarities, two important differences distinguish the use of strategy groups from the use of achievement groups. First, strategy groups typically last for only a few periods before children are regrouped for instruction on new strategies. Second, not all children will require instruction in the targeted areas. As a result, you should plan to use other activities with children who are not placed in a skill or strategy group.

Whole-Class Patterns

Whole-class experiences are especially valuable when they take advantage of the diversity inherent in any classroom. There are several types of **whole-class patterns** with which to organize literacy instruction.

strategy groups An intraclass organizational pattern in which children are grouped for a short period of time according to their skill or strategy needs.

whole-class patterns Whole-class experiences can be valuable in many instances of reading instruction. They are especially useful when they take advantage of the diversity inherent in any classroom.

MODEL LESSON

Using Cooperative Learning Groups in Bill Graham's Class

Bill often uses reading workshop with his sixth-grade class. He has reader-based beliefs about *what* to teach; prior knowledge components are much more important to him than decoding knowledge. In addition, he has a holistic language learning perspective about *how* to teach, believing that most of his students learn best when they direct their own learning activities. He is concerned, though, that reading workshop limits interactions among children. Bill is coming to believe that his students benefit both socially and intellectually when they work together more often on joint projects. Consequently, Bill has decided to spend 2 weeks during each 9-week marking period in cooperative learning groups.

The Teacher Defines a Learning Task. Bill's class is studying Europe in social studies and he decides to integrate social studies, reading, and writing for several weeks by using cooperative learning groups. He explains to the class that each group will study one European country in detail, exploring the history of the country as well as its economy, geography, political system, and famous people. Bill is especially excited about the potential this project has to motivate children to read newspapers and news magazines and to become acquainted with the European news locations on the WWW such as **CNN World News** (http://www.cnn.com/WORLD/index.html). Bill explains that each group will use Internet and library resources to locate information about its country and prepare a bulletin board display with a map of physical features and written reports on the country's history, economy, political system, and famous people. After the bulletin board displays are completed, Bill tells his students they will begin a keypal project in groups with children their own age from the country they studied. He plans to use **Web 66: Internations Schools Registry** (http://web66.coled.umn.edu/schools.html) and **Intercultural E-mail Classroom Connections** (http://www.stolaf.edu/network/iecc/) to locate schools in Europe who are interested in participating.

The Teacher Assigns Children to Groups. Bill puts up a list of European countries on the bulletin board and asks children to sign up for their three favorite countries. Using that list for guidance, he puts children together in groups of four or five.

Children Complete the Learning Task Together. For the next 2 weeks, each group gathers information and puts it together for a bulletin board display. Some groups work as a unit on each element of the task. Other groups split up, with one person responsible for the map and one person responsible for each of the reports. Bill encourages all groups to spend 10 minutes at the beginning of each work period sharing the information collected the previous day. He notices that children are gathering information for each other as they come across it in their reading. The last 2 days are a flurry of work, excitement, and debate as each group puts the finishing touches on its bulletin board display.

The Results of the Learning Task Are Shared with the Entire Class. On the final day, the recorder/reporter designated by each group makes a formal presentation to the class. Individual group members also contribute their expertise; then members of the class get to ask questions about the group's country.

Because he has reader-based beliefs about *what* to teach, Bill wanted to develop background knowledge about Europe his students could bring to their upcoming keypal experiences and to their independent reading of magazines and newspapers. A teacher with text-based beliefs would have directed children to find literal information about each of their countries.

Bill also has holistic language learning beliefs about *how* to teach. Consistent with these beliefs, he allows his students to select their country and he encourages each of the groups to develop their bulletin board presentation in their own way, including the information they find most appropriate. If he had a specific-skills perspective, Bill might have given each group a worksheet, specifying the information each group was required to find out about their country. Bill, more than his students, would have decided what each group would learn about their country.

---

thematic units Reading and writing experiences that include vocabulary study and discussions, all of which are organized around a theme.

As noted in chapter 6, **thematic units** are increasingly used in elementary and middle school classrooms. Thematic literacy experiences result when a teacher organizes reading and writing activities around a single theme. In addition, vocabulary study and discussions are used to expand on the theme and generate new understanding.

Thematic experiences can be organized in numerous ways: around a topic, such as solving problems, helping others, winter adventures, friendship, or animal pets; around an

MODEL LESSON

A Thematic Unit on Sharing in Bob Dewey's Class

Bob Dewey teaches fourth grade. He has an integrated belief about *how* to teach. He also has a reader-based belief about *what* to teach. Bob has organized a short integrated language arts unit on sharing for his class. Several reading selections form the core of the unit:

Maniac Magee by Jerry Spinelli

The Giving Tree by Shel Silverstein

The Gift by Helen Coutant

New Year's Hats for the Statues by Yoshiko Uchida

Before each reading selection Bob initiates a discussion about sharing that prepares children for the story. He also introduces new vocabulary words from the selection that might be unfamiliar to children. After each selection Bob uses cooperative learning groups to organize the discussion and response. He presents each group with a thought-provoking question about the story and asks them to respond to it in groups before sharing their responses with the entire class. After children read *The Giving Tree,* for example, he has cooperative learning groups consider the following:

> If you had been this apple tree, would you have acted the same way? Why or why not?

During this thematic unit Bob also conducts read-aloud sessions from the historical novel *Freedom Train* by Dorothy Sterling, a novel about the Underground Railroad and Harriet Tubman. He has his children complete response journal entries after each read-aloud. Afterward, volunteers share their entries with the class. He also uses Internet Workshop in his class (see Figure 13-4 on page 496), most notably these sites:

Harriet Tubman and the Underground Railroad (http://www2.lhric.org/pocantico/tubman/tubman.html)

The Underground Railway Quilt (http://www.beavton.k12.or.us/greenway/leahy/ugrr/index.htm)

Bob also introduces a writing experience to connect reading and writing. He suggests that everyone in class share an important idea for making the class a better place in which to learn and to grow. He encourages children to brainstorm a list of possible ideas and writes the list on the board. This gives everyone an idea about which to write. After children finish drafting, editing, and revising their work, Bob has them all read their papers aloud from the author's chair in the room. Their ideas generate lively discussion about improving the classroom. Finally, Bob posts each paper on a bulletin board labeled *Share a Great Idea.*

Teachers with a holistic language learning belief about *how* to teach would provide more student-directed learning activities, perhaps through the use of literature discussion groups during this unit instead of whole-class reading experiences with everyone reading the same works of literature. Teachers with a text-based or integrated belief about *what* to teach would focus on factual information in the reading selections, perhaps using a who, what, where, when, and why structure during discussion.

author, such as Daniel Pinkwater, Chris Van Allsburg, Paul Goble, or Laura Ingalls Wilder; or around a type of writing, such as science fiction, biographies, fables, or mysteries. Thematic literacy experiences focus on content. As a result, reading and writing experiences become more significant and functional. Children read, discuss, and write about a theme to learn more about it, not simply to learn how to read or write as shown above.

In a thematic unit the entire class usually reads the same selections so that all children share a similar body of content. However, these experiences often include cooperative learning group activities and individualized writing assignments to better accommodate individual differences.

Additional Whole-Class Patterns

Any activity that requires an audience is a perfect opportunity for a whole-class experience. Oral book reports, for example, can be presented by children when they finish

FIGURE 13-4

Harriet Tubman and the Underground Railroad (http://www2.lhric.org/pocantico/ tubman/tubman.html)), one of several locations on the WWW Bob Dewey used for Internet Workshop during his thematic unit on sharing

Note: Courtesy of Terry Hongell and Patty Taverna, Pocantico Hills School.

reading a book they think others might enjoy. Readers theater presentations are also especially appropriate, as are read-aloud response journal sessions.

Short sessions in which children are introduced to new materials are also perfect opportunities for a whole-class activity. You might conduct a book talk, for example, to introduce a new set of books in the reading corner. Or a child might introduce the author-of-the-week bulletin board and acquaint others with a favorite author. Perhaps a new activity at the reading/writing center could be explained. Each of these provides a useful literacy experience in a whole-class pattern.

Another opportunity for a whole-class experience may occur when you wish to teach a reading or writing strategy to all children together; for example, the use of references in the library, map reading before a field trip, the use of a thesaurus as a writing aid, or a new poetic form. Another opportunity comes with current events. You might have your class subscribe to a weekly newspaper so that children can read and discuss current events together. In addition, sustained silent reading (SSR), which is often incorporated into a daily reading schedule, is an important whole-class reading experience, while choral reading provides an entire class with an opportunity to appreciate rhythm, poetry, and the stylistic conventions of unique discourse forms.

Integrating Internet Experiences within a Single Computer Classroom: Special Organizational Strategies

Some schools are fortunate enough to have one, or several, computer clusters available to an entire class at a single time. Others have several computers linked to the Internet in each classroom. More typically, however, a classroom will have a single computer linked to the Internet. In this case, you will face the important organizational challenge

FIGURE 13-5

Mary Lou Balcom's weekly schedule for Internet use in her sixth-grade classroom, posted on the bulletin board next to the Internet computer in her classroom

	Monday	Tuesday	Wednesday	Thursday	Friday
8:30–9:00	Mikka	Mikka/Bobbi	Austin/Emily	Betina/Cara	Torrie/Sasha
9:00–9:30	Austin	John/Peter	Jeremy/Dave	Kati	Patti
9:30–10:00	**Internet Workshop**	Ben	Aaron	Lisa	Julia
10:00–10:30	Betina	**PE**	Paul	**PE**	Andy
10:30–11:00	**Library**	Mike	Scott	Faith	Melissa
11:00–11:30	Torrie	Matt	Curt	Linda	Sara
11:30–12:00	**Lunch**	**Lunch**	**Lunch**	**Lunch**	**Lunch**
12:30–1:00	Sasha	Dave	Peter	Cara	Emily
1:00–1:30	Bobbi	Jeremy	Ben/Sara	Mike/Linda	John
1:30–2:00	Matt/Curt	Aaron/Melissa	**Music**	Paul/Scott	**Class Meeting**
2:00–2:30	Kati/Lisa		Faith/Andy	Patti/Julia	

of providing equal and sufficient time for each child to access resources on the Internet to complete his or her required assignments.

A common solution to this situation is to assign each child to two, half-hour blocks of time each week on the Internet computer. Each child works independently during the first half-hour block and with a partner during the second half-hour block. This provides each child with at least 1 hour of Internet use each week. If children require more time on the Internet, they can often visit the media center or computer cluster at your school and use the connections there. Figure 13-5 presents the schedule used by Mary Lou Balcom at Edward Smith Elementary School for her class.

Ensuring sufficient access to Internet resources with only a single classroom computer requires a special accommodation, however. You must be willing to have individuals or pairs of children miss other activities in the classroom during their Internet time. In most elementary classrooms, this is not a large problem. Teachers usually find a time block for children during content-area instruction where they are strongest and can afford to miss a half-hour session. Thus, if a student is very strong in math, he or she would probably have a half-hour block during the time when math is regularly scheduled. When you set up such a system in your class, you will see that children quickly help one another to get caught up on any work they might have missed.

You should also note that a schedule like that in Figure 13-5 provides opportunities for you to put a weaker student together with a stronger student for at least a half-hour each week. This is often helpful during Internet experiences. It allows time for children to work together and exchange Internet strategies.

Using a Literacy Framework to Guide Decisions about Classroom Organization

Decisions about classroom organization are decisions about *how* you will teach. Will you use reading and writing workshop, literature discussion groups, interest groups, or thematic reading and writing experiences to provide student-directed experiences? Will you use guided reading groups and strategy groups to provide children with more direct instructional experiences, focusing on skill instruction? Or will you integrate guided reading and/or strategy groups with reading and writing workshop, literature discussion groups, interest groups, and thematic reading and writing experiences? Because organizational

TABLE 13-2

A summary of how a literacy framework can inform decisions about classroom organizational patterns

Issues and Beliefs in a Literacy Framework That Inform This Issue	Instructional Decisions That Are Informed by Your Beliefs
How Should I Teach?	
Children learn to read best by directing their own reading experiences. (Holistic language learning beliefs)	I should emphasize student-directed reading experiences and inductive learning. Reading experiences always take place in the context of authentic social contexts and always with authentic reading materials. I am most concerned about accommodating two individual differences that make a difference in reading: interests and background knowledge. Popular organizational patterns are those that allow for much student direction during learning experiences: the use of thematic units, literature discussion groups, interest groups, and reading and writing workshop activities. Internet Inquiry and Internet Project are often used.
Children learn best when teachers direct reading experiences, providing direct instruction in specific reading skills. (Specific-skills beliefs)	I should teach specific skills with direct instructional practices. I am most concerned about accommodating two individual differences that make a difference in reading: literacy achievement levels and literacy skills. Popular organizational patterns include those that focus on skill development: guided reading and strategy groups.
Sometimes children learn best by directing their own reading experiences, and sometimes children learn best when teachers direct learning experiences, providing direct instruction in specific reading skills. (Integrated beliefs)	I should create authentic learning environments for children to explore their own literacy insights and directly teach specific skills, depending on individual needs. I am most concerned about accommodating all four individual differences that make a difference in reading: interests, background knowledge, skills, and literacy achievement level. All organizational patterns are used to meet the widest range of individual needs. Internet Workshop, Internet Inquiry and Internet Project are used.

decisions determine how learning experiences will be structured, your beliefs about *how* to teach can be used as a guide. These relationships can be seen in Table 13-2.

If you have more of a holistic language learning belief about how to teach, you believe that reading is learned inductively as children engage in self-directed, meaningful, and holistic experiences with authentic literature. As a result, you are most concerned about accommodating two individual differences that make a difference in literacy: interests and background knowledge. Because you are most concerned about accommodating these two differences, you tend to favor certain types of intraclass organizational patterns. These include the use of thematic units for reading and writing, literature discussion groups, interest groups, and reading workshop. You would also use Internet Inquiry and Internet Workshop.

If you have a specific-skills belief about how to teach, you believe that differences in achievement levels and skills are most important to accommodate in your organizational plans. These differences are most important because you believe children learn best when they are directly taught specific literacy skills. As a result, you favor intraclass organizational patterns such as guided reading groups and strategy groups. These allow you to focus your attention on direct instruction of specific literacy skills.

If you have an integrated belief of how to teach, you think that all four types of individual differences are important to consider: reading interests, background knowledge, reading skills, and reading achievement level. This is because you believe children learn best when they are exposed to authentic and holistic experiences with print and, at the same time, receive instruction in important skill areas. As a result, you favor all six types of intraclass organizational patterns: thematic units for reading and writing, literature discussion groups, interest groups, reading workshop, guided reading groups, and strategy groups. These allow you to accommodate all of the individual differences that are important to you. You would also use Internet Inquiry and Internet Workshop.

Of course, it is also important to recognize that the previous discussion represents three specific beliefs. If your beliefs about how children learn to read fall somewhere between any two of these beliefs, you will modify your organizational plans accordingly.

But how would teachers with these different beliefs actually organize their reading program during the year to accommodate the individual differences they find most important? The following section will describe how teachers with different beliefs might develop a **yearly plan** for their classroom. A yearly plan is often used by teachers to plan out how and when they will use different organizational patterns in their classroom for the entire year. The plans in Tables 13-3 through 13-5 on the following pages specify the primary grouping patterns for each week and indicate how much time will be devoted to other organizational patterns such as read-aloud response journals, sustained silent reading, individualized reading, and reading/writing center activities.

yearly plan A schedule of organizational patterns to be used during the year to accommodate individual differences.

TABLE 13-3

An organization plan for one year consistent with a holistic language perspective

Week	Getting Started in Reading
1 & 2	Introduce and begin read-alouds and response journals Introduce and begin reading/writing center activities Introduce the Internet and go over the acceptable use policy Collect reading interest information from an interest inventory and discussions Collect background knowledge information with informal assessment Administer informal assessment (IRI and running records) Check cumulative files for additional assessment information

Week	Primary Grouping Pattern	Additional Experiences
3–6	Thematic unit #1: Human rights and responsibilities (whole class—60 minutes)	Read-aloud response journals (30 minutes, alternate days) Sustained silent reading (30 minutes, alternate days) Internet Inquiry/Internet Project (1 hour per week) Reading/Writing center activities (as time permits)
7–9	Thematic unit #2: The African-American experience (whole class—60 minutes)	Read-aloud response journals (30 minutes, alternate days) Sustained silent reading (30 minutes, alternate days) Internet Inquiry/Internet Project (1 hour per week) Reading/Writing center activities (as time permits)
10–12	Thematic unit #3: The Asian experience (whole class—60 minutes)	Read-aloud response journals (30 minutes, alternate days) Sustained silent reading (30 minutes, alternate days) Internet Inquiry/Internet Project (1 hour per week) Reading/Writing center activities (as time permits)

Continued

TABLE 13-3

Continued

Week	Primary Grouping Pattern	Additional Experiences
13–15	Literature discussion groups (small groups—60 minutes)	Read-aloud response journals (30 minutes, alternate days) Sustained silent reading (30 minutes, alternate days) Internet Inquiry/Internet Project (1 hour per week)
16–18	Interest groups/Reading Workshop (small groups—60 minutes)	Read-aloud response journals (30 minutes, alternate days) Sustained silent reading (30 minutes, alternate days) Internet Inquiry/Internet Project (1 hour per week)
19–21	Thematic unit #4: The Hispanic experience (whole class—60 minutes)	Read-aloud response journals (30 minutes, alternate days) Sustained silent reading (30 minutes, alternate days) Internet Inquiry/Internet Project (1 hour per week) Reading/Writing center activities (as time permits)
22–24	Literature discussion groups (small groups—60 minutes)	Read-aloud response journals (30 minutes, alternate days) Sustained silent reading (30 minutes, alternate days) Internet Inquiry/Internet Project (1 hour per week)
25–27	Interest groups/Reading Workshop (small groups—60 minutes)	Read-aloud response journals (30 minutes, alternate days) Sustained silent reading (30 minutes, alternate days) Internet Inquiry/Internet Project (1 hour per week)
28–30	Thematic unit #5: The meaning of friendship (whole class—60 minutes)	Read-aloud response journals (30 minutes, alternate days) Sustained silent reading (30 minutes, alternate days) Internet Inquiry/Internet Project (1 hour per week) Reading/Writing center activities (as time permits)
31–33	Literature discussion groups (small groups—60 minutes)	Read-aloud response journals (30 minutes, alternate days) Sustained silent reading (30 minutes, alternate days) Internet Inquiry/Internet Project (1 hour per week)
34–36	Interest groups/Reading Workshop (small groups—60 minutes)	Read-aloud response journals (30 minutes, alternate days) Sustained silent reading (30 minutes, alternate days) Internet Inquiry/Internet Project (1 hour per week)

TABLE 13-4

An organization plan for one year consistent with a specific-skills perspective

Week	Getting Started in Reading
1 & 2	Check cumulative files for assessment information Introduce and begin reading/writing center contracts Introduce and begin read-alouds and response journals Collect reading interest information from an interest inventory and discussions Administer informal assessment (IRI and running records)

Week	Primary Grouping Pattern	Additional Experiences
3–6	Achievement groups with a published reading program (whole class—60 minutes) (regroup as necessary)	Read-aloud response journals (30 minutes, alternate days) Sustained silent reading (30 minutes, alternate days) Reading/Writing center activities (Contracts)
7–9	Achievement groups with a published reading program (whole class—60 minutes) (regroup as necessary)	Read-aloud response journals (30 minutes, alternate days) Sustained silent reading (30 minutes, alternate days) Reading/Writing center activities (Contracts)
10	Strategy groups (small groups—60 minutes)	Read-aloud response journals (30 minutes, alternate days) Sustained silent reading (30 minutes, alternate days) Reading/Writing center activities (Contracts)
11–18	Achievement groups with a published reading program (whole class—60 minutes)	Read-aloud response journals (30 minutes, alternate days) Sustained silent reading (30 minutes, alternate days) Reading/Writing center activities (Contracts)
19	Strategy groups (small groups—60 minutes)	Read-aloud response journals (30 minutes, alternate days) Sustained silent reading (30 minutes, alternate days) Reading/Writing center activities (Contracts)
20–27	Achievement groups with a published reading program (whole class—60 minutes)	Read-aloud response journals (30 minutes, alternate days) Sustained silent reading (30 minutes, alternate days) Reading/Writing center activities (Contracts)
28	Strategy groups (small groups—60 minutes)	Read-aloud response journals (30 minutes, alternate days) Sustained silent reading (30 minutes, alternate days) Reading/Writing center activities (Contracts)
29–36	Achievement groups with a published reading program (whole class—60 minutes)	Read-aloud response journals (30 minutes, alternate days) Sustained silent reading (30 minutes, alternate days) Reading/Writing center activities (Contracts)

TABLE 13-5

An organization plan for one year consistent with an integrated perspective

Week	Getting Started in Reading
1 & 2	Introduce and begin read-alouds and response journals Introduce and begin individualized reading Introduce and begin reading/writing center activities Collect reading interest information from an interest inventory and discussions Collect background knowledge information with informal assessment Administer informal assessment (IRI and running records) Check cumulative files for additional assessment information

Week	Primary Grouping Pattern	Additional Experiences
3–5	Thematic unit #1 with reading workshop: Diversity and difference (whole class—60 minutes)	Read-aloud response journals (30 minutes, alternate days) Sustained silent reading (30 minutes, alternate days) Internet Project/Inquiry/Workshop (1 hour per week) Reading/Writing center activities (as time permits)
6–9	Thematic unit #2 with reading workshop Planet Earth: Ecology (whole class—60 minutes)	Read-aloud response journals (30 minutes, alternate days) Sustained silent reading (30 minutes, alternate days) Internet Project/Inquiry/Workshop (1 hour per week) Reading/Writing center activities (as time permits)
10–13	Thematic unit #3 with reading workshop The Written Word: Literacy (whole class—60 minutes)	Read-aloud response journals (30 minutes, alternate days) Sustained silent reading (30 minutes, alternate days) Internet Project/Inquiry/Workshop (1 hour per week) Reading/Writing center activities (as time permits)
14–15	Literature discussion groups (small groups—60 minutes)	Read-aloud response journals (30 minutes, alternate days) Sustained silent reading (30 minutes, alternate days) Internet Project/Inquiry/Workshop (1 hour per week)
16–18	Interest groups (small groups—60 minutes)	Read-aloud response journals (30 minutes, alternate days) Sustained silent reading (30 minutes, alternate days) Internet Project/Inquiry/Workshop (1 hour per week)
19–22	Thematic unit #4 with reading workshop Medieval Europe (whole class—60 minutes)	Read-aloud response journals (30 minutes, alternate days) Sustained silent reading (30 minutes, alternate days) Internet Project/Inquiry/Workshop (1 hour per week) Reading/Writing center activities (as time permits)

TABLE 13-5

Continued

Week	Primary Grouping Pattern	Additional Experiences
23–25	Literature discussion groups (small groups—60 minutes)	Read-aloud response journals (30 minutes, alternate days) Sustained silent reading (30 minutes, alternate days) Internet Project/Inquiry/Workshop (1 hour per week)
26–27	Interest groups (small groups—60 minutes)	Read-aloud response journals (30 minutes, alternate days) Sustained silent reading (30 minutes, alternate days) Internet Project/Inquiry/Workshop (1 hour per week)
28–31	Thematic unit #5 with reading workshop The Meaning of Friendship (whole class—60 minutes)	Read-aloud response journals (30 minutes, alternate days) Sustained silent reading (30 minutes, alternate days) Internet Project/Inquiry/Workshop (1 hour per week) Reading/Writing center activities (as time permits)
32–34	Literature discussion groups (small groups—60 minutes)	Read-aloud response journals (30 minutes, alternate days) Sustained silent reading (30 minutes, alternate days) Internet Project/Inquiry/Workshop (1 hour per week)
35–36	Interest groups (small groups—60 minutes)	Read-aloud response journals (30 minutes, alternate days) Sustained silent reading (30 minutes, alternate days) Internet Project/Inquiry/Workshop (1 hour per week)

Holistic Language Learning Beliefs

Teachers with a holistic language learning perspective believe literacy ability develops as children engage in holistic, meaningful, and functional experiences with authentic literature and as children direct many of their own reading and writing experiences. A yearly plan for such a teacher would reflect those assumptions. Table 13-3 on pages 499–500 shows one possible arrangement.

The first two weeks of school typically are used by all teachers to develop an understanding of their students' strengths and needs in reading and writing. This time is also used to introduce children to some of the organizational aspects of the class. Note, for example, how this teacher introduces children to the Internet, read-alouds, response journals, reading workshop activities, and reading/writing center activities. Introducing these more independent activities also frees the teacher to conduct informal reading inventories (IRIs) or other informal assessments such as initial running records (see chapter 11).

Teachers with a holistic perspective would rely largely on four primary grouping patterns during the year: thematic units for reading and writing, literature discussion groups, interest groups, and reading workshop. Table 13-3 suggests how these primary grouping patterns might be scheduled during the year. Additional experiences would be provided through read-aloud response journal sessions, sustained silent reading, Internet Inquiry, Internet Project, and reading/writing center activities. Teachers with a holistic perspective would find these experiences to provide special opportunities for children to direct their own experiences in literacy learning.

Specific-Skills Beliefs

Teachers with a specific-skills perspective believe literacy develops as children learn specific skills through teacher-directed, deductive lessons. As a result, these teachers organize their classrooms to maximize instruction on specific literacy skills. A yearly plan for literacy instruction consistent with a specific-skills explanation is outlined in Table 13-4 (page 501). Teachers with a specific-skills perspective would rely largely on two grouping patterns during the year: guided reading groups and strategy groups. Each allows teachers with this belief to develop the specific literacy skills they find important.

As with all teachers, teachers with a specific-skills perspective want to spend the first 2 weeks getting acquainted with their children and letting children become familiar with the organization of their new classroom. These teachers might also introduce children to the Internet, read-aloud response journals, and reading/writing center activities. As children are working independently, these teachers might evaluate them individually with an IRI. They might also administer an interest inventory. At the same time, they would gather achievement information from children's cumulative files and use all of this information to make preliminary decisions about achievement groups.

Teachers with a specific-skills perspective would probably rely on a published reading program for the core of their reading instruction, thereby leading to the use of guided reading groups as their primary grouping pattern. According to Table 13-4, instruction would begin during week 3. Then, during weeks 3 to 6 these teachers would observe their children's performance and make any changes in group assignments by the end of week 6. They would also do the same type of observation and regrouping during weeks 7 to 9.

We can see from Table 13-4 that guided reading groups are used during the first 9-week period. After that, the first week in each 9-week block is devoted to strategy groups. Children would be regrouped according to their specific strategy and skill needs and provided with appropriate instruction. The final 8 weeks in each block are then spent in guided reading groups.

While guided reading groups and strategy groups are the primary grouping patterns used by teachers with specific-skills beliefs, other experiences will also be provided. Read-aloud response journals will be used on alternate days to make connections between reading and writing (see chapter 7). On other days, sustained silent reading will be used to help develop independent readers (see chapter 6). Throughout the week, reading/writing center activities will be used to provide independent practice opportunities for children. Here, a specific-skills teacher is likely to use contracts to monitor children's progress. Each week the center activity is changed, and children make a contract with the teacher to complete a certain number of activities during each 9-week period. There would probably be little Internet use, and when it is used it would be to practice specific literacy skills.

Integrated Beliefs

Teachers with an integrated explanation of development would include both holistic and specific-skills perspectives in their decisions about classroom organization. Table 13-5 (pages 502–503) shows one way in which an integrated classroom might be organized.

During the first 2 weeks, time would again be spent collecting achievement and interest data on the children and introducing them to the organizational patterns in the classroom. Notice, too, that many of the more independent activities are introduced during this time to permit individual assessment activities.

The primary grouping patterns used by teachers with integrated beliefs would include thematic units, literature discussion groups, and interest groups. Thematic unit reading experiences would be conducted along with reading workshop. This would provide specific-skills instruction for those who benefit from this assistance. Notice in Table 13-5 (pages 502–503) how this teacher weaves these different types of organizational patterns into the yearly plan.

Other experiences are also provided by teachers with integrated beliefs. Read-aloud response journals are used on alternate days to make connections between reading and writing (see chapter 7). On other days, sustained silent reading is used to help develop independent readers (see chapter 6). Throughout the week, Internet Workshop/Inquiry on Project would also take place (see chapters 2, 9, and 14). And reading/writing center activities are used to provide independent practice opportunities for children.

Use the self-test questions on http://www.prenhall. com/leukinzer to review the material presented in this chapter.

Major Points

▸ Reading instruction should attempt to meet the individual needs of each child in the classroom. Four types of individual differences are most important to reading instruction: background knowledge and experiences, interests, achievement levels, and skills.

▸ Schools accommodate the individual differences important to reading through interclass organizational patterns such as homogeneous grouping (tracking); departmentalized instruction; team teaching; cross-grade grouping; split-half classes; retention and acceleration; and assistance from reading specialists or special educators.

▸ Teachers accommodate the individual differences important to reading through intraclass organizational patterns. These include individualized patterns such as reading workshop, Internet Workshop, Internet Inquiry, reading/writing centers, cross-age tutoring, and paired reading. Small-group patterns include literature discussion groups, interest groups, cooperative learning groups, guided reading groups, and strategy groups. Whole-class patterns include thematic reading and writing experiences and other whole-class reading experiences.

▸ Teachers with a single Internet computer in their classroom will need to develop a schedule to provide equal access for each child.

▸ Because organizational decisions are based on how to structure learning experiences, your beliefs about *how* to teach can be used to guide decision making. A teacher with holistic language beliefs will favor organizational patterns that allow for much student direction during learning experiences: the use of thematic reading and writing units, literature discussion groups, interest groups, and reading workshop activities. A teacher with a specific-skills perspective will favor organizational patterns that focus on skill development: guided reading groups and strategy groups. A teacher with an integrated perspective will use all organizational patterns to meet the widest range of individual needs.

Making Instructional Decisions

1. Interview two children in an elementary-grade classroom. Find out as much as possible about their background knowledge and reading interests. Then interview their teacher and find out as much as you can about their reading achievement levels and needs. Write a description of each child (without using real names), comparing and contrasting these children in areas important to reading instruction: background knowledge, reading interests, reading achievement levels, and reading skills. What can you conclude about the nature of individual differences in a classroom of 25 children?

2. According to Harris and Sipay (1990), you can expect a minimum of 8 years' difference in reading achievement at the eighth-grade level. In reality, the difference is likely to be more than 8 years. Let's assume your school has departmentalized reading instruction for eighth grade and you are responsible for assigning children to

classes. You have begun by organizing three separate classes: one of lower-achieving readers, one of average-achieving readers, and one of higher-achieving readers. What is the minimum difference you should expect in reading achievement levels in each of your classes? Has a departmentalized reading program solved the challenge presented by individual differences? Why or why not?

3. Identify a thematic unit topic. Then, identify at least five different locations on the WWW that could be used during this thematic unit for Internet Workshop.

4. Use the data in Table 13-1 to form several different interest groups. Describe several different reading projects each group could complete together with appropriate Internet locations.

5. Using the information in cumulative files at the beginning of the school year is controversial. Some professionals argue that the use of this information biases a teacher's perception of a child and results in a self-fulfilling prophecy (Rosenthal & Jacobson, 1968). They consider this practice most damaging to the least able and suggest that achievement information in cumulative files not be used to form achievement groups. Others argue that achievement scores, used correctly, are just one source of information a teacher should consider. These professionals consider it inappropriate to ignore any information when making a decision as important as achievement group placement. Will you use the achievement information in a child's cumulative file? If you decide to use it, what might you do to reduce the possibility of creating self-fulfilling prophecies for your students?

6. Define your current literacy framework. If you were to begin teaching next week, which yearly plan would you follow in your classroom reading program? Describe how you would meet your children's individual differences in background knowledge, reading interests, achievement levels, and reading skills.

Further Reading

Berghoff, B., & Egawa, K. (1991). No more "rocks": Grouping to give students control of their learning. *The Reading Teacher, 44* (8), 536–541.

The authors describe grouping practices from a holistic language learning perspective. They present an excellent table describing a variety of whole class, small group, and independent patterns and explain how each supports literacy development and self-directed learning experiences.

Caserta-Henry, C. (1996). Reading buddies: A first grade intervention program. *The Reading Teacher, 49* (6), 500–503.

Describes the positive results in one classroom resulting from a reading buddy program. The article takes you through a school year, explaining how to establish a successful program with reading buddies.

Jacobs, G., & Gallo, P. (2002). Reading alone together: Enhancing extensive reading via student-student cooperation in second language instruction. *Reading Online.* Available: http://www.readingonline.org/articles/art_index.asp?HREF=jacobs/index.html

Describes an approach that combines extensive independent reading and cooperative discussion with others useful for a wide range of student populations.

Keegan, S., & Shrake, K. (1991). Literature study groups: An alternative to ability grouping. *The Reading Teacher, 44* (8), 542–547.

Describes the use of literature study groups, an approach to organizing classroom learning based on literature, discussions, and writing experiences. The article describes the importance of preparing students for these more independent experiences. Several useful ideas for the classroom are presented, including the use of a dialogue journal between the group and the teacher.

Staab, C. (1991). Classroom organization: Thematic centers revisited. *The Reading Teacher, 68,* 108–113.

Shows how the use of thematic reading centers can be used to engage students in meaningful literacy experiences within the classroom and promote self-directed learning.

References

Anderson, R. C., Hiebert, E. H., Scott, J. A., & Wilkinson, I. A. G. (1985). *Becoming a nation of readers: The report of the commission on reading.* Washington, DC: National Institute of Education.

Berghoff, B., & Egawa, K. (1991). No more "rocks": Grouping to give students control of their learning. *The Reading Teacher, 44* (8), 536–541.

Caserta-Henry, C. (1996). Reading buddies: A first grade intervention program. *The Reading Teacher, 49* (6), 500–503.

Harp, B. (1989). When the principal asks: "What do we know now about ability grouping?" *The Reading Teacher, 42* (6), 430–431.

Harris, A. J., & Sipay, E. R. (1990). *How to increase reading ability* (9th ed.). New York: Longman Publishing Group.

Hiebert, E. H. (1983). An examination of ability grouping for reading instruction. *Reading Research Quarterly, 18* (2), 231–255.

Keegan, S., & Shrake, K. (1991). Literature study groups: An alternative to ability grouping. *The Reading Teacher, 44* (8), 542–547.

Rosenthal, R., & Jacobson, J. (1968). *Pygmalion in the classroom.* New York: Holt, Rinehart & Winston.

Sharpley, A. M., & Sharpley, C. F. (1981). Peer tutoring—A review of the literature. *Collected Original Resources in Education, 5* (3), 7–11.

Slavin, R. E. (1987). Ability grouping and student achievement in elementary schools: A best evidence synthesis. *Review of Educational Research, 57* (3), 293–336.

Snow, C., Burns, M., & Griffin, P. (Eds.). (1998). *Preventing reading difficulties in young children.* Washington, DC: National Academy Press.

Staab, C. (1991). Classroom organization: Thematic centers revisited. *The Reading Teacher, 68,* 108–113.

Topping, K. (1989). Peer tutoring and paired reading: Combining two powerful techniques. *The Reading Teacher, 42* (7), 488–494.

Tunnell, M. O., & Jacobs, J. S. (1989). Using "real" books: Research findings on literature based reading instruction. *The Reading Teacher, 42* (7), 470–477.

CHAPTER 14

Supporting Literacy with Computers and Related Technologies

 E-mail from the Classroom

Subject: Getting Started
From: Sylvia Brundy, brun@vanderbilt.edu

I have used computers all the way through high school and college. Then, IM was my life!—Who needed a phone? It's hard to believe that some people are still a bit frightened about technology and don't use the Internet much!

However, even though I use computers a lot, it was mainly for IM, games, and music, and I didn't know too much about what to do with technology in my teaching. I didn't want to learn to program. But then I started getting on some teacher listservs and looked at some online support pages, did some reading, and found that there were lots of really good ways to integrate technology into my teaching, and to prepare my students for this "new literacy."

In addition to teaching with computers and the Internet, my students and I put together a home page for our classroom—it isn't all that hard to do. Our classroom home page gives my students a motivating place to share their work, and they now use the Internet to do all sorts of activities that help their literacy learning.

My advice is to just go ahead and try it. See you on the Internet!

—Sylvia

Key Concepts

application software	listserv
CD-ROM	managing learning with computers
drill-and-practice software	multimedia
graphics	network
hardware	program
hypertext	simulations
Internet	(speech-based) software
learning about thinking with computers	tutorial software
learning with computers	videodisc

After reading this chapter, you should be able to:

1. Implement an appropriate model for using computers and related technologies to enhance literacy instruction.
2. Choose and evaluate software for use in your literacy program.
3. Address issues related to child safety and your own professional development related to Internet use.
4. Integrate Internet and other technology resources into your literacy teaching.

⌨ Teach for Children's Literacy Futures: A Principle of Effective Literacy Instruction

As you consider the changes in what it means to be "literate" now as opposed to even 5 years ago, it should be clear that literacy demands are changing. Both leisure and work activities have come to incorporate technology and the Internet as a part of life, and effective use of technology is increasingly becoming part of being a literate individual. Communication ability now includes, but goes beyond, traditional paper-and-pencil environments. Therefore, teachers of literacy must consider two issues: how to use technology to further their work in teaching children, and how to teach children the necessary requirements for the literacies of their future. Thus, the final principle of effective literacy instruction, as noted in chapter 1, is:

12. **Teach for children's literacy futures.** Integrating computer and Internet technologies in literacy instruction allows children to use their emerging literacy abilities in the most current literacies that are valued in society and can enhance children's learning of both conventional and emerging literacies (Labbo, 1996; Leu & Kinzer, 2000; Reinking, 1998). Teaching in ways that prepare children for emerging communication and literacy demands is important. This principle is part of each chapter in this book and is emphasized in chapter 14.

This chapter will show you how to address both of the areas noted above. It presents a discussion to help you apply what may be already considerable knowledge about technology to your teaching, and will show you how to integrate technology into your teaching of the various components of the reading process.

Check your ongoing understanding of chapter concepts by using the guided review for this chapter on http://www. prenhall.com/leukinzer

If we believe that literacy serves communicative and meaning-making functions, then the Internet, and its use by children, must be considered in definitions of literacy and in literacy instruction. As Instant Messenger and children's personal home pages become ever more prevalent, and as children use the Internet to help complete traditional school assignments, we are being sent clear signals about what children view as important and everyday functions of literacy in their lives. Clearly, teachers must help to prepare children for the literacies that will become increasingly important in our children's futures.

⌨ Categories of Technology Uses

In chapter 1, you read about the need to consider the changing literacy demands your students will encounter as they leave your classroom. Throughout this book, you have read about how the Internet and other technology tools will help you to teach children to become literate. And you know from your coursework and from reading this text that you will be teaching at an exciting time—a time that will allow you to use resources from around the world to help you teach children to become independent readers and writers.

Two closely related tools—the classroom computer and the Internet—are transforming the teaching and learning of literacy. Nonetheless, some believe that computers and related technology are an expensive fad that adds little to the literacy curriculum and that technology is threatening the human qualities required for teaching. Others view computer technology as a force that will radically change instructional practice, almost replacing teachers.

Neither of these views adequately reflects the potential benefits of a thoughtful implementation of technology in the literacy curriculum. Computers are an educational tool that can be well used or badly misused, like all other technology and teaching materials. For example, neither published reading programs nor the use of children's literature provides any greater guarantee of effective instruction than do computers. In all cases, teachers must make appropriate instructional decisions and appropriately use instructional tools.

TABLE 14-1

A classification system of computer use

Classification	Examples
Learning with computers	*Simulations:* Includes software that models a real-world situation and attempts to enhance problem-solving abilities.
Learning about thinking with computers	*Problem solving:* Includes the potential influence on children's thinking skills that results from working with computers and some types of software.
Learning from computers	*Drill and practice:* Includes most games and tutorial software.
Managing learning with computers	*Classroom management:* Includes record-keeping, filing, gradebook, and other such functions.
Learning about computers	*Computer literacy:* Includes learning about the equipment as well as learning programming languages. Although you will have to provide basic knowledge about using the equipment in your classroom and the rules you have for its use, this category typically is applied to computer literacy classes.

To help teachers understand the range of potential uses of computers, Goldberg and Sherwood (1983) presented a five-part model of computer use, highlighted in Table 14-1.

This classification allows teachers to be more aware of the multiple appropriate uses of computers in classrooms. It also enhances the awareness that software and computer use should occur in each category. More recently, the Internet has provided a wide range of resources and tools for both teachers and students. These resources and tools can also be classified according to Goldberg and Sherwood's categories of use. As you encounter and evaluate software and explore the Internet for ways to enhance your children's literacy learning, keep in mind that an effective use of technology will include all the aspects shown in Table 14-1.

Learning with Computers

Software in this category provides a rich context for the child in the form of **simulations,** models of real-world events or situations. Simulations place students in situations that are similar to those they would experience in reality; simulations also model events and processes.

simulations
Presentations of events similar to those found in the real world.

Although simulation software is less prevalent in reading education than in other subject areas, it holds tremendous potential. For example, *Oregon Trail 5,* a simulation intended for social studies that uses 3-D animations and environments, might be used to build background knowledge before students read stories about settlers on the U.S. frontier. *Oregon Trail 5* puts the child in the place of an explorer moving through the frontier to a fort. Decisions must be made about where and how to travel, what supplies to buy, when and where to camp, and how to deal with dangers confronted along the way. Thus, relevant computer simulations can result in increased background knowledge and heightened interest in related, print-based stories. Because simulations can be used as

While some classrooms have older computers, Internet capabilities can make such equipment extremely useful for a wide variety or individual and group activities.

FIGURE 14-1

Sample screen from the Reporter Project software

Note: Courtesy of Charles Kinzer.

small- or large-group activities, discussion is facilitated and class time is effectively used to meet prereading activity goals.

Simulations might also put students in the world of a newspaper reporter who is sent out to get a story (see Figure 14-1). This Reporter Project software teaches writers about main ideas and details, point of view, and the importance of audience awareness in writing. By using a newspaper format, the child-reporter is placed in a situation where choices must be made about which section of the paper the story is targeted toward. This influences the way the story must be written, and which facts need to be highlighted. For ex-

FIGURE 14-2

Sample record-keeping screen from the Reporter Project software

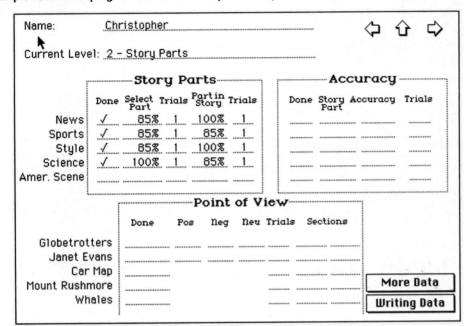

Note: Courtesy of Charles Kinzer.

ample, if a reporter is covering a sports story for the sports section, details about the game, the players, and the score are most important. Yet the same game, covered for the "People and Style" section of the paper, would highlight the dignitaries attending, some fashion information, and so on, with the game being less central. A specific objective of this software is to teach who, why, what, when, where, and how questions (Kinzer & Leu, 1997).

Initially, the child is a reporter who searches for pertinent facts and writes the story; later the reporter becomes a writer who writes and submits the story to the editor (the computer), who checks key words in the story to determine whether the appropriate facts have been presented. The editor then provides feedback about the logic of the facts chosen and gives hints about rewriting the story. Also, because real news footage was used (courtesy of NBC News), children can compare their stories to the story that was actually read by the news anchorperson. The Reporter Project software also allows children to print their stories for binding or display.

Simulation software often has a recordkeeping system that captures information about student progress so that teachers can provide specific help and additional instruction on aspects that appear to need more support than the software can provide (see Figure 14-2 for the record keeping system used in the Reporter Project software).

Simulations generally use all of the color, sound, and graphics capabilities available to the computer. However, you will need to decide whether the content is appropriate to your students' needs and to your instructional program.

Learning about Thinking with Computers

There have been claims that working with computers and with certain programming languages enhances the problem-solving strategies of the user. Among the main advocates of the potential of computers to influence thinking and problem-solving abilities are Seymore Papert and his colleagues, developers of the Logo computer language (Papert, 1980, 1984).

Simulations may also be a part of this category of computer usage. They traditionally have been developed to teach specific content, yet they require students to make decisions and anticipate the consequences of their actions. It may be that general thinking skills are also developed as children move through a simulation; thus, simulation software goes beyond simply imparting information.

Many Internet uses can also be classified in this category. As you involve your students in gathering information to include on your classroom's web page, as you discuss how to change your web page design to make it more accessible, as your children begin to anticipate the questions and uses that others will make of your page, and as they create products and display them using application or presentation software, they are learning to think with computers. Also, Internet sites such as Nova's **Curse of the T-Rex** (http://www.pbs.org/wgbh/pages/nova/trex/notalone.html), which places students in the world of dinosaurs while teaching them about thinking, fit into this category.

Learning from Computers

In this category, the computer acts as an instructor, with communication essentially operating as a one-way affair—from computer to student. Simply reading information to learn what is presented on the screen is an example of learning from computers, as is the use of **drill-and-practice software** and **tutorial software.**

Both drill-and-practice software and tutorial software can appear as fairly formal programs that require reading and question-answering activities; game-like formats are also used. Often, drill-and-practice programs in the younger grades target learning letters, sound symbol relationships, or vocabulary and spelling. These, along with programs such as **Integrated Learning Systems,** are becoming increasingly available for schools across subject areas and must be supplemented with other software that range across the other categories previously noted.

Because of the unique features of **game-like software** and concerns that have been voiced by parents and teachers, this format is considered as a separate category.

Drill-and-Practice Software. Drill-and-practice software often presents children with a series of questions. A correct response results in some form of feedback and a new question; an incorrect response results in feedback and the opportunity to try again. If the answer is still incorrect, most drill-and-practice programs give the answer and move on to a new question. Such software usually keeps track of a child's responses and provides the child, the teacher, or both with the overall score. Drill-and-practice software is available in all areas of reading from decoding to vocabulary to main idea comprehension and so on.

By definition, drill-and-practice software does not teach. Like paper-and-pencil worksheets, it only allows students to practice what has already been taught. The question for teachers is whether drill-and-practice programs, which are often little more than computerized worksheets, offer an advantage over a regular worksheet.

In the drill-and-practice area, computers may have at least three advantages over worksheets, although each drill-and-practice program must be evaluated to see whether these features are present.

1. *Motivational presentation.* Computers appear to stimulate and motivate children to a greater extent than workbooks do. Even when tasks are similar, children spend more time on computer drill-and-practice activities than they do on worksheets. It is possible that this increased attention is a response to novelty rather than to some inherently motivational aspect of the computer.
2. *Recordkeeping functions.* The computer can quickly capture and tabulate student scores, which are then usually placed in a file where teachers can easily see who has done well and who might need additional instruction. Thus, computerized recordkeeping can provide information needed for instructional decisions, thereby relieving you of the need to check children's answers manually.
3. *Branching capabilities.* The computer can present drill-and-practice activities more closely matched to children's ability levels than those presented in a workbook. For example, if a child answers three consecutive problems incorrectly, software can "branch" to similar items of less difficulty. It can also branch to items of greater difficulty if a child responds correctly a given number of times.

drill-and-practice software Nonteaching programs that present activities intended to reinforce knowledge.

tutorial software Programs that attempt to teach as well as reinforce concepts.

Integrated Learning Systems Available for all subject areas, these programs usually start with a computer-based assessment, which results in specific content to be taught, usually in small units that are followed by assessment and additional instruction or remediation.

game-like software Computer programs that use games or game-like formats to teach and reinforce concepts.

An additional advantage of some drill-and-practice software is that teachers can customize what is presented, thereby more closely matching instructional objectives. For example, you could enter the set of words to be presented in a vocabulary or spelling lesson, vary the rate of presentation and the number of repetitions, and so on. While these benefits may be present, overuse of drill and practice, as always, must not be the sole focus of an instructional program.

Tutorial Software.   Tutorial software is designed so that a child can learn as well as practice. It goes beyond a simple presentation of items to which a student responds. The critical difference between drill-and-practice software and tutorial software is that tutorial programs are written so that a concept or fact is first taught and then practiced. This type of software almost always includes explanations of concepts, feedback, and branches that change the difficulty of items or that provide additional instruction, depending on the child's performance.

Although tutorial software is preferred to simple drill-and-practice offerings, it, too, can be misused. The computer can patiently present a tutorial, but it cannot decide whether that tutorial includes content important to a child's reading development. You will need to decide whether software content, format, sequencing of concepts, pacing, and other factors are appropriate to the instructional program, the reading process, and reading instruction in general.

Game-like Software.   Most game-like software uses the color, sound, and animation capabilities of computers to catch and hold students' attention. Such software presents instruction in a format that allows children to play against others or the computer while learning. Students are challenged to compile a high score. As computers continue to enhance their graphics and sound capabilities, animations, short video clips, and high-quality sound are becoming standard on all models sold. This, in turn, has led to game-like software that is visually appealing, motivating, and engaging. Although teachers need to be careful that the concepts presented are not overshadowed by the peripheral aspects of the presentation, well-constructed game-like software can be pedagogically sound and is popular with both children and teachers.

Awareness of several problems associated with game-like software should help ensure that it is chosen for its educational use rather than its game-like value:

- Game-like software may have violent overtones. These programs must be carefully evaluated and their consequences considered.
- Problems with reinforcement can occur if getting a wrong answer is more interesting than getting a correct one. For example, seeing something explode in full color and with sound could motivate errors.
- Game-like software is sometimes used far beyond its value. Students who like to play a particular game may continue to use the software long after mastering its concepts. In that case, instructional time would be used inappropriately because students should have moved on to new items.
- Game-like software often involves eye-hand coordination and reflexes to use a joystick or control buttons, which may prompt incorrect responses due to factors unrelated to the reading process. This may also make the software inappropriate for use by children with certain physical handicaps.

Managing Learning with Computers

As you think about how to use your classroom computer, remember that it is not only for students' use. Don't forget that technology, including the Internet, can be used to make your job easier. An increasing amount of software is available to keep student records, indicate children's progress, track lunch money, write letters to parents, find information and references useful for lesson development, and help with a variety of other time-consuming functions. Even readability analyses of books considered for purchase

FIGURE 14-3

Sample entries in a computerized filing system

AUTHOR	Silverstein, Shel
TITLE	Where the Sidewalk Ends
GENRE	Poetry
RDGLEVEL	All
DESCRIPTOR	Appropriate for all students.
COMMENT	No reading level or descriptors because the book has a variety of poems. In previous use, has been of high interest across all students/grades.

STUDENT	Alex Smith
AGE	8
INTERESTS	Pets, Science Fiction, Poems, Cars, TV
RDGLEVEL	3.0
COMMENTS	Likes to read aloud to friends—especially poems.

can be quickly and easily performed with computers (see, for example, http://www.interventioncentral.org/htmdocs/tools/okapi/okapi.shtml). Many people have written about readability software (much of this writing occurred in the mid- to late 1980s; see, for example, Standal, 1987).

When coupled with filing system software, a computer can be used to keep track of anything that would normally require entries on file cards. For example, a classroom library can be easily and quickly entered into a computerized filing system, including information about author(s), title, reading difficulty level, topic area(s), genre, and so on. Similarly, a file can be made of students' attitudes and interests, as collected on attitude/interest inventories. Figure 14-3 illustrates two computerized file cards—one pertaining to books, the other to students.

Such a file system allows a teacher to quickly and easily choose or recommend reading material. For example, the computer could search for any books in the class library about pets or for any children who might be interested in pet stories. Using such a system, a teacher can more quickly and easily personalize supplementary reading for any child or group of children in the class. The class as a whole might decide on the categories to be included in the file system and might enter the data if that information is not confidential. If students are too young to enter data, older students might enjoy a real-world activity as part of their computer class assignment and might help set up the class database and enter the data. As Reinking and Watkins (1997) have pointed out, a database is ideal for storing student-constructed book reports. The categories generated by peers are useful, and the database becomes a resource that is truly used by children.

Facilitating Parental Involvement with Technology.   Technology can be especially helpful in communicating with parents. Several schools have purchased automatic telephone dialing equipment interfaced with a computer. Such a system is used by teachers and administrators to leave messages for parents; the computer can be set to dial a parent's phone number within certain hours and to keep dialing periodically until contact is made. In this way parents can be told of upcoming field trips, student tardiness, and so on. With this technology, parents also have an opportunity to leave messages for teachers.

Even without a computerized system, some schools have devised an effective alternative. Telephone lines are purchased for each grade level or each classroom and a low-cost answering machine is hooked up to each telephone line. (Schools have been relatively successful at partnering with businesses and telephone companies to provide

MODEL LESSON

Implementing Telephone Technology in Emily Dodson's School

It was just 2 years ago that I talked to our principal early in the school year about getting some additional telephone equipment. She agreed to contact the telephone company about a line for the second-grade teachers if we could find the funds to buy an answering machine. The three of us decided to contact several local businesses about the possibility of donating one to the school. We put together a brief but fairly detailed description of how the machine would be used and what it would do for us. Happily, three separate businesses agreed to donate it—two department stores and the bank our school uses. Therefore, we asked the bank to buy the machine and the two stores to underwrite the cost of the telephone line for a year. They agreed, and we promised to report back at the end of the school year to let them know how it had worked out. Our principal was thrilled not to have to spend any school funds for our project.

Now that we've had our system operating for 2 years, we all wonder how we ever managed without it. Just this morning I listened to the messages several parents left for me last night. One parent said that her son was becoming interested in the basketball playoffs, and she wondered if I could suggest any books for him. So before school started, I entered that information into our computer's filing system and found we had several appropriate books right in our own classroom library. I also made a note to tell him about the **National Basketball Association** site at http://www.nba.com/. Another parent had called to say that his daughter had the chicken pox and wouldn't be in school for about a week. I called him back at lunch time and talked about catch-up activities. This family has a home computer and Internet connection, so the class will compose and send a group "get well" e-message. Right now I've just finished writing out the message I'm going to put on tonight's tape:

This is Emily Dodson. Our class will soon be reading a set of stories about pets, and I'll be asking students to bring pictures of their pets to school. If your family doesn't have a pet, your child can cut out magazine pictures of a pet he or she might like to have. I have some magazines that I can send home with your child if you would like. Just let me know. It would also help if you could discuss with your child his or her feelings about your family pet and/or the responsibilities that having a pet brings. I'll be sending home a few short stories about pets, and you might want to talk about those with your child, too.

Today I've asked the students to finish writing stories that were started in class. You might ask to see the story and have your child tell you what it's about. The story should be finished by Friday, and you might suggest that your child draw a picture to go along with it. If you would like your child to bring home some crayons, please leave me a message.

In about a month we'll have a unit on Egypt. Please let me know if you or someone you know has traveled to Egypt and could share some pictures or could come and tell us about the trip.

Thanks for your support.

---

these resources at substantial discounts.) Each day teachers record a message about their students—for example, upcoming assignments, homework, or class achievements—and parents can listen to the messages at their convenience, leaving their own messages if they wish.

Bauch (1989, 1990, 1997) has studied the use of inexpensive answering-machine technology in a variety of schools. Without such technology, he notes that the national average of parent-to-teacher contacts is approximately two per day in schools averaging 300 students. Bauch's data indicate that a telephone message system increases that average to approximately 60 per day. An additional and important finding is that parents from low socioeconomic levels call just as often as do parents from average and above-average socioeconomic levels. Low-socioeconomic and single parents often have great difficulty finding time to see teachers in person, yet are concerned that their children achieve success. This is a use of technology that is cost-effective and easy to implement.

Of course, more and more parents (and children) have their own e-mail accounts; therefore, teachers can communicate with those parents and students more directly. This requires that e-mail account information is collected as part of the informational material captured at the beginning of each year, and as new children enter the class.

Be careful, however, not to disadvantage those parents who do not have computer access by also providing information through newsletters, notes, and telephone technology as previously discussed.

Using the Internet in Literacy Instruction

Although the computer and appropriate software can have tremendous benefits to literacy instruction and can help to make you be more efficient in your work, it is through networking that the computer realizes its greatest potential (see, for example, Leu & Kinzer, 2000; Reinking, 1995). Computer networks are structures that link computers to each other, so that information and communication can occur with other individuals who use computers linked to the same network. The largest computer network is the Internet/World Wide Web, and it is the most powerful network tool available to you. However, two other networks are commonly found in schools.

A local area network (LAN) is a number of computers in close proximity (usually within a room or a building) that are connected to each other through a **server,** or central computer dedicated to maintaining the LAN connection.

server A computer dedicated to serving as the "administrator" for linking other computers. The server must remain on at all times.

Each connected computer can send or receive messages through the server. A LAN is commonly used to link the computers in a computer lab or to link more than one computer in a classroom. It allows users to share files across computers that run the same software and is useful when multiple authors are working on the same project or when sharing information in electronic rather than paper-copy form. It also allows you to put information that you may want all students to access and work with on the server, rather than having to duplicate this information on all of the computers in the lab, classroom, or school.

A wide area network (WAN) links single computers, or groups of computers, to each other. It usually contains more computers spread over greater distances. Often, they also include different kinds of machines—perhaps both Macintosh and IBM-compatible hardware. WANs allow children in different schools to work on related projects and share their information or to be classroom penpals with children in different locations. Because different software and different machines are used in different locations, WANs are complex, having to format messages and data in ways that can be understood by all connected computers and having to route the information in different ways to different places. Because of the logistics (and the great demand) for WANs, commercial companies provide WAN service (these companies are usually called Internet Service Providers, or ISPs). The Internet is also a WAN, but it is a noncommercial, public WAN. ISPs allow their customers access to their own WAN as well as to others, including the Internet. What this means is that customers can send and receive information to and from individuals who are not customers of the same Internet Service Provider.

Finding What You Need: Searching the Internet

browser Software that facilitates searching the Internet and displaying Internet sites that include video, audio, animations, graphics, text, and full color.

Browser software allows you to see what is available on the Internet, to search for locations and information on the Internet, and to go directly to locations that you have previously identified.

Several browsers are available—the most well known and popular are Netscape Communicator/Navigator and Internet Explorer. Both of these browsers are available for use on Macintosh and Windows-compatible computers. Either of these browsers will allow you to view text files as well as multimedia (graphics, audio, video, and animations) that have been posted to the Internet. We encourage you to look at one of the many books available that describe the features of these and other browsers.

search engine A search engine allows the input of words and phrases that identify locations and sites where desired information can be found.

Each browser has a selection of **search engines** that allow you to enter words and phrases that form the core of your search. Popular search engines include Google, Yahoo, Lycos, AskJeeves, and AltaVista. When you activate a browser, one of the options is a box where you can type in a search request and a button that activates one of the search engines.

Classrooms with internet connections and telephone lines allow children to extend their learning activities in many ways.

E-mail from the Classroom

Subject: The Internet
From: Diana Thompson, dinathompson@HOTMAIL.COM

It seems like just a short time ago, the only thing I knew about technology was how to turn on the computer! My knowledge was limited to Microsoft Word, which I used as a word processor. The whole idea of using the World Wide Web completely overwhelmed me, but I was very excited about the prospect.

Therefore, I hooked up my home computer to the Internet, and now I feel very comfortable jumping online and looking for information when I need it. I also enjoyed searching for my 10 favorite websites (something a friend and I have been doing) because I found so many places I can go for ideas. Certainly a lot more than 10!

Based on my experiences, I encourage all teachers, regardless of their level of computer knowledge, to get on a computer and explore the Internet to find topics of interest. Then you'll be "hooked" and will quickly see the benefits for your students, as well as yourself!

One of the things that I like is getting ideas from other people. Here's one that I'd like to share with you. To give credit where credit is due, I've included the whole message:

> **From: RICHARDSJ@EDU-SUU-LIFAC.LI.SUU.EDU**
> **Organization: Southern Utah University**
> **Subject: Internet Searching**
> **To: RTEACHER@LISTSERV.SYR.EDU**
>
> If any of you are interested in teaching Internet skills to your students, here is a site that may be of interest to you.
>
> **Integrating the Internet** has primary resources, units of study, and tutorials to help you plan projects and class home pages (http://integratingtheinternet.com/).

I think it's great to "meet" other people and share ideas, and the Internet is opening up a whole new way to do so!

—Diana

To initiate a search, enter in the space provided the word or phrase that describes what you want to find and push the "enter" key. The "hits," or number of sites found, will be displayed. Clicking on one of the locations takes you to that site. Browsers typically include a "back" button that will return you to the previous screen, where you can choose to go to one of the other sites found by your search. When you find a valuable site—one that you or your students will want to return to—you can "bookmark" that location. Once stored, you can go directly to a given location. If you know a site's address but have not stored it, browsers allow you to type in a location's address and will take you there directly.

Often, a good way to begin a search for information on the Internet is through the use of central sites, discussed in chapter 2. These locations contain many links to related sites on a similar topic. Beginning with a central site can save time, and bookmarking such sites for children's use allows them to experience success quickly, even as they continue to develop their own knowledge of search strategies. A list of central sites across subject areas appears on page 50. Additional central sites include:

KidInfo (http://www.kidinfo.com/Index.html)—Includes links, information, and resources across a range of subject areas and issues. This site is useful for children, teachers, and parents.

JB Pinchbeck's Homework Helper (http://school.discovery.com/homeworkhelp/bjpinchbeck/bjreference.html)—A part of Discoveryschool.com, this link provides many resources that help students find needed information across topics.

Kathy Schrock's Guide for Educators (http://school.discovery.com/schrockguide/arts/artlit.html)—This address links to the Literature/Language Arts area of Kathy Schrock's site. As stated on the home page, this site is "a categorized list of sites useful for enhancing curriculum and professional growth. It is updated often to include the best sites for teaching and learning." This site is part of Discoveryschool.com.

Child Safety and Censorship Issues

Because the Internet is a public forum, it has evolved into a place where anyone can post information accessible to those with a computer and connection capabilities. Although the vast majority of sites on the Internet are appropriate, it also contains sites that include content not suitable for viewing by children. These sites include those that have sexually oriented content; that attempt, illegally, to solicit money or personal information; that provide instructions for using materials that might be hazardous; and that include propaganda or material that is untrue but that might not be recognized as such by developing readers.

Thus, parents and others are concerned that classroom computers and Internet assignments might result in inappropriate material being accessed by children. This can occur accidentally because Internet search engines return "hits" to sites that include both appropriate and inappropriate material.

However, there are ways to restrict access to certain sites without having to restrict individuals' rights to post information on the Internet. Schools are now required to implement policies related to "blocking" or filtering software, such as **Net Nanny 4** (http://www.netnanny.com/home/home.asp) or products by **SurfControl** (http://www.surfcontrol.com/). Blocking software usually contains a listing of sites and key words that are expressly locked out and cannot be accessed from the computer where the software is installed. System administrators can update the list of inappropriate sites and teachers can request that sites be blocked or unblocked.

Another way to address the issue of child safety is to ensure that children can only access a list of approved sites that have been "bookmarked" for your children's use, or to use sites that screen out inappropriate material. **Berit's Best Sites for Children** (http://www.beritsbest.com/), which includes a "safe surfing" section (http://www.beritsbest.com/SafeSurfing/KidsSearchSites/index.shtml), and **Yahooligans** (http://www.yahooligans.com/) are two such sites.

In addition to the use of blocking software and bookmarking sites that you feel are most appropriate, you should discuss with your class the fact that some information on the Internet is not intended for their age group and that your classroom environment does not allow the use of the classroom computer for searching such sites. Making sure your classroom is structured so that you can see the computer screen(s) from where you typically sit or stand is also a useful strategy. Placing computers so that the monitor screen is pointed away from the teacher may result in inappropriate exploration by some children. Knowing that you can see what is on the screen will guide their computer use in appropriate directions.

One other strategy is commonly used to ensure that children and their parents are aware of your expectations for computer and Internet use. This involves the use of an informational "contract" signed by children and their parents or guardians. Often called an "acceptable use policy," the form states your expectations and rules and informs parents about the steps you have taken to mitigate any inappropriate use of the computer, including positioning of the monitors and blocking software. It also reminds parents to discuss their family's expectations with regard to computer use and to remind children to immediately exit pages they have accidentally accessed if they believe the site is inappropriate or makes them uncomfortable. Many school districts have acceptable use policy forms that are sent home to parents early in each school year. You should check with the principal of your school about your district policy in this area.

Creating a Classroom Home Page

It is likely that one or more of your students (or their parents) will ask if your classroom has a home page on the Internet. Home pages are relatively easy to create and facilitate communication with classrooms and children from around the world. Children exhibit great excitement when they post some of their work on the classroom home page and receive unsolicited reactions and comments about their work. Home pages are also beneficial for communication with parents.

There are four steps to creating a home page. First, you must decide what you will place on the home page. Second, you must decide on a design. Third, you must enter the information into a format appropriate for the Internet. And, fourth, you must place your home page on a server that is connected to the Internet. Each of these is easily done and can provide wonderful opportunities for children's input and for cooperative group activities.

A classroom home page will usually include information about your school and classrooms, where they are located, and related information. There usually is a place for others to look at students' work that you post to the home page and a place where messages can be left for the class by people who would like to contact them. One caution, however, should be stated: Parental permission should be obtained before placing any child's picture on the class home page.

Once you and your students have agreed on the information to be placed on the home page, you might want to visit other sites to get ideas about an appropriate design (Figure 14-4 on page 522 shows an example). You are then ready to enter the information into a format appropriate for the Internet.

This is not difficult because most current word processors include formatters that allow you to enter information in the same way you enter text and graphics into the word processor, followed by a command that translates what you have entered to **HTML code.**

HTML is the programming language most often used to design home pages; software is available that is specifically intended for writing home pages in HTML code, and browsers often include such tools as well. These Internet locations explain the steps involved in creating a home page as well as provide useful tutorials for doing so:

A Beginner's Guide to HTML (http://www.ncsa.uiuc.edu/General/Internet/WWW/)

HTML code A programming language used to design pages for the Internet and the World Wide Web.

FIGURE 14-4

Home page for Mrs. Renz's fourth-grade class' website (http://www.redmond.k12.or.us/patrick/renz/)

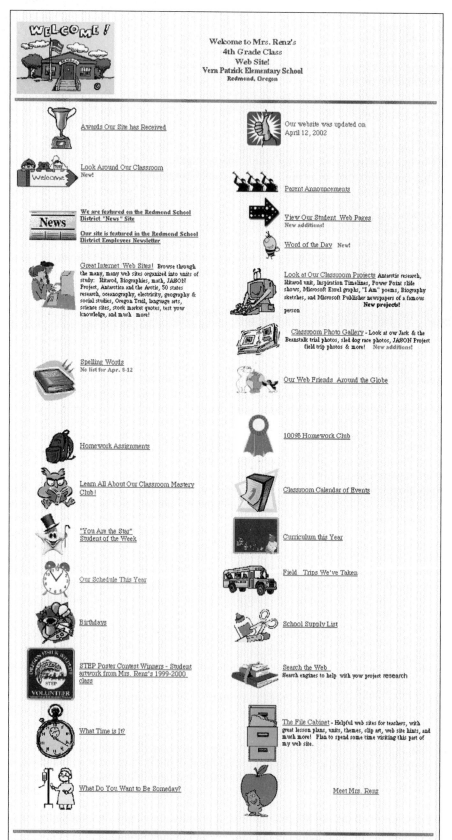

FIGURE 14-5

Sample from the **American School Directory** (http://www.asd.com/), showing the page allowing users to search for any school with an ASD home page

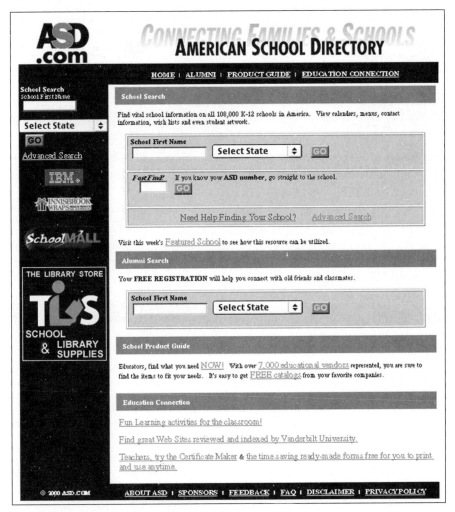

Note: Courtesy of American School Directory.

HTML Tools (http://www.utoronto.ca/webdocs/HTMLdocs/misc_tools.html)

Building a School Web Site (http://www.wigglebits.com/home.html)

The final step in creating your home page is placing it on a server so that it is part of the Internet. This is most easily done in one of two ways. If your school or school district has a server already dedicated to Internet use, then ask to have your home page placed on that server. Another way is to use sites such as the **American School Directory (ASD)** (http://www.asd.com/), which has a mission to provide an Internet home page location for every school in the United States. If your home page has been placed on another server (perhaps your school's or school district's server), telling ASD your home page address will allow ASD to enter your address into its search engine so that your site can be accessed from this central resource page.

Figure 14-5 provides information about the ASD site. Simply submit on paper or on disk your home page information and ASD will provide the server space for your home page. ASD will also provide e-mail addresses for all parents in the nation—free of charge. This takes away the necessity of parents owning a home computer or paying for a commercial server to receive e-mail. Any computer—at a library, community center, church, school, or work—can be used by parents to check their e-mail. ASD feels this is one way to close the gap for parents who cannot afford personal computers for their homes.

Continuing Your Professional Growth through the Internet

The Internet is also a powerful tool for your own professional development and curriculum activities. One way to continue your growth as a professional is to join one of the many listservs or mailing lists where you get responses to your questions from others who subscribe. The large number of people subscribing to a listserv ensures that many others will read your message, and it is very likely that creative solutions to problems can be found and shared.

One of the most useful and popular listservs for teachers of literacy is the listserv supported by the International Reading Association as part of *The Reading Teacher*—a journal intended for teachers in elementary grades (see chapter 3 for information about joining this listserv). You may also wish to visit one of these Internet sites containing master lists and conduct a search for a list that meets your specific needs:

Liszt Select (http://www.liszt.com)—This is probably the most comprehensive WWW site for mailing lists, containing over 50,000 lists as well as a search engine to search the extensive database.

TileNet (http://tile.net/lists/)—This is another extensive set of mailing lists. It also contains an excellent search engine.

IFLANET (http://www.ifla.org/I/training/listserv/lists.htm)—From the International Federation of Library Associations and Institutions, this site contains background information about mailing lists and how they are used, as well as list directories.

Of course, a key professional use of the Internet is to help you in developing lessons for your class. Throughout this book, you have found sites and procedures for using the Internet as a resource to find information pertaining to children's literature, content-area reading, facilitating the teaching and learning of comprehension, and other areas related specifically to literacy. The following general resources are also valuable:

ERIC (http://ericir.syr.edu/)—An online, free service that allows you to search for topics in education. An "ask ERIC" function allows you to enter specific questions and requests and provides e-mail replies.

Lesson Plans and Teaching Ideas (http://www.teachnet.com/)—Teachnet is a wonderful resource that contains information for teachers of all subject areas, disseminates information on educational issues, provides hints for teachers on management, and includes ideas and lesson plans for every content area.

🖮 Specific Applications of Technology

A Reminder about Appropriate Method Frameworks

Recall that chapter 2 detailed three important method frameworks that will help you to integrate Internet activities into your literacy program: Internet Workshop, Internet Project, and Internet Inquiry. We will not discuss method frameworks in detail here, but will instead present the procedural steps for each of the four frameworks as a summary and reminder of their importance.

Internet Workshop allows students to share information and to learn from each other. Because the importance of social interaction in learning is well known and because children are very motivated to share the outcomes of their Internet Project and Internet Inquiry, both of these methods frameworks should be combined with Internet Workshop. Generally, Internet Workshop is a regularly scheduled time set aside each week for children to share what they have learned, ask questions about issues they do not understand, and seek information that will help them in upcoming work. The workshop may focus on content or on search or navigation strategies. Below, we briefly summarize the procedural steps for Internet Project and Internet Inquiry and provide suggestions for using each with an Internet Workshop. More details about each of these

NIKKI'S

COMMENTS FROM THE CLASSROOM

Over the last few years, technology has embedded itself in my teaching. The students use computers regularly at home or in the library, so it's a natural fit for them in the classroom. The more comfortable I become with computers, the more I find ways to utilize them in meaningful ways. For instance, we use technology in several ways when we cover the Holocaust.

As a class we read *I Never Saw Another Butterfly: Children's Drawings and Poems from Terezin Concentration Camp, 1942–1944* by Hana Volavkova, which is a collection of work written by, or drawn by, children in the camp. It's very moving.

Each student chooses his or her own book for independent reading. To try to touch on everyone's interests, I offer historical fiction as well as nonfiction. I generate a list of possible titles with a CD-ROM by Tunnell, Jacobs, and Darigan called *Children's Literature Database: A Resource for Teachers, Parents and Media Specialists* that provides so many search fields, including award winners, that I can be sure to select a list of really good titles that will cover the span of reading abilities. This year we used *Touch Wood: A Girl in Occupied France* by Renee Roth–Hano; *Never Forget: The Jews of the Holocaust,* a book of journal entries, interviews, and records by Milton Meltzer; *Number the Stars* by Lois Lowry; *Anne Frank Remembered: The Story of Miep Gies Who Helped Hide the Frank Family;* and, of course, *The Diary of a Young Girl,* by Anne Frank.

Then the students work, some in pairs and some individually, on written projects. Many go to the Internet to gather information. I recommend sites like the **United States Holocaust Memorial Museum** (www.ushmm.org), which has a lot to offer, including a link under "education" for students, which covers some history, provides activities, and walks students through the museum's exhibits. Another site I sent them to is the **Teacher's Guide to the**

Holocaust (fcit.coedu.usf.edu/holocaust/default.htm). Just searching Google under "holocaust" allows students to see how the events are viewed and remembered by dozens of different countries.

Some students conduct an interview; one takes the point of view of someone related to the events of WWII while another is the interviewer. Others write one-act plays, or journal entries. Many write poems, probably because of the powerful material in *Butterfly*.

The projects go through many revisions and rewrites. First the students share their work with other students, who make written comments. The next draft is shared with me, and I also provide written comments. Each student keys in his or her final product, which we publish as a class book.

I remember worrying that I would never really be comfortable with computers, and particularly with the Internet, but I just had to give myself some time and really tool around on the web for a while. With just a bit of time and research, there are excellent resources available for the classroom.

PRACTICAL TEACHING STRATEGIES

Using Internet Workshop

Sadako and the Thousand Cranes. After older students (sixth or seventh grade) have read this touching story, have them visit **A-Bomb WWW Museum** (http://www.csi.ad.jp/ABOMB/index.html), a website developed at the Hiroshima Peace Park. Ask them to read the information at several links, including stories from survivors, and bring this to Internet Workshop for a discussion. Develop an Internet Workshop page where they can record the information they find.

Chris Van Allsburg. During a thematic unit on this wonderful author, where students read a number of his works, have them visit at least two sites containing biographical information. These might include **Ask the Author: Chris Van Allsburg** (http://www.eduplace.com/rdg/author/cva/question.html) and **About the Author: Chris Van Allsburg** (http://www.eduplace.com/rdg/author/cva/). Have students take notes on an Internet activity page and bring this to Internet Workshop where everyone can share information they have discovered about the author.

The Very Hungry Caterpillar. After reading this delightful story to younger children, invite them to visit several locations to gather information about the author, such as **Biographical Notes on Eric Carle** (http://www.eric-carle.com/bio.html) and **Caterpillar Express: A Newsletter from Eric Carle** (http://www.eric-carle.com/catindex.html). Have them record this information in an activity page or in a journal and share what they discovered during Internet Workshop.

Combining Internet Workshop with Internet Projects

Laura Ingalls Wilder Internet Book Club. If your class is reading at least one book by this outstanding author, invite several other classes to join you in an Internet Project. You might wish to exchange responses to chapters in a common book or reviews of different books she has written. You could also exchange useful websites with information about the author and her books such as **Laura Ingalls Wilder—Frontier Girl** (http://webpages.marshall.edu/,irby1/laura.htmlx). During Internet Workshop, share the correspondence from your project partners and develop messages you wish to send to them. You might wish to have each child in participating classrooms develop a short essay and share it with other participating classrooms, "What the Little House Books Mean to Me." Advertise for partner classrooms at **Global School Net's Internet Project Registry** (http://www.gsn.org/pr/index.html).

Women of NASA. During a thematically organized unit on space, have your class participate in the Internet Project **Women of NASA** (http://quest.arc.nasa.gov/women/intro.html). This experience is developed to encourage more young women to pursue careers in math, science, and technology. During Internet Workshop, share the results of the chat sessions with astronauts and other scientists describing their work as well as other experiences located at this site.

important Internet method frameworks are provided in chapter 2. Within Internet Workshop, you might use these basic steps:

1. Locate a site, or several sites, on the Internet with content related to a classroom unit of instruction and set a bookmark for the location(s).
2. Develop an activity inviting students to use the site(s).
3. Assign this activity to be completed during the week.
4. Have students share their work, questions, and new insights at the end of the week during Internet Workshop.

Internet Projects are of two types: website projects and spontaneous projects. Website projects are coordinated at a specific website; to participate, you will simply log on to a site that contains a project and follow the instructions. Spontaneous projects are developed by teachers who share an idea and advertise for collaborating classrooms to complete the projects. Spontaneous projects generally follow these procedural steps:

1. Develop a clear description of your project.
2. Post the project description and timeline.

PRACTICAL TEACHING STRATEGIES

Combining Internet Workshop with Internet Inquiry

Learning Fairs. If you use Internet Inquiry in your classroom, consider using a learning fair to share all the wonderful information your students have discovered during their inquiry projects. This is similar to a traditional science fair where children create a poster presentation of their inquiry question and the answers they discovered as they researched this issue. On a designated day, have children set their poster presentations up in your classroom and invite other classrooms to visit and discuss the projects with your students. Use Internet Workshop to support students at each phase of their inquiry projects.

Navigational Workshops. Use Internet Workshop during Internet Inquiry to help children with navigational strategies for the Internet as well as your school library. Invite students to come to each session prepared to share at least one informational strategy they recently learned and at least one problem they are having about how to find information. The exchange between children about successes and challenges can be informative for everyone.

---

3. Arrange collaboration details with teachers in other classrooms who agree to participate.
4. Complete the project, exchanging information with your collaborating classrooms.

Internet Inquiry is best used with children who have some experience using the Internet. It allows individuals or groups an opportunity to identify an important question and gather information to answer that question. Internet Inquiry places much of the responsibility for learning with the child, and consists of these five steps:

1. Question
2. Search
3. Analyze
4. Compose
5. Share

Another method framework is called a WebQuest. Information about webquests is found at http://webquest.sdsu.edu/webquest.html. In a WebQuest, students define a topic, find materials on the web, publish their results, and complete an evaluation. The seven steps to creating a WebQuest are:

1. Pick a fruitful, appropriate TOPIC and GOAL.
2. Select a TASK that engages higher-level thinking.
3. Start creating the WEBPAGE.
4. Develop an EVALUATION.
5. Flesh out the PROCESS.
6. Write documentation for other TEACHERS.
7. Test it. REVISE as needed.

These steps are detailed here: http://webquest.sdsu.edu/roadmap/index.htm, and various tools are provided as well. For example, templates for the various steps are provided—such as several templates for step 3 (Start creating the WEBPAGE).

Classroom Organization to Ensure Access

You may wonder how to fairly distribute access to only one or two computers among 25 or more students. In such situations you can allow students to work at the computer in much the same way they work at other learning centers in your classroom. In fact, the resulting discussion within the small group as problems are encountered and solved is valuable and can enhance learning. Small-group work is especially valuable when simulation software is used.

With the availability of projection devices that are useful for classrooms, you can project the computer screen and use software as a basis for discussion in whole-group situations. Consider how a discussion is enhanced if a simulation was projected, children were given different aspects or points of view to think about, and then various opinions were entered and played out within the simulation. This requires children to read and discuss within cooperative groups as part of the simulation and decision-making process and is most appropriate for content-area reading and research assignments.

Whether classroom computers are used in a whole-class structure or within a learning center structure (with individual students), you will need to guard against allowing some children more access to the computer than other children. For example, it is poor practice to allow computer time as a reward for finishing assigned work. Because more advanced students often complete assignments faster than average or below-average achievers, there is a danger of increasing the gap between high and low groups. Inequities in computer use can also occur between males and females as well as between students at high and low socioeconomic levels. In addition, be watchful of children with computers at home who may monopolize computer time in the classroom simply because of a greater comfort level with the technology.

Finally, keep in mind that the computers are appropriate for use at any grade level; they are not solely the domain of students in intermediate grades and above. Younger students may have some difficulty using keyboards to input information, but most software allows the use of a mouse or a touchpad that can be easily handled by younger children. In any case, keyboarding skills should not be the major concern in deciding whether to use a computer. More important is the appropriateness of the material presented by the software, the task itself, and the literacy skills required.

Using Word-Processing Software in Your Literacy Classroom

applications software
Programs that are useful in everyday life; for example, word-processing software.

Although much software is available, specifically for use in literacy instruction, **applications software** intended for a wide range of everyday tasks is also valuable.

For example, word-processing software can be used in language experience applications. As the children dictate a story, it can be typed directly into the computer and then quickly printed for each student. A word processor also allows students to revise or add to their stories easily. Changes can be incorporated into the original and a "clean" copy provided promptly. Printed stories can then be illustrated, posted in the classroom and on your home page, and bound into class books. Later, you can create vocabulary lessons from the words children use in their language experience stories.

Despite these software applications, however, students should still be provided with many opportunities to see you write directly on paper. Using a word processor in language experience activities should supplement—not replace—the more traditional procedure. Many teachers first write their students' stories on chart paper or notebook paper and then transcribe them into the computer for distribution. At higher grade levels, students often enjoy entering their stories themselves. Word-processing software is available for varying degrees of sophistication, and even kindergartners enjoy using the computer to write and print their stories.

Children can also use word-processing software to create their own stories or to access and read stories written by other class members. They might then leave messages to the other students, using the computer as a form of bulletin board. They can share their reactions to other students' stories or simply leave conversational messages. As children read and respond to such messages, they develop audience awareness in their writing and are highly motivated to read any further messages written specifically to them. Consider, for example, such a use as discussed by Myers (1993), who describes this activity with undergraduate students. Note, however, that this description could apply at any grade level:

> Undergraduates in my teacher education courses form inquiry groups to explore a topic of their choice. . . . Over the semester, they . . . discuss self-selected readings and past experiences, and write an article. Their articles are compiled into a book which we all buy,

read, and discuss. . . . This curricular structure supports students' connections between ideas, similar to the intertextual linking of students in literature circles (Short, 1992). (Myers, 1993, p. 251)

Word-processing software has uses other than typing stories, however. For example, it can help you make cloze tests (see chapter 11) if specific software for that purpose is unavailable. You can simply type a passage and then replace specific words with a blank, using a word processor's search-for-and-replace function. Word-processing software that checks spelling can also be used to help generate spelling lessons. You can make note of the words children misspelled and use those lists as the basis for periodic spelling lessons. In addition, some word processors have the capability of performing a readability analysis.

In the younger grades, students often enjoy software that allows them to easily draw illustrations for their stories or that allows them to print notes, banners, and cards that can be given to their friends and classmates. Software such as *KidPix Deluxe 3* allows even young children to easily manipulate icons and "stamps" that can form elaborate illustrations as well as allowing the addition of accompanying text. Labbo (1996) has described the benefits of using such software with kindergarten children in their development of sign/symbol knowledge and points out the value of such activities to enhance children's development as readers and writers. Examples of students' work created with *KidPix* software appear in Figure 14-6.

Using Spreadsheet Software in Your Literacy Program

Spreadsheet software can also be successfully used in literacy instruction. Spreadsheets present the user with a series of rows and columns. The information entered in those rows and columns can then be manipulated in several ways. Mathematical formulas can be applied to numerical entries, allowing spreadsheets to be used as a gradebook or for other purposes that require numerical information. For literacy instruction, however, the mathematics functions are less important than the row-and-column format.

One part of reading instruction is teaching the relationships among items. The rows and columns of a spreadsheet allow students an opportunity to classify in easily visible categories and to easily correct errors. For a lesson on action words, for example, the teacher might write on the chalkboard (or on a piece of paper beside the computer) a series of words containing both action and nonaction words. Then, at various times during the day, students could use the spreadsheet to sort the list of words into appropriate columns headed "Action Words" and "Not Action Words." They can be encouraged to add several of their own words to each column in addition to adding words from various selections they read throughout the day.

Video and Multimedia Technology in the Classroom

In 1922, Thomas Edison stated:

The motion picture is destined to revolutionize our educational system . . . in a few years it will supplant largely, if not entirely, the use of textbooks. . . . We get about two percent efficiency out of schoolbooks as they are written today. The education of the future, as I see it, will be conducted through the medium of the motion picture . . . where it should be possible to obtain one hundred percent efficiency. (Cuban, 1986, p. 9)

Edison's prediction did not come to pass, yet there is increasing evidence that television and video technology can play an important role in education and may have an increasing impact in the future.

One reason film did not have a significant impact is that it is a relatively linear medium. Even though students could watch an event occurring, it was difficult to revisit specific scenes for class discussion or to study in depth a specific item within a film. Even videotape—because of the time required for rewinding, inaccurate access to specific scenes, and poor freeze-frame capabilities—does not really allow more than a simple run-through of an entire film.

FIGURE 14-6

Samples of students' work

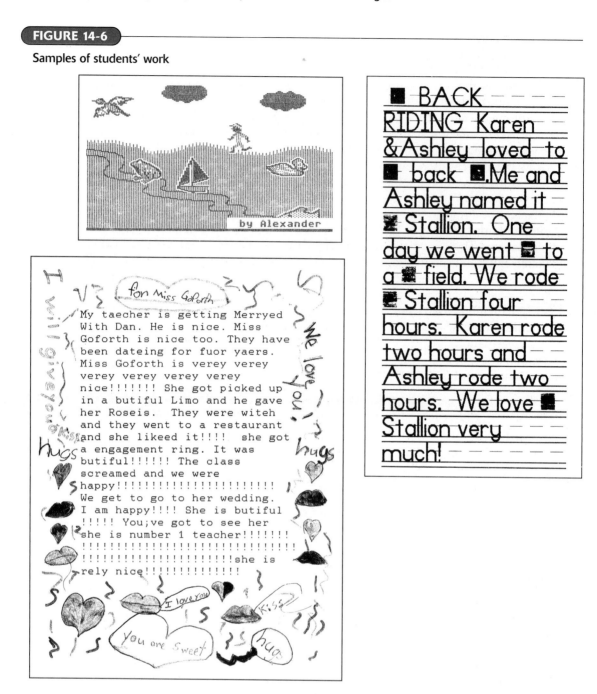

CD-ROM and DVD technology, however, has become available for educational purposes. These digital storage media hold large quantities of multimedia data (video, audio, text, and so on) and allow rapid, random access to any part of a disk. It also allows clear freeze-frame of images. Some schools may also have videodisc players available for classroom use. Videodiscs look like large CD-ROMs, and function in the same way. However, stand-alone videodisc players have been superseded by CD-ROM readers, which are standard equipment in modern computers. Inexpensive external units can be connected to older machines that do not have built-in CD-ROM players.

Many titles are now available on CD-ROM and DVD: National Geographic, Nova, and NASA all have CD-ROM offerings. General movies are available and can often be adapted for instructional use. In addition, specific instructional materials can frequently be applied to areas other than those for which they were created. For example, CD-ROMs and DVDs intended for social studies or science can also be used in literacy instruction to enhance background knowledge and to have students search for information relevant to literacy assignments.

Although CD-ROMs and DVDs can be played through stand-alone equipment on television screens, their power for educational uses is enhanced when they are linked to a computer. Integrated packages that are CD-ROM based and that incorporate a computer's multimedia capabilities to teach literacy include *The Little Planet Literacy Series* and *Wiggleworks*. Such CD-ROM-based programs merge video, audio, software, print materials, and publishing tools to help teach literacy.

Just as videodiscs are being replaced by CD-ROMs, however, CD-ROMs are also evolving. In the near future, Digital Video Disc (DVD) players will replace CD-ROM drives in computers. While still able to play current CD-ROMs, DVD players will allow the equivalent of a full-length movie to be placed on one disc. In addition, new compression standards continue to enhance movie-quality, full-screen video to be played on computer screens. These improvements mean that even more—and better—multimedia applications will be available for your classroom in the near future.

Hypermedia and Hypertext

Hypermedia and hypertext are often used synonymously, although hypertext implies a text-only presentation while hypermedia implies text together with graphics, video, audio, and animation. Both terms, however, refer to two common characteristics of the materials that they present to a potential reader. First, the materials in a hypertext or a hypermedia system are stored electronically, in what can be thought of as a relational database. The material is structured, searchable, and linked in some way. Second, a hypertext or hypermedia presentation allows the reader to jump, or link, across the contents of the document under user control and in no fixed path. This means that readers can move through a document in their own way—potentially, no two readers will read exactly the same document, as one might decide to skip certain links while another reader might branch to links that are of interest and only return to the central document after exploring other, related items.

HyperCard was among the first **hypermedia authoring programs** available to teachers who wished to create hypertext for use by their students. Still available for the Apple Macintosh, HyperCard has been supplanted by other programs that are more fully featured; for example, *Hyperstudio, Macromedia Director*, and Microsoft's *PowerPoint*, all of which are available for Macintosh and Windows operating systems.

With these programs, items appearing on individual computer screens usually are called cards or pages; an entire program is called a stack or book. After the stack has been created, users can pick and choose what part to look at, where to go next, and so on. Moreover, these programs can control CD-ROM and DVD players, allowing text and video to interact, as described earlier. The general term hypermedia often is used to refer to programs that combine text and video in graphics-based animated presentations.

Hypermedia authoring programs include the use of tools to draw graphics, and programming at a basic level is relatively easy. Thus, teachers can create simple, personalized lessons for their classes or can purchase hypermedia software. A number of stacks are available that move through pieces of literature, such as *Charlotte's Web*. These stacks are often free or distributed at a low cost, and children find them highly motivating.

Hypertext refers to text that has links to further information or that allows readers to move through it in a nonlinear sequence. For example, a hypermedia/hypertext program that presents children's literature and illustrations on the screen might allow readers to use the mouse to click on words, phrases, or pictures to receive more information about the item or to move to an entirely new topic or related issue. This feature provides the reader with on-line support and might well enhance background knowledge (since more information about a concept can be presented at the time of reading), but it also has an interesting side effect. Because different readers might proceed through a text in different sequences or jump to different related topics, students will not all have read the same text in the same way. Indeed, it is possible that children might begin a text, ask for

hypermedia A nonlinear, electronic text that can include graphics, video, audio, and animation.

hypermedia authoring programs A programming language that creates documents and presentations that allows users to follow their own nonlinear paths through the material.

Celebrating Diversity

Using the Classroom Computer and the Internet

Computers hold great potential for meeting the needs of learners who are diverse in terms of ability, ethnicity, and language. Consider that the branching possibilities of computer programs allow children to work at their own level and at their own pace. Students who wish to discover more about their own history or heritage can use the Internet to link with others who share their heritage. Students with diverse language backgrounds can listen to text in their own language, receive immediate translation to English, and begin to bridge the two while reading texts that are read by the rest of the class. Students with limited background knowledge can be supported through the use of computer-controlled video, while hypertext programs that incorporate multimedia can take students into topics in depth, or might show students new horizons that will develop into strong interests.

related information, become fascinated with a related topic, and never return or finish the original item. This creates interesting issues that are just beginning to be discussed for assessment and instruction (Kinzer & Leander, 2003). The differential support that hypertext might provide good and poor readers and the effect of hypertext on classroom discussion require further research but have much potential (Alexander, Kulikowich, & Jetton, 1994).

A special case of hypermedia applications in literacy are what some have called "talking books" (e.g., see McKenna, Young, & Gatliff, 2001). Here, talking books mean books available on CD-ROM or the Internet, where the story might include supports for struggling readers. This support can come in several ways. For example, the entire story can be read by the computer, with phrases highlighted as the reading occurs, while the child follows along. Or, the child can click on a word, phrase, or chapter for definitions, explanations, or to hear the section read, during guided reading. These books also offer the capability for the text to change into another language, or for the definitions of words clicked by the child to be read and defined in another (perhaps the child's native) language. Thus, possibilities for support, including support for children who come from different language backgrounds, are provided on an "as needed" basis. McKenna and his colleagues note that these supports have many benefits to the child. CD-ROM-based books are available in catalogs of traditional children's or educational book publishers.

Finding, Choosing, and Evaluating Software

Literally thousands of software programs are marketed for literacy instruction. Some software is intended for use on a single computer, as part of a larger reading program. Other packages are advertised as core reading programs and require a number of computers in a laboratory or a classroom.

One such program that you are likely to find in elementary schools is Accelerated Reader (AR). AR is, in essence, an assessment tool and recordkeeping system that provides teachers (and students) information about books read, their difficulty level, and comprehension of the material. Children choose books on their own, from a set of leveled materials (there are literally more than 25,000 titles on the AR list), and take a test about the book when they are ready to do so. Books are assigned point values, generally based on the number of words in the book and on the book's reading difficulty as determined by readability analysis. Point values are assigned to the student based on his or her performance of a comprehension test (usually 10 to 20 multiple choice items), and student must score at least 60 percent on the test to receive any points at all.

AR has become very popular with teachers, parents, and children. Parents and teachers seem to like the automated testing function, as well as the fact that the books are of high quality children's literature. However, concerns have been raised about AR when teachers

The capacity to cut and paste from several documents allows children to share their work in collaborative projects.

use it as their reading management system and when the goal of the activity is to achieve points on the test. Also, while many children enjoy the motivational value of the point system, other, perhaps less-able readers, may worry about the test-taking aspect. Teachers who use AR successfully usually ensure that there is quality discussion about the books being read, both in individual teacher-student conferences and in whole groups, rather than relying only on the AR testing system to engage readers in reading. Topping (1999) presents a discussion of AR, including its structure, goals, advantages, and possible disadvantages in a readable and interesting forum: http://www.readingonline.org/past/past_index. asp?HREF = ../critical/topping/index.html. Click on the arrow at the bottom of the screen to move interactively through Topping's moderated discussion.

As is true with all materials, software packages and programs must be evaluated carefully to determine if they are appropriate for your students' needs and to your instructional goals. We often hear teachers ask where they can find programs appropriate for their classrooms. As a starting point, search the many catalogs held in the school library. Also, most school district teacher resource centers have software catalogs, demonstration programs, and evaluations by teachers who have used specific programs.

Most educational book publishers also produce software and include those offerings in their general as well as specialized catalogs. Such catalogs briefly describe available educational software, but usually do not evaluate what is listed. They are available from publishers on request and are automatically sent to school and university libraries and to curriculum and resource centers. Journals, too, often list and evaluate educational software. The following publications feature new product announcements, software evaluation, or similar columns about computer use in schools.

The Reading Teacher

The Journal of Adolescent and Adult Literacy

Reading Online (http://www.readingonline.org/)

T.H.E. Journal (Technological Horizons in Education)
(http://www.thejournal.com/)

Also, search the Internet for comments about software you are considering from teachers who have tried it.

After finding software that interests you, you will have to decide whether it is appropriate for your students and your instructional program. Some software publishers will send a program (or a compressed demonstration copy) on approval so that it can be evaluated; others offer demonstration versions that can be downloaded from their Internet site. However, most publishers do not allow the return of used software. Thus, you should try to find one or more independent reviews of the software before ordering it. Reviews and articles are available in the previously listed journals. The Internet can also be used to ask others' opinions regarding an intended software purchase or to find compilations of reviews. Additionally, most state departments of education and many school districts have collected software evaluations and make them available to teachers.

Of course, the most relevant evaluation is the one you will do yourself. When considering software, you should assess two things. First, you must ask whether the software is appropriate to your hardware; that is, the equipment. Second, you must consider aspects of the software itself as they relate to your instructional program. Before you order any software, work through the following hardware-specific evaluation checklist (modified from Kinzer, Sherwood, & Bransford, 1986). It can help identify inappropriate software before further time, effort, and money are expended and it does not require that the software be in hand (the questions usually can be answered from information provided in catalogs or advertising brochures).

Hardware-Specific Software Checklist

1. Is the software available in your diskette format? For example, if your computer accepts only 3.5-inch diskettes, is the software available on such diskettes or is it available only on CD-ROM or through a direct on-line download from the publisher?
2. Does the software require a certain amount of unused hard disk space to operate? Sometimes hard disks are too full to allow temporary files to be written that are required by some software.
3. Is the software compatible with your particular computer? For example, some software requires that computers operate at a given speed. Thus, even if the software is available for your particular brand of computer, it still must be compatible with the model that you have (perhaps a model that incorporates a Pentium III or higher-speed processor).
4. Is the software compatible with your particular computer's operating system? For example, does the software require Windows 2000 or higher, or Macintosh system X to run? Even if the software is compatible with a particular computer platform (Apple, Windows, or Linux, for example), the version of the operating system must also be compatible with software requirements.
5. Does the software require a certain amount of computer memory? Some software must be loaded into memory before it can be used and may require additional memory during use. Find out how much memory is required for operation and whether your computer has the necessary amount. Memory requirements for video memory as well as "normal" random access memory must be considered.
6. Does the software require any specific input device? Are programmable, function, or special keyboard keys needed by the program? Is a special or enhanced keyboard or graphics tablet necessary? Is a joystick, touchpad, or other special input or control device required?
7. Does the software require any specific output device? Some software sends output directly to a printer and stops or "hangs up" if a printer is unavailable. Is the software really only appropriate with a color printer, or will a black and white printer be adequate?
8. Does the software require any specific output capabilities? A printer with graphics capabilities, an external speaker, or a high-level color monitor is sometimes required before the full capabilities of the software are available.

After determining that the targeted software is suitable for your classroom computer system, answer the questions in the list below (adapted from Kinzer, Sherwood, & Bransford, 1986). They require that you have the software in hand and will help you examine it carefully. Some software may be inappropriate for the reading level or typing skills of your students. In other cases, the computer's graphics and sound capabilities may draw attention to wrong answers, thus motivating children to input inappropriate responses. If your school district or school library catalogs software evaluations, you should forward yours for inclusion when it is completed. (Be sure to include title and version, publisher and address, and perhaps cost.) Additionally, because some software is developed and distributed without adequate field testing, you should send any suggestions for improvements or complaints regarding the software to the publisher so that modifications can be made. Hands-on evaluation is your only real safeguard.

Questions for Evaluating Reading and Writing Instructional Software

1. Do you have the proper equipment to run the software?
2. What aspects of literacy are developed, according to the publisher? Do you agree?
3. Are the skills developed by the software appropriate to your students and to your curriculum? For how many of your students would the software be useful?
4. What is the intended age/grade level, according to the publisher? Do you agree?
5. How do you intend to use the software? What would its purpose be in your overall program?
6. How many of your students are at a level at which the software would be useful?
7. In what area does the software fall: (a) learning from computers, (b) learning with computers, (c) managing learning with computers, or (d) some other area or combination of areas?
8. Does the software do more than a text could do in the same skill area? In what way?
9. Would the software be easy for your students to use and understand? Are the commands, required typing skills, or complexity of screen displays within your students' abilities?
10. Does the software make appropriate use of graphics, color, and sound to enhance motivation and learning? Are these elements necessary, given your intended use of the software?
11. Does the software make use of branching to provide instruction when errors are made? Is branching necessary, given your intended use?
12. How long would it take one of your students to go through the program? Is that an appropriate amount of time, given your goals and instructional situation?
13. Would your students have to go through the entire program, perhaps in some predetermined sequence, or would they be able to stop and start at various points?
14. Does the software provide a pretest so that students can begin at an appropriate level of difficulty? Is there a posttest to measure learning? Are these tests important, given your intended use?
15. Could your students load and use the software by themselves? How much teacher support would be needed? Is that involvement appropriate to your instructional situation?
16. Does the software provide a dictionary or glossary to explain words and/or concepts that students find difficult? Could students ask the computer for a more detailed explanation if they did not understand a word? Does the software provide help if commands are not easily understood?
17. Does the software use the computer's sound capabilities to provide speech support for unknown words? For example, can the user highlight a word or a larger part of the text and ask that it be read? If yes, which form is used: synthesized (more difficult to understand) or digitized (a good approximation of natural speech)?
18. If the software targets longer pieces of text, does it use selections that are interesting and/or drawn from good children's literature?
19. Does the software score students' work and file the results by individual names for later access by the teacher (that is, does it include recordkeeping capabilities)?
20. Can the software be used by more than one student at a time? Would this usage detract from your intended use?
21. Is there overt gender, racial, or socioeconomic bias in the software?
22. What suggestions for improvement should be communicated to the publisher?

⌨ Enhancing Basic Computer Technology

A computer, printer, and Internet access connection are the basic needs to implement the uses of technology that have been discussed throughout this book. However, other items can extend or enhance your use of computer technology in literacy instruction. Scanners, digital cameras, and CU–SeeMe technologies are becoming more available for classroom use.

A scanner is similar to a photocopy machine, except that copied items are digitized (placed in a format that can be manipulated electronically) and appear on a computer screen rather than on paper. A scanner is useful to scan students' artwork into a computer, to scan pictures of class projects or pictures supplied by students (pets are always a favorite) into a computer, or to scan other items that you or your students might want to incorporate into a classroom web page or into a project that will be created using the computer. Once scanned, the copy can be resized, enhanced in terms of color, and manipulated in other ways using software supplied with the scanner. Thus, students who write a story about their pet can incorporate a picture or drawing, which then prints normally on your classroom printer. Scanned items can also be sent to electronic penpals and can be wonderful discussion starters.

A digital camera captures images and stores them digitally rather than on film. Once pictures have been taken, the camera is linked to a computer by a cable, or the camera's storage medium (usually a small card or "wafer" that stores images but is removable) is placed into a card reader, where the images are transferred to a computer for storage. Having multiple storage cards for a camera means that the camera can be used while moving pictures into the computer. The storage card can then be erased and is ready to store more images. Digital cameras are useful when taking a class on field trips or to take pictures of general school or classroom life.

Children also can use the school or class camera to illustrate projects (for example, to incorporate pictures of trash in a pollution report) or to place photos on the class (or personal) web page. Once stored in the computer, images can be manipulated in the same way as can images from items that were scanned. Thus, inexpensive (or single-use) cameras can be provided to children to take pictures and then desired images can be scanned into the computer. However, this involves recurring costs for film, processing, and "wait time" before a project can be completed. Digital cameras are made by all major camera manufacturers (for example, Kodak, Canon, Nikon, Olympus, Fuji, and so on). When deciding on a camera purchase for your classroom, you will need to decide if you will want to print the pictures on paper, or use them only on a web page. Cameras with relatively low resolution create images that look wonderful on computer screens, but do not print well. These cameras are much cheaper than higher-resolution cameras that can be used for both web and print purposes.

CU–SeeMe technology, developed by Cornell University, allows two or more computers to project moving or still images, as well as audio, to each user. This technology often is used for videoconferencing, where both parties want to see each other. If the linked computers have video in-and-out capabilities (your computer manual will tell you this), you can plug a standard videotape camera into your computer and, using software that can be downloaded from various shareware sites (for example, http://www.tucows.com/ or http://www.zdnet.com/downloads/), can see the people you are talking to. You can also see artwork or student projects that the camera focuses on, providing opportunities for real-time discussion by children about their work and for opportunities for immediate discussion and questions and answers from keypals around the world. Computers without video in-and-out capabilities can use small cameras specifically made for desktop computer users. Usually, these cameras will come with appropriate software as well.

All of the items previously discussed are relatively inexpensive and are becoming increasingly available throughout homes and schools. Scanners and cameras come in a range of prices, with the most competitive prices appearing at large computer "warehouse" stores or through mail-order outlets. When evaluating scanners or cameras, your primary consideration should be your intended use. The least expensive scanners and cameras will be best for placing images on computer screens, perhaps for web pages, but will not be able to provide satisfactory output to a printer. Higher quality (and thus more expensive) scanners and cameras can be appropriate for both uses. Your school or district technology consultant is a good resource to answer questions about appropriate equipment and costs. You may be surprised, however, at how inexpensive a scanner or camera can be.

Wireless and Handheld Computing

In the past, many schools had difficulty connecting computers to an internal building network or to the Internet because wiring existing buildings was very expensive. However, technological advances now allow wireless Internet connections, through the use of relatively inexpensive transmitter/receiver "hubs" and a card that can fit inside laptop and desktop computers. These hubs are always active, and any computer with a wireless connection card will connect to the network or the Internet whenever a user clicks on an appropriate software program—for example, clicking to open browser software will automatically connect you to the Internet. Wireless computing in homes, businesses, universities, and schools is becoming common.

Also becoming common are handheld devices that initially served as organizers and appointment calendars, but that are now including cell phones, cameras, modem connectivity, and (depending on their location and the availability of a hub) wireless Internet access all in a handheld device that is much smaller than a paperback book. The most popular of these devices (usually called PDAs, or Personal Digital Assistants) are made by Palm, Inc., maker of Palm Pilot devices; and Handspring, Inc., maker of the Visor. These handheld devices run using a proprietary operating system, but other manufacturers, for example, Casio (maker of the Cassiopeia) and Sony (maker of the CLIE), are creating small, handheld computers that run truncated but very functional versions of Microsoft's operating system and business software.

As these handheld devices become cheaper and incorporate even more functions, they are becoming increasingly interesting for instructional applications. There are, at this time, many e-books available for download that can be directly loaded into these devices and read on their screens rather than on paper. There are typing and handwriting tutors available for the Palm and Visor devices, and there are numerous probes and other attachments that are useful in science and other content areas. Games and instructional programs in decoding, vocabulary, and other areas also abound—many of them available as inexpensive shareware. For example, at the time of this writing, going to http://www.zdnet.com/downloads/ (the download section of **ZDNet.com**), entering "vocabulary practice" in the search field, and choosing "Palm Operating System" resulted in literally pages of shareware programs of flashcards, dictionaries, predetermined vocabulary lists, and so on. These handheld devices, and their evolving wireless capabilities, will soon become incorporated into published reading programs and into literacy instruction in general.

Using a Literacy Framework to Guide Technological Applications

Your use of technology and the Internet will lead you to choose activities and sites that most closely match your decisions about what to teach and how you will do so. For example, in deciding what to teach, if you have reader-based beliefs, you may choose software that develops the meanings readers bring to texts and inferential experiences such as predicting outcomes and drawing conclusions. If you hold text-based beliefs, you may choose software that emphasizes decoding knowledge and literal-level meaning. If you hold interactive beliefs, you will choose a range of software categories and types of activities to develop all of the knowledge sources you have discovered throughout this book: syntactic, metacognitive, and discourse knowledge as well as decoding, vocabulary, and

Featured Teacher

Mrs. Barnard

Paula Barnard teachers fourth grade in Arlington, Washington. Her award-winning classroom website includes navigation buttons that we urge you to explore. See Figure 14-7 for her home page at http://www.asd.wednet.edu/EagleCreek/Barnard/Launcher.html. Mrs. Barnard has included samples of her children's work, links to resources for students and parents, WebQuests and Web Lessons, and hints to others about creating such web pages. Mrs. Barnard is a wonderful example of how teachers can integrate technology and the Internet into their classrooms.

FIGURE 14-7

Paula Barnard's home page (http://www.asd.wednet.edu/EagleCreek/Barnard/Launcher.html)

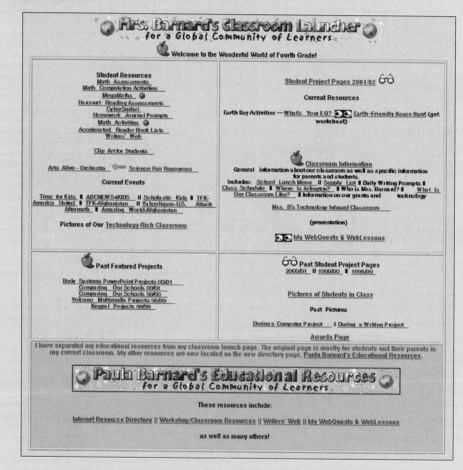

other aspects of the reading process. And you will do so in an integrated manner as appropriate for your individual students.

In deciding how to teach, holistic language learning beliefs would lead you to choose simulation applications that integrate video, audio, text, and other multimedia capabilities. These beliefs would also lead to the use of Internet Workshop, Internet Projects and Internet Inquiry.

If you have specific-skills beliefs, you will choose software that includes student recordkeeping functions that will help you to understand students' mastery of the specific skills they are learning and will use Internet strategies that enhance the development of the skills taught.

If you have integrated beliefs about how to teach, you will range across the method frameworks and software types that were discussed in this chapter and will choose both inductive and deductive experiences to teach the children in your classroom.

Computers are simply tools for teachers to use in reading instruction. They are governed by the same kinds of philosophical considerations that we applied to printed materials earlier. With both new and traditional technologies, you will be on the forefront of educational opportunities. Supported by the concepts, theories, and methods suggested throughout this text and guided by your own personal literacy framework, you are ready to become a professional and effective teacher of literacy.

Use the self-test questions on http://www.prenhall.com/leukinzer to review the material presented in this chapter.

Major Points

- The use of computers in literacy instruction falls into five general categories: learning with computers, learning about thinking with computers, learning from computers, managing learning with computers, and learning about computers.
- The Internet is a powerful and appropriate tool for use in literacy instruction, and method frameworks such as Internet Project, Internet Inquiry, Internet Workshop, and WebQuests are effective strategies.
- Issues of child safety and professional growth are important to your students and to you as a professional.
- In addition to computers and their software, various other technologies—including CD-ROMs and DVDs, answering machines, and handheld devices—are useful in reading instruction. These other technologies can be effectively used independently or can be linked to computers.
- All types of software—including drill-and-practice, tutorial, game-like, simulation, and programming—can have a place in reading instruction, if appropriately used.
- If thoughtfully applied, software intended for use in other areas can also be used in reading instruction.
- Teachers should carefully evaluate software before using it in reading instruction.

Making Instructional Decisions

1. Explain the difference between Internet Inquiry and Internet Project method frameworks, and how these can be incorporated into Internet Workshop.
2. Interview several teachers who use computers and the Internet in their literacy instruction. Ask how they use the system specifically in their literacy lessons and how they perceive the computer in comparison to more traditional instructional practices, such as workbooks.
3. Interview several children who have been allowed to use computers and the Internet as a part of their reading instruction. Ask how they feel about these technology tools and how they have helped them learn.
4. Your curriculum library or computer laboratory probably has software marketed as appropriate for literacy instruction. (If not, check a computer store.) Evaluate several software packages using the checklists in this chapter. How might the software be used in reading instruction?
5. Some, including legislators who are concerned about the appropriateness of material on the Internet and point to very real child safety and general security issues, argue that the Internet should be regulated with regard to what can appear for general access. Others argue that this public forum is invaluable, that the free exchange of ideas must take precedence, and that restricting the free flow of ideas is dangerous and violates constitutional issues and safeguards as they relate to freedom of speech and expression. As a future teacher who will use the Internet in your classroom, how do you feel about restricting what can be placed on the Internet? What

will you say to parents about restricting access to certain sites for the children in your classroom?

6. How might computers and related technologies fit into your instructional program and, specifically, your literacy framework?

Further Reading

Burnishke, R. W. (2001). *Literacy in the cyberage: Composing ourselves online.* Newark, DE: International Reading Association.

A short paperback that discusses how classroom teachers can expand instruction so that electronic literacy becomes an essential component in literacy instruction. Explains nine interrelated literacies that build on one another to enhance understanding of literacy in an electronic environment.

Dillner, M. (1994). Using hypermedia to enhance content-area instruction. *Journal of Reading, 37,* 260–270.

Discusses the procedures and decisions a teacher made to create a hypermedia lesson and gives some examples of how students used that lesson. Incorporates interesting ideas for developing lessons using hypermedia.

Grabe, M., & Grabe, C. (1998). *Learning with Internet tools: A primer.* New York: Houghton Mifflin.

A very short, readable, introductory-level publication to the Internet for novices.

Kinzer, C. K., & Leu, D. J., Jr. (1997). The challenge of change: Exploring literacy and learning in electronic environments. *Language Arts, 74*(2), 126–136.

Describes several multimedia projects that have been successful in classrooms and discusses design and use issues.

Labbo, L. D., Sprague, L., Montero, M. K., & Font, G. (2000, July). Connecting a computer center to themes, literature, and kindergartners' literacy needs. *Reading Online, 4*(1). Available: http://www.readingonline.org/electronic/labbo/ [accessed 2/14/02].

Used ongoing observations in a kindergarten classroom to design thematically connected, literature-based computer-related activities to meet the varying literacy needs of the children in the classroom

Leu, D. J., Jr., & Leu, D. D. (2000). *Teaching with the Internet: Lessons from the classroom* (3rd ed.). Norwood, MA: Christopher-Gordon.

A very readable and comprehensive resource book for teachers. Covers major subject areas, provides many suggestions from practicing teachers, and lists a wealth of Internet sites.

References

Alexander, P. A., Kulikowich, J. M., & Jetton, T. L. (1994). The role of subject-matter knowledge and interests in the processing of linear and nonlinear texts. *Review of Education Research, 64,* 201–252.

Bauch, J. P. (1989). The TransPARENT school model: New technology for parent involvement. *Educational Leadership, 47*(2), 32–34.

Bauch, J. P. (1990). The TransPARENT school model: A partnership for parent involvement. *Educational Horizons, 68,* 187–189.

Bauch, J. P. (Ed.). (1997). *The bridge project: Connecting parents and schools through voice messaging (report on the pilot projects).* Nashville, TN: Betty Phillips Center on Parenthood Education.

Berger, C. (1984, April). *Assessing cognitive consequences of computer environments for learning science: Research findings and policy implications.* Paper presented at the National Association for Research in Science Teaching, Lake Geneva, WI.

Bransford, J. (1984, April). Personal communication.

Bransford, J. D., Kinzer, C. K., Risko, V. J., Rowe, D. W., & Vye, N. J. (1989). Designing invitations to thinking: Initial thoughts. In S. McCormick & J. Zutell (Eds.), *Cognitive and social perspectives for literacy research and instruction* (38th NRC Yearbook, 35–54). Chicago, IL: National Reading Conference.

Bransford, J. D., Sherwood, R. D., Hasselbring, T. S., Kinzer, C. K., & Williams, S. M. (1990). Anchored instruction:

Why we need it and how technology can help. In D. Nix & R. Spiro (Eds.), *Cognition, education, and multimedia,* (pp. 115–141). Hillsdale, NJ: Lawrence Erlbaum Associates.

Bransford, J. D., Vye, N. J., Kinzer, C. K., & Risko, V. J. (1990). Teaching thinking and content knowledge: An integrated approach. In B. F. Jones & L. Idol (Eds.), *Dimensions of thinking and cognitive instruction,* (pp. 381–413). Hillsdale, NJ: Lawrence Erlbaum Associates.

Cuban, L. (1986). *Teachers and machines: The classroom use of technology since 1920.* New York: Teachers College Press.

Goldberg, K., & Sherwood, R. D. (1983). *Microcomputers: A parent's guide.* New York: Wiley.

Guglielmo, C. (1994). What's happening on CD-ROM: Encyclopedias. *MacWeek, 8*(31), 45–46.

Hasselbring, T. S., & Cavanaugh, K. (1986). Computer applications for the mildly handicapped. In C. K. Kinzer, R. D. Sherwood, & J. D. Bransford (Eds.), *Computer strategies for education: Foundations and content-area applications.* Columbus, OH: Merrill.

Kinzer, C. K. (1986). A five-part categorization for use of microcomputers in reading classrooms. *The Reading Teacher, 30,* 226–232.

Kinzer, C. K., with the Cognition and Technology Group at Vanderbilt. (1990). Anchored instruction and its relationship to situated cognition. *Educational Researcher, 19,* 2–10.

Kinzer, C. K., & Leander, K. (2003). Technology and the language arts: (Implications of an expanded definition of literacy). In J. Flood, J. M. Jensen, D. Lapp, & J. R. Squire (Eds.), *The Handbook of research on teaching the English language arts.* Mahwah, NJ: Lawrence Erlbaum Associates.

Kinzer, C. K., & Leu, D. J. (1997). The challenge of change: Exploring literacy and learning in electronic environments. *Language Arts, 74*(2), 126–136.

Kinzer, C. K., Sherwood, R. D., & Bransford, J. D. (Eds.). (1986). *Computer strategies for education: Foundations and content-area applications.* Columbus, OH: Merrill.

Labbo, L. D. (1996). A semiotic analysis of young children's symbol making in a classroom computer center. *Reading Research Quarterly, 31*(4), 356–385.

Labbo, L. D., & Reinking, D. (2000). Once upon an electronic story time. *New Advocate, 13,* 25–32.

Leu, D. J., & Kinzer, C. K. (2000). The convergence of literacy instruction with networked technologies for information, communication, and education. *Reading Research Quarterly, 35*(1), 108–127.

Luehrmann, A. (1983). *Computer literacy: A hands-on approach.* New York: McGraw-Hill.

McKenna, M. C., Young, T., & Gatliff, J. (December, 2001). *Creating and using talking documents with struggling second-grade readers.* Paper presented at the National Reading Conference annual meeting, Scottsdale, AZ.

Myers, J. (1993). Constructing community and intertextuality in electronic mail. In D. J. Leu & C. K. Kinzer (Eds.), *Examining central issues in literacy research, theory and practice.* Forty-second yearbook of the National Reading Conference (pp. 251–262). Chicago, IL: National Reading Conference.

Papert, S. (1980). *Mindstorms: Children, computers, and powerful ideas.* New York: Basic Books.

Papert, S. (1984). New theories for new learnings. *School Psychology Review, 13*(4), 422–428.

Poock, M. M. (1998). The Accelerated Reader: An analysis of the software's strengths and weaknesses and how it can be used to its best potential. *School Library Media Activities Monthly, 14*(9), 32–35.

Reinking, D. (1995). Reading and writing with computers: Literacy in a post-typographic world. In K. A. Hinchman, D. J., Leu, & C. K. Kinzer (Eds.), *Perspectives on literacy research and practice.* Forty-fourth yearbook of the National Reading Conference (pp. 17–33). Chicago, IL: National Reading Conference.

Reinking, D. (1998). Synthesizing technological transformations of literacy in a Post-typographic world. In Reinking, D., McKenna, M., Labbo, L. D., & Kieffer, R. (Eds.). *Handbook of literacy and technology: Transformations in a post-typographic world.* Mahwah NJ: Lawrence Erlbaum Associates.

Reinking, D., & Watkins, J. (1997). *A formative experiment investigating the use of multimedia book reviews to increase elementary students' independent reading* (Research Report). University of Georgia, University of Maryland: National Reading Research Center.

Short, K. G. (1992). Intertextuality: Searching for patterns that connect. In C. K. Kinzer & D. J. Leu (Eds.), *Literacy research, theory, and practice: Views from many perspectives.* Forty-first yearbook of the National Reading Conference (pp. 187–197). Chicago, IL: National Reading Conference.

Taylor, R. P. (Ed.). (1980). *The computer in the school: Tutor, tool, tutee.* New York: Teachers College Press.

Topping, K. (1999). Formative assessment of reading comprehension by computer: Advantages and disadvantages of the Accelerated Reader software. *Reading Online,* http://www.readingonline.org/past/past_index.asp?HREF=../critical/topping/index.html.

Whitaker, B. T., Schwartz, E., & Vockell, E. (1989). *The computer in the reading curriculum.* New York: McGraw-Hill.

Wresch, W. (1997). *A teacher's guide to the information highway.* Upper Saddle River, NJ: Merrill/Prentice Hall.

Appendix A

Award-winning children's literature: Newbery medal winners

Year	Title	Author
2002	A Single Shard	Linda Sue Park
2001	A Year Down Yonder	Richard Peck
2000	Bud, Not Buddy	Christopher Paul Curtis
1999	Holes	Louis Sachar
1998	Out of the Dust	Karen Hesse
1997	The View From Saturday	E. L. Konigsburg
1996	The Midwife's Apprentice	Karen Cushman
1995	Walk Two Moons	Sharon Creech
1994	The Giver	Lois Lowry
1993	Missing May	Cynthia Rylant
1992	Shiloh	Phyllis Reynolds Naylor
1991	Maniac McGee	Jerry Spinelli
1990	Number the Stars	Lois Lowry
1989	Joyful Noise: Poems for Two Voices	Paul Fleischman
1988	Lincoln: A Photobiography	Russell Freedman
1987	The Whipping Boy	Sid Fleischman
1986	Sarah, Plain and Tall	Patricia MacLachlan
1985	The Hero and the Crown	Robin McKinley
1984	Dear Mr. Henshaw	Beverly Cleary
1983	Dicey's Song	Cynthia Voigt
1982	A Visit to William Blake's Inn: Poems for Innocent and Experienced Travelers	Nancy Willard
1981	Jacob Have I Loved	Katherine Paterson
1980	A Gathering of Days: A New England Girl's Journal, 1830–32	Joan W. Blos
1979	The Westing Game	Ellen Raskin
1978	Bridge to Terabithia	Katherine Paterson
1977	Roll of Thunder, Hear My Cry	Mildred D. Taylor
1976	The Grey King	Susan Cooper
1975	M. C. Higgins, the Great	Virginia Hamilton
1974	The Slave Dancer	Paula Fox
1973	Julie of the Wolves	Jean Craighead George
1972	Mrs. Frisby and the Rats of NIMH	Robert C. O'Brien
1971	Summer of the Swans	Betsy Byars
1970	Sounder	William H. Armstrong
1969	The High King	Lloyd Alexander
1968	From the Mixed-Up Files of Mrs. Basil E. Frankweiler	E. L. Konigsburg
1967	Up a Road Slowly	Irene Hunt
1966	I. Juan de Pareja	Elizabeth Borton de Trevino
1965	Shadow of a Bull	Maia Wojciechowska
1964	It's Like This, Cat	Emily Neville
1963	A Wrinkle in Time	Madeleine L'Engle
1962	The Bronze Bow	Elizabeth George Speare
1961	Island of the Blue Dolphins	Scott O'Dell
1960	Onion John	Joseph Krumgold
1959	The Witch of Blackbird Pond	Elizabeth George Speare
1958	Rifles for Watie	Harold Keith
1957	Miracles on Maple Hill	Virginia Sorenson
1956	Carry On, Mr. Bowditch	Jean Lee Latham
1955	The Wheel on the School	Meindert Dejong
1954	. . . and now Miguel	Joseph Krumgold
1953	Secret of the Andes	Ann Nolan Clark
1952	Ginger Pye	Eleanor Estes

Appendix B

Award-winning children's literature: Caldecott medal winners

Year	Title	Illustrator	Author
2002	The Three Pigs	David Wiesner	David Wiesner
2001	So You Want to Be President?	David Small	Judith St. George
2000	Joseph Had a Little Overcoat	Simms Taback	Simms Taback
1999	Snowflake Bentley	Mary Azarian	Jacqueline Briggs Martin
1998	Rapunzel	Paul O. Zelinsky	Paul O. Zelinsky
1997	Golem	David Wisniewski	David Wisniewski
1996	Officer Buckle and Gloria	Peggy Rathmann	Peggy Rathmann
1995	Smoky Night	David Diaz	Eve Bunting
1994	Grandfather's Journey	Allen Say	Allen Say
1993	Mirette on the High Wire	Emily Arnold McCully	Emily Arnold McCully
1992	Tuesday	David Wiesner	David Wiesner
1991	Black and White	David Macaulay	David Macaulay
1990	Lon Po Po: A Red-Riding Hood Story from China	Ed Young	Ed Young
1989	Song and Dance Man	Stephen Gammell	Karen Ackerman
1988	Owl Moon	John Schoenherr	Jane Yolen
1987	Hey, Al	Richard Egielski	Arthur Yorinks
1986	The Polar Express	Chris Van Allsburg	Chris Van Allsburg
1985	Saint George and the Dragon	Trina Schart Hyman	Margaret Hodges
1984	The Glorious Flight: Across the Channel with Louis Bleriot	Alice and Martin Provensen	Alice and Martin Provensen
1983	Shadow	Marcia Brown	Blaise Cendrars
1982	Jumanji	Chris Van Allsburg	Chris Van Allsburg
1981	Fables	Arnold Lobel	Arnold Lobel
1980	Ox-Cart Man	Barbara Cooney	Donald Hall
1979	The Girl Who Loved Wild Horses	Paul Goble	Paul Goble
1978	Noah's Ark	Peter Spier	Peter Spier
1977	Ashanti to Zulu: African Traditions	Leo and Diane Dillon	Margaret Musgrove
1976	Why Mosquitoes Buzz in People's Ears	Leo and Diane Dillon	Verna Aardema
1975	Arrow to the Sun	Gerald McDermott	Gerald McDermott
1974	Duffy and the Devil	Margot Zemach	Harve Zemach
1973	The Funny Little Woman	Blair Lent	Arlene Mosel
1972	One Fine Day	Nonny Hogrogian	Nonny Hogrogian
1971	A Story—A Story	Gail E. Haley	Gail E. Haley
1970	Sylvester and the Magic Pebble	William Steig	William Steig
1969	The Fool of the World and the Flying Ship	Uri Shulevitz	Arthur Ransome
1968	Drummer Hoff	Ed Emberley	Barbara Emberley
1967	Sam, Bangs & Moonshine	Evaline Ness	Evaline Ness
1966	Always Room for One More	Nonny Hogrogian	Sorche Nic Leodhas
1965	May I Bring a Friend?	Beni Montresor	Beatrice Schenk de Regniers
1964	Where the Wild Things Are	Maurice Sendak	Maurice Sendak
1963	The Snowy Day	Ezra Jack Keats	Ezra Jack Keats
1962	Once a Mouse. . .	Marcia Brown	Marcia Brown
1961	Baboushka and the Three Kings	Nicolas Sidjakov	Ruth Robbins
1960	Nine Days to Christmas	Marie Hall Ets	Marie Hall Ets & Aurora Labastida
1959	Chanticleer and the Fox	Barbara Cooney	Translated by Barbara Cooney
1958	Time of Wonder	Robert McCloskey	Robert McCloskey
1957	A Tree Is Nice	Marc Simont	Janice May Udry

Year	Title	Illustrator	Author
1956	Frog Went A-Courtin'	Feodor Rojankovsky	Retold by John Langstaff
1955	Cinderella, or the Little Glass Slipper	Marcia Brown	Charles Perrault
1954	Madeline's Rescue	Ludwig Bemelmans	Ludwig Bemelmans
1953	The Biggest Bear	Lynd Ward	Lynd Ward
1952	Finders Keepers	Nicholas Mordvinoff	William Lipkind
1951	The Egg Tree	Katherine Milhous	Katherine Milhous
1950	Song of the Swallows	Leo Politi	Leo Politi
1949	The Big Snow	Berta and Elmer Hader	Berta and Elmer Hader
1948	White Snow, Bright Snow	Roger Duvoisin	Alvin Tresselt
1947	The Little Island	Leonard Weisgard	Golden MacDonald
1946	The Rooster Crows	Maud and Miska Petersham	Maud and Miska Petersham
1945	Prayer for a Child	Elizabeth Orton Jones	Rachel Field
1944	Many Moons	Louis Slobodkin	James Thurber
1943	The Little House	Virginia Lee Burton	Virginia Lee Burton
1942	Make Way for Ducklings	Robert McCloskey	Robert McCloskey
1941	They Were Strong and Good	Robert Lawson	Robert Lawson
1940	Abraham Lincoln	Ingri and Edgar D' Aulaire	Ingri and Edgar D' Aulaire
1939	Mei Li	Thomas Handforth	Thomas Handforth
1938	Animals of the Bible	Dorothy P. Lathrop	Helen Dean Fish

Name Index

Subject Index

Internet Index